PSYCHOLOGY LIBRARY EDITIONS:
MEMORY

Volume 22

NEW DIRECTIONS IN MEMORY AND AGING

T0347150

NEW DIRECTIONS IN MEMORY AND AGING

Proceedings of the George A. Talland Memorial
Conference

Edited by
LEONARD W. POON, JAMES L. FOZARD,
LAIRD S. CERMAK, DAVID ARENBERG
AND LARRY W. THOMPSON

Ψ **Psychology Press**
Taylor & Francis Group
LONDON AND NEW YORK

First published in 1980

This edition first published in 2014
by Psychology Press
27 Church Road, Hove, East Sussex BN3 2FA, UK

and by Psychology Press
711 Third Avenue, New York, NY 10017

Psychology Press is an imprint of the Taylor and Francis Group, an informa business

First issued in paperback 2015

British Library Cataloguing in Publication Data
A catalogue record for this book is available from the British Library

ISBN 978-1-84872-321-4 (Set)
eISBN 978-1-315-77503-6 (Set)
ISBN 978-1-84872-417-4 (hbk) (Volume 22)
ISBN 978-1-138-97707-5 (pbk) (Volume 22)
ISBN 978-1-315-77488-6 (ebk) (Volume 22)

Publisher's Note
The publisher has gone to great lengths to ensure the quality of this book but points out that some imperfections from the original may be apparent.

Disclaimer
The publisher has made every effort to trace copyright holders and would welcome correspondence from those they have been unable to trace.

NEW DIRECTIONS
IN MEMORY AND AGING

Proceedings of the
George A. Talland Memorial Conference

Edited by

LEONARD W. POON
JAMES L. FOZARD
LAIRD S. CERMAK
DAVID ARENBERG
LARRY W. THOMPSON

LAWRENCE ERLBAUM ASSOCIATES, PUBLISHERS
1980   Hillsdale, New Jersey

Lawrence Erlbaum Associates, Inc., Publishers
365 Broadway
Hillsdale, New Jersey 07642

Library of Congress Cataloging in Publication Data

George A. Talland Memorial Conference, Boston, 1978.
    New directions in memory and aging.

    Includes bibliographical references and index.
    1. Memory—Congresses.   2. Aging—Congresses.
I. Talland, George A.   II. Poon, Leonard W.
III. Title.
BF371.G4 1978   155.67'1   79-27548
ISBN 0-89859-035-3

Printed in the United States of America

Contents

KEYNOTE
Memory and Age: A Perspective View
Alan T. Welford

PART I
LOCALIZATION OF DECLINE AND
THE ROLE OF ATTENTION IN MEMORY
David Arenberg

EPILOGUE
New Directions in Memory and Aging Research
Leonard W. Poon and James L. Fozard

Preface

The major objective of this volume is to stimulate research toward a more comprehensive understanding of age related differences in memory. Further, we hope to provide direction for the application and utilization of research findings in the evaluation and treatment of memory complaints and memory difficulties experienced by the elderly.

To accomplish these objectives, the chapters in the present volume were prepared and reviewed jointly by experimental psychologists currently active in research on memory and those currently performing research on memory with specific interest in the area of adult aging. The objective of all the authors was to identify the most promising areas for advancing research in memory as it relates to aging. The result is a merging of contemporary thought on research in memory and aging and current ideas in the parent field of psychological research on memory. The authors and reviewers include scientists well known for their research, as well as scientists new to this area of research.

In the clinical arena, experimental and clinical psychologists addressed jointly the application of research findings to the diagnosis and treatment of memory problems of older adults. The present volume brings together for the first time a careful review of many of the contemporary efforts of psychologists to improve memory for adults of all ages, and suggests refinements and improvements in these procedures that will have a direct practical application.

This book fills a need not typically addressed by review chapters and journal articles. It is designed to provide the reader with a rich array of scientific concepts and testable hypotheses which can be transformed into research programs, and also which in the opinion of the editors will have a lasting and positive effect both on advances in research on memory and aging and on the practical application of such information.

The present volume is intended for two broad groups of scientists. The first consists of researchers in the psychology of memory, and those currently active in the research on aging. It is anticipated that the material will be of special interest to beginning scientists seeking to identify fruitful areas for research, and to developmental/life-span psychologists interested in viewing parallels between applications of general research on memory to adults and applications of such research to children or other special groups. The second group for whom the book will be of interest consists of persons concerned with applying current research findings to the diagnosis and treatment of problems of memory. A portion of the material presented in this volume reviews the conventional approaches to assessment of cognitive dysfunctions with psychometric devices or established neuropsychological procedures; the major focus however, is to identify problems in available instruments and to suggest more procedures based on experimental studies and to link them to effective assessment treatment techniques.

The book is organized into three parts: (1) Localization of Decline and the Role of Attention in Memory; (2) Age Related Changes in Memory Processes; and (3) Testing and Mnemonic Strategies. Each part is introduced by its editor and contains a number of chapters and reviews. A keynote chapter introducing the contents and an epilogue chapter summarizing the contents are included as well.

The most effective way to achieve an overall perspective of the book is to first examine the keynote chapter and the three section introductions. These materials were designed to guide the readers toward the various pertinent issues and to emphasize the fair amount of interchange and cross referencing among the presentations and discussions developed in the chapters. Finally, the epilogue chapter will help the reader to consolidate the various issues and hypotheses presented in the volume.

This book is dedicated to the memory of George A. Talland, who has made a significant contribution to the area of aging and memory. Dr. Talland was a colleague and friend of several of the contributors. His many efforts to relate applied problems of memory to ongoing experimental research, to identify the applications of research, and to teach young investigators are consistent with the goals of this book.

The concept of a memorial conference and an edited volume honoring the contributions of Dr. Talland was enthusiastically endorsed by Thomas G. Hackett, M. D., Chairman of the Psychiatry Department at Massachusetts General Hospital and by Gerald Borofsky, Ph.D., Chief Psychologist at the Psychiatry Department. Dr. Talland spent a large portion of his psychological research career in this department. James L. Fozard Ph.D., and Leonard W. Poon, Ph.D., who continued the direction of aging research established by George Talland, organized the conference by identifying the conference themes, chapter topics, and contributors for the conference and the edited volume.

The conference organizers wish to acknowledge the many individuals and institutions that made possible the memorial conference and this book. We wish to acknowledge the continual encouragement and cooperation of Thomas Hackett, M.D.; Gerald Borofsky, Ph.D.; Howard Chauncey, Ph.D., D.M.D., Associate Chief of Staff/Research and Development, Veterans Administration Outpatient Clinic; and William H. Kelleher, Clinic Director, Veterans Administration Outpatient Clinic, Boston. The technical advice and assistance from Lawrence Erlbaum, publisher, contributed significantly to the overall integrity of the book.

The implementation of the conference was made possible by Conference Grant 1R13 AG00972 01 from the National Institute on Aging. The administrative and scientific support from Walter Spieth, Ph.D., is especially appreciated.

We also wish to acknowledge the staff of the Mental Performance and Aging Laboratory, whose dedication and effort paved the way to a smooth conference and the completion of the book: Susan Carroll, Brian Dailey, Julie Demeter, Alice Graham, Don Kimball, Dale Paulshock, Leslie Walsh-Sweeney, and Diane Williams.

The conference organizers, editors, publisher, contributors, and participants are especially grateful for the managerial and editorial assistance from William R. (Billie) Poon, M.A., whose tenacity, diplomacy, and patience made the conference and this edited volume possible. She deserves a full share of credit for the conference and this edited book.

Finally, this product stems primarily from the impetus and enthusiasm generated by the active contributors and 120 invited conference participants who traveled from Australia, England, Scotland, Canada, and all over the United States to take part. They came to listen, to discuss, to present, to relentlessly challenge, and to probe every issue. If George Talland were alive today, he would beam in approval; he too would have thoroughly enjoyed this conference on memory and aging, which was held in his honor.

Leonard W. Poon

GEORGE A. TALLAND

George A. Talland was born in Budapest in 1917. After receiving B.A. and M.A. degrees in Economics at Cambridge University, he studied at the University of London, where, in 1953, he earned his Ph.D. In 1954, Talland joined the staffs of the Psychiatry Departments of Harvard Medical School and the Massachusetts General Hospital, remaining at these posts until his death in 1968.

Dr. Talland creatively applied the tools and hypotheses of general experimental psychology to the study of cognitive functioning associated with brain pathology, normal aging, and psychoactive drugs. Erich Lindemann (1963) described him as "a quiet, unassuming, but extremely purposeful and tenacious investigator."

Talland's best known personal contributions to the study of cognitive dysfunction in Korsakoff's syndrome is "The amnesic syndrome: A psychological study," for which Talland was awarded the annual monograph prize of the American Academy of Arts and Sciences in 1961, and *Deranged Memory: A Psychonomic Study of the Amnesic Syndrome,* 1965. Summaries of Talland's prolific research in aging are contained in his chapters "Initiation of Response, and Reaction Time in Aging, and with Brain Damage" in *Behavior, Aging and the Nervous System* (1965), edited by A. T. Welford and J. E. Birren, and "Age and the Span of Immediate Recall" in *Human Aging and Behavior* (1968), edited by Talland.

In addition to his own research, Talland systematically worked to unite outstanding clinicians and researchers in analyses of cognitive functioning associated with brain pathology and with normal aging. The most prominent examples are *The Pathology of Memory,* co-edited with N. C. Waugh, and *Human Aging and Behavior* (1969). The present volume continues the tradition associated with George Talland.

REFERENCES

Lindemann, E. Curriculum Vitae and Bibliography of Dr. George Talland, Assistant Professor of Psychology in the Department of Psychiatry, submitted to the Committee on Senior Fellowships, 1963.

Talland, G.A. "The amnesic syndrome: A psychological study" was awarded the 1961 Monograph Prize in the Physical and Biological Sciences by the American Academy of Arts and Sciences.

Talland, G. A. *Deranged Memory: A Psychonomic Study of the Amnesic Syndrome.* New York, New York, Academic Press, 1965.

Talland, G. A. "Initiation of Response, and Reaction Time in Aging and with Brain Damage," in A. T. Welford and J. E. Birren (Eds.), *Behavior, Aging, and the Nervous System.* Springfield, Illinois. Charles C. Thomas, 1965.

Talland, G. A. "Age and the span of immediate recall" in G. A. Talland (Ed.), *Human Aging and Behavior.* New York, New York. Academic Press, 1968.

Talland, G. A., & Waugh, N. C. *The Pathology of Memory.* New York, New York. Academic Press, 1969.

Contributors To This Volume

Marilyn Albert, Ph.D. Veterans Administration Medical Center, Boston and Department of Neurology, Boston University School of Medicine, Boston, Massachusetts

David Arenberg, Ph.D. Learning and Problem Solving Section, Gerontology Research Center, National Institute on Aging, National Institute of Health, Baltimore, Maryland

Robin Barr, Ph.D. University of Oxford, Oxford, England

Nelson Butters, Ph.D. Veterans Administration Medical Center, Boston and Department of Neurology, Boston University School of Medicine, Boston, Massachusetts

Laird S. Cermak, Ph.D. Veterans Administration Medical Center, Boston and Department of Neurology, Boston University School of Medicine, Boston, Massachusetts

Fergus I. M. Craik, Ph.D. Department of Psychology, Erindale College, University of Toronto, Mississauga, Ontario, Canada

Robert G. Crowder, Ph.D. Department of Psychology, Yale University, New Haven, Connecticut

Richard C. Erickson, Ph.D. Veterans Administration Medical Center, Portland, Oregon

James L. Fozard, Ph.D. Patient Treatment Services, Veterans Administration Central Office, Washington, D.C. and Department of Psychiatry, Massachusetts General Hospital and Harvard Medical School, Boston, Massachusetts

John Frederiksen, Ph.D. Information Sciences Division, Bolt Beranek & Newman Inc., Cambridge Massachusetts

Michael Gilewski, A.M. Ethel Percy Andrus Gerontology Center, University of Southern California, University Park, Los Angeles, California

Mitchell A. Grossberg, Ph.D. U.S. Department of Transportation, Transportation Systems Center, Human Factors Division, Cambridge, Massachusetts

Terence M. Hines, Ph.D. Veterans Administration Outpatient Clinic, Boston and Departments of Psychiatry, Massachusetts General Hospital and Harvard Medical School, Boston, Massachusetts

David F. Hultsch, Ph.D. Division of Individual and Family Studies, College of Human Development, The Pennsylvania State University, University Park, Pennsylvania

Edith Kaplan, Ph.D. Veterans Administration Medical Center, Boston and Department of Neurology, Boston University School of Medicine, Boston, Massachusetts

Marcel Kinsbourne, B.M., B.Ch., D.M. Neuropsychology Research Unit, Hospital for Sick Children, Toronto, Canada

Janet L. Lachman, Ph.D. Department of Psychology, University of Houston, Houston, Texas

Roy Lachman, Ph.D. Department of Psychology, University of Houston, Houston, Texas

Raymond S. Nickerson, Ph.D. Information Sciences Division, Bolt Beranek & Newman Inc., Cambridge, Massachusetts

Clyde A. Pentz, Ph.D. Division of Individual and Family Studies, The Pennsylvania State University, University Park, Pennsylvania

Marion Perlmutter, Ph.D. Department of Psychology, University of Minnesota, Minneapolis, Minnesota

Leonard W. Poon, Ph. D. Mental Performance and Aging Laboratory, Geriatric Research, Educational and Clinical Center, Veterans Administration Outpatient Clinic, Boston, and Departments of Psychiatry, Massachusetts General Hospital and Harvard Medical School, Boston, Massachusetts

Michael Prasse, B.A. Ethel Percy Andrus Gerontology Center, University of Southern California, University Park, Los Angeles, California

Elizabeth Robertson-Tchabo, Ph.D. College of Education, University of Maryland, College Park, Maryland

Timothy Salthouse, Ph.D Department of Psychology, University of Missouri-Columbia, Columbia, Missouri

Anne Sandoval, M.S. Department of Psychology, Brandeis University, Waltham, Massachusetts

Elliot Simon, Ph.D. Department of Psychology, Emory University, Atlanta, Georgia

Anderson Smith, Ph.D. School of Psychology, Georgia Institute of Technology, Atlanta, Georgia

Larry Squire, Ph.D. Veterans Administration Medical Center, La Jolla, California and Department of Psychiatry, University of California at San Diego, San Diego, California

Larry W. Thompson, Ph.D. Ethel Percy Andrus Gerontology Center, University of Southern California, University Park, Los Angeles, California

David Walsh, Ph.D. Ethel Percy Andrus Gerontology Center, University of Southern California, University Park, Los Angeles, California

Leslie Walsh-Sweeney, M.Ed. Veterans Administration Outpatient Clinic, Boston, Massachusetts

Nancy Waugh, Ph.D. University of Oxford, Oxford, England

Alan T. Welford, Sc.D. Department of Psychology, The University of Adelaide, Adelaide, South Australia

Arthur Wingfield, Ph.D. Department of Psychology, Brandeis University, Waltham, Massachusetts

Elizabeth Zelinski, Ph.D. Ethel Percy Andrus Gerontology Center, University of Southern California, University Park, Los Angeles, California

KEYNOTE
Memory and Age:
A Perspective View

Alan T. Welford
University of Adelaide, South Australia

IN MEMORIAM

George Talland's premature death 10 years ago deprived psychological gerontology, and indeed psychology in general, of one whose achievements were already substantial and who, had he lived, would by now have been one of the very brightest stars in the aging and human performance firmament. He brought to the study of aging a profound research interest and expertise in the field of cognitive pathology, the main thrust of which is shown in his book *Deranged Memory* (1965a). The quality of his mind is admirably displayed in his *Disorders of Memory and Learning* (1968b) published posthumously. Here we see a man who could rise above minutiae of methodology and petty theoretical squabbles to look his problems straight in the face, applying logic and common sense to the results of acute observation, and stating his conclusions with simplicity, penetrating insight, and a refreshing touch of humanity. This is the stuff of which great scientists in any discipline are made—qualities not always endearing to those who like their ideas to remain well ordered, but which are the means of driving a subject forward, freeing it from an endless round of ever more trivial details.

Talland's combining of interest in clinical disorders of memory and aging is understandable. Difficulties of learning and memory among older people are well recognized, and it is an obvious question to ask whether these can be regarded as due to mild forms of certain clinical syndromes. We do not attempt to deal with this question here, but instead look at the general situation of memory in relation to aging as understood in the 1960s, and at certain developments since that time. We then turn attention to some of the

1

wider ramifications of memory in skilled performance and thinking—areas where ignorance is as yet more prominent than knowledge, but where Talland's interests were obviously leading him and to which he provided some valuable pointers.

ROTE MEMORY, SIGNAL, AND NOISE

The theoretical position in the 1960s regarding memory and age is well exemplified in the contributions by Craik, Canestrari, Eisdorfer, and Talland himself in the book *Human Aging and Behavior*, which he edited (1968a). It was substantially influenced by two ideas. One, for which I must accept responsibility (Welford, 1956), was that the main loci of difficulty for older people in learning and memory are in the short-term retention which forms an essential link between perception and long-term registration, and in the process of search among memory traces at the time of recall: With age, the former become more liable to disruption by any shift of attention, and the latter become inefficient. The other idea was that proposed by Waugh and Norman (1965), who distinguished an ephemeral *primary memory* from a more enduring *secondary memory*, both of which they held to be involved in what is commonly regarded as short-term memory. They suggested that items are fed into the primary memory system until it is full, and then as further items arrive the earlier ones are either transferred to the secondary memory system or are lost. The immediate recall of some items can also displace others from primary memory. Of these two ideas, I now believe the first to be almost certainly wrong for reasons that will, I trust, become clear shortly. The second, despite a number of attacks, seems to stand up fairly well.

The substantial data now available regarding short-term memory in relation to age are confusing and not easy to interpret (for a review see Craik, 1977). However, it seems clear that the memory span in the sense of the number of items that, when presented, can immediately be repeated back without error falls little if at all with age, at least until the sixties. The same is true of the running memory span—the number of items that can be repeated from the end of a series longer than the ordinary memory span (Talland, 1965b). It is reasonable to assume, therefore, that the capacity of primary memory is little affected by age. However, older people do tend to recall less well than younger if the number of items to be recalled exceeds the span. For example, Smith (1975a) presented the numbers 1 through 8 in order each followed by a word, and then gave subjects the numbers in a different order, asking them to recall the appropriate word for each. He found that the last two words, if asked for first, were recalled equally well by subjects aged 20–39, 40–59, and 60–80. The older subjects' recall was, however, poorer of words presented earlier, which were liable to have been displaced from primary memory by the presentation of later numbers and words. Their recall was also poorer of the last two words presented if they were not recalled first and had thus been liable to have been displaced from primary memory by earlier recalls. In all these cases recall, when it occurs, is presumably from secondary memory, and the poorer recall of the older subjects could be due either to difficulty in recovering items from secondary memory or to the items not having been well recorded there. Other results to be considered shortly make the latter possibility the more likely, and support indications that failure of older people to recall is due basically to failure to pass material from primary to secondary memory (Drachman & Leavitt, 1972; see also Craik, 1977). It should be noted in passing that immediate recognition declines less with age then does immediate recall, presumably indicating that recognition has a less disruptive effect on primary memory (Craik, 1971; Smith, 1975b).

An important step forward in the study of memory was taken in the mid 1960s when signal detection theory was applied to recognition. The early work has been reviewed by Banks (1970). Items are presented for learning and are then presented again mixed with other items (distractors). On the second occasion, the subject is asked to indicate which of the items were presented before and which are new. The tendency of any item to be so indicated is assumed to vary from moment to moment due to some kind of random central activity or "neural noise" so that, over a period of time, the strength of tendency forms a roughly normal distribution. Presentation of an item for learning is assumed to add a constant to this tendency. The distributions for the items in the recognition list that have and have not been presented in the learning list can, therefore, be envisaged as those on the right and left sides respectively of Fig. K.1. The subject is assumed to fix a cutoff point and to treat any item with a momentary tendency at the time of recognition, which is

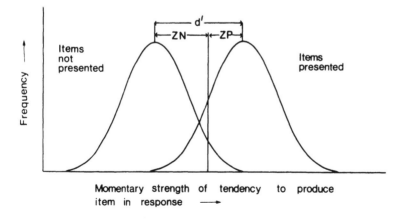

FIG. K.1. A signal detection theory model for recognition and recall.

above (to the right of) this cutoff, as having been presented before, and any item with a momentary tendency below the cutoff as new. The cutoff divides the distributions so as to produce the two pairs of proportions or probabilities necessary for signal detection theory analysis: (1) the probabilities that an item presented before will be recognised as such or will be regarded as new, and (2) the probabilities that a new item will be recognised as such or be regarded as having been presented before. If normality and equal variances of the distributions are assumed, d' can be calculated as a measure of recognition by summing the normal deviates (Z scores) corresponding to the first and to the second pairs of probabilities (e.g., McNicol, 1972). We shall denote these as ZP and ZN respectively as shown in Fig. K.1. The point of cutoff can be represented as β, that is the ordinate corresponding to ZP divided by that corresponding to ZN.

The importance of this application is partly that it provides a metric for learning and memory, but much more that it links memory to concepts of signal and noise already established in other fields of human capacity. In particular, it is known that the signal-to-noise ratio in discrimination tends to be lower in older people (Gregory, 1974; Vickers, Nettelbeck & Willson, 1972), due partly to sensory deficits which reduce signal levels and partly to increases of neural noise in the sense organs, afferent pathways, and brain. Application of these concepts to memory does not imply that memory deficits are attributable to poorer perception of material to be learned or in relation to which recall is required, but that memory itself depends on the signal-to-noise ratios of memory traces.

The theory is more difficult to apply to recall because we do not usually know how many effective distractors are operating, but it can be applied to a limited extent and doing so produces some important implications. We may consider by way of example the relationships between recognition and recall shown in an experiment by Bruning, Holzbauer, and Kimberlin (1975).

They presented visually to their subjects four lists of words, each once. Two of the lists were of high imagery words and two of low. One of each pair had to be recalled immediately after presentation, the other after a delay of 20 sec. Twenty-four hours later, subjects were asked to recall as many as they could of the 16 words they had seen, and were then given the 16 mixed randomly with a further 16 in a recognition test. The results are shown in Table K.1. The scores for short-term recall do not concern us, except to note that the proportion of words recognised correctly after 24 hr was in all cases within the range of the proportions recalled immediately or after 20 sec, and can reasonably be taken as the proportion that originally entered secondary memory.

The recognition results permit a rough calculation of d' and β, and these are given in Table K.1. Both scores fall with age. The fall of β can perhaps be regarded as a means of compensating to some extent for the fall of d',

TABLE K.1
Probabilities of Recall and Recognition of Words[a]

Age Group	High Imagery Words			Low Imagery Words		
	18–27	65–79	80–94	18–27	65–79	80–94
Recall at						
0 sec	.900	.738	.488	.863	.638	.338
20 sec	.825	.463	.200	.663	.325	.075
24 hr	.369	.131	.019	.213	.031	0
Recognition at 24 hr						
Correct	.834	.509	.488	.709	.444	.334
False	.044	.206	.263	.106	.225	.206
d'	2.68	.84	.60	1.80	.62	.39
β	3.07	1.40	1.22	1.87	1.32	1.27
Recall at 24 hr						
ZP	−.33	−1.12	−2.08	−.80	−1.87	<−2.50
Estimated ZN	3.01	1.96	2.68	2.60	2.49	>−2.89[b]

[a]Calculated from data reported by Bruning et al. (1975). Each entry is the mean for 20 subjects.

[b]This figure could not be calculated in the same way as the others in the row because none of the 80–94 age group recalled any words at 24 hr. It is based on the argument that if 20 subjects were trying to recall 8 words each, their cutoff would have to be at or above the point on the Presented Words distribution where $p = 1/(20 \times 8)$, i.e., .00625. This point is 2.50 standard deviations from the mean of the distribution. Therefore $ZN > 2.50 + .39 = 2.89$.

5

improving the chance of achieving correct recognitions at the risk of making more false ones. As regards recall at 24 hr, we can represent the proportion of words correctly recalled as a cutoff on the right-hand distribution of Fig. K.1, somewhat further to the right than the cutoff for recognition because the proportion recalled was less than that recognised. We can also calculate ZP. We have no means of calculating ZN, but since $ZN = d' - ZP$, we can estimate ZN from d' for recognition if we can assume that d' is the same for both recognition and recall. Experiments by the author, as yet unpublished, indicate that the assumption is justified provided most of the distractors used in the recognition task are in some way associated with the items to be recognised—for instance words which are semantically or phonemically similar to those presented. The assumption is further justified by experiments using a known familiar set of distractors—numbers from 10 to 99 (Davis, Sutherland & Judd, 1961; Welford, unpublished). Even if d' is not the same for recognition and recall, ZN for recall estimated by subtracting ZP for recall from d' for recognition may still be useful as a basis for comparing one recall with another, as will be seen later. It should be noted that when, as in the present case, correct recall is less than 50%, ZP is negative so that ZN is greater than d'.

The point of interest and importance is in the last line of Table K.1, which shows that ZN for recall estimated in this way does not, with one exception, differ greatly. The relative constancy of ZN suggests that subjects of all ages set their cutoff for recall at a point high enough to prevent all but a small proportion of false recalls, and that the poorer recall as well as the poorer recognition by older subjects can be attributed to a lower signal-to-noise ratio in their memory traces: It is not necessary to postulate any special difficulty of retrieval among older subjects.

The constancy between different groups of subjects of ZN for recall estimated in this way has been confirmed in further experiments not concerned with age (Felgenhaur, 1976; Welford unpublished), and is supported by findings that numbers of false recalls are also roughly constant including, as Talland (1968a) showed, those for different age groups.

To the extent that ZN for recall is constant, we can use ZP as an estimator of d' in recall. Especially if data are available for proportions of correct recalls over a number of trials, *differences* of ZP between earlier and later trials can be used to estimate the extent to which d' rises in the course of learning. An example, using data obtained by Witte and Freund (1976), is shown in Fig. K.2. The task was learning a series of 10 paired associates composed of one- or two-syllable words. Two groups of 60 subjects with mean ages of 65 and 19 were compared. The numbers of correct recalls reported by the authors for the first ten trials were converted to ZP scores and plotted against the square root of the number of trials. The square root was used because of the finding by Swets, Shipley, McKey, and Green (1959) that d' rose approximately linearly with the squre root of the number of exposures in a discrimination

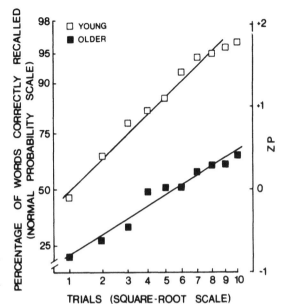

FIG. K.2. Percentages of words correctly recalled and corresponding values of ZP in 10 successive trials. Calculated from data reported by Witte and Freund (1976). The regression lines are fitted by least squares.

task. The theory is that, since d' is a measure of signal-to-noise ratio defined for a single presentation as $(\bar{X}_{S+N} - \bar{X}_N)/\sigma$, d' after several presentations will become

$$N(\bar{X}_{S+N} - \bar{X}_N)/\sqrt{N}\sigma^2 = \sqrt{N}(\bar{X}_{S+N} - \bar{X}_N)/\sigma$$

where $\bar{X}_{S+N}$ and $\bar{X}_N$ are the means at first presentation of the left-hand and right-hand distributions respectively of Fig. K.1, σ is their standard deviation, and N is the number of repetitions. It can be seen from Fig. K.2 that the increase of d' with the square root of the number of trials was roughly linear.

Two comments on the results shown in Fig. K.2 are pertinent:

1. The rate of learning by the older subjects was clearly lower, and the slopes of the regressions appear to provide a more elegant measure of this than trials to criterion or numbers of errors.

2. If the regression lines are extrapolated back to zero trials, that for the older subjects cuts the ordinate about four-tenths of a Z score unit below that for the younger. This suggests that although ZN may be constant over trials within either age group, it is higher for the older than for the younger.[1] The

---

[1] The author has shown in the unpublished experiments already referred to that the point at which the regression cuts the zero trials ordinate gives an estimate of ZN for recall independent of d' for recognition. Since at zero trials $d' = 0$, and $d' = ZP + ZN$, at zero trials $ZN = -ZP$. The slope of the regression is therefore a measure of d' for recall. It is accurate only if the number of false recalls does not change in later trials, but a method of correcting for such changes is available.

results are thus in line with those of Korchin and Basowitz (1957), who found that, during a series of trials at a rote learning task, older subjects tended to respond accurately or not at all—a tendency implying a high cutoff. The discrepancy between these results and those of Bruning et al. (1975) seems to merit further research. Meanwhile, it seems plausible to suggest that during learning the avoidance of false recalls is a wise strategy for older subjects as the errors they make tend to become ingrained and difficult to eliminate (Kay, 1951). Once learning is finished, however, a high cutoff will prevent correct as well as false recalls so that there is no advantage in a cutoff higher than that adopted by younger subjects.

Looking more generally at the implications of regarding memory in terms of signal-to-noise ratio, three further points may be made:

1. Since the effective strength of any memory trace varies from time to time, it is easy to see that it may sometimes fall below cutoff level so that the memory is unavailable, and at other times rise above it so that remembering is easy. The converse of this is that inappropriate items may sometimes rise above cutoff level and appear as slips of the tongue or as false yet confident recalls. All these effects are the subject of complaints by many older people and would follow from a low signal-to-noise ratio.

2. Registration in memory should be better if, when the material is presented, the signals are strong than if they are weaker—striking events tend to be remembered better than less impressive ones. Also, since effective signal strength can be accumulated over time, registration should be improved by taking more time to learn. It has been shown in the case of discrimination that the signal-to-noise ratio of older and younger subjects becomes equal if the older take more time than the younger (Vickers et al., 1972) and it is reasonable to suppose that an unconscious attempt to do the same in other performances leads to much of the slowness characteristic of older people (Welford, 1977b). One may wonder whether much of the forgetfulness and inability to learn, of which those in later middle age complain, are due to the pressures of life at its most responsible period preventing them from spending long enough to register events firmly. Certainly, extra time to learn has been shown to benefit older people in several laboratory tasks (see Arenberg & Robertson-Tchabo, 1977, pp. 426–428). So also have certain programs of training, especially the *discovery method* whereby the trainee is left, after a minimum of instruction, to find out for himself the way to work a machine or perform an operation (R. M. Belbin, 1965, 1969). Such conditions not only secure close attention to the task—thus producing stronger signals—but allow more time if this is needed. Under such conditions, middle-aged trainees have sometimes attained results equal to or better than those of younger ones (E. Belbin, 1958; E. Belbin & Downs, 1966; E. Belbin & Shimmin, 1964; Naylor & Harwood, 1973).

3. Accumulation of data over time is likely to occur at recall as well as during registration. In this way, a trace which over a short period may prove too weak to reach the criterion of recall might do so given more time to accumulate. If so, the many findings (see Arenberg & Robertson-Tchabo, 1977) that older people benefit substantially more than younger when longer times for recall are allowed are again explicable on the view that their memory traces are weaker, and it is not necessary to postulate any greater difficulty of searching material in store. Since forgetting usually appears not to be more rapid in older than in younger people, the weakness of the traces is presumably due to the poorer initial registration already discussed.

SOME EXTRAPOLATIONS

Traditional studies of rote memory using words, syllables, numbers, pictures, or designs clearly deal with only a part of human memory. In particular, they neglect four aspects which are of importance either theoretically or practically or both; (1) the fact known since the early years of the century that memory is schematic; (2) the acquisition of motor skills; (3) recent concepts of *working memory;* and (4) the holding of data in mind while thinking. We now consider these in turn.

Schematic Memory

This follows directly from the treatment of rote memory outlined here if two points are acknowledged. First, memory holds not only words, numbers, names, and sensory impressions of objects, but also a range of less tangible abstractions and inferences from them such as style, trends and expectations. Second, most learning consists in the selection for a particular purpose of items already registered in memory where they have a wealth of associations with other items along lines of similarity, sequential probability, desires, and fears. If signal-to-noise ratio is low but recall is nevertheless demanded, the subject may lower his cutoff point. If he does so, these associations will be likely to appear in the recall, filling gaps and producing a result which is plausible and coherent even if not wholly accurate. Such tendencies would account for the distortions of memory towards convention and familiarity noted by Bartlett (1932). Distortions along these lines would seem likely to increase with age because of both weaker traces and a wider network of associations gained in the course of long experience.

Motor Skills

Talland seems to have been fascinated by the fact that some of his patients with severe deficiencies of memory were nevertheless able to perform sensory-motor tasks quite well, and by the finding of Milner and her associates (Corkin, 1968; Milner, 1970) of patients who could not retain words or numbers but could nevertheless learn motor skills. Somewhat different mechanisms appear to be involved in verbal and motor learning and memory. However, many principles seem to be common to both. For example, the schematic quality of memory for narrative and events has its counterpart in motor skills where learned actions are tailored to their context, so that although in a sense they are repeated on different occasions, they are never exactly the same twice. Again the effects of spaced practice, progressive part learning, and rehearsal seem to be similar for both verbal and motor learning. A thoroughgoing attempt to compare and contrast the learning and memory of different types of material seems to be overdue. Meanwhile, it is reasonable to ask whether motor learning also can be considered relevantly in terms of signal-to-noise ratio.

Direct comparison between verbal and motor learning is usually difficult because the criteria of performance and methods of measurement are different. With material such as words or numbers, the relationship usually

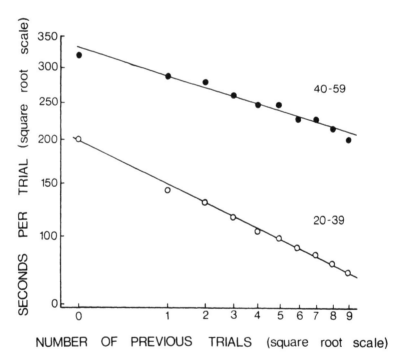

FIG. K.3. Times taken by subjects aged 20–39 and 40–59 to write the figures 1–9 and letter x so that they appeared normal when seen in a mirror. Ten trials were given. The subject's hand was hidden from direct vision but could be seen in the mirror. Data obtained by Szafran (see Welford, 1958, p. 137).

studied is between amount of practice and accuracy of reproduction, while time is either held constant or ignored. The same is true in some cases of motor learning, but in most cases practice is related to the time taken to perform the task to a roughly uniform level of accuracy. Can this case be treated in a way analogous to that of Fig. K.2? Tentatively the answer appears to be "yes." It can be argued that if the processes involved in motor performance work on a signal-to-noise ratio principle and to a given level of accuracy, data must be gathered until a criterion level of signal-to-noise ratio has been reached before action is triggered, and that the accumulation will rise as the square root of the time taken. If so, it can be further argued that the accumulation may come from two sources: first, the gathering of data during the actual trial concerned; and second, data carried by memory traces from previous trials—an amount depending on the square root of the number of previous trials. If these assumptions are correct, time spent on any trial and amount of previous practice should be compensatory, in the sense that if the square root of the first is plotted against that of the second, the result should be a straight line. Data by Szafran (see Welford, 1958/1973, p. 137) plotted in this way in Fig. K. 3 look promising, and suggest that further studies would be worthwhile. It can be seen that linearity is good for both age groups, with the older showing a somewhat lower rate of learning than the younger.

Working Memory

Talland conducted many experiments on sensory-motor performance in relation to age. These were largely an extension of an interest in Parkinsonism, but they seem to have been connected with his works on memory in that most of the tasks either obviously involved, or had been claimed by previous workers to involve, an element of memory, or were designed to study performance in which memory was specifically excluded (e.g., Talland, 1962, 1965c, 1966). The former can be regarded as elementary laboratory examples of what has come to be termed *working memory*. This involves the holding of data in mind in order to guide action until a task is complete, whereupon they are completely dismissed. Talland seems to have recognised that the memory involved is often more robust than primary memory, but is nevertheless ephemeral and therefore not to be regarded as a form of long-term memory, although it may be a selection of material held there. He noted evidence that a fairly protracted activity in the limbic system—up to two days in mice—is required for permanent registration to occur, and that the type of intermediate-term memory required could perhaps be attributed to activity in the limbic system which did not continue through to long-term registration. Such a view is perhaps supported by the finding that uncompleted tasks tend to be better remembered than completed ones— the so-called *Zeigarnik* effect: If the task is not finished, the data assembled for it remain in working memory for a longer time and thus have more chance of permanent registration.

Whatever the mechanism involved, working memory can be broadly divided into two types. First are rules of procedure illustrated in an elementary form by relationships of varying complexity between signals and responses in reaction-time tasks, and in more complex forms by the procedures in the skills of work and everyday life. Second is the keeping of a tally on developing events. This has been studied in elementary forms in the laboratory and is important at a more complex level for operators of process plants such as oil refineries, paper mills, and mechanised bakeries (Bainbridge, 1975; Beishon, 1967; Crossman, 1960). In these latter cases, the operator not only has to keep a tally of what is happening in different parts of the plant, but there is usually also an element of planning in that future events must be anticipated and a tally kept of what actions will be required to meet them. A somewhat similar tally is needed for complex manual operations in order to keep place in a sequence, remembering what has been done and what remains to be done. Indeed, a tally of this kind is the essence of all orientation in time.

Laboratory studies of working memory in relation to age have so far been fragmentary and not very conclusive. It has repeatedly been found that complex relationships between signals and responses in reaction-time tasks produce disproportionate slowing, error rates, or both in older subjects, and that the extent of the disproportion rises with the degree of complexity (see Welford, 1977a). However, it is not certain how far the difficulty lies in retaining the rule clearly, and how far it is due to inability to apply the rule quickly and accurately. On the other hand, Broadbent and Heron (1962), who required subjects to cross out certain digits on sheets of random numbers according to various complexities of rule, found no change between groups with mean ages of 20 and 52, although when the task was combined with one of identifying which of a string of 10 letters heard had occurred twice, the older subjects tended to neglect the additional task, implying that it overloaded their available storage capacity. The memory loads imposed in this task were, however, small compared with those of many process plants and other industrial and everyday tasks.

A difficulty of studying relationships between working memory and age in more realistic settings is that age brings experience which in turn brings better coding of signals and actions. Since memory seems to deal not so much with raw data as with coded units of information, better coding will effectively reduce the memory load of any task, so that the load may be effectively less for older people than for younger. If an introspective example is admissable, 40 years ago, if I was giving a lecture I had to write out every word in advance. Twenty years ago the points to be made had usually been well thought through and codified so that a lecture could be given using only a few notes indicating which points were to be made and in what order. Now, once again,

I like to use a fully prepared script because, although the coding has if anything improved, it is difficult to hold its full complexity in mind at any one moment, so that details and nuances tend to be forgotten in the heat of delivery. The lesson seems to be that in many practical situations making substantial demands on working memory, it is important to assess both capacity and efficiency of coding among older participants, because expert coding could sometimes obscure an incapacity of working memory which might be serious if unfamiliar or unexpected events such as plant failures occurred.

Thinking

When I was a student, one of the practical exercises we had to do was to think for 2 min about propositions such as "If you were given £1000 to spend within 24 hours, what would you do with it?" or "If there are more people in Birmingham than there are hairs on any one person's head, does it follow that there are two people in Birmingham with the same number of hairs on their heads?" When the two minutes were up, we had to dictate to a fellow student as full an account as possible of all that had passed through our minds during the period. The experiment was designed to test the claims made during the early years of the century that thought was mediated by sensory images, against those of the Wurtzburg School who held that thought was imageless. Years later, pondering over the task and many instances of thinking in everyday life, it seemed that both parties to the controversy had been right. Certainly thinking commonly involves a wealth of imagery, but the essential leaps from one stage to another seem to be devoid of images—they "just come" suddenly. Imagery seems to appear between the leaps and to store the results so far achieved while the next stage is being prepared outside consciousness. The amount of data capable of being stored in such images must be substantial: It does not typically consist of single items such as words or discrete objects, but of whole organised structures. For instance, one can store a considerable amount of data from an experiment in one's head and work on them in thought while out walking or lying awake at night. The amount that can be held upon occasion is far greater than a digit or word span and appears, in fact, to be a form of working memory.

Storage of a mass of data in this way seems to be easily disrupted by any distraction of attention. The images are mainly visual or auditory, or motor in the form of sub-overt movements, and it is perhaps significant that when thinking intensely we tend to shut our eyes, seek quiet, and either keep still or engage in very simple rhythmical actions. In other words, we cut down stimulation which might impair the signal-to-noise ratio of the imagery.

Be this as it may, there is clear evidence that temporary storage is often a source of limitation in problem solving, especially among older subjects. They have little difficulty, compared with younger subjects, at tasks such as adding where, in essence, the solution involves relating A to B to make C, then relating C to D to make E, and so on. The difficulty cannot, therefore, be due to inability to make the leap that A + B = C. Rather, difficulty appears when the task involves an operation such as relating A to B to make C and then holding C while D is related to E to make F, which has then to be related to C. The difficulty seems to arise with the intermediate storage. Older people have been found in a number of problem-solving tasks to forget intermediate solutions or data held while gathering further data. As a result, they may have to obtain the same data several times before reaching a solution (for examples, see Jerome, 1962; Welford, 1958, Chapter 8). It is possible that the same kind of difficulty caused the failure of many older subjects—and some younger ones—to solve complex logical problems set by Allan (see Welford, 1958, pp. 194–198). These required the subject to make deductions based on five separate statements in such a way that the implications of all of them had to be considered simultaneously. Failures were marked not so much by false deductions as by the making of comments on the statements separately without attempting to relate them together. Did the statements and their implications together exceed the available storage capacity?

Storage during thinking poses the same problem in relation to age as other forms of working memory in that, if the experience of age leads to better coding, older people may be able to achieve a given result with less storage capacity than younger. A converse problem is posed by speed: If the thinking processes take longer in older people, the load imposed on storage may be increased. The relationships among storage, coding, speed, and age are important because, if storage is the source of limitation, it should be possible to mitigate its effects by developing aids such as note-taking. Such aids are sometimes devised and used spontaneously by older subjects. For example, in a problem-solving task which involved arranging counters on a checkerboard to add up to marginal totals on rows and columns simultaneously, older subjects often marked a row or column to which they needed to refer later, by moving a counter slightly out of place (Clay, 1954). When talking to older people, it often seems that depth and penetration of insight are well preserved, but that the ability to sustain a *chain* of reasoning is impaired. Could the length of chain be increased by suitable training in the use of external aids to storage?

THE PRESENT POSITION

Looking over the current situation of learning and memory in relation to age, it seems fair to suggest four points. First, as regards basic principles of rote memory, our present knowledge appears to be reasonably coherent and complete, although new methods of measurement could lead to some clarification and there is still need for a good deal of mopping-up.

Second, the treatment of learning and memory set out here may seem stark. What about the subtleties of different strategies, varying situations, experience, education, health, and other variables? The importance of these is not denied, but it is suggested that their effects are of relatively few types—the subject's signal-to-noise ratio may be affected by a change of either signal or noise level, he can raise or lower his criterion, take more time or adopt other means to secure registration in secondary memory, maximize the use of primary memory, or restrict the range of potential distractors, but can do little else. In each case, the treatment proposed enables the effects to be measured in terms that transcend particular studies.

Third, although much less is known about the effects of age on learning motor skills, the main objectives for research and lines of advance are fairly obvious, and the time seems ripe for a determined and sustained attack.

The real challenges remaining appear to be in the area of working memory and thinking. Here is territory still largely uncharted, not only for gerontology but for psychology in general. It is fair to suggest that gerontological theory, with its simultaneous emphasis on both biology and behavior, is in a better position than more specialized branches of experimental psychology to lead the way. The challenge is all the greater because the endeavor does not, at least for the present, require large resources of either apparatus or facilities. The main requirement is an acute observer with a structured yet still open mind, with courage to look past methodological purism to follow hunches, and with a human sensitivity to appreciate the subtleties and details which tend to be flattened out in the experiments most of us do. In fact, the need is for just those qualities of mind that can be discerned in the work of the man in honor of whose memory this volume is dedicated.

ACKNOWLEDGMENT

I am grateful to Drs. L. W. Poon, J. L. Fozard, and T. M. Hines for valuable comments on an earlier draft of this chapter.

REFERENCES

Arenberg, D. and Robertson-Tchabo, E. A. Learning and Aging. In J. E. Birren & K. W. Schaie (Eds.), *Handbook of the psychology of aging.* New York: Van Nostrand Reinhold, 1977.

Bainbridge, L. The representation of working storage and its use in the organisation of behaviour. In W. T. Singleton & P. Spurgeon (Eds.), *Measurement of human resources.* London: Taylor & Francis, 1975.

Banks, W. P. Signal detection theory and human memory. *Psychological Bulletin,* 1970, *74,* 81–99.

Bartlett, F. C. *Remembering.* Cambridge University Press, 1932.

Beishon, R. J. Problems of task description in process control. *Ergonomics,* 1967, *10,* 177–186.

Belbin, E. Methods of training older workers. *Ergonomics,* 1958, *1,* 207–221.

Belbin, E., & Downs, S. Teaching paired associates: the problem of age. *Occupational Psychology,* 1966, *40,* 67–74.

Belbin, E., & Shimmin, S. Training the middle aged for inspection work. *Occupational Psychology,* 1964, *38,* 49–57.

Belbin, R. M. *Training methods for older workers.* Paris: O.E.C.D., 1965.

Belbin, R. M. *The discovery method: An international experiment in retraining.* Paris: O.E.C.D., 1969.

Broadbent, D. E., & Heron, A. Effects of a subsidiary task on performance involving immediate memory by younger and older men. *British Journal of Psychology,* 1962, *53,* 189–198.

Bruning, R. H., Holzbauer, I., & Kimberlin, C. Age, word imagery, and delay interval: Effects on short-term and long-term retention. *Journal of Gerontology,* 1975, *30,* 312–318.

Clay, H. M. Changes of performance with age on similar tasks of varying complexity. *British Journal of Psychology,* 1954, *45,* 7–13.

Corkin, S. Acquisition of motor skill after bilateral medial temporal-lobe excision. *Neuropsychologia,* 1968, *6,* 255–265.

Craik, F. I. M. Age differences in recognition memory. *Quarterly Journal of Experimental Psychology,* 1971, *23,* 316–323.

Craik, F. I. M. Age differences in human memory. In J. E. Birren & K. W. Schaie (Eds.), *Handbook of the psychology of aging.* New York: Van Nostrand Reinhold, 1977.

Crossman, E. R. F. W. *Automation and skill.* D.S.I.R. Problems of Progress in Industry (No. 9). London: H.M.S.O., 1960.

Davis, R., Sutherland, N. S., & Judd, B. R. Information content in recognition and recall. *Journal of Experimental Psychology,* 1961, *61,* 422–429.

Drachman, D. A., & Leavitt, J. Memory impairment in the aged: Storage versus retrieval deficit. *Journal of Experimental Psychology,* 1972, *93,* 302–308.

Felgenhaur, D. *Mental Health and retardation: Effects on short term and long term retention.* Unpublished thesis at the Department of Psychology, University of Adelaide, 1976.

Gregory, R. L. *Concepts and mechanisms of perception.* New York: Charles Scribner's Sons, 1974.

Jerome, E. A. Decay of heuristic processes in the aged. In C. Tibbitts & W. Donahue (Eds.), *Aging around the world.* Proceedings of the Fifth Congress of the International Association of Gerontology, San Francisco, 1960. New York: Columbia University Press, 1962.

Kay, H. Learning of a serial task by different age groups. *Quarterly Journal of Experimental Psychology,* 1951, *3,* 166–183.

Korchin, S. J. & Basowitz, H. Age differences in verbal learning. *Journal of Abnormal and Social Psychology,* 1957, *54,* 64–69.

McNicol, D. *A primer of signal detection theory.* London: Allen & Unwin, 1972.

Milner, B. Memory and the medial temporal regions of the brain. In K. H. Pribram and D. E. Broadbent (Eds.), *Biology of memory.* New York: Academic Press, 1970.

Naylor, G. F. K., & Harwood, E. Music for the elderly: Acquiring instrumental skill— Demonstration. *Proceedings of the Australian Association of Gerontology,* 1973, *2,* 26.

Smith, A. D. Aging and interference with memory. *Journal of Gerontology,* 1975, *30,* 319–325. (a)

Smith, A. D. Partial learning and recognition memory in the aged. *International Journal of Aging and Human Development.* 1975, *6,* 359–365. (b)

Swets, J. A., Shipley, E. F., McKey, M. J., & Green, D. M. Multiple observations of signals in noise. *Journal of the Acoustical Society of America,* 1959, *31,* 514–521.

Talland, G. A. The effect of age on speed of simple manual skill. *Journal of Genetic Psychology,* 1962, *100,* 69–76.

Talland, G. A. *Deranged memory.* New York: Academic Press, 1965. (a)

Talland, G. A. Three estimates of the word span and their stability over the adult years. *Quarterly Journal of Experimental Psychology*, 1965, *17*, 301–307. (b)

Talland, G. A. Initiation of response, and reaction time in aging, and with brain damage. In A. T. Welford and J. E. Birren (Eds.), *Behavior, aging, and the nervous system.* Springfield, Ill,: Charles C. Thomas, 1965. (c)

Talland, G. A. Visual signal detection as a function of age, input rate, and signal frequency. *Journal of Psychology*, 1966, *63*, 105–115.

Talland, G. A., ed. *Human aging and behavior.* New York: Academic Press, 1968. (a)

Talland, G. A. *Disorders of memory and learning.* Harmondsworth, England: Penguin, 1968. (b)

Vickers, D., Nettelbeck, T. & Willson, R. J. Perceptual indices of performance: The measurement of "inspection time" and "noise" in the visual system. *Perception*, 1972, *1*, 263–295.

Waugh, N. C. & Norman, D. A. Primary memory. *Psychological Review*, 1965, *72*, 89–104.

Welford, A. T. Age and learning: Theory and needed research. *Experientia*, Supplementum IV, 1956, 136–143.

Welford, A. T. *Aging and human skill.* Westport, Conn.: Greenwood Press, 1973. (Originally published by Oxford University Press for the Nuffield Foundation, 1958.

Welford, A. T. Motor performance. In J. E. Birren & K. W. Schaie (Eds.), *Handbook of the Psychology of Aging.* New York: Van Nostrand Reinhold, 1977. (a)

Welford, A. T. Causes of slowing of performance with age. *Interdisciplinary Topics in Gerontology*, 1977, *11*, 43–51. (b)

Witte, K. L. & Freund, J. S. Paired-associate learning in young and old adults as related to stimulus concreteness and presentation method. *Journal of Gerontology*, 1976, *31*, 186–192.

I LOCALIZATION OF DECLINE AND THE ROLE OF ATTENTION IN MEMORY

Edited by
David Arenberg

This section is divided into two parts. The first part examines age-related changes in encoding, storage, and retrieval processes, and includes chapters by Smith (Chapter 1) and by Salthouse (Chapter 2) and discussions by Arenberg (Chapter 3), and Hultsch and Pentz (Chapter 4). The second part examines the role of attention in these processes. Chapters by Craik and Simon (Chapter 5) and by Kinsbourne (Chapter 6) are included with discussions by Fredericksen (Chapter 7), Wingfield (Chapter 8), and Barr (Chapter 9).

Smith (Chapter 1) reviews the evidence for localization of age deficits in memory in the processes of encoding, storage, and retrieval. He points out that due to the sequential aspect of these processes, age deficits in any one make questionable conclusions about subsequent processes. It is concluded that evidence for an age deficit in encoding is substantial, nonexistent for storage, and difficult to evaluate for retrieval due to the dependence of successful retrieval on adequate encoding. Smith reviews recent studies using orienting tasks in incidental learning to explore age deficits in depth and elaboration of encoding processes, and states that the results confirm that the old use different processing strategies and tend to organize spontaneously less than young adults.

Salthouse (Chapter 2) identifies four potential sources of research strategies for understanding age deficits: memory theory, memory data, aging theory, and data on aging. He points out that most of the reported research on memory and aging stems from memory theory. He further suggests that the inconsistencies in findings of studies attempting to localize age deficits in encoding, storage, or retrieval may be due to an incorrect assumption, i.e., that theories of memory are appropriate for identifying dimensions on which old and young differ. From data on aging and behavioral slowing, he proposes that memory deficits with age are attributable to slower rehearsal speed. He presents a study to test this hypothesis, and the results are supportive.

Arenberg (Chapter 3) discusses control processes and structural mechanisms and how they may relate to age differences in encoding and in incidental learning with semantic orienting tasks. In his view, encoding deficits are primarily in the domain of control processes and should be amenable to memory training, whereas age differences in recall with semantic orienting tasks are more likely to result from structural impairment and are unlikely to be ameliorated by memory training. In response to Salthouse's vexing question about why older people shift to encoding procedures which are less effective, Arenberg offers the possibility that there may be no shift; that is, low-effort encoding that suffices for adequate performance in young adults may become less effective with age. He also suggests that Smith's rejection of increased susceptibility to interference with age is premature. Arenberg agrees that evidence for age-related interference effects in secondary memory is virtually nil, but believes that age differences in interference are likely in primary memory with concurrent distraction.

Hultsch and Pentz (Chapter 4) point out that encoding, storage, and retrieval processes are components of multistore models of memory consistent with an organismic world view, and that aging in this view results in biological degeneration and behavioral decrement. In a contextual world view, memory is a byproduct of events and their contexts, and remembering is a reconstruction of past events. Aging in this view results in change, but includes growth as well as decrement reflecting both biological and environmental influences. A contextual view of memory and aging emphasizes meaning rather than accuracy, broad rather than narrow contexts, and historical and life events as well as age changes.

In the second part of this section, Craik and Simon (Chapter 5) call attention to the movement in recent thinking about information processing from emphases on components and subsystems in flow systems (e.g., encoding, storage, and retrieval) to more holistic views such as depth of processing. They review recent ideas about depth of processing and describe the concepts of elaboration, congruity, and distinctiveness in that context. They discuss the results of several recent studies which, in general, provide evidence that the old process events less deeply and elaborately than do young adults as a consequence of reduced "processing resource." A similarity between aging and divided attention, according to Craik and Simon, is that processing resource is reduced in both. Effort is proposed as one reason that older people process less deeply and elaborately. Several research directions within the framework of depth of processing are suggested to improve our understanding of memory and aging.

Kinsbourne (Chapter 6) begins by observing that existing theoretical models of cognitive impairment with age have reached an impasse. He discusses opponent processes in the brain and how they determine attention. Asymmetric neuronal depletion, Kinsbourne points out, can result in imbalances in opponent processes leading to attentional impairment; locus, distribution, and duration of attention depend upon the integrity of opponent processes. Some attentional imbalances, such as impulsiveness versus perseverative compulsivity, can be corrected with psychoactive drugs which are already used with children (highlighting the need for individual assessment of cognitive deficits for the impaired elderly). He states that the most pervasive effect of neuronal depletion in the aged is to limit selective attentional processes. Kinsbourne discusses state dependence and how it relates to aging and memory. He also discusses divided attention and relates it to the functional cerebral distance principle, suggesting that functional cerebral distances become shorter with advanced age and cortical thinning, resulting in increased interference between concurrent tasks. He concludes with the observation that "encoding deficits are deficits of attending."

Frederiksen (Chapter 7) stresses the need for psychometric validation of concepts and laboratory measures of memory and attention before using them to explain age differences in performance. With the chapters of Craik and Simon and Kinsbourne specifically in mind, Frederiksen urges that the concept of general attentional deficit be put to test by demonstrating convergent and discriminant validity. He points out that recent studies do not demonstrate a general attentional factor in young adults, but rather suggest several components of processing limitations in time-sharing tasks. It remains to be seen whether, in older people, these components are substantially correlated, thus providing evidence for "a general loss of attentional resources."

Wingfield (Chapter 8) identifies some advantages and disadvantages of the shift in Craik's model from a fixed-order hierarchy of processing to a more flexible but more complex position involving elaboration as well as depth of processing. He points out the similarity of Craik and Simon's ideas involving encoding specificity to Kinsbourne's arguments for state-dependent processes, and expresses excitement and hope about "the development of a single position within functional and neuropsychological frameworks." Failures to process deeply by the elderly, according to Wingfield, may not represent limited attentional resources so much as differential allocation strategies. He notes a need to add "speed of processing" to the other aspects of processing, for "elaboration, depth and attentional processing all lie along temporal dimensions." He points out that, although memory deficits, in both old people and in children, are attributable to problems in encoding specificity and in using appropriate retrieval cues, the vast difference in experience between the old and the very young may make it possible to disentangle fixed resource limitations from optional strategies.

Barr (Chapter 9) discusses his attempt to establish a taxonomy of performance measures with different age functions, a goal he found unattainable at this time. When he reviewed the dichotic-listening literature, he found consistent linear declines in performance on second half spans. Age curves for other learning, memory, and problem-solving tasks, however, were quite varied with many showing age differences only late in life. Barr pointed out that if Craik and Simon's suggestions concerning processing resource are correct, then as processing demands of a task increase, the age function should become more like the linear functions found in divided-attention tasks such as dichotic listening.

The reader is invited to proceed to the chapters which follow in this section, and to savor the wealth of knowledge and ideas contained in them. It will be a satisfying and enriching experience.

1 Age Differences in Encoding, Storage, and Retrieval

Anderson D. Smith
Georgia Institute of Technology

To remember something requires three things. First, the information must be encoded or learned; second, the information must be stored during a retention interval anchored by original encoding on one end and the time of test on the other; and third, the information must be retrieved at the time memory is tested. In investigating the relationship between adult age and memory, a popular research endeavor has been to assign age differences on memory tasks to one of these three stages in the memory process. A series of studies can be found in the literature, each addressing some part of the overall question, are older subjects primarily deficient in encoding, in storage, or in retrieval?

A simple answer to this question, however, is difficult to give. Different researchers at different times have implicated all three stages in their attempts to specify the locus of the memory deficit seen in older age groups. Some researchers have attributed the age deficit to processing differences during learning (e.g., Eysenck, 1974), others have suggested that older persons are more susceptible to interference during the storage stage (e.g., Welford, 1958), and still others have concluded that the differences are due to greater retrieval difficulty in the older age groups (e.g., Craik, 1977). The purpose of this chapter is to review a sample of studies that either support or fail to support these three hypotheses and, in addition, to point out some of the problems and issues inherent in this research approach. The studies to be discussed by no means exhaust the literature, but only serve to illustrate the research being conducted and the conclusions being reached. The three hypotheses that localize age differences at either encoding, storage, or retrieval will be considered in the historical sequence of their popularity in the literature.

THE STORAGE STAGE: TRACE RETENTION

The storage stage refers to the interval of time between encoding at input and retrieval at output when the information is held in memory. Effects on memory during this stage would be caused by intervening events that somehow "interfere" with the maintenance or storage of the to-be-remembered information. If susceptibility to interference varies as a function of age, then differences in storage could account for many of the memory differences seen between age groups. This was a popular view among early investigators of age effects (Cameron, 1943; Kay, 1959; Welford, 1958). During that era, interference theory was the accepted account of forgetting, and so it was logical to assume that differences in forgetting between age groups were due to differences in the effects of interference. However, there is very little empirical evidence to support this view. Kausler (1970) has pointed out that many of the early investigations failed to equate learning ability between age groups, and that differential forgetting across the retention interval was probably due to differences in the levels of original learning. In addition, recent attempts to produce differences in interference between age groups have not been successful.

Interference effects can be either proaction, interference from previously learned material, or retroaction, interference from tasks interpolated between the input and recall of the to-be-remembered information. Several different experiments have found no increased effect of proactive interference in older age groups (Craik, 1968; Fozard & Waugh, 1969; Talland, 1968). Proactive interference was found, but the nature of the effect was the same for both young and old subjects. Because interference from previous learning experiences could have affected the processing at input, it is not clear that differences in proaction could be assigned to the storage stage anyway.

Differences in retroactive interference, however, would reflect storage differences. But, as with proactive interference, differences in retroactive interference are not typically seen between age groups (Gladis & Braun, 1958; Smith, 1974; 1975a). In fact, Craik (1977) concluded after reviewing the literature on retroactive interference and age: "Despite the popularity of this view, ... there is *no* good evidence to back it up [p. 407]."

Taub and his associates (Taub, 1968; Taub & Grieff, 1967; Taub & Walker, 1970) have suggested that the older age groups might be unduly affected by a specific kind of retroaction, response interference—the inability to maintain information in memory while simultaneously making a response. In his experiments, larger age differences were seen in the recall from the second half of a recall sequence. However, in a recent experiment looking at response interference in a more systematic fashion, differential age effects were not found. Using the paired-associate probe technique (Tulving & Arbuckle, 1966) , Smith (1975a) factorially combined the position of stimulus–response pairs at presentation and recall such that across lists and subjects, every combination of input position and output position was examined individually. By using this method, the effects of response interference could be examined as a function of the input position of the pairs during presentation. By examing the relationship between output position and serial position at input, the method allowed a separation of response interference effects primarily due to primary memory from ones due to secondary memory (Arbuckle, 1967). Taub's studies often did not distinguish between these two effects. For response interference to be an adequate account of age differences in memory, secondary memory effects should be found. The results of the Smith (1975a) experiment are presented in Fig. 1.1. For the portions of the input list assumed to be recalled primarily from secondary memory (Input Positions 1, 2, 3, 4, 5, and 6), there was no interaction between age and the

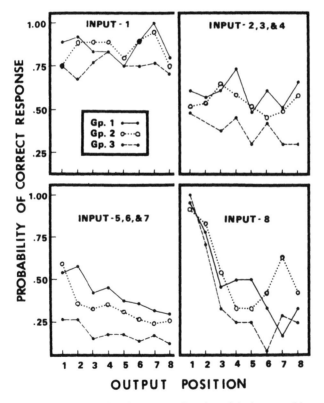

FIG. 1.1. The probability of recall as a function of the input position and output position of each pair in an eight-item paired-associate list. Input positions are represented in separate frames of the figure. The age groups are: Group 1, 20–39 years; Group 2, 40–59 years; and Group 3, 60–80 years (from Smith, 1975a).

output positions of the pairs. For the recency portion of the list, age effects were found, but only at the later output positions. This interaction (e.g., Input Position 7 and 8) probably had nothing to do with differential response interference in secondary memory, however, but rather was due to the transient nature of primary memory. Age effects are typically not seen in primary memory (e.g., Botwinick & Storandt, 1974), and thus an interaction between age and output position for the recency portion of the list reflects the decreasing role of primary memory in the recall of the responses. By delaying the recall to late in the response sequence, the probability of recalling the response from secondary memory increases and so do the age differences.

In summary, little evidence supports the view that older age groups are more vulnerable to interference effects. The storage hypothesis assumes that something happens to the memory trace as time passes, or as other activity occurs during the retention interval. Even when the retention intervals are very long, forgetting over the intervals is very similar in different age groups. Warrington and Silberstein (1970), for example, found little change in the magnitude of age differences when the retention interval was extended to as much as 18 months for recognition of news events. There were no differences between the age groups at either 6, 12, or 18 months. If older persons were more susceptible to interference, one would expect larger and larger age differences with longer and longer retention intervals. This was not found, however.

THE RETRIEVAL STAGE: TRACE UTILIZATION

By the late 1960s, the interference or storage hypothesis was replaced in popularity by the retrieval hypothesis. Instead of the memory trace being changed or lost during the retention interval, the retrieval hypothesis attributed the memory deficit to a failure of accessibility at the time of test, cue-dependent forgetting rather than trace-dependent forgetting (Tulving, 1974). A variety of experimental techniques have been used by the memory researcher to assess the retrieval process, and these techniques have been adopted for use in aging studies. A list of these procedures is presented in Table 1.1. One method of isolating retrieval has been to manipulate only the conditions at the time of test, as in the first two procedures listed in the table. If the experimental treatment can be kept constant until the time memory is tested, then differences in performance should reflect only the conditions of retrieval. Therefore, by using memory tests that minimize the retrieval requirement (e.g., recognition or cued recall), age differences should be reduced to the extent that they reflect differences in retrieval difficulty. For the third method listed in the table, different dependent variables that are assumed to be differentially sensitive to the different stages of memory can be

TABLE 1.1
Procedures Used to Examine Retrieval as a Separate Stage
of Memory

1.	Comparison of recall and recognition
2.	Comparison of free and cued recall
3.	Comparison of recall of units (NC) and items within units (IPC)
4.	Manipulation of the study and test requirements of the task
5.	Manipulation of variables known to affect retrieval differently

used. The fourth method involves manipulation of the relative importance of storage and retrieval as requirements in the task, by varying the amount of study and test in the learning task. In the last method listed in the table, variables assumed to affect retrieval differently from the other stages are manipulated to determine possible interactions with the age variable. All of these techniques have been used in age research and will be considered separately.

Schonfield and Robertson (1966), in an often cited and important study, showed that age differences were not found when recognition was used to test memory rather than recall. Because the items are provided at the time of test, recognition is assumed to be less sensitive to retrieval problems. The interaction between age and method of test (recall versus recognition) has been replicated in other experiments in the literature (e.g., Craik, 1971; Smith, 1975b), and while some investigators have found significant age differences in recognition, the effects are typically much smaller than differences in recall (e.g., Erber, 1974). Comparison of recall and recognition has also been used recently by White (reported in Craik, 1977) to test a retrieval interpretation of age effects seen in orienting task studies. The large effect of age on recall following a semantic orienting task was reduced when recognition was substituted for recall as the method of test. Again, age differences were minimized by using recognition tasks.

Similar effects have been shown with comparisons of free and cued recall. When categorical labels as retrieval cues are provided at test, age effects are greatly reduced if not eliminated (Hultsch, 1975; Laurence, 1967; Smith, 1977). In one conflicting experiment, however, Drachman and Leavitt (1972) failed to find reduced age differences in cued recall. In their experiment, the initial letter of each word was used as the retrieval cue and age differences in cued recall were similar to age differences in free recall. In a later experiment, Smith (1977) found that the relative effectiveness of the different cues was probably the reason for Drachman and Leavitt's failure to find an interaction between age and the presence of retrieval cues. Smith (1977) found that age groups were differentially sensitive to the presence of semantic categorical cues, but not to the initial letter cues like the ones used by Drachman and Leavitt.

One interesting finding in the Smith (1977) experiment was that providing the semantic cues at presentation, even when they were not provided at recall, was sufficient to improve recall of the older subjects to the level of the younger subjects. These data are presented in Fig. 1.2. While the results might be accounted for by a retrieval hypothesis indirectly, by stressing the importance of encoding retrieval cues during presentation, this interpretation implicates retrieval only as a byproduct of faulty processing at input. By providing category labels to the subjects during presentation, the older subjects processed the items more like younger subjects. Thus, the processing deficit was overcome and the age effect reduced.

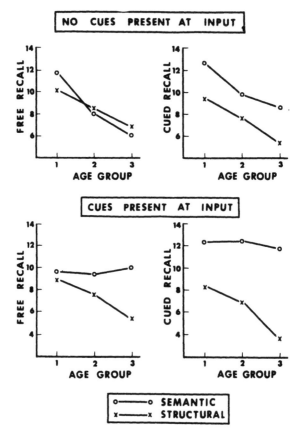

FIG. 1.2.   Free and cued recall performance with either semantic (category labels) or structural (initial letters) cues for three age groups: Group 1, aged 20–39; Group 2, 40–59; and Group 3, 60–80 (from Smith, 1977).

A third way to separate retrieval from the other stages of memory is to use different dependent measures. For example, Craik and Mansani (1969) found that age effects on recall of a categorized list were due to differences in the number of different categories represented in the recall protocols of the subjects. No age differences were found in the number of items recalled per category, given that a category was recalled. Recall of the categories as higher-order units is assumed to be determined by the retrieval plan (Tulving & Pearlstone, 1966). More recently, Hultsch (1975) replicated the age differences in category recall, supporting the retrieval hypothesis, but unlike Craik and Masani, he also found differences in the number of items recalled per category. This finding indicates that young subjects might also be organizing more information into categories when the list is being presented.

The next method isolates retrieval by varying the requirements of the task. This method was first used by Tulving (1967) and more recently used by Hogan and Kintsch (1974). The subject either receives three study trials followed by a single recall of the list (SSST), or one single study trial followed by three successive recall trials (STTT). The four-trial cycle is then repeated several times in a multitrial task. Using college-aged subjects, Tulving (1967) found no differences between SSST and STTT in the overall learning of a word list, pointing out the importance of retrieval in the test trial for improvement during learning. The test trial had the same effect on learning as did a further presentation of the list. In an unpublished Masters thesis from our laboratory, Crew (1977) used this method with two different adult age groups (aged 20-50 and 51-80 years). Each subject received four cycles for a total of 16 trials, followed by one further study and test trial. The results of this experiment are presented in Fig. 1.3. For the younger subjects, the original Tulving (1967) results were replicated. It made little difference whether the SSST or the STTT condition was used. In the older group, however, performance was worse with the STTT condition. One could argue that the STTT condition requires a greater reliance on retrieval, and when the retrieval component was emphasized in the task, the older group did not do as well. In other words, a retrieval deficit in the older group kept them from taking full advantage of the test trials in the STTT condition.

However, as with the cued-recall study discussed earlier, an alternative interpretation is tenable. One could also argue that only one study trial per cycle was insufficient for the older subject to encode the material effectively. When three encoding opportunities are provided prior to test, the older subject then performs at a level comparable to the young.

The final method listed in Table 1.1 involves the manipulation of variables that are assumed to affect retrieval differently from the other stages of memory. For example, list length is one such variable, since the probability of finding a word in memory decreases as the number of words in the list increases (Shiffrin, 1970, 1976). A variable like presentation rate, on the other

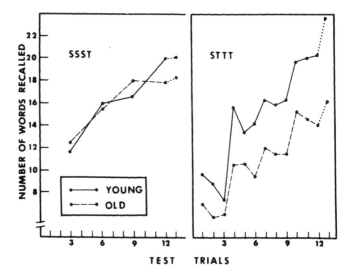

FIG. 1.3.   Mean number of correct words recalled across 16 acquisition trials for two age groups in each of two presentation conditions: (1) SSST—three study sessions followed by a single test session; and (2) STTT—three tests following a single presentation of the list.

hand, should affect the processing stage of memory. Presentation rate determines the amount of study time available to encode and rehearse the items. Smith (1976) manipulated these two variables, presentation rate and list length, together with adult age. As predicted, there was no interaction between presentation rate and age, replicating earlier research (e.g., Monge & Hultsch, 1971). But unexpectedly, there was also no interaction between list length and age. If list length had interacted with age as predicted by the retrieval hypothesis, a function of greater slope would have been found for the older age group. Craik (1968) had earlier reported such an interaction between age and list length—larger age effects were found with longer lists. However, Craik included list lengths in this study that were well below the immediate memory span. The interaction with age, therefore, could have been caused by the increasing role of secondary memory in recall as list lengths were increased to levels above the span of primary memory.

One conceptual problem with the list-length variable is that increasing the number of items to be remembered not only makes retrieval more difficult, but also increases the number of items that are interpolated between the presentation and recall of any single item in the list. While a problem of interference with storage seems unlikely in light of the research discussed earlier, an additional experiment was recently completed in our laboratory to clarify the relationship between age and the number of items presented in a list. Using the "delayed-recall" method developed by Shiffrin (1970), list length was varied in two ways by asking the subject to recall, not the list just seen, but the list that occurred prior to the one just presented. In other words, another to-be-recalled list always was interpolated between the presentation of any list and its subsequent recall. Two effects of list length could then be separated, the length of the list being recalled (retrieval) and the length of the list interpolated between presentation and recall (storage). The effects of list length as an interfering activity was assessed separately from the effects of list length on retrieval. Each list was either 10, 20, or 40 items long, and each subject was tested on 11 lists in one of the following two list orders:

Order 1: 20–10–20–20–40–20–10–10–40–40–10
Order 2: 20–20–40–40–10–40–20–20–10–10–20

The first 20-item list served only as a practice list and was not included in the analyses. The results of the experiment are presented in Fig. 1.4. The length of the list during the retention interval was significant, but this variable did not interact with age, in that all subjects recalled a smaller proportion of the longer lists regardless of age. List length, as interference with storage, does not seem to be important in determining age differences, supporting the conclusions made earlier.

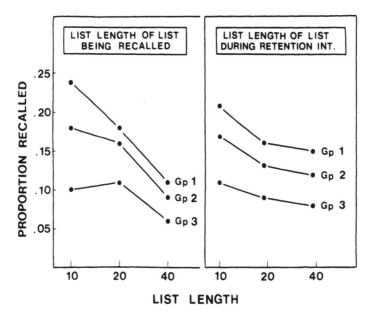

FIG. 1.4. The mean proportion of words recalled in three age groups is plotted as a function of the two list length variables using the Shiffrin (1970) delayed-recall procedure. The age groups are: Group 1, 20–39 years; Group 2, 40–59 years; and Group 3, 60–80 years.

There was a significant interaction, however, between age and the length of the list being recalled. This interaction is seen in the left panel of Fig. 1.4, but reflects a greater effect of age on recall from the shorter lists. Even though an interaction between age and list length was found, the results do not seem to support the retrieval hypothesis as originally proposed. The retrieval hypothesis predicted an interaction in the opposite direction of the one obtained. Larger age effects should have been found with the longer lists. Instead, age had larger effects on the shorter lists.

As with much of the research discussed so far, the results of the list-length study do not seem to support the retrieval hypothesis directly. The interaction, however, can be explained by proposing age differences in processing at the time of input. To recall information successfully, it must be encoded and later retrieved, and because recall depends on gaining access to the items at the time of test, a strategy that maximizes accessibility would be best for recall. One such strategy is organization, the process of interrelating items at the time of presentation. In other words, retrieval depends on organizational encoding, and if the older subjects engaged in less spontaneous organization, they would be less affected by list length. Increasing the list length makes organization more difficult. With a single presentation of a 40-item list, for example, effective organization would be difficult, if not impossible. The reason for the interaction between list length and age might be the dependency of the younger group on organizational processing during encoding, a strategy that becomes less and less effective as list length is increased. Older subjects are affected less by increases in list length because they rely less on organization as an encoding strategy.

To see if the obtained interaction between age and list length is reliable, the effects of list length were examined without the complicated Shiffrin (1970) procedure. Subjects of different ages either received 15 or 30 items followed by immediate recall. Because different list lengths are being compared, the number of items recalled is confounded with the number of items presented. Proportion scores, computed by dividing the number recalled by the number presented, are better dependent measures in these experiments (Shiffrin, 1971). As can be seen in Fig. 1.5, list length again had a larger effect on the younger subjects than on the older subjects, replicating the interaction. The same analysis could be performed on Craik's (1968) data and greatly change the nature of his interaction. Craik had used the absolute number of words recalled as his dependent measure. If list lengths below the immediate memory span were removed and proportion scores were used, the list length effects reported by Craik might have been considerably different.

As indicated by the discussion so far, many of the results dealing with the retrieval hypothesis are equivocal in terms of interpretation. There seems to be an alternative hypothesis which assumes that older subjects are deficient in organizational processing. One problem with the research dealing with

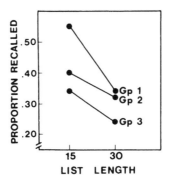

FIG. 1.5. The results of the Smith (1976) study reanalyzed in proportion scores to show the list-length effect in three different age groups: aged 20–39, 40–59, and 60–80 years.

retrieval as a separate entity is that retrieval is primarily a reconstruction of the encoding situation (Tulving & Thompson, 1973). For this reason, deficits attributable to faulty or ineffective retrieval could be due to different encoding strategies used at the time of learning. In other words, retrieval problems may exist, but they are caused by the different ways in which the age groups encoded the items during input.

For example, differential age effects on recall and recognition are usually attributed to retrieval differences. This conclusion, however, is based on the assumption that all the conditions of the experiment are held constant up to the time of test. This assumption is questionable when a subject variable, such as age, is manipulated. If the subjects differ in processing strategy, which is the conclusion of this discussion, then the conditions of encoding are certainly not constant, and differences between recall and recognition performance could be due to differences in processing for the two tasks.

In fact, recent studies in the memory literature have demonstrated differences between recall and recognition in sensitivity to various processing strategies (e.g., Connor, 1977; Griffith, 1975; Winograd & Smith, 1978). Organizational processing is appropriate for recall and might be inappropriate for recognition (Eagle & Leiter, 1964). When recognition memory is used to test memory, organizational strategies sometimes lead to poorer performance (Griffith, 1975). If older subjects engage in less organizational processing, then their recall would be poorer, but not recognition since it is not as sensitive to differences in organizational processing.

The same argument could be made for cued recall. Not only are the conditions of the experiment different at the time of test when different age groups are used, but in the cued recall paradigm, organizational cues are typically provided at input which would increase organizational encoding in the older age group, and thus attenuate the age effect in the cued recall condition. In Fig. 1.2, no difference was found in free recall when the cues were provided at input. Likewise, Hultsch (1969) has shown that specific organizational instructions to older subjects reduces age differences in recall performance. Older subjects do not spontaneously organize, but they can organize when instructed to do so.

To summarize, experiments originally designed to investigate potential retrieval deficits in older subjects seem to suggest an alternative hypothesis. Older subjects may not be processing the information in the same manner as younger subjects.

THE ENCODING STAGE: TRACE FORMATION

Current research in human memory emphasizes the encoding stage, a trend in part due to the "depth of processing" ideas of Craik and his associates (Craik & Lockhart, 1972; Craik & Tulving, 1975; Jenkins, 1974). The research approach typically used is to vary processing at input by manipulating instructional conditions. Subjects are told to do different things before or during presentation, and then the effects of the different instructions or processing tasks on memory performance are determined. Three different modes of processing will be considered: (1) organization, the encoding of the relationships among the different items in a list; (2) elaboration, the degree of verbal encoding for each individual item; and (3) imagery, the encoding based on visual rather than verbal attributes.

The discussion so far has focused on the hypothesis that older subjects engage in less organizational encoding during learning than younger subjects. Because organizational processing is influenced by the specific instructions to the subjects, the structure of the list, and the experimental conditions, organization can be studied in different ways.

First, the degree of organization can be directly measured in the recall protocols of the subjects. However, direct attempts to measure organizational deficits in older age groups have produced conflicting findings. In an often cited experiment, Laurence (1966) reported that while young and old subjects differed in recall performance, they displayed the same amount of organization in their recall protocols as measured by Tulving's (1962) index of "subjective organization." Using a different measure, however, Hultsch (1974) found age differences in organization. Hultsch used Bousfield and Bousfield's (1966) measure of intertrial repetition, and pointed out that the measure used by Laurence (1966) penalized the younger subjects for learning more rapidly. In a recent paper by Sternberg and Tulving (1977), comparisons were made between the different measures of subjective organization that have been used in the literature, and the "pair frequency" measure was found to be the most reliable and valid of the ones available. In their paper, Sternberg and Tulving reanalyzed the organization data collected by Laurence in another study she conducted with children and found age

TABLE 1.2
Mean Subjective Organization in Three Age Groups

Age Group	Trials			
	1–2	2–3	3–4	4–5
Group 1 (aged 20–39)	2.55	4.37	8.56	11.60
Group 2 (aged 40–59)	2.49	4.46	7.63	9.60
Group 3 (aged 60–80)	1.61	2.27	3.63	5.59

differences in organization with the "pair frequency" measure even though Laurence had reported none.

In a recent study completed in our laboratory, subjective organization was measured in different adult age groups using the method suggested by Sternberg and Tulving (1977). A 60-word list was presented to different age groups for five trials. The results of this experiment are presented in Table 1.2. The results show clear differences in organizational scores between the age groups. In addition, the growth in organization across trials was greater in the younger age group.

Organization has also been studied by manipulating instructions or the experimental conditions of the task in an attempt to control the degree of organizational processing during encoding. Hultsch (1971), for example, had subjects sort the words into categories prior to the memory task, a technique developed by Mandler (1967) to control organizational encoding. Half of Hultsch's subjects were instructed to sort words into from two to seven categories prior to recall (Organization condition). The remaining subjects simply inspected the words before testing (Control condition). Hultsch found no differences in sorting performance; all subjects used approximately the same number of categories while sorting. Even though sorting behavior was the same, differences were found in later recall performance. There was also an interaction between age and condition. Although age differences were found in recall following the sorting task, larger age effects were found for subjects in the Control condition who were not encouraged to organize the material. This interaction suggests that age decrements in recall could be due to organizational differences, even though no differences were found in the original sorting task.

The fact that Hultsch (1971) found that the sorting task reduced the age differences seen in recall performance suggests that the age deficit in organization might only be a "production deficit" problem (Reese, 1976). In other words, the older subjects fail to organize, but not because they cannot perform the organization carried out by younger subjects. In another experiment mentioned earlier, Hultsch (1969) found that providing the proper instructions can compensate for the organizational deficit. Subjects in each of three age groups were assigned to one of three different instructional conditions. In one condition, subjects were given standard free recall instructions. In a second condition, subjects were given nonspecific instructions to organize the words. A third group was given a specific means of organizing. Hultsch found that the age decrement was reduced with the specific organizational plan. The older subjects were "compensated" by the specific instructions which helped them to organize efficiently.

In addition to organizational processing, there is evidence to suggest that older subjects are deficient in verbal elaboration, the effective processing of each individual item. Verbal elaboration is usually studied by giving subjects different orienting tasks to perform during presentation that are assumed to differ in the amount of elaboration required to perform them. In general, the more semantic the task, the more elaborate the processing, and the better the recall. For example, Craik and Tulving (1975) have shown that a category placement task (i.e., deciding whether or not the to-be-remembered word belongs to a particular category) leads to better memory than a task requiring a decision about some physical feature of the word (e.g., deciding whether the word contained the letter "e"). The semantic task is assumed to lead to a more elaborate encoding of the item, and more elaboration leads to a better and more stable memory trace.

If the level of elaboration reached by older subjects is less than the level reached by younger subjects during encoding, then a resultant weaker memory trace could account for much of the observed age difference in memory performance.

In one experiment examining age differences with the orienting task procedure, Eysenck (1974) found support for the elaboration-deficit hypothesis. Different age groups were given different orienting tasks to perform, after which they were tested by free recall. Eysenck observed greater age differences when the orienting task involved elaborative processing. It seems that the older group was especially disadvantaged when elaborative processing was required. Using a procedure similar to Eysenck's, White (as reported in Craik, 1977) looked at the effects of orienting tasks on different age groups, but used recognition in addition to recall. She presented young and old subjects a list of 64 words. The first 48 words were presented under incidental learning instructions. Subjects were required to perform three different orienting tasks, a different task for each 16 of the words:

1. Is the word in capital letters? [structural]
2. Does the word rhyme with _____? [phonemic]
3. Does the word belong in _____category? [semantic]

The remaining 16 words in the list wre presented under intentional instructions. Subjects were then tested on the entire list, first by recall and then by recognition. The recall results replicated Eysenck's (1974) findings: Age decrements were substantial under two instructional conditions, the semantic orienting task and standard instructions. With the recognition test, however, age differences were not seen with the semantic orienting tasks but were found with the standard instructions. White contends (in Craik, 1977) that the older subjects processed the category items at a semantic level (normal elaboration), but were unable to recall as well as young adults because of a retrieval deficit. This finding has been replicated by Craik (see Craik & Simon, this volume, Chapter 5) and by Perlmutter (1978). The finding of substantial age deficits in recognition following standard instructions, however, is surprising in light of the other recognition studies discussed earlier (e.g., Craik, 1971; Schonfield & Roberston, 1966). This discrepancy with the other recognition studies in the literature might be due to the fact that instructional conditions were manipulated "within subjects" in both White's and Perlmutter's experiments. In a within-subject design, it is possible that encoding cannot be properly controlled when instructional conditions are being manipulated. For example, the processing of the last 16 words in White's experiment (Standard condition) was most likely affected by the type of processing done in the earlier incidental orienting tasks.

In an experiment by Mason (1977), the variables of age, orienting task, and type of test were manipulated between subjects, and the results of this experiment are quite different from the results of White and of Perlmutter. An age difference in elaboration was demonstrated in both recall and recognition performance. When subjects in Mason's experiment were given standard instructions with no orienting task, there were no age differences in recognition. With the semantic orienting task, however, age differences were found with both recall and recognition. Future research will have to resolve the conflicting results with recognition, but the results with recall are clear. Large age differences are seen with the more elaborate processing tasks.

The story suggested by these data is that age differences in recall are due to the spontaneous use of different processing strategies by young and old subjects. This is the same interpretation given for the retrieval studies reported earlier. It is suggested that young subjects tend to organize in anticipation of recall and that older subjects engage in less spontaneous organization. Mason's (1977) data suggest that older subjects are also not elaborating as well as younger subjects, but this conclusion is clouded by conflicting results.

If young and old subjects are differentially affected by the orienting task requirements because young adults have a greater tendency to interrelate list items, then orienting tasks should have similar effects across age groups when stimulus materials are not easily organizable. When pictures of faces are used

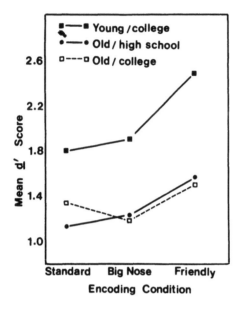

FIG. 1.6. Face recognition after different orienting tasks as a function of age and educational level (after Smith & Winograd, 1978).

instead of words, for example, the task should involve less organizational encoding. Smith and Winograd (1978) tested face recognition after various orienting tasks in two different age groups: college students and adults aged 50-80 years. Pictures of faces were selected from a British casting directory and were of adults of all ages, half male and half female. Subjects were assigned to one of three different encoding conditions. In one condition, subjects attended to a structural feature of each face by indicating whether the face had a big nose. Another group had to determine whether or not the face was friendly (elaborative task). A third group was given standard learning instructions. After all 50 faces were presented, 30 target faces were randomly selected for test with 30 new faces. The older age group was divided according to the highest educational level achieved, but as can be seen in Fig. 1.6, educational level made little difference.

While the young group correctly recognized more faces than older subjects, there was no interaction between age and orienting task. Friendliness judgments were associated with better memory than the structural task of rating nose size or the standard instructions in both age groups. When subjects categorize faces as friendly or unfriendly, they are more likely to integrate the details of each face; and a task which encourages subjects to elaborate upon items is more effective for recognition (Warrington & Ackroyd, 1975).

In the orienting studies with words, young subjects were disproportionately benefited by an elaborative task. In addition, Mason (1977) found a significant age decrement when recogntiion was tested following a semantic task, even though old subjects recognized as many words as young subjects following standard instructions. It seems, therefore, that the young subjects receive the greatest benefit from the semantic tasks because, under standard instructions, they tend to use an encoding strategy better suited for recall. Young subjects spontaneously organize the items together. Therefore, it was hypothesized that an elaborative task would be of equal benefit to young and old subjects when the opportunity for interrelating the list items was minimized. This hypothesis was supported by the results of the face recognition experiment. The fact that age differences were found in overall recognition performance with the faces could be due to several reasons. First, the young subjects are not spending time inappropriately on organizational processing, and because of this, the difference in face recognition reflects a better estimate of true age differences in elaborative encoding. And because organizational processing is not involved with this task, the elaboration difference does not seem to be modified by the instruction to perform different orienting tasks. Another reason for the difference between word and face recognition, however, could simply be the difference between verbal and visual encoding.

There is evidence to suggest that older subjects are deficient in visual encoding as well as verbal encoding. Abstract terms such as "love" and "truth" tend to evoke only verbal encoding, while concrete terms such as "tree" and "house" arouse both verbal processing and nonverbal images. According to Paivio's (1971) "dual-coding" theory, images can serve as an additional coding system. Because items differ in the ease of evoking images, visual encoding can be experimentally manipulated in two different ways. First, the type of learning material can be manipulated (e.g., concrete versus abstract words), and second, as with verbal encoding, instructions can be varied to control processing during learning.

Hulicka and Grossman (1967) suggest that the elderly are deficient in the spontaneous use of visual encoding. In their study, young and old subjects were given a variety of different instructions in paired-associate learning. Without imagery instructions, older subjects reported using visual mediators less often than did younger subjects. When the older subjects did report the use of visual mediators, they seemed to be inappropriate. When subjects were instructed to use visual imagery, the reported use of mediators increased for all subjects and there was a corresponding improvement in recall scores. While the old improved more than the young subjects, they did not attain the same high level of performance. Learning scores were highest for the older subjects when they were instructed to develop their own associations between the items in the pair. Treat and Reese (1976) also found that self-generated imagery mediators were more beneficial than experimenter-provided mediators. In their study, age differences in a paired-associate task were eliminated when the anticipation interval was extended and when subjects were told to form their own visual mediators.

Unfortunately, the use of the paired-associate task tends to confound imagery as an elaborative encoding operation with imagery as an organizational aid. In the paired-associate task, the subject must link the stimulus with the response. An association or organizational linkage is required to gain access to the response at the time of test. In an experiment by Mason and Smith (1977), imagery instructions were varied in a free recall task, a better procedure to study imagery as elaboration. Three age groups were presented a list of 10 concrete and 10 abstract nouns. Half of the subjects were given standard instructions and the other half were given instructions to image each word as it was presented. The results of this experiment are presented in Table 1.3. Concrete words were recalled better than abstract words in all age groups, and imagery instructions tended to improve recall. However, there was an interaction between age and instructions. Neither the youngest nor the oldest group were aided by the instructions to use imagery. The interaction resulted from the effect of imagery instructions in the middle-aged group. The performance of this group was similar to the old group under standard conditions, but similar to the young group after imagery instructions. It seems that the middle-aged subjects can be encouraged to use imagery and are benefited by such instructions. Young adults tend to use imagery spontaneously as evidenced by their high level of recall under both instructional conditions.

Although the oldest group seems less able, or less willing, to respond to imagery instructions, one cannot necessarily conclude that they are unable to use visual imagery. A greater number of concrete words was recalled than abstract words for all age groups. Maybe older subjects are just less willing to adopt experimenter-provided instructions, as Treat and Reese suggest, and this is the reason why imagery instructions were ineffective. Possible age

TABLE 1.3
Mean Number of Words Correctly Recalled
As a Function of Word Type and Imagery Instructions[a]

	Imagery Instructions		Standard Instructions	
Age Group	Concrete Words	Abstract Words	Concrete Words	Abstract Words
1 (20–39)	6.25	4.91	6.07	5.27
2 (40–59)	6.06	5.22	5.49	4.14
3 (60–80)	5.22	3.89	5.02	4.00

[a]After Mason and Smith, 1977.

deficits in imagery are discussed more fully by Winograd and Simon in Chapter 27.

To summarize the effects of age on the encoding stage of memory, the literature seems to indicate (a) a clear organizational deficit in the older age group, (b) a possible verbal elaboration deficit, and (c) a possible deficit in the use of visual imagery, but a problem that might be caused by the unwillingness of the older subjects to follow general instructions to alter their learning strategies.

Future research should focus on qualitative differences as well as quantitative differences in processing between age groups. Much of the research that has been discussed suggests that older subjects are using different encoding strategies, qualitative differences between the age groups. The best evidence supporting qualitative differences in processing is the common finding that encoding can be influenced by instructions and orienting tasks. With organization (e.g., Hultsch, 1967), older subjects were taught to behave more like younger subjects by inducing a strategy change through instruction.

Further, the nature of possible processing deficits should be specified in a more precise fashion. A processing-deficit hypothesis seems able to make two predictions, depending on whether the deficit is an inability to process in a particular way (i.e., mediational deficiency) or simple disuse of an available strategy (i.e., production deficiency) (Reese, 1976). If the second prediction is correct, then older subjects should improve when instructions are used. If, on the other hand, older subjects are incapable of processing in a particular fashion, instructions should have no effect.

In Eysenck's (1974) orienting-task experiment, support for the processing hypothesis was provided by the fact that the largest age difference was seen when the more elaborative semantic task was used. Because the older subjects were deficient in elaborative processing, the largest effect was seen with the elaborative task. However, the processing hypothesis also could predict the opposite. Because the older subjects do not use elaborative processing, providing them with a semantic task compensates for this deficit and reduces age differences. The distinction between these two predictions depends on whether instructions and/or processing tasks are "compensation" conditions or not (Rohwer, 1976)—that is, whether the effect is a mediation or a production deficiency.

There are some other conceptual problems with the overall research endeavor of assigning age differences to different memory stages. For example, there is a tendency for researchers to collapse the three stages into two. Storage to some means encoding and to others means the maintenance of information during the retention interval. There is also the tendency of memory researchers to pit one stage of memory against another. The stages are treated as "oppositions" or as alternative hypotheses. Eysenck (1977) has correctly pointed out that this research approach is "limiting conceptually" because more than one stage of memory may be affected by age. Paradigms and procedures should be used in which the stages of memory can be empirically separated, and yet simultaneously examined.

Another problem is the assumption of many of the experiments that the experimental conditions can be kept constant until the time retrieval is tested. As mentioned earlier, this is the basic assumption underlying the comparison of recall and recognition and the comparison of free and cued recall. This assumption is difficult to justify, however, when a subject variable such as age is defined as one of the independent variables. If the different age groups use different acquisition strategies, which is probable if one accepts the conclusions of this chapter, then the conditions of learning are not held constant, even though the experimenter-controlled procedures do not vary. Once processing differences have been established, then it becomes difficult, if not impossible, to assess the subsequent stages of memory. Initial processing determines what characteristics of the material are stored, and the nature of storage would determine the stability of memory during the retention interval. In fact, Kausler's (1970) criticism of early interference studies was that the learning conditions were not held constant between the age groups. Retrieval is also dependent on encoding strategy. It becomes difficult to decide whether differences at test are due to retrieval problems in the older age group, or due to the sensitivity of the various test procedures to the processing strategies used at the time of original encoding.

CONCLUSION

The purpose of this paper was to evaluate the various hypotheses that localize the age deficit in memory performance to one or more of the stages in the memory process. Because the stages of memory are difficult to untangle empirically, however, a simple conclusion is difficult. The weight of the evidence does suggest that processing differences exist, storage deficits do not exist, and retrieval deficits may exist but are difficult to measure because of encoding differences between the age groups.

It is interesting to speculate why older subjects fail to engage in the same encoding operations as young people. It may be that certain encoding strategies, such as organization, are nurtured by formal education, and as one becomes older and further removed from the educational milieu, the reliance upon these encoding strategies is altered. Everyday remembering may not involve the active, strategic encoding emphasized in academic remembering. However, this is only one possible reason for the encoding differences suggested in this chapter.

ACKNOWLEDGMENTS

The preparation of this paper was supported in part by a National Institutes of Health research grant No. AG-00445 from the Institute on Aging. I wish to thank Ms. Audrey Fullerton for her help in the preparation of the manuscript.

REFERENCES

Arbuckle, T. Y. Differential retention of individual paired-associates within an RTT "learning" trial. *Journal of Experimental Psychology*, 1967, *74*, 433–451.

Botwinick, J. & Storandt, M. *Memory, related functions, and age.* Springfield, Ill.: Charles C. Thomas, 1974.

Bousfield, A. K., & Bousfield, W. A. Measurement of clustering and of sequential constancies in repeated free recall. *Psychological Reports*, 1966, *19*, 935–942.

Cameron, D. E. Impairment at the retention phase of remembering. *Psychiatric Quarterly*, 1943, *17*, 395–404.

Connor, J. M. Effects of organization and expectancy on recall and recognition. *Memory and Cognition*, 1977, *5*, 315–318.

Craik, F. I. M. Short-term memory and the aging process. In G. A. Talland (Ed.), *Human aging and behavior.* New York: Academic Press, 1968.

Craik, F. I. M. Age differences in recognition memory. *Quarterly Journal of Experimental Psychology*, 1971, *23*, 316–319.

Craik, F. I. M. Age differences in human memory. In J. E. Birren & K. W. Schaie (Eds.), *Handbook of the psychology of aging.* New York: Van Nostrand Reinhold, 1977.

Craik, F. I. M., & Lockhart, R. S. Levels of processing: A framework for memory research. *Journal of Verbal Learning and Verbal Behavior*, 1972, *11*, 671–684.

Craik, F. I. M., & Mansani, P. A. Age and intelligence differences in coding and retrieval of word lists. *British Journal of Psychology*, 1969, *60*, 315–319.

Craik, F. I. M., & Tulving, E. Depth of processing and the retention of words in episodic memory. *Journal of Experimental Psychology: General*, 1975, *104*, 268–294.

Crew, F. F. *Age differences in retention after varying study and test trials.* Unpublished Masters thesis, Georgia Institute of Technology, August, 1977.

Drachman, D. A., & Leavitt, J. Memory impairment in the aged: Storage versus retrieval deficit? *Journal of Experimental Psychology*, 1972, *93*, 302–308.

Eagle, M., & Leiter, E. Recall and recognition in intentional and incidental learning. *Journal of Experimental Psychology*, 1964, *68*, 58–63.

Erber, J. T. Age differences in recognition memory. *Journal of Gerontology*, 1974, *29*, 177–181.

Eysenck, M. W. Age differences in incidental learning. *Developmental Psychology*, 1974, *10*, 936–941.

Eysenck, M. W. *Human memory: Theory, research, and individual differences.* Oxford: Pergamon Press, 1977.

Fozard, J. L., & Waugh, N. C. Proactive inhibition of prompted items. *Psychonomic Science*, 1969, *17*, 67–68.

Gladis, M., & Braun, H. W. Age differences in transfer and retroactive as a function of intertask response similarity. *Journal of Experimental Psychology*, 1958, *55*, 25–30.

Griffith, D. Comparison of control processes for recognition and recall. *Journal of Experimental Psychology: Human Learning and Memory*, 1975, *1*, 223–228.

Hogan, R. M., & Kintsch, W. Differential effects of study and test trials on long-term recognition and recall. *Journal of Verbal Learning and Verbal Behavior*, 1974, *13*, 512–521.

Hulicka, I. M., & Grossman, J. L. Age-group comparisons for the use of mediators in paired-associate learning. *Journal of Gerontology*, 1967, *22*, 46–51.

Hultsch, D. F. Adult age differences in the organization of free recall. *Developmental Psychology*, 1969, *1*, 673–678.

Hultsch, D. F. Adult age differences in free classification and free recall. *Developmental Psychology*, 1971, *4*, 338–342.

Hultsch, D. F. Learning to learn in adulthood. *Journal of Gerontology*, 1974, *29*, 302–308.

Hultsch, D. F. Adult age differences in retrieval: Trace-dependent and cue-dependent forgetting. *Developmental Psychology*, 1975, *11*, 197–201.

Jenkins, J. J. Can we have a theory of meaningful memory? In R. L. Solso (Ed.), *Theories in cognitive psychology: The Loyola Symposium*. Potomac, Md.: Lawrence Erlbaum Associates, 1974.

Kausler, D. H. Retention–forgetting as a nomological network for developmental research. In L. R. Goulet & P. B. Baltes (Eds.), *Life-span developmental psychology*, New York: Academic Press, 1970.

Kay, H. Theories of learning and aging. In J. E. Birren (Ed.), *Handbook of aging and the individual*. Chicago: University of Chicago Press, 1959.

Laurence, M. W. Age differences in performance and subjective organization in free recall learning of pictorial material. *Canadian Journal of Psychology*, 1966, *20*, 388–399.

Laurence, M. W. Memory loss with age: A test of two strategies for its retardation. *Psychonomic Science*, 1967, *9*, 209–210.

Mandler, G. Organization and memory. In K. W. Spence & J. T. Spence (Eds.), *The psychology of learning and motivation* (Vol. 1). New York: Academic Press, 1967.

Mason, S. E. *The effects of orienting tasks on the recall and recognition memory of subjects differing in age*. Unpublished doctoral dissertation, Georgia Institute of Technology, 1977.

Mason, S. E., & Smith, A. D. Imagery in the aged. *Experimental Aging Research*, 1977, *3*, 17–32.

Monge, R. H., & Hultsch, D. F. Paired-associate learning as a function of adult age and the length of the anticipation and inspection intervals. *Journal of Gerontology*, 1971, *26*, 157–162.

Paivio, A. *Imagery and verbal processes*. New York: Holt, Rinehart, & Winston, 1971.

Perlmutter, M. What is memory aging the aging of? *Developmental Psychology*, 1978, *14*, 330–345.

Reese, H. W. The development of memory: Life-span perspectives. In H. W. Reese (Ed.), *Advances in child development and behavior* (Vol. 11). New York: Academic Press, 1976.

Rohwer, W. D. Jr. An introduction to research on individual and developmental differences in learning. In W. K. Estes (Ed.), *Handbook of learning and cognitive processes* (Vol. 3). Hillsdale, N.J.: Lawrence Erlbaum Associates, 1976.

Schonfield, D., & Robertson, B. A. Memory storage and aging. *Canadian Journal of Psychology*, 1966, 20, 228–236.

Shiffrin, R. M. Forgetting: Trace erosion or retrieval failure. *Science*, 1970, *168*, 1601–1603.

Shiffrin, R. M. Retrieval failure or selective attention? *Science*, 1971, *173*, 1040–1041.

Shiffrin, R. M. Capacity limitations in information processing, attention, and memory. In W. K. Estes (Ed.), *Handbook of learning and cognitive processes* (Vol. 4). Hillsdale, N.J.: Lawrence Erlbaum Associates, 1976.

Smith, A. D. Response interference with organized recall in the aged. *Developmental Psychology*, 1974, *10*, 867–870.

Smith, A. D. Aging and interference with memory. *Journal of Gerontology*, 1975, *30*, 319–325. (a)

Smith, A. D. Partial learning and recognition memory in the aged. *International Journal of Aging and Human Development*, 1975, *6*, 359–365. (b)

Smith, A. D. Aging and the total presentation time hypothesis. *Developmental Psychology*, 1976, *12*, 87–88.

Smith, A. D. Adult age differences in cued recall. *Developmental Psychology*, 1977, *13*, 326–331.

Smith, A. D., & Winograd, E. Age differences in recognizing faces. *Developmental Psychology*, 1978, *14*, 443–444.

Sternberg, R. J., & Tulving, E. The measurement of subjective organization in free recall. *Psychological Bulletin*, 1977, *84*, 539–556.

Talland, G. A. Age and the span of immediate recall. In G. A. Talland (Ed.), *Human aging and behavior*. New York: Academic Press, 1968.

Taub, H. A. Age differences in memory as a function of rate of presentation, order of report, and stimulus organization. *Journal of Gerontology*, 1968, *23*, 159–164.

Taub, H. A., & Grieff, S. Effects of age on organization and recall of two sets of stimuli. *Psychonomic Science*, 1967, *7*, 53–54.

Taub, H. A., & Walker, J. B. Short-term memory as a function of age and response interference. *Journal of Gerontology*, 1970, *25*, 177–183.

Treat, N., & Reese, H. W. Age, imagery, and pacing in paired-associate learning. *Developmental Psychology*, 1976, *12*, 119–124.

Tulving, E. Subjective organization in free recall of "unrelated" words. *Psychological Review*, 1962, *69*, 344–354.

Tulving, E. The effects of presentation and recall of material in free-recall learning. *Journal of Verbal Learning and Verbal Behavior*, 1967, *6*, 175–184.

Tulving, E. Cue-dependent forgetting. *American Scientist*, 1974, *62*, 74–82.

Tulving, E., & Arbuckle, T. Y. Input and output interference in short-term associative memory. *Journal of Experimental Psychology*, 1966, *72*, 145–150.

Tulving, E., & Pearlstone, Z. Availability and accessibility of information in memory for words. *Journal of Verbal Learning and Verbal Behavior*, 1966, *5*, 381–391.

Tulving, E., & Thomson, D. M. Encoding specificity and retrieval processes in episodic memory. *Psychological Review*, 1973, *80*, 352–373.

Warrington, E. K., & Ackroyd, C. The effect of orienting tasks on recognition memory. *Memory and Cognition*, 1975, 3, 140–142.

Warrington, E. K., & Silberstein, M. A questionnaire technique for investigating very long term memory. *Quarterly Journal of Experimental Psychology*, 1970, *22*, 508–512.

Welford, A. T. *Aging and human skill*. New York: Oxford University Press, 1958.

Winograd, E., & Smith, A. D. When do semantic orienting tasks hinder recall? *Bulletin of the Psychonomic Society*, 1978, *11*, 165–167.

2 Age and Memory: Strategies for Localizing the Loss

Timothy A. Salthouse
University of Missouri

Encoding, storage, or retrieval—at which stage is the age decrement in memory localized? The evidence on this issue is becoming more confusing with each additional increment in information. Rather than detailing all of the relevant arguments, only the major positive evidence is summarized here to illustrate the complexity of the problem. In favor of an encoding deficit is the evidence that older adults utilize imagery less often and effectively than younger adults (e.g., Hulicka, 1967; Hulicka & Grossman, 1967; Rowe & Schnore, 1971; Treat & Reese, 1976) and that they exhibit less organization of to-be-remembered items than younger subjects (e.g., Craik, 1968a; Craik & Masani, 1967; Denney, 1974; Hultsch, 1969, 1974). The reports that age differences in retention are eliminated when the age groups are equated for initial learning (e.g., Gladis & Braun, 1958; Hulicka, 1967; Hulicka & Weiss, 1965; Moenster, 1972; Wimer & Wigdor, 1958) can also be interpreted as supporting an encoding deficit. Evidence for a storage deficit is reported by Gordon and Clark (1974) in the finding that older adults exhibit less retention of single items across successive learning trials than do younger adults. Retrieval problems have also been implicated in the reports that age differences are reduced where retrieval requirements are minimized, such as recognition tests (e.g., Craik, 1971; Schonfield & Robertson, 1966) or cued-recall tests (e.g., Hultsch, 1975; Laurence, 1967; Smith, 1977).

  The confusion with respect to localizing the age deficit to one stage concerned with encoding, storage, or retrieval led Craik (1977) to conclude: "There is no point in prolonging the debate on whether age differences are due to acquisition or retrieval. Undoubtedly some situation can be found in which acquisition is the major problem . . . while in others, retrieval will be the major source of difficulty [p. 408]." Such pessimism about the possibility of localizing the age deficit to one critical stage in memory is, in my opinion, fully warranted. The available evidence concerning age differences in specific hypothetical stages or processes in memory is so heterogeneous and contradictory that one can have little confidence that a solution will be soon forthcoming to the problem of identifying the stage or stages responsible for the age impairment in memory.

Part of the difficulty may be that much of the past research concerned with age differences in memory has relied exclusively on one strategy that may not be the most appropriate for localizing age losses in memory. The major focus of the present paper is to consider alternative strategies for specifying the nature of the impairment in memory with increased age. In the process of discussing alternative research strategies, a promising and powerful new interpretation of age differences in memory will be presented.

For the current purposes, a research strategy will be defined as the procedure by which an investigator typically obtains his research hypotheses. If an investigator derives all of his hypotheses from a single source such as a particular type of theory or a specific set of data, he may be considered to be employing a single research strategy. Since the combined fields of memory and aging yield two potential types of theory and two distinct sets of data, four possible strategies for investigating age differences in memory are to derive hypotheses from: (1) memory theory; (2) memory data; (3) aging theory; and (4) aging data.

GENERATING RESEARCH HYPOTHESES
FROM MEMORY THEORY

The first strategy, that of deriving hypotheses from existing theories or models of memory, has dominated most of the previous research on age and memory. The prevalence in the aging literature of such terms as interference, short-term memory, long-term memory, stages of encoding, storage, and retrieval, and more recently levels of processing, is one indication of the influence of normative theories in aging research. Indeed, all of these conceptualizations of memory have served to provide an "explanation" for the age deficit in memory, as over the past 20 years this phenomenon has been attributed to an age-related: (1) increase in interference (e.g., Welford, 1958); (2) reduction in long-term or secondary memory but not in short-term or primary memory (e.g., Craik, 1968 a, b); (3) impairment in retrieval but not encoding or storage (e.g., Schonfield & Robertson, 1966); and (4) decrease in depth of processing (e.g., Craik, 1977).

Much of the research inspired by mainstream memory theories has been of high quality, and thus the overall impact of the strategy has been positive. A problem exists, however, in that researchers seldom consider other strategies for investigating age differences in memory. This is particularly unfortunate when one realizes that it is only an assumption that the hypothetical mechanisms that serve to describe the performance of young adults will also serve to distinguish young adults from older adults. That is, merely because a model or theory has been found to provide an adequate description of the behavior of one population of subjects does not mean that the model or theory will be capable of identifying the dimensions along which two populations of subjects differ in that behavior. In fact, the inconsistency in the literature on age differences in encoding, storage, and retrieval may be interpreted as signifying that the encoding–storage–retrieval trichotomy is inappropriate for characterizing age differences in memory.

It is important to point out that I am not arguing that researchers abandon the strategy of borrowing concepts from current theories of memory to investigate age differences. I am merely advocating that alternative strategies should also be pursued. Obviously, because nearly every theorist seems to introduce one or more new concepts in his theoretical descriptions of memory, no one would seriously maintain that the researcher concerned with age and memory be exhaustive in investigating age differences in every possible theoretical mechanism. I am only suggesting that the researcher also not be exclusive in limiting his investigations to those derived from a particular strategy.

GENERATING RESEARCH HYPOTHESES FROM MEMORY DATA

One alternative strategy for attempting to isolate the locus of age differences in memory is to let the hypotheses for the age deficit emerge from the data base relevant to a particular memory phenomenon. The first step in this approach is to select a well investigated memory paradigm that has several possible effects, i.e., patterns of results, that could be observed. The second step is to compile a list of factors producing each type of effect. A third step is to locate (or conduct) an aging study to determine which of the possible effects is produced by the factor of adult age. The fourth and final step involves examining all factors producing the same effects as the age factor in an attempt to discover a common mechanism. If a mechanism common to all factors producing the same type of performance difference as the age factor can be identified, one might then hypothesize that that mechanism is also responsible for the age differences in memory.

An obvious objection to this strategy is that similarity of effects does not necessarily imply similarity of mechanism. That is, merely because two factors produce the same pattern of results does not mean that the two factors operate in the same manner. This objection is quite valid; however, the strategy can be effective when used primarily as a source of hypotheses rather than the sole basis for a conclusion.

As an example of this strategy, consider the phenomenon of free-recall memory analyzed in terms of the serial position of the to-be-remembered items at input. The serial position function in free-recall memory has been extensively investigated and thus it possesses a very large data base. Moreover, at least three possible effects of a factor may be determined, as researchers have identified three distinct segments of the function that are differentially influenced by a variety of manipulations.

A highly schematic illustration of the three segments of the serial position function is presented in Fig. 2.1. The solid line in each panel represents the typical pattern obtained in free-recall experiments, and the dotted line indicates the pattern produced by the manipulation of specific factors. There are substantial differences in effect magnitude across different factors, and therefore the patterns portrayed in Fig. 2.1 should be interpreted only qualitatively and not quantitatively.

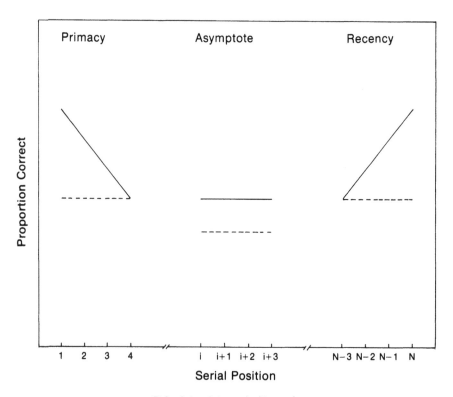

FIG. 2.1. Schematic illustration
of serial position effects.

The major factor that has been demonstrated to influence the primacy segment of the serial position function is rehearsal strategy. If subjects are instructed to rehearse an item only when it is being presented (e.g., Brodie & Prytulak, 1975; Fischler, Rundus, & Atkinson, 1970; Glanzer & Meinzer, 1967; Gorfein, 1970; Welch & Burnett, 1924), or if the task is disguised in an incidental learning design such that rehearsal is minimized (e.g., Marshall & Werder, 1972), the primacy segment is much reduced or eliminated.

A large number of factors have been found to influence the asymptote segment of the function relating item recall probability to item position at input. Among these factors are: presentation rate, such that faster rates decrease asymptote (e.g., Bernbach, 1975; Brodie, 1975; Brodie & Murdock, 1977; Brodie & Prytulak, 1975; Craik & Levy, 1970; Gianutsos, 1972; Glanzer & Cunitz, 1966; Glanzer & Razel, 1974; Leicht, 1968; Murdock, 1962; Raymond, 1969); list length, such that longer lists decrease asymptote (e.g., Deese & Kaufman, 1957; Lewis-Smith, 1975; Murdock, 1962; Postman & Phillips, 1965); interpolated activity between items, such that greater activity decreases asymptote (e.g., Baddeley & Hitch, 1974; Baddeley, Scott, Drynan, & Smith, 1969; Bartz & Salehi, 1970; Glanzer & Meinzer, 1967; Gorfein, 1970; Marshall & Werder, 1972; Murdock, 1965; Richardson & Baddeley, 1975; Silverstein & Glanzer, 1971); depth of encoding, such that deeper encoding increases asymptote (e.g., Glanzer & Koppenaal, 1977; Seamon & Murray, 1976); and item pronounceability, such that less pronounceable items have lower asymptote (e.g., Meunier, Stanners, & Meunier, 1971). A variety of factors that might be termed organizational have also been discovered to influence the asymptote segment. For example, the asymptote is higher with: greater item meaningfulness (e.g., Deese & Kaufman, 1957; Glanzer & Razel, 1974; Raymond, 1969); greater semantic relatedness (e.g., Bruce & Crowley, 1970; Craik & Levy, 1970; Glanzer, 1976; Glanzer, Koppenaal, & Nelson, 1972; Glanzer & Schwartz, 1971); greater acoustic similarity (e.g., Bruce & Crowley, 1970; Craik & Levy, 1970; Glanzer, Koppenaal, & Nelson, 1972; Watkins, Watkins, & Crowder, 1974); and greater word frequency (e.g., Raymond, 1969; Sumby, 1963).

Factors identified as influencing the recency segment of the serial position function include: presentation modality, yielding greater recency with auditory than with visual presentation (e.g., Craik, 1969; Murdock & Walker, 1969; Richardson & Baddeley, 1975; Watkins, 1972); post-list activity, yielding smaller recency with greater activity (e.g., Bartz & Salehi, 1970; Brodie, 1975; Brodie & Prytulak, 1975; Glanzer & Cunitz, 1966; Glanzer, Gianutsos, & Dubin, 1969; Glanzer & Schwartz, 1971; Postman & Phillips, 1965; Raymond, 1969; Shuell & Keppel, 1968); and order of output, yielding less recency when the last input items are recalled last (e.g., Craik, 1969).

The next step in this approach to generating hypotheses is to determine the effects of adult age upon the three segments of the serial position function. A search of the literature on memory and age revealed three studies that conducted serial position analyses, but none is entirely suitable for the present purposes. One (Raymond, 1971) did not include an appropriate young adult control group against which the performance of the older adults could be compared, and another (Craik, 1968b) did not present the serial position functions, but merely reported several theoretical measures derived from the functions. A third study (Arenberg, 1976) did present complete serial position functions but only conducted statistical analyses on the data from the primacy and recency segments of the function. A reasonable conclusion on the basis of these studies, particularly Arenberg's (1976) study, is that the asymptote segment of the function is reduced in older adults compared to younger adults, but that primacy and recency effects, at least judged in relation to the asymptote, are essentially equivalent across age groups. This indicates that, according to the steps outlined above, future efforts should be directed at discovering a mechanism responsible for asymptote effects in serial position functions.

Identifying a mechanism common to all the factors that produce a shift in the asymptote segment of the serial position function is a difficult problem in view of the variety of factors involved. Indeed, it is quite likely that no single mechanism is responsible for all asymptote effects. Nevertheless, we can proceed optimistically in the hope that one or two major mechanisms can be identified and investigated.

One likely candidate for a mechanism responsible for producing at least some of the asymptote effects is the time available for rehearsal of each item. Obviously, increasing the item presentation rate directly reduces the available rehearsal time, but many of the other factors may have similar indirect effects. For example, if earlier list items are rehearsed in alternation with current items, increases in list length will lead to decreases in rehearsal time per item because more earlier items are present in longer lists. Further, activity interpolated between the presentation of items will necessarily reduce the amount of time that can be devoted to rehearsing each item if the activity itself requires time. The various organizational factors might also operate by facilitating rehearsal time for single items or groups of items. Meunier, Stanners, and Meunier (1971) even interpreted their findings with item pronounceability in a similar fashion: "The easier an item is to pronounce, the faster it can be pronounced and the more material can be rehearsed per unit time [p. 123]."

Additional support for the importance of rehearsal time as a mechanism contributing to memory performance is provided by several recent studies utilizing overt rehearsal procedures. Rundus (1971) found a striking positive relationship between number of rehearsals per item and item recall probability, and he even demonstrated that the number-of-rehearsals–recall-probability relationship held across manipulations of item distinctiveness and interval between repetitions of the same item. Brodie and Prytulak (1975) recently postulated that rehearsal time along with retention interval can account for much of the data on free recall, and they provided impressive evidence in support of this hypothesis. Briefly, their results, which were largely replicated by Brodie and Murdock (1977), indicated that the primacy effect is caused by more rehearsal time allotted to early list items, and that the recency effect is caused by shorter retention intervals of late list items. In addition, both series of studies demonstrated that slower presentation rates led to greater rehearsal time per item than did faster presentation rates, and that the asymptote segment in particular was higher with slower presentation rates.

If amount of time for rehearsal is the mechanism common to most or all factors that lead to changes in the asymptote segment of the serial position function, then we can hypothesize that rehearsal time is also the mechanism responsible for the observed age differences in memory. That is, older adults may have less efficient rehearsal processes than younger adults because they require more time for each rehearsal, and thus can complete fewer rehearsals in a given period of time than can the younger individuals. An experiment providing a test of this hypothesis is described later in this paper.

As far as could be determined, the possibility that there are age differences in rehearsal efficiency would not have been generated from current theories of memory. In this respect, therefore, the strategy of attempting to speculate about the nature of age-related memory loss by beginning from the empirical data rather than existing theories of memory appears to be successful in that it generates novel hypotheses about the locus of the age difficulty in memory.

GENERATING RESEARCH HYPOTHESES FROM AGING THEORY

The third possible strategy listed earlier, that of generating hypotheses about the cause of age differences in memory from theories of aging, may be impractical at the current time. There presently do not appear to be any well established behavioral theories of aging, and thus it is premature to attempt to borrow any ideas or concepts from such theories. When these theories are developed, however, the approach would be similar to the memory theory approach except that the concepts from the aging theory rather than the memory theory would be used to formulate hypotheses about the age differences in memory.

GENERATING RESEARCH HYPOTHESES
FROM AGING DATA

The fourth strategy for deriving hypotheses about the locus of age differences in memory is to examine the data base in aging in order to determine whether known age differences in nonmemory functions could also account for the age differences in memory. Only two steps are involved in this approach. The first is simply to select some phenomenon that has been documented to have a substantial age effect. The second is to attempt to use that age-related phenomenon, or its underlying mechanisms, to speculate about causes for age differences in certain memory functions. If the speculation is plausible, specific testable hypotheses concerned with age differences in memory processes should be deducible.

In order to illustrate this strategy, the general slowing of behavior with increased age is utilized here as the aging phenomenon that might serve as a source of hypotheses concerning age differences in memory. Nearly every textbook in the psychology of aging cites loss of speed as one of the principal manifestations of increased age (e.g., Birren, 1964; Botwinick, 1973; Bromley, 1974; Elias, Elias, & Elias, 1977), and recent reviews cite dozens of studies demonstrating this phenomenon (e.g., Hicks & Birren, 1970; Welford, 1977).

Although a variety of explanations have been proposed (see Botwinick, 1959; Welford & Birren, 1965), there is still much controversy about the reason for the age change in speed. One of the most interesting hypotheses at the present time is what I call the Birren Hypothesis. Birren (e.g., 1956, 1964, 1970, 1974) has repeatedly suggested that the loss of speed associated with increased age is not merely a performance factor that is irrelevant to cognitive abilities, but rather is a reflection of a fundamental change in nervous-system activity. He argues that the slowing affects every event in the nervous system and not just peripheral processes concerned with sensory input or motor output. This has not been a popular argument, as both Birren (1956, 1964, 1974) and Welford (1959) have noted that many psychologists are reluctant to admit that brain mechanisms are involved in age losses in speed because of the implication that the central nervous system deteriorates with increased age. (A related objection, expressed by one of the participants at the conference where this paper was first presented, is that this type of explanation is "theoretically uninteresting" because it offers little opportunity for remedial intervention.) The currently available evidence, however, strongly suggests that nonperipheral factors are involved in the age-related speed loss, and thus the inference that the central nervous sysem is less efficient with increased age seems inevitable.

The Birren Hypothesis of the slowing phenomenon leads to an interesting implication concerning age differences in memory functioning. If all neural events are slowed with age, then one would expect that all time-dependent processes involved in memory functioning would also exhibit age differences. That is, all memory mechanisms that are sensitive to temporal parameters should lead to poorer performance in older adults because of the underlying speed loss that is associated with increased age. This hypothesis is quite different from the more limited view considered by some earlier investigators, in that it maintains that all processes are slowed with age, not merely those concerned with stimulus registration or response production. In other words, age differences would be expected from this hypothesis even when a self-paced task with unlimited response time was employed as long as some internal process is involved that is dependent upon speed. The critical difference between this hypothesis and other speed hypotheses is that it considers age-related speed loss to be an explanatory, rather than a to-be-explained, phenomenon.

Although not absolutely necessary at the current time, eventually the central-nervous-system speed loss must itself be explained. One possibility is that an increase in neural noise might be responsible. The neural noise concept was first introduced by Crossman and Szafran (1956) and later elaborated by Gregory (1957) and Welford (1958). The essential idea is that the loss of functional brain cells associated with increased age either lowers the strength of neural signals, or increases the level of random background activity, such that the internal signal-to-noise ratio is much reduced with increased age. In order to compensate for this lowered signal-to-noise ratio, it is postulated that the older nervous system integrates neural information over a longer period of time than the younger nervous system. Although still quite speculative, the neural noise concept does provide one conceivable mechanism by which a general central-nervous system slowing, such as that proposed by Birren, could occur.

The well established sensitivity of older adults to the rate of presentation on tests of verbal materials (e.g., Arenberg, 1965, 1967; Canestrari, 1963, 1968; Eisdorfer, Axelrod, & Wilkie, 1963; Kinsbourne & Berryhill, 1972) is consistent with this central speed loss interpretation. In addition, age differences in organization (e.g., Denney, 1974; Hultsch, 1969, 1974) and depth of encoding (e.g., Eysenck, 1974) could be explained with the speed-loss mechanism if it is assumed that the processes of organization and deep encoding require time which is less available in older adults. The existence of age differences in backward memory span, dichotic listening, and divided attention tasks (see Craik, 1977) might also be attributable to a slower attention switching time in older adults. Even interactions between age and type of memory test (e.g., Craik, 1971; Hultsch, 1975; Laurence, 1967; Schonfield & Robertson, 1966; Smith, 1977) might be explained by assuming that recognition and cued-recall tests do not require as strong a memory trace as recall tests and hence are more within the capability of older adults who generally have weaker memory traces because of slower rehearsal processes.

Finally, several experiments (e.g., Anders, Fozard, & Lillyquist, 1972; Anders & Fozard, 1973; Eriksen, Hamlin, & Daye, 1973) employing the Sternberg memory-scanning procedure have provided direct evidence that older adults are slower at searching through memory than younger adults.

The great generality of the speed explanation suggests that it might also encompass phenomena previously attributed to a reduction in "capacity" with increased age (e.g., Welford, 1959). Indeed, it is my contention that rate and speed measures are the best indices of processing capacity presently available. Therefore, until better indices can be developed, this speed interpretation can be considered to be functionally equivalent to interpretations suggesting that some vaguely defined "processing capacity" is reduced with increased age.

It is important to note that the present speed explanation is proposed to account for age differences in memory, and not memory per se. The current speculations therefore do not deny the relevance of mainstream memory models for characterizing the performance of older adults; they merely suggest that the *difference* between young and old adults is best described in terms of a slowing of all time-dependent processes.

AN EXPERIMENTAL TEST OF SPEED INFLUENCES ON MEMORY

The applicability of the Birren Hypothesis to memory performance was investigated in an experiment I recently conducted with Ruth Wright. Following the arguments presented earlier in this paper, we postulated that the memory process that would most likely be affected by age-related speed loss was rate of rehearsal. A speculative model indicating the manner in which rate of rehearsal might affect memory performance is illustrated in Fig. 2.2. Assumptions implicit in the processes portrayed in Fig. 2.2. are:

1. That rehearsal of items is continuous with both fast and slow rehearsal;
2. That item strength increases a fixed amount with each rehearsal and decays at a constant rate between rehearsals regardless of rehearsal speed; and
3. That the strength of an item trace accumulates if residual strength remains from the preceding rehearsal.

As can be seen in the two panels of the figure, these assumptions lead to items rehearsed at a fast rate having a greater trace strength over the same period of time as items rehearsed at a slow rate.

Our test of this proposed mechanism involved two converging operations. The first was based on the reasoning that if the age difference in memory was indeed produced by a slower rehearsal in older adults, then another factor that also affected speed of rehearsal should produce the same pattern of results as the age factor. We selected number of syllables per item as our other

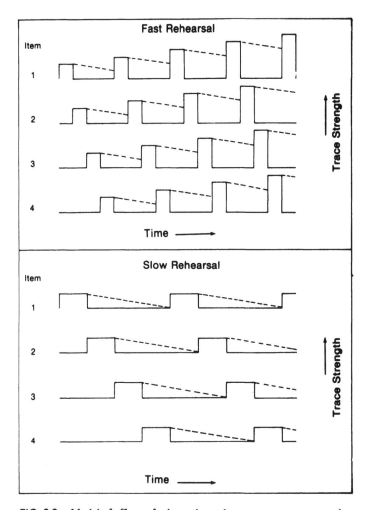

FIG. 2.2.   Model of effects of rehearsal speed on memory trace strength.

factor, believing that three-syllable items would take longer to say or rehearse than one-syllable items. If rehearsal speed is the mechanism common to both the age and syllable factors, then the difference between three- and one-syllable words should be qualitatively similar, across the three serial position segments, to the difference between old and young adults.

The second operation that we utilized to test the rehearsal-speed explanation involved the measurement and comparison of rehearsal speed for young and old adults with one-syllable and three-syllable words. According to our hypothesis, measures of rehearsal speed should be faster for young subjects than for old subjects, and faster for one-syllable items than for three-syllable items.

An indirect measure of reheasal speed was employed because of a suspicion that direct measures, such as those obtained from overt rehearsal procedures (e.g., Rundus, 1971), might be particularly disruptive to the memory performance of the older subjects. The indirect procedure consisted of asking subjects to repeat items to themselves once, twice, or three times and then using the slope of the function relating rehearsal time to the number of rehearsals as the estimate of speed of rehearsal.

Sixteen females and eight males with a mean age of 22.8 years served as the young subjects, and 13 females and 11 males with a mean age of 71.1 years served as the old subjects. The mean years of education was 16.0 for the young subjects and 18.1 for the old subjects. The mean Wechsler Adult Intelligence Scale vocabulary raw scores were 63.6 for the young subjects and 70.4 for the old subjects. All subjects reported themselves to be in good health and were community residents.

Ninety-six one-syllable words and 96 three-syllable words were selected from the A category of the Thorndike–Lorge word frequency count. The words were taken from all parts of speech, and an attempt was made to equate the one- and three-syllable words on a subjective basis for imagery and association value. Twelve rehearsal lists of three words each and five memory lists of 12 words each were constructed with both the one-syllable and three-syllable words. The assignment of words to lists was varied across subjects in a balanced fashion.

The words were prepared on cards and presented in one field of a Gerbrands G-1130 three-field tachistoscope with automatic card changers. The presentation duration was 1.5 sec with a 2.0-sec interval between words. Unlimited time was allowed for recall at the end of each list, but most subjects took less than 1 min.

All subjects began the session with 12 rehearsal lists, six containing one-syllable words presented in alternation with six containing three-syllable words. Instructions stated that the three words in the list should be silently rehearsed one, two, or three times and then repeated aloud one time. A Hunter Klockounter Model 120-C was used to measure the time between the presentation of the third word in the list and the first overt repetition of a word from the list. Half of the subjects started with four trials of three covert repetitions, followed by four trials with two covert repetitions and four trials with one covert repetition. The other half of the subjects proceeded in the reverse order.

The one-syllable and three-syllable memory lists were presented alternately, with half of the subjects in each age group starting with the one-syllable words and half starting with the three-syllable words.

The remaining 12 rehearsal trials were administered following the last memory trial. The procedure was the same as in the first 12 trials except that the sequence of the number of covert repetitions for each subject was reversed.

An analysis of variance was conducted on the recall percentage data with age, number of syllables, and serial position segment (i.e., primacy—

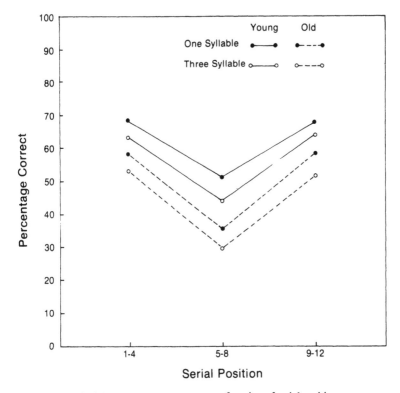

FIG. 2.3.   Percentage correct as a function of serial position.

positions 1 to 4, asymptote—positions 5 to 8, and recency—positions 9 to 12) as factors. All three main effects were significant [age, $F(1, 46) = 24.62$, $p < .01$; number of syllables, $F(1, 46) = 26.17$, $p < .01$; and segment, $F(2, 92) = 45.20$, $p < .01$], with no statistically significant interactions (i.e., all $Fs < 1.0$). The pattern is illustrated in Fig. 2.3. This figure in conjunction with the absence of an interaction between age and segment or between number of syllables and segment suggests that the age and syllable factors had very similar effects. Both factors lowered the overall level of recall, but did not change one segment of the serial position function more than any other segment.

Rehearsal time was measured as the slope of the least-squares regression line relating total rehearsal time to the number of rehearsals of the list. The fastest and the slowest times from the four trials with each number of rehearsals for one-syllable and three-syllable words were omitted to reduce variability. Since the lists consisted of three items each, the slope measures were divided by three to obtain rehearsal time per item. The mean rehearsal time per item and mean correlation coefficients indicating the fit of the regression functions to the data are displayed in Table 2.1. The excellent fits of the linear regression equations to the rehearsal time data suggest that

TABLE 2.1
Rehearsal Time Parameters

	Young	Old
Rehearsal Time per Item (in sec)		
One Syllable	.32	.43
Three Syllable	.37	.45
Correlation Coefficient[a]		
One Syllable	.96	.96
Three Syllable	.97	.95

[a]Mean correlations computed using the r-to-z transform.

subjects were following instructions and varying the number of subvocal rehearsals in the desired manner. This finding therefore supports the validity of the measures of rehearsal time. One indication of the reliability of these rehearsal time estimates can be obtained by examining the correlations across subjects for the rehearsal times of one- and three-syllable words. These correlations were + .79 for the young subjects and + .78 for the old subjects, suggesting a fairly high degree of consistency across the two estimates.

An analysis of variance conducted on the rehearsal-time measures revealed a significant effect of age [$F(1, 46) = 6.35, p < .01$] and number of syllables [$F(1, 46) = 8.21, p < .025$], but no interaction ($F < 1$).

The estimates in Table 2.1 are considerably slower than the estimates obtained by Clifton and Tash (1973) in a similar task, as their times were 185 msec and 260 msec for one-syllable and three-syllable words, respectively. One possible reason for this difference is that their subjects had received 10 previous sessions of experience with a much smaller set of stimuli (only 10 different words with each syllable number) than that employed here. The current data are in line with the rate of 3 items per sec mentioned by Sperling (1969) as being typical in memory experiments with unpracticed young subjects.

The rehearsal-speed hypothesis of age differences in memory is generally supported in these results as increased age and increased number of syllables had very similar effects on the rehearsal time measure and the recall percentage measure. An implication of these results is that older individuals have poorer memories because they are slow, i.e., they take longer to rehearse items than do younger individuals. This interpretation does not deny the existence of other factors also contributing to the age difference in memory— indeed, there is some evidence in the present study that older subjects are less adept at the strategy of recalling last input items first—but the interpretation does maintain that the major factor responsible for adult age differences in memory is a slower speed of rehearsal in older adults. According to this view, therefore, the phenomenon of a 65-year-old college professor complaining of a failing memory is due to the same mechanism as that responsible for a 35-year-old athlete complaining of loss of eye–hand coordination.

CONCLUSION

The possibility that encoding, retrieval, and perhaps even storage deficits can be predicted from the speed-loss mechanism suggests that this interpretation of age-related memory problems has more generality than the memory-stage interpretation. Moreover, even if a stage analysis approach were successful at isolating the age difference in a single stage, no explanation of why the older adults are impaired in that stage and not some other stage would be available unless some fundamental mechanism such as age-related speed loss was postulated.

The similarity in the predictions from the two alternative research strategies illustrated above is undoubtedly partly a reflection of this author's bias, but the time required to perform simple mental operations does seem to be a reasonable candidate responsible for many individual differences in memory performance. In fact, if we accept the implication that the central nervous system is functioning at a slower rate in older adults, mental operation time may be the principal mechanism behind age differences in nearly all aspects of cognitive functioning. It certainly seems more reasonable and parsimonious to suggest that the elderly are doing the same things as the young but merely at a slower rate, than to suggest that for some unknown reason they have shifted to a strategy of utilizing less imagery, less organization, or less depth of encoding.

Since Birren's writings have obviously influenced the ideas that I have expressed here, it is perhaps appropriate to summarize these ideas in Birren's own words (1964):

> Clearly, it is overreaching at present to force all the facts of age changes in behavior into a single explanation involving the speed of a primary neural event. However there is an indication that many of the facts may be attributable to an age change in speed of neural activity [p. 128–129].

ACKNOWLEDGMENTS

This research was supported by a research grant from the University of Missouri Joint Centers for Aging Studies. I wish to thank D. Kausler, J. Mueller, J. Rankin, and R. Wright for their comments on earlier versions of this chapter.

REFERENCES

Anders, T. R., & Fozard, J. L. Effects of age upon retrieval from primary and secondary memory. *Developmental Psychology*, 1973, *9*, 411–415.

Anders, T. R., Fozard, J. L., & Lillyquist, T. D. Effects of age upon retrieval from short-term memory. *Developmental Psychology*, 1972, *6*, 214–217.

Arenberg, D. Anticipation interval and age differences in verbal learning. *Journal of Abnormal Psychology*, 1965, *70*, 419–425.

Arenberg, D. Age differences in retroaction. *Journal of Gerontology*, 1967, *22*, 88–91.

Arenberg, D. The effects of input condition on free recall in young and old adults. *Journal of Gerontology*, 1976, *31*, 551–555.

Baddeley, A. D., & Hitch, G. Working memory. In G. Bower (Ed.), *The psychology of learning and motivation* (Vol. 4). New York: Academic Press, 1974.

Baddeley, A. D., Scott, D., Drynan, R., & Smith, J. C. Short-term memory and the limited capacity hypothesis. *British Journal of Psychology*, 1969, *60*, 51–55.

Bartz, W. H., & Salehi, M. Interference in short- and long-term memory. *Journal of Experimental Psychology*, 1970, *84*, 380–382.

Bernbach, H. A. Rate of presentation in free recall: A problem for two-stage theories. *Journal of Experimental Psychology: Human Learning and Memory*, 1975, *104*, 18–22.

Birren, J. E. The significance of age changes in speed of perception and psychomotor response. In J. E. Anderson (Ed.), *Psychological Aspects of Aging*. Washington, D. C.: American Psychological Association, 1956.

Birren, J. E. *The psychology of aging*. Englewood Cliffs, N.J.: Prentice-Hall, 1964.

Birren, J. E. Toward an experimental psychology of aging. *American Psychologist*, 1970, *25*, 124–135.

Birren, J. E. Translations in gerontology: From lab to life: Psychophysiology and speed of response. *American Psychologist*, 1974, *29*, 808–815.

Botwinick, J. Drives, expectancies and emotions. In J. E. Birren (Ed.), *Handbook of aging and the individual*. Chicago: University of Chicago Press, 1959.

Botwinick, J. *Aging and behavior*. New York: Springer, 1973.

Brodie, D. A. Free recall measures of short-term store: Are rehearsal and order of recall data necessary? *Memory & Cognition*, 1975, *3*, 653–662.

Brodie, D. A., & Murdock, B. B. Jr. Effect of presentation time on nominal and functional serial-position curves of free recall. *Journal of Verbal Learning and Verbal Behavior*, 1977, *16*, 185–200.

Brodie, D. A., & Prytulak, L. S. Free recall curves: Nothing but rehearsing some items more or recalling them sooner? *Journal of Verbal Learning and Verbal Behavior*, 1975, *14*, 549–563.

Bromley, D. B. *The psychology of human aging*. Middlesex, England: Penguin, 1974.

Bruce, D., & Crowley, J. J. Acoustic similarity effects on retrieval from secondary memory. *Journal of Verbal Learning and Verbal Behavior*, 1970, *9*, 190–196.

Canestrari, R. E. Paced and self-paced learning in young and elderly adults. *Journal of Gerontology*, 1963, *18*, 165–168.

Canestrari, R. E. Age changes in acquisition. In G. A. Talland (Ed.), *Human aging and behavior*. New York: Academic Press, 1968.

Clifton, C., Jr., & Tash, J. Effect of syllabic word length on memory-search rate. *Journal of Experimental Psychology*, 1973, *99*, 231–235.

Craik, F. I. M. Short-term memory and the aging process. In G. A. Talland (Ed.), *Human aging and behavior*. New York: Academic Press, 1968. (a)

Craik, F. I. M. Two components in free recall. *Journal of Verbal Learning and Verbal Behavior*, 1968, *7*, 996–1004. (b)

Craik, F. I. M. Modality effects in short-term storage. *Journal of Verbal Learning and Verbal Behavior,* 1969, *8,* 658–664.

Craik, F. I. M. Age differences in recognition memory. *Quarterly Journal of Experimental Psychology,* 1971, *23,* 316–319.

Craik, F. I. M. Age differences in human memory. In J. E. Birren & K. W. Schaie (Eds.), *Handbook of the psychology of aging.* New York: Van Nostrand, 1977.

Craik, F. I. M., & Levy, B. A. Semantic and acoustic information in primary memory. *Journal of Experimental Psychology,* 1970, *86,* 77–82.

Craik, F. I. M., & Masani, P. A. Age differences in the temporal integration of language. *British Journal of Psychology,* 1967, *58,* 291–299.

Crossman, E. R. F. W., & Szafran, J. Changes with age in the speed of information-intake and discrimination. *Experimentia Supplementum, IV,* Birkhauser, Basel, 1956.

Deese, J., & Kaufman, R. A. Serial effects in recall of unorganized and sequentially organized verbal material. *Journal of Experimental Psychology,* 1957, *54,* 180–187.

Denney, N. W. Clustering in middle and old age. *Developmental Psychology,* 1974, *10,* 471–475.

Eisdorfer, C., Axelrod, S., & Wilkie, F. L. Stimulus exposure time as a factor in serial learning in an aged sample. *Journal of Abnormal and Social Psychology,* 1963, *67,* 594–600.

Elias, M. F., Elias, P. K., & Elias, J. W. *Basic processes in adult developmental psychology.* St. Louis: Mosby, 1977.

Eriksen, C. W., Hamlin, R. M., & Daye, C. Aging adults and rate of memory scan. *Bulletin of the Psychonomic Society,* 1973, *1,* 259–260.

Eysenck, M. W. Age differences in incidental learning. *Develomental Psychology,* 1974, *10,* 936–941.

Fischler, I., Rundus, D., & Atkinson, R. C. Effects of overt rehearsal procedures on free recall. *Psychonomic Science,* 1970, *19,* 249–250.

Gianutsos, R. Free recall of grouped words. *Journal of Experimental Psychology,* 1972, *95,,* 419–428.

Gladis, M., & Braun, H. W. Age differences in transfer and retroaction as a function of inter-task response similarity. *Journal of Experimental Psychology,* 1958, *55,* 25–30.

Glanzer, M. Intonation grouping and related words in free recall. *Journal of Verbal Learning and Verbal Behavior,* 1976, *15,* 85–92.

Glanzer, M., & Cunitz, A. R. Two storage mechanisms in free recall. *Journal of Verbal Learning and Verbal Behavior,* 1966, *5,* 351–360.

Glanzer, M., Gianutsos, R., & Dubin, S. The removal of items from short-term storage. *Journal of Verbal Learning and Verbal Behavior,* 1969, *8,* 435–447.

Glanzer, M., & Koppenaal, L. The effect of encoding tasks on free recall: Stages and levels. *Journal of Verbal Learning and Verbal Behavior,* 1977, *16,* 21–28.

Glanzer, M., Koppenaal, L., & Nelson, R. Effects of relations between words on short-term storage and long-term storage. *Journal of Verbal Learning and Verbal Behavior,* 1972, *11,* 403–416.

Glanzer, M., & Meinzer, A. The effects of intralist activity on free recall. *Journal of Verbal Learning and Verbal Behavior,* 1967, *6,* 928–935.

Glanzer, M., & Razel, M. The size of the unit in short-term storage. *Journal of Verbal Learning and Verbal Behavior,* 1974, *13,* 114–131.

Glanzer, M., & Schwartz, A. Mnemonic structure in free recall: Differential effects on STS and LTS. *Journal of Verbal Learning and Verbal Behavior,* 1971, *10,* 194–198.

Gordon, S. K., & Clark, W. C. Adult age differences in word and nonsense syllable recognition memory and response criterion. *Journal of Gerontology,* 1974, *29,* 659–665.

Gorfein, D. Effects of intralist activity on free recall performance. *Psychonomic Science,* 1970, *20,* 331–333.

Gregory, R. L. Increase in "neurological noise" as a factor in ageing. *Proceedings of the 4th Congress of the International Association of Gerontology,* Merano, Italy, 1957.

Hicks, L. H., & Birren, J. E. Aging, brain damage, and psychomotor slowing. *Psychological Bulletin*, 1970, *74*, 377–396.

Hulicka, I. M. Age differences in retention as a function of interference. *Journal of Gerontology*, 1967, *22*, 180–184.

Hulicka, I. M., & Grossman, J. L. Age-group comparisons for the use of mediators in paired-associate learning. *Journal of Gerontology*, 1967, *22*, 46–51.

Hulicka, I., & Weiss, R. Age differences in retention as a function of learning. *Journal of Consulting Psychology*, 1965, *29*, 125–129.

Hultsch, D. F. Adult age differences in the organization of free recall. *Developmental Psychology*, 1969, *1*, 673–678.

Hultsch, D. F. Learning to learn in adulthood. *Journal of Gerontology*, 1974, *29*, 302–308.

Hultsch, D. F. Adult age differences in retrieval: Trace dependent and cue-dependent forgetting. *Developmental Psychology*, 1975, *11*, 197–201.

Kinsbourne, M., & Berryhill, J. The nature of the interaction between pacing and the age decrement in learning. *Journal of Gerontology*, 1972, *27*, 471–477.

Laurence, M. W. Memory loss with age: A test of two strategies for its retardation. *Psychonomic Science*, 1967, *9*, 209–210.

Leicht, K. L. Differential rehearsal and primacy effects. *Journal of Verbal Learning and Verbal Behavior*, 1968, *7*, 1115–1117.

Lewis-Smith, M. Q. Short-term memory as a processing deficit. *American Journal of Psychology*, 1975, *88*, 605–626.

Marshall, P. H., & Werder, P. R. The effects of the elimination of rehearsal on primacy and recency. *Journal of Verbal Learning and Verbal Behavior*, 1972, *11*, 649–653.

Meunier, G. F., Stanners, R. F., & Meunier, J. A. Pronounceability, rehearsal time, and the primacy effect of free recall. *Journal of Experimental Psychology*, 1971, *88*, 123–127.

Moenster, P. A. Learning and memory in relation to age. *Journal of Gerontology*, 1972, *27*, 361–363.

Murdock, B. B., Jr. The serial position effect of free recall. *Journal of Experimental Psychology*, 1962, *64*, 482–488.

Murdock, B. B., Jr. Effects of a subsidiary task on short-term memory. *British Journal of Psychology*, 1965, *56*, 413–419.

Murdock, B. B., Jr., & Walker, K. D. Modality effects in free recall. *Journal of Verbal Learning and Verbal Behavior*, 1969, *8*, 665–676.

Postman, L., & Phillips, L. W. Short-term temporal changes in free recall. *Quarterly Journal of Experimental Psychology*, 1965, *17*, 132–138.

Raymond, B. Short-term and long-term storage in free recall. *Journal of Verbal Learning and Verbal Behavior*, 1969, *8*, 567–574.

Raymond, B. J. Free recall among the aged. *Psychological Reports*, 1971, *29*, 1179–1182.

Richardson, J. T. E., & Baddeley, A. D. The effect of articulatory suppression in free recall. *Journal of Verbal Learning and Verbal Behavior*, 1975, *14*, 623–629.

Rowe, E. J., & Schnore, M. M. Item concreteness and reported strategies in paired-associate learning as a function of age. *Journal of Gerontology*, 1971, *24*, 470–475.

Rundus, D. Analysis of rehearsal processes in free recall. *Journal of Experimental Psychology*, 1971, *89*, 63–77.

Schonfield, D., & Robertson, E. A. Memory storage and aging. *Canadian Journal of Psychology*, 1966, *20*, 228–236.

Seamon, J. G., & Murray, P. Depth of processing in recall and recognition memory: Differential effects of stimulus meaningfulness and serial position. *Journal of Experimental Psychology: Human Learning and Memory*, 1976, *2*, 680–687.

Shuell, T. J., & Keppel, G. Item priority in free recall. *Journal of Verbal Learning and Verbal Behavior*, 1968, *7*, 969–971.

Silverstein, C., & Glanzer, M. Difficulty of a concurrent task in free recall: Differential effects on STS and LTS. *Psychonomic Science*, 1971, *22*, 367–368.

Smith, A. D. Adult age differences in cued recall. *Developmental Psychology*, 1977, *13*, 326–331.

Sperling, G. Successive approximations to a model for short-term memory. In R. N. Haber (Ed.), *Information-processing approaches to visual perception.* New York: Holt, Rinehart & Winston, 1969.

Sumby, W. H. Word frequency and serial position effects. *Journal of Verbal Learning and Verbal Behavior*, 1963, *1*, 443–450.

Treat, N., & Reese, H. W. Age, imagery, and pacing in paired-associate learning. *Developmental Psychology*, 1976, *12*, 119–124.

Watkins, M. J. Locus of the modality effect in free recall. *Journal of Verbal Learning and Verbal Behavior*, 1972, *11*, 644–648.

Watkins, M. J., Watkins, O. C., & Crowder, R. G. The modality effect in free and serial recall as a function of phonological similarity. *Journal of Verbal Learning and Verbal Behavior*, 1974, *13*, 430–447.

Welch, G. B., & Burnett, C. T. Is primacy a factor in association formation? *American Journal of Psychology*, 1924, *35*, 396–401.

Welford, A. T. *Ageing and human skill.* New York: Oxford University Press, 1958.

Welford, A. T. Psychomotor performance. In J. E. Birren (Ed.), *Handbook of aging and the individual.* Chicago: University of Chicago Press, 1959.

Welford, A. T. Motor performance. In J. E. Birren & K. W. Schaie (Eds.), *Handbook of the psychology of aging.* New York: Van Nostrand, 1977.

Welford, A. T., & Birren, J. E. (Eds.). *Behavior, aging and the nervous system.* Springfield, Ill.: Charles C. Thomas, 1965.

Wimer, R. E., & Wigdor, B. T. Age differences in retention of learning. *Journal of Gerontology*, 1958, *13*, 291–295.

3 Comments on the Processes That Account for Memory Declines with Age

David Arenberg
National Institute on Aging, NIH

Drs. Smith and Salthouse take quite different approaches to reviewing and discussing memory processes and aging. Dr. Smith's chapter is an excellent review of recent research in the field with heavy emphasis on several of the studies conducted in his laboratory. A major part of Dr. Salthouse's chapter presents an innovative set of proposed strategies for understanding memory and aging. The four sources of his strategies are theory from memory research in psychology, data from memory research, theory from aging research, and data from aging research.

Because of this dissimilarity, it seems virtually impossible to discuss and integrate the ideas and concepts from these two chapters. Instead, I attempt to set forth what I see as the current status of encoding, storage, and retrieval in aging and to add some comments about a few specific points raised in the two chapters.

One consistent story has been emerging over the past several years of research in memory and aging. The old recall less; and they encode less effectively. Retrieval is so dependent upon successful encoding that characterizing age deficits as encoding or retrieval seems to be a matter of preference. One could say that the major locus of age deficits in memory is encoding; old people encode less or encode less effectively and, therefore, remember less. On the other hand, one could say that the major locus of age deficits in memory is retrieval; old people retrieve less because they encode less or less effectively. I prefer the second description because it places emphasis on retrieval failure as the performance deficit, while at the same time identifying the encoding deficit as a major source of the retrieval problem.

The identification of an encoding deficit as a major source of impaired memory performance in the old is rather encouraging. Whenever we focus our attention on action ("intervention" seems to be the term currently in vogue), i.e., what can be done to improve performance in the older individual, it is important to maintain the distinction between structural and control processes. Cell loss and central-nervous-system dysfunction are structural aspects of memory; I do not expect behavioral scientists to implement changes in these areas. Fortunately, however, encoding deficits are primarily in the domain of control processes. It should be possible to modify encoding behavior in older individuals in order to improve memory performance. Mnemonics, for example, are essentially encoding procedures which are designed to enhance retrieval. A specific mnemonic well suited for list learning by the elderly has been demonstrated to be effective for older people (Robertson-Tchabo, Hausman, & Arenberg, 1976).

Evidence from the incidental-learning studies, however, is not so encouraging, for a structural impairment seems to be implicated. The recall findings from studies in which depth of processing has been manipulated by orienting tasks in the incidental-learning paradigm are consistent; i.e., the old do not benefit as much as the young from a semantic orienting task. In other words, a situation which induces high recall (frequently as good as with intentional learning) for the young does not induce high recall for the old. If we are dealing only with a failure to encode spontaneously by the old (a production deficiency), and if the orienting task is assumed to induce semantic encoding, then the old should benefit at least as much as the young from a semantic orienting task. If this does not occur, and much of the evidence says it does not, then this appears to be more than a failure to encode, in the sense of a control process, but rather a system breakdown, i.e., a structural impairment.

At this stage, for purposes of application to memory deficits of the aged, we need to identify procedures which augment encoding and result in improved memory. It may be that some older people are impaired primarily by poor control processes, whereas others are impaired structurally. If so, then findings in which the old benefit more than the young from encoding instructions would be attributable to the subgroup of poor control processors, and findings of poor performance in semantic orienting tasks would be attributable to the subgroup with structural impairment. This would suggest that studies which induced encoding so successfully that the old performed as well as the young included few if any old subjects with structural impairment. On the other hand, it may be that changes in structure with age limit the repertoire of available control processes, and the procedures used in those studies were compatible with the elderly's reduced set of usable control processes.

If there are two subgroups of old, then we need to identify which is which. Those whose performance is largely attributable to poor control processes should be candidates for appropriate memory training; those whose performance is due largely to structural impairment may need training of a different kind, perhaps compensatory behaviors such as list making and other strong reminders.

It is on this basis that I disagree with Dr. Salthouse's conclusion that age impairment at a particular memory stage requires postulating "some fundamental mechanism such as age-related speed loss [p. 61]." This is likely only if all age impairment in memory is due to structural mechanisms. Control processes, however, surely contribute to memory impairments with age and probably account substantially for age deficits in encoding which much of the current evidence supports. If all age deficits in memory are attributable to a fundamental mechanism such as age-related speed loss, it would seem that greater improvements in the memory of older individuals relative to young adults could occur only by affecting some aspect of speed— the basic mechanism or some process intervening between the speed mechanism and the memory performance. If, by enhancing encoding of the material to be remembered, a mnemonic procedure improves memory for an old person more than for a young adult, would we seek the explanation through a basic speed mechanism or through implicating faster encoding, search, or retrieval? I doubt it. Speed would seem to be an outcome rather than an explanation. It is more likely that a procedure which induces proficient encoding leading to improved performance *results in rather than from* faster encoding, search, and retrieval.

Dr. Salthouse does pose a thorny problem as he argues for slowing as the source of age-related memory impairment. He asks, "Why do the old shift to less effective encoding?" Pehaps they do not. Assuming that individuals encode less efficiently with age, perhaps they are doing the same things they did earlier in their lives, but those behaviors do not work so well anymore. In other words, it may be that one can get by with low effort encoding when young, but less-than-optimal encoding leads to increasingly poor performance with age. Whether encoding habits change with age, or as people age they suffer greater consequences from poor encoding habits, Dr. Salthouse identifies a vexing problem for cognitive research in aging.

Although Dr. Smith seems ready to abandon susceptibility to interference as a contributor to memory deficits in aging, I am not yet prepared to do so. My reluctance is based, in part, upon personal experience and a comparison of experiences of colleagues who are age peers with those who are younger. There is also some scientific evidence for increased susceptibility to interference with age (e.g., Arenberg, 1967), although as Smith points out, that evidence is scanty.

Dr. Smith focussed his discussion of interference on storage deficits. I would look elsewhere for age differences in susceptibility to interference, and believe they are most likely to be found in primary memory. Although substantial evidence indicates primary memory is virtually unaffected by aging, the fragility of information in primary memory may well be exacerbated with age. An older person may encounter no more difficulty remembering an unfamiliar telephone number than a young adult, but I would be surprised if the frequency of survival of a number following an interruption between locating it and dialing it would be as high for the older caller.

Dr. Smith might say that failure to recall a number after an interruption is a secondary memory effect rather than an interference effect. Perhaps distracting stimuli are deleterious only when they are interpolated between input and recall; then secondary memory can be invoked. It may be helpful to separate interference due to interpolated distraction from interference due to concurrent distraction. Dr. Smith apparently prefers to conceptualize effects due to an interpolated distraction as a secondary memory deficit. But there is extensive literature showing that the elderly encounter more difficulty in divided-attention tasks than do young adults. Divided-attention tasks typically involve concurrent distraction; during the performance of one task, another action is required. Secondary memory is not implicated. I think of divided attention as a type of interference involving concurrent distraction.

It may be that the older person is particularly susceptible to concurrent distraction only if it requires a response. In dichotic listening, each channel of information is a concurrent distraction for the other channel. Postcued dichotic listening requires attending to both channels but recalling the one that is cued after presentation. A failure to recall the postcued information cannot be attributed to secondary memory or to response interference. The evidence (see Inglis, Sykes, & Ankus, 1968) indicates that the old perform as well as the young for the information cued first. To the extent that the noncued half list in this dichotic paradigm is a distraction, concurrent distraction with no requirement to respond to the distracting stimulus before the primary response does not affect the old more than the young. Apparently concurrent distraction is particularly deleterious to performance of the older person when a response to the distracting task precedes responding to the primary task (and, I suspect, when the distracting task requires processing before the response to the primary task).

One technical point I would like to make concerns the use of proportion correct as a measure when list length is an independent variable. Although Dr. Smith advocates this measure, I am not comfortable with it when applied to entire lists. I am not convinced that proportion correct solves more problems than it creates, especially when an interaction hypothesis is of primary interest. Until convinced, I am not prepared to interpret interactions between age and list length which show that old groups decline less in proportion correct than do young groups (especially when the middle-aged group declines the least).

For age studies in which list length is an independent variable, I believe it is more informative to plot proportion correct at each presentation position. Then it is possible to compare what happens to the first few items of a list at the various list lengths, and to compare the last few items of the lists. It may be elucidating to look at a few items in the middle of each list, too. This approach seems preferable to using either number correct or proportion of total items correct when list length is varied. Proportion correct at specific presentation positions avoids some of the problems inherent in these other potential dependent measures and also provides an opportunity to compare separately primary memory performance and secondary memory performance.

Both Drs. Smith and Salthouse doubt the utility of the continued quest for "the" one process which accounts for age differences and changes in memory, and I agree; but where do we go from here? Dr. Smith suggests we focus on qualitative differences in processing. Dr. Salthouse prefers that we increase our use of rate and speed measures as indices of processing capacity to further our understanding of memory changes with age. I would like to add the suggestion that more of our research be directed at improving memory for older people. I believe we have enough knowledge from our laboratory research at least to begin developing procedures that are effective memory enhancers.

REFERENCES

Arenberg, D. Age differences in retroaction. *Journal of Gerontology,* 1967, *22,* 88–91.

Inglis, J., Sykes, D. H., & Ankus, M. N. Age differences in short-term memory. In S. Chown & K. F. Riegel (Eds.), *Interdisciplinary topics in gerontology* (Vol. 1). New York: Karger, 1968.

Robertson-Tchabo, E. A., Hausman, C. P., & Arenberg, D. A classical mnemonic for older learners: A trip that works! *Educational Gerontology,* 1976, *1,* 215–226.

4

Encoding, Storage, and Retrieval in Adult Memory: The Role of Model Assumptions

David F. Hultsch
C. A. Pentz
Pennsylvania State University

In recent years, scientists have become increasingly aware of the fact that theories and research are articulated within the context of metamodels[1] (Kuhn, 1962, Pepper, 1942). The assumptions outlined by such metamodels define the basic parameters of theory and research such as the nature of the questions to be asked and the truth criteria to be applied (Hultsch & Hickey, 1978; Overton & Reese, 1973; Pepper, 1942; Reese & Overton, 1970). Further, the value of metamodels is specifically found in their usefulness rather than the extent to which they can be found to be "true" (Pepper, 1942; Reese & Overton, 1970).

Such a view of science is clearly relativistic rather than absolute. This relativistic perspective encourages a tradition of scientific pluralism involving the application of multiple models, theories, research designs, and data analysis techniques to phenomena of interest (Baltes & Willis, 1977; Lerner & Ryff, 1978). In addition, it leads to the recognition that science itself is a product of transactions between the scientist and the sociocultural context at all levels (Buss, 1975; Riegel, 1972, 1977).

From such a perspective, descriptions of the learning and memory process will vary depending on the particular metamodel in which the theory and

---

[1]There are a number of metamodels based on various root metaphors. Pepper (1942), for example, distinguishes four basic hypotheses labeled formism, mechanism, organicism, and contextualism. Two of these, organicism and contextualism, appear particularly relevant for cognitive theory at the present time (Reese, 1976). Detailed analyses of the assumptions of these metamodels are available elsewhere (Kaye, 1977; Pepper, 1942; Overton & Reese, 1973; Reese & Overton, 1970). Rather than reviewing this literature in detail, we direct your attention to these references for further clarfication.

research are rooted (Reese, 1973b, 1976). Further, since the salience of various metamodels fluctuates over historical time, it follows that descriptions of the learning and memory process will also fluctuate over historical time. In our view, much of the confusion concerning the usefulness of encoding, storage, and retrieval as constructs for understanding adult learning and memory is related to these changes in our basic assumptions. Accordingly, in this chapter we briefly examine several historical shifts in research on adult learning and memory. Three approaches are reviewed within the context of their underlying metamodels: the associative, multistore information processing, and contextual approaches. Within this framework, emphasis is placed on the contextual approach as a useful perspective for future research. It should be noted that such an effort to examine the metatheoretical roots of learning and memory research is not unique (Jenkins, 1974; Kvale, 1977; Liben, 1977; Reese, 1973b, 1976), although the stress on contextualism from a developmental perspective receives more emphasis. It should also be noted that the purpose of this comparison is not to suggest that one approach to learning and memory is correct while the others are incorrect. Rather, consistent with the relativistic approach outlined previously, emphasis is placed on the need for pluralism in theory and method.

ASSOCIATIVE APPROACHES

From an associative perspective, learning involves the formation of stimulus–response (S–R) bonds, and the contents of memory are defined by such associations. The act of remembering involves emitting previously acquired responses under appropriate stimulus conditions. Changes in learning and memory are seen as quantitative rather than qualitative. Acquisition may occur as a function of increases in the number of S–R associations or as a function of a strengthening of existing associations through processes such as repetition. It follows that forgetting is a function of the loss or weakening of associative bonds through processes such as decay or interference.

  Associative approaches to learning and memory are consistent with the mechanistic metamodel (Reese, 1973b). This metamodel derives its constructs from the concept of a machine. Within this view, the human organism is reactive from a basic state of rest. Activity is a result of external stimulation. Complex activities such as problem solving and affective behavior are viewed as ultimately reducible to simple phenomena governed by material or efficient causes. Given such a framework, the mechanistic metamodel stresses the analysis of elements and the discovery of antecedent-consequent relations. As a result, development is seen as consisting of behavior change, and is continuous in that later behaviors are reducible to or predictible from previous antecedents (Overton & Reese, 1973; Reese & Overton, 1970).

Historically, associative views dominated work on learning, memory, and aging until the late 1950s (Jerome, 1959; Kay, 1959). By and large, the research derived from this framework has provided a relatively pessimistic perspective on the learning and memory capacities of middle-aged and older adults. For example, one major hypothesis derived from the associative framework suggested that the aged might be more susceptible to interference than younger individuals (Welford, 1958). With some exceptions (Gladis & Braun, 1958), this view found empirical support (Arenberg, 1967; Cameron, 1943; Wimer & Wigdor, 1958). Cameron (1943), for instance, compared groups of younger and older adults on a digit recall task. The difference between the age groups was greater when an interpolated task, presumably a source of interference, was included between the presentation and recall of the digits. The antecedents of such interference effects were generally postulated to stem primarily from material causes related to the biological degeneration of the aging organism (Inglis, 1965). Thus, associative approaches to learning and memory tend to project an irreversible decrement view of aging and learning/memory performance in which the principle antecedents are biological.

MULTISTORE INFORMATION-PROCESSING APPROACHES

Multistore information-processing approaches to learning and memory are based on the concepts of storage structures and control operations (Atkinson & Shiffrin, 1968; Murdock, 1967). The former constitute the "location" of memory traces, while the latter constitute the processes which transfer material from one storage structure to another. Typically, three storage structures (sensory stores, short-term store, long-term store), and an indeterminant number of control processes (attention, rehearsal, organization) are postulated.

Stimuli are received and registered in the sensory stores. Sensory memory is part of the peripheral sensory system, and items are represented as literal visual or auditory copies. These representations persist only for a brief time, decaying in the absence of further processing. Information is retrieved from the sensory stores by attending to it, thereby entering it into the short-term store. Here items are coded in terms of their phonemic or visual features. The capacity of the short-term store is small, with information being lost principally by displacement. The duration of primary memory from the short-term can be extended by rehearsal, or the material can be transferred to the long-term store by processing the items in terms of their semantic content. Retrieval from the long-term store is dependent on the development of a retrieval plan based on elaboration or organization of the material. The long-term store has unlimited capacity and the duration of secondary memory is lengthy, if not permanent. The concepts of encoding, storage, and retrieval, then, are fundamental to this view. In effect, the various stores are specifically defined by different encoding, storage, and retrieval characteristics.

Within multistore approaches, the control processes that transfer material from one storage structure to another produce qualitative changes in the material. While some of these processes appear to be automatic, others are clearly under the control of the individual. Thus, unlike the associative approach, multistore approaches assume the individual actively transforms the material and that what is learned and recalled is largely a function of these transformations. That is, what is learned and remembered is not a set of stimulus-response associations, but a totality—the organization of which is imposed by the individual through the various processing mechanisms.

Multistore views are clearly "cognitive" in nature, and Reese (1973b, 1976) has argued that they are consistent with an organismic metamodel. This metamodel derives its constructs from the concept of a living organism. Within this view, the organism is seen as an active totality, and change is qualitative as well as quantitative. Although material and efficient causes may have some effect on the various quantitative and qualitative changes, fundamental causation is teleological in nature. Given such a framework, determining principles of organization, rather than studying component parts, becomes the fundamental inquiry. As a result, development is seen as consisting of structural change, and is discontinuous in that later states are not reducible to or predictable from previous states (Overton & Reese, 1973; Reese & Overton, 1970).

In some respects, the multistore approach outlined previously does not fit neatly into the organismic framework (Reese, 1973b, 1976). First, while the concept of structure is present, it refers to a collection of transformed inputs. As such, it lacks, to some degree, the overall holistic character of organismic structures. Second, multistore theorists have typically not incorporated any teleological principles within their models, although they generally postulate the development of a permanent memory trace. Nevertheless, despite such issues, multistore approaches with their emphasis on active processing and qualitative change are inconsistent with the mechanistic metamodel and may be viewed, reinterpreted, or extended within an organismic framework (Reese, 1973b, 1976).

Historically, multistore views have dominated work on learning, memory, and aging from the early 1960s until the late 1970s (Craik, 1977; Walsh, 1975). Research based on these approaches has suggested that age differences in sensory and short-term storage capacity are minimal (Botwinick & Storandt,

1974; Craik, 1968; Raymond, 1971; Talland, 1968), although the rate at which information can be retrieved from the short-term store may decline (Anders, Fozard, & Lillyquist, 1972). However, when the material to be learned and remembered exceeds the capacity of the short-term store, large age differences are observed, thereby implicating acquisition or retrieval difficulties in secondary memory. Thus, while the adequacy of registration may be sufficient to support immediate recall, the more elaborate coding involved in secondary memory may not be completed as effectively by older individuals.

Essentially, within multistore models, acquisition depends on factors such as the organization of the material, which transforms it in some meaningful way and enters it into the long-term store. There is considerable empirical support for the hypothesis of age differences in these processes. Generally, the older adult's difficulty appears to be of the production deficiency or inefficiency variety. That is, older adults do not spontaneously use organizational strategies as extensively as younger adults, or if they do, use them less effectively (Canestrari, 1968; Eysenck, 1974; Hulicka & Grossman, 1967; Hulicka, Sterns, & Grossman, 1967; Hultsch, 1969, 1971, 1974; Laurence, 1966; Walsh, 1975). However, when various organizational strategies are built into the situation, the performance of older adults improves significantly, sometimes equaling that of the younger adults (Canestrari, 1968; Hulicka & Grossman, 1967; Hultsch, 1969, 1971).

It has also been suggested that the poorer memory performance of older adults is a function of deficits in the retrieval processes of secondary memory. That is, the older adult's difficulty is postulated to be accessibility to already stored information. According to this analysis, age differences should be exacerbated by the absence of retrieval cues at the time of recall and attenuated by their presence. This appears to be the case (Craik, 1968; Hultsch, 1975; Laurence, 1967). Consistent with these findings, age differences on recognition tasks are sometimes absent, or typically smaller, than on recall tasks (Schonfield & Robertson, 1966; Smith, Chapter 1). However, since multistore approaches often view the memory trace as permanent, and retrieval plans as a mechanism for the reproduction of original encoding, such retrieval effects may reflect inappropriate or inefficient encoding at the time of learning (Smith, Chapter 1).

Thus, multistore views of learning and memory have emphasized active processing on the part of the individual, and have suggested age-related decrements in such processing. However, in contrast to associative approaches, they have stressed the modifiability of these decrements via manipulation of variables such as the organization of the material, instructions, and the like. In this sense, multistore models tend to project a decrement-with-compensation view of aging and learning/memory performance. Within this framework, however, multistore approaches to learning and memory have been primarily descriptive. In particular, the focus has been on the specificiation of age differences in performance, and their locus within the encoding, storage, and retrieval processes of the various stores. Much of our recent work, as reviewed by Smith (Chapter 1), has been directed toward this goal.

A CONTEXTUAL APPROACH

In 1932, Bartlett published a book entitled *Remembering* in which he described a series of experiments on the retention of meaningful text materials. For example, in one study, participants attempted to recall an unusual Indian folk tale on several occasions over a period of months. Bartlett reported that there was a high proportion of inaccuracy in the participants' recall, and that they appeared to be unaware of the extent of this inaccuracy. Further, the inaccuracy resulted not only from omission and condensation but from transformation of the original material. These elaborations appeared to be efforts to recast the unusual tale into a form compatible with the participants' cultural knowledge and social conventions. These results led Bartlett (1932) to suggest that we form schemata or concepts of the world based on past experience. During learning, new information is integrated with existing schemata. When the material to be remembered conflicts with existing schemata, as in the case of the unusual folk tale used by Bartlett, recall is distorted. Thus, memory is viewed as an active process involving reconstruction and elaboration of the original information. Although Bartlett's work was published almost 50 years ago, it was essentially ignored for many years. Recently, however, many of the issues raised by Bartlett have re-emerged as researchers have begun to formulate a contextual approach to learning and memory (Cofer, 1977; Jenkins, 1974; Meacham, 1977; Shaw & Bransford, 1977).

The contextual approach to learning and memory is rooted in the contextual metamodel. This model derives its constructs from the concept of a historic event. Within this view, all experience consists of events. Like organicism, contextualism is a synthetic position, in that events have a quality or meaning as a whole. The quality of events is the result of transactions between the organism and its context. Change and novelty are accepted as fundamental to contextualism and the duration of an event is central to it. Organicism also emphasizes change, but it is change toward some particular end state. Unlike organicism, the contextual model denies the existence of absolute or final cause. Thus, the essence of substance is continuous activity and change. The task is to identify and describe these transitions in context.

Such an approach yields a different conceptualization of learning and memory than either the associative or multistore views. The contextual approach does not view learning and memory as involving associative bonds or storage structures and control processes. Rather, the focus is on the nature of the events the individual experiences. What is learned and remembered depends on the total context of the event: for example, the physical, psychological (perceptual, linguistic, semantic, schematic), social, and cultural context in which the event was experienced, the context in which we ask for evidence of remembering, and so forth. Contextually based approaches, then, view learning and memory as a byproduct of the transaction between the individual and the context. Because of this focus on cognition as a byproduct, learning and memory are not seen as isolated processes. Rather, the emphasis is on the interface of the various perceptual, linguistic, inferential, problem-solving, personality, social, and cultural processes that contribute to understanding events. Finally, because of the emphasis on a continuing transaction between the individual and the context, contextually-based approaches do not assume the retrieval of a permanent memory trace. Rather, remembering is a reconstruction of past events. This depends, in large measure, on the degree to which the material has been articulated with past experience during acquisition. In addition, memory also depends on events occurring following acquisition. Thus, the individual continually constructs and reconstructs events as the context changes.

It is important to note that there is no one contextual model of learning and remembering. Indeed, it may be said that there are no models at all but, rather, frameworks consistent with the contextual perspective. A partial listing might include the levels of processing (Craik & Lockhart, 1972; Lockhart, Craik, & Jacoby, 1975), constructive (Cofer, 1977), stage-setting metaphor and re-creation metaphor (Bransford, McCarrell, Franks, & Nitsch, 1977), and dialectical (Kvale, 1977; Meacham, 1977) approaches.

One significant dimension which distinguishes these approaches from one another is the scope of the context attended to. Some of them emphasize contexts proximal to the event while others emphasize contexts distal to it. Thus, emphasis may be placed on the context of the material itself (Craik & Lockhart, 1972; Jenkins, 1974; Kintsch, 1974), the individual's preexperimental knowledge (Brockway, Chmielewski, & Cofer, 1974; Dooling & Christiaansen, 1977), the individual's expectations and goals (Cofer, 1977; Kintsch, 1978), or the sociocultural context (Kvale, 1977; Meacham, 1972, 1977). From a contextual perspective, all of these contexts are potentially important. Indeed, for the contextualist, there is no complete definition of context (Hultsch & Hickey, 1978; Pepper, 1942). All analyses eventually move "outward" from the event into more extensive contexts. The level of analyses used is based on pragmatic criteria. Jenkins (1974) comments: "What makes an analysis good or bad for us is its appropriateness for our research and science and its utility in our pursuit of understanding and application [p. 787]."

There are other significant differences among the various contextual approaches. However, fundamentally, the views noted above (e.g., levels of processing, constructive, dialectical) appear to represent a "family" of approaches rooted in the contextual metamodel. What do these approaches suggest about learning and remembering during adulthood?

Learning

Associative and multistore approaches typically divorce the problem of learning from the problem of memory. However, since events are continually changing, and therefore novel, a contextual perspective does not view memory as an isolated activity. Rather, it is intimately related to other activities such as perceiving and learning. These activities involve the articulation of novel information with past experience (Bransford et al., 1977). Bransford and his colleagues suggest that past experience "sets the stage" for the integration and differentiation of new events.

The importance of this integration and differentiation may be illustrated by the effects of context on comprehension. For example, some passages of prose are not comprehended or remembered very well unless the person is given explicit information concerning what the passage is about (Bransford & Johnson, 1972; Dooling & Lachman, 1971; Dooling & Mullett, 1973). In the Dooling and Lachman (1971) study, for instance, subjects were given passages which, while grammatically correct, were vague and difficult to understand in isolation. For example:

> With hocked gems financing him, our hero bravely defied all scornful laughter that tried to prevent his scheme. "Your eyes deceive," he had said, "an egg not a table correctly typifies this unexplored planet." Now three sturdy sisters sought proof, forging along sometimes through calm vastness, yet more often over turbulent peaks and valleys. Days became weeks as many doubters spread fearful rumors about the edge. At last from nowhere welcome winged creatures appeared signifying momentous success [p. 217].

Subjects given this passage alone found it difficult to comprehend and remember. However, subjects who were given the title, "Christopher Columbus Discovering America," prior to reading the passage were better able to do so. The information presented in the title proved a context for the passage and engaged knowledge about the topic which the individuals already possessed. The passage could then be articulated with this knowledge.

From the contextual perspective, however, past experience is not simply a set of stored memories against which new input is matched. Rather, past experience provides a set of "boundary conditions" for the integration and differentiation of information (Bransford et al., 1977). One formulation of such "boundary conditions" is the concept of a schema (Bartlett, 1932; Cofer, 1977; Kintsch, 1978). A schema may be viewed as an organized representation of an event. It is a prototype or norm which specifies what is known and what is to be expected. Several strands of research may be interpreted within this framework (Bartlett, 1932; Cofer, 1977; Dooling & Christiaansen, 1977; Kintsch, 1978). For instance, Kintsch (1978) has argued that when an individual reads a story, he or she attempts to articulate the story within a certain schema. Thus, if an individual reads a story with a familiar structure, he or she should find it easier to comprehend than one for which they do not have the right schema. Within the Western cultural tradition, simple stories are formed as a series of episodes, each of which contains an exposition, a complication, and a resolution. Typically, events are ordered temporally and related causally (van Dijk, 1977). Stories from some other cultural traditions, however, are structured differently. For example, according to Kintsch (1978), Apache Indian stories are, "held together by a 'principle of fours': there must be four episodes, four actors, using four instruments, etc. [p. 51]." American college students, when presented with stories from these two traditions, were better able to comprehend and abstract the Western-culture stories than the Indian-culture stories. This was the case even though the individual sentences of the two types of stories did not differ in ratings of comprehensibility, imagery, and bizarreness. Thus, out of context, the sentences of the Indian story provided no difficulty. In the absence of the proper schema, however, it was difficult to comprehend the story they told.

The articulation of new information with past experience also allows the individual to go beyond the information given. This is illustrated by research demonstrating that inferences are made from what is read or seen and that these inferences are retained (Brockway, Chmielewski, & Cofer, 1974; Frederiksen, 1975; Johnson, Bransford, & Solomon, 1973; Keenan & Kintsch, 1974; Loftus & Palmer, 1974). For instance, in a series of studies, Keenan and Kintsch (1974) presented subjects with short texts in which certain propositions were either explicitly or implicitly expressed. For example:

Explicit: A carelessly discarded burning cigarette started a fire. The fire destroyed many acres of virgin forest.
Implicit: A burning cigarette was carelessly discarded. The fire destroyed many acres of virgin forest [p. 155].

After reading either the explicit or implicit version of the paragraph, subjects were given the task of verifying a test sentence corresponding to the implicit proposition (e.g., A discarded cigarette started a fire). Keenan and Kintsch (1974) found that subjects were able to recognize the test sentences as true even when they were not explicitly stated. On an immediate test, this judgment was rendered more quickly if the sentence was explicit rather than implicit. On a delayed test, however, verification times for the two types of sentences were the same. These results suggest that regardless of whether the test sentences are explicitly given in a text, the reader will infer the corresponding proposition and store it in memory.

There are many levels at which new input may be articulated with past experience. That is, acquisition processes may be conceptualized as a hierarchy of levels of processing involving wider and wider contexts. Thus, articulation may occur as a function of analysis of the physical, lexical, syntactic, semantic, schematic, functional, or social aspects of the input (see Craik & Lockhart, 1972; Kintsch, 1978 for illustration). Within this context, it is asumned that processing does not involve discrete and unidirectional steps. Rather, analysis occurs simultaneously at multiple levels and involves complex interactions among levels. Integration and differentiation occur from the "bottom up" and from the "top down" (Kintsch, 1978).

Thus, from a contextual perspective, acquisition may be seen as the articulation of inputs with past experience both in terms of their similarity and their uniqueness. Integration and differentiation does not involve matching new information with previously stored information. Rather, past experience provides the boundary conditions for determining the meaning of the event. The differentiation and integration process may be viewed as occurring within a hierarchy of levels which reflect wider and wider contexts.

Remembering

Associative and multistore approaches assume the existence of permanent bonds or traces. Remembering, then, consists of emitting previously acquired responses or retrieval of previously encoded and stored traces. However, the concept of "retrieving" stored items is inconsistent with the contextual metaphor which emphasizes continual change. Rather, from this perspective, remembering may be viewed as the re-creation of previous events (Bransford et al., 1977). On what basis are previous events reconstructed?

One issue involves the extent to which the input has been articulated with past experience during acquisition. In this regard, remembering the meaning of an event is enhanced to the extent to which the event has been integrated with previous knowledge. As we have seen, this may be defined by the extent to which the event has been integrated with various levels of a hierarchy of contexts (Craik & Lockhart, 1972; Kintsch, 1978). For example, research on incidental learning as a function of various orienting tasks illustrates this point (Jenkins, 1974). In these studies, free recall or recognition is superior following an orienting task which requires the use of a semantic unit than following an orienting task which requires a structural analysis of the word. Similarly, Bransford et al. (1977) report a study in which they presented subjects with sentences composed of proper names in the subject and object position (e.g., John is talking with Sally; Bill is helping Sam). Following a single acquisition trial, the subjects were provided with the subject nouns (e.g., John, Bill) and asked to recall the sentence. Bransford et al. report that subjects do very poorly on this task. However, if the acquisition sentences contain names of people with which the subjects are well acquainted, recall improves markedly.

Second, one's ability to remember a particular event will depend on the context of other events in which it was embedded during acquisition. Thus, remembering is a function of a total set of experiences to which a particular event belongs. From this perspective, it is not important whether recall is accurate or inaccurate. Remembering may be reproductive, constructive, and reconstructive at the same time (Kintsch, 1976). The focus is on the conditions under which one or the other of these activities predominates. Thus, in many contexts, increasing integration of the event with preexperimental knowledge enhances remembering of the total event but not the specific components of the event. For example, in some studies, individuals falsely recognize as "old" complex sentences which represent integrations of the simple sentences presented (Bransford, Barclay, & Franks, 1972; Bransford & Franks, 1971). Similarly, recall for text materials becomes increasingly reconstructed over time as the individual integrates the text event into preexisting knowledge (Bartlett, 1932; Dooling & Christiaansen, 1977; Kintsch, Kozminsky, Streby, McKoon, & Keenan, 1975). For example, Kintsch et al. (1975) asked subjects to read two types of texts of varying familiarity: unfamiliar topics from natural science, or familiar topics from classical history. Immediate recall for both types of paragraphs was largely reproductive. However, when recall was delayed for one day, this pattern changed drastically for the familiar texts. Subjects were unable to differentiate between what they read and what they knew, and mentioned many things which they knew about the topic that were not part of the original material.

Re-creation also depends on events following acquisition—events during the interval between acquisition and remembering and at the time of remembering (Anderson & Pichert, 1978; Dooling & Christiaansen, 1977; Loftus, 1975). For example, Dooling and Christiaansen (1977) asked subjects to read a short passage about a "fictitious" person. However, at various points in time, some of the subjects were informed of the true identity of the actually famous main character of the passage. One group received this information immediately before reading the passage; the second group immediately after reading the passage; and the third group immediately prior to the recognition test which occurred one week later for all subjects. Dooling and Christiaansen (1977) report that all three groups informed of the true identity of the main character made more thematic errors than the control group.

Similarly, Frederiksen (1975) has also reported that constructions are a characteristic activity of readers. Frederiksen (1975) considered four different types of constructions: overgeneralizations, pseudodiscriminations, inferences, and elaborations. An overgeneralization occurs when a subject recalls a more generic concept than the one used in the text; for example, "flat island" is recalled as "island." A pseudodiscrimination occurs when a subject recalls a more specific concept than the one used in the text; for example, "administrator" is recalled as "government administrator." An inference occurs when a subject recalls a concept which, although unstated in the text, is logically related to two or more stated concepts; for example "rich ranchers" is recalled when the text only mentions "rich senators" and the fact that all senators are ranchers. Finally, an elaboration occurs when a subject introduces a concept which is not directly related to the text; for example "senators are elected" is recalled although the text says nothing at all about the manner in which senators are chosen. Frederiksen (1975) hypothesized that the first three types of constructions occur during input and are not regarded as errors by the subject. Thus, when multiple study and recall trials are given, these constructions should remain constant or increase rather than decrease as errors would. Frederiksen reports that this was the case. Elaborations, on the other hand, decreased over trials, suggesting that these concepts may be a function of recall rather than comprehension. These data, then, suggest evidence for both constructive processes at the time of comprehension and reconstructive processes at the time of recall.

Thus, from a contextual perspective, remembering may be seen as the reconstruction of previous events. Event reconstruction depends in large measure on the extent to which material has been articulated and integrated with past knowledge and experience during acquisition. As we have seen, this articulation and integration is dependent on the total set of experiences to which the event belongs. In addition, remembering also depends on events occurring following acquisition. The individual continually constructs and reconstructs events as the context changes.

Future Directions

The contextual perspective draws our attention to a number of issues which have typically been neglected in the study of adult learning and memory.

Past Experience And Multiple Contexts. Traditionally, we have attempted to eliminate the impact of past experience on our research by using impoverished materials such as nonsense syllables. From a contextual perspective, such a strategy is unproductive because the articulation of novel information with past experience is the central feature of understanding.

For example, little attention has been directed toward the role of world knowledge. From a contextual perspective, differences in such knowledge will have a significant effect on the comprehension and reconstruction of events (Dooling & Christiaansen, 1977; Kintsch, 1976). That different age or cohort groups will differ in such knowledge is obvious from the fact that they have experienced different individual, cultural, and historical events (Baltes, Cornelius, & Nesselroade, 1979; Hultsch & Plemons, 1979). The importance of these differences is probably crudely indexed by age changes and cohort differences in crystallized intelligence (Baltes & Labouvie, 1973; Horn, 1970; Schaie & Labouvie-Vief, 1974). Gardner and Monge (1977), for instance, have recently demonstrated significant age/cohort-related differences in knowledge in such domains as transportation, disease, slang, finance, religion, fashion, art, hobbies, sports, and current affairs. A recent study by Poon and Fozard (1978) illustrates the point specifically. These investigators presented young, middle-aged, and old adults with stimuli varying in both their uniqueness and datedness. Subjects were asked to name the objects as quickly as possible. The results indicated that speed and accuracy of retrieval from long-term memory was a function of the relative familiarity of the materials to members of the cohort. Thus, older subjects were faster in retrieving the names of unique, dated stimuli (e.g., churn), while younger subjects were faster in retrieving the names of unique, contemporary stimuli (e.g., calculator). Older individuals were also faster in naming the dated version of common stimuli (e.g., telephone) than younger individuals, while no age differences were found in the case of the contemporary version of the same common stimuli. These results emphasize the importance of past experience and world knowledge in adult memory.

Further, little attention has been paid to the relationship of acquisition and remembering to other activities: i.e., intellectual, personality, and social processes. Work examining such multiprocess relationships in adulthood is very limited (Botwinick & Storandt, 1974; Fozard & Costa, 1977; Horn, 1978; Hultsch, Nesselroade, & Plemons, 1976). What little work is available, although derived from noncontextual frameworks, suggests that such relationships may be of importance. For example, Hultsch, Nesselroade, and Plemons (1976) found age/cohort-related differences in patterns of ability-performance relationships on a free-recall task. Memory abilities were more predictive of performance for older adults than for younger adults, while the reverse was true for fluency abilities. Similarly, Fozard and Costa (1977) found age differences in patterns of personality-performance relationships on tasks measuring the speed of retrieval from primary, secondary and tertiary memory.

Finally, we have paid little attention to the individual's goals. Learning and remembering are means to ends as well as ends in themselves (Meacham, 1972, 1977). Further, it is likely that the goals of learning and remembering change markedly over the life span. For example, there is some evidence to suggest the importance of remembering in constructing personality in late life (Butler, 1963; Meacham, 1977). Several studies have reported a relationshp between reminiscence and various indices of adjustment (Boylin, Gordon, &

Nehrke, 1976; Costa & Kastenbaum, 1967; Havighurst & Glasser, 1972). Such a perspective reinforces the importance of memory in reconstructing the individual and the social context (Meacham, 1977).

Thus, from a contextual perspective, attention to multiple and broad contexts is essential. Context is not simply a variable to be manipulated. It is basic. Bransford et al. (1977) comment:

> The basic problem of understanding involves grasping the significances of inputs, and significances are uniquely specified as a function of the *relationship* between a contextually induced framework and the particular input . . . understanding involves relationships; it is an *activity* rather than a *thing* [p. 438].

The adequacy with which these relationships are represented determines the basic validity of the research from a contextual world view (Hultsch & Hickey, 1978).

Meaning. Traditionally, we have also focused on verbatim recall. A contextual perspective, however, draws our attention away from accuracy and toward meaning. Although remembering may be accurate, a contextual perspective emphasizes that the knowledge one gains from experience goes beyond what is shown in accurate recall or recognition. Memory for an event is likely to be far more complete and longer lasting than memory for the "surface" characteristics of the event (Bartlett, 1932; Cofer, 1977; Dooling & Christiaansen, 1977; Frederiksen, 1975; Kintsch, 1976). Obviously, accuracy is important. However, we have probably placed too much emphasis on it. Dooling and Christiaansen (1977) conclude:

> What we remember is enormous. And even more remarkably, most of what we remember has been learned effortlessly and naturally. Our memories seem built for giving high priority to memory codes which have wide generality and importance. We seem to put stress on memory information that will allow us to be approximately correct most of the time, though rarely exactly perfect in terms of rote retention [p. 36].

The potential contrast between meaning and accuracy in adult memory is illustrated by Walsh and Baldwin's (1977) recent study. These investigators presented Bransford and Franks' (1971) linguistic abstraction task to younger and older adults (average ages 18.7 years and 67.5 years). Their general findings with the sample replicated those of Bransford and Franks. More interestingly, Walsh and Baldwin (1977) found no age differences in the integration of semantic information. A free-recall task administered to the same subjects, however, showed significant age differences, with the older adults recalling only about half as much as the younger adults.

Similarly, a number of researchers have shown that older adults are able to recall factual information as well as or better than younger adults (Lachman

& Lachman, Chapter 18; Perlmutter, 1978). Perlmutter (1978), for instance, found that her older subjects were better able to answer questions based on historical events occurring between 1890 and 1969 than were her younger subjects. Perlmutter (1978) also failed to find age-related differences in metamemorial processes—an individual's understanding of his or her own memory. There were no age differences on measures of memory knowledge (e.g., Is it easier to remember visual things than verbal things?), memory strategy use (e.g., How often do you write reminder notes?), and memory monitoring (e.g., prediction of the number of items that would be recalled following incidental and intentional memory tasks).

In our view, the emphasis on meaning its particularly important from an adult developmental perspective because of its relationship to ecological validity (Bronfenbrenner, 1977; Schaie, 1978). That many of our traditional learning and memory tasks lack meaning for older adults is apparent to anyone who has observed their behavior in the laboratory situation. The incidence of older adults' questions concerning the relevance of such tasks and refusals to continue participation is striking compared to that of younger adults. Such behaviors may reflect something more basic than general anxiety or uncooperativeness on the part of older adults. Thus, Schaie (1977) has suggested that there may be qualitatively different stages of adult cognitive functioning, with acquisitive processes dominating in early adulthood and reintegrative processes dominating in later adulthood. These latter processes emphasize the meaningfulness of cognitive demands. Schaie (1977) states:

> The cognitive response...is one of achieving more selective attention to cognitive demands which remain meaningful or attain new meaning. Thus problem solving now no longer occurs as a simple response to a competence-motivation linked stimulus situation, but requires meaning and purpose within the immediate life situation of the individual, or within the more cosmic interests of selected older individuals who exemplify what folk myth describes as the "wisdom of old age" [p. 135].

To the extent that these observations are useful, it is important to modify our strategies for examining remembering in adulthood—including the development of a taxonomy of age and cohort-specific life situations in which remembering occurs (Schaie, 1978; Siegel, 1977).

CONCLUSION

We have summarized three different perspectives on learning and memory—each of which is rooted in a different metamodel and each of which paints a different picture of these processes in adulthood. Further, the root assumptions of these different perspectives cannot be judged as true or false.

Instead, they may only be judged as more or less useful (Pepper, 1942; Reese & Overton, 1970). How is one to respond to such diversity?

From a pluralistic position, it may be argued that all three perspectives are potentially useful and should be retained (Baltes & Willis, 1977; Hultsch & Hickey, 1978; Lerner & Ryff, 1978). Essentially, we agree with this position. However, in our view, current trends in the field of gerontology suggest the potential usefulness of applying a contextual perspective to the study of adult learning and memory at the present time.

In the recent past, aging prototheory has been dominated by extensions of maturational growth models consistent with organicism (Labouvie-Vief, 1977; Reese, 1973a). Within such models, development is seen as biologically based, and is characterized by unidirectional, irreversible, and universal sequences directed toward some end state (Harris, 1957). When extended into adulthood, such maturational growth models focus on intrinsic aging processes which result in the biological degeneration of the aging individual. Behaviorally, this has led to an emphasis on either a "decrement" or "decrement with compensation" view of cognition (Labouvie-Vief, 1977; Schaie, 1973). In the former instance, the emphasis is on the irreversible nature of change, while in the latter instance this emphasis is modified by an examination of environmental conditions which may ameliorate the deterioration. In both instances, however, the focus is on intrinsic processes which reflect "true" aging.

More recently, aging prototheory has been influenced by life span models consistent with contextualism (Baltes & Willis, 1977; Riegel, 1976). These views emphasize multidirectional change and multiple influences in development. That is, change during adulthood is assumed to involve different directions (incremental, decremental) and different forms (linear, curvilinear). As a result, interindividual differences tend to increase over the life span as intraindividual change functions become increasingly divergent. This concept departs sharply from the maturationally based view because it suggests a significant potential for growth during adulthood. Further, a contextually based perspective calls attention to multiple sources of influence on development, including both biological and environmental at both individual, and cultural levels. Baltes, Cornelius, and Nesselroade (1979), for instance, specify three major influence patterns that control development: normative, age-graded influences, normative, history-graded influences, and nonnormative influences. The first two of these covary with time. On the one hand, normative, age-graded influences are highly correlated with chronological age, while, on the other hand, normative, history-graded influences are highly correlated with biocultural history. Influences from both systems may include biological as well as environmental variables (e.g., age changes in brain metabolism or social interaction; historical changes in the gene pool or in the educational system). The third system—nonnormative influences—is not directly indexed by time since they do not occur universally for all people. In addition, when they do occur, they are likely to differ in terms of their clustering, timing, and duration. Nonnormative influences consist of various life events (e.g., illness, divorce, promotion).

To date, our research on adult memory has focused almost entirely on normative, age-graded sources of variance. Undeniably, performance differences between adults of different ages do occur, and typically, these reveal poorer performance on the part of older adults. However, in many respects, our research on adult memory has been inadequate with respect to the issue of multiple sources of influence—both methodologically and conceptually. Methodologically, there is little longitudinal data available on adult learning and memory which would allow the examination of change—the fundamental concern of developmentalists—and still less which uses any form of sequential analyses to partially distinguish age-graded and history-graded sources of influence (Arenberg & Robertson-Tchabo, 1977; Gilbert, 1936, 1973). More data are required in order to examine these issues. We are not suggesting that all research must use sequential designs. Examining multiple sources of influence cannot be accomplished solely by applying a particular methodology (Baltes, Cornelius, & Nesselroade, 1979). That is, from a contextual perspective, history-graded and nonnormative sources are important conceptually as well as methodologically. This does not mean that normative, age-graded sources of influence are unimportant. However, other non-age-related sources of influence such as historical changes in educational patterns are also likely to be critical. From a contextual perspective, such historical variables are just as "developmentally relevant" as age-graded variables. Further, our own hunch is that the more we emphasize meaning rather than accuracy and the role of broader contexts in learning and memory, the more significant history-graded and nonnormative influences will become.

OVERVIEW

It has been argued that whether the course of cognitive development is characterized by growth, stability, or decline is less a matter of "fact" than a matter of the metamodel on which the theories and data are based. Three historical shifts in basic research on adult learning and memory have been reviewed. The associative approach, dominant until the late 1950s, is rooted in the mechanistic metamodel. Within this approach, learning and memory are seen as the formation and dissolution of stimulus-response bonds. The associative approach has projected an irreversible decrement view of aging and learning/memory performance. The multistore information-processing approach, dominant from the early 1960s until the late 1970s, is rooted in the organismic metamodel. Within this approach, learning and memory are governed by storage structures and control processes, and active processing on the part of the learner is emphasized. The multistore view has projected a decrement with a compensation view of aging and learning/memory performance. Finally, it has been argued that a contextual approach is emerging in the present historical context.

A contextual perspective appears to emphasize the activities of perceiving, comprehending, and remembering, rather than encoding, storage, and retrieval. Acquisition is seen as involving the articulation of input with past experience which sets the boundary conditions for perceiving and comprehending the new material. This differentiation and integration are viewed as occuring within a hierarchy of levels which reflect wider and wider contexts. Remembering is seen as the reconstruction of previous events. Event reconstruction depends, in large measure, on the extent to which original events are differentiated from and integrated with past experience during acquisition. In addition, event reconstruction also depends on events occurring following acquisition. Such a contextual perspective on acquisition and remembering leads to several suggestions for examining these activities during adulthood, including an emphasis on past experience, multiple contexts, and meaning.

REFERENCES

Anders, T. R., Fozard, J. L., & Lillyquist, T. D. The effects of age upon retrieval from short-term memory. *Developmental Psychology*, 1972, *6*, 214-217.

Anderson, R. C., & Pichert, J. W. Recall of previously unrecallable information following a shift in perspective. *Journal of Verbal Learning and Verbal Behavior*, 1978, *17*, 1-12.

Arenberg, D. Age differences in retroaction. *Journal of Gerontology*, 1967, *22*, 88-91.

Arenberg, D., & Robertson-Tschabo, E. A. Learning and aging. In J. E. Birren & K. W. Schaie (Eds.), *Handbook of the psychology of aging*. New York: Van Nostrand Reinhold, 1977.

Atkinson, R. C., & Shiffrin, R. M. Human memory: A proposed system and its control processes. In K. W. Spence & J. T. Spence (Eds.), *The psychology of learning and motivation* (Vol. 2). New York: Academic Press, 1968.

Baltes, P. B., Cornelius, S. W., & Nesselroade, J. R. Cohort effects in developmental psychology. In J. R. Nesselroade & P. B. Baltes (Eds.), *Longitudinal research in the study of behavior and development*. New York: Academic Press, 1979.

Baltes, P. B., & Labouvie, G. V. Adult development of intellectual performance: Description, explanation, and modification. In C. Eisdorfer & M. P. Lawton (Eds.), *The psychology of adult development and aging*. Washington, D. C.: American Psychological Association, 1973.

Baltes, P. B., & Willis, S. L. Toward psychological theories of aging and development. In J. E. Birren & K. W. Schaie (Eds.), *Handbook of the psychology of aging*. New York: Van Nostrand Reinhold, 1977.

Bartlett, F. C. *Remembering*. Cambridge: Cambridge University Press, 1932.

Botwinick, J., & Storandt, M. *Memory, related functions, and age*. Springfield, Ill.: C. C. Thomas, 1974.

Boylin, W., Gordon, S. K., & Nehrke, M. F. Reminiscing and ego integrity in institutionalized elderly males. *Gerontologist*, 1976, *16*, 118-124.

Bransford, J. D., Barclay, J. R., & Franks, J. J. Sentence memory: A constructive versus interpretive approach. *Cognitive Psychology*, 1972, *3*, 193-209.

Bransford, J. D., & Franks, J. J. The abstraction of linguistic ideas. *Cognitive Psychology*, 1971, *2*, 331-350.

Bransford, J. D., & Johnson, M. K. Contextual prerequisites for understanding: Some investigating of comprehension and recall. *Journal of Verbal Learning and Verbal Behavior*, 1972, *11*, 717-726.

Bransford, J. D., McCarrell, N. S., Franks, J. J., & Nitsch, K. E. Toward unexplaining memory. In R. Shaw & J. D. Bransford (Eds.), *Perceiving, acting, and knowing: Toward an ecological psychology*. Hillsdale, N.J.: Lawrence Erlbaum Associates, 1977.

Brockway, J. P., Chmielewski, D., & Cofer, C. N. Remembering prose: Productivity and accuracy constraints in recognition memory. *Journal of Verbal Learning and Verbal Behavior*, 1974, *13*, 184-208.

Bronfenbrenner, U. Toward an experimental ecology of human development. *American Psychologist*, 1977, *32*, 513-531.

Buss, A. R. The emerging field of the sociology of psychological knowledge. *American Psychologist*, 1975, *30*, 988-1002.

Butler, R. The life review: An interpretation of reminiscence in the aged. *Psychiatry*, 1963, *26*, 65-76.

Cameron, D. E. Impairment at the retention phase of remembering. *Psychiatric Quarterly*, 1943, *17*, 395-404.

Canestrari, R. E. Age changes in acquisition. In G. A. Talland (Ed.), *Human aging and behavior*. New York: Academic Press, 1968.

Cofer, C. N. On the constructive theory of memory. In F. Weizman & I. C. Uzgiris (Eds.), *The structuring of experience*. New York: Plenum, 1977.

Costa, P. T., & Kastenbaum, R. Some aspects of memories and ambitions in centenarians. *Journal of Genetic Psychology*, 1967, *110*, 3-16.

Craik, F. I. M. Short-term memory and the aging process. In G. A. Talland (Ed.), *Human aging and behavior*. New York: Academic Press, 1968.

Craik, F. I. M. Age differences in human memory. In J. E. Birren & K. W. Schaie (Eds.), *Handbook of the psychology of aging*. New York: Van Nostrand Reinhold, 1977.

Craik, F. I. M., & Lockhart, R. S. Levels of processing: A framework for memory research. *Journal of Verbal Learning and Verbal Behavior*, 1972, *11*, 671-684.

Dooling, J. D., & Christiaansen, R. E. Levels of encoding and retention of prose. In G. H. Bower (Ed.), *The psychology of learning and memory* (Vol. 11). New York: Academic Press, 1977.

Dooling, J. D., & Lachman, R. Effects of comprehension on retention of prose. *Journal of Experimental Psychology*, 1971, *88*, 216-222.

Dooling, J. D., & Mullett, R. L. Locus of thematic effects in retention of prose. *Journal of Experimental Psychology*, 1973, *97*, 404-406.

Eysenck, M. W. Age differences in incidental learning. *Developmental Psychology*, 1974, *10*, 936-941.

Fozard, J. L., & Costa, P. T. *Age differences in memory and decision-making in relation to personality, abilities, and endocrine function: Implications for clinical practice and health planning policy*. Paper presented at Conference on Aging and Social Policy, Vichy, France, May, 1977.

Frederiksen, C. H. Effects of context-induced processing operations on semantic information acquired from discourse. *Cognitive Psychology*, 1975, *7*, 139-166.

Gardner, E. F., & Monge, R. H. Adult age differences in cognitive abilities and educational background. *Experimental Aging Research*, 1977, *3*, 337-383.

Gilbert, J. G. Mental efficiency in senescence. *Archives of Psychology*, 1936, *27*, 188.

Gilbert, J. G. Thirty-five-year follow-up study of intellectual functioning. *Journal of Gerontology*, 1973, *28*, 68-72.

Gladis, M., & Braun, H. W. Age differences in transfer and retroaction as a function of intertask response similarity. *Journal of Experimental Psychology*, 1958, *55*, 25-30.

Harris, D. B. (Ed.). *The concept of development*. Minneapolis: University of Minnesota Press, 1957.

Havighurst, R. J., & Glasser, R. An exploratory study of reminiscence. *Journal of Gerontology*, 1972, *27*, 245-253.

Horn, J. L. Organization of data on life-span development of human abilities. In L. R. Goulet & P. B. Baltes (Eds.), *Life-span developmental psychology: Theory and research*. New York: Academic Press, 1970.

Horn, J. L. Human ability systems. In P. B. Baltes (Ed.), *Life-span development and behavior*, (Vol. 1). New York: Academic Press, 1978.

Hulicka, I. M., & Grossman, J. L. Age group comparisons for the use of mediators in paired-associate learning. *Journal of Gerontology*, 1967, *22*, 46-51.

Hulicka, I. M., Sterns, H., & Grossman, J. Age group comparisons of paired-associate learning as a function of paced and self-paced association and response time. *Journal of Gerontology*, 1967, *22*, 247-280.

Hultsch, D. F. Adult age differences in the organization of free-recall. *Developmental Psychology*, 1969, *1*, 673-678.

Hultsch, D. F. Adult age differences in free classification and free recall. *Developmental Psychology*, 1971, *4*, 338-347.

Hultsch, D. F. Learning to learn in adulthood. *Journal of Gerontology*, 1974, *29*, 302-308.

Hultsch, D. F. Adult age differences in retrieval: Trace-dependent and cue-dependent forgetting. *Developmental Psychology*, 1975, *11*, 197-201.

Hultsch, D. F., & Hickey, T. External validity in the study of human development: Theoretical and methodological issues. *Human Development*, 1978, *21*, 76-91.

Hultsch, D. F., Nesselroade, J. R., & Plemons, J. K. Learning-ability relations in adulthood. *Human Development*, 1976, *19*, 234-247.

Hultsch, D. F., & Plemons, J. K. Life events and life-span development. In P. B. Baltes & O. G. Brim, Jr. (Eds.), *Life-span development and behavior* (Vol. 2). New York: Academic Press, 1979.

Inglis, J. Immediate memory, age, and brain function. In A. T. Welford & J. E. Birren (Eds.), *Behavior, aging, and the nervous system*. Springfield, Ill.: C. C. Thomas, 1965.

Jenkins, J. J. Remember that old theory of memory? Well forget it. *American Psychologist*, 1974, *29*, 785-795.

Jerome, E. A. Age and learning-experimental studies. In J. E. Birren (Ed.), *Handbook of aging and the individual*. Chicago: University of Chicago Press, 1959.

Johnson, M. K., Bransford, J. D., & Solomon, S. K. Memory for tacit implications of sentences. *Journal of Experimental Psychology*, 1973, *28*, 203-205.

Kay, H. Theories of learning and aging. In J. E. Birren (Ed.), *Handbook of aging and the individual*. Chicago: University of Chicago Press, 1959.

Kaye, H. Early experience as the basis for unity and cooperation of "differences." In N. Datan & H. W. Reese (Eds.), *Life-span developmental psychology: Dialectical perspectives on experimental research*. New York: Academic Press, 1977.

Keenan, J. M., & Kintsch, W. The identification of explicitly and implicitly presented information. In W. Kintsch, *The representation of meaning in memory*. Hillsdale, N.J.: Lawrence Erlbaum Associates, 1974.

Kintsch, W. *The representation of meaning in memory*. Hillsdale, N.J.: Lawrence Erlbaum Associates, 1974.

Kintsch, W. Memory for prose. In C. N. Cofer (Ed.), *The structure of human memory*. San Francisco: Freeman, 1976.

Kintsch, W. On comprehending stories: In M. A. Just & P. A. Carpenter (Eds.), *Cognitive processes in comprehension*. Hillsdale, N.J.: Lawrence Erlbaum Associates, 1978.

Kintsch, W., Kozminsky, E., Streby, W. J., McKoon, G., & Keenan, J. M. Comprehension and recall of text as a function of content variables. *Journal of Verbal Learning and Verbal Behavior*, 1975, *14*, 196-214.

Kuhn, T. S. *The structure of scientific revolutions*. Chicago: University of Chicago Press, 1962.

Kvale, S. Dialectics and research on remembering. In N. Datan and H. W. Reese (Eds.), *Life-span developmental psychology: Dialectical perspectives on experimental research*. New York: Academic Press, 1977.

Labouvie-Vief, G. Adult cognitive development: In search of alternative interpretations. *Merrill-Palmer Quarterly*, 1977, *23*, 227-263.

Laurence, M. W. Age differences in performance and subjective organization in the free recall of pictorial material. *Canadian Journal of Psychology*, 1966, *20*, 388-399.

Laurence, M. W. A developmental look at the usefulness of list categorization as an aid to free recall. *Canadian Journal of Psychology*, 1967, *21*, 153-165.

Lerner, R. M., & Ryff, C. D. Implementation of the life-span view of human development: The sample case of attachment. In P. B. Baltes (Ed.), *Life-span development and behavior* (Vol.1). New York: Academic Press, 1978.

Liben, L. S. Memory from a cognitive-developmental perspective: A theoretical and empirical review. In W. Overton & J. Gallagher (Eds.), *Knowledge and development* (Vol. 1). New York: Plenum, 1977.

Lockhart, R. S., Craik, F. I. M., & Jacoby, L. L. Depth of processing in recognition and recall: Some aspects of a general memory system. In J. Brown (Ed.), *Recognition and recall*. New York: Wiley, 1975.

Loftus, E. Leading questions and the eyewitness report. *Cognitive Psychology*, 1975, *7*, 560-572.

Loftus, E. F., & Palmer, J. C. Reconstruction of automobile destruction: An example of the interaction between language and memory. *Journal of Verbal Learning and Verbal Behavior*, 1974, *13*, 585-589.

Meacham, J. A. The development of memory abilities in the individual and society. *Human Development*, 1972, *15*, 205-228.

Meacham, J. A. A transactional model of remembering. In N. Datan & H. W. Reese (Eds.), *Life-span developmental psychology: Dialectical perspectives on experimental research*. New York: Academic Press, 1977.

Murdock, B. B. Recent developments in short-term memory. *British Journal of Psychology*, 1967, *58*, 421-433.

Overton, W. F., & Reese, H. W. Models of development: Methodological implications. In J. R. Nesselroade & H. W. Reese (Eds.), *Life-span developmental psychology: Methodological issues*. New York: Academic Press, 1973.

Pepper, S. C. *World hypotheses*. Berkeley: University of California Press, 1942.

Perlmutter, M. What is memory aging the aging of? *Developmental Psychology*, 1978, *14*, 330-345.

Poon, L. W., & Fozard, J. L. Speed of retrieval from long-term memory in relation to age, familiarity, and datedness of information. *Journal of Gerontology*, 1978, *33*, 711-717.

Raymond, B. Free recall among the aged. *Psychological Reports*, 1971, *29*, 1179-1182.

Reese, H. W. Life span models of memory. *The Gerontologist*, 1973, *13*, 472-477. (a)

Reese, H. W. Models of memory and models of development. *Human Development, 1973, 16*, 397-416. (b)

Reese, H. W. Models of memory development. *Human Development*, 1976, *19*, 291-303.

Reese, H. W., & Overton, W. F. Models of development and theories of development. In L. R. Goulet & P. B. Baltes (Eds.), *Life-span developmental psychology: Theory and research.* New York: Academic Press, 1970.

Riegel, K. F. Influence of economic and political ideologies on the development of developmental psychology. *Psychological Bulletin,* 1972, *78,* 129-141.

Riegel, K. F. The dialectics of human development. *American Psychologist,* 1976, *31,* 689-700.

Riegel, K. F. History of psychological gerontology. In J. E. Birren & K. W. Schaie (Eds.), *Handbook of the psychology of aging.* New York: Van Nostrand Reinhold, 1977.

Schaie, K. W. Methodological problems in descriptive developmental research on adulthood and aging. In J. R. Nesselroade & H. W. Reese (Eds.), *Life-span developmental psychology: Methodological issues.* New York: Academic Press, 1973.

Schaie, K. W. Toward a stage theory of adult cognitive development. *International Journal of Aging and Human Development,* 1977, *8,* 129-138.

Schaie, K. W. External validity in the assessment of intellectual development in adulthood. *Journal of Gerontology,* 1978, *33,* 695-701.

Schaie, K. W., & Labouvie-Vief, G. Generational versus ontogenetic components of change in adult cognitive behavior: A fourteen-year-cross-sequential study. *Developmental Psychology,* 1974, *10,* 305-320.

Schonfield, D., & Robertson, B. A. Memory storage and aging. *Canadian Journal of Psychology,* 1966, *20,* 228-236.

Shaw, R., & Bransford, J. (Eds.). *Perceiving, acting, and knowing.* Hillsdale, N.J.: Lawrence Erlbaum Associates, 1977.

Siegel, A. W. "Remembering" is alive and well (and even thriving) in empiricism. In N. Datan & H. W. Reese (Eds.), *Life-span developmental psychology: Dialectical perspectives on experimental research.* New York: Academic Press, 1977.

Talland, G. A. Age and the immediate memory span. In G. A. Talland (Ed.), *Human aging and behavior.* New York: Academic Press, 1968.

van Dijk, T. A. *Text and context: Explorations in the semantics and pragmatics of discourse.* London: Longman, 1977.

Walsh, D. A. Age differences in learning and memory. In D. S. Woodruff & J. E. Birren (Eds.), *Aging: Scientific perspectives and social issues.* New York: Van Nostrand 1975.

Walsh, D. A., & Baldwin, M. Age differences in integrated semantic memory. *Developmental Psychology,* 1977, *13,* 509-514.

Welford, A. T. *Aging and human skill.* London: Oxford University Press, 1958.

Wimer, R. E., & Wigdor, B. T. Age differences in retention of learning. *Journal of Gerontology,* 1958, *13,* 291-295.

5

Age Differences in Memory: The Roles of Attention and Depth of Processing

Fergus I. M. Craik
Eileen Simon[1]
Erindale College, University of Toronto

In this chapter we wish to explore the roles of attention and depth of processing in the encoding of information, and how deficits in these two functions might underlie age decrements in memory and learning. In line with the aims of this volume, the stress will be as much on the types of work that may be carried out in the future as on work already completed. We will point to what we see as useful growth areas for the study of age differences in memory.

Whereas the dominant trend in models of information processing during the 1960s was to break down cognitive processes into their components, and study the characteristics of these isolated subsystems and their interrelations (e.g., Atkinson & Shiffrin, 1968; Broadbent, 1958), many recent theorists have argued for studying the cognitive system in a more holistic fashion (e.g., Craik & Lockhart, 1972; Norman, 1968). By this latter view, it is less likely that a cognitive deficit will be attributable to one "component" of the system leaving others intact (e.g., a dysfunction of short-term memory or of the attentional filter). Rather, deficits are likely to be widespread and permeate the whole system—although they may show up more clearly in some circumstances than in others. We suggest that many age decrements in memory are attributable to deficits in attention and depth of processing, attempt to show how these notions relate to each other, and speculate that the deficits will be observed in several related cognitive functions. In particular,

---

[1]Now with the Ministry of Transportation and Communications, Systems Research and Development Branch, Downsview, Ontario.

we suggest that encoding and retrieval processes are at least very similar, and perhaps even identical; if this is so, of course, a dysfunction in one process should be mirrored in the other.

Less radically, there seems good agreement that two major sources of age decrements in memory and learning are, first, situations involving division of attention and second, situations in which older people process information less "deeply" than do younger people. The first conclusion is based on some of Welford's (1958) findings, on the dichotic listening studies of Inglis and his colleagues, and on the results of other experiments examining age differences under conditions of divided attention summarized by Craik (1977a, pp. 391-392). All of this work points to the conclusion that older subjects are especially penalized when they must divide their attention between two input sources or between one input and some internal manipulation of the input. The second suggestion, that old subjects process information less deeply, is based on work by Eysenck (1974, 1977), Horn (1978), Lauer (1975), Perlmutter (1978a) and an experiment by White, reported by Craik (1977a). Some of these studies, and their implications, are discussed more fully later.

If these suggestions regarding two sources of memory deficit are confirmed by further work, the pattern of findings will clear up some of the confusion surrounding the question of whether older persons do or do not show a decrement in short-term memory functioning. As pointed out by Craik (1977a), it seems likely that previous conclusions to the effect that there is an age-related decline in short-term memory functioning were based on situations involving either divided attention or the need to manipulate the material held. When the task involves maintenance of a few items over a short time period, and no reorganization of the items is required, age differences are slight or nonexistent (Craik, 1977a, pp. 392-400). Although shallow levels of processing in the sense intended by Craik and Lockhart (1972) are not synonymous with short-term memory, it is nonetheless true that brief maintenance of small amounts of verbal material often appears to involve relatively shallow acoustic or articulatory codes. Thus the typical "primary memory" task (Waugh & Norman, 1965), involving neither divided attention nor manipulation of material, but allowing the use of "shallow" codes, should show no age decrements, and this is the result observed. However, both "working memory" tasks (Baddeley & Hitch, 1974) and secondary memory components of short-term retention, should show age decrements by the present view, since the first necessitates active reorganization and manipulation and the second requires the involvement of deeper, semantic codes for good performance. Again, observations are in line with this analysis.

The work and ideas discussed in the remainder of this chapter are concerned largely with secondary memory performance. The concepts of depth of processing and division of attention are examined more closely, and some speculations are offered on how attentional processes and "depth" may be related. In particular, we discuss ways in which the concepts may relate to observed deficits in cognitive functioning in the elderly.

Before turning to a consideration of age differences, some recent work on the levels-of-processing formulation will be described briefly. The ideas put forward by Craik and Lockhart (1972) have been added to and modified in various ways, and several of these changes are relevant to the subsequent discussion of age differences in memory.

RECENT WORK ON LEVELS OF PROCESSING

Craik and Lockhart (1972) suggested that the cognitive system was structured hierarchically and that operations are carried out by the system for the purposes of perception and comprehension; "shallow" levels of analysis are concerned with sensory and physical aspects of stimuli, whereas deeper levels of analysis are progressively concerned with abstract, semantic, associative processes. Further, it was suggested that the memory trace is the record of those operations, and that deeper processing is associated with more durable traces. Since 1972, this position has been added to and modified in various ways (Craik & Tulving, 1975; Jacoby & Craik, 1979; Lockhart, Craik & Jacoby, 1976). The major changes are now briefly summarized.

First, rather than thinking of the cognitive system as always analyzing stimuli from shallow to deep, with the attendant notion that stimuli must "pass through" intervening levels to reach deep levels, we now endorse recent notions of a more flexible, interactive system (e.g., Rumelhart, 1977). That is, both "bottom-up" sensory to semantic processing, and "top-down" schema-driven processing occur to facilitate perception and comprehension. The memory trace is still conceptualized as the record of those operations that have been carried out, but we have abandoned the notion of a fixed-order, bottom-up, processing system. By the present view, previous learning, in the form of expectations or "schemata," interacts with the current sensory input to give rise to perception and understanding.

Second, whereas "depth" is still an important concept, it is no longer the sole determinant of memory performance; in particular, the idea of "elaboration" has played a major role in recent formulations (e.g., Craik & Tulving, 1975). "Depth" refers to differences in the qualitative type of analysis and memory code, whereas "elaboration" refers to the extensiveness or richness of processing carried out at any level or depth. Certain tasks (e.g., proof-reading, color-matching) require rather extensive processing at shallow levels, whereas other tasks (e.g., reading for meaning) require minimal sensory analysis, but more extensive deep processing. Another example concerns practice effects: Early in practice, rather extensive operations must be carried out at various levels of analysis, but with increasing practice, fewer operations are necessary—again, however, it is suggested that the memory record of a specific performance will reflect the operations carried out on that particular occasion.

Third, further principles have been added to augment the ideas of depth and elaboration: The congruity of a stimulus with the cognitive system refers to its compatibility with the analyzing processes; thus a congruous event can be dealt with quickly and easily, it may be enriched by associative processes, and it can probably be reconstructed relatively easily at retrieval. The distinctiveness of an encoded event (Eysenck, 1979; Klein & Saltz, 1976) refers to the discriminability of the wanted event from others in the system. The suggestion is that deeper, more elaborately encoded events are likely to yield distinctive encodings which are then more discriminable and retrievable during recall or recognition.

Fourth, whereas the original ideas dealt exclusively with encoding, the framework has now been extended to describe retrieval also. The suggestion is that retrieval processes can be described in the same terms as encoding processes—thus, at retrieval the subject may or may not process retrieval information in a deep and elaborate fashion. In addition, we endorse the notion that retrieval operations must be compatible with the initial encoding operations for remembering to occur. This compatibility between encoding and retrieval is summed up as the encoding specificity principle (Tulving & Thomson, 1973) and was also proposed by Kolers (1973) in his work on repetition of operations. Our position differs from Tulving's, however, in that we argue for the necessity of both the encoding specificity principle and depth of processing (Fisher & Craik, 1977).

In summary, it is suggested that both the qualitative nature (depth) and extensiveness (elaboration) of processing lead to an event's being encoded in a more or less distinctive fashion. Distinctiveness confers *potential* memorability on the event, but for that potential to be realized it is necessary for retrieval processes to reinstate the same mental operations at the time of remembering. Memory may fail either (or both) because the event was not processed sufficiently deeply and elaborately in the first place to form a distinctive encoding, or because retrieval operations failed to match encoding operations (Jacoby & Craik, 1979; Moscovitch & Craik, 1976).

AGE DIFFERENCES IN DEPTH OF PROCESSING

How can the foregoing ideas be applied to age differences in learning and memory? One immediate implication is that it is no longer possible to split up encoding and retrieval phases so neatly as was implied by information flow models—encoding deficits are likely to be mirrored by retrieval deficits.

However, as detailed later in this section, it may be possible to "repair" inefficient processing by guiding the relevant operations in an optimal way; further, it appears possible to repair encoding and retrieval separately (although inefficient encoding will set a limit on performance that cannot be overcome even by optimal retrieval processing). Thus, in general, age decrements may be attributable either to an initial failure to encode the event deeply and elaborately, to a failure to process retrieval information deeply and elaborately, or (somewhat related to the second point) to a failure at retrieval to match retrieval processes to those carried out at input. Three lines of work relating depth of processing to age deficits in memory can be distinguished and these lines will now be described in turn.

The first set of ideas rests on the basic notion that deeper processing is more difficult and effortful to achieve, and that when processing resources are limited (as they plausibly are in older people) there is a consequent failure to utilize deeper, semantic levels. The evidence for the conclusion that deeper processing requires more effort or processing resource comes from studies by Eysenck and Eysenck (1979), Griffith (1976), Johnston and Heinz (1976), and Simon and Craik (1979). All these studies demonstrated that performance on a concurrent task declined as the primary task required deeper processing. Given that the achievement of greater depths of processing requires more effort, and on the assumption that older subjects are less able or less likely to make this greater effort, it follows that age decrements in memory might be attributable to a failure by older subjects to process stimuli to a sufficient depth to support good retention. Further, these ideas suggest that older subjects should not show a decrement in performance relative to young subjects when the initial task required only shallow processing; as the initial task necessitated progressively deeper processing, however, older subjects would be progressively less able to carry out the task as effectively and would thus show corresponding deficits in subsequent memory performance. That is, the ideas predict that, in retention, an interaction between age and the "depth" requirements of initial processing tasks should be found.

The predicted interaction was demonstrated by Eysenck (1974). He gave subjects various incidental orienting tasks that required the generation of either relatively shallow responses (counting letters or generating rhymes) or deeper responses (generating appropriate adjectives or images) to word stimuli. In a subsequent recall test, older subjects showed an increasing decrement, relative to a young control group, from letters to rhymes to adjectives to imagery. In a fifth condition, in which subjects were simply instructed to learn the group of words, old subjects showed the greatest decrement. This last result strongly implies that under relatively normal learning conditions, young subjects spontaneously employ deeper levels of processing whereas older subjects do not. Eysenck (1974, 1977) proposed such a "processing deficit hypothesis" of age decrements in memory to describe his results.

The second line of work relating aging to depth of processing starts with the speculative assumption that whereas older subjects do not spontaneously encode events in a deep semantic fashion, they are nevertheless capable of such processing. That is, it is suggested that older subjects exhibit a "production deficiency" in their encoding operations. If old subjects show a failure to process deeply when left to generate their own responses, but are still capable of carrying out more effective learning operations, it should be possible to overcome this apparent production deficiency by instructing them in the use of mediators (Hulicka & Grossman, 1967) or by *giving* them appropriate orienting tasks to perform.

The latter approach was taken by White (reported by Craik, 1977a). Subjects were asked to make either "case," "rhyme," or "category" decisions about common nouns (see Craik & Tulving, 1975, for details of the technique) or were asked simply to "learn" the words. White found substantial age decrements in recall for both the free learning task (where old subjects might be expected to exhibit a processing deficiency) and the semantic orienting task (where, by the argument above, little age decrement might be expected). However, in a subsequent recognition task for the same words, the age decrement remained for the free learning words, but was eliminated for those words processed in the semantic orienting task condition, as detailed in Fig. 5.1. Apparently, when processing is guided in an optimal fashion both at *input* (by means of an appropriate orienting task) and at *retrieval* (by using recognition) the age decrement in retention is minimized or even eliminated. It is important to note, however, that processing must be guided *both* at input and at retrieval before the age decrement is fully reduced.

In White's experiment, the recognition test followed the recall test within the same subjects. The study has since been replicated in Craik's laboratory, but with recall and recognition as a between-subject variable. Again, subjects were given case, rhyme, or category orienting tasks under incidental learning conditions, plus an intentional learning condition; again, the materials were unrelated words. The results are shown in Table 5.1.

Although in this case there were age decrements throughout, the pattern of findings is broadly similar to that reported by White. That is, the age decrement (taken here as the ratio of old/young scores) was least when orienting tasks were given during the acquisition phase and retention was tested by recognition. Age decrements were greater in recall, even when orienting tasks were used at acquisition, and were also greater in recognition following free-learning instructions. Again it may be concluded that old subjects fail to process deeply both at encoding and retrieval unless their processing is guided appropriately. The fact that older subjects' performance can be restored almost to the level attained by young subjects strongly supports the notion that the age deficit is a *production deficiency*—it is a failure to carry out operations which, nonetheless, the subjects are capable of carrying out.

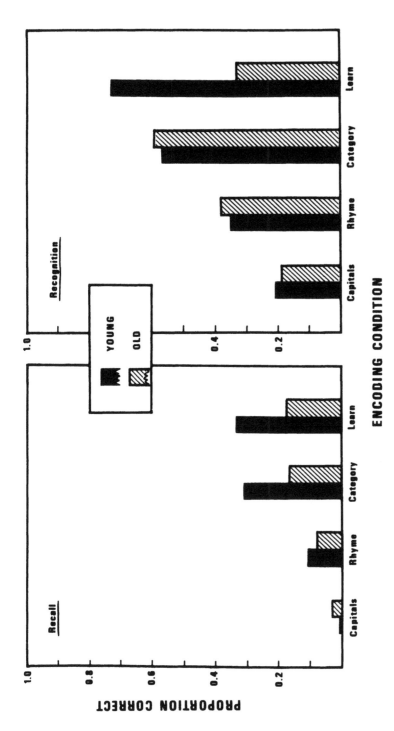

FIG. 5.1. Age differences in recall and recognition as a function of depth of processing (S. White, cited by Craik, 1977a).

101

TABLE 5.1
Mean Proportions Of Words Recalled And Recognized Following Various Orienting
Tasks

	Recall				Recognition			
	Case	Rhyme	Category	Learn	Case	Rhyme	Category	Learn
Young	.02	.08	.16	.45	.31	.49	.77	.83
Old	.01	.05	.12	.35	.26	.36	.69	.54

Two apparent differences between these results and previous studies in the literature may be attributed to the particular conditions of White's experiment and the replication just reported. First, why is there little sign of the age × depth interaction reported by Eysenck (1974)? The difference here may be that subjects in Eysenck's experiment were left free to generate their own responses, whereas in White's experiment processing was more constrained by the use of orienting tasks. In addition, in both White's experiment and the present replication, age decrements in *recall* tended to increase at deeper levels of processing (thereby confirming Eysenck's result), but there is no systematic pattern of decrement when *recognition* is used to assess retention. Second, why do both White's study and the replication show a large age decrement in the free-learning/ recognition condition—especially in light of several previous studies (e.g., Schonfield & Robertson, 1966) showing little if any age loss under such conditions? As a speculation, since the encoding manipulations were carried out within subjects in both present studies, the necessity to switch encoding operations from trial to trial, plus the large number of trials involved (64 in each study), may have led either to the older subjects processing "learn" words in a rather cursory manner, or to an attempt on their part to maintain some "learn" words by means of rehearsal for immediate recall at the time of test. The latter strategy, especially, would lead to reasonable levels of recall, but poor recognition.

The results of several other recent studies are broadly in agreement with the conclusion that a production deficiency in older subjects can be overcome by guiding processing both at input and retrieval. Studies by Lauer (1975) and by Zelinski, Walsh, and Thompson (1978) fall into this category. The results of an experiment by Perlmutter (1978b) are in even closer agreement with the present conclusions. As part of the study, Perlmutter examined age differences in recall and recognition for words after intentional learning and after an incidental semantic orienting task (generating free associations to each word). In line with the arguments and data discussed in this chapter, she found that the age decrement was least when recognition was coupled with a semantic orienting task. In a later study, Perlmutter (1978a) again concluded that an associative orienting task eliminated age differences between 20- and

60-year-olds' recognition, but not free or cued recall. In contrast, Mason (1979) found *greatest* age differences in both recognition and recall following a semantic orienting task. The difference between Mason's results on the one hand and those of White and Perlmutter on the other may be attributable to some difference in procedure. Just what that difference is, is unclear at present; one possibility to be discussed later is that older subjects require more time to achieve an adequate deep encoding, and that Mason's procedure (5 sec for each trial) did not provide sufficient time.

A third and somewhat different line of research, relating age decrements to current process-oriented views of memory, is illustrated by the work of Simon (1977, 1979). She obtained evidence on the types of processing carried out by older subjects by jointly manipulating processing at encoding and retrieval, and by studying the effectiveness of different retrieval cues. The rationale here follows from the encoding specificity principle of Tulving and Thomson (1973). In essence, this principle states that the memory trace reflects encoding operations and that, in turn, retrieval information must be compatible with trace information for the trace to be retrieved. In Simon's experiments, processing was guided at encoding by telling subjects, before list presentation, the nature of the retrieval cue. Then the relative effectiveness of different retrieval cues was compared, and inferences were drawn about the type of information in the trace. If older subjects do process less deeply, for example, it might be expected that, for them, relatively "shallow" cues would be more effective than "deeper" semantic cues.

In Simon's (1979) first experiment, subjects from three age groups were given intentional learning instructions for unrelated words, followed by different recall conditions. Subjects of all ages recalled more words when given a phonemic cue (the first two letters of the word) than when given no cues (free recall); however, the more informative contrast is between the phonemic cue conditions and a semantic cue condition in which synonyms of the target words were given as cues. If older subjects encode less deeply, a greater age decrement should be observed using semantic cues, and Fig. 5.2 (left panel) shows that this was so. In Experiment 2, a more semantic encoding was induced by presenting the words to be learned in the context of a sentence frame. In addition, subjects were instructed to study the specific meaning that was provided by each sentence frame in order to remember the words better. As in Experiment 1, subjects expected a memory test and knew, except with the context cues, the kinds of cue that would be given; in this case the cues were either phonemic, synonyms, or a re-presentation of the sentence context with the target word missing. The results are shown in the center panel of Fig. 5.2. The performance of older subjects was similar to that in Experiment 1 where words were presented in isolation, whereas the pattern of cue effectiveness for young subjects was quite different. In Experiment 2, semantic cues (synonyms and sentence frames) were excellent cues for young

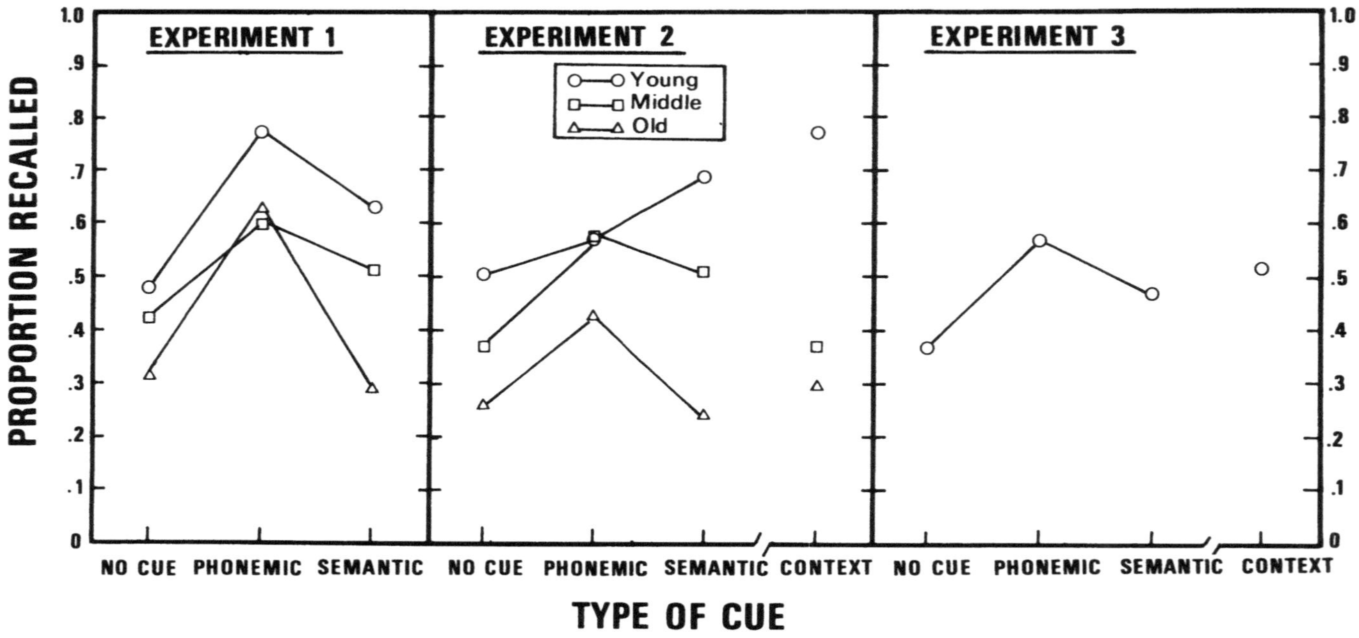

FIG. 5.2. Proportion of words recalled in three age groups as a function of type of cue (Simon, 1979).

subjects, whereas for the middle-aged and old groups the semantic cues were less effective than phonemic cues. It may be concluded that the encoded traces in young subjects contain more semantic information than do the corresponding traces in the two older groups. The sentence context was the best cue of all for young subjects, but was not particularly effective for the older groups, suggesting that one important age-related deficit is a failure to *integrate* fully each word with its meaningful sentence frame at encoding. More generally, it is interesting to speculate that perhaps older subjects do not integrate experienced events so well with the current context. Finally, in Experiment 3, the pattern of results obtained with older subjects in Experiment 2 was secured in young subjects by reducing presentation time from 8 sec per sentence to 4 sec (Fig. 5.2, right panel). The young subjects were apparently prevented from elaborating the words and integrating them with the sentence contexts, even though the information (namely meaningful sentences) and the instructions were compatible with such processing. Indeed, the pattern is similar to the pattern obtained in Experiment 1 where the same words were presented, to different subjects, without contextual information. Simon argued that these data do not illustrate the importance of time but, rather, the importance of focusing on the nature of the operations that underlie performance in different experimental conditions.

An important assumption underlies Simon's analysis of age differences within the levels-of-processing framework, and this distinguishes her approach from the studies reported by Craik (1977a) and Eysenck (1977). Simon's assumption is that orienting tasks probably do *not* control processing in cases where memory is deficient, such as in aging, alcoholic intoxication, and time restriction—or at least that orienting tasks exert much less control in such cases. Working with young adult subjects, Nelson (1979) and also Postman and Kruesi (1977) have pointed out that orienting tasks bias, rather than fully determine, the type of encoding actually carried out. It is a reasonable assumption that orienting tasks exert less control in, for example, older or intoxicated subjects. In these cases it is especially important to assess the encoding achieved under various input conditions by the use of different cues. In recognition tests, especially, it is unclear what information is being utilized; future work should attempt to clarify the picture by using procedures that guide processing more directly at both encoding and retrieval. Simon (1979) has speculated that perhaps older subjects perform well on recognition tests because they can rely on phonemic codes in that context.

A recent study by Simon and Craik further illustrates the use of different cues to assess age differences in processing operations. Old and young subjects were given sentences containing a word to be learned. The sentences biased a rather specific interpretation of the words, which always occupied the last position in the sentence. Two examples are:

The highlight of the circus was the clumsy BEAR.
The lock was opened with a bent PIN.

The cues used were either context-specific—in this case the qualifying adjective (e.g., "clumsy" or "bent")—or were general descriptions of the words with no reference to the sentence contexts (e.g., "wild animal" or "a fastener"). The rationale was that if young subjects' encodings of words are more influenced by the specific context and are more integrated into the sentence (Simon, 1979), then the adjective cues would be particularly effective. If older subjects encode events in a less context-specific manner, the general cues should be relatively more effective.

TABLE 5.2
Mean Proportions Of Words Recalled By Old And
Young Subjects

	General Cue (Category)	Specific Cue (Adjective)
Young	0.32	0.44
Old	0.31	0.22

Table 5.2 shows that the predicted pattern of results was obtained: Specific adjective cues were more effective for younger subjects, whereas the general descriptive cues were more effective for the old group. One reason for the generally observed superiority of semantic encoding in young adult subjects is that such encodings are rendered highly specific and distinctive by the encoding context (Jacoby, 1974; Nelson, 1979). If older subjects have a tendency to be less influenced by the context, to encode events in a similar way from occasion to occasion, it follows that they will benefit less from semantic encoding contexts.

FUTURE WORK ON LEVELS OF PROCESSING AND AGING

A number of issues present themselves for elucidation by future work. They are summarized briefly here.

If the suggestion that older people fail to process events deeply continues to be a reasonable description of the experimental findings, the question arises as to *why* this is so. Why do older subjects not process items deeply when, apparently, their processing can be repaired virtually to the level of young subjects by the use of orienting tasks and recognition procedures? It seems unlikely that they do not *know* what operations are effective for remembering (the type of explanation favored for production deficiencies in children); rather, it seems more likely that deep, elaborate processing is especially effortful, takes more "cognitive energy," and so such processing drops out first as the person ages. One goal of further work will be to explore the effort requirements for various types of processing and to determine how these requirements change with age. It is clear that any general relationship between depth and effort must be qualified by a person's expertise at a given task (Bransford, Franks, Morris, & Stein, 1979); deep processing that is highly practiced can probably be carried out with relatively little expenditure of effort. The interrelations among depth (in the sense of greater semantic involvement), expertise, and age will provide an interesting topic for further study.

A related question is whether the loss of "spontaneous" processing in older people can be fully reinstated by means of orienting tasks. The evidence from most studies, reviewed previously in the paper, is that it can, provided processing is repaired at both input and retrieval (although, admittedly, direct evidence from cuing studies is still lacking on this point). Results that are somewhat parallel to those found with older subjects have been obtained from experiments on memory and alcoholic intoxication (Craik, 1977b). In one recent study, Hartley, Birnbaum, and Parker (1978) found that intoxicated subjects could carry out various orienting tasks but still showed substantial decrements in recall. At first sight, these results provide a challenge to the levels-of-processing point of view which states that memory performance is a rather automatic function of the initial processing task. Two possibilities remain open within the levels-of-processing framework. First, it is possible that greater control of retrieval operations (by use of a cued recall test, for example) would reduce the decrement between intoxicated subjects and controls. Second, it is possible that although, nominally, the intoxicated subjects are carrying out the same orienting tasks, functionally, the processing of intoxicated subjects is less deep and extensive. This second possibility could be explored through the use of different retrieval cues. If it can be shown by the use of more direct procedures that intoxicated subjects do carry out mental operations that are as deep and elaborate as those performed by sober controls, it would seem necessary to postulate some further "consolidation" process between initial processing and memory performance. One exciting research issue is further exploration of the similarities and differences between the effects of aging and alcoholic intoxication on memory, especially the extent to which both deficits can be attributed to inefficient encoding and retrieval processes, or whether it is necessary to invoke the notion of consolidation.

If older subjects do suffer from some curtailment of processing, what is the nature of this reduction? Is it a failure to process each attended item so deeply and elaborately? A failure to enrich the item through association and inference (Till, 1978)? A failure to integrate the item with ongoing context (Simon, 1977, 1979)? A failure to relate items together (that is, a failure to organize)? Studies in progress in our own labs are directed at some of these questions.

What is the nature of retrieval inefficiencies in older people? Is it a failure to process retrieval information so deeply and elaborately or a failure to process information in the same way from time to time, so that a mismatch occurs between the encoded trace and the operations carried out at retrieval? Does the encoding specificity principle "interact" with age, in the sense that young subjects lay down more distinctive and discriminable traces and thus require highly specific retrieval information to match the traces? (That is, one possibility is that deeper, distinctive traces support higher levels of retention *potentially,* but require appropriate specific retrieval information before the potential can be realized).

Do time constraints give particular difficulty to older subjects? In the present volume, the chapters by Salthouse and by Waugh and Barr (Chapters 2 and 15 respectively) put a great deal of emphasis on temporal limitations in older persons' processing. We have somewhat mixed views on this question. On the one hand, work with young adult subjects shows that it is the qualitative nature of the encoding that is associated with later memory performance, not processing time as such (Kolers, 1973; Craik & Tulving, 1975). On the other hand, it is clear that time restrictions can limit the depth of processing, elaboration, or integration of an event with its context, and so lead to poorer memory (Paivio & Csapo, 1969; Simon, 1979, Experiment 3). One resolution of the debate on "time versus qualitative type of processing" is that type of processing is the critical determinant of retention but that older people require longer times to achieve equivalent encodings. The relations between time, processing type, and age provide another important focal issue for further work.

Although not strictly within the present framework, it seems likely that future work will have to take the distinction between episodic and semantic memory (Tulving, 1972) into account. Our own thinking here is that a dichotomy is too abrupt, and that episodic and semantic memories describe end-points of a *continuum,* with moderately specific generic memories lying between the extremes. Are there differential age losses in the ability to retrieve "semantic" and "episodic" information? The line of argument advanced in the present chapter suggests that context-specific episodic memories should be more vulnerable to the effects of aging (reflecting perhaps increasing complaints of absent-mindedness and forgetfulness as people grow older). In addition, recent studies have shown little or no impairment with age in the ability to retrieve and utilize factual knowledge (Lachman & Lachman, Chapter 18; Perlmutter, 1978b). There is some evidence, then, for an age-related decline in remembering episodic events, whereas utilization of general semantic knowledge is relatively unimpaired. However, Robert Crowder (Chapter 11) makes the interesting point that one major complaint of older people is that they have increasing difficulty in remembering names—semantic memory information in Tulving's terms. There is obvious scope here for a series of useful fact-finding studies.

In general, it seems that further work to examine age differences in memory within the levels-of-processing framework will aim to control various aspects of encoding, both at input and retrieval, and compare such controlled processing with that carried out during unrestricted tasks such as free learning and free recall. A major objective will be to determine how much of the loss is remediable through the use of guided procedures, and how much of the loss is permanent and irrecoverable.

DIVIDED ATTENTION

One research strategy that may illuminate the nature of the age decrement in memory is to examine the effects of other variables that appear to mimic aging in some respects. One such variable is division of attention between the primary task (for which later memory is assessed) and some secondary task. Some evidence points to the notion that divided attention and aging have similar effects on information processing and memory. In free recall, for example, both age (see Craik, 1977a) and divided attention (Murdock, 1965) are associated with substantial memory losses in secondary memory but little if any in primary memory. Second, Eagle and Ortof (1967) showed that divided attention (DA) was associated with an increase in phonemically related errors, suggesting shallower processing under DA conditions. Third, it is well established that the effects of age and DA interact, suggesting that some basic loss is being compounded. If the parallel holds, what similar processing deficits lie behind it? The most obvious is that both effects reflect a reduction in processing resource, and that this lack of resource leads to shallower and less elaborate encoding, as suggested earlier in this chapter (see also Simon & Craik, 1979).

We suggest further work can usefully be carried out to explore the parallel in greater detail—such work would illuminate both the nature of age decrements and possibly the relations between attention and memory. DA conditions can be contrasted with focused attention conditions at both input and retrieval; again the stress would be on the *qualitative nature* of the observed loss, not simply on the fact that performance is poorer under DA conditions. We are particularly keen to explore the notion that as attention is withdrawn, some cognitive activities can still be carried out, but perhaps in a less rich and elaborate fashion; presumably with greater removal of attention, fewer cognitive activities are possible.

How do the divided attention notions fit into the levels-of-processing framework? The most straightforward suggestion is that, in general, greater depths of processing require more attention (Griffith, 1976; Johnston & Heinz, 1976; Simon & Craik, 1979). However, it seems certain that this general relation must be qualified by the idea of expertise (Bransford et al., 1979)—that is, that highly practiced operations can be carried out quickly and relatively effortlessly even though they do involve deep processing. If the available amount of attention or processing resource is reduced (e.g., by a divided attention task and, possibly, by aging), there will no longer be sufficient "energy" to carry out deeper and more specific processing, although relatively automatic shallower processing (and also highly practiced operations) can still be accomplished.

SUMMARY

In summary, the present chapter has discussed ways in which recent formulations of memory processes might be applied to increase our understanding of age differences in memory. It was suggested that, due to a lack of processing resource, older people process events less deeply and elaborately and that the resulting memory traces are thus less distinctive and discriminable. Further work should attempt to clarify the nature of processing deficits at encoding and retrieval, and any age changes in the relations between encoding and retrieval processes. It seems particularly important to establish whether a curtailment in depth and elaboration is sufficient to explain age deficits (and to what degree such curtailment can be "repaired" by guiding processing), or whether such further notions as temporal slowing and differential consolidation are necessary. Finally, further light may be thrown on age deficits by studying the similarities between aging, divided attention, and perhaps other "abnormal" states such as fatigue, intoxication, and brain damage. A reduction in processing resource may be the common factor underlying the deficits in memory function associated with these conditions.

ACKNOWLEDGMENTS

The authors are grateful to Morris Moscovitch for helpful discussions of many of the issues treated in the present chapter. We are also grateful for research funds received from the University of Toronto and from the National Research Council of Canada (Grant A8261 to Fergus I. M. Craik).

REFERENCES

Atkinson, R. C., & Shiffrin, R. M. Human memory: A proposed system and its control processes. In K. W. Spence and J. T. Spence (Eds.), *The psychology of learning and motivation* (Vol. 2). New York: Academic Press, 1968.

Baddeley, A. D., & Hitch, G. Working memory. In G. H.Bower (Ed.), *The psychology of learning and motivation* (Vol. 8). New York: Academic Press, 1974.

Bransford, J. D., Franks, J. J., Morris, C. D., & Stein, B. S. Some general constraints on learning and memory research. In L. S. Cermak & F. I. M. Craik (Eds.), *Levels of processing in human memory*. Hillsdale, N.J.: Lawrence Erlbaum Associates, 1979.

Broadbent, D. E. *Perception and communication*. New York: Pergamon Press, 1958.

Craik, F. I. M. Age differences in human memory. In J. E. Birren & K. W. Schaie (Eds.), *Handbook of the psychology of aging*. New York: Van Nostrand Reinhold, 1977. (a)

Craik, F. I. M. Similarities between the effects of aging and alcoholic intoxication on memory performance construed within a "levels-of-processing" framework. In I. M. Birnbaum & E. S. Parker (Eds.), *Alcohol and human memory*. Hillsdale, N.J.: Lawrence Erlbaum Associates, 1977. (b)

Craik, F. I. M., & Lockhart, R. S. Levels of processing: A framework for memory research. *Journal of Verbal Learning and Verbal Behavior, 1972, 11,* 671–684.

Craik, F. I. M., & Tulving, E. Depth of processing and the retention of words in episodic memory. *Journal of Experimental Psychology: General, 1975, 104,* 268–294.

Eagle, M., & Ortof, E. The effect of level of attention upon "phonetic" recognition errors. *Journal of Verbal Learning and Verbal Behavior, 1967, 6,* 266–231.

Eysenck, M. W. Age differences in incidental learning. *Developmental Psychology, 1974, 10,* 936–941.

Eysenck, M. W. *Human memory: Theory, research and individual differences*. Oxford: Pergamon Press, 1977.

Eysenck, M. W. Depth, elaboration, and distinctiveness. In L. S. Cermak & F. I. M. Craik (Eds.), *Levels of processing in human memory*. Hillsdale, N.J.: Lawrence Erlbaum Associates, 1979.

Eysenck, M. W., & Eysenck, M. C. Processing depth, elaboration of encoding, memory stores, and expended processing capacity. *Journal of Experimental Psychology: Human Learning and Memory, 1979, 5,* 472–484.

Fisher, R. P., & Craik, F. I. M. The interaction between encoding and retrieval operations in cued recall. *Journal of Experimental Psychology: Human Learning and Memory, 1977, 3,* 701–711.

Griffith, D. The attentional demands of mnemonic control processes. *Memory and Cognition, 1976, 4,* 103–108.

Hartley, J. E., Birnbaum, I. M., & Parker, E. S. Alcohol and storage deficits: Kind of processing? *Journal of Verbal Learning and Verbal Behavior, 1978, 17,* 635–647.

Horn, J. L. *Final report on a study of speed, power, carefulness, and short-term learning components of intelligence and changes in these components in adulthood*. National Science Foundation Grant Number GB-41452, 1978.

Hulicka, I, M., & Grossman, J. L. Age-group comparisons for the use of mediators in paired-associate learning. *Journal of Gerontology, 1967, 22,* 46–51.

Jacoby, L. L. The role of mental contiguity in memory: Registration and retrieval effects. *Journal of Verbal Learning and Verbal Behavior, 1974, 13,* 483–496.

Jacoby, L. L., & Craik, F. I. M. Effects of elaboration of processing at encoding and retrieval: Trace distinctiveness and recovery of initial context. In L. S. Cermak & F. I. M. Craik (Eds.), *Levels of processing in human memory*. Hillsdale, N.J.: Lawrence Erlbaum Associates, 1979.

Johnston, W. A., & Heinz, S. P. *Attention: An integrative conceptual framework.* Paper presented at the annual meeting of the Psychonomic Society, St. Louis, November 1976.

Klein, K., & Saltz, E. Specifying the mechanisms in a levels-of-processing approach to memory. *Journal of Experimental Psychology: Human Learning and Memory,* 1976, *2,* 671–679.

Kolers, P. A. Remembering operations. *Memory and Cognition,* 1973, *1,* 347–355.

Lauer, P. A. *The effects of different types of word processing on memory performance in young and elderly adults.* Ph. D. thesis, University of Colorado, 1975.

Lockhart, R. S., Craik, F. I. M., & Jacoby, L. L. Depth of processing, recognition and recall: Some aspects of a general memory system. In J. Brown (Ed.), *Recall and recognition.* London: Wiley, 1976.

Mason, S. E. The effects of orienting tasks on the recall and recognition performance of subjects differing in age. *Developmental Psychology,* 1979, *15,* 467–469.

Moscovitch, M., & Craik, F. I. M. Depth of processing, retrieval cues, and uniqueness of encoding as factors in recall. *Journal of Verbal Learning and Verbal Behavior,* 1976, *15,* 447–458.

Murdock, B. B., Jr. Effects of a subsidiary task on short-term memory. *British Journal of Psychology,* 1965, *56,* 413–419.

Nelson, D. L. Remembering pictures and words: Appearance, significance, and name. In L. S. Cermak & F. I. M. Craik (Eds.), *Levels of processing in human memory.* Hillsdale, N.J.: Lawrence Erlbaum Associates, 1979.

Norman, D. A. Toward a theory of memory and attention. *Psychological Review,* 1968, *75,* 522–536.

Paivio, A., & Csapo, K. Concrete-image and verbal memory codes. *Journal of Experimental Psychology,* 1969, *80,* 279–285.

Perlmutter, M. *Age differences in adults' free recall, cued recall, and recognition.* Paper presented at the annual meeting of the Psychonomic Society, San Antonio, November 1978.(a)

Perlmutter, M. What is memory aging the aging of? *Developmental Psychology,* 1978, *14,* 330–345.(b)

Postman, L., & Kruesi, E. The influence of orienting tasks on the encoding and recall of words. *Journal of Verbal Learning and Verbal Behavior,* 1977, *16,* 353–369.

Rumelhart, D. E. Toward an interactive model of reading. In S. Dornic (Ed.), *Attention and performance VI.* Hillsdale, N.J.: Lawrence Erlbaum Associates, 1977.

Schonfield, D., & Robertson, B. A. Memory storage and aging. *Canadian Journal of Psychology,* 1966, *20,* 228–236.

Simon, E. *Age differences in human memory: A levels-of-processing analysis.* Ph.D. thesis, Queen's University, 1977.

Simon, E. Depth and elaboration of processing in relation to age. *Journal of Experimental Psychology: Human Learning and Memory,* 1979, *5,* 115–124.

Simon, E., & Craik, F. I. M. *Resource constraints on depth and elaboration of processing.* Manuscript in preparation, 1979.

Till, R. E. *Age differences in adult memory for implicational sentences.* Paper presented at the annual meeting of the American Psychological Association, Toronto, September 1978.

Tulving, E. Episodic and semantic memory. In E. Tulving & W. Donaldson (Eds.), *Organization of memory.* New York: Academic Press, 1972.

Tulving, E., & Thomson, D. M. Encoding specificity and retrieval process in episodic memory. *Psychological Review,* 1973, *80,* 352–373.

Waugh, N. C., & Norman, D. A. Primary memory. *Psychological Review,* 1965, *72,* 89–104.

Welford, A. T. Ageing and human skill. London: Oxford University Press, 1958.

Zelinski, E. M., Walsh, D. A., & Thompson, L. W. Orienting task effects on EDR and free recall in three age groups. *Journal of Gerontology,* 1978, *33,* 239–245.

6 Attentional Dysfunctions and the Elderly: Theoretical Models and Research Perspectives

Marcel Kinsbourne
University of Toronto

MODELS AND PRINCIPLES

Age-related impairments in mental function can be divided into those that arise for experiential reasons and those that arise for biological reasons. The former will vary with the social environment, and will exert their effects chiefly by influencing the older person's self-concept and therefore his motivation to perform. The latter are based on the probability, cumulative over time, that a person will sustain brain damage. They will vary with factors that affect the integrity of neuronal functioning.

The research to date on the biological determinants of age-related cognitive impairment has led us to an impasse. Recent studies validate and amplify what is already known, but no new research direction is apparent. When such a situation exists in a scientific field, it is usually because the existing theoretical models have been fully exploited and have outlived their usefulness. It is therefore opportune to consider what further models might offer heuristic possibilities.

Old people perform less well than young on many tasks (Botwinick & Storandt, 1974). Attempts have been made to identify particular modes of problem-solving (e.g., spatial rather than verbal) that are maximally vulnerable, or to identify processing stages (e.g., encoding rather than retrieval) that bear the brunt of age-related deficit. But the usual outcome of studies lends itself to the simpler interpretation that the impairment is a matter of degree, and involves no change in the pattern of behavior (e.g., Kinsbourne 1973a; Kinsbourne & Berryhill, 1972). Another conjecture was that learning that runs counter to overlearned information or habit is particularly difficult for the aged (Ruch, 1934; Korchin & Basowitz, 1957). But all the data produced for and against such notions are susceptible to a single simple generalization: "Fluid" as opposed to "crystallized" intellectual function is exceptionally vulnerable to aging (Horn, 1978; Kinsbourne, 1977a).

Most tasks call for some on-the-spot ingenuity in resolving novel or unexpected issues, as well as references to a long-accumulated fund of information or knowledge. Cattell (1957) called the former the fluid and the latter the crystallized aspect of intelligence. Different tasks call for these two components of intellect in different proportions. The more crucial the fluid component is, the more vulnerable is the performance of that task to age-related decrement. In contrast, the crystallized aspect seems to resist all but the most severe age-related brain deterioration. Although not all published data has been analyzed for this distinction, there is face validity to the effort to account for a wide range of disproportionalities in age-related performance decrements in this way. Take the apparent resistance to age-related decrement of verbal intelligence as an instance. As measured on the Wechsler Adult Intelligence Scale, verbal subscale scores hold up better with increasing age than do performance subscale scores. But the verbal tests rely extensively on fund of knowledge. When Elias and Kinsbourne (1974) used verbal and spatial tasks that were identical except with respect to whether the coding was verbal or representational, they found a comparable age-related decrement on both.

We can apply the fluid–crystallized distinction to memory, which is our present concern. Memory is classifiable into context-bound or context-free (Pribram, 1969), and into episodic or semantic (Tulving, 1972). We can argue that remembering unique conjunctions of circumstances or "episodes" exercises fluid intelligence to a greater extent than remembering much-rehearsed and overlearned items of information ("semantic memory"). The former is retrieved by means of contextual reconstruction; the latter is retrieved in so automatized a manner that contextual information is noncontributory. One would expect, and does find, that episodic memory lapses are the ones most frequently complained of by the old.

We are then left with a rather simple, ostensibly irreducible, proposition: The more difficult the fluid component is of any task, the more that task presents a problem to the old. Any new research direction in aging and cognition would have to qualify this proposition if it is not to lead back to well-worn paths.

We now introduce a further pertinent generalization. The widespread neuronal dysfunction and death that is often found in very old people may be caused by many different disorders, and each can vary in severity as well as in the particular distribution of its impact on the brain. This heterogeneity of pathology would be expected to lead to heterogeneity of "cognitive profile" (scatter of ability to perform in different problem-solving modes). With large subject samples, one would expect the skewing of various individual profiles to average out into a uniform decrement across modes, but with a substantially greater variance than obtains in younger populations (Kinsbourne, 1977a). Actually, in many studies that compare the performance of young and the elderly subjects, the expected variance differential is hard to find. It is counteracted by sampling biases that make for unrepresentative homogeneity within experimental groups. The use of volunteers, exclusion of the "unhealthy," restrictions with respect to socioeconomic status or race, and the loss from longitudinal studies of "drop-outs," tend to reduce within-group differences. Nevertheless, cognitive deficits in old people include a number of different subtypes, some of which we can now begin to explore.

Brain integrity may be compromised in old people in three general ways. There may be:

1. Diffuse neuronal depletion: This compromises the various cerebral "processors" to a comparable extent.
2. Topographically skewed neuronal depletion: This interferes with the proper balance and flexibility of opponent systems.
3. Intense focal damage: This generates specific neuropsychological symptoms.

The third of these categories is far from unique to the old, results from focal pathology (stroke, tumor, abscess, trauma, etc.) at any age, and is a concern of clinical neuropsychology. The first two, although also not unique to the old (they occur in presenile dementia during middle age, in the dementia of Down's syndrome in later adolescence, and in childhood in cases of progeria), are disproportionately prevalent among the old, and therefore are now further considered.

Localization of function in the cerebrum is no longer a contentious issue. It occurs, often to an exquisitely selective degree (e.g., Milner, 1974; Kinsbourne, 1976). But there has been no recent advance in our understanding of the effects on intellectual function of moderate diffuse neuronal loss. A simple model would predict in such a case a conglomeration of all possible neuropsychological syndromes in minor form. But Lashley and his students (Lashley, 1942) have evidence that certain aspects of intellect are not tied to particular brain loci, but rather depend on the integrity of wide cerebral areas. Diffuse impairment might leave specific functions intact, and yet render its victim sluggish in response, lacking in vigilance, and inert with respect to change of mental set. Such impairment implicates certain forms of attention, attentional modes that are determined by the state of specific opponent mechanisms.

Much central nervous function is controlled by opponent processes (e.g., Sherrington, 1906). There is mutually inhibitory interaction between opposing influences, offering the organism a range of possible settings, so that it can vary its behavioral style with a view to securing adaptive advantage across diverse situations (Kinsbourne, 1974b). But if some brain areas are more depleted of neurons than others, and it so happens that an opponent mechanism is asymmetrically implicated, then behavior will be biased toward the aspect contributed by the intact element, and the organism's range of behavioral options will become restricted. The abnormality is quantitative; some normal behaviors are used to excess, and others drop out of the repertoire.

Mature and efficient cognitive processes permit the selection for attention of particular stimuli or features of stimuli to the exclusion of others, the division or distribution of attention across a stimulus field, and flexibility with respect to the focus, locus, and maintenance of attention over time. We attribute the ability to select to general cerebral integrity. The ability to vary the locus, distribution, and duration of attention depends on the integrity of relevant opponent systems (Kinsbourne, 1974b). All these attentional capabilities are obviously pertinent to memory, in that they facilitate the encoding of critical features of the memorandum, thus providing a more salient and distinctive experience for subsequent retrieval. They are equally relevant to effective retrieval, for reasons that we now discuss in the context of a model for remembering.

A recent count (Roediger, 1978) listed more than 30 models of memory. Yet they had in common a dominant theme: "Traces are distributed in a hypothetical mental space and trace utilization involves a search for these traces." This type of theorizing, although it derives from a different subdiscipline of psychology, has the same heuristic limitations as does simplistic localizationism that conceives of the brain as a mosaic of differentially represented control centers for specific behaviors. Based on such a model, one can then ask, where in the brain is behavior A represented, where B, etc. In the case of memory, this approach leads into a will-of-the-wisp pursuit of the functional characteristics and brain location of the mental space that biases memory traces, and of the search processes that identify the correct address and thus retrieve the to-be-remembered item. These models prejudge the issue. No evidence for a memory store exists, and it is not at all clear that remembering is most usefully described as involving a search process.

Let us instead observe that there is no such thing as memory in the abstract. Instead, people remember events, gain information, acquire skills. These are processes in which, undoubtedly, particular brain areas play key roles. But it is one thing to localize mental operations (remembering), and quite another, to localize their product (memory) (cf. Bartlett, 1932).

A more economical model simply credits neural systems with a basic property, and specifies a process that is necessary to turn this property to adaptive advantage. The property is that when neuronal activity has once assumed a particular pattern, it will with more than chance probability once more function according to that pattern *if some critical portion of that pattern of activity is reinstated* (Beurle, 1956). Cueing is, experientially, the reproduction of some ingredient of the situation to be remembered. Neurologically, it reinstates some part of the patterned activity that prevailed during the event in question. By a process the fine detail of which eludes conscious awareness, the experience as a whole, in it essentials, "springs to mind." The brain has reassumed the relevant pattern of activity, and the previous experiences once more determine the individual's behavior. In organisms that do not mentally represent (i.e., many if not all animals and presumably the human infant), this reinstated pattern of neural unity necessarily triggers overt behavior; the organism reenacts its previous response. The same occurs in more mature humans when mental representation is not called for, i.e., when, by virtue of sufficient familiarity with salient aspects of the situation, response is automatic. But the ability to represent mentally greatly enlarges the organism's ability to respond differentially. While the episode is merely mentally represented, the organism is not yet committed to any specific action (unless the individual confuses mental representation with representation of ongoing events, i.e., hallucinates). Instead, the representation can be the focus of selective attention, the to-be-remembered item can be extracted, and the response limited accordingly, rather than determined by the total experience. So selective attention, unconstrained by crudely "salient" stimulus properties, is as much called for in processing a mental representation of a previous experience as in processing ongoing events.

If we provisionally accept, for heuristic purposes, the account of remembering described heretofore, we can readily specify the nature of the process that facilitates remembering. In order to remember (i.e., achieve a pattern of central activity that is not totally determined by the present stimulus situation), one must be able to dissociate the central state from salient but irrelevant stimulus influence, and also from existing but irrelevant states of mind. While the brain is protected from influences that would give rise to competing patterns of activity, it is optimally situated for purposes of remembering (given minimally sufficient cueing).

When a particular episode is repeatedly reexperienced, some of its characteristics gain in salience, whereas others cease to be mentally represented. Ultimately, a minimal cue will engender an invariant response with fluent preconscious automaticity, and without the need for mediation by reexperienced context. The item has entered the organism's information store (semantic memory). Its context (the circumstance under which it was initially experienced) is forgotten (Kinsbourne & Wood, 1975). The individual simply "knows" the answer to that question.

How then can remembering become more difficult due to diffuse damage of the brain? Based on the foregoing discussion, we would hesitate to incriminate damage to the hypothetical memory store or an equally hypothetical search mechanism. It seems implausible that the suggested propensity of neural systems to reproduce prior patterned states of activities when cued by elements of that activity would vary with either focal or general disease. Insofar as widespread and widely diverse areas of brain are active during different experiences, memory traces as a class cannot be localized to any one part of the brain. Instead, the remembering involves essentially the same parts of brain as did the initial experiencing. Focal lesions might limit the range and transform the nature of particular experiences, but they would not uniformly make all of episodic remembering more difficult. General or diffuse damage might deplete processors so as to render them capable of less fine resolution or specificity, but would not be expected to disturb the general pattern of neuronal activity. Instead, we suggest that both focal and diffuse damage that impair remembering exert their harmful effects by virtue of the attentional dysfunctions that they induce.

Damage to the limbic system (seen in sharp relief in the amnesic syndrome most commonly found in Korsakoff's psychosis—cf. Victor, Adams, & Collins, 1971) could interfere with its victim's ability to override the influence of his existing state of mind and of the stimuli that surround him, so as to attend selectively to the cues which will serve to reinstate the previous experience. Amnesics' difficulties with shift of mental set (Talland, 1968) and the ability to make spontaneous use of subtle changes in context for learning and recall can account for at least some of their difficulties as demonstrated in recent experimental studies (Kinsbourne & Winocur, in press; Kinsbourne & Wood, 1975; Winocur & Kinsbourne, 1978). In aging, diffuse damage could involve the limbic system among others, and thus generate similar though less severe difficulties.

But by far the most pervasive effects of diffuse neuronal depletion, as in aging, is likely to relate to limitations in selective attentional processes. Differences in selective attention alter the nature of experiences and affect the reproducibility of experiences. Specifically, old people who have suffered diffuse neuronal loss may have their experience of events more determined by details (including irrelevant details) of the events, and less by the event viewed in terms of the differentiations and categorizations which are habitually performed by people with intact cerebral functioning. Therefore the usual cues for remembering might not work. More concrete and specific cueing might be required. An understanding of the nature of possible attentional dysfunctions might suggest practical ways of helping old and intellectually impaired people to remember by supplying them cues which their impaired attentional systems can use.

POSSIBLE MECHANISMS OF
ATTENTIONAL DYSFUNCTION
DUE TO DIFFUSE CEREBRAL DAMAGE

Wholistic Perception

To some extent, the neuronally depleted brain may be like the immature brain of the same species or the less complex brain of a neurologically less specialized species. In children, the response repertoire is more limited and stereotyped (Gibson, 1969; Kinsbourne & Swanson, 1979a). "Prewired synergisms" found in the infant reappear in senile dementia. Similarly, attention dedifferentiates. Perception becomes more holistic and more tied to the perceptual hierarchy. "Salient" stimulus dimensions (e.g., color, form) trap attention and preempt awareness of more subtle parameters of perceptual differences.

In general, the elderly individual should be more constrained by biologically predetermined patterns of attending and performing. This loss of adaptive function must compromise his ability to extract from the environment just those cues which would most effectively support subsequent retrieval of specific information. The effect on remembering should be to reduce its specificity. Experiences merge into one another and only the most striking can be reconstructed. This issue, however, and the broader issue of the extent to which perception regresses to an immature (undifferentiated) state in senility have not yet been systematically investigated.

A potentially aggravating factor is anxiety, which restricts the "range of cue utilization" (Easterbrook, 1959). Anxious people base their responses on the most salient and familiar features, rather than on a more complete appraisal of the situation. State anxiety in old people is very common, particularly when they face what they fear are problems that they will be unable to solve. When old people behave in rigid and stereotyped ways, it may not be obvious to what extent biological variables and to what extent state anxiety are responsible.

State Dependence

An issue that arises in this connection, and that could conceivably be of major importance, is that of state-dependent learning (Overton, 1971; Swanson & Kinsbourne, 1979a). This describes the finding that material learned when an individual is in a particular distinctive (usually drug-related) state is better remembered when the person is in a similar than in a dissimilar state. In view of the high level of chronic drug use among the elderly, including psychoactive drugs, the issue of drug-state dependence calls for study. But state dependence transcends drug effects. For instance, the emotional coloring of an experience may constitute a "state" for purposes of learning, material being better retrieved when that emotion recurs than when the individual is in a different affective state. This variant of state-dependent learning could powerfully affect those old people who, on account of disinhibition of their affective responses through loss of cortical control, have become emotionally labile. But the phenomenon may have more general implications still. To illustrate this, we briefly turn to a topic in child development, childhood amnesia (Schachtel, 1947).

It is generally recognized that people remember little of their early childhood and virtually nothing of their infancy. Claims have been made for special situations that provide a context for remembering such early experiences, notably hypnotic regression. Both childhood amnesia and the efficacy of hypnotic regression (if validated) lend themselves to an explanation in terms of state dependence. Note first that the childhood amnesia involves only episodic memory. Learning (entry of information into "semantic memory") certainly does occur profusely during the very same stage of the life cycle. In other words, it is for context-bound information that amnesia prevails, not context-free. Now, the texture of experience in childhood is very different from that subsequently, both perceptually, as Piaget and others have illustrated, and emotionally, as has been much debated in the psychoanalytic literature. Perhaps only under extreme circumstances, such as hypnotic regression, can sufficient (presumably emotional) contextual cues be recovered to permit retrieval of some early experiences. Also, in the case of infants, who cannot yet mentally represent, one could not in any case expect events to be experienced with the richness that characterizes them at a later stage.

Now consider the possible parallel phenomena in aging. Again, learned material remains readily available. But the forgetting of episodes plagues the elderly. Presumably context-bound retrieval has become harder. Such retrieval difficulty could of course be due to limbic structural impairment as in the amnesic syndrome. But ill-encoded material is also harder to retrieve. If the perception of the elderly is like that of young children, more holistic rather than analytic, then perhaps experiences are encoded in such global fashion that splinter attributes can no longer perform their usual function of acting as cues for subsequent retrieval. Virtually the whole context would have to recur, a circumstance that would presumably be quite unusual.

The notorious disorientation that afflicts senile people when they find themselves in novel circumstances may be a state-dependent phenomenon. It would be of practical importance to investigate this as, if this is so, a systematic program of acquainting the individual with the new setting in a graduated, logical fashion could presumably be developed, and a favorable setting for further episodic remembering be reinstated (though it would presumably now be specific, i.e., context- dependent for the new environment).

Division of Attention

The element of selectivity in cognitive function is based on selective inhibition. Selective attention to a nonsalient aspect of a display must necessitate selective inhibition of response to salient features. The same must be true of analytic perception in general. One way of conceptualizing this is in terms of the functional cerebral distance principle (Kinsbourne & Hicks, 1978).

The phylogenetically most primitive nervous system was a nerve net (Sarnat & Netsky, 1974). This permits transmission of information, but without the element of adaptive selectivity. To some extent, selectivity can be achieved by preprogrammed channeling of information, through the fragmentation of the nerve net so as to make some connections exclusive; and this indeed happens in the evolution of brain. But such structural channeling makes no provision for learning from individual experience. For that purpose the channeling has to be functional, flexible, and continuously modifiable. Selective inhibition at intercalated neurons makes this possible.

When individuals observe or respond selectively, the inhibitory surroundings around the central focus of patterned activation cannot be fully impermeable. Adaptively irrelevant "spin-off" activities accompany the selected action. If one is righthanded, as one speaks, one's right hand gestures (Kimura, 1973). As one thinks verbally, one's eyes swivel; when thinking spatially, they swivel left (Kinsbourne, 1972). When one listens selectively to information from one of two concurrently transmitting head phones, the eyes swivel to the attended side (Kahneman, 1973). The wearing of laterally displacing prisms biases the ear asymmetry in the direction of displacement (Goldstein & Lackner, 1974). These are all instances of spread of focal activation to synergically linked (highly connected) neuronal facilities.

The functional cerebral distance principle proposes that the greatest overflow of excitation is to neighboring or highly interconnected loci. In the examples cited above, left-hemisphere verbal activity radiates to left auditory cortex and left frontal eye field. Also, lateral attending in the acoustic mode radiates to lateral attending visually.

When one divides attention (time-shares) between two tasks, the functional cerebral distance principle is again explanatory. The closer in functional distance the two relevant active loci are, the greater is mutual interference between orthogonal tasks. Thus in righthanders, vocalizing and right-hand performance mutually interfere more than vocalizing and left-hand performance (Kinsbourne & Cook, 1971; Kinsbourne & Hicks, 1978; Lomas & Kimura, 1976).

If the cortical thinning in old age depletes the individual's potential for selective central inhibition, then, from the perspective of this model, the various control centers in the brain effectively become closer to each other in functional distance. Overflow phenomena (and transfer of training—cf. Kinsbourne & Hicks, 1978) should then be enhanced. Interference between two concurrently attempted tasks should become more severe. Forms of interference that might compromise information pick-up and therefore encoding may be illustrated by a study performed by Treisman and Geffen (1968). They had subjects selectively shadow one of two concurrent continuous prose messages presented through head phones. At the same time, subjects were asked to respond to probe tones that occurred unpredictably on either channel. Pertinent to our discussion was the finding that subjects were better able to attend selectively (shadow efficiently and pick up tones) to the right than to the left auditory input. The functional cerebral distance model predicts this. Left-hemisphere activation caters better to verbal performance (in righthanders) and rightward attending. Verbal performance and leftward attending call for mutually incompatible activation levels (excitatory for the language area, inhibitory for the right frontal eye field) in adjacent cortical fields. Mutual interference results. We would expect such interference to be much more severe in the cortically depleted old person.

There would be practical implications for such findings for social engineering for the elderly. We often casually leave ourselves open to the concurrent challenges of diverse sources of input for processing because there appears to be no reason not to do so. For old people, there might be a rationale for so arranging the flow of pertinent information that it is restricted to one source and one category at a time, thus protecting the individual from gross between-task interference.

Finally, central inhibitory states are potentially under the influence of psychoactive drugs. The considerations discussed heretofore suggest behavioral paradigms that might be suitable for use when such drugs are appraised for possible beneficial effects on the elderly.

MECHANISM OF ATTENTIONAL DYSFUNCTION WITH UNEVEN CEREBRAL DAMAGE

Opponent mechanisms control the laterality of attention, the spatial dispersion of its focus, and its temporal persistence (concentration) on a particular display, performance, or train of thought. When wide areas of cortex are impaired, the impairment may happen to compromise one component of an opponent system more than another, throwing the mechanism out of balance.

Lateral Attention

The lateral distribution of attention is determined by the vector resultant of mutually inhibitory interaction between control centers in the two hemispheres, each primarily responsible for orientation toward contralateral space (Kinsbourne, 1974b; Melamed & Larsen, 1979). Severe damage to one component of this system results in the bizzare symptomatology of unilateral neglect of person and of space (Kinsbourne, 1977b). Minor instances may occur in old people without obvious neurological deficit. In such cases, information pick-up is spatially biased toward those features that are located at one end of a display. If so, these are the memoranda, not the whole display, and it is from these that retrieval cues should be chosen. Also, proper guidance of attention, by maneuvering what is to be remembered into the favored spatial location, would bring it to awareness and ready it for encoding.

Focus Of Attention

People can adjust the focus of their attention over a wide range, from exclusive attention to a point locus, to dispersion across the whole perceptual field. The opponent system involved appears to include parts of frontal lobe (for narrow aperture) and parts of parietal lobe (for wide aperture); Pribram & McGuinness, 1975). If the cortical thinning process preponderantly affects one of these two control mechanisms, the other will obtain virtually exclusive control of attention, leaving the individual either locked into focal attending, without ability to obtain an overview, or, conversely, restricted to a wide-ranging but superficial appraisal of a situation. Either defect compromises the efficient encoding of information, but each does so in a different way.

Duration Of Attention

Our preprogrammed approach tendencies toward objects of positive valence (Schneirla, 1959) are tempered by the intervention of a "stop" or "behavioral inhibition" system, which gives the organism pause while it computes a utility function (benefit versus cost) for the intended action (Swanson & Kinsbourne, 1979b). In healthy functioning, concentration is maintained on the source of information up to the point at which what is relevant has been noted, but not longer than that. If the computation is hastily done and prematurely concluded, impulsive behavior results, and too little may have been noticed to provide material for subsequent efficient retrieval. If the computation is unduly prolonged, hesitant behavior results, and the individual remains engrossed longer than necessary, to the detriment of his attention to whatever else is happening at the time.

In childhood, the impulsive responder is labelled hyperactive. In adolescence and early adulthood, he is a deliquent or psychopath or has "disordered impulse control." Among the aged, impulsive responding has been little recognized, perhaps both because it tends not to present as antisocial acting out, and because it may be mistaken for a consequence of diminished intellect. Yet accident-proneness, disordered behavior, and social ineptness on the part of old people, to mention but a few possible manifestations, could well result from a brain-based skewing of the relevant opponent system.

Depending on the vagaries of locus of maximal impact of the cortical loss, the opposite imbalance may occur. The individual is hesitant, compulsive, and perseverative. He restricts himself in his behavioral options far more than is justified by the state of his intellect. This is a character trait in some people from childhood on ("overfocusing"—see Kinsbourne & Caplan, 1979) but also can be acquired during aging as described.

These dichotomous possible outcomes of the aging process are particularly relevant not only because of their potential for impairing memory and other cognitive functions, but also because they could be correctable by psychoactive drug use. Stimulant drugs prolong concentration, sedatives and alcohol curtail it. Laboratory methods that have been developed for regulating the use of these agents in children could readily be adapted for use in the elderly, and the possibility exists that the ability of old people to concentrate effectively on material that they need to learn could be substantially enhanced by the judicious use of the appropriate medication.

In overview of this section, we note that whereas in some respects we may look for communality of behavioral deficit among old people, in other respects they would be expected to show pathologically extreme reactions in opposite directions. Rather than generalize about the aging brain, we need precise methods to determine individual deficit and meet individual need.

THE MEASUREMENT OF ATTENTIONAL CHANGE

Management methods for behavioral disorder attempt either to compensate for or to correct the patient's difficulty. In the case of attentional dysfunction, one might so engineer the environment as to guide the patient's attention toward the relevant cues, while stripping it of potential distractors. An adequate test for the success of such maneuvers is to note that the target material has in fact been noticed, e.g., that it is later remembered. Thus, the subject's strategies are held constant and the display varied. But if one aspires to *correct* the attentional dysfunction, one holds constant the material for encoding, and varies (with the customary double-blind precautions) the patient's state, e.g., drug versus placebo, different levels of drug, etc. Among possible remedies worth exploring are the use of certain drugs and certain manipulations of diet (Swanson & Kinsbourne, in press).

Insofar as attentional dysfunction seems to be based on underactivity of certain parts of the brain, it is conceivable that psychoactive agents might be identified which would selectively activate these areas. Insofar as opponent processes are out of balance, chemical agents might be found which enhance the activation of the underactive element in the opponent system.

The evaluation of therapies for pschopathology has typically been based on impressionistic information, gathered by involved rather than detached observers: relatives, institutional staff, or the patient. Observer error, biased expectations, and placebo effects confuse the assessment, both by implying spurious success and by concealing actual benefit. However much neurochemical insight is marshalled for selecting promising agents to correct attentional dysfunction, the results will be unreliable unless gathered under controlled laboratory conditions. Essentially, one must define the target behavior, develop a valid quantitative procedure to measure it, and obtain time-response and dose-response information with respect to each drug administration (or dietary manipulation). Rather than rely on the indirect evidence contained in observers' testimony, it is preferable to measure directly the patient's own performance in experimental and placebo states.

The following are necessary characteristics of dependent measures for acute behavioral change. The measure should be:

1. Quantifiable.
2. Not too time consuming.
3. Not too tiring for the subject.
4. Available in multiple alternate forms for repeated testing.
5. Subject to little or no practice effects after the initial familiarization period.
6. Ideally also simple, non-technical and inexpensive enough to lend itself to general use.

It is in principle feasible to develop measures that meet these specifications for each of the attentional variants we have discussed. In our laboratory, we have made a beginning with respect to the duration of attention ("concentration") and will quote some examples, although to date this work has been done with children rather than old people (Kinsbourne & Swanson, 1979b; Swanson & Kinsbourne, 1979a,b).

We have developed many alternate forms of a paired-associate learning task that requires subjects to associate color slides of various animals in zoo locations with a limited set of responses, e.g., north, east, south, west. The subject is shown the material time and time again until he has become able to respond without error on two successive trials. The dependent variable is the number of erroneous (or omitted) responses prior to achievement of critical performance.

After a familiarization period, the task is given to children referred for suspected organic hyperactivity at regular intervals, e.g., hourly, to measure the effect of the experimental intervention (drug or dietary challenge administration). The time-response characteristics of each challenge (active or placebo) are recorded, and the results permit conclusion about the efficacy of the challenge in either correcting or exacerbating a learning difficulty.

Paired-associate learning is accomplished on the basis of a succession of mental operations, of which maintained attention to the material is only the first. However, we have shown experimentally in hyperactive children responsive to stimulant drugs (methylphenidate, dextroamphetamine, pemoline) that at least some of the learning improvement that results from drug use is due to longer maintained concentration on the task.

Children were presented with stimulus–response pairs for a fixed total study time, but under three conditions of pacing: each pair for 4, 8, or 12 sec respectively. In the drug group, methylphenidate use improved learning under all three conditions, but more so the longer the presentation period (Dalby, Kinsbourne, Swanson, & Sobol, 1977). In the placebo condition, learning was best at the 4-sec pacing, worst at 12-sec pacing.

We conclude that, whereas on the drug children were able to maintain concentration on each item for as long as the longest duration called for (12 sec), on the placebo their concentration lapsed sooner. On the drug, they fully exploited the available study time. On the placebo, their concentration flagged and they did not.

This method should be adaptable to old people with concentration dysfunction. If their concentration is too soon suspended, the outcome should be the same as with the hyperactive children. If they have the opposite problem, delay in initiating attentional focus which is then well maintained, they should show the opposite effect, i.e., best performance at 12 sec pacing, worst at 4 sec pacing. If their learning difficulty is unrelated to dysfunctional concentration, then performance will not vary significantly across conditions.

Similar considerations apply to dietary effects, though the relevant studies have not yet been done. Given that artificial coloring substances in food are capable (in large doses) of impairing learning (Swanson & Kinsbourne, in press), then the question arises, is this due to attentional dysfunction? If so, then, when placebo and coloring challenge effects are compared, a concentration abnormality should reveal itself.

It is not difficult to envisage other measures for the maintenance of attention (e.g. continuous performance tests; Swanson, Barlow & Kinsbourne, 1979). The degree of dispersion of attention is a potentially fruitful issue for study, in that focus of attention is narrowed by anxiety, so that it could be maneuvered in one direction by antianxiety drugs and in the other by their antagonists. Clues for the design of other measures (e.g., of the elderly to overcome the distractor effect of salient irrelevancies) may be gleaned from the child development literature (e.g., Gibson, 1969).

In this discussion we have considered the relation of attentional variables to the encoding of information (which in turn is thought essential to its subsequent retrieval). The distinction between attention and encoding is not clear cut. If attention is the generation of observing responses patterned and tuned to be selective for attributes of adaptive relevance, then observing these attributes may be tantamount to encoding them. The associations that they conjure up may also preempt attention, and that awareness may also be tantamount to encoding them. We should be wary of regarding encoding as representing a distinct stage in processing, when it may amount to no more than information-theoretic jargon for observing (noticing) the material in question. In the sense of this discussion, encoding deficits are deficits of attending.

REFERENCES

Bartlett, F. C. *Remembering.* Cambridge: Cambridge University Press, 1932.

Beurle, R. L. Properties of a mass of cells capable of regenerating pulses. *Philosophical Transactions of the Royal Society of London,* 1956, *240,* 55–94.

Botwinick, J., & Storandt, M. *Memory, related functions, and age.* Springfield, Ill.: C. C. Thomas, 1974.

Cattell, R. B. *Personality and motivation structure and measurement.* New York: World Book, 1957.

Dalby, J. T., Kinsbourne, M., Swanson, J. M., & Sobol, M. P. Hyperactive children's underuse of learning time: Correction by stimulant treatment. *Child Development,* 1977, *4,* 1448–1453.

Easterbrook, J. A. The effect of emotion on cue utilization and the organization of behavior. *Psychological Review,* 1959, *66,* 183–201.

Elias, M. F., & Kinsbourne, M. Age and sex differences in the processing of verbal and non-verbal stimuli. *Journal of Gerontology,* 1974, *29,* 162–171.

Gibson, E. J. *Principles of perceptual learning and perceptual development.* New York: Appleton-Century-Crofts, 1969.

Goldstein, L., & Lackner, J. R. Sideways look at dichotic listening. *Journal of the Acoustical Society of America,* 1974, *55* (Suppl. S10).

Horn, J. L. Human ability systems. In P. B. Baltes (Ed.), *Life-span development and behavior* (Vol. 1). New York: Academic Press, 1978.

Kahneman, D. *Attention and effort.* Englewood Cliffs, N.J.: Prentice-Hall, 1973.

Kimura, D. Manual activity during speaking—I. Right-handers. *Neuropsychologia,* 1973, *11,* 45–51.

Kinsbourne, M. Eye and head turning indicate cerebral lateralization. *Science,* 1972, *176,* 539–541.

Kinsbourne, M. Age effects on letter span related to rate and sequential dependence. *Journal of Gerontology,* 1973, *28,* 317–319. (a)

Kinsbourne, M. The control of attention by interaction between the cerebral hemispheres. In S. Kornblum, (Ed.), *Attention and performance IV.* New York: Academic Press, 1973. (b)

Kinsbourne, M. Cognitive deficit and the aging brain: A behavioral analysis. *International Journal of Aging and Human Development,* 1974, *5,* 41–49. (a)

Kinsbourne, M. Lateral interactions in the brain. In M. Kinsbourne & W. L. Smith (Eds.), *Hemispheric disconnection and cerebral function.* Springfield: Thomas, 1974. (b)

Kinsbourne, M. The mechanism of hemispheric control of the lateral gradient of attention. In P. M. A. Rabbitt, & S. Dornic (Eds.), *Attention and performance V.* London: Academic Press, 1975.

Kinsbourne, M. The neuropsychological analysis of cognitive deficit. In R. G. Grenell & S. Gabay, (Eds.), *Biological Foundations of Psychiatry.* New York: Raven Press, 1976.

Kinsbourne, M. Cognitive decline with advancing age: An interpretation. In W. L. Smith, & M. Kinsbourne (Eds.), *Aging, dementia and cerebral function.* New York: Spectrum Press, 1977. (a)

Kinsbourne, M. Hemi-neglect and hemispheric rivalry. In E. A. Weinstein & R. P. Friedland (Eds.), *Hemi-Inattention and Hemisphere Specialization: Advances in Neurology.* Raven Press, 1977. (b)

Kinsbourne, M. & Berryhill, J. The nature of the interaction between pacing and the age decrement in learning. *Journal of Gerontology,* 1972, *27,* 471–477.

Kinsbourne, M., & Caplan, P. J. *Children's Learning and Attention Problems.* Boston: Little Brown, 1979.

Kinsbourne, M., & Cook, J. Generalized and lateralized effect of concurrent verbalization on a unimanual skill. *Quarterly Journal of Experimental Psychology,* 1971, *23,* 341–345.

Kinsbourne, M., & Hicks, R. E. Functional cerebral space: A model for overflow, transfer and interference effects in human performance. In Requin, J. (Ed.) *Attention and performance VII.* Hillsdale, Lawrence Erlbaum Associates, 1978.

Kinsbourne, M., & Swanson, J. M. Developmental aspects of selective orientation. In G. Hale, & M. Lewis (Eds.), *Attention and the development of cognitive skills.* New York: Plenum Press, 1979. (a)

Kinsbourne, M., & Swanson, J. M. Evaluation of symptomatic treatment of hyperactive behavior by stimulant drugs. In R. Knights & D. Bakker (Eds.), *Rehabilitation, treatment and management of learning disorders.* Maryland: University Park Press, 1979. (b)

Kinsbourne, M. & Winocur, G. Response competition and interference effects in paired-associate learning by Korsakoff Amnesics. *Neuropsychologia,* in press.

Kinsbourne, M., & Wood, F. Short term memory and pathological forgetting. In J. A. Deutsch (Ed.), *Short term memory.* New York: Academic Press, 1975.

Lashley, K. S. The problem of cerebral organization in vision. In *Biological Symposia* (Vol. 7). *Visual Mechanisms.* Lancaster, Pa.: Jacques Cattel Press, 1942.

Lomas, J., & Kimura, D. Intrahemispheric interaction between speaking and sequential manual activity. *Neuropsychologia,* 1976, *14,* 23–33.

Melamed, E., & Larsen, B. Cortical activation pattern during saccadic eye movements in humans: Localization by focal cerebral blood flow increases. *Annuals of Neurology,* 1979, *5,* 79–88.

Milner, B. Hemispheric specialization: Scope and limits. In F. Schmitt & F. Worden (Eds.), *The neurosciences: Third study program.* Cambridge, Mass.: M.I.T. Press, 1974.

Overton, D. A. Discriminative control of behavior by drug states. In T. Thompson & R. Pickens (Eds.), *Stimulus properties of drugs.* New York: Appleton-Century-Crofts, 1971.

Pribram, K. H. The amnestic syndromes: Disturbances in coding? In G. A. Talland & N. C. Waugh (Eds.), *The Pathology of Memory,* New York Academic Press, 1969.

Pribram, K. H., & McGuinness, D. Arousal, activation and effort in the control of attention. *Psychological Review,* 1975, *82,* 116–149.

Roediger, R. Paper to the Psychonomic Society, 1978.

Sarnat, H. B., & Netsky, M. G. *Evolution of the nervous system.* New York: Oxford University Press, 1974.

Schachtel, E. G. On memory and childhood amnesia. *Psychiatry,* 1947, *10,* 1–26.

Schneirla, T. C. An evolutionary and developmental theory of biphasic processes underlying approach and withdrawal. In M. R. Jones (Ed.), *Nebraska Symposium on Motivation.* Lincoln: University of Nebraska Press, 1959, 1–4.

Sherrington, C. S. *The integrative action of the nervous system.* New Haven: Yale University Press, 1906.

Swanson, J. M., & Kinsbourne, M. State-dependent learning and retrieval: Methodological cautions and theoretical considerations. In J. F. Kihlstrom, & F. J. Evans (Eds.), *Functional disorders of memory.* Potomac, Md.: Lawrence Erlbaum Associates, 1979. (a)

Swanson, J. M., & Kinsbourne, M. The cognitive effects of stimulant drugs on hyperactive (inattentive) children. In G. Hale & M. Lewis (Eds.), *Attention and the development of cognitive skills.* New York: Plenum Press, 1979. (b)

Swanson, J. M., & Kinsbourne, M. Food dyes impair performance of hyperactive children on a laboratory learning test. *Science,* in press.

Swanson, J. M., Barlow, A., & Kinsbourne, M. Task specificity of responses to stimulant drugs on laboratory test. *International Journal of Mental Health,* 1979, *8,* 67–82.

Talland, G. A. *Disorders of memory and learning.* Baltimore: Penguin, 1968.

Treisman, A., & Geffen, G. Selective attention and cerebral dominance in perceiving and responding to speech messages. *Quarterly Journal of Experimental Psychology,* 1968, *20,* 139–150.

Tulving, E. Episodic and semantic memory. In E. Tulving & W. Donaldson (Eds.), *Organization and memory.* New York: Academic Press, 1972.

Victor, M., Adams, R. D., & Collins, G. H. *The Wernicke-Korsakoff syndrome.* Philadelphia: Davis, 1971.

Winocur, G., & Kinsbourne, M. Contextual cues as an aid to Korsakoff amnesics. *Neuropsychologia,* 1978, *16,* 671–682.

7 Some Cautions We Might Exercise in Attributing Age Deficits in Memory to Attentional Dysfunctions

John R. Frederiksen
Bolt Beranek and Newman Inc. Cambridge, Massachusetts

I would like to preface my comments on the interesting chapters of Craik and Simon (Chapter 5) and of Kinsbourne (Chapter 6) with a few words about the perspective I am bringing to my task. Over the last few years, I have been engaged in studies of component processing skills in reading (Frederiksen, 1978, 1979). The goal of this work has been to find out if concepts derived from information-processing models and experiments could serve as reliable measures of individual differences in component reading skills. While the methods we have employed have been those of experimental psychology, the evidence for success in establishing such measures has been their ability to meet a set of criteria that are *psychometric* in nature. Thus, I have striven to develop several independent measures of each component process using a variety of experimental tasks, and have then used the correlations among measures of component skills as a means for establishing the *convergent* and *discriminant validity* of my measures. Convergent validity establishes the cross-situational applicability of the component process. Discriminant validity establishes the independence of processing performance when two tasks do not share a component process.

Now, the reason I bring up all of these matters is that I strongly feel that any concepts drawn from cognitive psychology must be submitted to the kind of psychometric validation I have referred to, if they are to be used as explanatory concepts in accounting for (1) individual differences in human performance, or (2) developmental differences in performance, which of course includes (3) differences in performance associated with aging.

Let's take a concept central to both Craik and Simon's and Kinsbourne's chapters, that of *limitations in attentional resources*. The notion is that there are age differences in the ability of subjects to carry out the information-processing requirements of two tasks concurrently that are not evident when performance is evaluated for either task alone. These limitations are due to problems of resource allocation across tasks that occur within a limited-capacity central processor (Kahneman, 1973; Norman & Bobrow, 1975). A consequence of this inability to divide processing between two tasks is a lowered level of performance in the component tasks. In the context of memory experiments, this performance deficit can be seen, Craik and Simon point out, in a reduction in depth of analysis accorded to-be-remembered items at the time of their encoding. The deficit is reflected, according to Kinsbourne, in the inability of older subjects to select for processing particular stimuli to the exclusion of others. Deficits in attentional capacity are thought of as being extremely general in their impact on processing; they are "widespread and permeate the whole system," in Craik and Simon's words. And Kinsbourne believes that the neurological source of impairment is a diffuse brain damage due to general neuronal depletion associated with aging. According to this view, the cortical thinning in old age reduces "functional cerebral distance" and this increases interference between two concurrently attempted tasks. In both chapters, general attentional deficits are invoked to account for differences in memory associated with aging. According to Craik, lack of attentional capacity leads to shallower processing at input, and this, in turn, yields a more general encoding, less tied to contextually specific details. Kinsbourne brings out the same idea in saying that associated with the attentional deficit, there is a "de-differentiation" of perception (perception is less analytic). In both chapters, the compatibility between encoding and retrieval conditions is stressed under the labels of the encoding specificity principle (Craik & Simon) or state dependence (Kinsbourne).

Before we accept either of these accounts of age-related deficits in memory, however strong their explanatory appeal, I would like to suggest that the concept of "general attentional deficit" should first be put to a crucial test. Evidence for such a general attentional deficit comes from a demonstration that, in a series of time-sharing tasks, the drops in performance occasioned by the addition of a concurrent task correlate across task domains (this is evidence for *convergent validity*). In other words, if individuals are ranked according to their *drop* in performance on Task A when Task B is added, then they should be similarly ranked on the basis of their drop in performance on Task C when Task D is added. The only assumption that is required here is that Tasks A, B, C, and D all make sizeable demands on the same central processing resource. Evidence for *discriminant validity* comes from a demonstration (I would suggest by using confirmatory maximum-likelihood factor analysis; cf. Jöreskog, 1970) that measures of attentional deficit, such as those referred to above, correlate more highly with each other than they do with other component-specific measures of information-processing skill that do not involve the allocation of processing resources.

Well, to continue my cautionary tale, several such studies have been carried out, and I am afraid that we have here a case where the "tale should wag the theoretical dog" (to throw together an unpardonable set of puns). Sverko (1976) at the University of Illinois has, for instance, studied time-sharing using all possible concurrent pairings of five tasks. A total performance decrement score was calculated for each task pairing, and the intercorrelations among these decrement scores (measures of "time sharing") were analyzed. The obtained correlations in all cases were essentially zero, ranging from -.068 to .060. When performance measures obtained in the time-sharing tasks were factor analyzed, the only factors that could be extracted were clearly task-specific. No general factor, reflecting the common attentional resource-sharing component of Sverko's tasks, emerged. In fact, Sverko's conclusion was that, while no unitary, general time-sharing ability exists, at least three types of subskills that are related to attention are likely to be involved in dual-task performance: (1) an ability to process information from several sources in parallel; (2) an ability to re-allocate quickly processing resources in tasks where processing must be carried out serially; and (3) an ability to *automate* or remove from attentional control processing at some stage or stages. The degree of involvement of each of these factors depends upon the characteristics of the two tasks that are being performed concurrently. It should be clear that, if aging could lead to impairment in one or another of these subskills related to attention, then the causes of age-related impairment in memory might in reality differ from individual to individual. It is also clear that the mapping of such subskill deficits to the varieties of cerebral depletion discussed by Kinsbourne will be far from clear-cut.

Another search for the "time sharing ability" has been reported by Hawkins, Church, and DeLemos (1978), who studied dual-task performance in a careful series of experiments that illustrate how convergent validity might be evaluated through experimental means. Using the double-stimulation or psychological refractory period paradigm, they investigated how the processing requirements of an initial or leading task influence performance on a following or trailing task. They tested a number of propositions concerning the locus of interference effects of initial task performance on processing associated with the second task, among them the notion that response retrieval from memory constitutes the point of greatest demand (and competition) for attentional resources. Their results suggest that, while this factor is of importance, it is not the only source of interference when subjects perform two tasks concurrently. In fact, these authors were forced to conclude that time-sharing is not a single general ability, but rather is dependent upon several more specific, and perhaps independent, processing limitations. These include:

1) An inability early in practice to simultaneously select, or retrieve, multiple responses, from memory; 2) a persisting inability to initiate multiple

independent responses simultaneously; 3) an inability to process, or at least efficiently process, contiguous inputs from separate modalities owing to the need for a modality specific attentional focus; and 4) an inability to efficiently process multiple inputs from within the same modality owing to the existence of structural-interference [p. ii].

Ironically, memory retrieval has re-emerged here (under Point 1) as a factor underlying and explaining performance in the attention sharing tasks, and not vice versa!

In conclusion, without dampening spirits, I want to suggest that use of a general attentional deficit—a sort of latter-day Spearman's g-factor of human information processing—as a theoretical device for explaining effects of aging on memory should be reexamined. Perhaps we should wait until the evidence is in on the validity of such a capacity as a determiner of human performance, before we subscribe fully to the attentional dysfunction theory of age deficits in memory. The research program I should hope to see develop would employ a variety of tasks, carried out singly and concurrently, in order to isolate those aspects of resource sharing that are most often a source of deficit in the performance of older subjects. The question of how such deficits in dual-task performance may influence memory encoding and retrieval could then be addressed by comparing subjects who have specific and contrasting attentional deficits. Of course, it may well turn out that with old people, the several components of attentional dysfunction do go hand in hand and constitute what could properly be termed a general loss of attentional resources.

REFERENCES

Frederiksen, J. R. Assessment of perceptual, decoding, and lexical skills and their relation to reading proficiency. In A. M. Lesgold, J. W. Pellegrino, S. W. Fokkema, & R. Glaser (Eds.), *Cognitive psychology and instruction.* New York: Plenum, 1978.

Frederiksen, J. R. Component skills in reading: Measurement of individual differences through chronometric analysis. In R. E. Snow, P. A. Federico, & W. E. Montague (Eds.), *Aptitude, learning, and instruction.* Hillsdale, N.J.: Lawrence Erlbaum Associates, 1980.

Hawkins, H. L., Church, M., & DeLemos, S. *Time-sharing is not a unitary ability.* Technical Report No. 2. Center for Cognitive and Perceptual Research, University of Oregon, 1978.

Jöreskog, K. G. A general method for analysis of covariance structures. *Biometrika,* 1970, *57,* Part 2, 239-251.

Kahneman, D. *Attention and effort.* Englewood Cliffs, N.J.: Prentice-Hall, 1973.

Norman, D. A., & Bobrow, D. G. On data-limited and resource-limited processes. *Cognitive Psychology,* 1975, *7,* 44-64.

Sverko, B. *Individual differences in time-sharing performance.* Unpublished manuscript, University of Illinois, 1976.

8

Attention, Levels of Processing, and State-Dependent Recall

Arthur Wingfield
Brandeis University

The attempt to relate studies of attention, acquisition, and retrieval to the analysis of normal and deficient memory processes is as reasonable as it is ambitious. Indeed, the positions taken by Kinsbourne, and by Craik and Simon, each cover a sufficiently wide range of ideas and topics that a full discussion of either of these papers alone would be impossible in this limited space. The goal I have set myself, therefore, is first to highlight several of the points in each chapter which seem to offer immediate research promise, and second, to indicate what I see as a number of intriguing similarities between their views. This second goal is not without risk, since one can easily represent as a single view what is in fact a distorted version of both, and one which neither set of authors would claim as their own. The critical necessity to integrate these important ideas, however, may justify this risk.

ELABORATION VERSUS LEVELS OF PROCESSING

I should first make my own bias clear by applauding Craik and Simon's current position, which gives less weight than previously to a linear, fixed-order, "shallow-to-deep" sequence through which all stimuli must pass on the road to the "lofty depths" of semantic processing. Fixed-order hierarchies are often proposed early in model building, but just as quickly abandoned. The systems we hope to model are invariably more complex than we might at first wish them to be.

At the same time, the introduction of the initial "levels" argument (Craik & Lockhart, 1972) offered a more dynamic, and fully welcomed alternative to the early structural models of memory current throughout the 1950s and 1960s. It is certainly the case that the attendant explorations of possible relationships between depth of processing and degree of retention yielded a host of interesting and valuable studies. If Craik and Lockhart's goal was to offer a productive framework for memory research, it was one quite clearly achieved.

Caution regarding the question of a fixed hierarchy of levels, together with an acceptance of the importance of a compatibility between the manner of encoding and later retrieval cues, offers some protection from critics of the original "levels" argument (cf. Baddeley, 1978; Craik & Tulving, 1975; Morris, Bransford, & Franks, 1977; Stein, 1978). These concessions, however necessary, nevertheless cost the original formulation some specificity, a problem already perceived as an early weakness (Baddeley, 1978). Whether the contrast between "elaboration" and "levels" of processing will return some of this lost specificity remains to be seen. The question is whether these two admittedly descriptive terms can be viewed as truly orthogonal dimensions of encoding, or whether one is ordinarily an automatic consequence of the other. I am sure we can look forward to the development of this debate as research progresses.

ENCODING SPECIFICITY VERSUS STATE-DEPENDENT PROCESSES

At one level, the two chapters under review take very different approaches to the questions of attention, encoding, and retrieval, seeming only to share a lack of enthusiasm for the previously mentioned structural models of short- versus long-term memory. There is also a close and very important similarity, however, in their common emphasis on the critical relationship between encoding and retrieval processes for any complete understanding of memory function.

In Craik and Simon's case, we see encoding specificity, or more properly, a lack of it, as a potential culprit in poor memory performance in the aged. Generally, deeper processing leads to better retention, but further, the best chances for recall occur when the retrieval processes used most closely match those involved in initial encoding.

This current emphasis on the importance of congruity between encoding and retreival schemes is reflected in the variety of ways it has been conceptualized: a question of encoding specificity (Tulving & Thomson, 1973; Wiseman & Tulving, 1976), precision of encoding and test appropriateness (Stein, 1978), or a uniqueness of the link between the retrieval information and encoded items (Craik, 1977). The historical separation of experimental attacks on memory storage versus memory retrieval is thus being seriously questioned. Indeed, if we consider the possibility that storage of information and retrieval processing are so distributed in the brain that a common set of neuronal elements may subserve both (Nickerson, 1977, p. 716), then such a conclusion would become inevitable.

Seen in this context, Kinsbourne's arguments for state-dependent processes become especially interesting, as they inescapably lead to the same position as taken by Craik and Simon, even though the approach is from a very different direction. The development of a single position within functional and neuropsychological frameworks could bring with it an exciting and long overdue revolution in the study of memory. On a more specific level, both seem to be suggesting that past research on aging and memory may have been retarded by earlier attempts to frame the question within a functionally dichotomous storage-versus-retrieval framework. This, it seems to me, is no trivial point.

The general notion of state-dependent processes has appeared in the literature for a number of years, but primarily in the context of simple learning tasks in lower animals. Overton (1964), for example, reported that tasks learned by rats in a drugged state (injection of sodium pentobarbital) did not transfer when the animals were in a nondrugged state. Reintroduction of the animals to the original drugged state, however, brought a demonstrated "reactivation of the habit." A similar state of affairs can be obtained for tasks learned in a nondrugged state, and then tested in drugged and nondrugged conditions. Acquisition and utilization can thus be described as "drug-state specific" (Hilgard & Bower, 1966, p. 475).

This historical antecedent to the work under discussion is especially interesting when we remind ourselves of some of the early explanations offered. Such results were often attributed to a chemically induced sensory distortion, in which the animals "saw something" in the stimulus relevant to its encoding in one state which was not seen in the other. It seems a modest step to relate this argument to subsequent studies of the effectiveness of "contextual cues" in recall in human subjects (e.g., Dallett & Wilcox, 1968; Strand, 1970), and, in the present context, to encoding specificity arguments. It was suggested also that the drugs may have served to modify threshold and firing patterns of neurons, with different neural circuits becoming active in one state from those activated in another state (Hilgard & Bower, 1966).

Kinsbourne's introduction of state-dependent processes in the context of aging, however, breaks fresh ground and will, I am sure, encourage active research interest. The central position shared by Kinsbourne and by Craik and Simon remains. Recall performance will be best when retrieval circumstances (broadly defined) most closely approximate those present at the time of acquisition.

Kinsbourne's position, of course, raises an obvious question. If recall ability is state-dependent, then why are early memories ordinarily better recalled by the elderly than recent memories, since the latter were presumably acquired and recalled in more nearly similar states? Perhaps Kinsbourne would argùe that this question is put too simply for an adequate answer, without a detailed analysis of the types of recent versus early memories we mean. One notes his recommended caution regarding the distinction between much used, overlearned material in semantic memory versus episodic memory where contextual information presumably plays a greater role in retrieval. Although Tulving's (1972) original distinction between semantic and episodic memory may have been, in Craik and Simon's words, too abrupt a dichotomy, they too signal the likely differential vulnerability characteristics of context-specific memory versus general knowledge to aging effects. This should continue to be a dimension of interest in future aging studies.

ATTENTION, DEPTH, AND PROCESSING TIME

Craik and Simon's emphasis on "shallow" processing as a possible source of memory impairment in the elderly is accompanied by a recognition that deep processing requires considerable attentional capacity which may represent a strain on limited resources. The central question, however, is whether one should see the problem in terms of limited resources, per se, or in terms of differential allocation strategies as the elderly attempt to distribute finite resources among several potential inputs and/or cognitive operations. One sees a hint of both possibilities in both Craik and Simon's and Kinsbourne's chapters, and the difference is amenable to empirical test.

An additional research question emerging from the chapters both of Craik and Simon and of Kinsbourne centers on the question of time. If we assume that deep or elaborative processing requires time as well as attentional resources, we cannot help but note the extensive literature on reduced speed of processing in a variety of cognitive tasks in the aged (see, for example, reviews in Jordan & Rabbitt, 1977, and in Welford, 1958). One consequence of slowed processing would be a loss of poorly encoded material through rapid decay or competitive interference before it receives more than superficial processing. That is, elaboration, depth, and attentional processing all lie along temporal dimensions.

Although from a different conceptual framework, one could anticipate the effects under discussion from earlier reports of a reduced tendency in the elderly to exploit potential "mediators" in learning (e.g., Hulicka & Grossman, 1967), and in the results of numerous experiments relating poor memory performance in very young or retarded children to poor encoding and rehearsal strategies and the availability of processing time (e.g., Murray & Roberts, 1968; O'Connor & Hermelin, 1965). The potential importance of this temporal factor in depth of processing can also be seen in the more recent studies cited by Craik and Simon (Chapter 5). We must, I believe, add to our terminological escalation the question of "speed of processing" to join the existing list of "depth," "spread," "specificity," "precision," and "elaboration."

The notion of speed of encoding may, for example, save us from too unidimensional an analysis of encoding specificity and predictive extremes such as a proposition that "shallow" processing followed by "shallow" retrieval in the elderly should imply better recall performance than one ordinarily expects to see. If we assume a slowness of processing, perhaps compounded by less effective utilization of limited attentional resources, sufficient depth, elaboration, or specificity would not be reached prior to loss of the information or its distortion over time or through interference from competing stimulus inputs. The temporal parameters of attentional and elaborative processing should also receive considerable research attack over the next few years.

MEMORY AND AGE

A final similarity between these two chapters is the shared recommendation that we look carefully and critically at comparisons between memory processes in the aged and performance in other states such as drug and alcohol effects, focal brain damage, and memory performance in children.

There is certainly a very extensive literature on attentional, encoding, and retrieval strategies in young children, which includes attempts to enhance performance through training, and studies of the influence of time available for encoding, and effectiveness of encoding strategy (e.g., Belmont & Butterfield, 1969, 1971; Flavell, Beach, & Chinsky, 1966; Kingsley & Hagen, 1969). To the extent that the dual principles of encoding specificity and utilization of appropriate retrieval cues are involved in limiting memory performance in both children and the aged, it is equally clear that the question of competence through experience is quite different. This may in fact be the clue we need to begin to unravel the question of fixed resource limitations versus optional strategies, and the part played by each in observed performance.

The issues raised in these two chapters are fundamental ones, and as such, they have a long history in the experimental study of memory processes. Both

Craik and Simon, and Kinsbourne, however, bring to these older questions a fresh viewpoint, and one which promises the potential for a reevaluation of these earlier studies in a new and theoretically powerful light. Such a reanalysis is long overdue.

ACKNOWLEDGMENT

The preparation of this discussion was facilitated by PHS Grant NS-14662 from the National Institutes of Health.

REFERENCES

Baddeley, A. D. The trouble with levels: A reexamination of Craik and Lockhart's framework for memory research. *Psychological Review*, 1978, *85*, 139–152.

Belmont, J. M., & Butterfield, E. C. The relations of short-term memory to development and intelligence. In L. P. Lipsett & H. W. Reese (Eds.), *Advances in child development and behavior* (Vol. 4). New York: Academic Press, 1969.

Belmont, J. M., & Butterfield, E. C. Learning strategies as determinants of memory deficiencies. *Cognitive Psychology*, 1971, *2*, 411–420.

Craik, F. I. M. Depth of processing in recall and recognition. In S. Dornič (Ed.), *Attention and performance VI*. Hillsdale, N.J.: Lawrence Erlbaum Associates, 1977.

Craik, F. I. M., & Lockhart, R. S. Levels of processing: A framework for memory research. *Journal of Verbal Learning and Verbal Behavior*, 1972, *11*, 671–684.

Craik, F. I. M., & Tulving, E. Depth of processing and the retention of words in episodic memory. *Journal of Experimental Psychology: General*, 1975, *104*, 268–294.

Dallett, K., & Wilcox, S. G. Contextual stimuli and proactive inhibition. *Journal of Experimental Psychology*, 1968, *78*, 475–480.

Flavell, J. H., Beach, D. R., & Chinsky, J. M. Spontaneous verbal rehearsal in a memory task as a function of age. *Child Development*, 1966, *37*, 283–299.

Hilgard, E. R., & Bower, G. H. *Theories of learning* (3rd ed.). New York: Appleton-Century-Crofts, 1966.

Hulicka, I. M., & Grossman, J. L. Age-group comparisons for the use of mediators in paired-associate learning. *Journal of Gerontology*, 1967, *22*, 45–51.

Jordan, T. C., & Rabbitt, P. M. A. Response times to stimuli of increasing complexity as a function of aging. *British Journal of Psychology*, 1977, *68*, 189–201.

Kingsley, P. R., & Hagen, J. W. Induced versus spontaneous rehearsal in short-term memory in nursery school children. *Developmental Psychology*, 1969, *1*, 40–46.

Morris, C. D., Bransford, J. D., & Franks, J. J. Levels of processing versus transfer appropriate processing. *Journal of Verbal Learning and Verbal Behavior*, 1977, *16*, 519–533.

Murray, D. J., & Roberts, B. Visual and auditory presentation, presentation rate, and short-term memory in children. *British Journal of Psychology*, 1968, *59*, 119–125.

Nickerson, R. S. Crossword puzzles and lexical memory. In S. Dornič (Ed.), *Attention and performance VI*. Hillsdale, N.J.: Lawrence Erlbaum Associates, 1977.

O'Connor, N., & Hermelin, B. Input restrictions and immediate memory decay in normal and subnormal children. *Quarterly Journal of Experimental Psychology*, 1965, *17*, 323–328.

Overton, D. A. State-dependent or "dissociated" learning produced by pentobarbital. *Journal of Comparative and Physiological Psychology*, 1964, *57*, 3–12.

Stein, B. S.   Depth of processing reexamined: The effects of the precision of encoding and test appropriateness. *Journal of Verbal Learning and Verbal Behavior,* 1978, *17,* 165–174.

Strand, B. Z.   Change of context and retroactive inhibition. *Journal of Verbal Learning and Verbal Behavior,* 1970, *9,* 202–206.

Tulving, E.   Episodic and semantic memory. In E. Tulving & W. Donaldson (Eds.), *Organization of memory.* New York: Academic Press, 1972.

Tulving, E., & Thomson, D. M.   Encoding specificity and retrieval processes in episodic memory. *Psychological Review,* 1973, *80,* 352–373.

Welford, A. T.   *Ageing and Human Skill.* London: Oxford University Press, 1958.

Wiseman, S., & Tulving, E.   Encoding specificity: Relation between recall superiority and recognition failure. *Journal of Experimental Psychology: Human Learning and Memory,* 1976, *2,* 349–361.

9 Some Remarks on the Time-Course of Aging

Robin A. Barr
University of Oxford

I have been searching through the literature on aging to try to answer a perennial question—when do we grow old? In my survey of the literature my hope was to establish a taxonomy of different tasks, mapping out performance as a function of age in each of them. In that way I hoped to find out whether we begin to show signs of aging in some tasks before we do so in others and whether there are still other tasks in which no decline or an improvement with age is reported. I was encouraged in my search by a remark of Talland (1968):

> Results of tests of verbal learning, and more especially of STR (short-term retention) offer a wide variety of curves, including examples of relative stability as well as of declining proficiency over the span of maturity. Differences between these curves throw light on the mechanisms that deteriorate with advancing age and that should be considered as distinct components of the complex functions involved in learning and memory [pp. 95–96].

Unfortunately, no ready taxonomy of different curves has proved possible. First, probably the majority of investigators (myself included) have tested only two age groups—"young" and "old"—so no map of the time-course of aging can emerge. Second, studies which have employed more than two age groups occasionally have yielded results which seem inconsistent with one another. Also, too few studies have investigated within-subject changes in behavior by means of longitudinal testing. Instead, most have relied on cross-sectional comparisons of different groups of subjects. Nevertheless, with these cautionary notes sounded, my survey has brought certain noteworthy features to light. I discuss these here, and then relate them to some points made by Craik and Simon in the present volume (Chapter 5).

Old age strikes consistently early in divided attention tasks. To me, "old" usually has referred to groups over 60 (at least!), so it was surprising to discover that in one study of age and divided attention (Broadbent & Gregory, 1965) the *oldest* subjects were in the age group 45 and over.

The effects of aging on one divided attention task, dichotic listening, have been reported extensively in the literature (see Craik, 1977, for a review). I have plotted the results of four of these published studies in Figs. 9.1 and 9.2. The stimuli in all cases were digits between zero and nine. One set was presented to the right ear and the other set to the left ear. The instructions were varied within and between studies. In some conditions the subjects were required to recall digits heard on one ear before those heard on the other. Sometimes this instruction was given before presentation of the digits, sometimes after; while in other conditions the subjects were allowed to recall the digits freely. In the study by Schonfield, Trueman, and Kline (1972), retention was tested by recognition rather than by recall.

Inglis and Caird (1963) and Inglis and Ankus (1965) varied the number of pairs of digits presented to each ear. The results shown in Figs. 9.1 and 9.2 are the mean percentage recalled over all conditions. Craik (1965) also varied the rate of presentation of the digits (30 pairs per sec or 90 pairs per sec). The results shown are the mean of the two rates.

Figure 9.1 shows the percentage of the second set remembered as a function of age. Despite differences in instruction and in the method of test, the pattern

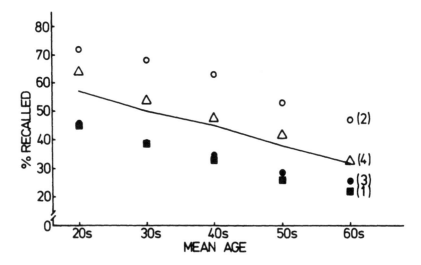

FIG. 9.1. The effects of age upon the percentage of the second set of digits remembered after dichotic listening: (1) Inglis and Caird (1963); (2) Craik (1965); (3) Inglis and Ankus (1965); (4) Schonfield, Trueman, and Kline (1972).

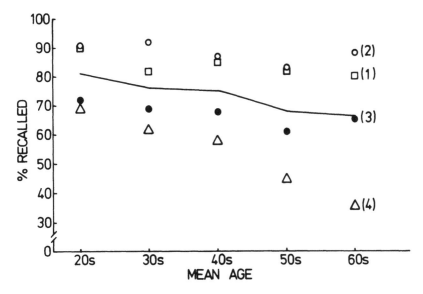

FIG. 9.2. The effects of age upon the percentage of the first set of digits remembered after dichotic listening: (1) Inglis and Caird (1963); (2) Craik (1965); (3) Inglis and Ankus (1965); (4) Schonfield et al. (1972).

of results in the four studies is very uniform. Performance declines linearly with age and at very similar rates in all four studies. The percentage of the first set of digits remembered is shown in Fig. 9.2. These results are not as straightforward as those for the second set. In three out of the four studies (Inglis & Caird, 1963; Craik, 1965; Inglis & Ankus, 1965), performance declines only slightly or not at all from the 20s to the 60s. In the fourth study (Schonfield et al., 1972), retention of the first and second set of digits declines at similar rates.

Thus the decline in performance of this divided attention task is observed most clearly in the second set remembered and is linear or nearly linear throughout adulthood in most published studies. By contrast, the majority of studies on memory or learning loss have concentrated on differences in performance in the 50s, 60s, and 70s. Relatively few studies have investigated performance in the 30s and 40s. Those studies which have investigated performance in early middle age have yielded a considerable variety of functions.

Arenberg (1967) published cross-sectional analyses of the performance of men of different ages on serial and paired-associate learning. The analyses revealed relatively small age differences prior to 60 but considerably larger differences after this age. Arenberg and Robertson-Tchabo (1977) discussed longitudinal comparisons of the same group of subjects. At the short anticipation interval, the youngest subjects (initially 30 to 38) improved slightly on a paired-associate task after a 6.8 year interval. The performance of the other groups all declined. Again, however, the decline was greatest for the oldest age group (initially 69 to 76).

In a test of visual retention employing both cross-sectional and longitudinal analyses, Arenberg (1978) found that the most striking changes with age occurred in the oldest group. Arenberg (1974) also reported data on differences in problem-solving ability at different ages. The task required subjects to discover certain logical relationships amongst a display of lights. In the cross-sectional comparisons he reported no differences with age below 60 but a decline after this age in the number solving the problem. However, he did report an increase between the 30s and 40s in the number of uninformative inputs used to solve the problem.

Thomas, Waugh, and Fozard (1978) used a Sternberg memory search task (Sternberg, 1975) to investigate the effects of age on memory. Thomas et al. varied the familiarity of the to-be-remembered set of letters (a–b–c–d–e–f versus p–g–k–t–r–i) and measured reaction time (RT) to determine whether a probe item was a member of the positive set. The effects of age on time to respond to the familiar set were slight. However, the effects of age on RT to the less familiar set were more marked. Subjects in their 60s and 70s responded more slowly to the probe item than subjects in their 30s, 40s, and 50s. In a second study measuring RT, Waugh, Thomas, and Fozard (1978) found that time to remember a very recently presented item (retrieval from primary memory) increased most sharply between the 50s and 60s. RT to remember a less recently presented item (retrieval from secondary memory) increased more steadily throughout the adult years. However, the youngest group that Waugh et al. tested were in their late 30s. Accordingly, this function is not directly comparable to those observed in the dichotic listening studies, in which the youngest subjects were in their early 20s.

Thus the studies cited so far do reveal a similar underlying function in which performance declines only slightly during the middle adult years but the decline is accelerated in old age. However, a number of results have been published which are not entirely consistent with this conclusion.

Talland (1968) required subjects to serially recall nine-digit sequences. He used two methods of scoring: (1) the number of complete sequences correctly recalled, and (2) the number of digits recalled correctly prior to the first error. The number of complete sequences recalled declined linearly from the 20s to the 60s. On the other hand, the number of digits recalled before the first error declined only slightly between the 20s and 50s and then sharply in the 60s.

A few studies seem to indicate that substantial decrements can be found in the performance of the middle-aged relative to younger groups. Hultsch (1971) discovered that such subjects recalled substantially fewer words after a classification task than those in their 20s. Schonfield and Robertson (1966) required subjects to recall bisyllabic nouns or adjectives. Again, those in their

40s recalled fewer words than those younger than they. Inglis and Ankus (1965) reported a study on the serial learning of nonsense syllables. In this task the major decrement with age seemed to be almost complete by the time subjects were in their 40s.

A number of other investigators have published results from which it is possible to plot performance as a function of age throughout the span of maturity (e.g. Brinley, Jovick, & McLaughlin, 1974; Craik, 1968; Moenster, 1972; Smith, 1975; Taub, 1975). The majority of these results yield a function in which performance declines most steeply in late middle and old age. However, the exceptions which already have been cited caution against concluding that there is little or no difference in memory or learning ability throughout the middle years and a more marked decline in the 60s and 70s. Rather, we must attempt to establish which tasks consistently do yield the linear function observed in the divided attention studies and which other tasks yield a function in which performance is stable throughout the middle years.

Craik (1977) and Simon (Chapter 5, this volume) have suggested that a major cause of memory and learning differences with age is a loss of processing capacity in older subjects. Their lack of overall capacity causes them to process information less deeply than younger subjects and so to perform less well in certain memory and learning tasks. Craik and Simon have suggested that *young* subjects' poor performance in dichotic listening and other divided attention tasks can be attributed to lack of processing resources; they attribute this deficit to the requirement to perform more than one task simultaneoulsy. Hence, they argue, when older subjects are required to perform divided attention tasks, a basic loss is compounded and their performance falls dramatically relative to younger subjects.

Continuing their logic, it should follow that, as the processing demands of *any* task increase, the function relating performance on that task to age should approximate increasingly the linear function found in dichotic listening—a divided attention task.

As the ambiguities in the research reviewed above indicate, there is little clear evidence to show whether the regression of performance in a task on age increasingly does approximate the function found in dichotic listening as demands on processing capacity increase. However, it does seem possible to test the hypothesis. Craik and Simon (Chapter 5, this volume) have suggested that deep processing is more effortful than shallow processing. They cite the published work of Eysenck (1974, 1977), and Simon (1979) and several unpublished studies to support the proposal that older subjects do process information less deeply than younger ones. Accepting their definition of deeper and more elaborative processing, then, in tasks requiring such processing, differences in performance with age should be evident throughout adult lifespan (as is the case in dichotic listening), rather than emerge only in the 50s, 60s, and 70s as is true of the majority of studies of memory and learning.

In conclusion, my attempt to find a taxonomy by which to classify the time-course of aging in different tasks so far has proved unsuccessful. However, it may be found that tasks requiring deeper processing do reveal differences in performance at earlier ages than those requiring less deep processing. If this is the case, then my attempt to classify the time-course of aging may yet have a happier outcome.

REFERENCES

Arenberg, D. Regression analyses of verbal learning on adult age at two anticipation intervals. *Journal of Gerontology*, 1967, *22*, 411–414.

Arenberg, D. A longitudinal study of problem solving in adults. *Journal of Gerontology*, 1974, *29*, 650–658.

Arenberg, D. Differences and changes with age in the Benton Visual Retention Test. *Journal of Geronthology*, 1978, *33*, 534–540.

Arenberg, D., & Robertson-Tchabo, E. A. Learning and aging. In J. E. Birren & K. W. Schaie (Eds.), *Handbok of the psychology of aging*. New York: Van Nostrand Reinhold, 1977.

Brinley, J. F., Jovick, T. J., & McLaughlin, L. M. Age, reasoning and memory in adults. *Journal of Gerontology*, 1974, *29*, 182–189.

Broadbent, D. E., & Gregory, M. Some confirmatory results on age differences in memory for simultaneous stimulation. *British Journal of Psychology*, 1965, *56*, 77–80.

Craik, F. I. M. The nature of the age decrement in performance on dichotic listening tasks. *Quarterly Journal of Experimental Psychology*, 1965, *17*, 227–240.

Craik, F. I. M. Short-term memory and the aging process. In G. A. Talland (Ed.), *Human aging and behavior*. New York: Academic Press, 1968.

Craik, F. I. M. Age differences in human memory. In J. E. Birren & K. W. Schaie (Eds.), *Handbook of the psychology of aging*. New York: Van Nostrand Reinhold, 1977.

Eysenck, M. W. Age differences in incidental learning. *Developmental Psychology*, 1974, *10*, 936–941.

Eysenck, M. W. *Human memory*. New York: Pergamon Press, 1977.

Hultsch, D. F. Adult age differences in free classification and free recall. *Developmental Psychology*, 1971, *4*, 338–342.

Inglis, J., & Ankus, M. N. Effects of age on short-term storage and serial rote learning. *British Journal of Psychology*, 1965, *56*, 183–195.

Inglis, J., & Caird, W. K. Age differences in successive responses to simultaneous stimulation. *Canadian Journal of Psychology*, 1963, *17*, 98–105.

Moenster, P. A. Learning and memory in relation to age. *Journal of Gerontology*, 1972, *27*, 361–363.

Schonfield, D., & Robertson, B. A. Memory storage and aging. *Canadian Journal of Psychology*, 1966, *20*, 228–236.

Schonfield, D., Trueman, V., & Kline, D. Recognition tests of dichotic listening and the age variable. *Journal of Gerontology*, 1972, *27*, 487–493.

Simon, E. Depth and elaboration of processing in relation to age. *Journal of Experimental Psychology: Human Learning and Memory*, 1979, *5*, 115–124.

Smith, A. D. Aging and interference with memory. *Journal of Gerontology*, 1975, *30*, 319–325.

Sternberg, S. Memory scanning: New findings and current controversies. *Quarterly Journal of Experimental Psychology*, 1975, *27*, 1–32.

Talland, G. A. Age and the span of immediate recall. In G. A. Talland (Ed.), *Human aging and behavior*. New York: Academic Press, 1968.

Taub, H. A. Mode of presentation, age and short-term memory. *Journal of Gerontology*, 1975, *30*, 56–59.

Thomas, J. C., Waugh, N. C., & Fozard, J. L. Age and familiarity in memory scanning. *Journal of Gerontology*, 1978, *33*, 528–533.

Waugh, N. C., Thomas, J. C., & Fozard, J. L. Retrieval time from different memory stores. *Journal of Gerontology*, 1978, *33*, 718–724.

II AGE-RELATED CHANGES IN MEMORY PROCESSES

Edited by
Laird S. Cermak

The ordering of the chapters in this section falls into the general framework of those dealing with short retention intervals, followed by those testing retention intervals that can be subsumed within an experimental testing session, to those which tap preexisting knowledge. The first three chapters concentrate upon deficits observed in the aging population immediately following stimulus presentation. New techniques for such assessment as well as results from previously utilized procedures are presented. Walsh and Prasse (Chapter 10) explore age related differences in immediate retention following visual presentation, an area traditionally referred to as iconic memory. Then Crowder (Chapter 11) makes a parallel type of search through the area of echoic memory deficits following auditory stimulus presentations. Finally, Wingfield and Sandoval (Chapter 12) review theories of attentional resources and describe the phenomena surrounding perceptual processing for meaning. Grossberg (Chapter 14) concentrates upon a critique of iconic and echoic memory, while Thompson (Chapter 13) focuses upon a discussion of the processing of meaning.

The second division of this section is primarily concerned with an analysis of those processing tasks that can be studied in the laboratory and involve retention beyond the sensory memory level. Waugh and Barr (Chapter 15) argue persuasively that aging eventuates in a slowing of mental processing almost regardless of the nature of the task. Cermak (Chapter 16), on the other hand, proposes that the quality of processing needs further exploration, and presents a model that has been applied to the study of amnesia. Hines (Chapter 17) critiques both these papers and presents a parallel-processing-of-features model as an alternative to a "strict" serial-processing-of-features model.

The last division of this section concentrates upon assessments of the subject's retrieval of material acquired throughout his individual lifespan. J. Lachman (with R. Lachman, in Chapter 18) presents an interesting study of the individual's "World Knowledge" in which she discovers that the aged fare quite well. R. Lachman (with J. Lachman, in Chapter 19) describes the individual's ability to retrieve information from long-term memory in order to perform naming tasks. In their critiques, Perlmutter (Chapter 20) and then Nickerson (Chapter 21) present intriguing questions, interesting data, and insightful comments concerning the nature of the older person's memory deficit.

Throughout this section the emphasis is placed upon a careful analysis of the subject's ability to "process" information as well as to retrieve it. Thus, it is the entire spectrum of information processing that comes under investigation and not just the ability to store material in specialized memory boxes. This approach, which has become the hallmark of modern-day theories of memory, has also become popular in applied research. From the content of these chapters, it seems this approach might continue to provide the framework for research on memory in the aged for some time to come.

10 Iconic Memory and Attentional Processes in the Aged

David A. Walsh
Michael J. Prasse
University of Southern California

In 1960, George Sperling published his investigations of the information available in brief visual presentations. One of the major findings was the existence of a brief visual storage that lasts for a few tenths of a second. Neisser (1967) labeled this visual storage "iconic memory," and the label has become well accepted. In the pages that follow we review the history of iconic memory research with the goal of outlining the experimental procedures that have been used in its study. Using this foundation, we examine studies of age differences in iconic memory and make suggestions for future investigations. The remaining sections discuss some attentional components involved in experimental tasks that have been employed to study iconic memory. Finally, we report the results of work on age differences in attention mechanisms and propose some problems for further investigation.

HISTORY OF ICONIC MEMORY RESEARCH

The question Sperling (1960) set out to investigate was: How much can be seen in a brief visual exposure? This question has relevance to our normal mode of seeing, which resembles a series of brief exposures as, for example, in reading where the eye assimilates information only in the brief pauses between its quick saccadic movements. Many researchers prior to Sperling had investigated this question, and they found that when stimuli consisting of a large number of letters were presented tachistoscopically to subjects they could report only four letters, but subjects insisted more letters could be seen. Sperling was able to gain new insight into this enigma with some clever methodology.

Researchers before Sperling had used a whole report methodology: Subjects viewed a tachistoscopic flash of a stimulus array and were asked to report all of the letters presented. The usual result of such studies is that only four or five letters can be reported even though many more letters may have been presented. This limit on the number of items reported suggests a memory limit, and it has been called the span of immediate-memory (cf. Miller, 1956). A novel aspect of Sperling's work was the use of a partial report procedure. Subjects were given an instruction immediately after the tachistoscopic presentation. The instruction specified only a part of the display to be reported. The difference between partial and whole report results was dramatic: Subjects were able to report about 80% of all the information included in complex displays immediately after presentation. Fig. 10.1 shows the results for partial and whole report conditions used by Sperling (1960).

An ingenious aspect of Sperling's work was the use of a precisely timed auditory signal as the instruction for which part of the visual display to report. Subjects would view the tachistoscopically presented stimulus for 50 msec

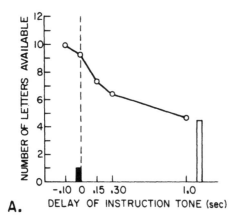

A.

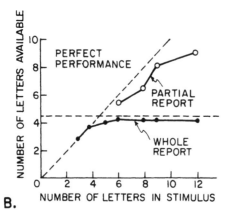

B.

FIG. 10.1. Large capacity and decay of information in iconic memory as shown by Sperling's (1960) partial report. (A) shows the decay of information with increasing tone delay, and (B) shows the accuracy of whole report and partial report data as a function of the number of letters in the stimulus displays. (Adapted from Sperling, 1960. *Psychological Monographs: General & Applied,* 74(11), 1-28. Copyright 1960 by the American Psychological Association. Reprinted by permission.)

and would hear immediately thereafter either a high, low, or medium frequency tone. On each experimental trial subjects would see three rows of letters with either three or four letters (consonants) in each row. The high tone indicated the top row of letters was to be reported, the low tone indicated the bottom row, etc. While the use of these tones was important in establishing that many more than four or five letters can be *seen* in a brief glance, they were equally useful in examining the rate at which information is lost after it is seen.

Sperling was able to study the rate of loss by presenting the tone instructions at accurately timed intervals after the tachistoscopic presentation. Fig. 10.1 presents Sperling's findings. While subjects were able to report about 80% of the information when the tone immediately followed the display, their accuracy of report dropped rapidly with increases in tone delay. With 1 sec of delay, subjects were no more accurate in the partial report condition than when whole reports were given. However, when delays of 150 and 300 msec were used, most subjects performed above their own whole report levels. These results suggest that: (1) Subjects can see much more in a brief presentation than they can report; and (2) much of this extra information remains available for a few hundred msec following the presentation.

Sperling conducted a number of experiments to assess the nature of the brief store of information his experiments had uncovered. The introspective accounts of subjects in Sperling's experiments suggested that the store was in the visual modality. Most subjects reported that they could still see and read the tachistoscopic displays when the tone occurred 150 msec after the tachistoscopic flash. Sperling tested the hypothesis that information was briefly stored in the visual modality by manipulating a variable known to affect visual performance. The standard conditions used in Sperling's experiments presented subjects with dark fields before and after the stimulus display. Baxt (1871), and many investigators since, demonstrated that a lighted poststimulus field reduces the clarity of the stimulus field. Sperling used a lighted post field in combination with immediate and delayed (150 msec) tones in a partial report task. His findings were that the response accuracy of subjects decreased by half when a lighted field followed the stimulus. The ability of a homogeneous visual field to affect the available information is evidence that the memory store depends on a persisting visual image of the stimulus.

Another experiment reported by Sperling suggests that iconic memory is preperceptual or noncategorized, as well as visual. Sperling presented subjects with mixed displays composed of both letters and digits. The subject's task called for a partial report, but the instruction was given before the tachistoscopic presentation and specified that either letters or digits were to be reported. Performance on the partial report by category task was much poorer than on partial report by location. The partial report by category performance was similar to performance on the whole report task. These results are consistent with the idea that iconic memory is a visual persistence of the stimulus display. Iconic memory seems to hold visual information which can be read (or recognized), but which has not yet undergone these perceptual analyses. An instruction that identifies categories of information is not useful because each element of the visual store must be perceived and categorized before it is identified as an element to be reported. The poor performance in the category partial report condition suggests that the processing time to identify the elements of complex displays exceeds the duration of iconic persistence. However, the partial report by location instruction is useful because it directs the subject's attention to a row of three or four elements which can be read, identified, and stored in primary memory before iconic memory has decayed.

The partial report by category experiments are very important for reasons other than their demonstration that iconic memory is preperceptual. These experiments suggest that the perceptual analyses necessary to identify elements in iconic memory take some amount of time. Neisser (1967) has seen this as an important point and suggested an alternative explanation of the limit of four items retained when subjects are asked to make whole reports. Sperling and many others have interpreted the whole report limit as the result of a limit on how many letters or digits can be held in primary memory. Sperling assumes that subjects have seen (and perceived) all of the elements, but that only four can be held in primary memory. This assumption seems wrong, since the partial report by category task shows that subjects are unable to read (perceive) nine or 12 elements in the time afforded by iconic persistence. Neisser's interpretation seems more consistent with these data and explains the whole report limits as a limit on perceptual rather than primary memory processes. Neisser (1967) hypothesizes that the time required to perceive (identify, recognize) four letters is equal to the duration of iconic memory; the icon has faded before a fifth or sixth letter can be perceived. Thus, Neisser's explanation suggests partial report by location improves performance by reducing the perceptual processing time to a level within the limits of iconic persistence.

A further implication of Neisser's analysis is the difficulty of measuring iconic persistence with the partial report procedure. These measures will usually be an underestimate of icon duration. Let us consider what a subject must do when he is presented with a partial report task. He views a tachistoscopic flash which produces an iconic memory with some persistence. At some point in time, either immediately after or a fraction of a second later, the subject hears a tone which indicates which stimulus row to report. He must focus his attention to the indicated row of elements and, if Neisser is correct, then identify each element in the row. It is clear from this analysis that two processes are operating in opposition to one another. Iconic memory is rapidly fading, while a series of processes consuming some unknown time are laboring to transform the visual information of iconic memory into a more permanent primary memory representation. These considerations suggest we cannot measure iconic persistence by determining when partial report performance has decreased to the level of whole report performance, as we suggested could be done in examining Fig. 10.1. Such a measure is an underestimate of icon duration.

ACCURATE MEASUREMENT OF ICONIC PERSISTENCE

Two separate approaches have been taken to establish measures of iconic persistence which are not confounded by attention and readout processing times associated with the partial report task. One approach has involved the measurement of the processing times associated with these processes and has used these measures to correct iconic measures. The second approach has sought to develop direct measures of iconic persistence, measures which do not involve attention and readout processes.

Averbach and Coriell (1961) reported a series of experiments which used a backward masking methodology to measure the processing time for attention and readout components of the partial report task. The Averbach and Coriell experiments use a partial report procedure that differs from Sperling's experiments in that the instruction of what to report was presented visually. These researchers used a television tachistoscope that allowed successive visual fields to be presented. Fig. 10.2 shows a typical sequence from these experiments. Subjects viewed a bright (70 foot-lambert) uniform screen with a fixation point in the center. An array of 16 letters (two rows of eight letters) was presented for 50 msec and then a bar marker was presented for 50 msec. The marker appeared either over or under one of the letters, and it was delayed for one of eight different time intervals.

Fig. 10.3 shows the results of the Averbach and Coriell studies. Subjects were able to report about 70% of the letters (11.2 items) when the visual instruction occurred just as the tachistoscopic display turned off. When the marker was delayed for 200 msec, performance had dropped to a level of 30% (4.8 items). These results replicate those of Sperling and provide further support for the existence of a brief visual storage.

A number of the results reported by Averbach and Coriell support the idea that iconic memory is a brief visual store. Fig. 10.4 shows the accuracy of report as a function of the position of each letter in the array. Subjects were most accurate in reporting letters in the center of the viewing field (Positions 4, 5, 12, and 13) and those at the outer edges (Positions 1, 8, 9, and 16). The shape of this function (the W-shape) has been explained as the result of lateral

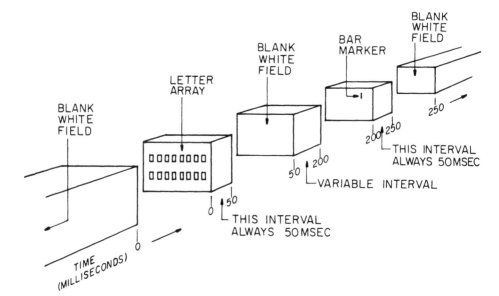

FIG. 10.2. Stimulus sequence from a typical trial in the Averbach and Coriell (1961) investigations. (Copyright 1961 by the American Telephone and Telegraph Company. Reprinted by permission from the *Bell Systems Technical Journal.*)

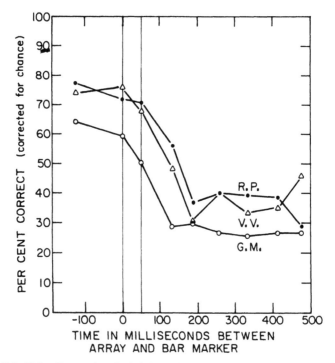

FIG. 10.3. Decay of available information for three subjects in the Averbach and Coriell (1961) partial report task. (Copyright 1961 by the American Telephone and Telegraph Company. Reprinted by permission from the *Bell Systems Technical Journal.*)

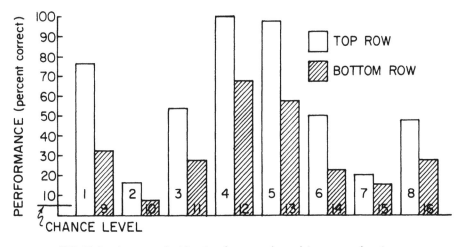

FIG. 10.4. Accuracy of subjects' performances in partial report as a function of position in array, averaged over all time intervals between array and marker (from Averbach & Coriell, 1961). (Copyright 1961 by the American Telephone and Telegraph Company. Reprinted by permission from the *Bell system Technical Journal.*)

inhibitory effects in the visual system: The outer positions have letters (contours) inhibiting their registration on only one side, while letters in the center positions fall within the foveal area which is less sensitive to lateral inhibitory processes. The W-shape function provides further evidence that iconic memory is affected by properties of the visual system. The high accuracy of report for letters in the center position is an important source of evidence against recent reports by Sakitt (1976) that the primary source of storage for iconic memory is in the rods. The fovea is a rod-free region from .5° to 1° of visual angle in radius. The displays used by Averbach and Coriell were 4° vertically by 5° horizontally, and each letter subtended 1° vertically by .5° horizontally. Our calculations show that the four center letters in Averbach and Coriell's displays must have fallen almost completely within the rod-free area of the fovea. However, contrary to Sakitt's hypothesis, which would predict little or no iconic store for these center letters, performance was highest for these items. Clearly, in the Averbach and Coriell experiments the most effective source of iconic storage was not in the rod photoreceptors of the retina, as Sakitt has suggested is the case for all iconic information.

The important point of the Averbach and Coriell experiments is their use of backward masking procedures to obtain measures of the processing time necessary to locate the bar marker and read out the target letter. Backward masking occurs when two visual stimuli follow one another with a very short interval of time separating them. The second stimulus works backward in time and erases the first stimulus which was presented earlier. There is a large literature that examines the backward masking phenomena and, like most areas of psychological research, there is far from complete agreement as to the explanation of masking effects. The investigations of Averbach and Coriell (1961), Turvey (1973), and Hellige, Walsh, Lawrence, and Prasse (1979) provide substantial evidence that two different mechanisms operate to produce masking effects. The first mechanism involves the combination of the two visual stimuli into a single preperceptual visual store; the luminance of each of the two stimuli are averaged together and while the contour information of both stimuli is included in the single icon, the contrast ratio between these contours and their background is reduced. The second mechanism involves the *replacement* of contour information in the first stimulus by contour information of the second stimulus. The contour replacement is local or specific to subareas within the viewing field, rather than a global replacement of all of the first viewing field by the second. Furthermore, the replacement depends on similarity of contours between the two stimulus fields. Averbach and Coriell used this second type of backward masking to control the amount of time subjects had available to process visual displays.

Averbach and Coriell (1961) measured readout rate by presenting arrays of letters simultaneously with a bar marker indicating which letter to report and then presenting a circle mask a short time afterwards which stopped the processing of the marked letter. The subject's performance under these conditions is used as a measure of how well he can detect the marker and read the letter when given only the time interval between the onset of the array with marker and the subsequent onset of the circle. The results of this experiment show that subjects required between 200 and 270 msec to detect a marker and read the designated letter. These results provide evidence that the decay curves seen in partial report tasks incorporate two effects: (1) icon duration, and (2) readout time. Averbach and Coriell used the readout-time measurements to correct for this latter factor and solve for icon duration. The computed estimates of icon duration involve correcting the partial report decay functions by subtracting out increments in performance that result from nonselective readout of the correct letter before it is designated by the marker and adding in the loss of performance that results from the time required to read out the designated letter after the marker appears. The estimates obtained by Averbach and Coriell suggest that iconic memory persists for durations of 250 to 300 msec.

Other researchers have tried to avoid the confounding influence of visual detection of a marker and readout time by using other tasks to assess iconic persistence. Eriksen and Collins (1967) used what they termed "stimulus halves." As shown in Fig. 10.5, each stimulus half (upper two panels) appears to be a random collection of dots. When they are overlayed as in the lower panel, however, the halves combine to form the nonsense syllable "VOH." Eriksen and Collins reasoned that if one stimulus half was followed by

FIG. 10.5. An example of "stimulus halves." The upper two dot
patterns, when superimposed, result
in the bottom stimulus pattern in
which the nonsense syllable VOH
can be read. (From Eriksen &
Collins, 1967. *Journal of Experimental Psychology, 74*, 470–484.
Copyright 1967 by the American
Psychological Association. Reprinted by permission.)

presentation of the second stimulus half after some delay, subjects would be
able to identify the nonsense syllable only if that delay was shorter than the
iconic duration of the first stimulus half. They found that the ability to
identify the nonsense syllable decreased from about 90% at a delay interval of
0 msec to 30% at a delay of 300 msec. Further increases in the delay produced
no further decrements in identification accuracy. The 300-msec value Eriksen
and Collins obtained for the length of iconic storage agrees rather well with
the estimate obtained by Averbach and Coriell (1961) and Sperling (1960).

The Eriksen and Collins "stimulus halves" method eliminates the subject's
task of selecting among multiple elements, as is the case in partial report
tasks, but it does not eliminate the need for subjects to read the stimulus word.
Three other tasks have been reported by Haber and Standing (1969, 1970)
that provide direct measures of iconic persistence. One task involves "viewing
a camel through the eye of a needle." Subjects were seated in front of a
rectangular piece of cardboard that contained a narrow slit and which had a
black-on-white circle immediately behind. The slit was oscillated back and
forth in front of the circle at varying speeds until the subject perceived the
illusion of seeing the whole circle. The idea behind this task is that the
portions of the circle viewed through the slit create iconic memories which are
integrated into a whole perception once the slit is moving fast enough to
refresh all iconic images before any one decays. Haber and Standing found
storage times of about 325 msec when the moving slit task was used.

A second task also required subjects to make subjective judgments about
the persistence of a form, but a complete form was shown on each trial. Fig.
10.6 shows the logic behind this task. A circle is presented tachistoscopically
at regular intervals and its rate of presentation is under the control of the
experimenter. Each presentation creates an icon which begins to decay. If the
next presentation of the circle occurs before the icon from the first has faded,
then subjects should perceive the illusion of a continually present form.

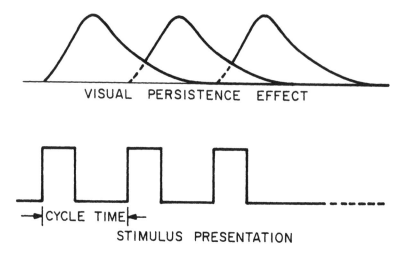

FIG. 10.6.   A hypothetical view of visual persistence as a result of a repeating stimulus. The subject's response of continuity or discontinuity is based upon whether he judges the persistence reached zero from the first flash before the second flash occurred (from Haber and Standing, 1969).

However, if the second presentation is delayed until the icon from the first has faded, then the subject will perceive the appearance, disappearance, and reappearance of the circle. By varying the interval between successive presentations of the circle and having subjects report if they perceive a continuous or discontinuous form, Haber and Standing were able to measure iconic persistence. These measures are direct in that the same form reappears in the same visual field location: Subjects do not have to search for the form nor recognize it, rather they only need to judge if it disappears for some brief instant. Using this persistence of form task, Haber and Standing obtained measures indicating a mean storage time of about 275 msec. Further investigations used the same persistence of form task, but varied whether the circle was presented monoptically (to one eye) or dichoptically (to one eye, then the other). The interesting finding was that subjects perceived the form as continuous whether it was presented every 270 msec to the same eye or alternated between eyes. This finding has been interpreted by many investigators as evidence for a central locus for the effects of visual persistence. Sakitt (1976), however, has suggested the locus of visual persistence is in the rods.

There is considerable evidence against Sakitt's hypothesis that the *rods* provide the main locus of iconic storage. However, we do not believe the Haber and Standing finding for dichoptic presentations is evidence against a hypothesis such as that proposed by Sakitt. The photoreceptors of the retina (rods and cones) could serve as the primary locus of storage for iconic memory, and one might still predict the effect observed by Haber and

Standing. This idea assumes the mechanism for perception of the icon is located centrally. The dichoptic findings can be explained by assuming the central perceptual mechanism will "see" a continuous form whenever it receives uninterrupted neural input from either eye. Thus, stimulating the photochemical storage of either retina every 250 msec would provide information for the central perception of form.

One other task designed to make a direct measure of visual persistence has been used by Haber and Standing (1970) and other investigators (Sakitt, 1976; Sperling, 1967). This method requires a subject to adjust an auditory "click" to coincide with the perceived onset and offset of a visual flash. The difference in time settings between the two clicks is used as a measure of visual persistence. This method sounds straightforward, but we have found it extremely difficult to perform reliably. Haber and Standing used only two subjects who were highly trained. They report that at least 4 hr of practice were necessary before their subjects were able to reliably make the "click settings."

The Haber and Standing (1970) investigations provide some important information about the effects of stimulus duration and the use of lighted or dark pre- and postfields on iconic persistence. With dark pre- and postviewing fields, subjects adjusted the clicks so that 400 msec separated their perceived onset and offset of an array of nine letters presented tachistoscopically for 20 msec. With lighted pre- and postfields, a 20-msec stimulus resulted in a perceived icon of only 200 msec in duration. A surprising result of the Haber and Standing investigation was the effect of varying target duration on icon persistence. They found that as the duration of the target increased, the time interval set by subjects remained about constant. For example, when the 20-msec target presented with dark pre- and postfields was increased to 300 msec, subjects continued to set the interclick interval to 400 msec. These data suggest that iconic persistence begins with the onset of the tachistoscopic presentation, rather than at its offset. When stimulus durations were set at or above 500 msec, subjects set the interclick interval to correspond with the stimulus duration: There appears to be no visual persistence following the offset of stimuli with more than 500-msec duration.

Before we begin a discussion of investigations of iconic memory and aging, it seems appropriate to discuss more fully the recent work by Sakitt (1976). Sakitt, in a series of investigations, has presented strong evidence that the rods may serve as the locus of iconic storage. Her evidence consists of (1) showing that a subject with only rod vision (rod monochromat) has iconic memory; and (2) that the spectral sensitivity for producing 500-msec icons is that of the rods in normal subjects. Unfortunately, we believe Sakitt has made unwarranted claims about her evidence as support for the hypothesis that the icon is predominantly a rod phenomenon. The following evidence and arguments suggest to us that Sakitt's conclusion is unwarranted.

1. All of her subjects were run under conditions of strong dark adaptation. She presents no evidence that the rods play any role in iconic persistence for non-dark-adapted subjects.
2. The acuity gradient reported by Averbach and Coriell, discussed earlier, shows their subjects performed best on the partial report task for letters presented to the fovea—the rod-free area of the retina.
3. Banks and Barber (1977) have presented clear evidence that color information is available throughout the course of iconic memory. The rods cannot, therefore, be the sole locus of iconic storage.

ICONIC MEMORY AND AGING

Few studies of age differences in iconic memory have been reported. Abel (1972) attempted to look at age differences in iconic memory using the procedure employed by Sperling (1960). Arrays of letters arranged in three rows of three items were presented tachistoscopically. Subjects reported only a single row of three letters; the row to be reported was designated by a tone presented either simultaneously with the letters or delayed for various durations after the letters.

Abel found only marginally significant age differences in accuracy of report. Furthermore, no age differences were found in the rate of decline of partial report accuracy. Fig. 10.7 presents these findings. An important point in Fig. 10.7 is the equivalent difference between old and young groups at all delay periods from 0 to 1200 msec. This finding might suggest that the storage capacity of sensory memory declines with age, while the rate of decay remains unchanged. The latter conclusion is supported by the finding of equal rates of decline in accuracy with increasing delay periods for all age groups. The conclusion of decreases in storage capacity with age follows from the finding that older adults report fewer items than young even when the tone indicating which row to report occurs without delay. However, for methodological reasons, it is questionable that Abel's investigation really deals with iconic memory.

Abel found that it was necessary to use fairly long stimulus exposures in order to obtain an acceptable level of performance in the oldest sample. A stimulus duration of 500 msec was used. The work of Haber and Standing (1970) suggests that no visual persistence should follow the offset of tachistoscopic presentations as long as those used by Abel. In fact, many of the subjects in her investigation reported that they were not reading an image when they heard the tone instruction, but rather had to "remember what items were presented where." Also, the small drop in performance between the 0-msec delay and 1200-msec delay conditions shown in Fig. 10.7 is inconsistent with other partial report investigations: Young and old subjects show only a

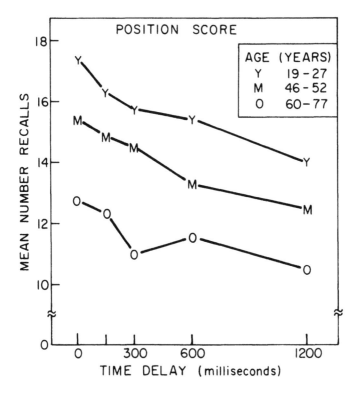

FIG. 10.7. The number of letters reported from tachistoscope arrays as a function of time-delay of a signal indicating what to report. Items were scored as correct only if their spatial position was known. (Adapted from J. Botwinick, *Aging and Behavior*, 2nd ed., Fig. 17.1. Copyright © 1978 by Springer Publishing Company, Inc., New York. Reprinted by permission.)

20% drop in performance across this time range. We have more to say later about the necessity of using 500-msec stimuli in Abel's investigation. For the moment, we feel it safe to conclude that the differences seen in Fig. 10.7 reflect age differences in primary memory performance.

A number of years ago, Walsh and Thompson (as reported in Walsh, 1975) began a series of investigations of age differences in iconic memory. Their first approach was to use a partial report task similar to that used by Averbach and Coriell. Subjects were shown arrays of eight letters (two rows of four letters) for 50-msec durations. After 16 delay intervals ranging from 0 to 700 msec, subjects saw a marker for 50 msec that indicated a single letter to report. Each trial began with a fixation point displayed for 2 sec at a luminance about 200 times dimmer than the stimulus array. The viewing fields of the binocular tachistoscope remained dark between the letter and marker stimuli and between test trials. Before beginning the test trials, each subject was practiced in a no-delay condition until he could report 75% of the target letters.

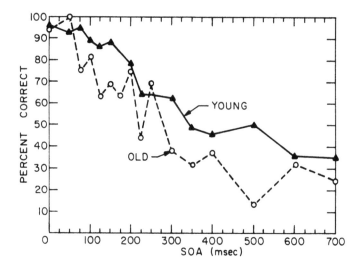

FIG. 10.8. The percentage of letters reported as a function of the delay between an array and marker.

Walsh and Thompson found a dramatic difference between the performance of the 18-31-year and 60-72-year-old samples. The partial report task was easy for the young subjects. On their first series of partial report trials, they could report more than 75% of the target letters. In contrast, the old subjects had great difficulty with the task, and 80% of the old subjects were not able to reach the 75% performance criterion in the no-delay condition despite many hours of practice. Walsh and Thompson did find, as did Abel (1972), that increasing the stimulus duration to 500 msec increased the performance of many of the old subjects who could not perform the partial report task at 75% accuracy when 50-msec stimulus displays were presented. Fig. 10.8 presents the data from 10 young subjects and two old subjects who exceeded the criterion of 75% partial report performance at 0 msec delay between letters and marker stimuli. Although these two old subjects are atypical of persons their age, the performance difference between these two subjects and the young sample was statistically reliable.

We believe the most interesting aspect of the Walsh and Thompson investigations was the difficulty of the partial report task for eight of the 10 older subjects tested. All of these subjects showed good tachistoscopic performance when single letters were displayed on each trial. They were also able to perform the partial report task when the letter array and marker were shown simultaneously for 500 msec or 1 sec. These findings suggest the difficulty of the partial report task was not the result of test anxiety, inability to see the arrays, or misalignment of the letter arrays and marker. Two other explanations for their difficulty seem more plausible to us:

1. The duration of iconic memory may decrease with age to a point where the readout processing time of the partial report task exceeds the reduced icon duration.
2. The processing times required for the readout component of partial report tasks may increase with age, and these increased processing times may be longer than the persistence of iconic memory.

It is possible that both of these explanations are correct; older adults may have both shorter-duration iconic memory stores and require longer processing times to read out letters in a partial report task. These explanations are consistent with the findings of Abel (1972) and Walsh and Thompson (as reported in Walsh, 1975) that old subjects need 500-msec stimulus presentations in order to perform well at partial report tasks. The work of Haber and Standing (1970) shows the use of 500-msec stimulus durations results in longer periods of available information than does a 50-msec exposure. This increased period of available information might be expected to compensate for either shorter icons or longer readout times for old subjects performing a partial report task.

Walsh and Thompson (1978) used a direct measure procedure reported by Haber and Standing (1969) to examine age differences in iconic memory duration. This procedure presents subjects with repetitive flashes of the letter 0 which are separated by varying dark time intervals controlled by the experimenter. The subject's task is to report whether he/she sees the 0 completely disappear for an instant or whether it remains continually present. The logic behind this task was shown in Fig. 10.6. The experimental conditions included three stimulus durations (10, 50, and 90 msec) and two viewing conditions (monoptic and dichoptic). In each condition, subjects viewed two ascending and two descending sequences of trials. On the ascending trials, the dark period between flashes was increased in 25-msec steps from less than 100 msec to the point where subjects could perceive the 0 disappear and reappear. In the descending series, the dark period between flashes was decreased in 25-msec steps from 525 msec or longer to the point where subjects could no longer perceive the 0 disappear and reappear. The dependent variable recorded for each condition was an average of the longest intervals at which the subject saw the circle as continuous.

Table 10.1 presents the results from the Walsh and Thompson (1978) investigation. The only significant effect was the age of subjects: The iconic memory of the young persisted for 289 msec, as compared to 248 msec for the old sample. The data of Table 10.1 show that alternating the stimulus presentations between the two eyes (dichoptic condition) did not result in different periods of perceived persistence than when the same eye (monoptic condition) viewed the repetitive stimulus presentations. These data suggest that the perceptual mechanism which creates the icon is a central mechanism

TABLE 10.1
The Persistence of Visual Storage from Stimulus Offset to Stimulus Onset
CONDITIONS

		Monoptic			Dichoptic			
		Target Duration (msec)						
		10	50	90	10	50	90	Marginal Means
YOUNG	Mean	284	306	295	269	290	288	289
	SD	31.5	38.6	44.7	30.5	27.4	64.5	
OLD	Mean	255	254	230	244	255	246	248
	SD	57.0	66.2	86.0	68.8	83.9	61.	
Marginal Means		269	280	262	257	273	267	

mediating neural input from both eyes. However, we do not believe that these data provide any strong evidence for the idea that the locus of iconic storage is central. The proposal that the locus of iconic storage may be in the rod and cone receptors of the retina (as Sakitt [1976] has suggested) seems reasonable to us. However, this proposal is still compatible with the idea that some central perceptual mechanisms create the iconic image by operating on neural inputs stored in the retina. Whether the locus of iconic storage is peripheral and the perceptual mechanism is central or whether both are central, the data from the Walsh and Thompson (1978) investigation show that these mechanisms function similarly in young and old adults.

The data presented in Table 10.1 also show that varying the duration of the stimulus flash across the range of 10 to 90 msec did not affect the perceived stimulus persistence for either age group. These data are consistent with the findings reported by Haber and Standing (1969), which show no variation in persistence across a range of stimulus durations from 4 to 200 msec using a similar persistence of form task.

The results of the Walsh and Thompson investigation do show a small (41 msec) difference in iconic persistence between young and old adults. However, iconic memory for these samples does not seem to be affected differentially by variation in stimulus duration or viewing conditions. The persistence of form task has one limitation in that it provides no estimate of how much information is available in the iconic store. We have more to say about this limitation later when we discuss age differences in some attentional processes required in partial report performance. Sakitt (1976) has suggested a number of other limitations of the persistence of form task used in the Walsh and Thompson investigation. Her major criticism is that the task measures critical flicker frequency (CFF) rather than iconic persistence. We feel this is an unwarranted criticism. The critical flicker frequency task is a measure of the longest pulse rate at which subjects can no longer detect any variation from a steady luminance when a stimulus is cycled off and on. The persistence of form task is a measure of the longest pulse rate at which subjects cannot detect the disappearance of contour information. The difference in typical CFF and persistence of form task data underline this difference. Typically, measures of CFF in young populations show interpulse duration of 25 msec, whereas the Walsh and Thompson data show interpulse durations of 289 msec in the persistence of form tasks.

Kline and his colleagues (Kline & Baffa, 1976; Kline & Orme-Rogers, 1978) have used the Eriksen and Collins procedure of "stimulus halves" to examine age differences in visual persistence. Kline and Baffa (1976) presented two age groups (older group mean age = 55.6 years; young group mean age = 21.3 years) with two stimulus halves which together formed one of five three-letter words. The stimulus halves were separated by ISI values ranging from 0 to 150 msec in 30-msec steps. Kline and Baffa found that the younger subjects were more accurate than older subjects across all ISI values in identifying the target word. Although this result indicates that iconic memory in the elderly is shorter in duration than in the young (as was also found by Walsh and Thompson, 1978), Kline and Baffa argue that the stimuli used in their study may have disadvantaged the elderly subjects. Their stimulus halves were composed of black dots on a white background. Integrating these dots into a perceptual whole may have been more difficult for the older subjects than for the young (Basowitz & Korchin, 1957, as cited by Kline & Baffa, 1976); the poorer performance by the elderly may have been due to an inability to integrate the dots into a perceptual whole rather than as a result of shorter duration icons. This argument, like those presented above, emphasizes the difficulty of assessing age differences in iconic memory when task performance involves cognitive processes, such as pattern recognition and/or component integration.

Kline and Orme-Rogers (1978) replicated the Kline and Baffa (1976) experiment with one major exception: Each stimulus half was constructed of straight line segments that connected together to form the target words. In addition, the duration of each stimulus half pair was presented at either a 20- or 40-msec duration. The results of this study were opposite to those obtained in Kline and Baffa (1976). Older subjects did much better in identifying the target word than did the young subjects when two halves were separated by ISIs of 60 and 120 msec. Furthermore, stimulus duration was inversely related to accuracy: In both age groups, subjects were more accurate at the 20-msec duration than at the 40-msec duration. Kline and Orme-Rogers suggest these results support the idea that iconic memory persists longer in old than in young adults. This conclusion is based on the idea that the icon of the first stimulus half must persist until the second half is presented in order for successful identification to occur. Thus, the "stimulus halves" task is believed to involve the integration of two separate icons into a single whole.

This review of the research examining age differences in iconic memory does not produce any simple conclusion. It is clear, however, that adults over 60 years of age have a very difficult time in performing partial report tasks and that these tasks are probably not appropriate for studying age differences in iconic memory. The possibility is considered later that age differences in attentional mechanisms may explain the difficulty with partial report tasks. The investigations of Kline and Baffa (1976) and Walsh and Thompson (1978) provide evidence for shorter iconic persistence in 60-75-year-olds than in 18-30-year-old adults. However, the Kline and Orme-Rogers (1978) results suggest the opposite, that iconic memory persists longer in older adults. In either case, it is clear that any differences in duration are small and, we believe, unlikely to have any important effect for registration of information in later memory stages.

There are many differences between the Walsh and Thompson (1978) work and that of Kline and his colleagues. For instance, the luminances employed were different: Walsh and Thompson used luminances of 72 cd/m^2, whereas Kline and Baffa and Kline and Orme-Rogers used stimulus presentations of about 6 cd/m^2. The Kline and Baffa task involved some perceptual closure in that words had to be perceived from dot patterns, while the Kline and Orme-Rogers study reduced closure requirements. However, both of the Kline investigations involve readout processes: Subjects must identify the integrated "stimulus halves" before the composite icon fades. In contrast, the Walsh and Thompson (1978) study involves neither perceptual closure nor readout components. The estimates of icon duration are also very different: Estimates for young subjects vary from 289 msec in the Walsh and Thompson work to 120 msec in the Kline and Baffa (1976) and Kline and Orme-Rogers (1978) investigations. We feel more research will be necessary to resolve the issue of age differences in icon duration. Further research would do best to avoid the use of partial report tasks or other measures of icon duration which include attentional components. We feel a productive next step would be to compare performance of adults who vary in age on the "stimulus halves" task and persistence of form tasks in a single investigation. Such an investigation should use a range of luminance values and also employ stimuli consisting of black contours on white background and vice versa. The combination of these tasks and the contour factor in a single investigation would clarify the extent to which the "stimulus halves" and persistence of form tasks measure similar components of iconic memory and clarify the directions of age differences in iconic memory duration.

ATTENTIONAL PROCESSES
AND PARTIAL REPORT

The efforts of Averbach and Coriell (1961) to measure the time taken to locate a visual marker and read out the indicated letter in a partial report task were discussed earlier. Their masking procedure did not allow them to distinguish between the separate times associated with locating the marker and the time associated with reading the letter. The possibility of separating these processing times is suggested by Neisser's (1967) analysis of the partial report task. Neisser hypothesized that iconic memory consists of unidentified features that specify information about each element (letter, digit, etc.). According to Neisser, these clusters of features are assembled in parallel by feature detection mechanisms in the perceptual system. Neisser has hypothesized that pattern recognition processes are carried out sequentially, one element at a time, and operate on the clusters of features held in iconic memory.

As discussed earlier, Neisser's analysis leads to the hypothesis that the limit on whole report performance is a limit on the rate at which target elements can be read from a rapidly fading icon. The increased percentage of information reported in partial report tasks, according to Neisser, results from reducing the pattern recognition processing requirements of the task to a time frame consistent with the duration of iconic memory. The reduction in processing load is accomplished by indicating a small set of elements that are selectively attended to and recognized for later report. These processes proposed by Neisser (1967) can be summarized as three stages: (1) parallel processing of visual features which produces iconic memory—a collection of segregated features which are not yet identified; (2) selective attention, a process which allows a shift of processing capacity to a subarea of iconic memory; and (3) focal attention, the concentration of processing capacity on the selected element so that pattern recognition can be completed.

Other researchers have proposed models similar to that of Neisser (1967). Turvey (1973) has outlined in more detail the stages involved in creating the icon. Peripheral perceptual processes are hypothesized to operate in parallel and to be responsible for detecting context-independent features such as contour shape, size, and orientation. The rate of peripheral processing has been shown by Turvey to be affected by stimulus energy: As stimulus energy decreases, the rate of peripheral processing decreases exponentially. Central perceptual processes assemble the context-independent features detected by peripheral processes into context-dependent features—features that arise from the relationships between lower level features such as parallel or perpendicular lines. Central processes have been demonstrated by Turvey to require a constant amount of time, unaffected by either stimulus energy or duration. Peripheral and central processes seem to be related in a concurrent but contingent fashion. Early steps in peripheral processes must be complete before the first stages of central processes can begin, but since there are many stages of both peripheral and central processes, the two can operate in parallel as long as peripheral processes are completed more quickly than central processes. However, if stimulus energy is very low, then central processes must await the completion of peripheral processes at each step of analysis. The output of the peripheral and central stages of analysis is hypothesized by Turvey (1973) to be iconic storage.

Turvey's concept of iconic storage is similar to Neisser's (1967); it is believed to be a set of features that are available to pattern recognition processes for identification. Thus, processing stages subsequent to iconic memory formation are believed necessary to complete recognition processes. The Turvey (1973) model of peripheral and central processes is useful in understanding some of the diverse measures of readout rate from iconic memory reported by various researchers.

Numerous investigations since the work of Averbach and Coriell (1961) have been conducted to examine the factors affecting both selective attention and the processes involved in reading out elements from iconic memory. We now briefly review some of the findings related to readout rate and selective attention and then discuss some research from our laboratory that has begun to examine age differences in these processes.

READOUT RATE FROM THE ICONIC STORE

Many of the investigations of readout rate have used a backward masking methodology. Baxt (1871) presented multielement arrays for periods of 5 msec that were followed by a bright flash of light. Baxt assumed that the flash of light terminated readout from the letter display and that the delay between its presentation and the letter array should represent the amount of time needed to read out the elements which were recognized. Using this procedure, Baxt found that he could recognize a single letter with a delay of 10 msec and an additional letter for every 10-msec increase in the duration of the delay.

However, Sperling (1963) questioned Baxt's assumption that a bright flash of light following a visual stimulus terminated processing of the stimulus. In his replication of Baxt's experiment, Sperling discovered that the effect of the flash of light was to create a negative afterimage, from which the letter array could be clearly read after termination of the flash. Consequently, Sperling reasoned that Baxt's value of 10 msec per letter reflected something other than readout rate. To rectify this situation, Sperling again replicated Baxt's procedure, but replaced the flash of light with a random noise field of less intensity than the letter array. Sperling felt that such a noise field would terminate the processing of the letter array without producing a negative afterimage. Nevertheless, Sperling's results replicated those of Baxt: Readout rate was again found to be about 10 msec per letter.

Despite the replication of Baxt's original estimate, the Sperling study was questioned by Eriksen and Spencer (1969) on methodological grounds. Eriksen and Spencer questioned whether the random noise field Sperling used in his experiments terminated processing as Sperling had assumed, or whether it combined with the letter stimuli to form a degraded, but still somewhat readable, "double exposure" iconic representation.

To reduce these problems, Eriksen and Collins (1969) used a masking methodology in which each successive stimulus masked the previous stimulus. They presented the numbers 1 through 9 in the center of a visual field. On each trial, eight of the nine numbers were sequentially presented in their numerical order (e.g., 8, 9, 1, 2, etc.) at luminance of $1.75 \text{ cd}/\text{m}^2$. Each letter was presented for a duration of 10 msec, with the experimenter varying the delay between successive letters. The subject's task was to indicate which number had not been presented. Eriksen and Collins reasoned that identifying which number had not been presented required processing of the numbers which had been presented, and therefore, manipulating the rate at which the numbers were presented would give an indication of the processing time for a single digit. They found that a rate of one digit every 200 msec resulted in 100% accuracy in identifying the missing digit.

Similarly, Eriksen and Eriksen (1974) presented sequences of three successive stimuli to subjects. The stimuli were letters (either A or H), numbers (either 5 or 8), and arrows (pointing either up or down). One stimulus from each of these stimulus categories was presented on a trial, illuminated at $3.18 \text{ cd}/\text{m}$ and presented for an average duration of 5 msec. Once again, a delay of 200 msec between stimulus presentations was found to be necessary for 100% accuracy in identifying all three stimuli.

How can the dramatically different estimates of Sperling (1963) and Eriksen and his colleagues be explained? We believe these differences are best explained by Turvey's model of peripheral and central perceptual processes. The masks used by Baxt (1871) and Sperling (1963) are most likely to interfere with perceptual processes only at the peripheral level of context-independent feature extraction. Turvey has shown that masks must have features similar to those of the target stimuli if central perceptual processes are to be affected. Thus, the Sperling and Baxt investigations probably reflect only the time necessary to complete peripheral processes. The studies by Eriksen and his colleagues used successive target stimuli to mask previously presented stimuli. This condition maximizes target and mask feature similarity and should affect all stages of readout. However, there are a number of important points to consider before we conclude that reading out each element from a multielement display requires 200 msec.

First, Eriksen and his colleagues used very low stimulus energies, a condition which should exaggerate the time required to complete peripheral perceptual processes. Work by Turvey (1973) and Walsh (1976) has demonstrated that young adults require about 75 msec to complete all stages of perceptual processes when high energy stimulus presentations are used. Furthermore, Walsh (1976) has shown that adults 60 to 70 years of age require 25 msec longer processing times than young adults to complete readout processes for single letter displays.

Second, it is important to realize that Eriksen's investigations presented single targets sequentially. Thus, for each presentation, peripheral, central, and pattern recognition processes had to be carried out. In multielement displays, the peripheral and central perceptual processing stages would, according to Turvey, be carried out in parallel; the time required to complete central and peripheral processing for many elements should be no longer than the time required for single elements. However, recognition processes operate serially such that reading out a second, third, or fourth element should require additional processing times. Unfortunately, Eriksen's investigations do not allow us to separate peripheral and central processing times from pattern recognition processing times.

We are now in the process of collecting data in an experiment designed to eliminate the weaknesses of previous investigations and provide measures of the processing time required by 18-20- and 67-72-year-old adults to read out letters from multielement displays. Our investigation uses a backward masking methodology. The experimental conditions are designed to ensure that central perceptual processing time can be controlled. One-, two-, and three-letter displays are presented dichoptically with a pattern mask composed of line segments identical to the target letters. Both target and

TABLE 10.2
The Average Processing Times Required By Subjects to Report Four
Successive Stimulus Displays

			Number of Letters in Display		
			1	*2*	*3*
Average Age of Subjects	18.8 years	X̄	61.12	79.73	101.94
	(n = 18)	SD	18.8	25.6	31.0
	69.5 years	X̄	85.4	114.2	153.06
	(n = 9)	SD	28.7	34.6	54.9

masking stimuli are presented at high luminance levels (72 cd/m^2) to maximize peripheral processing speed. Table 10.2 presents the preliminary findings from this research. The data show that 18-22-year-old subjects require about 60 msec to complete the readout processes for a single letter. Each additional letter requires about 20 msec more processing time. The 67-72-year-old subjects require about 85 msec to read out a single letter, whereas each additional letter requires another 35 msec. These findings suggest that aging is associated with slower rates of readout from visual displays and that a substantial portion of this slowing is attributable to pattern recognition processes.

SELECTIVE ATTENTION

One of the more amazing aspects of the Sperling (1960) and Averbach and Coriell (1961) investigations with the partial report task was the finding that subjects could switch their attention in a few hundred milliseconds to the elements indicated for report. Eriksen and his colleagues have reported many investigations designed to examine aspects of multielement displays that affect selective attention performance. Eriksen and Spencer (1969) presented subjects with circular arrays of letters in which each letter was located an equal distance from a central fixation point. The letters were presented sequentially at rates from one letter every 5 msec to one letter every 3000 msec. The number of letters presented per trial was also varied with either one, three, five, or nine letters presented. Finally, the position in which the target letter appeared was also varied (first, middle, or last position). Eriksen and Spencer found that the number of letters presented was the only variable which affected performance. The more letters presented, the less accurate subjects were in detecting the target letter. However, if an indicator specified either that a letter just presented in a series was the target or that no target appeared in the series, the number of letters presented in the series no longer affected performance. These results suggest to us that selective attention requires substantial amounts of processing effort and that processing capacity diminishes as the number of elements to which one must attend increases.

Eriksen and Rohrbaugh (1970) investigated the effect of spatial location on the identification of a designated letter. Circular arrays of four, eight, or 12 letters were presented under two conditions. In the distributed condition, letters were separated by at least one letter "space." In the grouped condition, letters were immediately adjacent. Furthermore, a probe indicating which letter to report was presented 100 msec before, simultaneous with, or 50 msec after presentation of the array. Eriksen and Rohrbaugh found that accuracy varied inversely with the number of letters presented, and was worse overall in the grouped, rather than spaced, condition. In addition, accuracy decreased as the ISI for presentation of the probe stimulus went from 100 msec before, to 50 msec after the letter array was displayed. To account for these results, Eriksen and Rohrbaugh suggested that attention may act much like the lens of a camera. With a wide field of view, more items may be attended to, but the individual details of each item are degraded or "out of focus." However, when the attentional mechanism focuses on a smaller field of view, the number of items attended to decreases, but the resolution for each item is much better. Thus, when the probe occurred before presentation of the array, the attentional "lens" had sufficient time to focus on the target position, resulting in better accuracy than when the probe occurred simultaneous with or 50 msec after the array was shown.

Further investigations of the effects of adjacent elements on selective attending to elements in multielement displays were reported by Eriksen and Hoffman (1972). They presented a single target letter simultaneous with its probe. This was followed after some ISI value by the remainder of the circular array, with the spacing of the letters in this array an independent variable. They found that reaction time for target identification was greatest when the separation between the target letter and the letters in the following circular array was less than 1° of visual angle. However, no differential reaction time as a function of this letter spacing was obtained for spacing greater than 1°. Eriksen and Hoffman concluded that the attentional focusing mechanism had a minimum resolution of 1° and, therefore, that both targets and nontargets separated by less than 1° would be processed equally well. Consequently, the subject would require more time to disentangle the target from the nontarget letter than when the letter stimuli are spaced such that the attentional lens could be focused on the single target letter.

The work of Eriksen and his colleagues represents only a small sample of the research literature in selective attention. Furthermore, there are many different models of how attention mechanisms operate and where in the flow of information processing they are located (cf. Schneider & Shiffrin, 1977; Shiffrin & Schneider, 1977). However, the work by Eriksen and his colleagues has uncovered some important variables that influence selective attention performance when subjects are asked to make partial reports from multielement displays. These variables may be useful in beginning to conceptualize why older adults have so much difficulty with the partial report task. For example, Eriksen's work shows that the use of an attentional cue requires at least 100 msec of processing time in young adults. Furthermore, the number of elements in a display and their proximity to one another impairs performance. An investigation conducted in our laboratory by Walsh, Vletas, and Thompson has begun to explore age differences in some aspects of selective attention.

The goal of the Walsh, Vletas, and Thompson (in preparation) investigation was to measure age differences in the processing time taken to perform a partial report task like that used by Averbach and Coriell (1961). We have previously discussed an unsuccessful attempt by Walsh and Thompson to use a similar partial report task to examine age differences in iconic memory. That investigation suggested that Walsh, Vletas, and Thompson would not be able to use the masking methodology employed by Averbach and Coriell (1961) to measure the processing time their subjects required to locate a visual marker and read out a single letter from an array. Averbach and Coriell's procedure depended on subjects' ability to perform the partial report task with a high level of accuracy, whereas previous work shows adults 60-70 years of age are unable to do so. Walsh, Vletas, and Thompson circumvented these problems by simplifying the subjects' task and doing so in a way designed to isolate separate components of selective attention and pattern recognition processes.

The experimental design of this investigation involved the use of a backward masking procedure to control visual processing time. Subjects' performance was measured on three visual tasks when they were allowed between 0 and 300 msec to process the visual displays. All visual displays contained only a single target element. Walsh, Vletas, and Thompson chose single-element displays as a starting point because of the need to bypass problems that might arise from age differences in the effects of adjacent items on readout processes. One display presented a single letter in the center of the viewing field. This condition was selected to provide a measure of how much processing time was required by subjects of different ages to recognize a target letter when they knew where it would appear so that no attention shift was required. (On every trial in each condition, subjects viewed a fixation point that appeared in the center of the visual field 2 sec before a stimulus was presented.) The second display condition presented a visual marker in one of four corners of the visual field. The position chosen for the marker was determined randomly on each trial. The subject's task was to report where the marker was presented. This condition was selected to measure how much processing time was required by subjects to locate a visual marker. The third viewing condition presented one target letter, but the letter appeared in one of four randomly chosen corners of the visual field. This condition was selected to measure the amount of processing time subjects required when their task involved both locating the item and identifying it.

Before discussing the results of this investigation, it is important to emphasize that the visual exposures were very brief—only 10 msec in duration. It was not possible for subjects to move their eyes in searching the visual field for either the marker or target letters. Furthermore, the processing time was controlled in this experiment by using a central masking procedure:

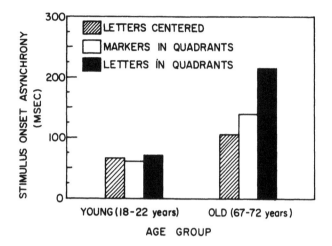

FIG. 10.9. The processing time required by subjects to correctly report 75% of the target items.

The target displays and mask were presented dichoptically, and the features of the mask were similar to those of the target.

Fig. 10.9 presents the results of this investigation. The 12 young subjects (mean age 19 years) required about 65 msec to complete each processing task. In contrast, the 15 old subjects (mean age 68 years) needed longer processing times to reach the same level of perceptual performance as the young. Most interesting, however, is the finding that the 68-year-old sample required different amounts of processing time for the three tasks, whereas the young subjects did not. As Fig. 10.9 shows, the old sample required about 100 msec to identify single letters that appeared in the center of the viewing field, 140 msec to locate a visual marker, and 220 msec to carry out the combined task of locating where a letter appeared and identifying what it was. These results make it easy to understand why 60-70-year-old adults have so much more difficulty with a partial report task than do young subjects. Young subjects appear able to complete both a visual search and recognition process in the length of time that they are able to complete either task alone. However, the time old subjects require to complete a combined visual search and recognition task is about the sum of the time required to do each task alone. We believe these findings are important in that they suggest major age differences in selective attention processes.

It is important to emphasize that even these results may underestimate the selective attention deficit associated with age, because these investigations minimize selective attention problems; that is, only single-element displays were presented. The disparity of processing times found for young subjects in the Walsh, Vletas, and Thompson experiment and those found by Averbach and Coriell provide an indication of the increased load associated with multielement displays. Averbach and Coriell estimated that attentional shift and readout processes require about 200-270 msec, whereas the Walsh, Vletas, and Thompson measures are about 70 msec for young subjects.

The Walsh, Vletas, and Thompson investigation represents only a first step in examining age differences in attention. The effects of increasing the number of elements in displays and the spacing between elements on age differences in performance are questions we intend to explore in future investigations. But even these investigations will represent only a beginning step toward understanding what may be important age changes in attention. Iconic memory has been given an important role in many information processing models of human memory. Theorists such as Neisser (1967) and Atkinson and Shiffrin (1968) have suggested that iconic memory is the initial stage of storage for visual information and that later stages of memory are encoded from the iconic store. Changes with age in iconic memory duration may affect the amount of information stored in later stages of memory. However, we believe that age differences in the speed and efficiency with which information can be attended to and read out of the iconic store will play a more important role in determining the amount of information encoded into later memory stages.

ACKNOWLEDGMENTS

Original research reported in this chapter was supported by a research grant (5 R01 AG 00521) and a Research Career Development Award (5 K04 AG 00017) from the National Institute on Aging.

REFERENCES

Abel, M. *The visual trace in relation to aging.* Unpublished Ph.D. dissertation, Washington University, 1972.

Atkinson, R. C., & Shiffrin, R. M. Human memory: A proposed system and its control processes. In K. W. Spence & J. T. Spence (Eds.), *The psychology of learning and motivation: Advances in research and theory* (Vol. 2). New York: Academic Press, 1968.

Averbach, E., & Coriell, A. S. Short-term memory in vision. *Bell Systems Technical Journal,* 1961, *40,* 309-328.

Banks, W. P., & Barber, G. Color information in iconic memory. *Psychological Review,* 1977, *84,* 536-546.

Basowitz, H., & Korchin, S. J. Age differences in the perception of closure. *Journal of Abnormal and Social Psychology,* 1957, *54,* 93-97.

Baxt, N. Ueber die Zeit welche nötig ist, damit ein Gesichtseindruck zum Bewustein kommt und uber die grosse (extension) der bewussten wahrnehmung bei einem gesichtseindrucke von gegenbener dauer. *Pfluger's Arch. ges Physiol.,* 1871, *4,* 325-336.

Eriksen, B. A., & Eriksen, C. W. Effects of noise letters upon the identification of a target letter in a nonsearch task. *Perception and Psychophysics,* 1974, *16,* 143-149.

Eriksen, C. W., & Collins, J. F. Some temporal characteristics of visual pattern perception. *Journal of Experimental Psychology*, 1967, *74*, 476-484.

Eriksen, C. W., & Collins, J. F. Visual perceptual rate under two conditions of search. *Journal of Experimental Psychology*, 1969, *80*, 489-492.

Eriksen, C. W., & Hoffman, J. E. Temporal and spatial characteristics of selective encoding from visual displays. *Perception and Psychophysics*, 1972, *12*, 201-204.

Eriksen, C. W., & Rohrbaugh, J. W. Some factors determining efficiency of selective attention. *The American Journal of Psychology*, 1970, *83*, 330-342.

Eriksen, C. W., & Spencer, T. Rate of information processing in visual perception: Some results and methodological considerations. *Journal of Experimental Psychology Monograph*, 1969, *79*, 1-16.

Haber, R. N., & Standing, L. G. Direct measures of short-term visual storage. *Quarterly Journal of Experimental Psychology*, 1969, *21*, 43-54.

Haber, R. N., & Standing, L. G. Direct estimates of apparent duration of a flash. *Canadian Journal of Psychology*, 1970, *24*, 216-229.

Hellige, J. B., Walsh, D. A., Lawrence, V. W., & Prasse, M. Figural relationship effects and mechanisms of visual masking. *Journal of Experimental Psychology: Human Perception and Performance*, 1979, *5*, 88-100.

Kline, D. W., & Baffa, G. Differences in the sequential integration of form as a function of age and interstimulus interval. *Experimental Aging Research*, 1976, *2*, 333-343.

Kline, D. W., & Orme-Rogers, C. Examination of stimulus persistence as the basis for superior visual identification performance among older adults. *Journal of Gerontology*, 1978, *33*, 76-81.

Miller, G. A. The magical number seven, plus or minus two: Some limits on our capacity for processing information. *Psychological Review*, 1956, *63*, 81-97.

Neisser, U. *Cognitive psychology*. New York: Meredith Publishing, 1967.

Sakitt, B. Iconic memory. *Psychological Review*, 1976, *83*, 257-276.

Schneider, W., & Shiffrin, R. M. Controlled and automatic human information processing: I. Detection, search, and attention. *Psychological Review*, 1977, *84*, 1-66.

Shiffrin, R. M., & Schneider, W. Controlled and automatic human information processing: II. Perceptual learning, automatic attending, and a general theory. *Psychological Review*, 1977, *84*, 127-190.

Sperling, G. The information available in brief visual presentations. *Psychological Monographs: General & Applied*, 1960, *74*(11), 1-28.

Sperling, G. A model for visual memory tasks. *Human Factors*, 1963, *5*, 19-31.

Sperling, G. Successive approximations to a model for short-term memory. *Acta Psychologica*, 1967, *27*, 285-292.

Turvey, M. T. On peripheral and central processes in vision: Inferences from an information-processing analysis of masking with patterned stimuli. *Psychological Review*, 1973, *80*, 1-52.

Walsh, D. A. Age differences in learning and memory. In D. S. Woodruff & J. E. Birren (Eds.), *Aging: Scientific perspectives and social issues*. New York: D. Van Nostrand Co., 1975.

Walsh, D. A. Age differences in central perceptual processes: A dichoptic backward masking investigation. *Journal of Gerontology*, 1976, *31*, 178-185.

Walsh, D. A., & Thompson, L. W. Age differences in visual sensory memory. *Journal of Gerontology*, 1978, *33*, 383-387.

Walsh, D. A., Vletas, S., & Thompson, L. W. Age-related differences in visual search and selective attention. Manuscript in preparation, 1979.

11 Echoic Memory and the Study of Aging Memory Systems

Robert G. Crowder
Yale University and Haskins Laboratory

As far as I know, no one has yet investigated whether echoic memory changes with advancing age, although there have been studies at the younger end of the developmental continuum. As we wait for this effort to materialize, I cannot be held responsible for reviewing a literature that does not exist. Instead, I take this opportunity to do several things: First, I review the logic of how echoic memory is demonstrated. Second, I consider some special relationships between the inferential problems in the first section and inferences about age decrements. Finally, I point out a promising approach to measuring echoic memory declines associated with aging and make some guesses about what we ought to expect from such research.

Throughout this chapter, I consider echoic memory more as a "model system" for aging research on memory than as an urgent priority for either applied or theoretical psychology. Indeed, I have the suspicion that changes in sensory memory with age are not very interesting. One reason for being guarded about the possibilities of theoretically interesting age effects in echoic memory is that they are likely to be small on a priori grounds. If echoic memory is as closely tied to the processing of auditory sensations as I claim (Crowder, 1978c), it should escape the sorts of general impairment that slow down the truly higher mental processes in aging. On the other hand, there are grounds for believing echoic memory to be sufficiently central not to suffer degradation through deafness. (About this, I have a few more words to say at the end of this chapter.) Another reason for considering the subject matter of this chapter as a model system rather than an urgent research priority is that echoic memory appears to play only a small, supplementary role in conventional memory tasks. There may be other circumstances in which echoic memory is more centrally involved (perhaps the registration of prosodic information in speech perception; see Crowder, 1978a), but these remain to be discovered. Thus, this review is being undertaken mainly to allow scrutiny of the problems that arise when one wishes to study age effects in a small, simple, and isolated memory system. The hope is that these inferential problems will become clearer in this narrow context than they are when we grapple with the intimidating overall phenomenon of the aging human mind.

DIRECT AND INDIRECT MANIFESTATIONS
OF MEMORY STORES

In this first section, I review briefly some of the methods that have been proposed for demonstrating auditory sensory storage (echoic memory). In doing so, I take pains to distinguish between direct and indirect manifestations of the store. It will develop that the indirect methods—where the existence of a store is inferred from poor performance as a result of an experimental operation—are not ideal for demonstrating memory stores. Because I have prepared extensive reviews of the experimental literature on demonstrations of echoic memory in two different places (Crowder, 1976, 1978c), I do not repeat anything like a complete review here. Instead I just illustrate the organization proposed on this field with what I think are particularly apt and clear examples.

In the following memory demonstrations it will be shown that there is a direct relation between performance and the inference that the memory store is manifested. That is, we infer the presence of echoic memory from the observation of good performance in the crucial experimental condition. (With the indirect methods, it is the disruption of performance that is taken as evidence for the presence of the proposed store.)

Sampling. The sampling method is an application of Sperling's (1960) research logic in demonstrating sensory memory in the visual system. The subject is hit with too much information to be categorized on the spot; this sets up the possibility that we may sample the precategorical information he may have available, for a while, following stimulus offset. The experimenter provides a cue to the subject which notifies him which particular part of the stimulus array he is to report. The diagnostic pattern of results is when performance on this cued stimulus information is better than it would have been if no cue had been presented. In other words, we look to see whether partial report, cued by a definition of some target information, is better than whole report, where the subject must try to encode everything. We know that directing attention to a part of a real stimulus array produces selection; but in this paradigm we look to see whether the same selectivity can be applied to a stimulus array after the physical stimulus has been terminated. If so, then there must be sensory memory remaining.

However, we need slightly more than the advantage of partial over full report to make our inference. It must also be shown that the cue works only when it points to a truly precategorical stimulus property—such as a position within a physical layout—and not when the cue describes a selection criterion which itself requires categorization to use (for example, report all items that come after G in the alphabet). Still further, it has to be shown that the cuing operation works only if the cue is presented soon after the delay. The partial-report advantage disappears if too long a delay separates the stimulus and the cue, which allows us to infer that the sensory memory representation necessary for the cue to work is fading.

In the auditory domain, we do not have a clear demonstration of all these circumstances at once. But an experiment by Glucksberg and Cowan (1970) illustrates the general approach. In this experiment, subjects listened to two separate streams of words—one in each ear—over headphones. One of these two channels was to be repeated, or shadowed, and the other was to be ignored. (Thus, in addition to presenting too much information to be categorized, these authors specifically directed attention away from one portion of the stimulus array.) Every once in a while a single digit was mixed into the words presented on the ignored side. From time to time, the whole shadowing task was interrupted and subjects were asked whether they had recently heard a digit on the channel they were supposed to be ignoring. The independent variable was the length of a separation existing between the actual occurrence of a digit on the ignored channel and when the subject was asked about it. The assumption was that since subjects were ignoring the channel containing digits, they would have to be consulting a sensory memory trace of the ignored channel in order to have a chance of reporting any digits there might have been on it recently.

The results showed a systematic decay in accuracy for reporting the digits as this delay was extended to several seconds. Furthermore, the subjects almost never reported that they had heard a digit on the ignored channel and then were incorrect in reporting which digit it was. This is all consistent with the hypothesis that subjects were actually categorizing the digit at the time of the query, listening to an echoic trace of a stimulus that had occurred in the past. If they were perceiving the digits on the spot, there would have been errors of commission more frequently.

This study illustrates the direct method of showing echoic memory. Subjects tell us they have such a memory representation through their ability to retrieve information which, we have reason to believe, could not have been other than precategorical.

Continuation. Huggins (1975a,b) has performed experiments on temporally segmented speech that afford another look at echoic memory through a direct method of inference. The observation starts with the finding that when 63 msec bursts of speech are interrupted with periods of silence lasting from about 100 to 500 msec, there is a loss in intelligibility down to about 55%; this is true even though there is no loss of stimulus information per se, just insertion of silent gaps. When the lengths of the silent gaps were further reduced below about 125 msec, however, Huggins found a sharp improvement in intelligibility (measured by shadowing accuracy), until the intervals of silence were as short as 60 msec, at which point performance was too good to detect whatever further improvements there might have been.

Huggins calls this improvement found as the 63-msec segments of speech are moved closer and closer together, from 125 to 60 msec gaps, the "gap-bridging result," and he properly considers it a manifestation of echoic memory. If two speech segments, each individually capable of supporting shadowing performance only at a level of 55%, are allowed to reside together in echoic memory, then some higher order processing system can draw information from them, together, in support of some perceptual category state. But if the first of these two segments has already departed from echoic memory before the second arrives, whatever categorization is done must happen individually for each one. Thus, the presence of echoic memory is directly inferred from performance in that improved shadowing indicates the operation of the store.

Repetition. Treisman (1964) performed a particularly useful experiment on dichotic shadowing which provides another illustration of the direct strategy of demonstrating echoic memory. Her subjects listened to two different verbal streams, coherent prose in this case, one in each ear. The two messages were actually identical, but one was delayed by a constant amount relative to the other one. The task was to shadow one of the two, either the leading version or the lagging version. It was assumed that the shadowed version was being categorized and that the nonshadowed one was being ignored.

The variable in this experiment was the amount by which the two messages were offset. Our interest is in the minimum delay at which subjects were able to report that the two messages were in fact the same. Consider first when the leading version, the one that arrives first, is on the channel being attended. What memory residue is this leading, attended, message likely to leave that could be matched up with the lagging message in order to support perception of identity? There are two sources of such information, the precategorical or echoic memory for the sounds of the leading message and the postcategorical information resulting from its deliberate processing. The finding was that subjects could recognize identity of the messages in the two ears when they were separated by as much as 4.5 sec, provided the first version to arrive was the one to which they were attending.

On the other hand, now we should consider what information is available to support a matching when the first version to arrive is the one that subjects are charged with ignoring. In this case, it should be only the precategorical information that survives from the first version, because the postcategorical system was busy with the shadowing task on the other channel. Treisman found that when the leading message was ignored, the two versions could be separated by only 1.5 sec and still be recognized as repetitions of each other. In other words, with only precategorical or echoic information about the leading message, the lag could not be nearly as great as when both pre- and postcategorical information were present for the leading message. Again, it is the ability of subjects to use echoic information in the ignored-leading condition that directly provides the basis for their having echoic information available at all.

The Indirect Methods

The backward masking technique has been used in both audition and vision to establish the properties of precategorical memory systems. In backward masking, some target episode is presented and then followed by some unrelated event after a variable delay period. The harmful consequences of the second stimulus on performance related to the first stimulus are the results of interest. In the auditory domain, both Crowder and Morton (1969) and Massaro (1970) have used the fact of backward masking to argue that the masked information was precategorical. This inference is indirect, in that it is the loss of information caused by the mask that is taken to support the presence of the memory store in question. We now are inferring the existence of the store by an operation that makes performance worse than it otherwise would have been.

Backward Masking Of Tones.   Massaro (1970) studied the effects of a masking tone on recognition of a prior target tone as having been "high" (870 Herz) or "low" (770 Herz), the masking tone being set between the two possible targets (820 Herz). The delay between one of the two targets and the mask was varied between 0 and 500 msec.

The main result was that performance was only slightly better than chance when 40 msec or less separated the target and mask. However, performance improved with longer delays, out to an asymptote of around 250 msec. Massaro was willing to conclude that this pattern of results established a system of echoic memory. His reasoning was that the two tones were far too short to have been identified during their actual presentation, which lasted only 20 msec, and that therefore information contributing to their identification must have been available during the delay following presentation. The fact that occurrence of the masking tone disrupted performance is consistent with the notion that the time following presentation had been necessary for extracting this stimulus information from an echoic trace.

The large size of the masking effect at short interstimulus intervals and the smaller effects at longer intervals were pointed to as showing the decay of echoic memory in this experiment. Thus, the index of whether or not echoic memory is there is being made on the basis of destruction of performance, that is, indirectly.

The Stimulus Suffix Effect. Another method that has been proposed for the inspection of echoic memory is also a backward masking situation, but this time disguised as a conventional memory-span test. Crowder and Morton (1969) were the first to propose that echoic memory, or, in their terminology, Precategorical Acoustic Storage (PAS), is responsible for an interference effect observed when auditory presentation of a short memory list is followed by a redundant word. They demonstrated this by comparing two conditions in which a memory list of span length is presented out loud. In the control condition, the subject is simply told to recall the list items in order when the list has been presented; sometimes a nonverbal cue such as a tone is the cue for when to begin recall. In the experimental condition, everything is the same except that the cue for recall, presented after the memory items, is a word of some kind. The word "RECALL" is quite adequate for this purpose.

The control and suffix conditions are about the same, as far as correct recall goes, except for performance on the last one or, sometimes, the last few items, where the condition with the suffix word leads to higher error rates. Research that is discussed in Crowder (1976, Chapter 3) has established that the meaning of the suffix word makes no difference whatever in the occurrence or magnitude of this effect. On the other hand, nonverbal cues presented at the same temporal position as the suffix word leave performance unaffected. Suffixes that occur in a physically discrepant channel from the one for the memory list—such as a different voice or the same voice located differently in apparent space—produce an intermediate suffix effect.

The hypothesis for the action of the stimulus suffix upon performance for the last part of the stimulus list unites the suffix effect and another property of immediate memory, namely, the modality effect. Here, the finding is that auditory presentation of immediate memory lists leads to better recall than visual presentation, but only for the last positions in the series. In fact, the suffix and modality effects produce essentially identical graphs: In both cases, there are two serial position curves displaying the classic bowed shape, but one with a large recency effect and the other with only a slight recency effect.

Morton and I proposed that in the auditory presentation condition of the modality comparison, performance on the last item is so good because it enjoys two sources of information, the regular short-term memory that results from ordinary encoding of each item as it is heard (no matter what the input modality is) and, secondly, the contents of a special echoic memory store, PAS, that exists for the auditory modality only. This PAS was conceived to be comparable to Sperling's iconic memory, except that it is characterized by considerably longer decay time. The longer life of the precategorical acoustic store, as compared with its visual counterpart, makes it potentially useful for such leisurely tasks as immediate memory. Our assumption was that the auditory advantage occurred only at the end of the list because the PAS system was in some way strictly limited in capacity through a masking rule—each new entry into the PAS system masked the contents there from previous items. Thus, following list presentation, only the last item remains registered in PAS, the others having been masked by their successors.

Our explanation of the suffix effect followed from this masking rule. Just as each item in line was masked by the next item to be presented, the last item in the list would be masked by the suffix on trials when there was a verbal suffix. This masking by the suffix would deprive performance of the extra advantage inherent with auditory presentation, returning performance to where it would have been with visual presentation in the first place.

There are other observations to be made on the suffix effect that are important for its interpretation. I shall pass these up now, because I have made the point that the PAS interpretation is at least one conceivable interpretation of the phenomenon. In Crowder (1976, Chapter 3; also 1978b) may be found considerable prose supporting this interpretation in preference to other possible hypotheses. For the moment, it suffices to note, once again, that this suffix experiment is fundamentally a masking situation. The last item in the list is being masked by the suffix. In principle, we would need only two items, the target item and the mask, to do the experiment. But in practice, there would never be any errors with a memory list of one, so it is necessary to add all of the other memory items. Again, the inference is indirect, in that we conclude that PAS is active in a situation because the suffix makes performance worse than in a control with no suffix.

The Trouble with the Indirect Methods

Here, I argue that for most purposes the indirect methods of demonstrating echoic memory are inherently more problematic than the direct methods. This is ironic since the two major research programs that exist on echoic memory are those stemming from the Crowder and Morton (1969) paper, employing the suffix technique, and from the research on recognition backward masking of tones by Massaro (1970). The direct demonstrations that I cited initially are very largely single-shot experiments that make their points more or less cleanly but that have not been the focus for major cumulative research efforts. Thus, most of the evidence pertaining to echoic memory comes from the indirect strategy of backward masking.

The Locus Of The Store. Those interested in sensory memory stores are preoccupied with demonstrating their locus, that is, in demonstrating the logical level of abstraction at which the storage in question occurs. A very peripheral store might be located somehow in the relevant sense organ, whereas a more central store might itself be subsequent to considerable information processing yet still lie ahead of actual categorization (which I take to mean the first contact of sensory input with stable response categories in long-term semantic memory).

The problem with masking as a means of elucidating precategorical memories is that the level at which masking occurs could be different from the level at which the source of the information being masked resides. For example, the sensory store, iconic or echoic memory, might lie quite within the sensory machinery, peripherally, and yet the masking we observe could be coming from a locus much more central.

There is considerable interest now in exactly this indeterminacy within the study of iconic memory. Turvey (1973) has shown clearly that backward masking in vision can be demonstrated on two levels, one relatively peripheral and the other relatively central. The peripheral masking occurs only if the target and mask are presented monoptically, that is, to the same eye. The peripheral masking effect is furthermore directly associated with the total energy possessed by the mask, integrating its intensity over time. The central type of masking occurs dichoptically, when the target and mask are presented to different eyes, and its magnitude is associated with the time between onsets of the target and mask, rather than their energy relations to each other. These and other arguments in Turvey's paper leave little doubt that two very distinct phenomena are in question here.

On the other hand, Sakitt (1976) has recently turned in a set of elegant experiments converging on the conclusion that the iconic store may well be exclusively located in the rod photoreceptors. Her arguments and evidence have been cited in the Walsh and Prasse (Chapter 10). Unfortunately, not all workers are happy with the inferences she has made, but we are forced by the possibility of a retinal locus for the icon to consider an important hypothesis: If the source of iconic information is on the retina, it could still be possible to observe masking of information based on the icon at more than one site on the way toward the categorization machinery. One must picture a flow of information from the icon towards categorization, but passing through numerous intermediate centers on the way. Masking could occur at any one of these. It follows that we may not conclude anything about the locus of the memory store from observing what properties the masking phenomenon reveals. If experimenters had been unlucky enough not to have hit on methods for monoptic masking, they might have been tempted to conclude that the icon occurs after the information from the two eyes is integrated. This might still be the case, but masking experiments will never give us satisfactory evidence for the proposition.

In echoic memory experiments, it has been shown that neither tonal recognition masking nor the suffix effect occur when the mask used is a noise stimulus as opposed to another tone or another speech sound, respectively. One would be tempted to conclude, as I have, that this requires a locus for echoic memory beyond a stage in auditory information processing at which tones and words are shunted in different subsystems. But, as we have seen, this is not a legitimate inference (though it may be true); the parameters of the system could be such that a backward mask does not catch up with information from the target until both have reached a higher stage at which speech and noise are separated, but the source of the echoic information might still be peripheral.

The Tangled Web.   I believe it is a general premise that negation is less specific than affirmation. Except in extraordinarily contrived situations, positive instances convey more information than negative instances. In a certain sense the direct methods, as defined here, depend on affirmative information, and the indirect methods depend on negation. This logical point is not without practical implications for the strength of the experiments I have been reviewing in this survey: If I ask a subject to read out, selectively, specific information from a stimulus array that has already been terminated, he can do so only through a sensory trace of that array. If, on the other hand, I present some target stimulus and then a masking event, it is hard to know what aspect of the system the mask has affected. For example, had I the means for delivering some overwhelmingly disgusting odor a few instants after the last item in a memory list, I might well observe a selective impairment for performance on the last item in the presentation sequence. But I need a far more complicated web of arguments than this in order to be persuasive in the claim that masking occurs in sensory memory.

What is needed to document that the masking occurs within a sensory system at all is a complex pattern of interactions that usually involve selective interference. Selective interference refers to an interaction between at least two kinds of memory information and the effects of two kinds of interfering material. The idea is to set up two situations in which a presumptive case exists for different amounts or different kinds of sensory memory. If a mask, or interference task, is truly selective on the sensory memory system in question, there should be different effects on the two formats. It is best of all to have two different masking agents as well as two different memory preparations. This is all well illustrated in an experiment by Bower (1972) on visual imagery in memory.

In Bower's experiment, people learned lists of paired associates under instructions either for visual imagery or for mediation through repetition (the former an excellent strategy and the latter a miserable one). During the period when people were trying to learn the list, they were required to perform a concurrent tracking task. There were two versions of this tracking task, a visual version and a tactual one. In the first version, people looked directly at the target, and in the second version they were blindfolded and could follow it only by feel. (The target in this case was a raised sandpaper line embossed on a moving paper band.) The finding was that, under repetition instructions, the two versions of the tracking task were equally harmful to performance on the paired-associate list. However, when the imagery instructions were used, performance was worse under the visual tracking task than under the tactual tracking task. This is consistent with the inference that the visual modality was somehow involved with processing in the imagery instructions condition and that it was impaired by the simultaneous visual processing demanded by the visual version of the tracking task. Notice that without all four conditions, the two instructional sets and the two distracting activities, Bower would not have been justified in making his inference about the joint dependence of imagery learning and visual tracking on common information processing machinery.

It is inherent with the masking methods that such patterns of interaction must be built up. In masking experiments designed to elucidate echoic memory, both Crowder and Morton (1969, Experiment II) and Massaro and Kahn (1973) have found it necessary to show that a visual mask and an auditory target do not interact; otherwise, they would have had little justification for associating their experiments with the auditory modality at all. Experiments on the suffix effect (Crowder, 1976, Chapter 3) have shown a consistent pattern of which suffix characteristics are important for the effect and which are irrelevant. The general thrust of these results is that the semantic identity of the suffix has utterly no influence on how much disruption is caused by the suffix. Thus, when semantic similarity between the memory targets and the suffix is varied, nothing happens. On the other hand, the physical similarities that may exist between the suffix and the memory targets are very important: If the suffix occurs in a different voice than that used to deliver the memory lists, or in a different position within apparent auditory space, the effect is much attenuated.

Of course, clever controls are necessary in any research program, whether the methodology is direct or indirect in the sense used here. But my claim is that more of these controls are necessary when we are dealing with the nonspecific indirect methods than when we are dealing with the direct methods. There are many reasons a particular operation can disrupt performance, whereas if the analytic targetting of a particular piece of information is successful, there is only a much more limited number of possible mechanisms.

The Indeterminacy Of Decay Rate. A vexing drawback to the masking methods for demonstrating echoic memory is their inability to produce estimates of the decay rate of the system in question. We may easily delay the time of the mask relative to the time of the target and, indeed, the masking effect is always smaller after more time is allowed separating it from the target. However, it is not possible to separate two reasons for the enchanced performance with a delayed mask: One is that there is less masking after the delay because indeed the sensory memory has faded during the target-mask interval. The other possibility is that during the delay the subject is extracting the information from the sensory store so that by the time it is masked, it has already been promoted into some more advanced storage format. (See Kaleman & Massaro [1978] and Crowder [1978c] for more on this point.) For all these reasons, it is clear that the indirect methods are logically cumbersome, and if we are interested in establishing the properties of echoic memory, it would be a better idea to pay more attention to the direct methods.

The direct and indirect methods are similar, however, in one more basic respect. They both are defined by experiments comparing a condition presumed not to reflect sensory memory with another condition, which is presumed to reflect it. In the direct methods, such as analogues of Sperling's visual experiments, it is the condition where no sampling cue is presented that shows the absence of the sensory contribution; the cue is presumed to add the beneficial contribution of the sensory store. In the indirect methods, it is the condition *with* the extra cue, a suffix or a mask, that shows performance without the sensory contribution. To recall my earlier remark, there are more ways a cue can nonspecifically hurt performance than there are ways a cue can specifically help performance, and therein lies the advantage of the direct methods.

ADDED STAGES IN AGING RESEARCH

In this section, the notion is developed that much of the work on age deficits in memory has been predicated on finding older people performing worse than younger people in more difficult conditions and nearly as well as the young in the easier conditions. This pattern of results has been used to infer that the age deficit lies with whatever process it is that is more challenged in the harder condition than in the easier condition. However, there is a very strong tendency in the literature on age effects for older people to do selectively worse in any hard condition. This is true even when there is no particular reason to expect that the harder condition contains any particularly different information processing than the easier condition, just more of it.

When the added stage is beneficial to performance, as in the echoic memory experiments of both types, poorer performance in the harder condition leads us to infer more of the extra beneficial added stage. This is because older people then show a bigger gain from the added stage. When the added stage is a complicating factor in performance, such as having to do a search or retrieval pass as well as a recognition judgment, we conclude from poorer performance in the harder condition that older people have a special deficiency in the added stage.

The Added Stage That Complicates

The standard and proper approach to finding out about the changes in memory that occur with age is to apply contemporary theoretical analyses of the phenomena of memory to the design of analytic experiments. A common realization of this strategy is to test the hypothesis that older people suffer decrements in some, but not all, processing stages. To test this general proposition, it is minimally necessary to devise two tasks, or conditions, one with and one without that stage in which it is suspected that old people are deficient. Then both tasks are measured on both old and young people. If indeed the older population is failing in the processing stage that differentiates the two tasks, there will be a larger age decrement on the task or condition with both Stages A and B, let us call them, than in the task or condition with only Stage A. If it turns out that both tasks suffer to the same extent, we conclude that the age decrement is associated with Stage A and not Stage B.

Examples Of This Strategy. Let me cite a few well known experiments that subscribe to this approach. Schonfield (1965) was interested in applying Tulving's distinction between availability and accessability to age decrements in memory. He started from the then-accepted proposition that recall entails two stages—a retrieval stage in which candidates for recall are extracted from permanent memory, and a recognition stage in which these candidates are edited for evidence that they occurred in the experimental context. It was hypothesized that older subjects are selectively weak in the former, search, component of recall; then they would suffer in tests of free recall but not in tests of recognition, where only the editing stage is necessary. This was the result obtained; older subjects were at a disadvantage in recall but not in recognition, when compared with younger subjects. I won't attempt to comment on the current status of this result as an empirical controversy, because it is mentioned here only as an example of the additive-complicating-factor logic in aging research. In fact, Hultsch (1975) has failed to confirm the conclusion of Schonfield's study in an experiment comparing cued and noncued recall; the age changes seemed to occur equally for cued and noncued recall, with respect to words correct.

A recent study by Thomas, Fozard, and Waugh (1977) illustrates the same approach in a totally different context. These authors were interested in age-related decrements in the time required to name objects. They found that when the name of the pictured object had recently been primed, the age difference was minimized compared with when it was not primed. The assumption is that there are two stages involved in naming pictured objects. One included retrieving the lexical item, and the other consists of the interface operations of perceiving the visual pattern and producing the motor response. The selectively larger age effects when retrieval was necessary, on top of the routine input and output processes shared by the two conditions, seemed to indicate a selective impairment in retrieval from lexical memory.

The Pitfalls

These experiments employing the additive logic have produced many stimulating and informative results. However, they are subject to a dangerous pair of inferential pitfalls. If the age-related changes are the same in the task containing both Stages A and B as in the task containing only Stage A, we have not learned anything. All that can be said is that performance decreases with age, which everyone knew more or less all along. Now of course there are some positions on aging, such as the one that identifies the problem simply as a slowing down of neuronal transmission or a loss of brain cells, that find comfort in across-the-board losses. However, these results dash our hopes of achieving a theoretical language for describing age changes that is faithful to our best theoretical concepts in basic memory and information-processing research. The second pitfall inherent with this method is that if the result is positive in the sense of showing a larger age effect when Stages A and B are posited to occur than when only Stage A is occurring, then performance is more sensitive to age in the harder of the two tasks or conditions.

Ceiling Effects. There are, of course, many dangers that accompany ceiling effects on performance. One must always be sensitive to the possibility that age differences could be absent in the easier condition primarily because everyone does nearly perfectly on this condition, whatever his age. I don't mean to say that the data on age changes in memory are free from simple ceiling effects; it is just that the problem is so transparent that it requires no further discussion.

An Empirical Law? Beyond transparent ceiling effects, there is, I believe, a tendency for age effects to be larger in harder conditions anyway. I think this is not always attributable to the presence of more processing stages or components in harder than in easier tasks. I shall try to show some examples where this is very probably not the case. Yet, in a surprising quantity of the data I have seen, older people suffer disproportionately when the going gets harder. I hesitate to declare this to be an empirical law, for I have seen too many exceptions and in some cases, it depends on whether performance decrements are measured as difference scores or as ratios. Furthermore, I have not been able to think of any nongratuitous theoretical proposition for why it should be the case.

I offer the following rationale for why age changes should be disproportionate in difficult tasks, anyway; it is not a general hypothesis for the effect, and I see little possibility of an independent test. However, it provides a framework in which to think about the problem. We assume, with Norman and Bobrow (1975), that the allocation of attention and performance may be considered a reciprocal operating characteristic. If a general tendency exists for younger subjects to underallocate attention to easy tasks, it might be expected that older subjects can "catch up" by investing more of their attention capacity in it. When the difficulty is increased, younger subjects are working closer to capacity and the older subjects, with a chronically inferior operating characteristic, are no longer able to overtake the youngsters by spending more of their already taxed capacities.

If anything like this principle is correct, it should make no difference whether we make a task more difficult by concatenating information-processing stages or by increasing the burden without adding stages. Therefore, we should look for cases where older people suffer disproportionately even though the harder version of the task is quite unlikely to contain basically different processing demands.

Some Examples. The first data I ever saw on aging and human performance were in the volume by that name published by our keynoter, Professor Welford, while I was an undergraduate at the University of Michigan (Welford, 1958). On page 250 and following, in that book, some experiments by Kay are discussed on a pioneering short-term memory task. In Kay's task, the subject worked at extinguishing light bulbs with a corresponding set of keys. In the easiest condition, he simply pressed a key to turn off the light paired with it. In the more interesting conditions, the keypress was directed at extinguishing lights that had gone off one back, two back, three back, or even four back in the sequence. In other words the subject had to be keeping a running span of items, responding to an event several steps back into the series but also encoding the currently new stimulus. I bring up this task because it seems very likely that the continuous increase in difficulty caused by increasing the span separating the current light and the one to be responded to constitutes a case where we are increasing the difficulty of a task while not adding significantly different components. The general result of a number of comparisons with this task was that the difference between older and younger subjects increased the more the span between the current stimulus and the one to be responded to increased. In the easiest condition there seems evidence for a regular ceiling effect, but not in the other comparisons.

There are data of the systematic sort we need here in the chapter by Talland (1968) delivered at an earlier conference on the subject of this text. Talland's chapter contains a wealth of information and some data displays that tend to violate the conclusion I am pushing here. However, I think that when the floor and ceiling effects that occur in those data are discounted, there is no real contradiction. In one of his experiments, reported on page 122, Talland simply compared age changes in various forms of memory span test as a function of whether subjects were responding to lists of digits or to lists of letters. As has long been known, immediate memory is better for digits than for letters, and Talland showed a reliable effect of this kind. It is also obvious from the data that performance declined with age much more in the condition with letters being remembered than in the condition with digits being remembered. Performance losses with age were markedly larger in the more difficult condition than in the easier condition, even though no one has remotely suggested that any different theoretical mechanisms were entailed by the two stimulus populations.

Craik (1968) has also contributed several bodies of data that illuminate this same issue. In one study (page 146), he simply compared free recall of unrelated words for young and old subjects. The lists varied in length, either 10 words or 30 words. It is safe to assume that basically similar processes are used in the two list lengths, even though it is harder to remember a given proportion of a long list than of a short list. The age effect was significant at both list lengths, but it was a much larger effect with the long lists, both numerically—an age effect of 1.05 words for the shorter lists and of 2.75 words for the longer list—and statistically—ts of 2.84 versus 6.14. This was not a scaling effect, because the number of words correct was quite similar for the two conditions. In another experiment, Craik (1968, p. 161) examined list-length effects for old and young subjects with four different kinds of memory stimulus materials—digits, county names, animal names, and unrelated words. Here, the interest was in how rapidly performance changed as lists of these four categories were increased in length. The general finding was that old subjects gained new recall successes more slowly, as the lists were lengthened, than did younger subjects. We are interested in how this relationship changed as a function of the four kinds of stimulus used. Both groups found digits easiest, in the sense that the slope of items recalled against items presented was highest for them. By this same measure, unrelated words were hardest; subjects recalling unrelated words achieved the least payoff in terms of new words recalled from increased list length. The losses in slopes with age—that is, how much less sharply words recalled regressed on words presented—were directly related to the difficulty of the stimulus classes. The easiest stimuli, digits, showed the least loss with age. The next easiest stimuli, county names, showed the next largest loss with age. The third easiest stimuli, animal names, showed the third largest loss with age. Finally, the unrelated words, which had the shallowest slopes to start with, were most affected by age. Again, unless one has a theory of why these tasks should contain different components, one is tempted to conclude simply that age effects are largest in tasks that are inherently most difficult.

At this point, I should remind you that the data displayed by Anderson Smith (Chapter 1) seem to present a case that goes against my empirical generalization. He showed that age decrements were larger with a list of 15 items than with a list of 30. I do not want to brush aside this nonconforming observation. However, I must point out that this result depends on using the proportion of items correct as the response measure. If a different performance index were used—number of words correct—the length-by-age interaction would not look the same. Of course, which measure to pay most attention to is an extremely heavy question with no clear answer.

In a final example, Adamowicz (1976) presented subjects with various kinds of abstract visual patterns (checkerboard figures with randomly filled and unfilled cells) and measured their recall after either 3, 6, or 12 sec of viewing time. Performance in terms of correctly recalled cells was not near the performance ceiling. The young subjects performed about equally at all three levels of exposure duration; however, the older subjects improved dramatically as they were allowed more time to look at the stimulus. At the longest display duration, there was no difference as a function of age, whereas at the shorter intervals there was a significant age decrement.

All of these examples are consistent with the possibility that we should expect age decrements to an increasing degree the harder the task being measured. One notion of why this should be true is that with easy tasks young and old subjects can achieve equal performance so long as the older subjects are working close to their capacity and the younger subjects are not. When the task demands capacity performance even from the younger subjects, there is a measurable decrement for the older subjects.

Artifacts Raised By The Difficulty–Age–Loss Law

The admirable objective we all have is to learn about aging in terms of analytic experiments that isolate specific deficits. The canons of our method require that this be done through experimental arrangements that contrast conditions differing by the presence of one or more stages. Against this program, we have seen that there is a potentially disturbing artifact—that older subjects lose more in going from a simple to a difficult condition than younger subjects do. This is understandable in terms of attention allocation, without recourse to processing stages.

The artifacts that these two circumstances, together, can produce depend on the particular sort of added stage being examined in an experiment. If the added stage is beneficial to performance, generally, the age–difficulty artifact will make it look like older subjects actually have more of whatever capacity is indexed by the added stage. This is because the harder condition is one without the extra beneficial stage. If older people show a larger decrement in the harder condition, it will then appear that they *benefit* more from the added factor than younger subjects do.

In echoic memory demonstrations, the extra factor under consideration is a beneficial contribution to performance from sensory memory. The artifact just outlined will lead to the conclusion that older people have better echoic memories than younger people. In the suffix experiment, for example, the age–difficulty decrement relation dictates that older subjects will show a bigger loss in the suffix condition—which is harder—than in the control condition—which is easier. Since the size of echoic memory is guaged by the difference between these two conditions, we might be fooled into thinking that the echoic store grows with age. Of course, if there is no difference between the size of the suffix decrements for two ages, it could be the case that the age–difficulty decrement artifact is working the opposite direction from a true loss in echoic memory, with age, resulting in no measured difference.

When the added factor is a complication for performance, such as an additional error-prone stage of processing, the artifact works in the opposite direction. Here, scores will generally be worse in the condition with the added stage, for everyone. Following the rule that older subjects show a bigger decrement in harder conditions than in easier ones, we should expect to find a *disproportionate* loss caused by the added stage for older subjects. The tempting conclusion would then be that we have located one specific source of aging decrements in memory—whatever stage provided the added complication in the experimental demonstration.

The logic of the recognition-retrieval class of experiments fits exactly within this summary and so I do not have to repeat it once again. The point of this section is to observe that the consequences for inference of the artifact are opposite depending on whether the added stage is helpful or harmful to performance. The argument to this point is illustrated in a series of outline sketches in Fig. 11.1.

A Warning.   At this point, it is necessary to issue a rather technical warning about the measurement of the suffix effect. Part of the argument that

I. *Direct and Indirect demonstrations of Echoic Memory*

A. *Direct (Sampling à la Sperling)*   B. *Indirect (Suffix or Masking)*

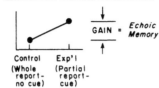 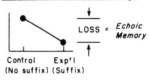

A Problem:

Many nonspecific agents (a kick in the shins) can produce a performance *loss* and mimic masking; however performance *gains* are usually specific.

II. *Direct and Indirect methods both reveal Beneficial Added Stage*

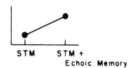

III. *The situation when the Added Stage complicates*

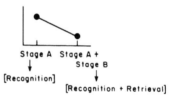

IV. *An Empirical Generalization:*

The difference between older and younger subjects is larger in difficult conditions than in easy conditions.

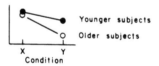

V. *Artifacts produced by IV depend on whether Added Stage is Beneficial or Complicating*

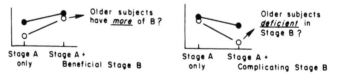

FIG. 11.1.   A summary of the arguments made concerning direct and indirect methods of establishing echoic memory, the relation between task difficulty and aging effects, and the relation between added stages and artifacts that can be produced in stage-analytic experiments.

the suffix has a selective effect on the PAS component of performance is that it is selective on the last item or last few items in the series. If this were not the case, it could be argued that absolutely anything that delays recall might make scores lower and that the suffix merely works as a source of general interference. Many things could raise or lower performance quite independently of the PAS action. Therefore, it has to be performance on the last item relative to performance elsewhere in the list that is our measure of PAS contributions to performance. The suffix could affect performance adversely, even by a large amount, yet if the relative advantage of the last item compared to the rest of the list were not affected, we could conclude that the suffix was ineffective. This is part of the "tangled web" that becomes the responsibility of experimenters who depend on the indirect approach of masking.

The best way to measure the suffix effect in a condition is to proportionalize the errors: Proportionalized errors are essentially the same as conditional probabilites, in that they express how likely an error is to occur at a given place in the series, provided that the error occurred somewhere. If 100 errors are made in one condition, 10 on the last serial position, and 350 errors are made in another condition, 35 on the last serial position, the two conditions have the same amount of recency, by this measure. We would conclude that if the latter had been a suffix condition and the former a control, no suffix effect had in fact occurred. This is despite the disastrously worse general performance in the suffix condition. In other words, recency has to be defined relative to performance elsewhere in the list, and the PAS theory is informative about this measure of relative recency. The proper index of performance is the proportion of errors that occur on the last position relative to all errors within a particular condition. This refinement of the performance index does not change the basic argument that I have been making about inferential logic and deconfounding it from prosaic performance-level artifacts.

THE PROBLEM OF DECAY RATE

The fact that indirect methods have been the only really extensively explored methods for analyzing echoic memory has had a destructive influence on the possibility of measuring the decay rate for it. It was mentioned earlier precisely why it is not sufficient to perform experiments which delay the onset of the masking stimulus (suffix or second tone) beyond the offset of the target information (last memory item or first tone). This was because one can't know whether a reduced masking effect comes because there is less information there to be masked or because the subject has been able to read out the useful information from the target before the mask occurs. Grossly discrepant estimates of the decay characteristics of echoic memory have been bandied about on the most irresponsible of evidential bases (Crowder, 1978c). One widely circulated estimate is based on the most casual of guesses Morton and I made (Crowder & Morton, 1969) that PAS might last about two seconds. Indeed this seems to be about the most widely mentioned of our points in that paper.

The impossibility of learning about decay of echoic memory through the masking methods has a consequence for our interest in speculating about the changes there might be in echoic memory with aging: Rather than simply determining whether echoic memory gets weaker with age, as one might try to do with a suffix experiment, another approach is to find out whether the rate of decay changes with age. A technique that permits unambiguous estimation of decay is the aim of the preliminary research described in the next section.

Estimating Decay Of PAS. Repp, Healy, and I (1979) have extended a method used by Pisoni (1973) for examining the echoic memory contribution to speech discrimination. We had subjects making "same–different" judgments for pairs of vowel tokens along a continuum including the vowel sounds in the words BEET, BIT, and BET. Through synthetic speech, we constructed a continuous transition among these sounds in 13 steps, producing many intermediate sounds. The purpose and design of our study are not important here. The basic logic used was that if subjects are to be able to tell two stimulus tokens apart, from this continuum, they must have either a phonetic basis for doing so or an auditory memory (echoic) basis for doing so. By measuring the application of phonetic labels to the stimuli in a pretest, we could estimate for particular pairs whether or not a phonetic basis would exist for telling them apart when they occurred together in the discrimination test. We reasoned that at least some discrimination performance would depend on echoic memory for the pairs with no easy phonetic basis for discrimination— if the subject could hold the sound of the first member of each pair in echoic memory until the second member was presented, he could compare them and reach a decision on an auditory basis.

We predicted that if some of the same–different discrimination is based on such direct auditory comparisons, it should be harder if a delay is imposed between the two vowel sounds than if little or no delay is imposed. This is because a delay means the subject must hold the echoic memory longer, and perhaps be limited by the decay rate of the store. By a similar argument, we expected that placing some irrelevant masking sound between the two tokens being judged would hurt performance, just as a suffix serves to mask echoic memory for a verbal target item in the memory paradigm. Both predictions were confirmed; both a delay and a mask between the two vowels impaired discrimination performance.

In a more recent experiment, an effort was made to use parametric variation in delay between the two vowel sounds being discriminated in order to construct a decay curve from which the life of echoic memory for these stimuli might be estimated. The stimulus continuum used has 13 steps, like the earlier study, but the continuum travelled through the region of vowel space in which the sounds heard in COT, CUT, and CAT are represented. The synthetic stimuli were 300 msec long and were contoured in fundamental pitch and amplitude to sound quite realistic. Identification data indicated that subjects had no trouble identifying these synthetic stimuli as the phonemes from the three example words used. The interval of time separating the offset of the first sound from the onset of the second sound was varied from 200 msec to 4,700 msec in 500 msec steps. Some of the pairs were actually identical to each other, and others differed by either two or three steps along the continuum.

The results are shown in Fig. 11.2, which combines both ways of being correct (calling different stimuli different and same stimuli same). There is a more or less regular decline in performance as the two tokens are separated,

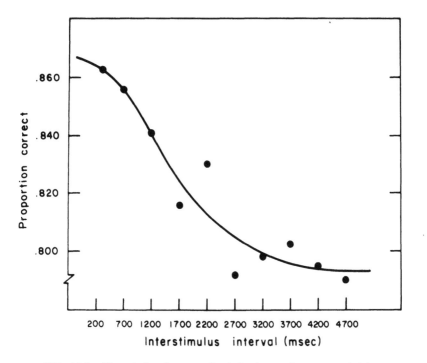

FIG. 11.2. The relation between discrimination performance and delay separating two steady-state vowels from a continuum connecting the vowel sounds in the words COT, CUT, and CAT.

just as we would expect if indeed echoic memory plays a role in this task and is also subject to decay with time. From these preliminary data, it looks as though the curves reach asymptote at somewhere between 2 and 3 sec.

The estimate just mentioned is not as important as the realization that the method holds promise for application to deviant populations, including the aged. Notice that the asymptote of the function can be estimated quite independently of the level of performance. It doesn't matter, in other words, whether older subjects have a harder time making their judgments altogether; we are just interested in when judgments seem no longer to be affected by the delay separating the two stimuli. Of course, the contribution of the performance-level artifact I harped on earlier in this chapter cannot be calculated for such hypothetical data.

SHOULD WE EXPECT
ECHOIC MEMORY TO CHANGE?

In this section, finally, I raise the main theoretical question of interest about aging and echoic memory: Will older people show reduced capacity in echoic memory, and why? It develops rapidly that I can only be raising and not settling anything related to this issue, and so this will be a very short section.

Deafness And The Peripherality Of Echoic Memory. One theoretical payoff from achieving answers to the questions surrounding aging and echoic memory could be new information on how peripheral a sensory memory store it is. If Sakitt (1976) is right, the iconic memory system in vision is actually a very peripheral store, being located on the retinal surface. It follows that various visual disorders, especially blindness due to retinal degeneration, should have marked consequences for iconic memory. If the retinal grain for resolving afterimages of objects is not there they cannot be registered during presentation at all and therefore of course cannot reside there later in the form of an icon.

There could be a representation of echoic memory so peripheral that it would display a similar decline with hearing degeneration caused by malfunction in the eighth nerve or even earlier in the system. But such changes would be relatively uninteresting—if the stimulus never gets represented in the first place in the sensory system, we should not get excited about finding it absent after stimulation has ceased. In any case, because there is a possible relation between deafness and echoic memory loss, a research strategy suggests itself to protect against what I am calling here an uninteresting change. The incidence of deafness is certainly related to aging but the correlation is very far from perfect because many other conditions besides age produce nerve deafness. To separate out the relevant factors, one should measure hearing acuity separately and then determine, afterwards, whether age contributes signifcantly to echoic memory performance (by some appropriate measure) after the contribution of hearing acuity is partialled out.

A more interesting set of speculations comes from considering echoic memory not as a place but rather as a residue of auditory information processing (see Crowder & Morton, 1969). Assuming the very peripheral sensitivity loss has been ruled out, we might be able to evaluate how peripheral the echoic store is by correlating losses in it with processing deficits during ongoing auditory perception. For example, Kaleman and Massaro (1978) consider the echoic store revealed by tonal recognition masking to be less central and less abstract than the echoic store revealed by the suffix type of experiment. If we can rule out deafness as a factor, then it would be interesting to observe a loss at the more central locus but not at the more peripheral locus, or vice versa. If, on the other hand, echoic-memory losses in the two paradigms were perfectly correlated across subjects of different ages, it would be some evidence that the two situations do, after all, measure the same thing. In fact, an aging population of subjects provides an excellent sample in which to test for correlation among the various methods proposed for measuring echoic memory. If the correlations obtained are low, relative to the measured reliabilities of the methods tested, we might conclude that there are a number of echoic memory systems, each tied, perhaps, to a different mode of information processing in the auditory system.

REFERENCES

Adamowicz, J. K. Visual short-term memory and aging. *Journal of Gerontology*, 1976, *31*, 39-48.

Bower, G. H. Mental imagery and associative learning. In Lee W. Gregg (Ed.), *Cognition in learning and memory*. New York: Wiley, 1972.

Craik, F. I. M. Short-term memory and the aging process. In G. A. Talland (Ed.), *Human aging and behavior*. New York: Academic Press, 1968.

Crowder, R. G. *Principles of learning and memory*. Hillsdale, N. J.: Lawrence Erlbaum Associates, 1976.

Crowder, R. G. Language and memory. In J. F. Kavanagh and W. Strange (Eds.), *Speech and language in the clinic, school, and laboratory*. Cambridge: MIT Press, 1978. (a)

Crowder, R. G. Mechanisms of backward masking in the stimulus suffix effect. *Psychological Review*, 1978, *85*, 502-524. (b)

Crowder, R. G. Sensory memory systems. In E. C. Carterette and M. P. Friedman (Eds.), *Handbook of perception*. (Vol. 9). New York: Academic Press, 1978. (c)

Crowder, R. G., & Morton, J. Precategorical acoustic storage (PAS). *Perception and Psychophysics*, 1969, *5*, 365-373.

Glucksberg, S., & Cowan, G. H. Memory for nonattended auditory material. *Cognitive Psychology*, 1970, *1*, 149-156.

Huggins, A. W. F. Memory for temporally segmented speech. *Perception and Psychophysics,* 1975, *18,* 149–157. (a)

Huggins, A. W. F. *Temporally segmented speech and "echoic" storage.* Paper presented at Symposium on Dynamic Aspects of Speech Perception, Einhoven, Netherlands, August, 1975. (b)

Hultsch, D. F. Adult age differences in retrieval: Trace-dependent and cue-dependent forgetting. *Developmental Psychology.* 1975, *11,* 197–201.

Kaleman, H. J., & Massaro, D. W. *Similarity effects in backward recognition masking.* WHIPP Report 4, Department of Psychology, University of Wisconsin, Madison, Wis., May, 1978.

Massaro, D. M. Preperceptual auditory images. *Journal of Experimental Psychology,* 1970, *85,* 411–417.

Massaro, D. M., & Kahn, B. J. Effects of central processing on auditory recognition. *Journal of Experimental Psychology.* 1973, *97,* 51–58.

Norman, D. A., & Bobrow, D. G. On data-limited and resource-limited processes. *Cognitive Psychology,* 1975, *7,* 44–64.

Pisoni, D. B. Auditory and phonetic memory codes in the discriminability of consonants and vowels. *Perception and Psychophysics,* 1973, *13,* 253–260.

Repp, B., Healy, A. F., & Crowder, R. G. Categories and context in the perception of isolated, steady-state vowels. *Journal of Experimental Psychology: Human Perception and Performance,* 1979, *5,* 129–145.

Sakitt, B. Iconic memory. *Psychological Review,* 1976, *83,* 257–276.

Schonfield, W. N. Memory changes with age. *Nature,* 1965, *208,* 918.

Sperling, G. The information available in brief visual presentations. *Psychological Monographs,* 1960, *74,* 1–29.

Talland, G. A. Age and the span of immediate recall. In G. A. Talland (Ed.), *Human aging and behavior.* New York: Academic Press, 1968.

Thomas, J. C., Fozard, J. L., & Waugh, N. C. Age-related differences in naming latency. *American Journal of Psychology,* 1977, *90,* 499–509.

Treisman, A. M. Monitoring and storage of irrelevant messages in selective attention. *Journal of Verbal Learning and Verbal Behavior,* 1964, *3,* 449–459.

Turvey, M. T. On peripheral and central processes in vision. *Psychological Review,* 1973, *80,* 1–52.

Welford, A. T. *Aging and human skill.* London: Oxford University Press, 1958.

12 Perceptual Processing for Meaning

Arthur Wingfield
Anne W. Sandoval
Brandeis University

Research within the past two decades has shown reliable age-related differences in a variety of cognitive activities. These include a lowered effectiveness in using organizational strategies during learning (Hulicka & Grossman, 1967; Hultsch, 1971; Talland, 1968), a slowness in scanning and retrieval from recent memory (Anders & Fozard, 1973; Anders, Fozard & Lillyquist, 1972), shifts in criterion value in sensory detection (Rees & Botwinick, 1971), and reports of unusual difficulty in dividing attention between two or more simultaneous inputs or activities (Fozard & Poon, 1976).

All of these observations are consistent with the generally accepted proposition that decrements in stimulus encoding and/or rapid semantic processing are more characteristic of normal aging than are corresponding difficulties in long-term retention or retrieval. The last of these observations, that of a special difficulty in tasks requiring divided attention, may in fact hold a critical key to the understanding of a wide variety of specific deficits which, to this point, have been studied only in isolation.

One of our goals in this chapter is to explore the twin concepts of processing capacity and attentional resources in an experimental setting, in order to tap the ways in which utilization of central processing capacity might interact with a range of such potential deficits. A second, related, goal is to recommend a reorientation of cognitive research in the elderly from the study of specific tasks in isolation (short-term memory, auditory detection, and so forth) to studies in a more ecologically valid framework (Neisser, 1976): ones in which subjects must engage in more than one activity at any one time. That is, in the course of every day events, people, old or young, remember, forget, and process incoming information in the face of a variety of competing activities, from several voices in a single room to distracting traffic noises, or the ever-present background of a TV set.

CENTRAL CAPACITY AND
PROCESSING FOR MEANING

Although the study of selective attention has been present in the research literature since the time of Titchener (1908), contemporary research really began with the pioneer work of Broadbent and the simple observation that it is difficult for subjects to accurately report verbal information from more than one source arriving at the ears simultaneously. This is true whether such information is presented dichotically as a different message to each ear (Broadbent, 1954), or binaurally, as two messages distinguishable only by voice quality (Moray, 1960).

In a typical experiment, subjects wore headphones and heard two simultaneously presented lists of three or four digits: one member of each pair spoken to the left ear and one member spoken to the right. Alternatively, subjects heard two different continuous prose passages, one to each ear. In the former case, the subject's task was to report as many of the digits as possible from both ears. In the latter case, subjects were required to continuously repeat, or "shadow," the content of the message in one ear, while ignoring the second message from the other ear.

The findings were robust, and, at least initially, apparently straight-forward. Subjects could easily report the content of one "channel"(one ear, one voice, etc.), while effectively "filtering" the information from the other channel. Monitoring one of several simultaneous messages yielded performance levels quite comparable to those under conditions of single-channel presentation. Attempts to simultaneously monitor several channels, or to switch attention back and forth between them, was invariably accompanied by major losses of information.

Following these early findings, the study of selective attention in general, and of dichotic listening in particular, became something of a cottage industry in British and American psychology. On the one hand, dichotic listening appeared capable of shedding some light on functional lateralization within the cortex, since it was sometimes found that the right ear (left hemisphere) was more sensitive in discriminating speech, while the left ear (right hemisphere) had an advantage for some nonspeech sounds (Berlin, 1976; Cullen, Thompson, Hughes, Berlin & Samson, 1974; Pisoni, 1975; Porter & Berlin, 1975; Zurif & Sait, 1970). On the other hand, studies of dichotic listening served also as a prime motivator behind the development of the so-called "filter" theories of selective attention (Broadbent, 1958, 1971;

Treisman, 1964a). Good reviews of this latter work can be found in, for example, Moray (1969) or Broadbent (1971).

Where Is Capacity Limited?

As we review the recent literature on models of attention, it is easy to sympathize with Titchener's (1908) observation that "the discovery of attention [by the psychologists] did not result in any immediate triumph for the experimental method. It was something like the discovery of a hornets' nest: the first touch brought out a whole swarm of insistent problems [p. 173]." On the one hand, we know, for example, that attention is a special problem in schizophrenia, where the ability to block out irrelevant stimuli seems especially difficult (McGhie & Chapman, 1961; McGhie, 1969). On the other hand, we know that attention in healthy young adults can seem extraordinarily absolute. Treisman (1966), for example, quotes an early study by Hovey (1928), who gave subjects an IQ test while trying to distract them with "seven electric bells, four buzzers, two organ pipes, a circular metal saw, a flashlight, and several peculiarly dressed people walking about carrying strange objects." These subjects did nearly as well as a control group taking the same test under quiet conditions (Treisman, 1966, p. 98).

Nevertheless, the recognition that there are upper-bound limits to normal processing capacity has not been questioned since the writings of William James (1890). The characterization of this limited capacity, however, has been variously seen in terms of limits on perception (Broadbent, 1958, 1971; Welford, 1952), short-term memory (Shiffrin, Pisoni & Casteneda-Mendez, 1974), or more general notions of resource allocation within a limited capacity central processor (Kahneman, 1973; Norman & Bobrow, 1975). Indeed, in the current literature alone, one can find over a dozen identifiably different theoretical models attempting to explain selective attention. Rather than attempting to offer an exhaustive review of this complete literature, we will instead examine a few of the more influential models and a representative sample of the experimental data, in order to give a flavor of the work and ideas they represent.

A Model Taxonomy

To give some organization to the diversity of theory existent in the field, we can begin by describing briefly two major views of the attentional process. The first of these can be referred to as *time-sharing models,* and the second as *capacity models* of divided attention. These models represent two general classes of explanation, each appearing in a variety of forms. Both recognize that the rapid handling of two or more simultaneous inputs creates difficulty when these stimuli (or required responses) are relatively simple, and becomes virtually impossible when they are complex. The dispute centers only on why this is so.

The Elements Of Time-Sharing.   The essence of time-sharing models of attention is the postulate of a limited-capacity processing system capable of accommodating only one meaningful input at a time (e.g., a single speech message). In order to attempt to cope with simultaneous inputs (e.g., two speech messages, one to each ear), time-sharing must be employed. This is analogous to the way in which a modern computer can switch its "attention" between any number of input terminals so rapidly as to give the impression that all are being simultaneously monitored. In fact, the information from only one terminal is ever being processed at any one time.

According to time-sharing explanations of divided attention, the central processor can either allocate full time to a single message or rapidly switch processing between several inputs (or their echoic representation) through brief temporal sampling. Attentional strategies, such as giving priority to one input over another, would be determined by the relative amount of time devoted to analysis of one signal versus the time devoted to the analysis of others. Broadbent's (1958, 1971) so-called "filter" theory and its modification by Treisman (1964a) are the best known examples, along with the notion of a perceptual dead-time in alternating stimulus sampling proposed by Cherry and Taylor (1954). The very important "single-channel" models of psychomotor skill also fall into this category (Welford, 1959, 1968, 1977).

The Elements Of Capacity Allocation.   The primary alternative to the time-sharing models of attention are the so-called "capacity" models. These models also assume a limited capacity central processor, but one which can receive several inputs simultaneously and which can process them, to one degree or another, in a parallel fashion. Since these processing resources are limited, if not fixed, the subject must allocate relative amounts of "space," or processing capacity, to the analysis of one input or another on a priority basis.

In this case, attentional strategies take the form of differential allocation of these limited processing resources among the various inputs, with some receiving more complete processing than others. Examples of this general class of explanation have included, for example, Moray (1967), Allport, Antonis, and Reynolds (1972), Kahneman (1973), Norman and Bobrow (1975), and McLeod (1977). As we shall see, however, there are major differences between these various capacity models. Related work can also be found in Posner and Boies (1971), Kerr (1973), and Posner and Snyder, (1975).

Depth Of Processing

To the extent that there has been a single historical weakness in attention research, it has been one alluded to earlier: namely, the tendency to study isolated processes independent of one another. Research and theory in selective attention became one specialty field within cognitive psychology, while the study of short-term, or primary, memory became another. This was especially true of the time-sharing models which were largely developed within the framework of distinct structural memory stores (cf. Shiffrin, 1976). Such a structural distinction could not but encourage the independent development of task specific models.

We would argue, however, that any limited capacity system must not allocate its resources merely to the analysis of incoming stimuli, but that different levels of processing, to include the interface between new and old memories, will place different concomitant demands on the system. This was a point recognized by Craik and Lockhart (1972), who argued for a levels-of-processing approach to memory processing. This general position is, of course, discussed at length elsewhere in this volume. As Norman (1976) put the position, one may have to allocate one's limited resources in many different ways, "concentrating sometimes on some aspects of the sensory input through the sense organs, sometimes on deep processing of internally generated ideas, and sometimes on preparing for a forthcoming acitvity.... Above all, there is some limit on how much processing can be performed at any one time [p. 80]."

To be sure, the issue of levels of processing and elaborative encoding is hardly closed (cf. Craik & Tulving, 1975; Morris, Bransford, & Franks, 1977; Winograd & Smith, 1978). Indeed, Baddeley (1978) has argued that the sort of dynamism we are arguing for here can be accommodated within the broad framework of a componential analysis of memory. Our intention, however, is not to try to resolve this question, especially as it relates to trace durability in retention and recognition tasks. Our intention is, rather, to extend the ideas of levels of processing to the study of attentional demands in stimulus analysis.

Our starting point for the research to be described here is the position that once a subject "attends" to one stimulus or another, the level of processing, and hence demands on a limited-capacity processor, must vary depending on whether the stimulus is merely identified as to location or voice quality, is simply shadowed, or whether it must be processed to a semantic level. That is, our ultimate goal must be to describe the cognitive system within which processing strategies—in encoding information, recognizing speech, organizing memory, and so forth—may begin to operate. The question of the extent to which some performance decrements with normal aging may have their locus in limits of, or allocation strategies within, such a limited-capacity system, remains a critical one.

MODELS OF ATTENTION

Time-Sharing Models Of Attention

Fig. 12.1 shows the basic structural elements of a representative time-sharing model of attention. Readers familiar with the work of Broadbent (1958, 1971) will recognize that we have borrowed heavily from his "filter" model, although taking some liberty with the labelling and characterization of some of its individual elements. In keeping with this earlier approach, we will describe the features of this model in terms of selective listening in the face of competing speech streams. The principle of time-sharing, however, could apply equally to divided attention between a variety of tasks.

The first element of the system, shown here as *discrimination and channel separation,* represents a feature-analytic device necessary to resolve complex stimulus inputs, such as multiple speech inputs, in order to segregate them into isolated *channels* (a,b,c,d). Channels represent classes of events, such as different voices, intensity differences, spatial localization, and so forth. This emphasis on physical characteristics for early discrimination was an important feature of early time-sharing models (Broadbent, 1958; Treisman, 1960, 1964b, 1964c; Treisman & Geffen, 1967), since they presumed that semantic analyses were performed only on signals selected for further processing. This is a critical point that formed the foundation of later criticisms of the model. Indeed, we now recognize that even the isolation of channels by spatial localization represents a process of considerable complexity (e.g., Mills, 1972).

The sensory information, now segregated by channel, is held temporarily in parallel in a rapid-decay *sensory register,* where it remains in store just long enough to be sampled for possible further processing, or not, as the case may be. Because of an estimated duration of 1 to 2 sec and its presumed precategorical nature, this store can be identified as *echoic memory* (Neisser, 1967). Although there is some disagreement about its parameters (Massaro, 1976b), some such preperceptual store is a logical requisite for the model.

The third element is the heart of the system, a so-called perceptual *filter* which selects between the input channels. A single input channel selected for further processing will receive analysis for meaning later in the system. Those not selected are gated by the filter and decay rapidly within the echoic store, unanalyzed as to meaning. The filter operates not unlike the channel selector of a TV set, allowing the viewer (listener) to see (process) only one channel at a time. Information selected by the filter then passes to a limited-capacity *short-*

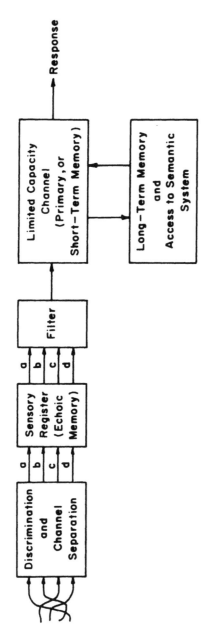

FIG. 12.1. Structural elements of a typical time-sharing model of attention.

term or *primary memory* where, through access to the remote system represented in *long-term memory,* it can be categorized, given meaning, and retained for an indefinitely long period depending on the degree of rehearsal (Peterson & Peterson, 1959; Waugh & Norman, 1965), elaborative rehearsal (Craik & Watkins, 1973), or "depth" of processing (Craik & Lockhart, 1972; Craik & Tulving, 1975).

The general model is an interesting one in that it attempts to account for a surprising amount of data within a very simple system. Thus, for example, when pairs of digits are presented simultaneously to the two ears in rapid succession, subjects have no difficulty reporting first the digits presented to one ear and then the digits presented to the other ear. The same small set of digits cannot be recalled as accurately, however, if the subject is required to report the digits pair-by-pair, in the order of arrival (Broadbent, 1954). This is also true for pairs discriminable on the basis of voice quality (Broadbent, 1956, 1957; Moray, 1960; Wingfield & Byrnes, 1972). To the time sharing, or "filter" model, only one channel (the information from one ear) can pass the filter at any one time for full analysis in the limited capacity short-term memory. That is, we can "attend" to the three digits of the left ear, report them, then switch to the echoic trace of the three digits from the right ear before they fade.

Assuming that it takes finite time for the filter to switch from one channel to another, the time required for switching between each for pair-by-pair report could exceed the presumed duration of the echoic store. This switching time was estimated by Cherry and Taylor (1954) to be on the order of a sixth of a second, based on their studies of alternated speech. (But see also the discussions in Wingfield & Wheale, 1975, and Wingfield, 1977).

The problem, according to this model, would not be encountered for slow rates of presentation because, presumably, there would be time for the filter to switch from one input trace to another before the arrival of subsequent pairs. In fact, at rates of presentation slower than 500 msec per pair, pair-by-pair performance can indeed become as good as reporting ear-by-ear (Broadbent, 1954; Moray, 1960). Similarly, one could follow two simultaneous conversations only by briefly sampling temporal segments of each, and relying on the inherent redundancy of language to allow one to reconstruct the elements of one conversation missed during the sampling of the other. It was the absence of redundancy in pairs of random digits that called Broadbent's attention to the split-span task as a critical test for his theory.

Processing Interactions In Time-Sharing. It is certainly the case that the model, as we have presented it, requires modification to be at all viable. Most important is the question of processing for meaning. It has been shown that both semantic content and linguistic structure can be as effective, or even more effective, in defining a channel than either voice quality or spatial location (e.g., Gray & Wedderburn, 1960; Treisman, 1960; Wingfield, & Klein, 1971). Since processing an input for meaning was thought to occur only after the input had been selected for analysis, one is hard pressed to say how meaning could be used as a basis for this selection.

In order to accommodate this problem, Treisman (1964a) offered a major variant to Broadbent's original version of all-or-none analysis on a time-sharing basis. She postualted a similar perceptual filter, but one which *attenuated,* rather than blocked, all but the relevant stimulus. Some information from secondary channels might pass the limiting filter, and, while attenuated, could be sufficient to allow meaningful recognition. This could occur if semantic context, probability, personal relevance, or some similar factors had lowered the detection threshold for the elements of that channel. Should this occur, the filter would switch to the channel conveying that information, with the input from all of the other channels now attenuated.

Treisman's modification advanced attention theory by suggesting the existence of levels of analysis in the processing of multiple inputs. The filter, nevertheless, remained a perceptual gate, however leaky this gate might be. The model began a shift in emphasis from the simple all-or-none time-sharing scheme to the more dynamic models to be discussed.

Alternative Explanations For The Split-Span Task.   While Broadbent's model in several variations held the field for a full decade, a very respectable period in this area of theory, alternative explanations for his supportive data were routinely reported. Some were even radical enough to dismiss the necessity of a perceptual filter with or without attenuation (cf. Deutsch & Deutsch, 1963; Yntema & Trask, 1963).

For illustrative purposes, let us take Broadbent's best known experimental paradigm, that of the split-span task. It was this task which first led Broadbent to postulate his perceptual filter theory (Broadbent, 1954, 1958). Some time ago, we replicated this classic experiment, following his original procedures as closely as possible (Wingfield & Byrnes, 1972). Subjects, university undergraduates, heard prerecorded lists of six random digits presented as three simultaneous pairs. The rate of presentation was one pair every 500 msec, the rate Broadbent found to be most critical. For convenience, we presented our lists with channel separation determined by voice quality, rather than spatial separation, with one member of each pair spoken by a male voice, and one by a female (Moray, 1960).

As in Broadbent's case, subjects were required to report the lists either successively (the three digits spoken by one voice, followed by the three digits in the other voice) or pair-by-pair (the first set of simultaneous digits, the second set, and so forth). There was, however, one major addition to our experiment. As the subjects heard each list and gave their responses, both list

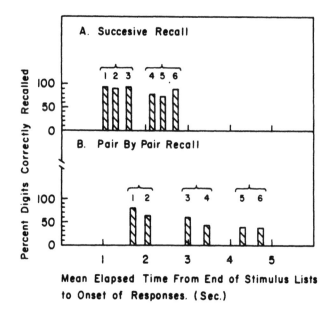

FIG. 12.2.   Accuracy of recall and response latency (mean elapsed time from end of stimulus lists to onset of responses) for each of the six serial positions in successive report and pair-by-pair report. (Data from Wingfield & Byrnes [1972]. Copyright 1972 by the American Association for the Advancement of Science. Reprinted by permission.)

and response were recorded on a second, good quality tape recorder. This recording was later used in conjunction with an ink-writing oscillograph which allowed us to measure accurately the delay and time pattern of the subjects' responses. The subjects, of course, were given no hint that the temporal pattern of their responses would later be analyzed, nor that this was our primary interest.

As one might expect, recall accuracy for successive recall was significantly better than for pair-by-pair report (87.4% versus 55.5%) [$F(1,5) = 29.31$, $p < .01$]. This is exactly what Broadbent found. Fig. 12.2 expresses these results in a more detailed way for successive versus pair-by-pair report. The height of the bars represents recall accuracy in terms of the percentage of digits correctly recalled for each serial position. The overall superiority of successive report is apparent, along with a tendency for a decline in recall accuracy toward the end of the lists, and a slight recency effect for the last digit in successive recall. Most striking is the very different temporal pattern of the responses under the two recall conditions. Successive report is characterized by a rapid output of the three digits of one channel, a delay, and then the three digits of the second channel in rapid succession. Pair-by-pair recall, on the other hand, shows a longer initial delay before report of the first digit, followed by the two members of the first pair in rapid succession, and so forth. These patterns were identical for all of the subjects tested.

At first glance, it might appear that alternating input analysis on a time-sharing basis could account for these results. The delay between each group of two digits in pair-by-pair report might represent switching time as the hypothetical filter selects the two responses from echoic memory for transfer to the output system, while the single interruption in successive recall might represent the one switch that would be involved. This explanation, however, would not account for the noticeably longer delay in pair-by-pair report before even the first digit of the response is produced. It would seem that some organization of the response is occurring even before the first digit in pair-by-pair report is produced.

Fig. 12.3 helps to resolve this question by plotting recall probability of each of the six digits in successive and in pair-by-pair recall as a single function of the total time elapsed between presentation of that digit, and the instant of response. There seems to be good fit to a single, monotonic decay function, similar in general form to memory decay for unrehearsed items presented as a single channel (Peterson & Peterson, 1959; Peterson, 1966). Pair-by-pair recall leads to longer average storage times before recall than successive report [$F(1,5) = 7.61$, $p < .05$], and hence distributes the responses along later points on the memory decay curve.

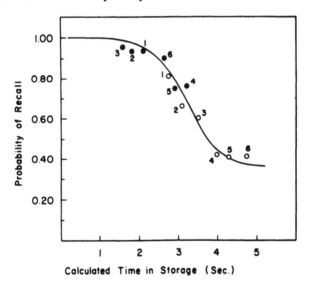

FIG. 12.3.   Probability of recall for successive report (filled circles) and pair-by-pair report (open circles) as a function of calculated time in storage. The small numerals indicate the actual serial order of responses. The curve is based on the equation $Y = (1 + at^n)/(1 + bt^n)$ where $a = 2.4 \times 10^{-4}$, $b = 7.0 \times 10^{-4}$, and $n = 6.5$. (Data from Wingfield & Byrnes, 1972.)

When these results were first reported, we interpreted them in terms of organizational strategies within memory, and readers interested in these arguments are referred to Wingfield and Byrnes (1972). The possible implications of these results for decay versus interference as a cause of loss from recent memory have also been discussed by Crowder (1976, pp. 178–180). The point we wish to make here, however, is that the classic split-span task originally used to support the notion of a perceptual filter is open to an alternative, more parsimonious explanation which makes no such assumptions. Further support for the view of split-span results in terms of memory processes, rather than perceptual gating, can also be seen in the work of Byrnes (1976), who used a memory-scanning probe paradigm. Other research originally seen as supportive of perceptual switching on a time-sharing basis (e.g., Cherry & Taylor, 1954) has also yielded to alternative interpretations (Huggins, 1964; Wingfield, 1977; Wingfield & Wheale, 1975).

The general concept of "switching time" in attention has not been completely forgotten, at least in studies involving number estimation of rapid clicks presented either in a single channel or as two channels alternating rapidly between the two ears. In the latter case, a performance decrement is often observed, leading some to support the idea of information loss with switching attention (e.g., Guzy & Axelrod, 1972; Massaro, 1976b; Treisman, 1971). There has, nevertheless, been little impetus to use these potentially important, but limited, findings to salvage time sharing models of attention in general.

Time-Sharing Models Reconsidered. One reason for this lack of impetus may have been the realization that the study of selective attention had become largely mired in a search for evidence of some postperceptual processing of information from "unattended" channels. Given the general agreement that conscious awareness could not serve as the sole criterion for the occurrence of such processing, a variety of imaginative attacks on the "fate" of information from secondary channels appeared in the literature.

Treisman and Geffen (1967), for example, had subjects shadow speech heard in one ear, while attempting to detect a specified target word embedded in speech presented to the other ear. The subjects merely had to tap a microphone the moment it was heard. They found that detection rates were significantly lower when a target word arrived in the unattended channel than in the attended one. To Treisman and Geffen (1967) and to Broadbent (1971), it seemed that shadowing the primary ear "required the filtering system to close off all inputs from the neglected ear [Broadbent, 1971, p. 151]."

Contrary evidence came from Lewis (1970), who showed that shadowing responses to words in one ear were often delayed when a semantically related word (a synonym) occurred simultaneously in the other ear. Similar evidence for some semantic analysis of unattended messages came from McKay (1973), who had subjects shadow ambiguous sentences, such as "They threw stones toward the bank yesterday," while the word "money" or the word "river" was simultaneously presented to the other ear. A later recognition test for the meaning showed that subjects who had the word "money" presented to the unattended ear were more likely to select the sentence, "They threw stones at the savings and loan association yesterday," while those having the word "river" presented were more likely to choose "They threw stones toward the side of the river yesterday."

Other workers employed verbal conditioning, in which a particular word was first paired with a mild electric shock until hearing the word alone produced a reliable GSR. When the conditioned word was later presented to an unattended ear during a shadowing task, a detectable GSR could often be observed. Indeed, there are also reports of GSR (of lesser magnitude) to the occurrence of words semantically related to the conditioned stimulus word (Corteen & Wood, 1972; Von Wright, Anderson, & Stenman, 1975).

To many, it seemed clear that material from an apparently unattended channel can receive analytic processing, and *semantic* processing at that. Performance decrements can be prevented by instructing subjects on the channel of priority, but some processing without conscious awareness seemingly occurs, even for material in the unattended channel. It could, of course, be argued that very rapid attention switching for brief sampling periods might account for these data, however strained an account this might be. But other fresher approaches to the general question of divided attention began to appear in the 1970s. These were the previously mentioned capacity models of attention, and they brought with them a major shift in perspective accompanied by the introduction of new experimental paradigms.

Capacity Models of Attention

The difficulty filter theories had in accounting for the experimental findings described above reduced the credibility of a simple linear, sequential-processing system. The apparent ability of subjects under some conditions to simultaneously process more than one incoming stimulus suggested that some attentional processes were more flexible than filter theories would ordinarily imply.

Filter theories claim that simultaneous inputs are processed by "switching" attentional focus on a time-sharing principle. Capacity models, on the other hand, propose that at least some simultaneous inputs can be processed in parallel on what might be termed a "space sharing" basis. These models describe a single pool of resources (capacity) that can be allocated proportionally to incoming stimuli. Task priorities are set by the individual, and resources are distributed accordingly. Interference among incoming stimuli occurs only when demands on capacity exceed the total pool of resources available. Incoming stimuli are seen, then, as varying concurrent demands on the organism's total capacity, with attentional processes allocating resources differentially for the processing of these stimuli.

While these are the fundamental features of capacity models of attention, several identifiably different versions of this basic model have evolved. Each model stresses slightly different aspects of the problem. Some address the central structures which accommodate multiple inputs, while others concentrate on the proposed operations which are applied to these inputs once they have entered the system. These are, however, differences more in emphasis than substance, such that most current capacity models share more elements than they debate.

Two general types of models, nonetheless, can be distinguished. The first, which we shall call "Comprehensive Capacity Models," describe a general, overall limit on attentional capacity which affects the processing and response to all concurrent stimuli. "Multiprocessor Capacity Models" assign a more circumscribed role to the limited capacity in which resources operate. Processing of different classes of events can co-occur in functionally separate, independent processors, with the limited attentional resources utilized primarily in keeping simultaneous responses separate.

These two models developed largely on the basis of dual-task interference studies, which assume that any two tasks that simultaneously require access to the same limited capacity system will interfere with one another. This interference would, in principle, be observable either in terms of accuracy or speed of response to one or both of the stimulus inputs. If a secondary task (e.g., shadowing a speech message) is added to a primary task (e.g., choice-reaction time, or visual tracking), and performance on the primary task remains equivalent to control performance on the primary task alone, changes in performance on the secondary task would reflect the extent of capacity demands required for performance on the primary task (Kerr, 1973). Although the interpretation of secondary task performance may be complex (Wickens, 1976), especially when using probe reaction time as such as a secondary task (McLeod, 1978), this essential paradigm has remained the method of choice for the study of multiple demands on a limited capacity system.

A Comprehensive, Variable-Capacity Model. Kahneman (1973) developed one of the first complete comprehensive capacity models. Noting the close relationship between physiological arousal and degrees of effort, Kahneman suggested a direct relationship between attention and effort, with resource availability a direct function of existing level of arousal. Thus, within the limits the nervous system places on stimulus processing, the capacity (effort) available to one or more tasks varies with the individual's state of arousal, with capacity and arousal covarying in response to the changing demands of ongoing activities. Kahneman's qualification, of course, is the well known deterioration of performance which accompanies exceedingly high arousal levels associated with stress: the so-called Yerkes-Dodson law (1908).

The completion of any mental activity is seen as depending upon two components: information specific to the structure of the stimulus or task, and a nonspecific component termed "attention" or "effort." Performance decrements may be due either to inadequate stimulus information, insufficient overall capacity, or when requisite capacity must be shared with some other activity.

Within this primary system, there exists a subsystem which evaluates processing demands, and allocates the amount of resources (effort) to be made available to various simultaneous tasks. Unlike time-sharing models, resource allocation is not all-or-none; several inputs can gain simultaneous access to these processing resources on a priority basis, provided the limited capacity is not exceeded. The system envisaged by Kahneman is a conservative one, in which total capacity is never fully consigned, such that spare capacity is always available for processing nonemphasized perceptual units. While attentional resources, or effort, can increase as task demands increase (within the limits of the Yerkes-Dodson law), Kahneman does see some absolute limit on attentional capacity.

Comprehensive, Fixed-Capacity Models.   Moray (1967) outlined a similar comprehensive capacity model, but one in which the limitations on capacity are fixed. He compared human processing capacity to a limited-capacity digital computer in which available data space is determined by the complexity of the operational program to be applied to these data. By analogy, Moray saw sensory input, and the operations to be performed on that input, competing for available capacity. For example, if the input signals are degraded or of poor quality, more capacity will necessarily be allocated to their detection. Conversely, task demands requiring complex cognitive operations on the input will leave less "space" for stimulus detection operations.

Parallel processing is assumed to be possible when the total capacity is not exceeded by task demands and when compatibility exists between the sensory input and the response to it. Moray uses "compatibility" in the usual sense of a relationship between stimulus and response in which the internal processing necessary to map the input function is of minimal complexity (Fitts & Seeger, 1953). More complex operations reduce capacity for both input and output processes.

The system proposed by Moray is one of great flexibility. It has a common pool of attentional resources subserving stimulus detection, storage, transmission, response selection, and execution. Several investigators have, however, questioned whether resource requirements of all such operations are equal and necessarily require access to this limited capacity (Kerr, 1973). Some theorists (Deutsch & Deutsch, 1963; Norman, 1968) have suggested that only response selection and execution require capacity, while Shaffer (1971) has offered the view that simultaneous stimulus input and response output processing can co-occur or overlap in time. Other investigators have concluded that a number of discreet operations may impinge on the central mechanism, but not all such operations. Posner and Boies (1971) conducted a series of experiments combining reaction time to a visual-letter-naming task with reaction time to an auditory stimulus. Both tasks required manual responses. Their results indicated that response selection and execution do absorb capacity, along with rehearsal (maintenance of the stimulus in some short-term store). Their data further indicated that encoding (stimulus reception and memory look-up) does not require space in the limited capacity system. The findings of Posner and Klein (1973) suggest that transformations (the computation of answers from stimulus material) may also require such space.

Data-Limited Versus Resource-Limited Processes.   We earlier alluded to the fact that experimental analyses of attentional allocation have relied heavily on the dual-task interference paradigm, in which the subject processes multiple stimuli and generates multiple responses. We also noted that inferences regarding capacity allocation based on the interaction of these responses can often be problematic. Norman and Bobrow (1975) have especially noted this problem, suggesting a possible framework in which to productively analyze the relationship between concurrent task performances.

Norman and Bobrow suggest that performance can be limited either by the amount of available resources (resource-limited), or by the quality of the stimulus data (data-limited). Capacity limitations, they argue, will be accurately reflected only in a resource-limited process, but not in a data-limited one. Their solution relies on the principle that mental operations continually provide output over the entire range of their analyses, such that it is possible, in principle, to compute performance–resource operating characteristics which would provide a graphic representation of the variation of one performance as a function of the other.

While the specific application of this general notion has been questioned (Kantowitz & Knight, 1976), the distinction between data-limited and resource-limited processes remains a potentially useful one (Norman & Bobrow, 1976). Performance decrements in a dual-task setting are not necessarily absolute indicators of differential resource allocation. They may reflect differential processing requirements determined solely by the quality of the stimuli.

Multiprocessor Capacity Models. As we have seen, comprehensive capacity models share the view that mental operations make differential demands on a single pool of processing resources which, whether fixed or variable, certainly do have some upper limit. Some operations, particularly those in the earliest stages of processing, may require little resource from the central mechanism. Latter-stage operations, such as transformations and response selection, appear to make considerable demands on capacity. Task interference will not occur until specific operations within each task simultaneously compete for this limited capacity.

A major alternative type of capacity model proposes a number of functionally independent processors which may operate on separate inputs in parallel (Allport, Antonis, & Reynolds, 1972; McLeod, 1977). Separate tasks may be performed concurrently with success so long as they do not require simultaneous access to the same processors. This model recognizes the reality of performance decrements that are invariably encountered when two or more tasks must be handled simultaneously. This decrement is presumed to occur as the processors are monitored by an executive controller which performs higher level functions such as keeping response performances separate. It is this executive controller which requires capacity.

The predictions of this model are not dissimilar from those of Posner and Boies (1971), Deutsch and Deutsch (1963), or Norman (1968), all of whom have argued that later stage operations such as response selection have major capacity requirements, while earlier input analyses do not. Multiprocessor capacity models, however, specify that interference observed in performance measures will occur not as a function of the absolute difficulty of the tasks, as would be predicted by a single comprehensive capacity model, but rather as a function of the similarity of the tasks in question. If the required responses are very much like one another, the monitoring function of the executive controller will require more capacity to keep the independent response streams separated. The more dissimilar the responses, the less capacity needed to segregate them.

Unlike the comprehensive capacity models, in which all stimulus processing and response generation reflect the characteristics of the limited capacity, the multiprocessor capacity model describes a system in which only very similar responses reflect the properties of that capacity. Brooks (1967), Allport, Antonis, and Reynolds (1972), and McLeod (1977) have all documented the greater interference between similar tasks than between dissimilar ones within this framework.

Allport and his colleagues found no decrement in shadowing performance when subjects were required to sight-read and perform an unfamiliar piece of music. Shadowing performance did deteriorate, however, when subjects were instructed to recall words presented either visually or vocally during the shadowing trials. On the other hand, presentations of pictures for recall had no significant effect on shadowing performance.

McLeod (1977) had subjects perform manual tracking tasks and concurrent reaction-time tasks in either a vocal or a manual mode. Dissimilar vocal responses were found to have no effect on tracking accuracy, while similar manual responses did interfere with tracking accuracy. More important, McLeod found that the two response streams in the dissimilar tasks were temporally independent, in that the temporal output pattern of the vocal response in no way predicted response production on the tracking task. On the similar tasks, however, a change in the timing pattern of the tracking task was affected by the manual reaction-time response. In this second case, unlike the first, the two tasks appeared to be interactive.

McLeod concluded that the tasks must have involved a number of independent processors. He refers to his findings as illustrative of a "response modality effect" in which responses in the same sensory modality always interfere with each other. If this effect obtains, it casts some doubt on Posner and Boies' interpretation of their findings, inasmuch as their subjects performed their two tasks in the same manual modality (McLeod, 1978).

Stimulus Demands and Depth of Processing

Both the comprehensive and the multiprocessor capacity models, like their time-sharing predecessors, address the central question of performance mechanisms in the face of potentially competing inputs and multiple response requirements. We have seen the differences in emphasis between time-sharing and capacity models largely in terms of the experimental paradigms used as vehicles for their development. Time-sharing models developed largely in the framework of task instructions requiring selective attention: experimental demand characteristics biased subjects to select a single input from among multiple inputs for a single response. Capacity models, on the other hand, created demand biases for multiple responses, no matter how poor the quality of one or more of these performances might be. It is important before we proceed, therefore, to briefly define those areas on which there seems to be general agreement, and those areas in which major questions remain. We next, in our discussion, concentrate primarily on current capacity models.

1. Resource Allocation. Capacity models of attention generally accept the basic concept of a limited-capacity system in which sensory inputs and various elements of response processing are handled in a simultaneous or "parallel" fashion. Some of these models (Kahneman, 1973; Moray, 1967; Norman & Bobrow, 1975) see an undifferentiated central processor in which all cognitive input receives processing, and among which limited capacity resources must be allocated. Posner and Boies (1971) accepted this basic notion, adding that not all components of a given processing task may necessarily require access to this limited-capacity system. All of these models, in other words, predict a performance decrement at some level of operations whenever two activities must be performed simultaneously.

2. Single Versus Multiple Processors.   A major exception to these ideas came from Allport, Antonis, and Reynolds (1972) and McLeod (1977, 1978), who raised the possibility of parallel processing co-occurring in separate processors for input-response operations involving different modalities. In principle, these multiple processors might each have their own fixed capacity, a feature which would not be apparent so long as their independent capacities are not reached. Thus, the model clearly predicts no interference between different tasks, but it need not necessarily exclude the possibility of performance decrements for sufficiently complex independent operations. As currently conceived, however, all performance decrements would be attributed to the operation of a limited-capacity "executive controller" monitoring the conduct of these parallel operations. It is this executive that introduces a limit on speed, accuracy, or quality of performance.

3. Fixed Versus Variable Capacity.   The notion that processing capacity may be limited, but is not necessarily fixed (Kahneman, 1973), does not seem to contradict the positions taken either in comprehensive or multiprocessor models. Capacity, or effort, could vary with task complexity or, in principle, with motivational factors affecting arousal level. Thus, at this stage of research, one must retain the possibility that, as resources become strained to capacity, additional effort on the part of the subject could increase resource capacity, thus minimizing a potential performance decrement. While Kahneman raised this possibility in terms of a comprehensive capacity model, the principle could apply as easily to multiprocessor theories.

4. Stimulus Demands.   The early time-sharing notions of attention gave considerable treatment to the quality or redundancy of stimulus inputs, because such redundancy was essential to any notion of stimulus sampling as an explanation of processing information from more than one source. Two sets of low-information (high-redundancy) inputs could be effectively processed on a time-sharing basis, while sets of high-information (low-redundancy) inputs could not.

With the exception of Norman and Bobrow's (1975) notion of data-limited processes, one weakness of both comprehensive and multiprocessor models currently in the literature is a concentration on the number of independent input channels, giving less attention to the demand implications of their quality. Poor stimulus quality, whether represented by degraded stimuli or an excessively high input rate, would be expected to increase processing demands within a central or multiple processors (Moray, 1967). Upper-based capacity limits would thus be reached sooner as a result of poor stimulus quality independent of the number of inputs, per se. An attempt to independently vary stimulus quality or structural complexity of each of a set of multiple inputs seems an important next step.

5. *Depth of Processing.*   In a similar way, both capacity and time-sharing models have placed little emphasis on differential demands potentially required by attentive processing options ordinarily open to subjects. For example, shadowing or recall of speech inputs, the traditional choice of early selective attention research, represents only a convenient testing paradigm easily understood by subjects. Shadowing hardly exhausts subjects' processing options in dealing with speech materials. Monitoring speech for physical characteristics, verbatim recall, or deep processing for meaning may all put differential demands on processing resources. Drawing from the ideas of Craik (1973, 1977; Craik & Lockhart, 1972), for example, this feature of attentional processing might be expected to interact with stimulus quality and structural characteristics. Stimulus features that allow rapid or efficient processing to a "deep" or semantic level might be expected to drain capacity to a lesser degree than those which do not. The flexibility of the system to adapt to the demand characteristics of experimental tasks makes this feature especially easy to overlook (cf. Baddeley, 1978; Craik & Tulving, 1975; Morris, Bransford & Franks, 1977; Stein, 1978).

A STRATEGY FOR ATTENTIONAL RESEARCH

Our goal at this point should not necessarily be to produce a single model which addresses all five of these fundamental issues. Rather, our goal should be to design experimental paradigms which recognize these alternatives and which allow for, and indeed encourage, the appearance of potential interactions derived from these parameters.

The following sections describe a series of three experiments which we hope will be illustrative of this approach. Taken together, the paradigms describe conditions in which a number of potentially critical elements of stimulus complexity and response demands are allowed to covary. By doing this we run the risk of raising more questions than we answer. On the other hand, the early acceptance of time-sharing explanations of divided attention suggests that the risk of premature closing of questions due to the use of too-limited paradigms may in fact be the more dangerous course.

Experiment I.
Stimulus Complexity and Dual Task Performance

The dual-task paradigm employed in this study makes use of two processing activities readily recognized by those familiar with the classical literature on aging research. One of these deals with speed of encoding of verbal materials, and the other with performance in a standard visual choice-reaction time task. Our goal was to select two activities which allowed the independent manipulation of task complexity of each.

The Tasks.   In the conduct of the experiment, subjects were seated before a bank of four neon lights which were placed in a horizontal row. Below these lights were four standard telegraph keys. The subjects' task was to constantly monitor the light array and to press, as quickly and accurately as possible, the corresponding key when one of the lights was suddenly illuminated (Hick, 1952; Hyman, 1953). The lights and keys were in circuit with an electronic clock, giving latencies from the onset of a light to the key response to 1 msec accuracy. All responses were made with the index finger of the preferred hand.

Three light conditions were employed in a blocked design. In one condition, subjects were told simply to monitor the extreme left-hand light and to press the extreme left hand key as soon as it was illuminated. In a second condition, two lights were indicated, with the instructions that either light might be illuminated and to press the corresponding key as quickly as possible. In a third condition, similar instructions were given for all four lights and four keys. For each light condition subjects received a total of 38 practice trials, followed by 80 experimental trials. The order of receiving each of these light conditions was varied between subjects in a counterbalanced designed.

For half of the trials in each light condition, subjects engaged only in the choice reaction time task. For the remaining half of the trials, subjects were required to perform this task while simultaneously shadowing short prose speech passages. Each of the passages was drawn from high school level texts on the general topics of literature and sociology. Each passage was 20 words long and was spoken by a native speaker of American English in normal intonation at an average rate of 190 words per minute. A total of 120 passages were prepared.

Complexity of the speech materials was varied by using electronic time-compression of the passages in an attempt to create "overload" conditions. Subjects would hear intelligible speech, but speech in which processing demands would be strained by the necessity of rapid encoding. There is general agreement that such time-compression makes comprehension difficult, not so much because of degradation of the speech signal, but because listeners are deprived of ordinarily available processing time (Aaronson, Markowitz, & Shapiro, 1971; Overmann, 1971; Wingfield, 1975a,b).

The compression technique employed was the "sampling method" in which small (20 msec) segments are periodically deleted from the speech signal with the remaining segments abutted in time. When played back at normal speed, the result is speech reproduced in less than normal time, but without the distortions in pitch or quality which would accompany tape-recorded messages played back at faster than normal speed. A Lexicon Varispeech II compressor/expander was used to compress the prose passages to 80, 65, and 55% of normal playing time, corresponding to speech rates of 228, 352 and 371 words per minute. Pilot studies had shown that even at 55% compression, at least 70% shadowing accuracy could be expected.

For each light condition, subjects were required to shadow an equal number of passages at normal speech rate and at each of the three compression ratios described. The particular passages heard at each speech rate, and under each light condition, were varied between subjects in a counterbalanced design. As each passage was presented, subjects were instructed to shadow that passage, giving that priority. They were also told, however, to monitor the light array and react by pressing the appropriate key as quickly as possible when the light (or one of the two or four lights) was illuminated. Subjects were told that only one visual stimulus would be presented per passage, and that it might occur at any time between the 12th and 18th word. The subjects were 12 university undergraduates.

Results And Discussion. The main results are summarized in Fig. 12.4a, which shows mean reaction times to key responses in the one-, two-, and four-light conditions when no speech was concurrently presented, and when subjects were required to simultaneously shadow speech presented at normal speech rate, and at each of the three increasingly difficult compression ratios (compression to 80, 65, and 55% of normal playing time). Errors in the choice reaction task were low (typically less than 10%) and did not systematically interact with the experimental conditions. Data points shown were based on correct responses only.

As one might have expected from early studies of choice reaction time (Hick, 1952; Hyman, 1953), reaction times showed an overall, monotonic increase as stimulus uncertainty was increased from ensemble sizes of one to four lights [$F(2,22) = 36.29$, $p < .001$]. We also see that the introduction of the concurrent speech task produced significant increases in reaction times to the visual choice task [$F(1,11) = 102.56$, $p < .001$]. This general performance decrement would also have been predicted from past dual-task interference studies.

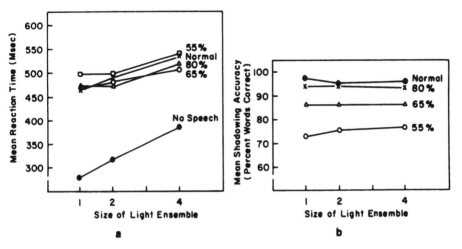

FIG. 12.4.   a. Mean reaction time as a function of size of light ensemble as subjects simultaneously shadowed speech heard at normal rate and at three compression ratios (reproduction to 80%, 65%, and 55% of normal time). Lowest function shows choice reaction times without concurrent speech task.   b. Mean shadowing accuracy (percentage of words correct) as a function of size of light ensemble for normal and time-compressed speech as subjects performed a concurrent visual choice reaction time task.

Two surprising features of the data, however, are also apparent in Fig. 12.4a. First, while choice reaction times increased with size of the light ensemble both with and without the concurrent speech task, the slopes of the two functions are clearly very different, with a significant light-conditions × speech interaction [$F(2,22) = 16.10$, $p < .001$]. That is, while reaction times increased with the size of the light ensemble both without speech [$F(2,22) = 69.33$, $p < .001$] and with speech [$F(2,22) = 17.89$, $p < .01$], the latter is relatively flat as compared with the former. This is surprising, since neither time-sharing, comprehensive, nor multiprocessor capacity models would have cause to predict other than higher but parallel functions as the speech task is added.

The second surprising feature in Fig. 12.4a is the absence of a systematic decrement in choice reaction times with increasing speech rate of the materials to be shadowed. Although there was an overall effect of speech rate [$F((3,33) = 4.93$, $p < .01$], this effect was attributable primarily to 55% compression at the one-light condition. There is no question, however, that increasing speech rate added to inherent complexity of the shadowing task. This is shown in Fig. 12.4b, where we see a significant, systematic decrease in the percentage of words correctly shadowed with increases in compression ratio [$F(3,33) = 49.19$, $p < .001$]. It is equally apparent, however, that the level of shadowing performance was independent of complexity of the choice reaction task. Each of the shadowing functions is relatively flat across one-, two-, and four-light conditions [$F(2,22) = 3.18$, n.s.]. In both cases, that of reaction time performance in Fig. 12.4a and shadowing performance in Fig. 12.4b, separate plots of individual subject data failed to show systematic differences suggestive of alternative strategies which might "cancel out" to produce the relatively flat functions shown for the group data.

This absence of mutual interference between shadowing and reaction-time performance is problematic for both time-sharing and for comprehensive, fixed-capacity models of attention. Reaction times were somewhat sensitive to concurrent demands of the shadowing task, showing a general decrement in performance, if not a specific effect of increases in speech rate. The decrement in shadowing performance with compression did not reflect varying demands of the visual tasks. Time-sharing models would predict a decrement in shadowing accuracy as the conditions of the visual task become more complex.

A multiprocessor model of the sort postulated by Allport, Antonis, and Reynolds (1972) and by McLeod (1977) would, on the other hand, predict this independence of shadowing and reaction-time performance. This is exactly the autonomy one would expect to see for independent processing of two response streams produced in different modalities, vocal and manual responses (McLeod, 1977). The general increase in reaction times with the addition of shadowing would be attributed to the overall draw on capacity as the executive monitor goes into operation, keeping the response streams separated. The model, stressing *mutual* independence of the response streams, would, however, provide no explanation for the very slight compression effect on reaction time observed at 55% compression. Since this effect was small, and may not be reliable, we must reserve judgment on this issue.

Intriguingly, the results are most consistent with Kahneman's (1973) original variable-capacity model which postulates increases in effort, and consequent attentional resources, as task demands increase. When subjects are forced to intensify effort as the number of light choices multiplies and to intensify effort as compression increases, the result would be a maintenance of constant performance level on the reaction time task with increasing compression, and on the shadowing task with increasing demands of the choice reaction task. This model could also account for the lack of parallel functions between speech and no-speech conditions on the choice reaction time task, if one presumed that an increase in demands from one to four lights in the speech task was partially offset by corresponding increases in effort and, hence, available resources. Resources, according to Kahneman, are limited, but not fixed.

Experiment II.
Depth of Processing and Dual Task Performance

It could of course be argued that the type of processing required by our two tasks was not sufficiently demanding to cause mutual task interference beyond the overall decrement in reaction time observed with the addition of the shadowing task. Shadowing certainly involves some measure of semantic or syntactic processing (Lackner & Garrett, 1972), but it is unlikely that it involves the depth of processing evidenced in normal speech perception. In fact, when questioned about the materials shadowed, our subjects were rarely able to give more than a limited report of their content. If, as Craik and Lockhart (1972) suggest, deeper processing does establish more elaborate and durable memory traces, then the processing conducted by our subjects must have been relatively shallow.

For this reason, we were curious to see the effect on reaction time performance when deep processing of the speech materials was specifically required, on the assumption that deeper processing would take a heavier toll in expending overall processing capacity (cf. Griffith, 1976). A number of methods have been used to vary depth of processing of speech materials in memory paradigms, such as those of Hyde and Jenkins (1969) and Craik and Tulving (1975). In our case, however, we felt a more appropriate insurance of deep processing would be to require subjects to paraphrase each passage after it had been heard and shadowed. Subjects would be required to restate the essential semantic content of each passage using words other than those contained in the original passage.

Our second experiment followed exactly the same conditions as those of Experiment I, except that, following the simultaneous shadowing and key response task, subjects were required to give a paraphrase of the sentence; they were instructed to state, in their own words, and in sentence form, what the passage had said. We also eliminated the 80% compression condition from the experiment, since the previous experiment had shown performance to be essentially equivalent to that for normal speech rate.

Results And Discussion.   The main results are again summarized in two graphs: Fig. 12.5a, which shows the effects of the concurrent speech task on choice reaction times, and Fig. 12.5b, which shows shadowing performance across light conditions. Again, shadowing performance decreased with increasing degrees of time compression $[F(2,10) = 26.78, p < .001]$, but there was no significant effect of light conditions on shadowing accuracy. (The slight trend observed for 55% compression was not statistically reliable.) Our attempt to score paraphrase performance also showed an effect of time compression but not an effect of light conditions. Thus, even the combined

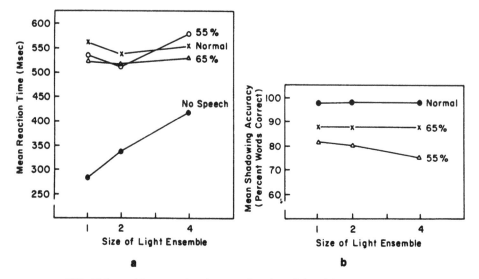

FIG. 12.5.   a. Mean reaction time as a function of size of light ensemble as subjects concurrently shadowed and formed paraphrases of normal and time-compressed speech. Lowest function shows reaction times obtained without speech task.   b. Mean shadowing accuracy (percentage of words correct) as a function of size of light ensemble as subjects performed a concurrent visual choice reaction time task and formed paraphrases of the passages.

demands of shadowing plus paraphrase requirements failed to show interference from the variable demands of the visual task.

In terms of reaction time performance in Fig. 12.5a, one again sees a significant general decrement with the addition of the concurrent speech task [$F(1,5) = 36.40, p < .01$], but this time there was no significant effect either of degrees of compression of the speech materials, or of light ensemble size once the concurrent speech task was required. Analysis of variance failed to show either effect to be significant.

Thus, while the increased load of shadowing combined with paraphrasing did not elicit differential reaction times among compressions, it did eliminate the light effect. To the extent that an absence of compression effects and a lack of parallel functions reflect increasing effort with increasing task demands, the absence of a light effect on reaction times can be seen as evidence that a significant draw on capacity was imposed by the task of paraphrasing. This combination of tasks influenced reaction-time performance in a way that shadowing alone did not.

This apparent failure of Hick's Law to hold under conditions of divided attention (the absence of a systematic increase in reaction time with light ensemble-size) is especially intriguing if viewed in the context of fast, parallel processing sometimes associated with "automaticity" in mental operations (e.g., Shiffrin & Schneider, 1977). In the past, automaticity and speed have been invariably associated, such that one would not ordinarily look for automatic, or parallel, processing in a slow-responding situation. In this experiment, the salience of the speech tasks and the combined load imposed by both shadowing and paraphrase requirements would be expected to produce an especially great draw of resources away from the choice reaction task. Were one to attribute the flat reaction-time functions in the speech conditions to parallel, automatic operations in the choice reaction task, this would raise interesting issue with the usual association between slow responding and serial processing versus parallel processing and fast responding. We are grateful to Marcel Kinsbourne for pointing out this possible connection.

Experiment III. Task Demands and Processing Load

We were intrigued by the absence of a light effect on choice reaction time performance under the conditions which reflected the additional load of two speech tasks, shadowing and paraphrasing, contrasted with shadowing alone. Consequently, we conducted a third experiment which was intended to reduce processing load closer to the conditions of Experiment I. The same choice reaction time task with one, two, and four lights was conducted, but this time subjects were required only to paraphrase each passage after it was heard. Thus, with shadowing eliminated, subjects needed only to silently monitor the speech passages as they performed the choice reaction task. Deep processing of the passages, however, would still be required because of the later paraphrasing requirement.

Results And Discussion.   Fig. 12.6a shows that the addition of the concurrent speech task again produced a significant decrement in reaction-time performance $[F(1,5) = 49.61, p < .001]$. This time, however, we observed a considerable effect of light conditions on reaction time in the speech conditions $[F(2,10) = 19.06, p < .001]$, with the speech and no speech functions more nearly parallel, at least for the more complex light conditions.

There was again, however, no systematic effect of increasing speech compression on reaction-time performance, nor was there an overall significant effect of compression on reaction time. (The slight effect at the one-light condition for 55% compression interestingly reappeared.) Fig. 12.6b shows our attempt to score paraphrase performance, and although we do not express great confidence in our scoring methods, there was clearly an effect of speech compression $[F(2,10) = 11.82, p < .01]$ and of light conditions. Paraphrase scoring was based on the number of semantic components correct. As in shadowing scores in the previous experiments,

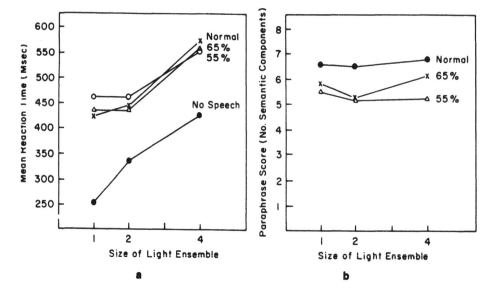

FIG. 12.6.   a. Mean reaction time as a function of size of light ensemble as subjects simultaneously formed paraphrases of normal and time-compressed passages. Lowest function shows reaction times obtained without the speech task.   b. Mean paraphrase scores as a function of size of light ensemble for normal and time-compressed speech as subjects simultaneously performed a visual choice reaction time task. Scores based on number of semantic components retained in paraphrases.

paraphrase performance again appeared to be independent of the visual task demands.

Except for the absence of a slight compression effect on reaction times obtained in Experiment I, the results of these two experiments are comparable; reaction times increased with increases in the number of visual alternatives, but remained unaffected by increased complexity of the speech task. The stability of the scores for the speech task implies adequate capacity allotment to that task and, possibly, independent processing.

CONCLUSION

We began our presentation by outlining four general models offered in the literature for selective attention and dual task interference studies. As we interpret our results, they seem to show elements of the predictions of multiprocessor models such as those of Allport and of McLeod. This can be seen in the effective independence of the level of speech-task performance from the variation in task demands imposed by the visual choice reaction tasks. The failure to observe increases in reaction time with increasing degrees of speech compression is also consistent with this autonomous processing principle. At the same time, the failure to reliably show parallel reaction time functions between speech and no speech conditions across all three experiments is at least suggestive of Kahneman's more general notion of flexibility between task demands, effort, and available resources. While time-sharing and comprehensive capacity models receive little support from these data, no single model offered to this point appears totally satisfactory.

The possibility of some form of alternation of attention cannot be completely dismissed so long as there remains a possibility that any two or more sets of simultaneous tasks can be effectively monitored by intermittent sampling, or that temporal grouping in response organization could be used to periodically leave the channel free for processing of the alternate stimuli. Both possibilities have been raised in opposition to divided attention models of the sort proposed by Allport (e.g., Fisher, 1975a,b; Welford, 1977). While potential stimulus and response timing interactions could not be easily analyzed in the discrete reaction time task employed here, a concurrent continuous visual tracking task could offer this capability, combined with appropriate temporal analyses of stimulus timing and response patterns related to shifting stimulus demands.

While failing to isolate a single model, these studies do suggest several directions for further research. Of the many questions which remain, one high on any list is that of the concentration of attention over prolonged periods of time. This is especially so in the context of aging. Contrasted with the relatively short durations of our experimental trials, one could employ considerably longer speech passages combined with concurrent continuous visual tracking for the entire duration of the speech passages. The use of longer speech passages would add an interesting "vigilance" dimension to those studies, while a continuous measurement of accuracy and latency in visual tracking could provide data for analysis of fluctuations in attention as a function of time, and of changes in processing demands imposed by the speech stimuli.

Our use of time-compressed speech and choice reaction times as a means of manipulating simultaneous task demands does not exhaust the possible range of potential variables which might be used. We have found in these tasks a convenient vehicle for our purposes of illustrating a promising paradigm. One feature of these tasks, however, is that they can easily be simplified for use with aged or patient populations. Simplifying the speech materials, reducing the degree of time-compression, or scaling down the choice reaction task, for example, would not diminish the essential features of the paradigm for interactive analysis of attentional processing.

While studies of choice reaction time analogous to ours have an established place in aging research (e.g., Rabbitt, 1964a,b), the use of time-compressed speech may offer special promise in extending these studies to work with aged populations. Existing evidence suggests that time-compression can be used to differentiate between young and aged listeners (Broca & Calearo, 1963; DiCarlo & Taub, 1972; Konkle, Beasley & Bess, 1977; Sticht & Gray, 1969). The small effects of compression observed with our subjects might well be amplified in interesting ways with older populations.

In one respect, we have attained the goal we set ourselves at the start of this research; we have certainly raised more questions than we have answered. As we introduced a paradigm in which processing demands of multiple tasks were systematically and independently varied, we appear to have aroused that hornets' nest of insistent problems to which Titchener referred some seventy years ago. The hornets, it would seem, have been there all the time. Our paradigm has simply served to give the nest another prod.

There is no question that attentional resources impose some "bottleneck" on the rapid processing of incoming information and that these resources, although flexibly applied, have some upper limit. As we pursue the question of dual-task performance in young adults, we will undoubtedly begin to define these limits, and to understand those optional processing strategies that give rise to this flexibility. These answers, we would argue, are a necessary prerequisite both for the understanding of information acquisition in normal memory processing and, potentially, for the corresponding analysis of debilitated function.

ACKNOWLEDGMENT

The research reported in this chapter was supported by PHS Grant NS-14662 from the National Institutes of Health to Arthur Wingfield.

REFERENCES

Aaronson, D., Markowitz, N., & Shapiro, H. Perception and immediate recall of normal and "compressed" auditory sequences. *Perception and Psychophysics*, 1971, *9*, 338–344.

Allport, D. A., Antonis, B., & Reynolds, P. On the division of attention: A disproof of the single channel hypothesis. *Quarterly Journal of Experimental Psychology*, 1972, *24*, 225–235.

Anders, T. R., & Fozard, J. L. Effects of age upon retrieval from primary and secondary memory. *Developmental Psychology*, 1973, *9*, 411–416.

Anders, T. R., Fozard, J. L., & Lillyquist, T. D. Effects of age upon retrieval from short-term memory. *Developmental Psychology*, 1972, *6*, 214–217.

Baddeley, A. D. The trouble with levels: A reexamination of Craik and Lockhart's framework for memory research. *Psychological Review*, 1978, *85*, 139–152.

Berlin, C. I. Dichotic listening. In N. J. Lass (Ed.), *Contemporary issues in experimental phonetics*. New York: Academic Press, 1976.

Broadbent, D. E. The role of auditory localization in attention and memory span. *Journal of Experimental Psychology*, 1954, *47*, 191-196.

Broadbent, D. E. Successive responses to simultaneous stimuli. *Quarterly Journal of Experimental Psychology*, 1956, *8*, 145-152.

Broadbent, D. E. Immediate memory and simultaneous stimuli. *Quarterly Journal of Experimental Psychology*, 1957, *9*, 1-11.

Broadbent, D. E. *Perception and communication*. London: Pergamon Press, 1958.

Broadbent, D. E. *Decision and stress*. New York: Academic Press, 1971.

Broca, E., & Calearo, C. Central hearing processes. In J. Jerger (Ed.), *Modern developments in audiology*. New York: Academic Press, 1963.

Brooks, L. R. The suppression of visualization by reading. *Quarterly Journal of Experimental Psychology*, 1967, *19*, 289-299.

Byrnes, D. L. Memory search of dichotically presented lists of digits. *Bulletin of the Psychonomic Society*, 1976, *8*, 185-187.

Cherry, E. C., & Taylor, W. K. Some further experiments on the recognition of speech with one and two ears. *Journal of the Acoustical Society of America*, 1954, *26*, 554-559.

Corteen, R. S., & Wood, B. Autonomic responses to shock-associated words in an unattended channel. *Journal of Experimental Psychology*, 1972, *94*, 308-313.

Craik, F. I. M. A "levels of analysis" view of memory. In P. Pliner, L. Krames, & T. M. Alloway (Eds.), *Communication and affect: Language and thought*. New York: Academic Press, 1973.

Craik, F. I. M. Depth of processing in recall and recognition. In S. Dornič (Ed.), *Attention and performance VI*. Hillsdale, N.J.: Lawrence Erlbaum Associates, 1977.

Craik, F. I. M., & Lockhart, R. S. Levels of processing: A framework for memory research. *Journal of Verbal Learning and Verbal Behavior*, 1972, *11*, 671-684.

Craik, F. I. M., & Tulving, E. Depth of processing and the retention of words in episodic memory. *Journal of Experimental Psychology: General*, 1975, *104*, 268-294.

Craik, F. I. M., & Watkins, M. J. The role of rehearsal in short-term memory. *Journal of Verbal Learning and Verbal Behavior*, 1973, *12*, 599-607.

Crowder, R. G. *Principles of learning and memory*. Hillsdale, N.J.: Lawrence Erlbaum Associates, 1976.

Cullen, J. F., Thompson, C. L., Hughes, L. F., Berlin, C. I., & Samson, D. S. The effects of varied acoustic parameters on performance in dichotic speech perception tasks. *Brain and Language*, 1974, *1*, 307-322.

Deutsch, J. A., & Deutsch, D. Attention: Some theoretical considerations. *Psychological Review*, 1963, *70*, 80-90.

DiCarlo, L., & Taub, H. The influence of compression and expansion on the intelligibility of speech by young and aged aphasic (demonstrated CVA) individuals. *Journal of Communicative Disorders*, 1972, *5*, 299-306.

Fisher, S. The microstructure of dual task interaction. 1. The patterning of main-task responses within secondary-task intervals. *Perception*, 1975, *4*, 267-290. (a)

Fisher, S. The microstructure of dual task interaction. 2. The effect of task instructions on attentional allocation and a model of attention-switching. *Perception*, 1975, *4*, 459-474. (b)

Fitts, P. M., & Seeger, C. M. SR compatibility: Spatial characteristics of stimulus and response codes. *Journal of Experimental Psychology*, 1953, *46*, 199-210.

Fozard, J. L., & Poon, L. W. *Research and training activities of the Mental Performance and Aging Laboratory*. Technical Report 76-02. Veterans Administration Outpatient Clinic, Boston, Massachusetts, 1976.

Gray, J. A., & Wedderburn, A. A. I. Grouping strategies with simultaneous stimuli. *Quarterly Journal of Experimental Psychology*, 1960, *12*, 180-184.

Griffith, D. The attentional demands of mnemonic control processes. *Memory and Cognition*, 1976, *4*, 103-108.

Guzy, L. T., & Axelrod, S. Interaural attention shifting or response. *Journal of Experimental Psychology*, 1972, *95*, 290–294.

Hick, W. E. On the rate of gain of information. *Quarterly Journal of Experimental Psychology*, 1952, *4*, 11–26.

Hovey, H. B. Effects of general distraction on the higher thought processes. *American Journal of Psychology*, 1928, *40*, 585–591.

Huggins, A. W. F. Distortion of the temporal pattern of speech: Interruption and alternation. *Journal of the Acoustical Society of America*, 1964, *36*, 1055–1064.

Hulicka, I., & Grossman, J. Age-group comparisons for the use of mediators in paired-associate learning. *Journal of Gerontology*, 1967, *22*, 46–51.

Hultsch, I. Organization and memory in adulthood. *Human Development*, 1971, *14*, 26–29.

Hyde, T. S., & Jenkins, J. J. The differential effects of incidental tasks on the organization of recall of a list of highly associated words. *Journal of Experimental Psychology*, 1969, *82*, 472–481.

Hyman, R. Stimulus information as a determinant of reaction time. *Journal of Experimental Psychology*, 1953, *45*, 188–196.

James, W. *Principles of psychology*. New York: Holt, 1890.

Kahneman, D. *Attention and effort*. Englewood Cliffs, N.J.: Prentice-Hall, 1973.

Kantowitz, B. H., & Knight, J. L. On experimenter-limited processes. *Psychological Review*, 1976, *83*, 502–507.

Kerr, B. Processing demands during mental operations. *Memory and Cognition*, 1973, *1*, 401–412.

Konkle, D. F., Beasley, D. S., & Bess, F. H. Intelligibility of time-altered speech in relation to chronological aging. *Journal of Speech and Hearing Research*, 1977, *20*, 108–115.

Lackner, J. R., & Garrett, M. F. Resolving ambiguity; Effects of biasing context in the unattended ear. *Cognition*, 1972, *1*, 359–372.

Lewis, J. L. Semantic processing of unattended messages using dichotic listening. *Journal of Experimental Psychology*, 1970, *85*, 225–228.

Massaro, D. W. Perceiving and counting tones. *Journal of Experimental Psychology: Human Perception and Performance*, 1976, *2*, 331–339. (b)

Massaro, D. W. Auditory information processing. In W. K. Estes (Ed.), *Handbook of learning and cognitive processes. Vol. 4: Attention and memory*. Hillsdale, N.J.: Lawrence Erlbaum Associates, 1976. (a)

McGhie, A. *Pathology of attention*. Baltimore: Penguin, 1969.

McGhie, A., & Chapman, J. Disorders of attention and perception in early schizophrenia. *British Journal of Medical Psychology*, 1961, *34*, 103–116.

McKay, D. C. Aspects of the theory of comprehension, memory and attention. *Quarterly Journal of Experimental Psychology*, 1973, *25*, 22–40.

McLeod, P. A dual task response modality effect: Support for multiprocessor models of attention. *Quarterly Journal of Experimental Psychology*, 1977, *29*, 651–667.

McLeod, P. Does probe RT measure central processing demand? *Quarterly Journal of Experimental Psychology*, 1978, *30*, 83–89.

Mills, A. W. Auditory localization. In J. V. Tobias (Ed.), *Foundations of modern auditory theory* (Vol. 2). New York: Academic Press, 1972.

Moray, N. Broadbent's filter theory: Postulate H and the problem of switching time. *Quarterly Journal of Experimental Psychology*, 1960, *12*, 214–220.

Moray, N. Where is capacity limited?—A survey and a model. *Acta Psychologica*, 1967, *27*, 84–92.

Moray, N. *Listening and attention*. Baltimore: Penguin Books, 1969.

Morris, C. D., Bransford, J. D., & Franks, J. J. Levels of processing versus transfer appropriate processing. *Journal of Verbal Learning and Verbal Behavior*, 1977, *16*, 519–533.

Neisser, U. *Cognitive psychology.* New York: Appleton-Century-Crofts, 1967.

Neisser, U. *Cognition and reality.* San Francisco: W. H. Freeman, 1976.

Norman, D. A. Toward a theory of memory and attention. *Psychological Review,* 1968, *75,* 522–536.

Norman, D. A. *Memory and attention. An introduction to human information processing* (2nd ed.). New York: Wiley, 1976.

Norman, D. A., & Bobrow, D. G. On data-limited and resource-limited processes. *Cognitive Psychology,* 1975, *7,* 44–64.

Norman, D. A., & Bobrow, D. G. On the analysis of performance operating characteristics. *Psychological Review,* 1976, *83,* 508–510.

Overmann, R. A. Processing time as a variable in the comprehension of time-compressed speech. In E. Foulke (Ed.), *Proceedings of the Second Louisville Conference on rate and/or frequency-controlled speech.* Louisville, Ky.: University of Louisville Press, 1971.

Peterson, L. R. Short-term verbal memory and learning. *Psychological Review,* 1966, *73,* 193–207.

Peterson, L. R., & Peterson, M. J. Short-term retention of individual verbal items. *Journal of Experimental Psychology,* 1959, *58,* 193–198.

Pisoni, D. B. Dichotic listening and processing phonetic features. In F. Restle, R. M. Shiffrin, N. J. Castellan, H. R. Lindman, & D. B. Pisoni (Eds.), *Cognitive theory* (Vol. 1). Hillsdale, N.J.: Lawrence Erlbaum Associates, 1975.

Porter, R. J., & Berlin, C. I. On interpreting developmental changes in the dichotic right ear advantage. *Brain and Language,* 1975, *2,* 186–200.

Posner, M. I., Boies, S. J. Components of attention. *Psychological Review,* 1971, *78,* 391–408.

Posner, M. I., & Klein, R. On functions of consciousness. In S. Kornblum (Ed.), *Attention and performance IV.* New York: Academic Press, 1973.

Posner, M. I., & Snyder, C. R. R. Attention and cognitive control. In R. Solso (Ed.), *Information processing and cognition: The Loyola Symposium.* Hillsdale, N.J.: Lawrence Erlbaum Associates, 1975.

Rabbitt, P. M. A. Set and age in a choice-response task. *Journal of Gerontology,* 1964, *19,* 301–306. (b)

Rabbitt, P. M. A. Age and time for choice between stimuli and between responses. *Journal of Gerontology,* 1964, *19,* 307–312. (a)

Rees, J., & Botwinick, J. Detection and decision factors in auditory behavior of the elderly. *Journal of Gerontology,* 1971, *26,* 133–136.

Shaffer, L. H. Attention in transcription skill. *Quarterly Journal of Experimental Psychology,* 1971, *23,* 107–112.

Shiffrin, R. M. Capacity limitations in information processing, attention, and memory. In W. K. Estes (Ed.), *Handbook of learning and cognitive processes. Vol. 4: Attention and memory.* Hillsdale, N.J.: Lawrence Erlbaum Associates, 1976.

Shiffrin, R. M., Pisoni, D. B., & Casteneda-Mendez, K. Is attention shared between the ears? *Cognitive Psychology,* 1974, *6,* 190–216.

Shiffrin, R. M., & Schneider, W. Toward a unitary model for selective attention, memory scanning and visual search. In S. Dorniĉ (Ed.), *Attention and performance VI.* Hillsdale, N.J.: Lawrence Erlbaum Associates, 1977.

Stein, B. S. Depth of processing reexamined: The effects of the precision of encoding and test appropriateness. *Journal of Verbal Learning and Verbal Behavior,* 1978, *17,* 165–174.

Sticht, T., & Gray, B. The intelligibility of time-compressed words as a function of age and hearing loss. *Journal of Speech and Hearing Research,* 1969, *12,* 443–448.

Talland, G. A. *Disorders of memory and learning.* Baltimore: Penguin Books, 1968.

Titchener, E. B. *Lectures on the elementary psychology of feeling and attention.* New York: Macmillan, 1908.

Treisman, A. M. Contextual cues in selective listening. *Quarterly Journal of Experimental Psychology*, 1960, *12*, 242-248.

Treisman, A. M. Selective attention in man. *British Medical Bulletin*, 1964, *20*, 12-16. (a)

Treisman, A. M. The effect of irrelevant material on the efficiency of selective listening. *American Journal of Psychology*, 1964, *77*, 533-546. (b)

Treisman, A. M. Verbal cues, language and meaning in selective attention. *American Journal of Psychology*, 1964, *77*, 206-219. (c)

Treisman, A. M. Human attention. In B. M. Foss (Ed.), *New Horizons in Psychology*. Baltimore: Penguin, 1966.

Treisman, A. M. Shifting attention between the ears. *Quarterly Journal of Experimental Psychology*, 1971, *23*, 157-167.

Treisman, A. M., & Geffen, G. Selective attention: Perception or response? *Quarterly Journal of Experimental Psychology*, 1967, *19*, 1-17.

VonWright, J. M., Anderson, K., & Stenman, V. Generalization of conditioned GSRs in dichotic listening. In P. M. A. Rabbitt & S. Dornič (Eds.), *Attention and performance V*. London: Academic Press, 1975.

Waugh, N. C., & Norman, D. A. Primary memory. *Psychological Review*, 1965, *72*, 89-104.

Welford, A. T. The "psychological refractory period" and the timing of high speed performance: A review and a theory. *British Journal of Psychology*, 1952, *43*, 2-19.

Welford, A. T. Evidence of a single-channel decision mechanism limiting performance in a serial reaction task. *Quarterly Journal of Experimental Psychology*, 1959, *11*, 193-210.

Welford, A. T. *Fundamentals of skill*. London: Methuen, 1968.

Welford, A. T. Serial reaction-times, continuity of task, single-channel effects and age. In S. Dornič (Ed.), *Attention and performance VI*. Hillsdale, N.J.: Lawrence Erlbaum Associates, 1977.

Wickens, C. D. The effects of divided attention on information processing in manual tracking. *Journal of Experimental Psychology: Human Perception and Performance*, 1976, *2*, 1-13.

Wingfield, A. Acoustic redundancy and the perception of time-compressed speech. *Journal of Speech and Hearing Research*, 1975, *18*, 96-104. (a)

Wingfield, A. The intonation-syntax interaction: Prosodic features in perceptual processing of sentences. In A. Cohen & S. G. Nooteboom (Eds.), *Structure and process in speech perception*. Berlin: Springer-Verlag, 1975. (b)

Wingfield, A. The perception of alternated speech. *Brain and Language*, 1977, *4*, 219-230.

Wingfield, A., & Byrnes, D. L. The decay of information in short-term memory. *Science*, 1972, *176*, 690-692.

Wingfield, A., & Klein, J. F. Syntactic structure and acoustic pattern in speech perception. *Perception and Psychophysics*, 1971, *9*, 23-25.

Wingfield, A., & Wheale, J. L. Word rate and intelligibility of alternated speech. *Perception and Psychophysics*, 1975, *18*, 317-320.

Winograd, E., & Smith, A. D. When do semantic orienting tasks hinder recall? *Bulletin of the Psychonomic Society*, 1978, *11*, 165-167.

Yerkes, R. M., & Dodson, J. D. The relation of strength of stimulus to rapidity of habit-formation. *Journal of Comparative Neurology of Psychology*, 1908, *18*, 459-482.

Yntema, D. B., & Trask, F. P. Recall as a search process. *Journal of Verbal Learning and Verbal Behavior*, 1963, *2*, 65-74.

Zurif, E. B., & Sait, P. E. The role of syntax in dichotic listening. *Neuropsychologia*, 1970, *8*, 239-244.

13 Periodic "Lapses" in Attentional Processes: A Possible Correlate of Memory Impairment in the Elderly

Larry W. Thompson
University of Southern California

The chapter by Wingfield and Sandoval has provided a concise and excellent summarization of the literature on divided attention. The authors' comparison of the numerous models developed over the years in this field is both informative and provocative. They have shown that, for the most part, models attempting to account for the operation of attention in processing information implicate a time-sharing or capacity notion.

Concentrating on the capacity models, Wingfield and Sandoval have highlighted five areas of importance to the study of divided attention and have depicted the varying amounts of agreement and disagreement among the different models. The points are:

1. There is a limited capacity in resources.
2. There may be single or multiple processors.
3. Although capacity may be limited, it can be variable depending on a number of other factors.
4. Stimulus quality may have importance in determining the capacity limits for attentional processes.
5. "Deeper" processing may require more capacity than shallow processing.

Wingfield and Sandoval examined some aspects of each of these areas in three cleverly conceived experiments, in which they varied components of stimulus tasks, reaction time and speech shadowing. Overall, shadowing and/or semantic processing had a definite incremental effect on slowing of reaction time. Compression of prose passages had no effect on reaction time, but did affect shadowing accuracy and paraphrase recall. On the other hand, shadowing and recall were not affected by the increased complexity of the reaction-time (RT) task. The authors concluded that the effective independence of the performance on the speech task from the changes in the task demands of the RT task supported the multiprocessor models. Two or more distinctly different classes of information could be processed fairly independently, and, depending on stimulus conditions, task priorities, etc., one operation could be carried out effectively, with negligible influences from other operations being performed simultaneously. The authors interpreted their data as particularly damaging to the time-sharing and comprehensive capacity models, but also pointed out that the results do not completely support any one specific model.

Wingfield and Sandoval are in the difficult position of arguing for independence of tasks—in part, at least, on the basis of negative results. To make their argument completely compelling, they should address a host of objections, most of which center around the sensitivity of their measures in detecting subtle influences, or, to a lesser degree, the adequacy of their manipulations in precipitating changes within measureable ranges. For example, although accuracy of speech shadowing seems independent of variations in reaction-time demands, some form of time lag measure might show that accuracy is constant only as a result of some trade-off with time. Such a finding would make it difficult to accept the notion of independence.

Whatever the case may be, scrutiny of the authors' data analysis and interpretation indicates theirs is a superb and timely paper—one that convincingly reminds us of the importance of attentional processes in cognitive function, and encourages us to incorporate similar experimental strategies into the study of cognitive processes in the elderly. Their emphasis on selective and divided-attention tasks as being more "ecologically valid" is welcomed and should be helpful in developing new possibilities for the investigation of attentional processes, particularly in the elderly.

Their proposed design for adding a vigilance component to a divided attention task should provide intriguing results in aging research, and certainly is consistent with the theme of making experimental tasks more reflective of practical situations. Not only is it often necessary to perform more than one task simultaneously, but it is also frequently necessary to sustain this attentive set to multiple tasks for prolonged periods. A four-light task similar to the one described in this chapter has already been used to examine hemispheric differences in vigilance performance (Dimond, 1976; Dimond & Beaumont, 1971, 1973). This suggests that such complex tasks can be used in a vigilance framework with the elderly, and direct comparisons with studies investigating hemispheric asymmetries may yield useful information concerning changes in brain function with age.

It is fitting that these authors have reminded us of the importance of vigilance measures at this time because George Talland (1966) was one of the first investigators to show that older individuals have increased difficulty maintaining sustained attention in continuous-scanning tasks. Evaluation of performance in complex cognitive tasks requiring sustained attention suggests even more substantial age differences (Harkins, Nowlin, Ramm, & Schroeder, 1974; Thompson, Opton, & Cohen, 1963). These latter studies employed a task which involved the presentation of numbers at 1-sec intervals over a 10-min period. Subjects were required to press a key every time they were aware of two odd or two even digits being presented in succession. Analysis of performance for 30-sec intervals across this time span revealed marked fluctuations in performance, ranging from 100% correct during some intervals, to a complete absence of correct responses in others (Harkins, Thompson, & Nowlin, unpublished manuscript). These variations tended to be periodic, and are somewhat reminiscent of the "blocking" principle referred to by Bills some years ago (Bills, 1931). Interestingly, older individuals performed as well as or better than younger individuals during some intervals, but overall age differences could be attributed to a greater number of low-performance intervals for the old than for the young. A similar trend was also observed on extremely simple vigilance tasks, though it was not as marked.

Thus, it appears that these periodic variations in performance or "lapses" in young and old are common to both simple and complex tasks when pacing is controlled by the experimenter. This suggests that some involuntary reorganization of processing resources may occur periodically, and the extent to which this affects performance is probably amplified by the demands being made concurrently on attentional mechanisms. It is noteworthy, however, that this reorganization may occur even when capacity has not been exceeded. Thus, this suggests the existence of yet another little-understood aspect of the dynamic process of attention, which may be changing with age.

REFERENCES

Bills, A. G. Blocking: A new principle of mental fatigue. *American Journal of Psychology,* 1931, *43,* 230–245.

Dimond, S. J. Depletion of attentional capacity after total commisurotomy in man. *Brain,* 1976, *99,* 347–356.

Dimond, S. J., & Beaumont, J. G. Hemisphere function and vigilance. *Quarterly Journal of Experimental Psychology,* 1971, *23,* 443–448.

Dimond, S. J., & Beaumont, J. G. Difference in the vigilance performance of the right and left hemispheres. *Cortex,* 1973, *9,* 259–265.

Harkins, S. W., Nowlin, J. B., Ramm, D., & Schroeder, S. Effects of age, sex and time-on-watch on a brief continuous performance task. In E. Palmore (Ed.), *Normal aging II*. Durham, N.C.: Duke University Press, 1974.

Harkins, S. W., Thompson, L. W., & Nowlin, J. B. Effects of age on attentional lapses in a brief continuous performance task. Unpublished manuscript.

Talland, G. A. Visual signal detection, as a function of age, input rate and signal frequency. *The Journal of Psychology*, 1966, *63*, 105–115.

Thompson, L. W., Opton, E., & Cohen, L. D. Effects of age, presentation speed and sensory modality on performance of a "vigilance" task. *Journal of Gerontology*, 1963, *18*, 366–369.

14

Individual Age-Related Differences in Sensory Memory

Mitchell Grossberg
U.S. Department of Transportation

This discussion concerns two earlier chapters that focused on experimental methods and results pertaining to human sensory memory: "Iconic Memory and Attentional Processes in the Aged" by D. A. Walsh and M. J. Prasse, (Chapter 10), and "Echoic Memory and the Study of Aging Memory Systems" by R. G. Crowder (Chapter 11). These chapters considered analogous mechanisms in vision and audition that allow a human subject to perceive a relatively unmodified copy of an external stimulus during a short interval of time after the stimulus is turned off. Research conducted within the last 15 years has strengthened and refined the view that under certain experimental conditions a subject extracts stimulus information primarily from such a sensory image (e.g., Sakitt, 1976), rather than from a categorized or encoded version of the stimulus (Holding, 1975). But research has not yet produced convincing evidence of systematic changes in sensory memory as a function of subject age; while experimental results for iconic memory are inconsistent, results for echoic memory are nonexistent. In fact, for sensory memory in both modalities, methodological questions outweigh other concerns when aging is the issue.

This discussion responds to the methodological difficulties reported in the two earlier chapters by suggesting an experimental tactic wherein each individual's sensory-memory functioning is measured while he or she performs diverse tasks, all of which have potential for significantly reflecting sensory memory, but which evidently differ in terms of the information retrieval processes (broadly defined) that the tasks invoke. Also, because investigators may wish to control task requirements while studying an individual's sensory memory functioning in both vision and audition, approximate task analogues are identified between the tasks described by Walsh and Prasse for studying iconic memory, and the tasks described by Crowder for studying echoic memory.

COVARYING AGE-RELATED EFFECTS IN ICONIC MEMORY STUDIES

Experiments reviewed by Walsh and Prasse illustrate a tendency for age effects to covary in such a way that measures of subject performance provide biased estimates of sensory memory characteristics. In three reviewed situations, inferred age differences in the duration of iconic memory were, or could have been, significantly biased by age-related effects in the speed of selective information readout from iconic memory, the relative ability to perceive particular stimulus patterns formed by a combination of successive stimulus halves, and the decision criterion adopted while judging the temporal continuity of a repeated stimulus pattern. These cases suggest a general difficulty—namely, that any single task we ask subjects to perform in an experiment on sensory memory can reflect the operation of other processes or stages in processing that might also vary systematically as a function of age. Such confounding of effects has, of course, been recognized in the literature by, for example, Saccuzzo (1977), who cites two types of confoundings: (1) An observed decrement in performance can occur because of a generalized, rather than a specific, deficit that affects performance; and (2) a decrement can be observed if a control task is less discriminating than the experimental task. Confounded age effects certainly challenge the ingenuity of investigators who study iconic memory, as is clear from the work reviewed by Walsh and Prasse. Three experimental situations that illustrate the biases cited previously will now be discussed to focus on pertinent details.

Sampling

Walsh and Prasse report that Walsh and Thompson have applied to the problem of aging the well documented partial-report task for studying iconic memory. In performing this task, subjects identified the letter occupying the stimulus array position that was designated at a controlled instant of time following termination of a brief stimulus. In contrast with 18–31-year-olds, 60–72-year-olds were unable to reach a criterion of 75% correct identifications, even when the position marker occurred concurrently with stimulus offset. Because the older subjects ultimately attained criterion performance when the stimulus duration was increased from 50 to 500 msec (which demonstrated that the subjects could perform the required task), the investigators hypothesized that the poor performance at 50 msec was due to either a relatively short iconic memory, a slow readout of information from iconic memory, or both. In other words, more than one underlying age effect could have been responsible for the observed results. Due to this impasse, the investigators turned to a very different task in order to estimate age-related changes in the duration of iconic memory.

Continuation

Another example of confounded age effects was described by Walsh and Prasse in reference to two experiments by Kline and his colleagues, who applied a method developed earlier with university students (Eriksen & Collins, 1967, 1968). Subjects identified a three-letter word formed by two complementary arrays of dots that were presented briefly, in succession, separated by a controlled interval of time. Apparently the image persists after termination of the first array, as it appears to be a random pattern when presented alone, but is completed perceptually by the second array when it is presented sufficiently soon after the first.

In the two experiments by Kline, elderly subjects performed either better or worse than young subjects, depending on whether the half-stimuli were constructed of connected line segments or dots. The better performance of elderly subjects on the line segments supported a prediction based on a number of other kinds of vision experiments (see Kline & Orme-Rogers, 1978), but, more importantly for our purposes, was in striking contrast with numerous experiments that show performance deficits with age. Nonetheless, the point most relevant to this discussion is that age effects were confounded in the two experiments; the processes responsible for better or worse performance by elderly subjects were not experimentally isolated.

Repetition

In another experiment described by Walsh and Prasse, Walsh and Thompson inferred that the duration of iconic memory is shorter for elderly subjects than for young subjects; the average difference between groups was 41 msec. Covarying age effects that might suggest another explanation were not apparent in the data, but the kind of judgment required of the subjects was conducive to significant differences among subjects in terms of their decision criteria. Because decision criteria have been found to vary with subject age (e.g., Gordon & Clark, 1974; Potash & Jones, 1977), the possibility of confounding between sensory (iconic memory) and judgmental (decision criterion) processes with age should be considered in this experimental context.

In the prototype experiment by Haber and Standing (1969), university students indicated when they saw interruptions in a stimulus pattern (a circle) that was presented repeatedly—the briefly exposed pattern alternated with a long-duration blank field. The purpose of this method was to estimate the image duration at which the image of the pattern faded sufficiently to produce a perceivable discontinuity. Group data were used to estimate the longest average duration for apparent persistence of the pattern. However, a number of remarks and analyses concerned differences among individual subjects, which were clearly of importance because there was no objectively correct judgmental response in the situation. Haber and Standing pointed out that although "subjects had a specific set to look for continuity or visual persistence, they were aware that perceived continuity was always illusory [p. 46]." Threshold durations of pattern persistence showed significant intersubject differences that were, however, regarded as "no larger than individual differences typically found in psychophysical studies [p. 49]."

Because reliable intersubject differences as a function of subject age have been found for the decision criteria that subjects adopt in various experimental situations (e.g., Gordon & Clark, 1974; Potash & Jones, 1977), it would be desirable to estimate explicitly both the criterion component and the sensory component of each subject's judgmental response when the Haber and Standing method is applied to measure age-related individual differences in iconic memory. An experimental paradigm used by Clark (1966) to study individual differences in critical flicker frequencies could be adapted for use with repetitive patterned stimuli. Clark's procedure allowed him to apply signal detection theory in analyzing subjects' judgmental performance. Specifically, the signal stimulus was an intermittent light that sometimes appeared to flicker, while the nonsignal stimulus was always a physically steady light. Clark used one rate of intermittency, but more than one could be used to vary signal strength. On each experimental trial, either a nonsignal or a signal was presented according to a quasirandom schedule, and the subject reported whether or not the light appeared to "flicker." This procedure produced "flicker" responses to signals (hits) and nonsignals (false alarms), permitting a contrast between the sensory and decision components of the subjects' performance.

An analogous procedure could be used to study pattern persistence. The nonsignal stimulus would have a relatively short interpattern interval for which the pattern sometimes appears to have a temporal discontinuity. The subject would report on each trial whether or not the pattern is "discontinuous," the same task that the subjects had in the prototype experiment by Haber and Standing and in the later age-oriented experiment by Walsh and Thompson.

Multiple Tasks for Studying Individual Differences

We have seen that experimental situations developed using young subjects may not be adequate, without additional control procedures, for estimating and understanding individual age-related differences in sensory memory.

When we infer that age-related differences in performance on a single task are mainly due to differences in iconic memory, we can easily be mistaken, because another process or stage in processing could be responsible. Confronted by subtle covarying age effects, we could increase our confidence that sensory memory differences are actually being estimated by having subjects perform diverse indicator tasks that impose logically different information-processing requirements. Investigators are, of course, using diverse indicator tasks as we have seen, but they are using separate groups of subjects with each task. Eventually, however, it would be desirable to study the correlation between different estimates of sensory memory functioning when the same subjects perform diverse tasks.

It would be asked whether the estimates of iconic memory obtained on one task have the same distribution among individuals as estimates obtained on another task. This consistency would give further assurance that a common inferred mechanism is responsible for the differences in observed performance. If this consistency exists, then we would also inquire whether the estimates are ordered systematically as a function of the individuals' ages. Haber and Standing (1969) aptly described the present state of our knowledge regarding individual differences in sensory storage times: "Until more attention is paid to individual differences in psychophysical tasks, further interpretation of the magnitude of this correlation is highly speculative [p. 49]."

MEASURING ECHOIC MEMORY
IN RELATION TO SUBJECT AGE

Not having data on echoic memory as a function of age, but anticipating various inferential difficulties, Crowder (Chapter 11) first considered general methodological problems pertaining to all subjects, then considered special problems pertaining to elderly subjects, especially task difficulty and hearing loss. While discussing hearing loss, Crowder made some remarks about the potential of "within-subject" correlational analyses which should be reemphasized. He suggested that an aging population of subjects provides an excellent sample in which to test correlations among the various methods proposed for measuring echoic memory. If the correlations obtained are low, relative to the measured reliabilities of the methods tested, we might conclude that there are a number of echoic memory systems, each tied, perhaps, to a different mode of information processing in the auditory system. But, as noted previously in the present discussion, we must allow in our thinking for the intrusion by other processes.

Crowder described for illustrative purposes three experimental situations that provide direct evidence of echoic memory functioning—direct in that a subject's response carries verifiable information extracted from the sensory image. Because investigators may wish eventually to compare individual differences in sensory memory functioning in audition and vision, apparent parallels between Crowder's three auditory situations and the three described visual situations need to be delineated. In order to facilitate this comparison, the rubrics used by Crowder for identifying the auditory situations, specifically sampling, continuation, and repetition, were used to label the analogous visual situations. One fundamental difference between the auditory and visual analogues would be that information is distributed temporally in audition and spatially in vision. Nonetheless, the information-processing requirements of the subject tasks appear similar in the analogous situations, as the following descriptions indicate.

Sampling

In the auditory sampling situation, a subject searches selectively in sensory memory for information to identify and report. The task requirement resembles the requirement in the visual partial-report situation, as Crowder has pointed out. The problem in vision is that iconic memory is brief compared with the time required by elderly subjects to extract information from iconic memory; the slow iconic readout by elderly subjects impedes application of the partial-report task to study aging effects. However, since auditory echoic memory, estimated by the sampling technique, lasts about 5 sec (Glucksberg & Cowen, 1970), while elderly subjects' word-pattern discrimination latencies are about 500 msec (Elias & Elias, 1976), the sampling technique might still provide useful estimates of echoic memory duration as a function of age.

Continuation

In the auditory continuation situation, a subject *recognizes* and repeats (shadows) continuous speech that is partitioned into successive segments separated by silent intervals which compel the subject to *combine successive segments perceptually*. In the visual situation, the subject recognizes perceptually combined stimulus halves.

Repetition

In the auditory repetition situation, a subject *compares categorized information* (shadowed) *with information* (received a short time earlier in the other ear) that is *stored in sensory memory*. In the visual situation, the subject presumably compares the fading iconic image of a stimulus pattern with an unfaded image, which represents the subject's concept of how the pattern looks when it is "continuous." Changing the visual situation so that it involves the simultaneous presentation of a "continuous" standard stimulus spatially adjacent to a possibly "discontinuous" comparison stimulus (depending on the interval between repeated presentations of the pattern) makes the visual situation more like the auditory dichotic situation. Even greater situational equivalence is attainable by making the auditory test materials more similar to the visual materials. For instance, Treisman (1964) has used stimulus materials in addition to coherent prose, such as random words, sequences of digits (also see Norman, 1969), and reversed speech which subjects could not repeat, but which they could compare as patterns.

Covarying Age Effects

In two of the auditory situations, sampling and repetition, a subject is asked to shadow input to one ear so that he attends only to this input and ignores, to the extent that he does not categorize, input to the other ear. An aging problem that could prove to be a source of intersubject variability in these situations was recently emphasized by Shonfield (1974). It is that older individuals tend to be more distractible, and thus have the "problem of excluding from attention material irrelevant to the task at hand [p. 799]." This tendency could affect the keystone assumption of these experimental situations, that the unshadowed input is in a relatively raw, unprocessed form before the subject focuses attention on the input to apply it in some way.

Fortunately, techniques to estimate subject distractibility in such situations have been used successfully with younger subjects and could be applied in research on aging. Glucksberg and Cowen (1970) asked subjects to report spontaneously whenever they heard digits in the unshadowed ear. Norman (1969) measured shadowing performance as a function of time with, and without, the presentation of material to the unshadowed ear. Measurement of shadowing performance in time could permit an investigator to index the attentional drifts elderly subjects might display. Applied in research on aging, these experimental techniques could yield data not only on sensory memory, but also on higher order processes associated with verbal behavior and attention. Significant covarying effects of aging on different underlying processes might then be disclosed and, hopefully, identified.

As suggested for research on iconic memory with age, varying the auditory information-processing task for the same subjects would permit us to have greater confidence that sensory memory effects are indeed responsible for observed age-related differences in subject performance.

ACKNOWLEDGMENT

This work was performed as a personal professional activity. It is not for a project sponsored and supported by the U.S. Department of Transportation.

REFERENCES

Clark, W. C. The psyche in psychophysics: A sensory-decision theory analysis of the effect of instructions on flicker sensitivity and response bias. *Psychological Bulletin,* 1966, *65,* 358–366.

Elias, J. W., & Elias, M. F. Matching of successive auditory stimuli as a function of age and ear of presentation. *Journal of Gerontology,* 1976, *31,* 164–169.

Eriksen, C. W., & Collins, J. F. Some temporal characteristics of visual pattern perception. *Journal of Experimental Psychology,* 1967, *74,* 476–484.

Eriksen, C. W., & Collins, J. F. Sensory traces versus the psychological moment in the temporal organization of form. *Journal of Experimental Psychology,* 1968, *77,* 376–382.

Glucksberg, S., & Cowen, G. N. Memory for nonattended auditory material. *Cognitive Psychology,* 1970, *1,* 149–156.

Gordon, S. K., & Clark, W. C. Adult age differences in word and nonsense syllable recognition memory and response criterion. *Journal of Gerontology,* 1974, *29,* 659–665.

Haber, R. N., & Standing, L. G. Direct measures of short-term visual storage. *Quarterly Journal of Experimental Psychology,* 1969, *21,* 43–54.

Holding, D. H. Sensory storage reconsidered. *Memory & Cognition,* 1975, *3,* 31–41.

Kline, D. W., & Orme-Rogers, C. Examination of stimulus persistence as the basis for superior visual identification performance among older adults. *Journal of Gerontology,* 1978, *33,* 76–81.

Norman, D. A. Memory while shadowing. *Quarterly Journal of Experimental Psychology,* 1969, *21,* 85–93.

Potash, M., & Jones, B. Aging and decision criteria for the detection of tones in noise. *Journal of Gerontology,* 1977, *32,* 436–440.

Saccuzzo, D. P. Bridges between schizophrenia and gerontology: Generalized or specific deficits? *Psychological Bulletin,* 1977, *84,* 595–600.

Sakitt, B. Iconic memory. *Psychological Review,* 1976, *83,* 257–276.

Schonfield, D. Utilizing information. *American Psychologist,* 1974, *29,* 796–801.

Treisman, A. Monitoring and storage of irrelevant messages in selective attention. *Journal of Verbal Learning and Verbal Behavior,* 1964, *3,* 449–459.

15 Memory and Mental Tempo

Nancy C. Waugh
Robin A. Barr
University of Oxford

Psychologists like dichotomies. They also like continua with clearly specifiable end-points. Nowhere is this more evident, perhaps, than in their attempts to explain failures of memory in old age. The deficit lies either in the storage or in the retrieval of traces that are either short-lived or long-term, episodic or semantic, auditory or visual, modality-specific or verbal. Attention is divided or focused. Information is encoded deeply or superficially. The hope seems to be that some peculiar combination of alternatives will uniquely specify the problem. Some investigators have indeed pointed to impoverished encoding of verbal information—a result of incomplete attention or inadequate rehearsal—as a probable candidate. Others cite the inefficient retrieval of episodic memories. Still others implicate a diminshed ability to recall anything at all after a filled delay. (For details, see Craik, 1977, and Eysenck, 1977.) Predictably enough, the search for a single clear-cut locus has led to no general systematic description of the nature of the memory deficit in aging. Nor, in our opinion, is it likely to do so.

An informal survey of the recent technical literature has forced us to that conclusion. We have encountered a jumble of facts, and even a fair number of reproducible facts. All too often, however, they seem to have very little to do with each other. We have wondered whether they were doomed to exist in isolation one from the other or whether they could be organized and interrelated according to some general rubric. We believe that they can. Our reasoning is as follows.

First, the efficiency of an operation by definition varies directly with the rate at which it is performed. Second, it is an unanswerable truth that the older we become, the longer it takes us to complete almost any mental operation. The evidence is well documented, pervasive, and compelling: Our

251

psychological tempo decreases from presto to largo as adolescence gives way to old age; and so does the speed with which we register or retrieve information. The customary distinctions between primary, secondary, and tertiary memory (Waugh, 1970a), or between episodic, semantic, and lexical stores, or between "deep" and "superficial" levels of processing are totally subsidiary to that fact. Those distinctions may be useful in other contexts, but they are of limited value in explaining the nature of the memory decrement in late adulthood.

Contemporary statements about what happens to memory in aging are generally qualitative and loose. They often fall short of the mark, moreover, because they fail to recognize the essential fact that the rates at which mental operations are performed uniformly decrease with age. Time is a critical but curiously neglected dependent variable. At the moment we lack accurate, systematic descriptions of how and to what extent people slow down as they get older. Yet it ought to be possible, given reliable data in sufficient numbers, to construct different sorts of chronometric functions according to which the time required to complete operation X, Y, or Z varies as a function of age. We put this endeavour forward as a potentially fruitful program. Furthermore, should anyone seek reductionist explanations, he will need a coherent and quantitative set of results to present to the neurophysiologist. Measurements of changes in mental tempo present an obvious choice.

We have tried to make two points so far.

1. Our current body of facts about progressive changes in memory throughout adulthood is ill-organized and has sometimes been subjected to premature interpretations of an either/or variety.
2. We believe that most observed age-related decrements in cognitive function—and specifically in memory—can be accounted for by age-related decrements in speed of performance.

In the remainder of this chapter, we attempt to substantiate this second point. We review recently published work, but only very selectively. (For useful comprehensive summaries, see Arenberg & Robertson-Tchabo, 1977; Craik, 1977; and Eysenck, 1977.) We also describe some work of our own which is consistent with the "slow tempo" principle. We now discuss in turn age-related changes in time to attend to, identify, encode, and retrieve information.

TIME TO PERCEIVE

It is impossible to dissociate memory from either perception or attention since we experience what we attend to, and we can remember only what we have experienced. Perception takes time even when memory load is minimal and decisions are straightforward. Depending on the complexity of a visual display, a subject in his 60s can take anywhere from 20 msec (Hertzog, Williams, & Walsh, 1976; Walsh, 1976; Walsh, Till, & Williams, 1978) to 200 msec (Eriksen, Hamlin, & Breitmeyer, 1970; Eriksen & Steffy, 1964) to 500 msec (Schonfield & Wenger, 1975) longer than a younger adult to identify a visual signal: He needs that much more time than a young subject to process sensory information to the same degree of accuracy. The older subject is similarly less readily able to integrate auditory signals over intervals of 50 to 500 msec (Corso, Wright, & Valerio, 1976) or to process time-compressed speech (Konkle, Beasley, & Bess, 1977). Elias and Elias (1976) have found that it takes 60-year-olds up to 200 msec longer than it takes 20-year-olds to identify words or pure tones, even when they are highly predictable.

The discrepancy between the perceptual performance of old and young becomes quite dramatic when (1) an auditory signal occurs at an unpredictable point in time, and (2) the subject must switch attention from one message source to another. In one experiment, we asked subjects to listen to two simultaneous messages presented to the same ear. One message was a meaningful sentence read at a normal rate and in a normal tone of voice. The other was a series of semantically unrelated words read in a monotone at a rate of one word per second. One message was spoken by a male and the other by a female. The subject listened for a predefined target word which might occur at any point in the sentence. As soon as he heard the target, he was to switch his attention to the unrelated words and report the latest member of the series.

The unrelated words were timed such that one of them began approximately 150 msec after the onset of the target. Two groups of subjects, one in their 20s and one in their 60s, were tested. Their performance is summarized in Table 15.1. On two-thirds of the trials, the young groups correctly reported the unrelated word that began just after the target. On over two-thirds of the trials, the older group instead reported the next word in the unrelated series—i.e. the word that actually began almost a full second after the target. The older subjects, then, were either much slower to identify the target in the one message, or to switch their attention to the other message, or to both identify and switch. We hope in future experiments to measure identification and switching times independently. Clearly, the times taken to

TABLE 15.1
Lag between Target and Reported Word

Group	Relative Position						
	-3	-2	-1	0	+1	+2	+3
Older	.01	.00	.00	.25	.69	.03	.01
Young	.00	.00	.00	.66	.34	.00	.00

perform these perceptual operations exert a considerable effect on performance.

SPONTANEOUS ORGANIZATION AND TIME TO ENCODE

Treat and Reese (1976) have provided a striking illustration of how the slow mental tempo of old age can exert pervasive effects on memory. They varied the length of both the anticipation and inspection intervals in a paired-associate learning task. They also manipulated the subject's use of imagery. In three separate conditions, they either: (1) gave the subjects no imagery instructions; or (2) provided a specific image with which to relate the paired associates; or (3) encouraged the subjects to employ their own imagery to link the two terms.

With a short anticipation interval, young subjects were able to make much better use of imagery (either experimenter- or subject-produced) than the old. However, with a long anticipation interval, the older group's performance improved markedly. In fact, when they provided their own imagery, they did as well as the young. Given proper instructions and enough time, then, the older subjects were able to reduce or even completely eliminate their memory "deficit."

We too have investigated older subjects' use of mnemonic strategies. Our own preference has been to infer organizational strategies from performance when information is presented at different rates.

One obvious way in which people organize a series of verbal items is to group them. Young adults tend spontaneously to chunk items into successive groups of three when they are presented aurally and in supraspan lists (Frankish, 1976). We have carried out an experiment to determine whether spontaneous grouping also occurs when supraspan lists are presented visually, and whether the elderly are as likely to group spontaneously as the young. We also wished to discover whether externally imposed temporal grouping differentially aids the older subject—and especially when presentation is visual. An older (mean age 67) and a younger (mean age 25) group of subjects listened to or looked at lists of nine digits, attempting ordered recall after each list. The lists were presented either over headphones or on the face of a visual display unit, one digit at a time. In each case, they were presented either at a constant rate of one digit every half second or in three successive groups of three separated by pauses. Total time was held constant. The results are shown in Table 15.2.

It is clear that both the older and the younger subjects recalled more auditory than visual items. It is also clear that both benefited from external grouping under the auditory condition. Younger subjects also recalled more

TABLE 15.2
Proportion of Errors as a Function of Serial Position for Four Kinds of List

	Serial Position								
	1	2	3	4	5	6	7	8	9
Y:AG[a]	.02	.06	.05	.15	.17	.08	.19	.19	.05
Y:AU	.03	.11	.10	.25	.29	.28	.35	.28	.06
Y:VG	.08	.13	.08	.21	.26	.16	.38	.43	.33
Y:VU	.09	.17	.14	.30	.36	.29	.44	.45	.29
O:AG	.06	.09	.09	.26	.26	.12	.29	.27	.08
O:AU	.06	.15	.13	.27	.35	.25	.37	.36	.07
O:VG	.13	.22	.16	.37	.43	.25	.57	.62	.47
O:VU	.09	.17	.11	.33	.34	.19	.53	.53	.44

[a]Key: Y = young; O = older; A = aural; V = visual; G = grouped; U = ungrouped.

visual items when they were externally grouped than when they were not; but older subjects actually remembered *less* when visual items were externally grouped. The pattern of errors-by-serial position indicates that both older and younger subjects spontaneously organized the ungrouped lists, both visual and auditory, into three triads. Older subjects in fact gave slightly more evidence of grouping spontaneously than did younger ones, perhaps because their overall error rate was higher.

The gross aspects of the data have been fitted by a quantitative model which assumes (a) that items are initially stored in a verbal code; (b) that acoustic input is translated more rapidly than visual input into a verbal code; and (c) that older subjects are slower than younger ones to make both kinds of translation. The model predicts that external grouping will be of no use as soon as items begin to arrive more rapidly than they can be handled (that is, translated into a verbal code).

We have accordingly been able to account for some initially rather puzzling and counterintuitive results with a hypothesis which states merely that the elderly take longer than the young to encode both visual and aural information. Such differences in encoding rates are not obvious when subspan lists of simple items are presented slowly (Taub, 1966, 1972). They do appear when supraspan lists are presented rapidly (Kinsbourne, 1973). It is not surprising that the older subject also encodes more complex verbal items more slowly than the young adult (Kinsbourne & Berryhill, 1972; Smith, 1976, 1977).

Clearly, then, it takes the older subject longer to process information of a simple sort at a primitive level. It also takes him longer to perform relatively sophisticated operations—for example, to classify verbal items as instances of categories (Eysenck, 1977), or to produce either free associates (Reigel, 1968) or visual images (Nebes, 1976). This may explain why the older subject is sometimes thought not to use imagery or verbal mediators in conventional learning-and-retention tasks. But he quite evidently can and does do given sufficient time (Elias & Hirasuna, 1976; Hulicka, Sterns, & Grossman, 1967; Monge & Hultsch, 1971; Rowe & Schnore, 1971; Treat & Reese, 1976).

TIME TO RETRIEVE

A currently popular belief, at least in some quarters, is that aging affects certain memory "stores" but not others. Specifically, it has been suggested that the elderly suffer from a differential impairment of retrieval from episodic but not semantic memory (Eysenck, 1975; 1977) or from secondary but not primary memory (Craik, 1977). (There are those who claim that there is no retrieval problem in aging. Anyone who does so seriously must be very young. There *is* a problem and it is a straightforward one: It simply takes us longer the older we get to recall almost any piece of information from any hypothetical mental warehouse.)

Data on naming-latencies (Thomas, Fozard, & Waugh, 1977) show that semantic memory is not completely immune to the "slow-tempo" effect: Older subjects take some 200 msec longer to retrieve the name of a pictured common object than do young ones. The difference is attenuated by practice, but it is by no means eliminated. Elderly subjects, moreover, are slow to remember both very recent and relatively remote experiences. Time to remember recent ones does not increase appreciably until subjects are in their 60s (Waugh, Thomas, & Fozard, 1978). The time taken to retrieve information that one has not thought about for a while, on the other hand, increases steadily throughout the adult years. A lower bound on retrieval time from secondary memory is approximately 600 msec for the young adult and over 1200 msec— twice as long—for the elderly individual (Waugh, Thomas, & Fozard, 1978; see also Waugh, 1970b). Given these facts, it should come as no surprise that anticipation as well as the inspection times in a paired-associate task both affect retention scores. Older subjects do not perform as competently as younger ones when they are given insufficient time to either encode or retrieve. Given sufficient time to carry out both operations, they perform equally well (Monge & Hultsch, 1971; Treat & Reese, 1976).

EXCEPTIONS TO THE RULE

As we have tried to illustrate thus far, the slowing of mental operations with age exerts pervasive effects on memory. We are aware of only two exceptions to the rule, which we shall describe shortly. We should like first, though, to point out that it is important to identify any tasks which older subjects perform as quickly as the young. Such tasks ought if possible to be included in retraining programs wherein the elderly can be taught to make maximal use of those abilities in which they show minimal deficit.

RETRIEVAL FROM LEXICAL MEMORY

Waugh, Thomas, and Fozard (1978) have reported that the time taken to retrieve information from secondary memory increases steadily throughout adulthood and that the time taken to retrieve information from primary memory increases most dramatically when subjects are in their 60s. In the same study, subjects were also required simply to read out words projected onto a screen, one at a time, as rapidly as possible. The interval elapsing between the presentation of the word and the beginning of the subject's response was termed retrieval time from lexical memory. Its mean value did not increase with age until subjects were in their late 60s or well into their 70s—and then only marginally.

We have recently begun to investigate the effects of age on retrieval time from lexical memory in more detail. Two groups of subjects (mean ages 25 and 61) saw words from four different frequency categories in the Thorndike–Lorge count (1-24, 25-49, A, AA). Within each frequency category, words were either one, two, or three syllables long. Again there was no observed age-related decrement in performance. In fact, the older group (mean RT = 396 msec) recognized the words slightly more rapidly than the younger group (mean RT = 415 msec). The data for the two age groups were therefore pooled.

Figure 15.1 shows the overall mean naming-latencies for the different sorts of words. Word length interacted with frequency in the same way for both groups. For the three higher frequency categories, response times did not vary with word length. However, for the very rare words, response times increased with number of syllables. It is as though very short or very common words can

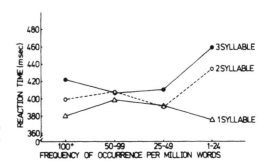

FIG. 15.1.   Mean naming-latencies as a function of word-frequency and number of syllables.

be apprehended in one glance, while words that are both long and unfamiliar need two or more glances to be taken in. Or the difference could arise from the need to initiate a relatively complex and unfamiliar motor program to pronounce a long, uncommon word.

GENERATION OF CATEGORY INSTANCES

Drachman and Leavitt (1972) and Eysenck (1975) have reported the results of another task in which there is little or no age-related temporal decrement or loss of efficiency. In both their studies, subjects were presented a category name and then had to generate appropriate instances of the category. Drachman and Leavitt required their subjects to generate as many instances of a category as possible within a given interval. Eysenck first presented his subjects with a category name (e.g., *fruit*) and then an initial letter (e.g., *A*). The subject's task was the generate an appropriate instance as soon as he saw the letter. In neither study was there any significant age-related decrement, either in mean time taken to generate a single instance (Eysenck) or to generate each of several successive instances (Drachman & Leavitt).

Both the "lexical memory" and the "category instance" tasks require the subject to produce highly familiar associates. Perhaps the long experience that older subjects have had in producing them compensates for whatever factors would otherwise slow down their performance. This explanation does not seem entirely adequate, however, because Thomas, Fozard, and Waugh (1977) have reported a substantial age-related decrement in a task (naming pictures of familiar objects) which also requires the subject to generate familiar associates. It may be of some significance that in the picture-naming task the associates were superordinate (category names), while in the other two they were subordinate (category instances). However, we clearly need an explicit comparison of the three tasks—picture-naming, retrieval from lexical memory, and generation of category instances—before drawing any firm conclusions.

In summary, we have tried to show that most age-related memory impairments described in the technical literature can plausibly be accounted for in terms of reduced speed of mental operations. It takes the older subject longer to attend to, perceive, register, and recall. Almost every component of the learning/ remembering process seems to be affected. We favor a general program which would (a) identify all those mental functions which slow down with age and (b) determine the rate at which they do so. Dichotomies such as "episodic" versus "semantic" or "primary" versus "secondary" or "deep" versus "superficial" may possibly prove useful in accounting for age-related memory decrements. They will surely not be sufficient. The "slow tempo" principle may even make them unnecessary.

ACKNOWLEDGMENTS

The research reported in this paper was supported by the Medical Research Council and the Social Science Research Council (U. K.).

REFERENCES

Arenberg, D., & Robertson-Tchabo, E. Learning and aging. In J. E. Birren & K. W. Schaie (Eds.), *Handbook of the psychology of aging.* New York: Van Nostrand, 1977.

Corso, J. F., Wright, N. H., & Valerio, M. Auditory temporal summation in presbycusis and noise exposure. *Journal of Gerontology,* 1976, *31,* 58–63.

Craik, F. I. M. Age differences in human memory. In J. E. Birren & K. W. Schaie (Eds.), *Handbook of the psychology of aging.* New York: Van Nostrand, 1977.

Drachman, D. A., & Leavitt, J. Memory impairment in the aged: Storage versus retrieval deficit. *Journal of Experimental Psychology,* 1972, *93,* 302–308.

Elias, J. W., & Elias, M. F. Matching of successive auditory stimuli as a function of age and ear of presentation. *Journal of Gerontology,* 1976, *31,* 164–169.

Elias, C. S., & Hirasuna, N. Age and semantic and phonological encoding. *Developmental Psychology,* 1976, *12,* 497–503.

Eriksen, C. W., Hamlin, R. M., & Breitmeyer, R. G. Temporal factors in visual perception as related to aging. *Perception and Psychophysics,* 1970, *7,* 354–356.

Eriksen, C. W., & Steffy, R. A. Short-term memory and retroactive interference in visual perception. *Journal of Experimental Psychology,* 1964, *68,* 423–434.

Eysenck, M. W. Retrieval from semantic memory as a function of age. *Journal of Gerontology,* 1975, *30,* 174–180.

Eysenck, M. W. *Human memory.* New York: Pergamon, 1977.

Frankish, C. R. Organizational factors in short term memory. Unpublished Ph.D. thesis, University of Cambridge, 1976.

Hertzog, S., Williams, M. V., & Walsh, D. A. The effect of practice on age differences in central perceptual masking. *Journal of Gerontology,* 1976, *31,* 428–433.

Hulicka, I., Sterns, H., & Grossman, J. Age-group comparisons of paired associate learning as a function of paced and self-paced association and response times. *Journal of Gerontology,* 1967, *22,* 274–280.

Kinsbourne, M. Age effects on letter span related to rate and sequential dependency. *Journal of Gerontology,* 1973, *28,* 317–319.

Kinsbourne, M., & Berryhill, J. The nature of the interaction between pacing and the age decrement in learning. *Journal of Gerontology,* 1972, *27,* 471–477.

Konkle, D. F., Beasley, D. S., & Bess, F. H. Intelligibility of time-altered speech in relation to chronological aging. *Journal of Speech and Hearing Research,* 1977, *20,* 108–115.

Monge, R. H., & Hultsch, D. F. Paired-associate learning as a function of adult age and length of the anticipation and inspection intervals. *Journal of Gerontology,* 1971, *26,* 157–162.

Nebes, R. D. Verbal-pictorial recoding in the elderly. *Journal of Gerontology,* 1976, *31,* 421–428.

Riegel, K. F. Changes in psycholinguistic performance with age. In G. A. Talland (Ed.), *Human aging and behavior.* New York: Academic Press, 1968.

Rowe, E. J., & Schnore, M. M. Item concreteness and reported strategies in paired-associate learning as a function of age. *Journal of Gerontology,* 1971, *26,* 470–475.

Schonfield, D., & Wenger, L. Age limitations of perceptual span. *Nature*, 1975, *253*, 377–378.

Smith, A. D. Aging and the total presentation time hypothesis. *Developmental Psychology*, 1976, *12*, 87–88.

Smith, A. D. Adult age differences in cued recall. *Developmental Psychology*, 1977, *13*, 326–331.

Taub, H. A. Visual short-term memory as a function of age, rate of presentation, and schedule of presentation. *Journal of Gerontology*, 1966, *21*, 388–391.

Taub, H. A. A comparison of young adult and old groups on various digit span tasks. *Developmental Psychology*, 1972, *6*, 60–65.

Thomas, J. C., Fozard, J. L., & Waugh, N. C. Age-related differences in naming latency. *Americal Journal of Psychology*, 1977, *90*, 499–509.

Treat, N. J., & Reese, H. W. Age, pacing and imagery in paired-associate learning. *Developmental Psychology*, 1976, *12*, 119–124.

Walsh, D. A. Age differences in central perceptual processing: A dichoptic backward masking investigation. *Journal of Gerontology*, 1976, *31*, 178–185.

Walsh, D. A., Till, R. E., & Williams, M. V. Age differences in peripheral perceptual processing: A monoptic backward masking investigation. *Journal of Experimental Psychology: Human Perception and Performance*, 1978, *4*, 232–243.

Waugh, N. C. Primary and secondary memory in short-term retention. In D. E. Broadbent and K. Pribram (Eds.), *Biology of memory*. New York: Academic Press, 1970. (a)

Waugh, N. C. Retrieval time in short-term memory. *British Journal of Psychology*, 1970, *61*, 1–12. (b)

Waugh, N. C., Thomas, J. C., & Fozard, J. L. Retrieval time from different memory stores. *Journal of Gerontology*, 1978, *33*, 718–724.

16 Memory as a Processing Continuum

Laird S. Cermak
Boston V. A. Medical Center and
Boston University School of Medicine

Research and theory in memory have undergone two radical changes within the last two decades that have changed not only the manner in which memory is investigated but the way in which psychologists have performed their research in general. These changes have given investigators the freedom to escape from the rigid confines of stimulus–response (S–R) behavioristic models of research to the more creative, less stereotyped techniques of the cognitive psychologists.

The first change occurred during the late 1950s and the decade of the sixties when psychologists began to emerge from the post-Hullian influence present in most American laboratories of the forties and fifties. Most of the terminology that had been used to this time in describing the memorization process bore the distinct trademark of conditioning paradigms. However, with the influence of British theorizing (especially Broadbent, 1957, 1958) leading the way and two classic experiments (Peterson & Peterson, 1959; Sperling, 1960) opening new vistas of research, a new conceptualization of the memory process began to emerge. Man began to be viewed as a processor of information, with information from the stimulus being analyzed and processed through a series of stages. This change in orientation brought with it a rash of theories describing memory as consisting of two or more compartments, each with its own set of characteristics, potentials, and limitations. Most of the research on memory at this time, consequently, was designed to further explore these characteristics and to evaluate more precisely the nature of each of these compartments.

Broadbent (1958) was one of the first to emphasize that memory was more than just the attaching of a response to a stimulus, and he proposed that several stages of processing probably intervened between the reception of information and an individual's permanent storage of that material. During the initial stage, he felt that certain stimuli in the total environment were chosen to be remembered. Then, because our capacity to process information was severely limited during an intermediate stage, some of this selected material still became lost before it could be processed in our permanent long-term memory (LTM). The limitation in our ability to take in information became an area of intense investigation starting with Sperling's (1960) demonstration that more can be taken in than used due to an extremely high rate of decay during storage of material in this stage of processing. This area of research became known as the study of sensory memory, sometimes also called iconic memory (IM) when the material was presented visually (Neisser, 1967), echoic memory when presented aurally (also Neisser), and occasionally preacoustic storage (Crowder & Morton, 1969) when its characteristics became more well-defined. The limitations on our ability to retain selected information to await further processing has also been highly researched primarily using a procedure introduced by Brown (1958) and the Petersons (1959) called the distractor technique. Basically, this procedure seeks to prevent rehearsal and further processing of an item after its presentation, until such time as retrieval is desired. Other similar techniques have also been used, but prevention of rehearsal and further processing remains the primary requisite of each (see Conrad, 1964; Waugh & Norman, 1965). This area of research has generally been called short-term memory (STM), though it, too, has had other labels.

The characteristics of long-term memory, the final memory stage in Broadbent's theorizing, had been investigated for some time prior to the late fifties but always from the vantage point of attempting to determine what variables prevented, or interfered with, retrieval from this storehouse of information. Interestingly enough, this attitude prevailed during most of the sixties as investigations of LTM continued to study the types of material most likely to prevent retrieval of the given information. Most research concluded that the major contributor to retrieval of verbal material from LTM was interference and not decay. Furthermore, this interference was of a semantic nature with the rule of thumb being that the more closely related semantically the desired item was to the interference, the less likely it would be retrieved (Adams, 1967).

Thus, at the beginning of the sixties at least three areas of research within memory existed, with most theories attempting to describe the properties of each of the three stores or stages (see Atkinson & Shiffrin, 1967; Broadbent, 1958; Murdock, 1967; Waugh & Norman, 1965). Most of these theories concluded (Cermak, 1972) that sensory memory was extremely limited and very subject to decay, while STM was limited to seven plus or minus two items being continuously recirculated and was subject to an interaction of decay and interference (primarily of an acoustic nature); and finally, LTM was unlimited and subject only to the effects of semantic interference.

The second major influence which changed the style of doing research in the area of memory is even more recent, beginning to emerge only after the publication of Neisser's (1967) *Cognitive Psychology* text. This change involved an increased emphasis on the role of the individual in controlling his own memorization process. This change in emphasis was stimulated by Atkinson and Shiffrin's (1967) inclusion of control processes in their model of memory (which structurally retained the three types of memory), and it had become a full-blown trend in the early seventies with the publication of Melton and Martin's (1972) volume on *Coding Processes, in Human Memory*, Tulving and Donaldson's (1972) *Organization of Memory*, and Craik and Lockhart's (1972) "Levels of Processing" framework for performing memory research. Gradually, the emphasis of memory research shifted from studying the characteristics of memory stores to studying the nature of the individual's role during information processing. Rather than investigating stages of memory, researchers now ask questions concerning how an individual analyzes and processes new information on the basis of the characteristics of the material, the length of the retention period, and the nature of the task. It is now realized that the individual has a great deal of control over this process and that his own expectations in large part determine how he will process the material and ultimately the probability that it will be recalled.

LEVELS OF PROCESSING

Melton (1963) was actually one of the first to suggest that memory need not be compartmentalized, but rather might be thought of as existing on a continuum in which retrieval probability is simply a function of the amount and type of interference present during recall. However, it was not until nearly a decade later that Cermak (1972) and Craik and Lockhart (1972) again pointed research in this direction. Craik and Lockhart emphasized that the type of interference that might at any one time be effective in preventing retrieval was largely dependent upon the way in which the to-be-recalled item itself was represented in memory. Phonemic interference would effectively block only material represented on the basis of its phonemic features, while not effectively preventing retrieval of semantically represented traces. The reverse would also be true, in that semantic interference would not prevent retrieval of phonemically represented material but would interfere with retrieval of semantically encoded information. Thus, Melton's original argument was modified to read that retrieval was a function of the amount and "level" (or similarity) of interference present during recall.

Craik and Lockhart (1972) went on to suggest that the adequacy of an item's representation in memory, quite apart from its probability of recall in the face of interference, is a direct function of the level of analysis performed upon that item during its presentation. Analysis of an item's semantic features ensures more effective storage and consequently a more durable representation in memory than does analysis of its phonemic features. Phonemic analysis, in turn, provides a longer lasting representation than does physical analysis. This conceptualization of a hierarchy of processing stages was referred to by Craik and Lockhart as "depth of processing," where greater "depth" implied a greater degree of semantic or cognitive analysis.

Based on this theory, memory could be viewed as being a sort of by-product of the extent, or depth, to which an item was analyzed. The greater the extent of analysis, the longer lasting and stronger the memory trace produced by it. The probability of retrieval was still felt to be dependent upon the number of similarly encoded (i.e., analyzed and stored) traces in memory, but the stronger a trace, the greater its chances of being present and able to overcome this interference.

It was already known that the more types of analysis performed upon a particular item of information, the more elaborate would be its encoding (Tulving & Madigan, 1970), but Craik and Lockhart (1972) next hypothesized that certain analytic stages had to precede others. They felt that the physical or sensory features of information such as its lines and angles, brightness, pitch or loudness probably preceded stages concerned with pattern recognition, auditory matching or extraction of meaning. At least these preliminary stages seemed to be completed prior to the completion of more cognitive stages as evidenced by the work of Posner and his associates (Posner, Boies, Eichelman, & Taylor, 1969; Posner & Mitchell, 1967). The initiation of the later stages of analysis seemed to await completion of the preliminaries; however, there is now some evidence to suggest that we begin deep levels of analysis even before completing logically prior analyses (Macnamara, 1972; Savin & Bever, 1970). Thus, differences in elaborative coding need not necessarily exist in a hierarchy, but might be better described as being a differential spread of encoding. However, the notion of depth still provides a good description of the type of encoding ultimately performed on a particular item, regardless of the path followed in attaining that analysis. Semantic analyses seem to give rise to more permanent traces than do phonemic analyses.

Memory was thus viewed as being a continuum of processing, from the transient products of sensory analyses to the highly durable products of semantic-associative operations. However, Craik and Lockhart pointed out that there is a second way in which stimuli can be retained. Retention can occur through the continual recirculation of information at any one level of processing. This type of processing, which they called maintenance processing, simply repeats the analyses already carried out and, although it does keep the item active in memory and available for recall, Craik and Lockhart proposed that the process did nothing to strengthen the item's memory representation. This state of affairs was contrasted with elaborative processing which involved deeper analyses of the item, thus improving its later retrieval probability through a strengthening of its representation. To the extent that a subject utilized elaborative processing, total study time improved retention; but when he relied upon maintenance processing, increased time did not appear to add to the strengthening of an item in memory (see also Cooper & Pantle, 1967; Stoff & Eagle, 1971).

SUPPORTING EVIDENCE

Naturally, there was some evidence in existence at the time these notions were first formulated which did, in part, substantiate the theoretical implications of "levels of processing." Most of these experiments systematically studied retention following different orienting tasks. For instance, Hyde and Jenkins (1969) and Johnston and Jenkins (1971) had shown that free recall of a list of highly associated words was superior when the subjects engaged in an orienting task which required the use of the words as semantic units compared to when they were required to treat each word structurally (checking for certain letters in the word). Bobrow and Bower (1969) and Rosenberg and Schiller (1971) showed that recall after an orienting task that required processing sentences to a semantic level exceeded that of recall of the same sentences when they were processed nonsemantically.

Using a somewhat different paradigm, H. G. Shulman (1971) had subjects scan a list of words for targets defined either structurally (such as words containing the letter A) or semantically (such as words denoting living things). Then, after the scanning task, subjects were given an unexpected recognition test. It was discovered that semantically defined target conditions produced better recognition performance than did the structurally defined conditions.

On a more rudimentary level, Moray (1959) showed that unanalyzed words presented in the unattended channel during a dichotic listening task were not subsequently recognized on a memory test. Neisser (1964) found that nontarget items in a visual search left no recognizable traces. Turvey (1967) found that repeated slides in a Sperling-type task were never recognized as repeats. This latter task also lent credibility to the hypothesis that trace strengthening does not occur when the same level of analysis is repeated (maintenance processing). No matter how often the slide occurred in Turvey's experiment, the subject still did not recognize it as having occurred previously.

Similar evidence that same-level processing does not increase durability of a trace came from Norman (1969), who found that repetition of unattended information during dichotic listening did not lead to improved memory for that material. Also, Tulving (1966) demonstrated similarly that repetition without intention to learn does not facilitate learning, and Glanzer and Meinzer (1967) demonstrated that overt repetition of items during free recall learning is a less effective strategy than that normally used by subjects (i.e., involving organization of list items in memory). Thus, whether or not rehearsal strengthens the trace or merely postpones forgetting seemed to depend entirely upon what the subject did during rehearsal. If he persisted in processing it at the same level, then forgetting was simply delayed; but if he performed deeper analyses on the material, then the trace was increasingly strengthened.

SUBSEQUENT RESEARCH

Since the introduction of the term "levels of processing" by Craik and Lockhart in 1972, an enormous amount of research has been generated. The Craik and Lockhart paper has been cited in well over 100 subsequent articles, and many later theoretical accounts have been influenced by levels-of-processing notions. The types of research that have been performed within this framework have been quite varied, but can be subsumed to some extent under four major categories: effects of differential encoding instructions, role of encoding time, rates of decay of levels, and nonverbal levels of analysis.

Effects Of Differential Encoding Instructions

It is true that experiments in this area were performed prior to the introduction of "levels" and, as just pointed out, were instrumental in the formation of the theory. However, the publication of the theory did much to stimulate highly productive research in this area, by providing a rationale and framework within which such explorations could flourish. In 1973, Hyde found that semantic orienting tasks produced incidental levels of recall that were as high as those found for a group instructed to intentionally learn the list, while nonsemantic orienting tasks produced lesser recall. Thus, incidental learning could be made to be as productive as intentional learning when the orienting task is appropriately semantic. Furthermore, the effect of a second variable, difficulty of the orienting task, had no effect on recall outcomes. These results were confirmed in another series of experiments by Till and Jenkins (1973), Walsh and Jenkins (1973), and Hyde and Jenkins (1973), as well as by Mondani, Pellegrino, and Battig (1973), Jacoby and

Goolkasian (1973), Till, Diehl, and Jenkins (1975), and Epstein, Johnson, and Phillips (1975).

Elias and Perfetti (1973) extended the results by showing that instructions to produce synonyms of words produced superior incidental recall of the words compared to instructions to form associates, which in turn exceeded a straight intentional learning condition, which in its turn exceeded recall of a group instructed to produce rhymes of the key words. Frase and Kamman (1974) found that answering specific questions (Is this word a vegetable?) produced superior recall to general questions (Is this word a type of food?). A. Schulman (1974) discovered that congruous semantic orientations (Is a bubble a sphere?) led to better retention than noncongruous questions (Is a chapter slippery?). Levy and Craik (1975) found that when subjects could be convinced to encode two codes for a word, recall was superior to the retention of either code alone. Finally, instructions to use a nonverbal level of analysis (commonly referred to as imagery) lead to better retention of words than did phonemic analysis (Paivio, 1971; Sheehan, 1971).

Role Of Encoding Time

Recently a very important modification of the differential encoding instructions paradigm has been made, with results that far exceeded even the original theory's expectations. H. G. Shulman (1971) had originally found that it took more time for subjects to make semantic comparisons of word pairs than it did to make phonemic comparisons, and that retention of the semantically analyzed words exceeded retention of the phonemic. Gardiner (1974) replicated this result and added the finding that the length of the retention interval did not interact with the type of processing. In other words, even for short intervals (such as those used in STM tasks), semantic analysis was superior.

The most extensive investigation within this area, and most recent, also revealed the most dramatic effect. Craik and Tulving (1975) discovered that the duration of analysis did not necessarily correlate with the probability of later retrieval. Prior to this finding, it had been thought that semantic analysis led to greater recall because, in taking longer to perform, the item was receiving more attention by the subject. However, Craik and Tulving presented an instance in which visual analysis instructions (e.g., asking the subject to respond to the question "Does the following word have this pattern of consonants and vowels—CCVVC?") took much longer to analyze than did a semantic analysis ("Does the following word fit into this sentence—The man threw the ball into the————?"). Yet, subjects still retained the semantically analyzed words better than the words analyzed on a physical level. Thus, depth of encoding, and not encoding time, was demonstrated as the primary factor associated with later retrieval.

Decay Of Levels

Given the hypothesis that deeper levels of encoding seemed to produce longer lasting memory traces, it was reasonable to attempt to trace the "decay" rate of information encoded along these different dimensions. An early investigation by Bregman (1968) found no differences in rate of decay for these two types of encoding. However, in his investigation the subjects were always aware that they would be asked to recall each word at the end of the list and therefore they may have optimized their probability of recall by analyzing the words in the list beyond the level desired by the researcher.

A later attempt to study the same effect of differential decay functions for phonemic and semantic analyses, by Jacoby (1974), attempted to correct for this potential contamination. Jacoby developed a procedure which he called the "looking-back" technique, in which the subject looked at a list of words with instructions to detect instances in which words shared particular features with preceding words. Decay of feature representation was then determined by changes in detection as a function of the number of intervening words. Despite these changes, Jacoby also found no differences in rate of feature-retention loss for the different levels of analysis. However, as Cermak and Youtz (1974) pointed out, this may have been because his rhyming words often looked alike (e.g., "rock" and "dock"), and thus visual presentation may have aided the phonemic task.

To correct this problem, Cermak and Youtz (1976) first presented the material aurally and then, in a later experiment, presented it visually, taking care that rhyming words did not also look alike (e.g., "news," "lose"). In both cases, they found that detection on the basis of phonemic features dissipated faster across intervening items than did semantic features, which included detection of category inclusion. That this differential feature loss probably represented a susceptibility to interference rather than to pure decay was then demonstrated in a subsequent experiment by Cermak, Youtz, and Onifer (1976), in which time and number of intervening items were parametrically manipulated within one investigation. From this it now appears that the superior retention of semantically analyzed information is largely a function of its being less susceptible to the effects of interference from other semantically analyzed information than phonemic analyses are to interference from other phonemic analyses.

Nonverbal Levels Of Analysis

To date, little has been done in the area of levels of processing of nonverbal material. What has been done has largely involved the retention of pictorial material. For instance, both Bower and Karlin (1974) and Warrington and Ackroyd (1975) varied the depth of processing of faces by having subjects either indicate the sex of the photographed face (a low level of analysis) or determine whether or not they liked the face or felt the person looked honest. Recognition was found to be greater for pictures judged for likableness or honesty than for pictures judged for sex. Later, Bower, Karlin, and Dueck (1975) found that people remember nonsensical pictures (doodles) better when they comprehend them than when they do not.

Bartram (1974) has suggested that at least three levels of encoding exist for pictures, at least for complex pictures, and interestingly enough, one of these is verbal. They are a visual code not unlike imagery, a nonverbal semantic code similar to grouping by category, and a name code. A similar conclusion was reached by Nelson and Reed (1975), who also found some verbal labeling in the retention of pictures. Thus, while the few preliminary studies seem to indicate that a levels-of-processing approach may provide a viable framework within which to study nonverbal retention, none has as yet definitively determined what processes are involved. The possible involvement of a verbal code does, however, warrant a great deal more investigation.

CONTROVERSIAL ISSUES

The levels-of-processing framework has not existed without controversy during its short lifespan. Indeed the notion of levels has served not only to stimulate and direct an enormous amount of research, but it has also provided an excellent foil against which others have been able to pit their own theories. There are at least two areas of research within which these latter theorists have been able to supply data forcing revision of the original "levels" formulation. The first of these areas concerns the relationship of the retention test to the original learning situation. The second questions the basic kernel of the theory that semantic encoding necessarily leads to better retention than phonemic encoding, which, in turn, leads to better retention than physical feature encoding.

Tulving (Thompson and Tulving, 1970; Tulving, 1978) was among the first to propose that there is an interaction between the encoding operations present at input and the circumstances (i.e., cues) present at retrieval. He proposed that the "level" of encoding is not as important as the degree of similarity between input and output cues. In other words, semantic encoding will only be useful if retrieval exists in the presence of those same semantic cues. If it does not, then the semantic encoding might actually prove debilitating, as in the case where a subject is cued at retrieval by a phonemic cue when originally the word was encoded in the presence of a category cue. Under these retrieval conditions, having encoded the word phonemically should produce a higher potential for retrieval than having encoded it semantically. Thomson and Tulving (1970) showed this to be true in a modified paired-associate (P–A) task, at least for weak versus strong associative cues. But, interestingly enough, it was Craik himself (Fisher & Craik, 1977) who provided the most direct test within the now-standard "levels" paradigm. He showed that retention levels were highest when the same type of information was used as a cue for a word at retrieval as had been used as the question for analysis at input. Thus, rhyme cues were more effective than semantic cues when the subject had been asked whether or not a word at input rhymed with another word. However, Fisher and Craik also found that rhyme encoding followed by rhyme cueing gave lower levels of performance than did semantic encoding followed by semantic cueing. Further, they found that this advantage of semantic encoding over phonemic encoding increased as the retrieval cue was made more and more compatible with the encoded trace. Thus, they proposed that the levels-of-processing notion had to be coupled with encoding specificity in order to explain results of this type; but "levels of processing" was still the dominant determiner of probability of retrieval. Tulving (1978) would argue this point, but, to date, it appears to be mostly a matter of theoretical emphasis, as paradigms can be devised to favor either alternative.

Other investigators who seem to favor the encoding specificity hypothesis are Bransford and Franks (Bransford, Franks, Morris, & Stein, 1978; Bransford, McCarrell, Franks, & Nitsch, 1977). In a series of experiments, these authors found that when the retention test is semantic, semantic learning leads to better performance than phonemic learning; but when the retention test is phonemic, a rhyming task performed during learning leads to better retention than a semantic task. Furthermore, subjects given orthographic coding (deciding whether or not a particular letter of a word is capitalized) perform better than those receiving semantic coding on a word recognition task when the task is to decide if the word has the same or a different letter capitalized. Naturally, when the recognition task involves a semantic task, semantic encoding is superior. Over all their tasks, however, Bransford and colleagues did find somewhat better retention on semantic tasks than on the others, but they suggested that this is because subjects have more experience with this type of task, and they did not attribute this superiority to anything inherent in the nature of semantic encoding per se.

Similarly, Nelson (1978) reports that interference occurs during the P–A learning when words share similar letters between lists. This was an especially powerful effect when the letters shared were the ones in the initial positions. This effect became most dramatic when long time intervals existed between lists containing these similar words for, on the basis of the "levels" framework, such orthographic analysis should dissipate rapidly. Further evidence for retention of such orthographic properties one year later comes from the work of Kolers (1975, 1978). He found the subjects could remember whether a sentence they had read had been printed upside down or not. Also, as Kolers (1978) points out, people do often remember where on a page they have read something and even remember often the color of the binding of a particular book. All of these remembrances are incidental to our semantic understanding and retention of the material.

From these studies one is forced to conclude both that:

1. "Depth" of processing does not necessarily lead to the optimum performance, as the nature of the retention task may interact with the probability of retrieval.
2. "Lower" levels of analysis do not necessarily enjoy shorter life spans than the higher levels of analysis.

These two modifications have been acknowledged by Craik (1979) in his analysis of the continuing development of the levels-of-processing framework, and they have now been partially absorbed into the processing framework.

APPLICATION OF THE LEVELS-OF-PROCESSING FRAMEWORK TO THE STUDY OF MEMORY DISORDERS

During the last few years, the levels-of-processing research framework has been applied to the study of amnesia, especially that seen in alcoholic Korsakoff patients. These patients have memory deficits in what has traditionally been called long-term memory as well as in short-term, and even sensory, memory. The only information that seems to be available to these patients is that which probably was learned prior to the onset of their brain dysfunction. Since they are so unable to learn and remember new information, it could be asked whether an information-processing deficit might not account, at least in part, for their memory disorder.

One of the first indications that this approach might prove viable came in a study reported by Cermak and Butters (1972), in which patients were asked to remember an eight-item list composed of two words from each of four taxonomic categories. Following the reading of the list, the patients were simply asked to recall the items in any order (free-recall condition), and the number of words they correctly recalled was recorded. The patients were then told they would receive a second list of eight words and, since the words were drawn from specific categories, they would be asked to recall the words category by category when so prompted by the experimenter. Patients were always informed what these categories would be prior to the reading of the list. While cueing by category in this manner did improve the control subjects' recall, the Korsakoff patients actually retrieved fewer words under cued recall than they did under free recall. This suggested the possibility that Korsakoff patients had not employed a semantic encoding strategy to the same extent as had the controls. Consequently, while the Korsakoff patients were able to recall the words on a rote basis in the free-recall condition, their performance deteriorated when they were called upon to recall the words on the basis of the semantic meaning of each word.

Further support for the hypothesis that Korsakoff patients tend to rely on less sophisticated analytic strategies than do normals came in a study based on Underwood's (1965) false recognition test. In this task, a 60-word stimulus list was shown to the patient at the rate of one word every 2 sec. The patient's task was to detect any repetitions presented within the list. While the list actually contained repetitions, it also contained several words that are acoustically identical (homonyms such as *bear* and *bare*), highly associated *(table* and *chair),* or synonymous *(robber* and *thief).* Whenever the patient indicated that a homonym, an associate, or a synonym was a repetition, it was scored as a false recognition. If the patient preferred to encode only the acoustic dimension of the words, then he would have falsely recognized some of the homonyms as being repetitions. Associative false recognitions would have indicated that an associative level of encoding had been achieved, and synonym false recognition would have indicated that a still more sophisticated level of encoding had been accomplished. Thus, the type of errors made by the Korsakoff patients were indicative of the extent to which they normally encoded information. The results showed that the Korsakoff patients falsely recognized more homonyms and associates as being repetitions than did the controls. On the other hand, they made as many correct identifications as the controls and made no more synonym or neutral-word false recognitions. These results suggested that the Korsakoff patients were encoding the words on acoustic and associative dimensions but were not encoding the semantic dimensions of the words to the extent that would allow the rejection of acoustically identical or highly associated words.

Further evidence for the existence of this phenomena was also provided by Cermak and Moreines (1976), employing a somewhat similar paradigm, but one in which features were supposed to be detected rather than "falsely" recognized. This test, which was first introduced by Cermak and Youtz (1974), requires that the patient listen to a list of words read at a constant rate and indicate when a word is repeated (repetition condition), or when a word rhymes with a previous word (phonemic condition) or when a word belongs to the same category as a preceding word (semantic condition). The patient does not have to indicate which previous word was the match, nor does he have to explain the rationale for his choice. All he has to do is indicate when the target word occurs. Memory for the particular features is then monitored by plotting the number of correct choices as a function of the number of words intervening between the initial and probe members of each pair.

The results revealed that Korsakoff patients consistently performed worse than the normals on the semantic task, and approximately the same as normals on all other tasks except where four items intervened during the phonemic task. This suggests that while Korsakoff patients may be capable of retaining verbal information in working memory on the basis of a phonemic code, they suffer when the capacity of this system is exceeded or when they are asked to make semantic judgments based on this code. This finding was later confirmed by a series of experiments using the distractor technique, to which we shall now turn.

While the above studies have all shown an impairment in Korsakoff patients' encoding strategies, the relationship between this deficit and their extreme sensitivity to the effect of interference with consequent failures in retrieval ability remains unspecified. At least two interactions between interference and encoding seemed plausible: (1) The two deficits could be totally independent of one another and may represent two separate deficits in the total alcoholic Korsakoff syndrome; or (2) the patients' increased sensitivity to interference may be a result of their lack of analysis of the semantic dimensions of information. To test this latter hypothesis, Wickens' (1970) technique of release from proactive inhibition (PI) was adapted for use with alcoholic Korsakoff patients (Cermak, Butters, & Moreines, 1974). Using a modification of the Peterson distractor technique, Wickens had discovered that the PI generated by the presentation of material from the same class of information on several consecutive trials can be released by the introduction of material from a new class of information. This finding was interpreted to mean that the extent of interference during STM recall is largely a function of the subject's ability to differentiate words in memory on the basis of their semantic features. It was predicted that if the Korsakoff patients' increased sensitivity to interference is related to their lack of semantic encoding, then the amount of PI release demonstrated by these patients should vary with the encoding requirements of the verbal materials. It was anticipated that Korsakoff patients would demonstrate normal PI release when the verbal materials involved only rudimentary categorizations (e.g., letters versus numbers), but when the stimulus materials involved more abstract semantic differences (e.g., taxonomic differences such as animals versus vegetables), the Korsakoff patients would show far less PI release. When the letter–number shift occurred on the fifth trial (experimental condition), the Korsakoff patients did show a complete release from PI. Their recall performance on the fifth trial of the experimental condition was just as good as their performance on the first trial of the same condition. When different taxonomic (animal–vegetable) categories were used, the alcoholic Korsakoff patients did not improve on shift trial.

The next question that was logical to ask was whether or not improved semantic processing would necessarily lead to improvements in Korsakoffs' retention. The paradigm chosen for this investigation was the precise one described by Craik and Tulving (1975). In this procedure, a patient's analysis of incoming information is directed by asking either an orthographic (e.g., is this word printed in capital letters), phonemic (e.g., does this word rhyme with "ring"), or semantic (e.g., does this word fit into the sentence "The man stooped down and picked up the ——") question. The rationale was that the higher the level of analysis required to answer, the greater the probability the item would later be recognized as having been presented. The results showed that this was true for the amnesic patients in a pattern similar to, but still far below, normal. Also, the effect only occurred with very short lists of words (12 items) and was easily washed out when many words (48) were presented. Thus, it was concluded that Korsakoff patients' retention can be somewhat affected by forcing them to analyze material beyond their apparently preferred phonemic level of operation.

Similar results have been demonstrated on a cued-recall task following essentially the same procedure, except that the patients were cued with either the same question used at input or one on a different level (see Fisher & Craik, 1977, for the procedure). The only beneficial condition for the Korsakoffs was when a semantic cue was given at both input and output suggesting an encoding specificity interpretation for at least that level of processing. In order to follow this notion further, the Thomson and Tulving (1970) procedure was adopted for use with Korsakoff patients.

In this procedure, the patients were given a list of 12 word pairs consisting of a capitalized to-be-remembered (TBR) word and an associated word printed in lower case letters above it. The patient was told to memorize each TBR word but to pay attention as well to the small related word as it might help him remember the TBR word. After the words were presented, the patient was given a sheet with the 12 cue words printed on it and a blank next to each and was told to write down the associated TBR words. This procedure was repeated five times, and five different input–output relationships were investigated:

1. S–S, in which a strongly associated cue word occurred at input and again at output.
2. W–W, in which the same weakly associated cue word occurred at input and output.
3. S–W, in which a strong associate was presented at input, but a weak associate at output.
4. W–S, in which a weak associate was present at input, but a strong one at output.
5. O–O, in which no cues were given.

A different list of TBR words was given for each condition and a condition was constant within a list.

The results shown in Table 16.1 depict an extremely interesting result. Unlike normals, Korsakoff patients were not so much affected by encoding specificity (as evidenced by the poor W–W recall) as they were by the presence

TABLE 16.1
Percentage of Target Words Correctly Recalled

Patient Group	S–S	W–W	W–S	O–O	S–W
Korsakoff	57	14	33	29	7
Alcoholic	91	75	63	57	24

of a strong associate at retrieval. That this was most obvious in the S–S condition argues for some retention of the encoding conditions, but apparently only when it reinforces something already existent in semantic memory (see also Cermak, Reale, & Baker, 1978), not when a new associate is formed. Indeed, W–W is worse than nothing at all, and W–S exceeds W–W, demonstrating the potential of high-associate elicitation of TBR words (but again no better than O–O).

From this one could conlcude that Korsakoff patients' retention can be improved by providing semantic contexts, but only if the semantic context at input and output is identical and does not represent "new or creative learning." That is to say, if the semantic context simply reestablishes remote learning, it may be facilitory; but when it necessitates cognitively reorganizing one's semantic network for purposes of retaining an episodic event, the outcome is abysmal.

APPLICATION TO MEMORY
AND THE AGING PROCESS

This same cognitive sluggishness which is seen in the extent to which Korsakoff patients spontaneously analyze, organize, and rehearse verbal input, as reflected throughout this attempt to apply information-processing paradigms to their disorder, may also prove to be a factor in the aging process relative to the loss of memorial skills. Naturally not precisely the same tests have to be given, as our line of reasoning in choosing paradigms has not followed a straight course. However, application of the research strategies suggested by the processing framework might well prove profitable to the study of memory and the aging brain, as it has for amnesia due to brain damage. In particular, it would seem that the relationship between learning and retentive ability ought to be fully investigated. It must be determined whether or not the aged tend increasingly to rely on, and profit from, the utilization of phonemic analysis–or whether it is the case that they profit as much as do younger subjects from semantic appropriate processing. If they do not do the latter, then it must be asked whether this is due to an inability to do so or to a simple failure to spontaneously incorporate such analysis as part of their memorizing experience. Knowledge gained in these areas might be beneficial in future planning of memory-retaining procedures for the elderly.

REFERENCES

Adams, J. A. *Human memory.* New York: Mc Graw-Hill, 1967.

Atkinson, R. C., & Shiffrin, R. M. *Human memory: A proposed system and its control processes.* Technical Report No. 110, Stanford University, 1967.

Bartram, D. J. The role of visual and semantic codes in object naming. *Cognitive Psychology,* 1974, *6,* 325-356.

Bobrow, S. A., & Bower, G. H. Comprehension and recall of sentences. *Journal of Experimental Psychology,* 1969, *80,* 455-461.

Bower, G. H., & Karlin, M. B. Depth of processing pictures of faces and recognition memory. *Journal of Experimental Psychology,* 1974, *103,* 751-757.

Bower, G. H., Karlin, M. B., & Dueck. A. Comprehension and memory for pictures. *Memory and Cognition,* 1975, *3,* 216-220.

Bransford, J. D., Franks, J. J., Morris, C. D., & Stein, B. S. Some general constraints on learning and memory research. In L. S. Cermak & F. I. M. Craik (Eds.), *Levels of processing in human memory.* Hillsdale, N.J.: Lawrence Erlbaum Associates, 1979.

Bransford, J. D., McCarrell, N. S., Franks, J. J., & Nitsch, K. E. Toward unexplaining memory. In R. E. Shaw & J. D. Bransford (Eds.), *Perceiving, acting and knowing: Toward an ecological psychology.* Hillsdale, N.J.: Lawrence Erlbaum Associates, 1977.

Bregman, A. S. Forgetting curves with semantic, phonetic, graphic, and contiguity cues. *Journal of Experimental Psychology,* 1968, *78,* 539-546.

Broadbent, D. E. A mechanical model for human attention and immediate memory. *Psychological Review,* 1957, *64,* 205-215.

Broadbent, D. E. *Perception and communication.* New York: Pergamon, 1958.

Brown, J. Some tests of the decay theory of immediate memory. *Quarterly Journal of Experimental Psychology,* 1958, *10,* 12-21.

Cermak, L. S. *Human memory: Research and theory.* New York: Ronald Press, 1972.

Cermak, L. S., & Butters, N. The role of interference and encoding in the short-term memory deficits of Korsakoff patients. *Neuropsychologia,* 1972, *10,* 89-96.

Cermak, L. S., Butters, N., & Moreines, J. Some analyses of the verbal encoding deficit of alcoholic Korsakoff patients. *Brain and Language,* 1974, *1,* 141-150.

Cermak, L. S., & Moreines, J. Verbal retention deficits in aphasic and amnesic patients. *Brain and Language,* 1976, *3,* 16-27.

Cermak, L. S., Reale, L., & Baker, E. Alcoholic Korsakoff patients' retrieval from semantic memory. *Brain and Language,* 1978, *5,* 215-226.

Cermak, L. S., & Youtz, C. *Differential resistance to interference of acoustic and semantic encoding.* Presented at the Psychonomic Society Convention, Boston, November 1974.

Cermak, L. S., & Youtz, C. Retention of phonemic and semantic features of words. *Memory and Cognition,* 1976, *4,* 172-175.

Cermak, L. S., Youtz, C., & Onifer, S. *Retention of semantic and phonemic features of words.* Presented at the Psychonomic Society Convention, St. Louis, November 1976.

Conrad, R. Acoustic confusions in immediate memory. *British Journal of Psychology,* 1964, *55,* 75-84.

Cooper, E. H., & Pantle, A. J. The total-time hypothesis in verbal learning. *Psychological Bulletin,* 1967, *68,* 221-234.

Craik, F. I. M. Conclusions and comments. In L. S. Cermak & F. I. M. Craik, (Eds.), *Levels of processing in human memory.* Hillsdale, N.J.: Lawrence Erlbaum Associates, 1979.

Craik, F. I. M., & Lockhart, R. S. Levels of processing: A framework for memory research. *Journal of Verbal Learning and Verbal Behavior,* 1972, *11,* 671-684.

Craik, F. I. M., & Tulving, E. Depth of processing and the retention of words in episodic memory. *Journal of Experimental Psychology: General,* 1975, *104,* 268-294.

Crowder, R. G., & Morton, J. Precategorical acoustic storage. *Perception and Psychophysics,* 1969, *5,* 365-373.

Elias, C. S., & Perfetti, C. A. Encoding task and recognition memory: The importance of semantic encoding. *Journal of Experimental Psychology,* 1973, *99,* 151-156.

Epstein, M. C., Johnson, S. J., & Phillips, W. D. Recall of related and unrelated word pairs as a function of processing level. *Journal of Experimental Psychology: Human Learning and Memory,* 1975, *104,* 149-152.

Fisher, R. P., & Craik, F. I. M. The interaction between encoding and retrieval operations in cued recall. *Journal of Experimental Psychology: Human Memory and Learning,* 1977, *3,* 701-711.

Frase, L. T., & Kamman, R. Effects of search criterion upon unanticipated free recall of categorically related words. *Memory and Cognition,* 1974, *2,* 181-184.

Gardiner, J. M. Levels of processing in word recognition and subsequent free recall. *Journal of Experimental Psychology,* 1974, *102,* 101-105.

Glanzer, M., & Meinzer, A. The effects of intralist activity on free recall. *Journal of Verbal Learning and Verbal Behavior,* 1967, *6,* 928-935.

Hyde, T. S. Differential effects of effort and type of orienting task on recall and organization of highly associated words. *Journal of Experimental Psychology,* 1973, *79,* 111-133.

Hyde, T. S., & Jenkins, J. J. Differential effects of incidental tasks on the organization of highly associated words. *Journal of Experimental Psychology,* 1969, *82,* 472-481.

Hyde, T. S., & Jenkins, J. J. Recall for words as a function of semantic, graphic, and syntactic orienting tasks. *Journal of Verbal Learning and Verbal Behavior,* 1973, *12,* 471-480.

Jacoby, L. L. The role of mental contiguity in memory: Registration and retrieval effects. *Journal of Verbal Learning and Verbal Behavior,* 1974, *13,* 483-495.

Jacoby, L. L., & Goolkasian, P. Semantic versus acoustic coding: Retention and condition of organization. *Journal of Verbal Learning and Verbal Behavior,* 1973, *2,* 324-333.

Johnston, C. D., & Jenkins, J. J. Two more incidental tasks that differentially affect associative clustering in recall. *Journal of Experimental Psychology,* 1971, *89,* 92-95.

Kolers, P. A. Specificity of operations in sentence recognition. *Cognitive Psychology,* 1975, *7,* 289-306.

Kolers, P. A. A pattern analyzing basis of recognition. In L. S. Cermak & F. I. M. Craik (Eds.), *Levels of processing in human memory.* Hillsdale, N.J.: Lawrence Erlbaum Associates, 1979.

Levy, B. A., & Craik F. I. M. The co-ordination of codes in short-term retention. *Quarterly Journal of Experimental Psychology,* 1975, *27,* 33-45.

Macnamara, J. Cognitive basis of language learning in infants. *Psychological Review,* 1972, *79,* 1-13.

Melton, A. W. Implications of short-term memory for a general theory of memory. *Journal of Verbal Learning and Verbal Behavior,* 1963, *2,* 1-21.

Melton, A. W., & Martin, E. *Coding processes in human memory.* New York: Winsten-Wiley, 1972.

Mondani, M. S., Pellegrino, J. S., & Battig, W. F. Free and cued recall as a function of different levels of word processing. *Journal of Experimental Psychology,* 1973, *101,* 324-329.

Moray, N. Attention in dichotic listening: Affective cues and the influence of instructions. *Quarterly Journal of Experimental Psychology,* 1959, *11,* 56-60.

Murdock, B. B., Jr. Recent developments in short-term memory. *British Journal of Psychology,* 1967, *58,* 421-433.

Neisser, U. Visual search. *Scientific American,* 1964, *210,* 94-102.

Neisser, U. *Cognitive psychology.* New York: Appleton-Century-Crofts, 1967.

Nelson, D. C. Remembering pictures and words: Appearance, significance, and name. In L. S. Cermak & F. I. M. Craik (Eds.), *Levels of processing in human memory.* Hillsdale, N.J.: Lawrence Erlbaum Associates, 1979.

Nelson, D. L., & Reed, V. S. *On the nature of pictorial encoding: A levels-of-processing analysis.* Presented at the Psychonomic Society Convention, Denver, November 1975.

Norman, D. A. Memory while shadowing. *Quarterly Journal of Experimental Psychology,* 1969, *21,* 85–93.

Paivio, A. *Imagery and verbal processes.* New York: Holt, Rinehart and Winston, 1971.

Peterson, L. R., & Peterson, M. J. Short-term retention of individual verbal items. *Journal of Experimental Psychology,* 1959, *58,* 193–198.

Posner, M. I., Boies, S. J., Eichelman, W. H., & Taylor, R. L. Retention of visual and name codes of single letters. *Journal of Experimental Psychology Monographs,* 1969, *79,* (1, pt. 2).

Posner, M. I., & Mitchell, R. F. Chronometric analysis of classification. *Psychological Review,* 1967, *74,* 392–409.

Rosenberg, S., & Schiller, W. J. Semantic coding and incidental sentence recall. *Journal of Experimental Psychology,* 1971, *90,* 345–346.

Savin, H. B., & Bever, T. G. The nonperceptual reality of the phoneme. *Journal of Verbal Learning and Verbal Behavior,* 1970, *9,* 295–302.

Schulman, A. Memory for words recently classified. *Memory and Cognition,* 1974, *2,* 47–52.

Sheehan, P. W. The role of imagery in incidental learning. *British Journal of Psychology,* 1971, *62,* 235–244.

Shulman, H. G. Similarity effects in short-term memory. *Psychological Bulletin,* 1971, *75,* 399–415.

Sperling, G. The information available in brief visual presentations. *Psychological Monographs,* 1960, *74,* Whole No. 498.

Stoff, M., & Eagle, M. N. The relationship among reported strategies, presentation rate, and verbal ability and their effects on free recall learning. *Journal of Experimental Psychology,* 1971, *87,* 423–428.

Thomson, D. M., & Tulving, E. Associative encoding and retrieval: Weak and strong cues. *Journal of Experimental Psychology,* 1970, *86,* 255–262.

Till, R. E., Diehl, R. L., & Jenkins, J. J. Effects of semantic and non-semantic cued orienting on associative clustering in free recall. *Memory and Cognition,* 1975, *3,* 19–23.

Till, R. E., & Jenkins, J. J. The effects of cued orienting tasks on the free recall of words. *Journal of Verbal Learning and Verbal Behavior,* 1973, *12,* 489–498.

Tulving, E. Subjective organization and effects of repetition in multitrial free recall learning. *Journal of Verbal Learning and Verbal Behavior,* 1966, *5,* 193–197.

Tulving, E. Relation between encoding specificity and levels of processing. In L. S. Cermak & F. I. M. Craik (Eds.), *Levels of processing in human memory.* Hillsdale, N.J.: Lawrence Erlbaum Associates, 1979.

Tulving, E., & Donaldson, W. *Organization of memory.* New York: Academic Press, 1972.

Tulving, E., & Madigan, S. A. Memory and verbal learning. *Annual Review of Psychology,* 1970, *21,* 437–484.

Turvey, M. T. Repetition and the preperceptual information store. *Journal of Experimental Psychology,* 1967, *74,* 289–293.

Underwood, B. J. False recognition by implicit verbal responses. *Journal of Experimental Psychology,* 1965, *70,* 122–129.

Walsh, D. A., & Jenkins, J. J. Effects of orienting tasks on free recall in incidental learning: "Difficulty", "effort," and "process" explanations. *Journal of Verbal Learning and Verbal Behavior,* 1973, *12,* 481–488.

Warrington, E. K., & Ackroyd, C. The effect of orienting tasks on recognition memory. *Memory and Cognition,* 1975, *3,* 140–142.

Waugh, N. C., & Norman, D. A. Primary memory. *Psychological Review,* 1965, *72,* 89–104.

Wickens, D. D. Encoding categories of words: An empirical approach to meaning. *Psychological Review,* 1970, *77,* 1–15.

17

Depth of Processing or Multiple Codes: An Explanation of Age-Related Decrements in Memory

Terence Hines
Geriatric Research, Educational & Clinical Center
VA Outpatient Clinic
and Harvard Medical School

In their discussion of memory and aging, both Cermak (Chapter 16) and Waugh and Barr (Chapter 15) take a hierarchical or serial processing point of view. They propose that prior to the time that a stimulus can be processed to some relatively "deep" level (i.e., the semantic level), it must first be processed on more peripheral, or shallow, levels (i.e., the orthographic and phonetic levels). Baddeley (1978) has questioned whether or not such a hierarchical model of memory is realistic and has concluded that it is not. This chapter briefly reviews some of the evidence that argues that the presentation of a stimulus results in the simultaneous activation of the several different representations or codes of that stimulus in memory. A more complete treatment of this issue is found in Posner (1978). The implications of this view of memory activation for problems of aging and memory are then considered.

One prediction made by a serial model of memory is that a manipulation that slows judgments which can be made at a relatively shallow level of processing will slow judgments that must be made at a deeper level. If, for example, a manipulation of some characteristic of a stimulus adds 50 msec to the time for activation of some peripheral level representation, then in a serial system, activation at a deeper level will also be slowed by at least 50 msec since activation at the peripheral level must take place before activation at the deeper level. Peripheral delays will be passed on, and the activation at deeper levels will be similarly delayed. Corcoran and Besner (1975) varied the size and contrast of letters in a visual letter matching task. In this task, subjects had to decide whether two visually presented letters were the same or different. These manipulations did slow physical-identity judgments, based on what a serial view would have to consider some relatively shallow physical representation of the letters. These manipulations did not, however, slow name-level judgments in which subjects had to respond that letter pairs sharing only a common name (i.e., A–a) were the same. Since these name-level judgments must be based on some deeper level representation, storing the letters' names, according to a serial model those judgments should also be slowed by differences in size and contrast. That only physical-level matches were slowed argues that the serial model is incorrect.

Posner (1970) reported a similar finding. In one condition in this study, subjects made a speeded vowel–consonant judgment on a pair of letters. In another condition, digits were added and the task required a letter–digit judgment. In the vowel–consonant condition certain letter pairs (B–b, D–d, G–g, Q–q) resulted in longer reaction times due to the confusability of items in the set (b and d being highly confusable) than other, less confusable, pairs (F–f, H–h, M–m, R–r). However, in the letter–digit condition there was no reaction-time difference between the confusable and nonconfusable letter pairs. Posner (1970) argued that subjects did not derive the name of a letter when making the letter versus digit discrimination. Subjects can access the category information needed for the judgment without any interference from activation of the name codes of the letters. Category and name activation, therefore, proceed in parallel.

Taylor (1978) has provided additional support for the parallel model of name and category retrieval. In Taylor's (1978) experiment, subjects made a name-level judgment of two sequentially presented stimuli. Considering only the case in which the first stimulus was a letter (in some cases it could be a digit), the second stimulus was, in one condition (called condition I), always a letter and in another condition (called condition IC) always a digit. Thus, in condition IC the name and category of the stimuli were redundant variables. This was not the case in condition I. A serial model predicts that, since the name judgments could be made without processing to the deeper category level, the redundancy of name and category information in condition IC should not speed reaction time. Taylor's (1978) findings show that reaction time was faster in condition IC than in condition I, supporting a parallel model of the process of identification and categorization.

Particularly interesting evidence for the model of parallel activation of different memory codes comes from work with brain-damaged patients suffering from phonetic or "deep" dyslexia (Marshall & Newcombe, 1973). These patients show two major symptoms. First, they are unable to pronounce orthographically regular nonwords (i.e., durnt). Second, they often make semantic confusions when asked to read real words. For example, one of the patients reported by Marshall and Newcombe (1973) responded "talk" when asked to read "speak." These errors are quite common in such patients, although they will also show orthographic and phonetic errors. Marshall and Newcombe (1973) believe that the basic deficit underlying these patients' impaired performance is an inability to use grapheme and phoneme conversion rules to derive the phonetic code of letter strings. However, the parallel orthographic route to meaning is relatively unimpaired.

Two recent papers (Patterson & Marcel, 1977; Saffran & Marin, 1977) have experimentally evaluated several deep dyslexics and have confirmed Marshall and Newcombe's (1973) conclusions. Patterson and Marcel (1977) showed that their patients could repeat, although not read, pronounceable nonwords. In a lexical decision task in which subjects must decide whether a string of letters forms a real word or not, normal subjects are slowed by psuedowords, letter strings that would be pronounced like a real word according to the pronounciation rules of English, but which are spelled unlike any real word (i.e., *proon*). This slowing of reaction time to such letter strings can be attributed to the conflicting information coming from the phonetic and orthographic representations activated by these letter strings. On the one hand, the phonetic code output to some decision mechanism indicates that the stimulus is a word since it sounds just like one. The orthographic code output, however, indicates that the letter string is not a word. Unlike normal subjects, semantic dyslexics are not slowed by the presentation of pseudo-words. This finding is consistent with their lack of ability to transform graphemes to phonemes. Thus, they base their lexical decisions only on the orthographic features of the stimuli and, since pseudowords don't look like real words, they are quickly rejected. These patients can, however, perform the lexical decision task with a very respectable rate of speed and accuracy. Therefore, they must be able to access the meaning of the words either directly or via the orthographic code.

Saffran and Marin (1977) examined a single semantic dyslexic. This woman could not pronounce pseudowords, make accurate rhyming judgments when orthography was not a cue to rhyme, or recognize pseudowords as phonetically identical to their real counterpart (i.e., bote and boat). Apparently she was severely impaired in her ability to analyze phonological features represented by a string of letters. Nevertheless, she could read even such complex words as "chrysanthemum." Patterson and Marcel (1977) have found that two semantic dyslexics could perform a lexical decision task. In this task, the subjects had to judge whether or not a string of letters was a real word or not. This ability suggests that alternate pathways to meaning, not involving the phonetic code, must be intact in these patients. This suggestion is, or course, incompatible with serial models in which either or both the orthographic and phonetic codes must be activated before meaning can be retrieved.

Results from a series of recent experiments with normal subjects indicate not only that meaning can be accessed from either the phonetic or orthographic code, but that it may be accessible directly from a minimal amount of primary visual processing of the stimuli. Allport (1977) has replicated some of the results characteristic of semantic dyslexics in normals by presenting a word and then masking it. In his paradigm, subjects often report that they did not see any word at all, but when forced to guess what word was presented, make the same sort of semantic errors as do semantic dyslexics. This, then, also appears to be an instance where neither the phonetic nor the orthographic codes have been activated, yet the subject still has some awareness of the meaning of the stimuli presented.

Marcel (in press) has recently provided an additional demonstration of direct meaning access without activation of phonetic or orthographic codes. Marcel used a lexical decision task in this study. In such a task, semantic facilitation occurs when two associated words are presented one after the other. Thus, subjects are faster to respond that *doctor* is a word if they have just judged that *nurse* is a word than if they have just judged that *butter* is a word. This facilitation is the result of spreading activation in semantic memory and apparently takes place automatically, as subjects do not have to be consciously aware of the presence of the associations for the effect to occur (Fishler, 1977). In his version of the lexical decision task, Marcel (in press) had subjects make a lexical decision about a letter string that had been immediately proceded by a prime word that was either a nonassociated word, an associated word, a masked nonassociated word, or a masked associated word. In the masked conditions, subjects were unaware (consciously) that a word had been presented preceding the word they were to make the lexical deicision about. In fact, they were unable to discriminate between the masked presentation of a word and the presentation of a blank field followed by the mask. Equivalent semantic facilitation was found for both the masked and the unmasked associated prime words. Thus, even when the subjects were unaware of the presence of the masked word, its meaning was activated and that activation had the same facilitating effect on reaction time as if the word had been presented unmasked. Thus, it appears that meaning can be contacted directly without activation of either the phonetic or the orthographic codes.

The results such as those just reviewed have implications for the issue of declining memory performance in the aged. It has been suggested that this decline in memorial abilities might be due to their failure, due to lack of willingness or ability, to encode material on sufficiently "deep" (i.e., semantic) levels (Craik, 1977). Unfortunately, only two studies have examined this point, and their results conflict. Eysenck (1974) has found that older subjects benefit, but to a lesser degree than younger subjects, from having to process words to a deeper level. Smith and Winograd (1978) found that younger and older subjects received equal benefit from having to make judgments of faces that presumably required a deeper level of processing. Although different stimuli were used and there were other differences in procedure between these two studies, these differences do not seem adequate to account for the different findings.

Regardless of the theoretical position that is taken, one must at some point ask why activation of the semantic code is seemingly impaired in the elderly. Several chapters in this volume stated possible reasons for such an impairment. Waugh and Barr (Chapter 15) have contended that the major factor in age changes in memory is an overall slowing of all cognitive processes with advancing age. It was argued earlier that activation of the semantic, orthographic, and phonetic codes of a stimulus takes place in parallel. This does not imply that all these codes take the same length of time to become activated. The semantic code seems to take longer to become activated. Thus, in a letter-matching task, physical matches (i.e., A–A) based on the orthographic code can be made faster than vowel–consonant matches or name matches, both of which may require activation of semantic or name codes (Posner, 1978). Any process, like the overall slowing proposed by Waugh and Barr, which adds a constant proportion of time to all cognitive processes will add, in absolute terms, more to initially longer processes. This would result in greater slowing of the time course for activation of the semantic code. However, this position is not totally satisfactory because it ignores the important question of why all (or at least many) cognitive processes are slowed with age in the first place. This view can serve as the basis for a more complete hypothesis for any deficit of the elderly to access the semantic code. While the activation of various memory codes can take place automatically (see Posner, 1978 for a review), it appears that attention to the activated codes is necessary for the establishment of easily retrievable memories. Since activation of semantic codes takes longer than the activation of orthographic or phonetic codes, it may also require more attention or attention sustained for longer periods of time. If, as Kinsbourne (Chapter 6, this volume) suggests, older subjects do suffer from attentional impairments, then the impairment in the activation of the semantic code of an item may be the result of such activation requiring more attention from persons who have a lessened attentional capacity. It remains the task of future research to experimentally examine the question of whether older persons actually are selectively impaired in their ability to activate semantic codes of stimuli and, if such an impairment is found, whether or not it is due to attentional factors.

REFERENCES

Allport, D. On knowing the meaning of words we are unable to report: The effects of visual masking. In S. Dornic (Ed.), *Attention and performance VI.* Hillsdale, N.J.: Lawrence Erlbaum Associates, 1977.

Baddeley, A. The trouble with levels: A reexamination of Craik and Lockhart's framework for memory research. *Psychological Review,* 1978, *85,* 139–152.

Corcoran, D., & Besner, D. Application of the Posner technique to the study of size and brightness irrelevancies in letter pairs. In P. Rabbitt (Ed.), *Attention and performance V.* London: Academic Press, 1975.

Craik, F. Age differences in human memory. In J. Birren & K. Schaie (Eds.), *Handbook of the psychology of aging.* New York: Van Nostrand Reinhold Co., 1977.

Eysenck, M. Age difference in incidental learning. *Developmental Psychology,* 1974, *10,* 936–941.

Fischler, I. Associative facilitation without expectancy in a lexical decision task. *Journal of Experimental Psychology: Human Perception and Performance,* 1977, *3,* 18–26.

Marcel, T. Unconscious reading. *Cognitive Psychology,* in press.

Marshall, J., & Newcombe, F. Patterns of paralexia: A psycholinguistic approach. *Journal of Psycholinguistic Research,* 1973, *2,* 175–199.

Patterson, K., & Marcel, A. Aphasia, dyslexia and the phonological coding of written words. *Quarterly Journal of Experimental Psychology,* 1977, *29,* 307–318.

Posner, M. On the relationship between letter names and superordinate categories. *Quarterly Journal of Experimental Psychology,* 1970, *22,* 279–287.

Posner, M. *Chronometric explorations of mind.* Hillsdale, N.J.: Lawrence Erlbaum Associates, 1978.

Saffran, E., & Marin, O. Reading without phonology: Evidence from aphasia. *Quarterly Journal of Experimental Psychology,* 1977, *29,* 515–525.

Smith, A., & Winograd, E. Adult age differences in remembering faces. *Developmental Psychology,* 1978, *14,* 443–444.

Taylor, D. Identification and categorization of letters and digits. *Journal of Experimental Psychology: Human Perception and Performance,* 1978, *4,* 423–439.

18

Age and the Actualization of World Knowledge

Janet L. Lachman
Roy Lachman
University of Houston

The research we describe in this chapter concerns the lifespan development of a person's ability to use permanent memory, i.e., knowledge about the world. Knowing about one's environment, both immediate and distant, is essential to effective coping in that environment. However, while possession of the relevant knowledge is necessary to successful coping, it is not sufficient. A person must be able to make effective use of that knowledge. At least three subcomponents of successful knowledge actualization can be identified: efficient retrieval, appropriate inference, and accurate metamemorial function. *Retrieval* is obviously central, since knowledge is of little use if one can't get at it. *Inference* involves the ability to construct new information from existing information. *Metamemory* is the name given to a constellation of memory control capacities, including the assessment of whether a particular piece of knowledge is available, how likely one is to access it, and how certain one is that it is accurate. Metamemorial control processes are posited as the hypothetical mechanisms that direct efforts to retrieve and to draw inferences; they are also assumed to figure in an individual's willingness to act on retrieved or constructed information. Optimal use of knowledge, therefore, depends partly on *metamemorial accuracy*. These three concepts are further elaborated in later sections.

PRETHEORETICAL CONCEPTIONS OF THE ORGANISM AND KNOWLEDGE

Before presenting the research, it makes sense to elaborate the conceptual orientation within which we work. We view the human information-processing system as one instance of a class of general symbol-manipulating

285

systems, describable in the same theoretical language that is appropriate to abstract automata (Newell & Simon, 1972, 1976). Hence, when the individual *knows* something, we presume he has a stored symbolic representation of it, and this representation may be accessed, concatenated, elaborated, and subjected to any operation that may be performed on logical symbols. The questions we find interesting, and the class of answers we seek, reflect this very central notion about the nature of human cognition (cf. Lachman, Lachman, & Butterfield, 1979, Chapter 4).

It is also useful to distinguish the term "knowledge" from other, related formulations. Three dichotomies in the cognitive psycholinguistic literature will help elucidate the conception of world knowledge that underlies the research to be reported: short- and long-term memory (STM and LTM), semantic and episodic memory, and dictionary versus encyclopedic knowledge.

STM And LTM.   The concept of long-term memory (LTM) has been used ambiguously in the literature on verbal learning, memory, and cognition. It has typically been contrasted with short-term memory (STM) because the retention interval is comparatively long. Nevertheless, most usages of the LTM concept are based on measures of retention for arrangements of verbal materials learned in a single laboratory session, usually tested minutes or hours after original learning. Atkinson and Shiffrin (1968) posited LTM as the theoretical terminus for information that had been output by a rehearsal-buffered short-term storage system in their three-stage memory model. Our conception of knowledge is closer to current conceptions of LTM content, such as those of Shiffrin and Schneider (1977) or Anderson (1976), that are derivatives of Hebb's (1949) notion of a LTM system with relatively permanent and stable content.

Episodic And Semantic Memory.   According to Tulving's (1972) conception, episodic memory is essentially autobiographical and preserves the temporal and spatial features of an individual's past experience, usually of recent origin. Semantic memory, in contrast, preserves people's general linguistic and world knowledge, without necessarily preserving the place and time of acquisition. The world knowledge under investigation in these studies is in the domain of semantic memory, although the conditions of acquisition may be retained occasionally for some world knowledge.

Dictionaries And Encyclopedias.   A distinction between information that is essentially linguistic and that which is essentially world knowledge has been drawn by philosophers, linguists, and psychologists (Frege, 1892; Katz & Fodor, 1963; Lyons, 1969; Miller, 1978). This distinction has also been incorporated into psychological research and theory (Clark & Clark, 1977;

Lachman, 1973; Smith, 1978). The requirement that *spinster* must refer to a woman, for example, is stored as a component of the word's meaning. Thus, the knowledge that spinsters are women, are unmarried, etc., is stored in an idealized internal dictionary. On the other hand, the knowledge that spinsterhood is relatively rare and that it has been regarded as a misfortune in most Western societies is stored in an idealized encyclopedia containing all such world knowledge. The studies we have done so far have used questions which, if the dictionary–encyclopedia distinction is maintained, are presumably answered by reference to the encyclopedia.

When we speak of the actualization of knowledge, then, we are referring to a vast information store in the brain that is the source of an enormous range of facts such as the location of the nearest supermarket, the name of one's maternal grandmother, the knowledge that it is unwise to walk alone late at night in most cities, the name of the current prime minister of Great Britain, and the fact that stars are part of galaxy systems. Some of the information is of high salience to one's daily life; some of it is of relatively academic interest. However, none of it was acquired for the express purpose of remembering it in the laboratory; it is part of the person's preexperimental informational repertoire. As such, it was originally acquired for motivations other than those which normally determine acquisition performance in experimental settings.

In summary, our concern is with knowledge and information that is relatively permanent, nonepisodic, nonlinguistic, has not been studied for the sole purpose of experimental remembering, but has been acquired during a lifetime of formal education and day-to-day experience.

THREE PROCESSES IN THE ACTUALIZATION OF KNOWLEDGE

When a person requires some information for some particular purpose, at least three types of cognitive processes can be brought into play. These are shown in Fig. 18.1. Locative processes are primarily non–attention-demanding retrieval routines set into motion when the organism requires specific information for some purpose. The retrieval of information from an individual's store of world knowledge is normally automatic, unconscious, and strategy-free, although on some occasions (e.g., tip-of-the-tongue experiences) it may become deliberate and attention-demanding. It is not clear at this time what overlap, if any, there is between permanent memory retrieval processes and the STM retrieval processes so intensively studied in the last decade (cf. Craik, 1977).

A second process is inference, whereby a person who does not know a particular fact can construct it if necessary. Inferential processes span a range

METAMEMORY CONTROL PROCESSES

(conscious or unconscious)

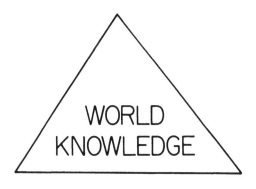

WORLD
KNOWLEDGE

LOCATIVE

(conscious or unconscious)

INFERENTIAL

(conscious or unconscious)

FIG. 18.1.   Hypothetical relationship among three subsystems implicated in
the retrieval of world knowledge.

of conscious awareness and deliberate control. Our concern is not with the
type of inference studied at length by metamathematicians and logicians. We
are interested in the kind of inferential process available to all normally
intelligent adults with a modicum of formal education, and perhaps others as
well. Even within these boundaries, at least two levels of automaticity can be
distinguished. On the one hand are inferences so rapid and automatic that
they may underlie general language comprehension. In such automatic
inference, the hearer must use his knowledge to fill in gaps in linguistic
messages (Clark & Clark, 1977; Kintsch, 1974, 1976; Lachman, Lachman, &
Butterfield, 1979; Schank, 1976); however, the hearer is normally not aware
of having done so. For example, if a person hears the comment, *John forgot
to let the dog out this morning,* the hearer will normally know without being
told that the dog was undesirably in. He might also infer that the dog being in
resulted in some untoward consequences, e.g., furniture or rug damage. These
small, everyday inferences do not require instruction; they seem to be part of
normal language comprehension and are available even to young children
(e.g., Paris, 1975; Paris & Carter, 1973). Although automatic inferences of
this type have only been studied in the context of language comprehension, it
is virtually certain that similar processes operate nonlinguistically, as for
example when we observe an empty driveway and garage and infer that a
house's occupants are not at home. A somewhat more deliberate and attended

kind of inference occurs when a person constructs new information from old in an effort to answer a question. Most people know that snowshoes sell poorly in Tahiti, for example, although few have troubled to memorize this fact. Such inferential processes are intuitive to the normal adult, but they are more conscious and deliberate than the linguistic inferences just described. Naturally, the dividing line between these kinds of inferences is not sharp. We draw the distinction only to accommodate the fact that various experimental paradigms for studying inference may initiate differentially automatic constructive processes.

A third process is metamemorial control. The term *metamemory* has been used to label a constellation of capacities concerned with knowledge about one's own memory processes and abilities (Flavell & Wellman, 1977). Our research has concerned one metamemorial process in particular, that which has been called "feeling-of-knowing" (Hart, 1965). This ability is best described in the context of an example. If one is asked the home telephone number of the Health, Education, and Welfare Secretary, for example, the likeliest response is, "I don't know." Most people would respond quickly, and if asked how sure they were that they didn't know, they would indicate they were quite sure. In contrast, if asked the HEW Secretary's first name, some people would be unable to retrieve it instantly; nevertheless, they could with great confidence state that they do in fact actually know the full name, could reject incorrect candidates, or would recognize it. This phenomenon of "knowing about knowing" is an important control process which guides the knowledge-retrieval system in making effective use of its time. It would be wasteful of time to persist in a long mental search for the HEW Secretary's phone number, given that it is definitely not available. However, continued efforts to retrieve the HEW Secretary's first name, given that it is in store, may be much more efficient than a trip to the library to find it in *Who's Who*. In fact, Hart (1965, 1966, 1967), Blake (1973), and Laughery, Thompson, and Band (1974) have shown that people can predict with considerable accuracy their ability to pick an answer from a set of alternatives when they cannot retrieve the answer directly from memory. The time they spend searching memory is also predictive of their recognition accuracy, with longer search times being associated with greater likelihood of correct recognition (Laughery, Thompson, & Band, 1974). Metamemorial processes, such as retrieval and the type of inference we are considering in this proposal, are normally rapid and effortless, do not demand attention, and are difficult to examine introspectively. Of course, appropriate instructions *can* render metamemory the object of deliberate scrutiny, as for example in several of Flavell and Wellman's (1977) studies. However, in the normal course of cognitive acitvity, such processes go unattended.

It is our view that metamemorial control processes guide both retrieval and inferential activity and the resultant behavioral output. When a person needs a particular piece of information—e.g., to answer a question—s/he attempts to retrieve it directly. Metamemorial processes return the information that an answer is or is not in store. If an answer is found, metamemorial control processes are involved in assessing its adequacy. If no answer, or an inadequate answer, is retrieved, the process of inference is set into motion. Again, metamemorial processes are called into play, to ascertain whether enough related information is in store to warrant an inference, and if one is made, to determine its likelihood of being sufficiently correct to be reported. Let us illustrate this scenario with an example. If a student entered our office and asked for a reference work on aging and memory, this would engender a search through memory for the existence of such a book. Easily and effortlessly we would find answers adequate for the student's purpose as we understand it, such as Birren and Schaie's (1977) *Handbook of the Psychology of Aging,* or Botwinick's (1978) textbook. Locating the existence of these books in memory would require little conscious attention, and would leave plenty of working memory space for anticipating the student's next question, planning how to avoid lending him our own copies, or whatever other ideation the arrival of such a student might initiate. On the other hand, suppose the student popped in and asked the proportion of Americans 65 and older whose liabilities exceed their assets. Search for a directly retrievable answer to this question would fail; however, sufficient related information would be available to attempt an inference. The resultant figure would be evaluated as to whether it is close enough for the purpose at hand, and if so it would be offered to the student, perhaps with a demurral as to its precision. If it is too imprecise or uncertain to be given, it would be withheld; and a routine for obtaining the information from a library or a well informed individual might be offered. Metamemorial processes, retrieval processes, and inference processes in the above sequence go on without conscious direction or attention, although any of the processes can be rendered attention-demanding and conscious under particular circumstances. For example, the idea of "Botwinick" could produce a tip-of-the-tongue experience for his name, in which case the retrieval process would become conspicuous through its failure. Or the inferential activity could become deliberate if one recalled reading several separate facts which, taken together, yielded a particular estimate of the number of insolvent people over 65; one might even take the trouble to write these down and compute the answer. The metamemorial processes could become conscious if one had an estimate that would be good enough for one purpose but not another, and one did not know what the student needed the answer for. Presumably one would ask for some additional information to guide the decision of whether to give the student a number or send him to the library.

Thus, our view of world knowledge retrieval in the human mind involves a complex interaction of search, metamemory judgment and control, and inference, all of which operate in even the most routine and ubiquitous of intelligent human behaviors.

KNOWLEDGE ACTUALIZATION
AND THE ADULT LIFE SPAN

With respect to older people, what might be the consequences of reduced retrievability, inferential capacity, and/or metamemory accuracy? Reduced retrievability would require the person to rely more and more on supplemental inference-making, to construct facts which are actually in store but inaccessible. Such inference-making probably takes more time than direct retrieval (Haviland & Clark, 1974), and would therefore slow down the person's functional rate of information-processing. To the extent that supplemental inference-making failed to construct the appropriate facts, the person's ability to use his or her existing data base would be impaired, even if retrieval ability remained intact. Lowered inferential capacity, especially if coupled with reduced retrievability, would further impair the person's ability to make effective use of existing knowledge to construct new facts. In conversation, this kind of impairment might make him or her appear dull and literal-minded. Metamemorial inaccuracy might affect adults and older persons in several ways. Unable to tell with certainty whether or not s/he knows a thing, a person might resort to a stereotyped "I don't know" whenever possible, withholding information that in fact he knows. He might use valuable mental time and effort trying to triangulate by inference many facts which should be directly retrieved with ease. Withholding information, or marginally improving accuracy by large increases in decision time, are aspects of caution, a trait that is often ascribed to the elderly (cf. Botwinick, 1973, Chapter 9). Alternatively, the person might volunteer information that he does not have (i.e., give wrong answers to questions). He might waste time in futile searches for nonexistent facts. Any of these consequences constitute suboptimal actualization of knowledge, and therefore suboptimal interactions with any environment relying on accumulated knowledge, or "crystallized intelligence" (Cattell, 1963; Schaie, 1970).

The long-range goals of our research program are twofold. We seek to validate empirically the conception of knowledge actualization just described; and we want to determine stable periods, peaks, and points of decline in the component processes. The first experiments concern the life-span course of retrieval efficiency.

Retrieval

Although considerable experimental work has been done under the rubric of "retrieval," much of it is of uncertain relevance to our present usage. Most laboratory studies examine the retrieval of experimentally learned materials, and therefore of "episodic" memories (Tulving, 1972). Retrievability of such memories depends strongly upon the relationship between acquisition context and retrieval cues (Anderson & Ortony, 1975; Tulving & Osler, 1968; Tulving & Thomson, 1973). Recallability of such material should therefore be considerably diminished after the subject (S) has left the laboratory. Our concern is precisely with knowledge which is recalled and used in a large variety of settings, as it must be if it is to support the individual's day-to-day functioning; therefore, the relevant studies are those concerned with retrieval of truly permanent, preexperimentally acquired information.

Such experiments are few, both in the general memory literature and that concerned with aging. For example, Craik's (1977) recent review of the literature on aging and memory mentions only four such studies. In one of these, Schonfield (1972) informally studied recall of the names of high school teachers by Ss varying in age from 20 to over 70. A decline in recall was obtained for that age range, from 67% correct recall for the youngest Ss to only 45% for the oldest. In a similar experiment, Bahrick, Bahrick, and Wittlinger (1975) studied recall and recognition of names and faces taken from high school yearbooks. Both name recall and face recognition were relatively stable for 15 years following graduation. Performance appeared to start declining 25 years after graduation and to fall precipitously 47 years later (S's calendar age approximately 65).

These studies leave unclear whether the age of the individual or the age of the information accounts for observed retrieval deficit. Other studies which controlled for item age produced conflicting results. Warrington and Silberstein (1970) found recall and recognition decrements with both age and retention interval for public events occurring 6, 12, or 18 months earlier. Warrington and Sanders (1971) extended the interval to 30 years, and found decrements with age and interval for the preceding five years; earlier events showed continued age effects but diminished interval effects. On the other hand, using only recall in an otherwise similar study, Botwinick and Storandt (1974) found no age effects on overall recall ability.

The picture is not clarified by adding another potentially useful sort of data, the Wechsler Adult Information Scale (WAIS). The WAIS information subtest is the one most closely related to this research. But a comparison of several related experimental studies (Bahrick, Bahrick, & Wittlinger, 1975; Schonfield, 1972; Warrington & Sanders, 1971; Warrington & Silberstein, 1970) reveals a contradiction: The experiments show age-related declines for adults, while information is generally held to be one of the least age-sensitive of the WAIS subtests.

This problem can potentially be resolved if attention is directed to the *efficiency*, rather than the *quantity*, of retrieval. The fallibility of an information-retrieval system may be described as some average number of breakdowns or errors per hour of processing time, or per some (large) number of operations or cycles. Because processing time is proportional to amount of information processed, retrieval fallibility is relative to the amount of information in storage that must be scanned. There is reason to believe that biological systems are subject to this general rule; while we do not know precisely what kind of information system human beings are, we do know that they are information systems in a nontrivial sense (cf. Lachman, Lachman, & Butterfield, 1979, Chapter 4). These considerations suggest that retrieval efficiency cannot be adequately determined in the absence of an estimate of the size of the data base from which particular informational elements are retrieved. In general, of course, we would expect a person's knowledge store to increase throughout his or her lifetime. Comparison of different-aged persons on sheer amount correctly recalled does not weigh in the size of the knowledge base from which a particular fact must be retrieved.

Suppose that we can estimate—even imperfectly—how much a particular person knows. A measure of information recall could then be weighted by the estimate of total information. One preliminary way to do this is to divide the amount of recall by the estimate of total knowledge; this yields a figure between 0 and 1 which can be taken as a measure of efficiency. Thus, for a given sample of information, the efficiency statistic would be:

$$E = R/K$$

where E is recall efficiency, R is the number of test items correctly recalled, and K is the number of items estimated to be in storage. In our experiments, K is the number of items answered correctly, either by recall or in a multiple-choice test, less empirically determined guesses. Because the E statistic adjusts for the size of the data base, it has the potential virtue of weighting recall performance by generational differences in acquired information. Inability to answer due to information never having been stored (in the young, primarily) is adjusted; and retrieval failures due to the size of the data base (in the elderly, primarily) are adjusted as well.

Two studies provide data on the efficiency measure. The first included 10 persons in each of four age groups, averaging approximately 20, 45, 60, and 75 years of age. The three older samples consisted of people who responded to a newspaper article about our research; the youngest group were college students. The questions in this study covered a wide range of topics, including current events, movies, sports, history, the Bible, and geography. There were 190 questions, in two sets of 95 each. Subjects each received one set of 95 items. In the first (recall) phase of the experiment, they were given a computer print-out of the questions in open-ended form, e.g., *What was the former name of Muhammad Ali?* They either wrote the answer or indicated "Don't know" or "Can't remember," whichever was appropriate. During a break, the experimenter scored the test, removing from the multiple-choice set those which the subject had answered correctly during recall. The subject then attempted to answer, in multiple-choice format, the remaining items. They were also asked to indicate if their selection was a wild guess.

The second experiment, which was undertaken to study metamemory, is sufficiently similar that the results can be combined with those of the first experiment in discussing retrieval efficiency. It included three groups of subjects, 12 at each of three age levels averaging 20.6, 46.9, and 68.9 years of age, respectively. Only one middle-aged group was used in this study, because the two middle-aged groups in the first study were indistinguishable from each other. The procedures were essentially the same, except that the stimulus questions were presented by slide projector, and recall efforts were timed. Otherwise, the same questions were used and the subjects came from the same populations as in the first experiment. In both studies, total knowledge was estimated by summing together the number of items answered correctly in the recall test and those selected correctly in the multiple-choice test. False positives were then subtracted; these were defined as correctly answered items that the subject indicated, during the recall phase, s/he did not know (as against could not remember), *and* designated as wild guesses in the multiple-choice phase. The subjects' dual self-report, first of not knowing and later, of guessing, is convergent validation. The efficiency statistic was computed by dividing the recall score by the estimate of total knowledge.

Results are presented for the two experiments combined. All middle-aged subjects (two groups in the first experiment, one in the second) are treated as a single group in these analyses. The resulting groups are: young ($N = 22$, $\bar{X} = 20.3$ years of age); middle-aged ($N = 32$, $\bar{X} = 52.0$ years of age); and elderly ($N = 22$, $\bar{X} = 71.4$ years of age).

Fig. 18.2 shows the total knowledge and efficiency statistic for these combined studies. The upper half of the figure shows that there is a significant increase in total knowledge from the 20s to the 50s; however, the function relating age and the efficiency statistic is essentially flat. As is commonly found, the oldest group shows the most variability. Fig. 18.3 plots recall as a function of total knowledge. In this graph, the steeper the slope, the better the efficiency—i.e., more increments in recall per unit of increment in total knowledge. A lower intercept reflects a smaller data base. As the figure shows, the poorest performance came from the young group, both in terms of overall knowledge and slope of the function. The middle-aged and elderly groups are almost indistinguishable from each other; however, the direction of the slopes and intercepts suggest superior performance by the oldest group. Given the considerable variability, judicious selection of a powerful statistical test is not likely to produce significant differences. However, there is certainly no reason

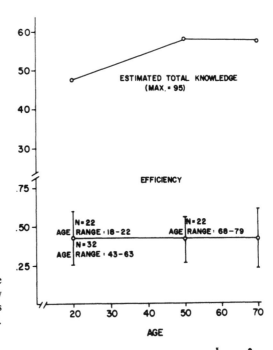

FIG. 18.2. Mean total knowledge estimates and retrieval efficiency scores for three age groups; results are of two experiments combined. Vertical bars indicate ±1σ.

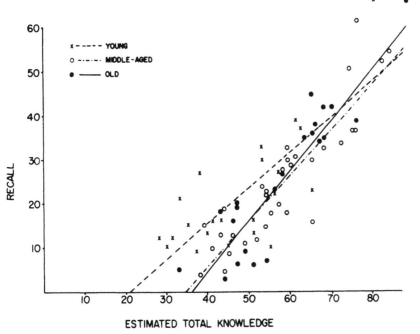

FIG. 18.3. Another way of looking at efficiency: recall as a function of estimated total knowledge for individuals in three age groups (two studies combined).

to think that retrieval efficiency *declines* with age—at least, not on the basis of these data.

In the two experiments just described, the three older groups may have been somewhat exceptional, relative to their generational cohorts. They read a news article in the feature section of a newspaper, called the psychology department to volunteer their services, drove themselves to the unfamiliar environment of the university, negotiated the troublesome parking situation, and located the laboratory. Although they were paid $6.50 for participating, most indicated they were not very interested in the money. We wondered whether these delightful individuals were really representative of their age-mates who did not read the newspaper, or skipped the article about our research, or read it but wouldn't dream of offering to participate. An examination of the older group's WAIS information subtest scores lent some credibility to this concern. The oldest group scored almost one standard deviation above the mean on that subtest, before any age correction was applied. Two possibilities exist: One is that age declines do not occur in bright people, and the other is that decline had already occurred but our groups had started so high that they still looked good compared to the young. A split-half analysis of our brighter and duller subjects did make it appear that age declines might be present in the less-bright half. We therefore wished to repeat the experiment, with better control over sampling procedures.

Anyone who has engaged in gerontological research knows that this is no minor problem. The vast majority of aging studies have used a sample of college sophomores as representative of "young adults." Older people have been found in rest homes, community centers, "Golden Age" clubs, and sometimes hospitals. There is no way of knowing whether these people are representative older persons, nor whether they are sampled from the same population as the college students. Our approach was to locate a population with relatively well-defined characteristics, containing individuals at all ages of the typical adult life span. We would then sample individuals at various ages exclusively from this population. Schoolteachers looked ideal for this purpose; the teacher population is both homogeneous and stable. For over 100 years, American schoolteachers have tended to originate in the lower-middle class, to be upwardly mobile, and to reach the middle- to upper-middle class. There is considerable comparability in the educational experience of teachers, whether educated recently or long ago. They are fairly homogeneous with respect to such relevant factors as intelligence, attitudes toward reading and learning, and health care. One can compare young and old teachers, and with at least a modicum of confidence, attribute obtained differences to age. What is more, the population of teachers in most major cities is quite large. In the Houston area there were over 14,000 teachers, educational administrators, and aides employed by the Houston Independent School District as of February, 1978. We therefore planned to repeat our study using practicing schoolteachers at three age levels. To further insure comparability of the age groups, the study included only white females, the majority subgroup of teachers. Trends that are true of teachers as a group may or may not be true of male teachers. And older black teachers, who achieved their education in spite of the institutionalized discrimination of 20 or more years ago, may differ from young blacks beginning their teaching careers in the last few years.

Subject recruitment efforts ran into immediate difficulties. The teachers overwhelmingly refused to participate in a one-hour session for $10. Attrition rate exceeded 80%, an unacceptable level because it left the problem of potentially unrepresentative sampling unsolved. Accordingly, the entire experiment was conducted by telephone, which reduced attrition to an acceptable level of 20%. However, to make a telephone study feasible, we had to reduce our 95 questions to only 20 per subject. In this subset, we were careful to include only items which were atemporal, or if time-dependent, involved events occurring only over the last 10 years. Forty questions were included, in two sets of 20 each.

A teacher was called and asked her age. If she was in one of the target ranges, she was asked if she would spend 10 or 15 minutes on the telephone answering questions. If she agreed, the recall portion of the test was administered. If the teacher had time, the multiple-choice portion was administered immediately; otherwise she was asked if we might call her back the next evening with more questions. No respondents refused at this point, and of course no indication was given that the questions would be the same ones in a different format. Again subjects were asked to indicate when their multiple-choice selection was a wild guess. However, no use was made of the "Don't know" versus "Can't remember" distinction used in the previous studies, because subjects prove to be very good at identifying wild guesses. The telephone study included 44 individuals in three age groups; mean ages of the groups were approximately 27, 43 and 61.

Results of the telephone study appear in Fig. 18.4. Total knowledge estimates, here based on a maximum of 20, show a similar relationship to age as in the previous experiments. Estimated total knowledge increases from the 20s to the 40s, but not thereafter. This is probably due to the 10-year limit on the age of time-dependent information. Efficiency also appears to increase from the 20s to the 40s; however, this may be an artifact. The small number of questions which could be asked on the telephone yielded asymptotic performance from some persons in the two older groups, which tends to inflate the efficiency measure. No asymptotic performances occurred among the young respondents, whose average efficiency score of .41 is quite comparable to the .43 of previous studies. The two older groups in the study both achieved average efficiency scores of .48, which is somewhat higher than previously obtained. Taken together, these observations suggest that the

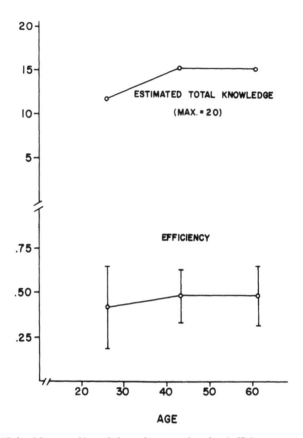

FIG. 18.4.   Mean total knowledge estimates and retrieval efficiency scores for three age groups of teachers. Vertical bars indicate ±σ.

apparent increase in efficiency in this study may be spurious. The efficiency of retrieval in the two older groups may reflect ceiling effects produced by the relatively small number of questions.

An interesting aspect of these data is that, with sampling controlled, the oldest group is not more variable than the younger groups. If anything, it is slightly less variable. It may be that the common experimental observation that old people are more variable than young ones is due to the common practice of drawing young samples from among college sophomores or other restricted populations. Perhaps these young people are more similar to each other than young people in general, whereas the older people sampled may more truly reflect the heterogeneity of their age group.

The absence of age effects was not what we expected. The preponderance of deficit findings in the aging literature, as well as the introspective reports of older persons, led us to expect an age decline in retrieval efficiency. However, we are coming to have some faith in our outcomes, and would predict (cautiously) that a "definitive experiment" will yield comparable results. Obviously, such an experiment remains to be done. It would have to use subjects sampled from a homogeneous population, enough questions to preclude asymptotically high or low performances in any age group, and enough subjects to insure that differences of an interesting size will be detected. Most importantly, attrition must be minimized to insure that sampling is representative. This latter requirement is costly, since it means people must be induced to participate in the experiment who would really rather not. Ethics limit an experimenter's choice of offers the subjects cannot refuse; however, money is a legitimate device for overcoming the resistance of the reluctant. Telephone questioning of the teachers suggested that $40 might improve attrition to about 40%, and $60 could potentially lower it to a quite acceptable level.

Meanwhile, we have been attempting to extend our initial conception of the efficiency statistic. It was developed to weight recall by an estimate of total knowledge, to bypass retrieval problems related to the size of the data base from which information was retrieved. However, E does not meet the formal requirements of a ratio: A plot of the proportion of recall to estimated total knowledge does not pass through the origin, and it may not be linear. This means that E does not weight recall by total knowledge equally at different performance levels. We cannot, for example, assume that all efficiency scores of .5 are equivalent.[1]

A somewhat different way of looking at the statistic held promise of solving both the formal problem and the pragmatic one of obtaining enough teachers. The points on the plot of Fig. 18.3 reflect the difficulty of our list to each subject as well as the retrieval capacity of that subject. Consider, for example, a subject who obtained a score of .40 on our list, answering 30 questions right in the recall test and an additional 45 on the recognition test $[30/(30 + 45) = .40]$. There must exist a list of questions so trivially easy that this person could answer all of them at recall, achieving a score of 1. As list difficulty increases, there will be some items answered correctly only in the recognition test, and thus the value R/K will decline. Very difficult lists, then, should be expected to produce very low E values. If all this is true, then few subjects tested on many lists ought to generate a plot similar to that of Fig. 18.3. This approach assumes that there is a relationship between intersubject and intrasubject difficulty—that the items on a "hard" list are unlikely to be answered, and if answered are likely to be recognized rather than recalled.

---

[1]The discussion following is based partly on exchanges and consultations with Prof. Juliet P. Shaffer, Dept. of Statistics, University of California, Berkeley, and Dr. Davis H. Howes, Neurology Service, VA Hospital, Boston. We are grateful for their input.

Fortunately, our existing data permitted us to test the validity of this assumption. We could look at those questions that few people answered correctly, and ascertain whether the rare individuals who got them right generally did so in the multiple-choice situation rather than the recall test. We took the data from the two experiments and constructed a new plot. For each of our 195 questions, we computed the percentage of all subjects who answered the question right, either at recognition or recall. This value was plotted against the percentage of people who recalled it, given that they could answer it. Despite appearances to the contrary, these values are potentially independent. The scatter diagram should tell us whether items that few people knew tended to be answered correctly only at recognition, by those who knew them. The resultant plot was exceedingly scattered, and no relationship was apparent on visual inspection. The two variables showed a low positive correlation, $r = .28$, accounting for only 7% of the variance in the data. Reaction time might provide a more sensitive measure of the relationship. If so, "difficult" items, which few people knew, would be answered relatively slowly by those who could answer them. We had question-answering latencies for subjects in the metamemory experiment, and thus could plot the mean latency to give the right answer as a function of the percentage of subjects who knew the answer. No relationship was found; the correlation was near zero. It appears that the retrievability of a piece of information for a person who knows it is not related to the proportion of people in the general population who do know it.

This most interesting, if unexpected, outcome complicates our efforts considerably. Clearly, it means that we cannot develop lists of questions whose intrasubjective difficulty is predictable from their intersubjective difficulty. We cannot construct an ordered set of lists so that a single subject will generate points along the lines of function like those plotted in Fig. 18.3. This is one pragmatic consequence of an extraordinarily interesting and complex question, which should be posed and addressed: What is it to "know" an answer and what makes a known fact "easy" or "difficult" to the person who knows it?

Answers to these questions may be unavailable until we have an adequate theory of knowledge. However, we are able to consider some of the factors that might have impact on the effort to retrieve some particular fact from memory. There are three sets of factors that are potentially relevant: those inherent in the data base, those inherent in the retriever, and those inherent in the fact itself. We have already mentioned that the size of the data base may exert a negative effect on retrieval efforts; this hypothesis derives from comparisons with information-processing machines considered as analogies or as formal automata. Other properties of the data base are also undoubtedly relevant, such as its organizational structure (cf. Lachman & Lachman [Chapter 19]), and the number and kind of related facts the person knows.

Experiments on propositional fan show that the number of sentences learned about a particular concept affects retrievability (Anderson, 1976; King & Anderson, 1976).

The retriever's characteristics are presumably implicated in a variety of ways. Some people are good retrievers; some are not. The functions plotted in Fig. 18.3 suggest positive acceleration; it may be that people who know a lot also tend to be those with a high proportion of recall to recognition. This is reasonable from several points of view. It is likely that people who are efficient retrievers are also facile in storing new facts. Or it may be that people who know a great deal are likely to know how to access their information effectively. This interpretation would require a modification of our previous prediction based on the size of the data base. It is possible that two competing vectors impact retrieval. Efficient retrievers may possess mechanisms that facilitate accretion to their knowledge store; but as the store grows, its size negatively impacts retrieval efficiency. This idea leads to a number of predictions, including an age change in retrievability that interacts with general intelligence. A test of the hypothesis requires the controlled sampling that we have been endeavoring to achieve.

A final impact on retrievability is inherent in the facts to be retrieved. Facts, of course, can vary in age and in frequency of occurrence, and these will surely influence retrievability. However, we mean to focus now on the relationship between particular facts and the person in whose memory they reside. Highly salient facts are likely to be easily retrieved, even though they may be infrequently accessed. To some extent, salience may be communal just as it is in the case of word-environment mappings (Lachman & Lachman [Chapter 19]). For example, people who were adults on December 7, 1941, are apt to find a number of personal memories about Pearl Harbor Day easy to access. However, in the case of facts, salience may also be highly idiosyncratic: The circumstances surrounding one's wedding and news events of that day may be salient only to one or two people. Presumably, the salience works by the same mechanism in both cases, but communally salient facts are also likely to benefit from frequency and/or recency. With respect to age of acquisition, no one knows if it influences retrievability of world knowledge as it does names (Carroll & White, 1973).

Metamemory

We have already introduced our conception of metamemory. Our interest is in knowledge about one's own information store, which is reflected in a subjective state called "feeling-of-knowing." Pioneering work on feeling-of-knowing was done by Hart (1965, 1966, 1967). Hart used general information questions similar to those we have used. Subjects were instructed to supply the correct answer if they could. Otherwise, they were asked to indicate whether or not they felt they would be able to select the correct answer from several wrong alternatives. The entire test was then re-administered in multiple-choice format. The results of the multiple-choice test showed that subjects could predict quite accurately which items are in storage.

The "feeling-of-knowing" procedure is one way of assessing metamemory. However, the kind of metamemorial process which figures in everyday information-processing is rapid, non-attention-demanding, and unconscious. The procedure used by Hart renders it the object of explicit attention and scrutiny on the subject's part. Ideally, one would also want a measure of metamemorial accuracy which did not require subjects to make an overt effort to attend to their metamemorial processes. In fact, such a measure is available in recall reaction-time. Laughery, Thompson, and Band (1974) found that latencies to respond "I don't know" during recall predicted recognition performance. The quicker the response, the less likely that subjects would select the correct answer in the multiple-choice test. This presumably reflects metamemory operation, in that the person knows he does not know the answer and therefore need not waste time searching his memory extensively for it. Longer times—even though the subject eventually said "I don't know"—were associated with higher probabilities of choosing a correct response, presumably reflecting the subject's use of his metamemorial information to prolong a potentially successful search. Since recall latency can be taken while the processes are still unconscious, prior to an overt feeling-of-knowing judgment, both latency and feeling-of-knowing were incorporated in the next experiment to be described (Lachman, Lachman, & Thronesbery, 1979).

To avoid contaminating the reaction-time metamemory measure during recall by the overt and deliberate feeling-of-knowing judgment, our experimental design blocked these procedures. All latencies were collected before any feeling-of-knowing judgments were made. The study was done in three phases. In the first phase, questions were presented by slide projector, on an apparatus designed to measure reaction time. The onset of the stimulus coincided with the start of a timer, and the timer was stopped by the subject's vocal response. The subject was instructed to supply the correct answer, or if he could not do so to say "I don't know" or "I can't remember," whichever was appropriate. After the entire set of questions had been presented, the subject then went through them one at a time giving a feeling-of-knowing judgment on a four-point scale. They said either that they definitely did not know the answer, maybe did not know the answer, could recognize the answer if shown it, or could recall the answer given more time and a few hints. These categories were intended to reflect an increasing feeling of knowing, without alerting subjects to the fact that a recognition test was coming.

Following a break, the subjects were again asked the questions to which they had previously responded "I don't know"; however, this time they selected the answer from a set of four alternatives as in the prior studies. These responses were not timed. The subjects were also asked for a confidence rating about each choice: wild guess, educated guess, probably right, or definitely right. After the multiple-choice test was completed, the subjects were administered a questionnaire concerning educational level, socioeconomic status, and reading practices, as well as the comprehension subtest of the WAIS.

Three age groups of age approximately 21, 47, and 69 were included in the study. The young group were college students and the two older groups responded to the newspaper article described earlier. The questions used were the same as in the first studies reported; in fact, the efficiency data in Figs. 18.2 and 18.3 includes these subjects. The issues addressed in this study were concerned with age changes in metamemory function. Do young people predict more or less accurately than older ones whether they will be able to answer a question? Do young and old differ in how well they match their search times to the probability of a correct response? Do young and old differ in after-the-fact confidence in their correct and incorrect choices in a multiple-choice situation?

In describing the results of this study, we have combined the two intermediate feeling-of-knowing categories. It is possible that our wording of the second category, "maybe do not know", was unfortunate; subjects tended to avoid use of that category. Consequently, Fig. 18.5 shows the percentage of "I don't know" items correctly answered for each of three rating categories: (1) "definitely do not know"; (2) an intermediate category including "maybe do not know" and "could recognize if told"; and (3) "could recall with hints and more time." All groups show metamemorial accuracy, replicating the findings of Hart (1965). This is reflected by a highly significant feeling-of-knowing category effect, and a strong linear trend. However, no group was more accurate than any other. Different slopes would have resulted from different accuracies, with steeper slopes reflecting better metamemorial judgments. There is also no age effect in these data.

Fig. 18.6 shows the response times for "I don't know" items as a function of rating category for the three age groups. Good metamemorial function would be represented here also by a steep slope. A steep slope would mean that subjects spent minimum time searching for answers to items they believed they did not know, and maximum time on items that they felt they could recall with more time. The two intermediate rating categories are again combined in the analysis. The overall slower response times of the middle-aged group were almost significant, $.05 < p < .06$. A significant effect of rating category and a strong linear trend reflect the fact that all subjects searched longer for those items they thought they might be able to recall. However, no age group allocated their search times more effectively than any other.

. Fig. 18.7 shows the accuracy of confidence ratings given by the subjects after they had selected an alternative in the multiple-choice test. All four of these categories were used extensively enough to include them in the analysis.

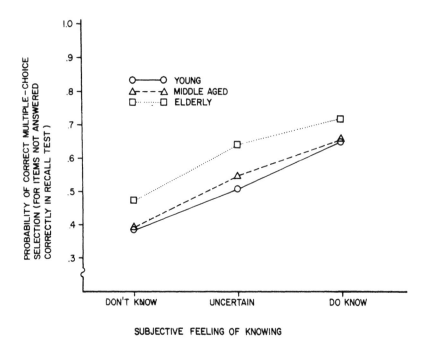

FIG. 18.5.   Metamemorial accuracy of three age groups: likelihood of correct performance in a multiple choice test as a function of subjective feelings of knowing. The feeling-of-knowing judgment was made after attempting to answer the question in open-ended form and before subjects knew the questions would be asked in multiple-choice form.

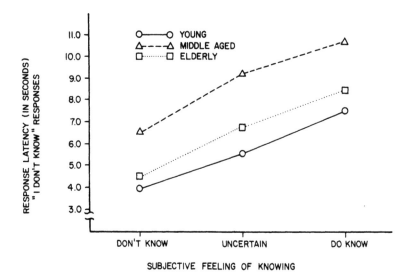

FIG. 18.6.   Metamemorial efficiency of three age groups: amount of time spent searching memory for the answer to an open-ended question as a function of subjective ratings of "feeling of knowing".

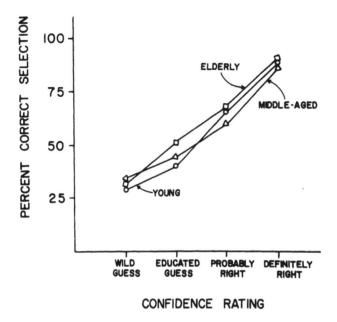

FIG. 18.7. Metamemory accuracy assessed through confidence ratings: percentage correct at each confidence level.

Subjects of all ages are quite accurate in this task. For items labeled "wild guess," they perform at about 30%—just slightly better than chance. On items labeled "definitely right," they perform between 85% and 90% correct. This good assessment of their own choices is reflected by a significant rating effect, with a powerful linear component. There are no age effects and no interaction of rating with age, indicating that all age groups performed the confidence rating task in a very similar fashion and equally accurately.

These three ways of looking at metamemorial accuracy, then, give no reason at all to suppose that metamemory function deteriorates with age in healthy individuals. The study, however, is subject to the sampling problem discussed previously. We hope to redo it using teachers, if we can provide sufficient inducements to bring them to the laboratory.

The results so far obtained suggest that this research program is tapping functions which do not decline with age. But there is a problem in substantiating such absences of change. It is essential that this problem be confronted in the area of cognitive gerontology. Aging research is taking on increased social importance as the average age of the population rises; asymmetries of outcomes in the literature will soon cease to be an in-house problem for professional researchers alone. And there is reason to suppose that the preponderance of deficit findings may reflect methodological asymmetries. Most research tasks are initially developed for use with college students, often taking into account their interests, motivations, and abilities.

When these are transferred to new populations, such as the elderly, three possibilities exist: The elderly will improve on the performance of the young, they will perform equally well, or they will perform more poorly. It is unlikely that the elderly will outperform the young on a task developed with the young in mind. If the groups perform equally well, the investigator is faced with reporting "negative results." Likeliest to appear in the literature, then, are studies in which the young do better than the old—inflating our impression of widespread age decline in healthy individuals for a large array of psychological tasks.

A possible solution to this problem is the use of power analyses. It is not possible, using Fisherian methods of research design and analysis, to assign a probability to the conclusion that no differences exist between groups. However, a conclusion of *minimal* differences can be reported within confidence intervals. Statistical power functions relate power (probability of finding a relationship given that it exists), degrees of freedom, alpha level, and effect size. Specification of any three of these values permits computation of the fourth. Thus, in any given experiment, an investigator can calculate the smallest effect which he had the power to detect at some designated significance level. If that effect size can be judged negligible, the researcher can conclude that if differences exist, they are small. At present, no conventional levels of power exist comparable to the widespread convention of .05 for alpha, and a judgment is required that some specified effect size is "small." However, the reporting of scientific studies is built on such judgments, whether or not conventions exist for making them. No convention exists, for example, for deciding how well an investigator's data fit his theory; yet, manuscript reviewers routinely make such evaluations. Capacities which do not decline with age may be of considerable theoretical and social relevance. It is a disservice to ourselves as scientists and to the aging population to withhold studies of such capacities. It would be preferable to report them, if it can be done in a manner which excludes poorly done experiments and those with insufficient power to detect sizable differences. Power analyses permit just such reporting. We plan to use such analyses in continued research on knowledge actualization.

Inference

To the extent that a person fails to engage in inference-making, that person's knowledge base will not be used effectively and intelligent behavior may be impaired. Comprehension of language and the understanding of nonlinguistic aspects of one's environment involve considerable supplementation of linguistically and perceptually available information. The source of this supplementation is previous knowledge.

We are concerned with the lifespan maintenance of inferential capacity, and its role in a theory of knowledge actualization. If it were possible to construct a set of questions which were "inferential" and another set which could only be answered by direct access, it would be possible to determine whether there are differential changes in the lifespan maintenance of direct-access retrieval and inferential constructive ability. Moreover, such a set of questions would provide a beginning in the categorization of various forms of world knowledge. However, unaided intuition is not necessarily a good guide to construction of inferential and direct-access items. It may be that one person's inference is another's direct access. The first question that must be answered, therefore, is whether it is possible to construct such sets of questions. If so, what empirical consequences emanate from the questions' inferential or noninferential character? These questions have been addressed in a master's thesis completed in our laboratory by Cameron Camp (1978) (see also Camp, Lachman, & Lachman, 1980).

Camp developed a technique for writing questions which is at least partly canonical. "Direct-access" questions were drawn largely from the previous studies. Camp selected those items which were infrequently answered in unaided recall, but readily answered with high confidence in the multiple-choice test. He reasoned that these items were known to the subject, but had been forgotten, and could not be reconstructed by inference. When the correct answer appeared among the multiple-choice alternatives, the subject presumably recognized it immediately as correct, thereby giving it a high confidence rating. Had the subject not really known the answer, but chose it inferentially by elimination, the confidence rating would have reflected some degree of doubt in the alternative's correctness. Several methods were used to write inferential questions. All were designed to produce questions that most people would not have encountered directly, but which could be answered by combining commonly known facts. One technique involved identifying an answer domain having a limited set of values, such as directions on a compass or musical instruments. Questions were then written which had one of these values as the answer. Examples of items generated by this approach are, "Which way does the Statue of Liberty face?" and "What musical instrument is made only of leather and metal?" (Answers: SE; cymbals.) Other items were generated by relating two previously unrelated topic areas, then framing a question whose answer involved discovery of the new relationship: for example, "Which horror-movie character might starve in Northern Sweden in the summertime?" (Answer: Dracula.) Another technique involved questions that required computation of temporal relationships, such as "What U.S. President was the first to see an airplane fly?" (Answer: Theodore Roosevelt.) Camp used several other techniques in developing his inferential questions (Camp, Lachman, & Lachman, 1980). Two sets of 30 questions each were written. Each set contained 15 direct access and 15 inferential items.

Each item consisted of a question and four alternative answers: the correct answer, a phonetically similar alternative, a semantically similar alternative, and an alternative which phonetically resembled the semantically similar alternative. Structuring of the alternatives permitted Camp to determine if different types of alternatives were "seductive" for different types of questions.

Two different tasks were used. The first task, called "multiple-choice," was designed to validate Camp's question-construction procedures, and to determine whether direct-access items really introduced direct-access retrieval, and whether inferential items really initiated inferential processing. Subjects received one question set, and chose the answer from among four alternatives. They then wrote a description of how they went about selecting their answer. They were given extensive instruction and practice to insure that they gave informative descriptions of their reasons. They were told, for example, to write "I learned that answer in History 433" as opposed to "I just knew that was the right answer." Likewise, they were instructed in how to describe inferential processes: "I knew that G was the seventh letter of the alphabet because I counted up to it" rather than "I just figured it out." Two judges, who did not know how the questions were intended to be answered, rated the "inferentialness" of the subject's description on a five-point scale where "one" was maximally direct access in nature and "five" was maximally inferential.

The second task, a reaction-time task, was designed to determine whether direct access and inferential processing take different amounts of time, and whether different kinds of distractors are seductive in the two kinds of item. Questions were presented by slide projector. Following the question, a single alternative was presented on the next slide, and the subject's task was to say "right" or "wrong." Latency was taken from the onset of the candidate answer to the onset of the subject's vocal response. The two tasks were counterbalanced as to order of presentation, and subjects received one set of questions in the multiple-choice task, the other in the reaction-time task.

Results of the multiple-choice task indicate that Camp had successfully written items that initiated direct access and inferential processing. Subjects' descriptions of their mode of answering direct-access questions received an average rating of 2.04 (where 1 is maximally direct). For inferential questions, the average rating was 4.10 (where 5 is maximally inferential). In the reaction-time task, direct-access items were answered significantly faster ($\bar{X}$ = 2.23 sec) than inferential items ($\bar{X}$ = 3.16 sec). Incorrect alternatives which phonetically resembled the correct answer were expected to be more seductive for direct-access questions, while semantic alternatives were thought to be more seductive for inferential questions. In fact, the data suggest that phonetic alternatives are generally not attractive; they were seldom incorrectly accepted by subjects. However, phonetic alternatives did take slightly longer to reject in direct-access questions, while semantic alternatives took longer for inferential questions. Thus, even when the subject does converge on the right answer, his mode of processing may be reflected in the kind of alternative which seems, even fleetingly, to be a viable possibility.

SUMMARY

The research program reported here is still in an early stage of development. There is much conceptual work to do in developing appropriate statistical and process models for the efficiency measure. The metamemory experiment will hopefully be extended using controlled sampling and larger Ns, so that power can be used in reporting small differences. The Camp thesis will be extended to middle-aged and elderly individuals.

We believe, on the basis of the data so far collected, that knowledge actualization may not decline with age in healthy individuals up to at least age 70. The convergence of several studies on this conclusion is compelling, although a definitive set of experiments has yet to be done. It is exciting to think that a task like question-answering, with its powerful ecological and face validity, may not be subject to the deficits so often found in gerontological experiments. Perhaps we in the academic world may yet look forward to our own futures without trepidation in a world that has set aside mandatory retirement.

ACKNOWLEDGMENTS

Work reported here was supported by NSF Grant - BNS 77-25657. We gratefully acknowledge the assistance of our graduate students, Don Taylor and Carroll Thronesbery, whose help has been invaluable in the completion and reporting of this work.

REFERENCES

Anderson, J. R. *Language, memory and thought.* Hillsdale, N.J.: Lawrence Erlbaum Associates, 1976.

Anderson, R. C., & Ortony, A. On putting apples into bottles—A problem of polysemy. *Cognitive Psychology,* 1975, *7,* 167–180.

Atkinson, R. C., & Shiffrin, R. M. Human memory: A proposed system and its control processes. In K. W. Spence & J. T. Spence (Eds.), *The psychology of learning and motivation* (Vol. 2). New York: Academic Press, 1968.

Bahrick, H. P., Bahrick, P. P., & Wittlinger, R. P. Fifty years of memory for names and faces: A cross-sectional approach. *Journal of Experimental Psychology,* 1975, *104,* 54–75.

Birren, J. E., & Schaie, K. W. *Handbook of the psychology of aging.* New York: Van Nostrand Reinhold, 1977.

Blake, M. Prediction of recognition when recall fails: Exploring the feeling-of-knowing phenomenon. *Journal of Verbal Learning and Verbal Behavior,* 1973, *12,* 311-319.

Botwinick, J. *Aging and behavior: A comprehensive integration of research findings.* New York: Springer, 1973.

Botwinick, J. *Aging and behavior: A comprehensive integration of research findings.* New York: Springer, 1978.

Botwinick, J., & Storandt, M. *Memory, related functions and age.* Springfield, Ill.: Charles C. Thomas, 1974.

Camp, C. J., III. Recognition processes in the multiple-choice test: Convergent validation of the constructs of direct access vs. inferential/constructive processing. Unpublished master's thesis, University of Houston, 1978.

Camp, C. J., III, Lachman, J. L., & Lachman, R. Direct access and inferential processes in question-answering. *Journal of Verbal Learning and Verbal Behavior,* 1980.

Carroll, J. B., & White, M. N. Word frequency and age of acquisition as determiners of picture-naming latency. *Quarterly Journal of Experimental Psychology,* 1973, *25,* 85-95.

Cattell, R. B. Theory of fluid and crystallized intelligence: An initial experiment. *Journal of Educational Psychology,* 1963, *105,* 105-111.

Clark, H. H., & Clark, E. V. *Psychology and language: An introduction to psycholinguistics.* New York: Harcourt Brace Jovanovich, 1977.

Craik, F. I. M. Age differences in human memory. In J. E. Birren & K. W. Schaie (Eds.), *Handbook of the psychology of aging.* New York: Van Nostrand Reinhold, 1977.

Flavell, J. H., & Wellman, H. M. Metamemory. In R. V. Kail, Jr. & J. W. Hagen (Eds.), *Perspectives on the development of memory and cognition.* Hillsdale, N.J.: Lawrence Erlbaum Associates, 1977.

Frege, G. On sense and reference. *Zeitschrift fur philosophie und philosophische kritik,* 1892, *100,* 25-50.

Hart, J. T. Memory and the feeling-of-knowing experience. *Journal of Educational Psychology,* 1965, *56,* 208-216.

Hart, J. T. A methodological note on feeling-of-knowing experiments. *Journal of Educational Psychology,* 1966, *57,* 347-349.

Hart, J. T. Memory and the memory-monitoring process. *Journal of Verbal Learning and Verbal Behavior,* 1967, *6,* 685-691.

Haviland, S. E., & Clark, H. H. What's new? Acquiring new information as a process in comprehension. *Journal of Verbal Learning and Verbal Behavior,* 1974, *13,* 512-521.

Hebb, D. O. *The organization of behavior.* New York: Wiley, 1949.

Katz, J. J., & Fodor, J. A. The structure of a semantic theory. *Language,* 1963, *39,* 170-210.

King, D. R. W., & Anderson, J. R. Long-term memory search: An intersecting activation process. *Journal of Verbal Learning and Verbal Behavior,* 1976, *15,* 587-605.

Kintsch, W. *The representation of meaning in memory.* Hillsdale, N.J.: Lawrence Erlbaum Associates, 1974.

Kintsch, W. Memory for prose. In C. N. Cofer (Ed.), *The structure of human memory.* San Francisco: W. H. Freeman, 1976.

Lachman, J. L., Lachman, R., & Thronesbery, C. Metamemory through the adult lifespan. *Developmental Psychology,* 1979, *15,* 543-551.

Lachman, R. Uncertainty effects on time to access the internal lexicon. *Journal of Experimental Psychology,* 1973, *99,* 199-208.

Lachman, R., Lachman, J. L., & Butterfield, E. C. *Cognitive psychology and information processing: An introduction.* Hillsdale, N.J.: Lawrence Erlbaum Associates, 1979.

Laughery, K. R., Thompson, B., & Band, T. *How do we decide to terminate a memory search?* Paper presented at the meeting of the Psychonomic Society, Boston, 1974.

Lyons, J. *Theoretical linguistics.* Cambridge: Cambridge Unviersity Press, 1969.

Miller, G. Practical and lexical knowledge. In E. Rosch & B. B. Lloyd (Eds.), *Cognition and categorization.* Hillsdale, N.J.: Lawrence Erlbaum Associates, 1978.

Newell, A., & Simon, H. *Human problem solving.* Englewood Cliffs, N.J.: Prentice-Hall, 1972.

Newell, A., & Simon, H. A. Computer science as empirical inquiry: Symbols and search. *Communications of the ACM,* 1976, *19,* 113–126.

Paris, S. G. Integration and inference in children's comprehension and memory. In F. Restle, R. M. Shiffrin, J. Castellan, H. Lindman, & D. Pisoni (Eds.), *Cognitive Theory,* Vol. 1. Potomac, Md.: Lawrence Erlbaum Associates, 1975.

Paris, S. G., & Carter, A. Y. Semantic and constructive aspects of sentence memory in children. *Developmental Psychology,* 1973, *9,* 109–113.

Schaie, K. W. A reinterpretation of age-related changes in cognitive structure and functioning. In L. R. Goulet & P. B. Baltes (Eds.), *Life-Span Developmental Psychology: Research and Theory.* New York: Academic Press, 1970.

Schank, R. C. The role of memory in language processing. In C. N. Cofer (Ed.), *The structure of human memory.* San Francisco: W. H. Freeman, 1976.

Schonfield, D. Theoretical nuances and practical old questions: The psychology of aging. *Canadian Psychologist,* 1972, *13,* 252–266.

Shiffrin, R. M., & Schneider, W. Controlled and automatic human information processing: II. Perceptual learning, automatic attending, and a general theory. *Psychological Review,* 1977, *84,* 127–190.

Smith, E. E. Theories of semantic memory. In W. K. Estes (Ed.), *Handbook of learning and cognitive processes.* (Vol. 5). Hillsdale, N.J.: Lawrence Erlbaum Associates, 1978.

Tulving, E. Episodic and semantic memory. In E. Tulving & W. Donaldson (Eds.), *Organization of memory.* New York: Academic Press, 1972.

Tulving, E., & Osler, S. Effectiveness of retrieval cues in memory for words. *Journal of Experimental Psychology,* 1968, *77,* 593–601.

Tulving, E., & Thomson, D. M. Encoding specificity and retrieval processes in episodic memory. *Psychological Review,* 1973, *80,* 352–373.

Warrington, E. K., & Sanders, H. I. The fate of old memories. *Quarterly Journal of Experimental Psychology,* 1971, *23,* 432–442.

Warrington, E. K., & Silberstein, M. A questionnaire technique for investigating very long term memory. *Quarterly Journal of Experimental Psychology,* 1970, *22,* 508–512.

19

Picture Naming: Retrieval and Activation of Long-Term Memory

Roy Lachman
Janet L. Lachman
University of Houston

THE GENERAL PROBLEM:
WORD DELIVERY AND LEXICALIZATION

Over a decade ago, Oldfield (1963) estimated that young, university-educated people know the meaning of about 75,000 discrete words, and that the range of identifiable words stored in the memories of such individuals is between 55,000 and 90,000. He later posed a major psychological problem approximately in this fashion: How is the store of words in memory organized and indexed, and how do we access them at the typical rate of normal speech production—two words a second (Oldfield, 1966)? Specific answers to these problems are as elusive today as they were at that time. The intervening years have seen much research and some progress, including a growing awareness of the complexity of the issues. Accessing words in an internal storage system is part of the larger problem of *lexicalization:* the attachment of meaning to words, and the appropriate use of those words in speech and speech-related behaviors.

Lexicalization has both learning and performance dimensions. It obviously is a central aspect of first-language learning, as the child comes to attach the conventional symbols of his language community to appropriate objects. However, lexicalization also underlies important adult abilities. It supports the capacity to name objects and events which, although not physically present, are appropriate to the context of discourse. Further, lexicalization is involved in the capacity to construct multi-word descriptors when no single word designates a concept the speaker wishes to mention. These adult capacities are the performance aspect of lexicalization and the focus of this research report.

313

Words are not equally accessible; some take longer to produce than others. It seems reasonable to suppose that this differential accessibility reflects the organizational structure of the cognitive system that stores lexical items internally and relates them to the concepts they designate. Presumably, that organizational structure is motivated by efficiency: Words of high salience should be readily available, while less salient words should be harder to access. But in order to develop and maintain efficiency, the system must contain some mechanism for accommodating changes in salience that may attach to particular lexical items. The variables that influence word production latency, then, should provide clues to two important questions. First, how is the lexical system organized to facilitate efficient word production? Second, how does the system reorganize itself to maintain efficiency in the face of changing patterns of word salience? The variables of interest fall into two broad classes.

One class of variables reflects the conventional nature of language—what people of a particular language community need to converse about. Frequency of particular items, the age at which they are learned, and the amount of consensus in their usage are three such variables that have been studied. These are communal variables, and must be measured by means of samples from the language community. Their impact on the individual language user may be estimated, indirectly, from the community's collective behavior. A second class of variables are those that have been directly manipulated. They are presumed to exert a direct effect on the internal computational processes occurring within the individual during the access of lexical items. Such variables include prior presentation of an event which should, in some specified fashion, alter the subsequent accessibility of a given word. This paper describes the research, the conclusions drawn from it, and insofar as possible, gives an analysis of the cognitive mechanisms responsible for locating words in memory and delivering them to the behavioral systems that use them.

THE LABORATORY ANALOGUE: PICTURE NAMING

We are ultimately interested in contributing to theories of lexicalization and speech production, human functions that undoubtedly involve virtually all the mechanisms underlying human language capacity. Proper selection of a laboratory analogue renders a complex system amenable to experimental study; but at the same time it limits the range of capacities subjects can demonstrate in the laboratory task, and hence the scope of inferences from the laboratory which are directly valid. An appropriate task would render complex psychological issues amenable to careful experimental control without losing touch with the natural system the experimental arrangements are intended to illuminate. Following others before us (e.g., Oldfield & Wingfield, 1965), we chose picture naming, for several reasons. The task is neither intractably complex nor too simple to offer any hope of generalizing to extra-laboratory performance. Picture naming excludes, insofar as possible, the poorly understood capacities that underlie syntactic processing. It permits the design of methodologically sound studies which can be expected to yield interpretable outcomes. At the same time, the task maintains a considerable degree of sufficiency and ecological validity. It taps into man's vast and complex language capacities, requiring as it does the mapping of an experiential reality onto a linguistic code. Neither the reality nor the code are simple structures in the speaker–hearer; and both must be taken into account in any explanation of their mapping. This mapping, while not the entirety of language use, must be handled by any adequate psycholinguistic theory.

A research task should also permit decoupling of the internal mechansims of interest from the vast network of human cognitive capacities. Lexical memory structures, for example, should be at least partially isolable from internal visual and conceptual codes if the effects of external variables are to be precisely localized and relevant stages of processing are to be specified. In a reaction-time task, this translates into the pragmatic requirement that an experimenter must know when conceptual access is complete and lexical access begins. Presenting a linguistic description of a concept to elicit its name is less satisfactory, because linguistic strings are processed serially and real-time measurement of memory access is not possible. A picture, in contrast, serves as a global definition of a concept; the picture is processed, if not completely in parallel, at least at high speed.

The picture-naming task, then, recommends itself as a laboratory analogue of speech production on several grounds: It is tractable, it is adequate to represent real human capabilities, and it is pragmatically useful. Let us now turn to some of the communal variables which influence rate of word production in the picture-naming task.

ENVIRONMENTAL SALIENCE
AND NAME ACCESSIBILITY

The major variables that influence accessibility of name-words are frequency, uncertainty, age of acquisition, and repetition. Frequency, usually estimated from word counts of printed language, refers to the frequency of occurrence of the name labels for pictures (Oldfield, 1966; Oldfield & Wingfield, 1965). Uncertainty, or codability, reflects the diversity of names given to an object (Lachman, 1973b; Lachman, Shaffer, & Hennrikus, 1974). Age of acquisition is based on estimates of how early in life an object's name is first encountered (Carroll & White, 1973). Repetition refers to re-responding, or the repeating of an object's name over short temporal intervals—hours or days. Frequency, uncertainty, and acquisition age are permanent vectors of lexical long-term memory (LTM) (Lachman et al., 1974). Repetition, in contrast, seems to produce transient changes in system sensitivity to activity- or task-determined changes in relative likelihood of specific word productions.

In an extensive series of studies on the role of frequency in picture-naming, Wingfield (1966) found that the time it takes to name an object is a linear function of the log frequency of occurrence of the object's name in written English (Oldfield & Wingfield, 1965). This result is readily replicated and the magnitude of the effect is sizeable. Objects with the highest frequency names have average latencies of about 600 msec, while those with the lowest have average latencies of 1300 msec. However, Oldfield and Wingfield (1965) selected pictures that met certain very strict conditions, one of which was that each stimulus picture possess a "single commonly-acknowledged name [p. 277]." It seems, however, that very-high frequency objects, such as *book, chair, shoe,* and *key,* are likelier to meet the condition of a single commonly acknowledged name than objects with low-frequency names, e.g., *stethoscope, gyroscope, bagpipe,* and *syringe.* To check these intuitions, students in a class were shown a series of pictures and asked to write the first name they thought of for each. As the frequency of the dictionary name went down, the number of different names the students supplied went up. For example, everyone responded "book" to a picture of a book; but to a gyroscope, they supplied "spinner," "top," "machine," "whirler," and "rotator," as well as "gyroscope." A series of formal studies exposed additional facts suggesting that frequency is not a unitary variable which alone determines reaction time. Most damaging was the fact that when high-frequency names were given to low-frequency objects, reaction times were generally indistinguishable from those for low-frequency names given to the same objects. In other words, the latencies to name a picture of a gyroscope were long whether the subject called it "gyroscope," which is low-frequency, or "machine," which is high-frequency. The long latencies for such pictures, then, must be determined at least as much by properties of the object as by properties of the name supplied. A variable such as frequency, which is defined entirely by properties of the linguistic code, cannot be solely responsible for differential naming latencies.

It seems likelier that different naming latencies do not stem exclusively from either object properties or name properties, but from the process by which people map language onto the categories that they find or impose upon the world. Brown and Lenneberg (1954), in their work on codability, recognized that words are labels for categorization processes. Category construction and labeling practices, in turn, ordinarily reflect the cultural importance of the categorized objects. Our working assumption is that the tightness of mapping—what Brown and Lenneberg called *codability*—depends on the social and biological salience of objects. The most salient objects have a one-to-one mapping with words; they are linguistically well coded. The most salient objects in Western cultures will include items of food, clothing, shelter, and such objects as are necessary for functioning in an advanced industrial society. In Western languages, these salient objects should have high-frequency, well coded names. Other objects, of low salience, are likely to have names of low written and spoken frequency—and the name-to-object mapping is apt to be many-to-one (many words to one object). This will be manifested by an increase in name diversity as object frequency declines—i.e., as the amount of commerce or interaction with the object becomes more rare. The conception of codability developed here is not inconsistent with B. L. Whorf's observations of language coding in diverse cultures (Carroll, 1956). Whorf reported, for example, that the Eskimo lexicon has three different names for snow. This may appear to be high name diversity associated with a highly salient category. The source of the confusion is that for the Eskimo, *snow* is not one category with three names; it is three categories with one name each. North Americans dwelling further south can treat all three categories as one with no untoward consequences; but the Eskimo needs all three, and a name for each. Our conception of codability implies that each Eskimo category should have a single, well agreed on name in the Eskimo lexicon; and each does.

Not only are people unlikely to agree on the names of poorly coded objects, such objects are also unlikely to have monolexemic (one-word) names. Highly salient objects, such as *autos, cups, chairs,* and *apples* in our culture, tend to have single-word names which most people know, and the names are apt to be short. Less salient objects, such as *Buddhas, pueblos* and *gyroscopes,* have names which are longer on average and generally less familiar to the average speaker. Some objects are of such low salience that, if there is a single-word name for it, most people do not know it. If they must communicate about such categories, they construct multiword descriptors. For example, a stapler has a flat metal plate running along its center between the front hinge and the depression where the staple is bent. Stapler manufacturers doubtless have a name for this piece of metal, but it is unknown to most people (ourselves included).

Objects of sufficient salience, then, have single-word names that are stored in the LTMs of virtually all mature and intact individuals in the language community and similarly applied. It is frequently necessary to communicate about such aspects of the environment, and they are designated by efficient linguistic codes: short, common, agreed on names. At the very low end of the codability dimension is an enormous number of visual configurations that have little or no importance to members of a culture. Most of these objects or patterns are not directly represented in the lexicon of the language, but are designated by multiword descriptors or by various single words that differ from individual to individual.

Codability must be measured normatively. When naming norms are collected under time constraints, common and salient objects are given the same name by all Ss. As salience and codability decrease, the object-to-name mappings become increasingly one-to-many. Rare, infrequent objects yield a distribution of various names. Such distributions of name diversity can be measured by several statistics such as the number of different names the object elicits, or the uncertainty (Shannon, 1948) of the name distribution. The two statistics are correlated, but we use the information-theoretic measure and report codability/uncertainty in *bits* because it is sensitive to individual word probabilities. Codability is a theoretical concept for object-to-language mappings; uncertainty is a quantitative, operational definition of codability.

The extensive discussion of codability is necessary to indicate why, in many of our studies, we have calibrated stimuli on uncertainty rather than the more familiar frequency measure. Name frequency is reflected in the computation of uncertainty, but not the reverse. In our view, it is object salience that determines both codability and facility of name production. Frequency, uncertainty, and acquisition age are all somewhat different estimates of the salience of a named object. However, of the three variables, uncertainty most reflects the mapping aspect of the picture-naming task and the speech production of which picture-naming is an analogue. In this sense, uncertainty is a coordinating definition for codability.

Having described our research focus, the picture-naming laboratory task, and our choice of variables, it is now time to lay out the processing model which has guided our research. We can then be in a position to describe empirical studies and our interpretation of their outcomes.

A PROCESSING MODEL
OF LEXICAL PRODUCTION

Every intact human baby has the capacity to acquire language, and a disposition to do so is generally held to be innate (Chomsky, 1968; Lenneberg, 1967). Among other things, this innate capacity eventually supports the ability to map arbitrary phonological codes onto internal representations of external events. There are, no doubt, universal and invariant structures which are part and parcel of language utilization, including naming. At the same time, the human language utilization system is responsive to experience. It acquires the language to which it is exposed, and hence the communal practices of the individual's language community come to be represented within the linguistic system of the individual. More subtly, the system appears to contain a mechanism for responding to environmental contingencies so as to organize its content efficiently. Somehow, it monitors the salience of environmental events, and arranges itself so that labels for highly salient events are highly accessible. The responsivity is evident from the fact that communally measured variables consistently and powerfully influence individual word production latencies. Naming latencies are presumed to measure accessibility and hence internal lexical organization patterns. The research of Oldfield and Wingfield (1965) suggests that internal access time is inversely proportional to the frequency of occurrence of name-words in the language. Relationships have also been demonstrated between naming latency and experimental manipulation of frequency (Williams, 1971), and age of name acquisition (Carroll & White, 1973). Our own work (Lachman, 1973a,b; Lachman, Shaffer, & Hennrikus, 1974) has repeatedly demonstrated that naming is independently affected by frequency, recency, uncertainty, and age of acquisition, and that none of these variables is reducible to the others. Frequency and uncertainty, and to a lesser extent recency and age of acquisition, can be viewed as present in both the collective practices of a language community and in the internal linguistic organization of the particular individuals who use the language. The collective practices, in turn, reflect the varying salience of aspects of the environment. Therefore, the internal representations and access procedures of interest will be determined both by structures characteristic of all human beings and those features of particular languages and experiences to which the mental or brain structures are sensitive. Insofar as environmental linguistic events influence the subsequent behavior of an individual, it must be that such events result in a change in the internal memory system of that individual. Each variable, therefore, must be described not only in terms of its occurrence in the language community, but also in terms of its effect on the cognitive structure of each person.

In constructing a working model of a system which can label the environment, and come to do so in an efficient manner, we have been guided both by data and by the demands on analogous automata (Lachman, Lachman, & Butterfield, 1979, Chapter 4). The resultant approximation model appears in Fig. 19.1. The figure represents one of a large family of equivalent models and is to be understood as didactic, not literal. Any such system that can supply names for visually presented environmental configurations must be able to construct a more-than-fleeting internal representation of the configuration to be named, and this representation must make contact with previously stored visual information to support recognition of the object. Contact must also be possible with an abstract and amodal representation—amodal in that it could also be accessed via other modalities such as a linguistic description or private thought processes. There

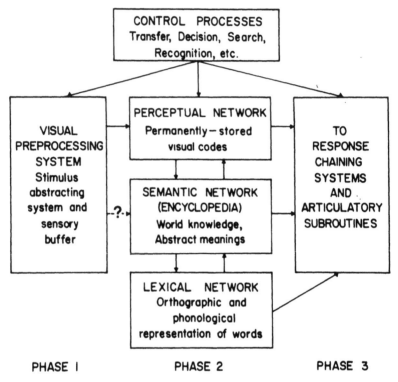

FIG. 19.1. Outline of a general processing system for picture naming representing one of an equivalent set of cognitive models.

must be, in addition, a route to the phonological representation of some appropriate name for the object. These requirements have suggested the preprocessing component and the intercommunicating perceptual, semantic, and lexical networks of Fig. 19.1.

Specification of particular characteristics for the three components may require years or even decades of research; however, there is reasonable evidence for the existence of all three, and for their partial isolability. We have elaborated the three systems in terms of hypothetical relationships and functions which are tentative and, in fact, tested in some of the research reported hereafter. One hypothetical sequence of processing in picture-naming is as follows: The visual processing system generates a transient visual code based on abstracted information from the picture stimulus. A recognition process matches the abstracted perceptual code with an internal perceptual code permanently stored in a perceptual (perhaps visual) network. Each permanently stored perceptual code has one or more corresponding conceptual codes in the semantic network, which is an encyclopedia and the repository of propositional world knowledge. This semantic network is further assumed to contain the "address" (content, path, or locative) to locations in the lexical network. Each concept node for which there is a name in the lexicon will contain access information to that name. Each network is now examined in somewhat greater detail.

The Perceptual Network. The assumption of a partially independent visual store has become more than a working hypothesis because considerable evidence has accumulated in its support. Part of this evidence comes from investigations of several different formulations of a dual-coding hypothesis (Paivio, 1971, 1975; Paivio, Rogers, & Smythe, 1968; Pellegrino, Siegel, & Dhawan, 1975; Snodgrass, Wasser, Finkelstein, & Goldberg, 1974). A second source of evidence comes from research on complex free-form figures which are difficult to code verbally. The retrieval of internal codes for such stimuli has been obtained under conditions where verbal labeling is unlikely (Cermak, 1971; Shepard & Cermak, 1973), which implies that all processing—both storage and retrieval—can occur in an independent visual memory system. Even if visual stimuli facilitate verbal coding, as do faces (Warrington & Shallice, 1972; Warrington & Taylor, 1973) and pictures of common objects and scenes (Cohen, 1973; Standing, 1973), the experimental findings suggest at least some independence between visual and auditory–articulatory storage systems. For one thing, there are well established differences in storage capacity for pictures and for words (Nickerson, 1965; Shepard, 1967). Second, there are well known processes associated with the memory of verbal materials, such as rehearsal and serial position. Although their interpretation is controversial, several studies (Loftus, 1974; Potter & Levy, 1969; Shaffer & Shiffrin, 1972) suggest no analogue for such processes in memory for pictures. Experiments using only visually presented words have also shown that subjects generate a visual code containing such information as typeface; this code is to some extent independent of the corresponding verbal code (Kirsner, 1973). The isolable character of visual and verbal subsystems has been carefully explored by Posner (Posner, 1973; Posner, Lewis, & Conrad, 1972). Finally, it is necessary to assume that the form of the permanent visual code is sufficiently abstract to permit matching of any physical stimulus token that is appropriate to the concept or category type with the concept's name, a performance that is ubiquitous and effortless in human beings.

The Semantic Network. Presentation of a visual pattern begins processes that can tap a vast array of world knowledge, including much of what the viewer knows about the stimulus object. Information that can be retrieved includes, among other things, the object's properties, its class affiliation, subordinates, superordinates, and coordinates; its various uses and relationships to other objects and events; and even its familiarity and frequency of use. To accommodate these links to world knowledge, a semantic memory network is posited. This network is also the assumed repository of indexing information, providing directions to the names of semantic categories stored in a separate lexical network.

It is only very recently that researchers in semantic memory have opted for putting some world knowledge into the representation of linguistic units (Lachman, Lachman & Butterfield, 1979). Smith, Shoben, and Rips (1974), for example, distinguish between defining and characteristic features for the concepts denoted by a word. Defining features correspond approximately to notions previously held by linguists, who argued for semantic representations which contained only the intrinsic and essential meaning of a word. The notion of characteristic features, postulated by Smith et al., (1974), brings in the full domain of world knowledge in the representation of a concept. The concept of *bird* in normal adults, for example, includes the understanding that while not all birds fly, most of them do, and moreover, those that do not are not especially good representatives of the class of birds. The work of Rosch (1975) on typicality in category membership and the recent increase in references to "fuzzy" logic in cognitive psychology argues that world knowledge cannot be evaded in any serious account of how people use words. Much current research and theory is directed at discovering the organizational structure of categories in semantic memory (for a review see Lachman, Lachman & Butterfield, 1979, Chapters 9 and 12). Translated into the hypothetical structures of Fig. 19.1, this amounts to discovering the internal organization of the semantic network.

The Lexical Network. The lexicon is the vocabulary store, the repository of acquired names for all perceptual or conceptual categories having a vocabulary code. The lexical network is not unlike the hypothetical lexicons of other theorists; however, most prior theorizing concerns comprehension rather than production. Kintsch (1974), for example, suggests that independent word storage is required by the act of comprehension. Words or their morphemic structure are stored in memory; sentences are decomposed into words along with syntax by the listener/comprehender. The "words" are approximately delineated by traditional orthography; that is, they roughly correspond to written words, with some multiple-word units belonging to a single node in the memory system (e.g., New-York-Yankees, Richard-M.-Nixon, ice-cream-cone, aircraft-carrier). With respect to picture naming, it is suggested that such "words" constitute the unit of storage immediately preceding the output response, along with their phonological representations. Our distinction between the semantic network and the lexicon is also similar to the differentiation between concepts and words in the semantic memory theory of Norman and Rumelhart (1975). In their system, the meanings of concepts are given by the relationships among them; however, the relationship between a concept and its corresponding name is of a different sort. In the present formulation, the semantic network is the locus of abstract conceptual representations underlying a name-word, and the repository of its meaning. But the phonological and graphemic representation is elsewhere, in the lexical network. This does not imply that the lexicon is the repository of final production subroutines or articulatory codes—rather, it contains the information that serves as input to a final speech production mechanism. Such a final system, we assume, takes lexical units as input, orders them, and produces a final well formed physical speech signal.

Although our separation of lexical and semantic information corresponds to the main distinction of the dictionary–network model of Loftus (1977), we make no claims about the organization of the lexicon relative to its phonological properties. The extant research is not clear as to the general organization of this system; however, it appears to be sensitive to name variance and frequency. This sensitivity constrains the class of search algorithms and organizational schemes that can be plausibly claimed for the lexical network. It also appears that retrieval of the phonological form of words from the lexicon is relatively labile compared to the retrieval of semantic information, as is evidenced in the familiar tip-of-the-tongue phenomenon (Brown & McNeill, 1966; Yarmey, 1973).

Effective Procedures.   In addition to storage systems for permanently represented information, the system must also have "effective procedures" for accessing the stored representations. To state that a picture is "associated with" its name is not to specify an effective procedure or algorithm for access, for it leaves unanswered all the questions of what internal events represent the picture, what internal events represent the name, what internal routes link the two, and what processes activate just these routes on presentation of a picture. The logical or analogical use of automata in theorizing requires that there be some internal representation and some access procedure.

The unit of storage or the form of access is unspecified and these must therefore be stipulated by assumption, pending empirical discoveries that constrain the possibilities. A similar situation obtains with respect to the procedures whereby the system internalizes information with regard to environmental salience. Presumably, the occurrence of an interaction with some piece of the environment results in an internal change in one or more of the component networks. The nature of the change, no doubt, depends upon the nature of the interaction: the modality in which it occurred and the networks accessed in the course of the interaction.

Independence Of The Three Components Of The Tripartite Model.   Few students of human cognition would find fault with the notion of a visual store which is to some degree separate from verbal capacities, but many theorists have chosen not to postulate separate conceptual and lexical stores. Several lines of evidence argue persuasively for the latter distinction, however. Extant research shows that they are differentially susceptible to neurological insult, and may be different in developmental pattern (Geschwind, 1967). Differential loss of information or accessibility seems also to occur for the two systems. For example, subjects often can recognize an object and recall its properties but not retrieve its name, although the name can be selected from a set. Thus, information-location procedures between visual and/or semantic memory systems and the lexical system can be interrupted, but they can be reestablished by an external word stimulus for the corresponding lexical item. The extreme form of this breakdown in search algorithms between the visual or semantic network and the permanent lexical store is seen in certain forms of aphasia. We do not preclude the possibility that the names for some words—e.g., those with high frequency of occurrence and low-uncertainty referents—may be stored directly in the semantic network. However, any claim that *all* names are stored in semantic memory must account for the striking instances of nominal aphasia in which well articulated, fluent speech is present but the patient has considerable difficulty and frequent failure in producing names for objects whose properties and uses he can understand and explain (Gardner, 1973, 1974; Geschwind, 1967; Schaff, 1973).

The distinction between a semantic network and a lexical store also has experimental corroboration. A long series of experiments by Loftus supported a dual-storage model in which attribute and name information are stored, organized, and retrieved separately from each other (Collins & Loftus, 1975; Loftus, 1977; Loftus & Cole, 1974). Moreover, virtually everyone has experienced tip-of-the-tongue difficulty for names, but so far no one with normal memory has reported experiencing it for property attributes or semantic information. This suggests that names and encyclopedic information must be given different status in any reasonable account of their access.

These arguments have often suggested a two-stage model of performance in the picture-naming task (Clark & Clark, 1977). In stage one, the object in the picture is identified, and an appropriate name-word is selected from an internal dictionary in stage two. In contemporary terms, stage one—perceptual identification—would be described as essentially parallel and fast. Stage two, lexical access, may be largely serial and slow. This view is intuitively appealing, and Wingfield (1967, 1968) has reported some empirical support for it. However, it seems necessary to separate the perceptual and conceptual networks from each other, as well as from the lexical network, to extend the model beyond picture-naming to other kinds of word production. And the two-stage model is probably too emphatically serial. We have postulated three "phases" (cf. Fig. 19.1), rather than two "stages," since we doubt that the networks are accessed in completely discrete temporal succession. Nevertheless, we believe they are amenable, at least partially, to experimental isolation. The experiments on localization, described shortly, were designed to accomplish such isolation.

Our research program's objectives are to extend, correct, and clarify the foregoing working model of endosomatic or internal codes in picture naming and word production. Many of the studies are efforts to localize the effects of specified variables in one or more of the hypothetical subsystems. Some experiments reflect an additional objective, that of characterizing the mechanism by which the complex of subsystems responds to salience, through exposure to communal linguistic variables such as frequency, uncertainty, and acquisition age.

THE EFFECT OF CODABILITY
AND ENVIRONMENTAL SALIENCE

For reasons mentioned earlier, we have used normative uncertainty (U) as a measure of codability, which in turn is a consequence of salience. It is correlated with and reflects both frequency and acquisition age of the name-word, and it represents the code-to-environment mapping that is the focus of our research program. This mapping reflects the individual's experience with his linguistic community. Butterfield & Butterfield (1977) found a developmental trend in children's naming consensus that converged on adult uncertainty values. As children mature, their coding of objects becomes increasingly like that of adults, presumably by virtue of their linguistic experience.

The adult's ability to produce a name to a picture depends on salience, and access time is related to uncertainty. Typical effects of uncertainty on naming latency are shown in Table 19.1 and the upper curve of Fig. 19.2. Pictures with zero uncertainty, for which everyone gives the same name, yield short latencies. At higher levels of uncertainty, where several names are given to the same object, latencies increase dramatically. Sophisticated subjects have reported that the names of some objects seem, in some fashion, to be directly accessed; other objects—usually uncommon ones—seem to engender a conscious and deliberate effort, and the name given is sometimes selected from several possible alternatives. These two modes of production occur disproportionately at low and high uncertainty: Low-uncertainty pictures tend to produce "automatic" naming, while high-uncertainty pictures are likelier to result in conscious searches. This observation led us to propose that names at low average uncertainty, $U < 2.0$ *bits,* are retrieved directly by an algorithmic process. But the concepts underlying high-uncertainty objects have no algorithm for locating a particular name, and hence one must be selected heuristically. Statistical evidence has been reported suggesting a

TABLE 19.1

Uncertainties, Reaction Times, And Examples Of Picture Names For Seven Sets Of 16 Stimuli[a]

Examples of Picture Names			Uncertainty (bits)		Reaction Time (msec)			
					Means of Medians[a]		Mean Reciprocal[b]	
			Median	Range	Trial 1	Trial 2	Trial 1	Trial 2
Apple	Glove	Zebra	0	0	825	713	1.21	1.38
Diamond	Hanger	Microscope	.56	.47–.63	1004	807	1.03	1.22
Clown	Hacksaw	Volcano	1.01	.95–1.05	1076	848	.949	1.16
Bracelet	Diver	Wasp	1.51	1.44–1.54	1235	965	.840	1.03
Coins	Knight	Syringe	2.06	1.91–2.12	1305	987	.805	1.02
Gears	Ram	Temple	2.51	2.37–2.66	1801	1208	.611	.840
Hourglass	Gondola	Pueblo	3.08	2.70–3.40	1995	1264	.563	.821

[a]From, Lachman, Shaffer, & Hennrikus (1974).
[b]Mean of 16 subjects for medians of 16 stimuli.
[c]Mean of 16 subjects for mean reciprocal of 16 stimuli.

326

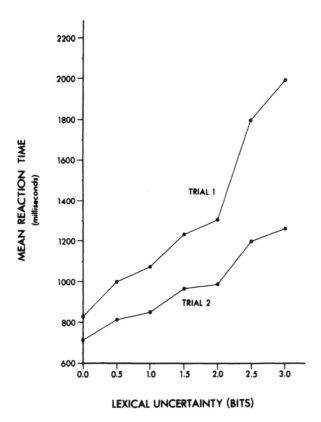

FIG. 19.2.   Naming latency as a function of uncertainty of the distribution of name-word responses obtained from a normative sample (from Lachman, Shaffer, & Hennrikus, 1974).

disjunction at $U = 2$ bits between direct, algorithmic access and heuristic name construction (cf. Lachman et al., 1974). Butterfield & Butterfield (1978) found that subjects of all ages can be divided into two groups: those who show a break in the curve relating uncertainty to naming latency, and those for whom the function is linear. Even for linear subjects, however, the increase in latency with greater uncertainty can be explained by the subjects' increasing use of deliberate search strategies. Whether or not there is a clear point of disjunction between algorithmic and heuristic retrieval processes, direct access of endosomatically stored names clearly decreases with higher values of uncertainty. This would be consistent with efficient retrieval. If heuristic or controlled capacity is costly or limited, it would make sense to allocate automatic processes to those environmental events which are likely to be labeled most often—highly salient and well-coded events.

It is interesting that aphasia is most evident at high uncertainty levels. Mills, Knox, Juola, and Salmon (1979) describe two relevant findings. Aphasic and normal subjects differ in naming-latency at high uncertainty levels, but not for low uncertainty. This seems to suggest that the aphasic's deficit selectively affects the systems that supply names for events of relatively low salience. The outcome is quite consistent with our speculation that high- and low-uncertainty stimuli are named by different processes. Mills et al. (1979) also found that uncertainty affects name production but not recognition performance. We have found several parallel results in our laboratory. Our research has employed a variety of experimental operations in which an object name is provided the subject for some judgmental task. The subject makes a decision such as whether the name is appropriate for a preceding picture, responding either "yes" or "no." In this task, the slope of the function relating uncertainty to reaction time is approximately zero. In another similar task, the subject is given a property (e.g., *has wings*) followed by a picture (e.g., *bird*), and must respond "yes" or "no" depending on whether the property is true of the picture. In still another version of this task, subjects indicate whether a line drawing which follows a color slide is of the same object or a different one. In all these tasks, which do not require name production, the effect of uncertainty on latency is essentially nil (see Fig. 19.3). Even word-reading latencies are insensitive to uncertainty. Occasionally there is a slight latency increase at the highest level of uncertainty ($U = 3$ bits), which is probably due to perceptual problems subjects (Ss) have with the most poorly coded items (e.g., geothermal steam). Typically, we remove such items from our stimulus ensembles. In general, when the experimental task requires the subject to produce a name-word autonomously, then and only then does latency increase with uncertainty.

The processes implicated in the uncertainty measure—those involving mapping words onto environmental categories—must therefore be located primarily in Phases 2 or 3 of Fig. 19.1, or perhaps both. What appears to be required for an uncertainty effect is either passive or directed search through an internal dictionary or encyclopedia. Uncertainty is, therefore, related to endosomatic cognitive processes that are localized in a lexical or conceptual network, but not directly in visual analogue storage. The subtleties suggested by the qualifier "not directly" will be made apparent shortly.

ISOLATION RESEARCH
AND SYSTEM UPDATING

When a set of pictures is named a second time, in a single experimental session, a substantial drop in latency occurs on the second naming. Fig. 19.2 shows the phenomenon: Naming-latencies drop about 100 msec at $U = 0$, and more than 800 msec at $U = 3$ *bits*. The effect is pervasive. It even occurs, though it is somewhat attenuated, when the language is shifted

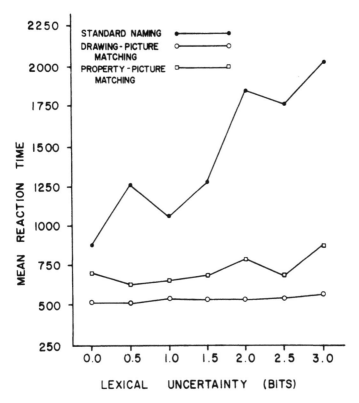

FIG. 19.3. Typical effects for naming latency as a function of lexical uncertainty in different experimental tasks. Uncertainty appears to yield a nonzero slope only when a name must be located endosomatically.

(English–German) from the first to the second naming (Lachman & Mistler-Lachman, 1976).

We believe that the repetition–speedup effect reflects a reordering of priorities within the semantic and lexical systems, in order to deal efficiently with concepts and words that have become topically more current. A word for a particular concept that has already occurred once in speech is likelier to be needed again soon. Conversation about some topic will typically contain multiple tokens for the name of the topic, and for various related or associated terms. The repetition–speedup effect may be one mechanism mediating the speed and efficiency of word production in fluent speech. The relationship between the repetition–speedup effect and the concept of "activation" will be considered later. For the moment, it will suffice to say that some underlying system or systems must be primed by the first presentation such that it facilitates the second. We turn now to studies that were designed to capitalize on the latency-drop to localize the effect in specific underlying networks, thereby also testing the adequacy of the three-network model.

When a person sees and recognizes a picture, contact is made with a visual code. If the viewer can report properties of the object, contact has been made with a conceptual or semantic code. If he can name the picture, contact has been made with a lexical code. This entire sequence happens faster the second time. The question, then, is this: which of the three networks was activated, or changed to a more accessible state, by previous presentation and naming of the picture? The data presented in Fig. 19.3 show that only tasks requiring internal name location yield uncertainty effects. This makes it appear that name location, rather than visual processing, is the locus of the uncertainty effect—that is, that longer latencies at high uncertainty reflect effortful name searches or constructions, rather than slower visual processing. Moreover, the repetition-effect data shown in Fig. 19.1 indicate that the repetition latency-drop is greater at high uncertainty levels than at low ones. Taken together, these observations lead to the conclusion that repetition priming effects are located in the word-finding process and the networks implicated in it. In other words, the occurrence of a picture-naming episode primes the lexical or semantic network, or both; it does not appear to affect the perceptual (visual) network.

A series of experiments was undertaken to test this view of the locus of system updating. We assumed that the picture-naming task activated all three networks: visual, semantic, and lexical. We further assumed that selective-activation tasks could be devised which would implicate only selected networks. Reading the name of an object aloud, for example, presumably requires a subject to activate only the lexical, and possibly the semantic, network. Judging the appropriateness of a property to a picture presumably activates the visual and semantic, but not the lexical, network. The general approach in the localization experiments was to use multiple-stage experiments in which such selective-activation tasks were administered in Stage 1, and Stage 2 was a standard, timed picture-naming task. The extent to which various subsystems contributed to the latency drop could then be assessed by comparing Stage 2 naming performance to conditions of no drop and total drop, as follows. If all three networks are activated in picture-naming, then renaming represents the condition of maximum drop. If the subject is totally naive with respect to the picture, his latency represents zero drop; this is the case in first-trial naming. Some slides, then, are named during Stage 1, and the mean latency gives an estimate of zero drop. Other slides appear in the selective-activation tasks. When all slides are named during Stage 2, the latency to name them reflects their history. Those slides that were named previously give an estimate of maximum drop; those that appeared in the selective-activation tasks are named with a speed reflecting the contribution to repetition-update of the networks experimentally activated. For example, consider the slides that appeared in the reading condition previously mentioned. In Stage 1, subjects would not see picture slides. Instead, they would read the name most commonly supplied for each by a normative group. In Stage 2, they would see the picture slides and name them. The Stage 2 naming latencies can be compared to two relevant measures: Stage 1 naming (the naive condition), and Stage 2 renaming of previously named slides. These conditions reflect no update and maximum update, respectively. If Stage 2 naming of slides in the reading condition is as rapid as Stage 2 naming in the renaming condition, we could conclude that the visual system played no role in the update effect. This would follow since the speed-up was the same whether or not the subject had actually seen the slide previously. Conversely, if slides in the reading condition are named no faster than those in the naive (Stage 1) naming task, we could conclude that the lexical system played no role in the latency drop. In summary, the rationale underlying these studies is this: If the final latency of some condition is like the standard on first naming, system updating is not occurring in the network(s) accessed by that condition. On the other hand, if the final latency of a treatment is as fast as the second naming in the standard condition, then the network(s) accessed by that condition plays a role in the updating or activation effect.

We started out by trying to isolate visual processing. The objective was to show that visual processing alone produces no repetition update, and conversely that the entire repetition effect can be produced without priming the visual network. In the first experiment, the critical treatment was presentation of slides in rapid succession, about 200 msec per slide. Two carousel projectors were mounted vertically and wired electronically to project and advance in tandem in order to achieve this presentation rate. Prior to this experimental treatment, the same Ss named a comparable set of picture slides in the standard naming condition. In the final stage, Ss performed the standard naming task on three groups of slides: Those which had been previously named, those which had been rapidly presented, and a new set never previously shown. The results (Lachman, Lachman, Thronesbery, & Sala, 1979) are shown in Fig. 19.4 in reciprocal reaction times. As expected, there was no latency drop for the rapid visual treatment. This was what we expected if Ss were not seeking names—and indeed, the phenomenological report was universal: "I saw the slides but they came too fast to name." To back up this introspection, we ran a fresh group of subjects but added a recognition test. The results were unexpected: Pictures previously named were correctly recognized as "old" near the 100% level. Likewise, new pictures yielded close to 100% correct "new" responses. But the fast-exposure slides yielded 48% correct performance: Just about half were designated "new" and half "old." This performance is chance—but it is not random. Fast presentation, at this 200-msec rate, does not leave the subject in the same condition as no presentation; it leaves something behind so the subject is unable to say surely whether he recently saw the picture or not. The outcome

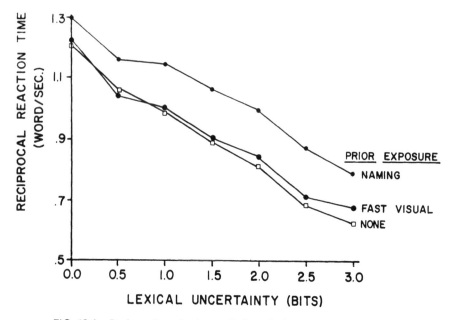

FIG. 19.4.   Reciprocal naming latency in Stage 2 of a two-stage experiment. Each curve represents a different Stage 1 treatment: naming, fast visual exposure, or none.

is actually not anomalous in the context of other studies on picture exposure duration (e.g., Potter, 1976; Shaffer & Shiffrin, 1972).

A stronger test of our initial hypothesis would require a presentation long enough for full visual "registration," but without introducing covert naming. The next study was designed to accomplish just this; however, we had to "trick" the subjects to prevent them from naming the pictures. Our vehicle was a mock visual-recognition experiment, the design of which is shown in Table 19.2. In the first stage of the study, a group of slides were named. In the second stage, a feigned recognition test included half of the previously named items, and an equal number of new items. It is this presentation that constitutes the experimental treatment; the slides are viewed long enough to decide if they are new or old, but since the subject thinks he is doing a recognition task, he has no reason to covertly name the slides. The ruse apparently worked, since subjects typically reported in a post-experimental interview, "I could immediately tell if I had seen the slide before . . . . No, I did not name the (new) slides—there was no reason to." In Stage 3 of the study, these experimental slides were named for the first time. In addition, the remaining half of the earlier-named slides were renamed, providing a baseline for the maximum repetition speedup, and a new group of slides—never

TABLE 19.2
Experimental Treatments Between Stimuli, Within-Subjects

	Experimental Stage			
	1	*2*		*3*
Objective Of		Recognition	(*Prior*	
Treatment	*Naming*	Test	Treatment)	*Naming*
Second Naming	Pictures	Pictures	Naming	Pictures
				Named
Control	Named	Omitted		Second Time
Recognition	Pictures	Recognition		Pictures
Foils	Named	"Old"	Irrelevant	Omitted
Priming Visual	Pictures	Recognition		Pictures
Network	Omitted	"New"	Visual	First Time
First Naming	Pictures	Pictures		Pictures
				Named
Control	Omitted	Omitted	None	First Time

shown before—were named to provide the no-repetition baseline. The slides which had been named initially and shown as "old" items in the mock recognition test were dropped from the study. The question was, would the experimental pictures—fully seen but not named—be named as rapidly as slides named for the second time or as slowly as those named for the first time? Our hypothesis, at the time we did the study, was that visual presentation without naming would produce no latency drop and that experimental slides would compare to those seen and named for the first time in Stage 3.

This did not happen. The results are shown in Fig. 19.5, in reciprocal reaction times. The reciprocal transformation tends to normalize the distribution of reaction-time data and reduce the correlation between means and variances. The conclusion under consideration here is the same if raw scores are analyzed. Prior processing of a picture that activates a visual code and primes the visual network, without necessarily disturbing lexical memory, produces a latency drop of 30 to 40% upon initial naming. This is not the outcome we expected or wanted. The identification phase of picture naming should be much faster than name finding. Visual identification, if it makes an independent contribution to the latency drop, should account for a rather small proportion of that drop. But priming the visual network appears to reduce subsequent naming latencies by as much as 40%. Several other studies are consistent with this conclusion. Bartram (1974) found clear reductions in latency due to prior visual processing, and Poon & Fozard (1978) showed that familiar pictures of objects are named faster than

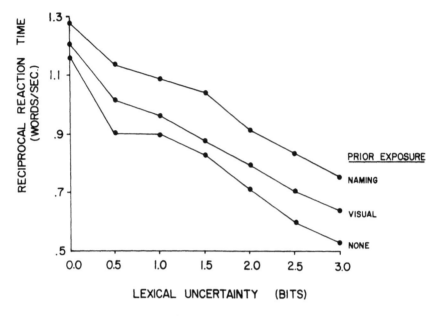

FIG. 19.5. Reciprocal naming latency in Stage 2. Stage 1 treatments were naming, negative instance in a recognition task (visual), or none.

unfamiliar exemplars. This convergence, and the tight design of our own study, led us to question our hypothesis that the visual system is not implicated in the repetition–speedup effect.

Still, it could be that the visual system exerts its effect indirectly, through the semantic or lexical systems. On this view, it is priming of semantic and/or lexical networks that produces the speedup effect; but with enough viewing time, the visual system "spills over," resulting in priming of one or both of these systems. Another possibility, one that seemed increasingly likely given the results shown in Fig. 19.5, was that each system that is primed makes an independent contribution to the repetition effect. A study was designed, therefore, to see how much of the latency drop could be produced without priming the visual system at all. The experiment was intended to isolate various subsystems to determine if they contributed to the update effect, and if so, how much.

In this experiment, several experimental conditions were introduced in a between-subject design, and compared to standard Trial 1 (naming) and Trial 2 (renaming). One group performed the standard naming and renaming tasks, providing the upper (no drop) and lower (full drop) baselines. One condition, reading, was designed to prime only the lexical network. In Stage 1, these Ss saw no pictures; they read names. The names were those most frequently supplied by a normative sample to pictures, and the pictures themselves were

TABLE 19.3
Examples of Stimuli Used In The Predicate-Name And
Predicate-Picture Conditions

First Slide (Predicate)	Second Slide (Word or Picture)	Subject's Response
Has Wings	Battery	No
Is Edible	Ham	Yes
Carries Passengers	Bus	Yes
Is Worshipped	Buddha	Yes
Burns Oil	Raccoon	No

named in Stage 2 by *S*s in the reading condition. A second experimental condition, predicate-name, was designed to prime the semantic and lexical networks together while excluding the visual system. In Stage 1, subjects judged whether a predicate (e.g., *has teeth*) was true of a category (e.g., *shark*). Again, the category names were those most frequently supplied to pictures, and the pictures themselves were named in Stage 2. Distractors were included, but not analyzed; the nature of the stimuli in this condition is shown in Table 19.3. Also shown in Table 19.3 is the third experimental condition, predicate-picture, designed to prime the visual and semantic networks without priming the lexicon. The predicate, e.g., *has teeth,* was followed by a picture of a shark rather than the word *shark,* and these *S*s also judged whether the predicate was true or false of the object.

The results of this study could thus show the effects on repetition update of priming the lexical system alone (reading), the lexical and semantic systems together (predicate-name), and the visual and semantic systems together (predicate-picture). Put in the obverse terms, it would show the effect of excluding ony the visual system (predicate-name), only the lexicon (predicate-picture), and possibly both, or excluding the semantic and perceptual systems (reading). The contribution of each system to the latency drop should be inferrable, approximately, from this and the previous experiments.

Fig. 19.6 shows the results, again in reciprocal reaction time. Stage 2 naming-latencies of subjects in each of the three isolating conditions were faster than first-trial naming and slower than renaming. Priming any of the three networks, or bringing two of the three types of code into working memory, facilitates performance when a picture is subsequently named, even if that picture was never seen before. The effect appears at every level of uncertainty. The mere articulation of a concept's name, in the reading

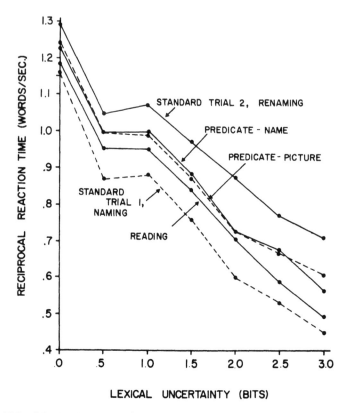

FIG. 19.6. Reciprocal naming latency in Stage 2 of a two-stage experiment. Prior treatments in Stage 1 were naming, predicate-picture matching, predicate-name matching, or name reading.

treatment, produces a subsequent speedup of picture naming; this occurs despite the universal polysemous character of individual words. But producing the word cannot alone account for the total naming-latency drop. If a given name has been previously linked to a predicate, which requires accessing the appropriate concept in semantic memory, the speedup is approximately half the maximum. This happens in the predicate-name condition without the S ever having seen the picture previously; but again it does not account for the entire effect. The predicate-picture condition, predictably from the results of the earlier study, produces a latency drop; this drop is about the same magnitude as that of the predicate-name condition.

It has been argued that it is virtually impossible to isolate a visual code, since the effects of semantic processing are ubiquitous (Klatzky & Stoy, 1978). Certainly meaning and understanding are a most potent variable in human information processing. However, semantic priming alone cannot account for our data. If semantic priming accounted for the entire latency drop, then any task involving the semantic network should produce the drop in its full magnitude. Obviously, this did not happen. The semantic network was plainly implicated in both the predicate-name and predicate-picture conditions, each of which resulted in a speedup about half the size obtained when all three networks were accessed in the naming condition. Apparently, the semantic network alone can account for at most half the repetition speedup effect. The visual and/or lexical systems must be invoked to deal with the remainder.

It is possible that the primary effects of visual and lexical network priming are roughly additive to produce the entire repetition speedup. But it is also possible that the subsystems interact. If this is the case, the relationship between the visual and lexical networks is not as independent as the two-stage theory, and our own initial views, would have it. The lexical network, and the semantic network as well, may develop in intimate congress with the perceptual system. This possibility is intuitively reasonable, since vision is phylogenetically and ontogenetically prior to language. What is more, humans—like other primates—are heavily dependent on vision for their knowledge of the environment, and the visual system may importantly determine semantic and lexical categories. Research we have conducted with coordinate bilingual subjects highlights the potential developmental intertwining of visual and lexical networks. Priming of the visual system alone produced a subsequent naming latency drop in the native language— but not as much in a second language learned after puberty (Lachman & Mistler-Lachman, 1976). This suggests that the visual system may be tied to linguistic long-term memory, but only that of the first language learned, the mother tongue. If this is correct, the visual system may produce its effects on later naming by virtue of "pulling in" semantic and lexical systems, rather than through a direct update of the visual code. But on the basis of research described thus far, a separate and independent effect within the visual network itself cannot be discounted.

How may we disentangle these alternative possibilities? It might yet be possible to do so, by the following logic. We assumed that the repetition–speedup effect is transient, and that in the absence of continued updating the system will return to its initial state. What if the networks return to their original state at different rates? We may yet be able to localize and explain the update effect if our various priming conditions produce different rates of return. We have heretofore completed only the first step in such a program, which is to identify the time-course of return to initial state of the total system combining the effects of all subsystems. The question is, how much time must elapse after a picture is named before it will be named with the same latency as originally—that is, without a latency drop?

The objective of the final experiment to be described was to answer that question. In this study only four levels of uncertainty were used, in order to have sufficient stimuli at each level for the various treatments. This is an experiment in which subjects saw and named pictures, and then renamed them at a series of delay intervals.

On the first day of testing, subjects saw 160 slides. Forty of these were renamed immediately after completion of the initial naming task. The subjects returned to the laboratory one day later and renamed a second set of 40. They then returned seven and 14 days later to rename the third and fourth sets. Thus, each subject named 160 slides twice: 40 at each of four delay conditions. Fig. 19.7 shows the outcome of the experiment for all uncertainty levels. Two aspects of the figure are surprising. One surprise is the continued reduction in latency from the immediate renaming to the one-day interval (recall that different slides were renamed at each delay interval).

We had seen this effect previously in pilot studies, but at the time dismissed it as noise. It occurs in nine out of 12 of our subjects. The "tuning" of the system as a result of a single naming experience appears to pick up momentum for a day or so following the experience! But the major result is the slow rate of return. The update effect is no on-again, off-again thing: It is very persistent. Subjects' latencies have only returned, on average, halfway to their original performance level two weeks after the first naming. Fig. 19.8 shows the return patterns for different levels of uncertainty. The two higher and the two lower levels appear to exhibit a somewhat different pattern of

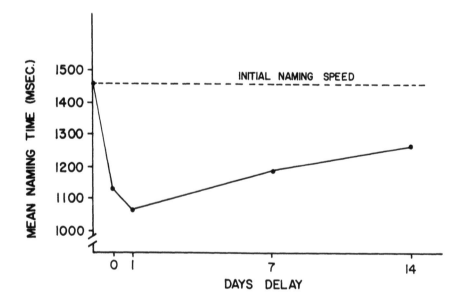

FIG. 19.7. Speed of second naming as a function of number of days delay after first naming (means of individual subject's median naming-latency).

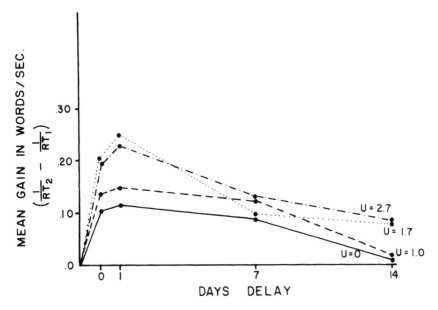

FIG. 19.8.   Difference in reciprocal naming-latency between original naming and renaming for four levels of lexical uncertainty.

return; by the end of two weeks $U = 0$ and $U = 1.0$ are near original average latency level. The differences among U levels, however, are not statistically significant.

We can only speculate about the meaning of these new data. One possibility has occurred to us: For some stimuli, the system may never fully return to its original state. It may be that the visual system, which behaved so intrusively in our earlier localization experiments, is profoundly subject to updating. Shepard (1967) long ago showed that memory for pictures seen only once is nearly perfect weeks later. Perhaps the visual system, once it has been exposed to a picture, is never again naive with respect to that picture. It may be only the lexical component of the latency drop that returns to its original state. Obviously, our next efforts will be to use priming tasks and delay conditions in an attempt to specify a rate of return for each network.

The outcome of this final study suggests that the update effect cannot be identified with the concept of "activation" (Anderson, 1976; Collins & Loftus, 1975; Posner & Snyder, 1975). The theoretical role assigned to activation requires that it be transient. It is invoked to predict, for example, that it will take less time to access information when related information has been accessed "a short time previously [Collins & Loftus, 1975, p. 419]." Spread-of-activation theory was formulated generally to accommodate semantic priming effects over relatively short intervals, and will not readily encompass effects lasting hours or days. But, whatever the precise allocation of the latency drop to specific networks, priming of a conceptual and/or lexical node by naming a picture clearly lasts beyond two weeks. The cognitive system would become intolerably noisy if activation, with its capability to spread, were maintained over such long intervals.

We are working with the tentative hypothesis that two system changes may occur when a word and its conceptual and/or visual referent is brought into working memory. One such change may correspond to activation: a transient, short-term memory effect that supports facile access of related content and dissipates over a time-course consistent with the decay intervals of short-term memory, less than 18 sec. The other change, corresponding to the latency update effect, is more durable. It may entail a frequency increment tag, or a system reorganization whose effects are detectable for weeks. The underlying mechanism would control long-range adjustment in network structures and information accessibility as a consequence of changes in environmental salience. The processes controlled are long-term incrementing and updating of conceptual and vocabulary information. While accommodating short-term memory effects, this interpretation leaves room for such activation to exert relatively long-lasting effects on the organizational structure of LTM, thus taking account of the effects of frequency and codability on accessibility from LTM. This kind of interpretation is in line with contemporary theories that view short-term memory as a temporarily activated portion of long-term memory (e.g., Shiffrin & Schneider, 1977).

To summarize the state of our research program, then, we believe that the localization studies we have completed support the general conception of the tripartite model. Each subcomponent we have postulated appears to be "primable" and to contribute to the repetition update effect alone or in combination with other systems. The independence of the networks is still ambiguous. We are planning to attack this issue by means of priming studies in which we chart the rate of dissipation of the update effect. The fact that the update effect dissipates so slowly has raised a new set of interesting issues, including the relationship of repetition update to the concept of activation. We hope that some of these questions will be answered soon.

ACKNOWLEDGMENTS

The final experiment reported and preparation of this paper were supported by NSF Grant BNS 77-25657. We gratefully acknowledge the assistance of our students, Don Taylor, Carroll Thronesbery, Cameron Camp, and former student Linda Sala, for collecting most of the data reported and assisting in statistical analyses. Thanks also to Laird S. Cermak for astute feedback.

REFERENCES

Anderson, J. R. *Language, memory and thought.* Hillsdale, N.J.: Lawrence Erlbaum Associates, 1976.

Bartram, D. J. The role of visual and semantic codes in object naming. *Cognitive Psychology,* 1974, *6,* 325–356.

Brown, R., & Lenneberg, E. H. A study in language and cognition. *Journal of Abnormal and Social Psychology,* 1954, *49,* 454–462.

Brown, R., & McNeill, D. The "tip of the tongue" phenomenon. *Journal of Verbal Learning and Verbal Behavior,* 1966, *5,* 325–337.

Butterfield, E. C., & Butterfield, G. B. *Retrieval strategies as a function of name uncertainty.* Unpublished manuscript, 1978.

Butterfield, G. B., & Butterfield, E. C. Lexical codability and age. *Journal of Verbal Learning and Verbal Behavior,* 1977, *16,* 113–118.

Carroll, J. B. (Ed.). *Language, thought and reality: Selected writings of Benjamin Lee Whorf.* Cambridge, Mass.: M.I.T. Press, 1956.

Carroll, J. B., & White, M. N. Word frequency and age of acquisition as determiners of picture-naming latency. *Quarterly Journal of Experimental Psychology,* 1973, *25,* 85–95.

Cermak, G. W. Short-term recognition memory for complex free-form figures. *Psychonomic Science,* 1971, *25,* 209–211.

Chomsky, N. *Language and mind.* New York: Harcourt Brace Jovanovich, 1968.

Clark, H. H., Carpenter, P. A., & Just, M. A. On the meeting of semantics and perception. In W. G. Chase (Ed.), *Visual information processing.* New York: Academic Press, 1973.

Clark, H. H., & Clark, E. V. *Psychology and language: An introduction to psycholinguistics.* New York: Harcourt Brace Jovanovich, 1977.

Cohen, G. How are pictures registered in memory? *Quarterly Journal of Experimental Psychology,* 1973, *25,* 557–564.

Collins, A. M., & Loftus, E. F. A spreading-activation theory of semantic processing. *Psychological Review,* 1975, *82,* 407–428.

Gardner, H. The contribution of operativity to naming capacity in aphasic patients. *Neuropsychologia,* 1973, *11,* 213–220.

Gardner, H. The naming of objects and symbols by children and aphasic patients. *Journal of Psycholinguistic Research,* 1974, *3,* 133–149.

Geschwind, N. The varieties of naming errors. *Cortex,* 1967, *3,* 97–112.

Kintsch, W. *The representation of meaning in memory.* Hillsdale, N.J.: Lawrence Erlbaum Associates, 1974.

Kirsner, K. An analysis of the visual component in recognition memory for verbal stimuli. *Memory and Cognition,* 1973, *1,* 449–453.

Klatzky, R. L., & Stoy, A. M. Semantic information and visual information processing. In J. W. Cotton & R. L. Klatzky (Eds.), *Semantic factors in cognition.* Hillsdale, N.J.: Lawrence Erlbaum Associates, 1978.

Lachman, R. Subject and stimulus data for research on the internal lexicon. *Catalog of Selected Documents in Psychology,* 1973, *3,* 40 (Ms. #339, 31 pages). (a)

Lachman, R. Uncertainty effects on time to access the internal lexicon. *Journal of Experimental Psychology,* 1973, *99,* 199–208. (b)

Lachman, R., Lachman, J. L., & Butterfield, E. C. *Cognitive psychology and information processing: An introduction.* Hillsdale, N.J.: Lawrence Erlbaum Associates, 1979.

Lachman, R., Lachman, J. L., Thronesbery, C., & Sala, L. *Object salience and code separation.* Manuscript in preparation, 1979.

Lachman, R., & Mistler-Lachman, J. L. Dominance lexicale chez les bilingues. In S. Ehrlich & E. Tulving (Eds.), *La memoire semantique.* Paris: Bulletin de Psychologie, 1976.

Lachman, R., Shaffer, J. P., & Hennrikus, D. Language and cognition: Effects of stimulus codability, name-word frequency, and age of acquisition on lexical reaction time. *Journal of Verbal Learning and Verbal Behavior,* 1974, *13,* 613–625.

Lenneberg, E. H. *Biological foundations of language.* New York: John Wiley and Sons, Inc., 1967.

Loftus, E. F. How to catch a zebra in semantic memory. In R. Shaw & J. Bransford (Eds.), *Perceiving, acting and knowing.* Hillsdale, N.J.: Lawrence Erlbaum Associates, 1977.

Loftus, E. F., & Cole, W. Retrieving attribute and name information from semantic memory. *Journal of Experimental Psychology,* 1974, *102,* 1116–1122.

Loftus, G. R. Acquisition of information from rapidly presented verbal and nonverbal stimuli. *Memory and Cognition,* 1974, *2,* 545–548.

Mills, R. H., Knox, A. W., Juola, J. F., & Salmon, S. J. Cognitive loci of impairments in picture naming by aphasic subjects. *Journal of Speech and Hearing Research,* 1979, in press.

Nickerson, R. S. Short-term memory for complex meaningful visual configurations: A demonstration of capacity. *Canadian Journal of Psychology,* 1965, *19,* 155–160.

Norman, D. A., & Rumelhart, D. E. *Explorations in cognition.* San Francisco: W. H. Freeman, 1975.

Oldfield, R. C. Individual vocabulary and semantic currency. *British Journal of Social and Clinical Psychology,* 1963, *2,* 122–130.

Oldfield, R. C. Things, words and the brain. *Quarterly Journal of Experimental Psychology,* 1966, *18,* 340–353.

Oldfield, R. C., & Wingfield, A. Response latencies in naming objects. *Quarterly Journal of Experimental Psychology,* 1965, *17,* 273–281.

Paivio, A. *Imagery and verbal processes.* New York: Holt, Rinehart and Winston, 1971.

Paivio, A. Perceptual comparisons through the mind's eye. *Memory and Cognition,* 1975, *3,* 635–647.

Paivio, A., Rogers, T. B., & Smythe, P. C. Why are pictures easier to recall than words? *Psychonomic Science,* 1968, *11,* 137–138.

Pellegrino, J. W., Siegel, A. W., & Dhawan, M. Short-term retention of pictures and words: Evidence for dual coding systems. *Journal of Experimental Psychology: Human Learning and Memory,* 1975, *104,* 95–102.

Poon, L. W., & Fozard, J. L. Speed of retrieval from long-term memory in relation to age, familiarity, and datedness of information. *Journal of Gerontology,* 1978, *33,* 711–717.

Posner, M. I. Coordination of internal codes. In W. G. Chase (Ed.), *Visual information processing.* New York: Academic Press, 1973.

Posner, M. I., Lewis, J. L., & Conrad, C. Component processes in reading: A performance analysis. In J. Kavanagh & I. Mattingly (Eds.), *Language by ear and by eye: The relationships between speech and reading.* Cambridge: M.I.T. Press, 1972.

Posner, M. I., & Snyder, C. R. R. Attention and cognitive control. In R. L. Solso (Ed.), *Information processing and cognition.* Hillsdale, N.J.: Lawrence Erlbaum Associates, 1975.

Potter, M. C. Short-term conceptual memory for pictures. *Journal of Experimental Psychology,* 1976, *2,* 509–522.

Potter, M. C. & Levy, E. I. Recognition memory for a rapid sequence of pictures. *Journal of Experimental Psychology,* 1969, *81,* 10–15.

Rosch, E. Cognitive representations of semantic categories. *Journal of Experimental Psychology: General,* 1975, *104*(3), 192–233.

Rosch, E., & Lloyd, B. B. *Cognition and categorization.* Hillsdale, N.J.: Lawrence Erlbaum Associates, 1978.

Schaff, A. *Language and cognition.* New York: McGraw-Hill, 1973.

Shaffer, W. O., & Shiffrin, R. M. Rehearsal and storage of visual information. *Journal of Experimental Psychology*, 1972, *92*, 292-296.

Shannon, C. E. A mathematical theory of communication. *Bell System Technical Journal*, 1948, *27*, 379-423, 623-656.

Shepard, R. N. Recognition memory for words, sentences, and pictures. *Journal of Verbal Learning and Verbal Behavior*, 1967, *6*, 156-163.

Shepard, R. N., & Cermak, G. W. Perceptual-cognitive explorations of a toroidal set of free-form stimuli. *Cognitive Psychology*, 1973, *4*, 351-377.

Shiffrin, R. M., & Schneider, W. Controlled and automatic human information processing: II. Perceptual learning, automatic attending, and a general theory. *Psychological Review*, 1977, *84*, 127-190.

Smith, E. E., Shoben, E. J., & Rips, L. J. Structure and process in semantic memory: A featural model for semantic decisions. *Psychological Review*, 1974, *81*, 214-241.

Snodgrass, J. G., Wasser, B., Finkelstein, M., & Goldberg, L. B. On the fate of visual and verbal memory codes for pictures and words: Evidence for a dual coding mechanism in recognition memory. *Journal of Verbal Learning and Verbal Behavior*, 1974, *13*, 21-31.

Standing, L. Learning 10,000 pictures. *Quarterly Journal of Experimental Psychology*, 1973, *25*, 207-222.

Warrington, E. K., & Shallice, T. Neuropsychological evidence of visual storage in short-term memory tasks. *Quarterly Journal of Experimental Psychology*, 1972, *24*, 30-40.

Warrington, E. K., & Taylor, A. M. Immediate memory for faces: Long- or short-term memory? *Quarterly Journal of Experimental Psychology*, 1973, *25*, 316-322.

Williams, J. D. Memory ensemble selection in human information processing. *Journal of Experimental Psychology*, 1971, *88*, 231-238.

Wingfield, A. *The identification and naming of objects*. Unpublished doctoral dissertation, University of Oxford, 1966.

Wingfield, A. Perceptual and response hierarchies in object identification. *Acta Psychologica*, 1967, *26*, 216-226.

Wingfield, A. Effects of frequency on identification and naming of objects. *American Journal of Psychology*, 1968, *81*, 226-234.

Yarmey, D. I recognize your face but I can't remember your name: Further evidence on the tip-of-the-tongue phenomenon. *Memory and Cognition*, 1973, *1*, 287-290.

20

An Apparent Paradox About Memory Aging

Marion Perlmutter
Institute of Child Development, University of Minnesota

This chapter concerns "knowledge actualization," a kind of memory described by Lachman and Lachman, in Chapter 18, as "knowledge and information that is relatively permanent, nonepisodic, nonlinguistic, has not been studied for the sole purpose of experimental remembering, but has been acquired during a lifetime of formal education and day-to-day experience [p. 287]." This kind of memory seems to focus explicitly on what is the implicit concern of most investigations of human memory: that is, functional or real world memory.

There have been relatively few experiments in which retention of information not specifically studied for the laboratory task has been examined. However, there is a fairly consistent pattern of results from available studies of knowledge actualization. For example, Botwinick and Storandt (1974), Lachman and Lachman (Chapter 18), and Perlmutter (1978) found age-related improvements in adults' factual knowledge actualization; Perlmutter, Metzger, Miller, and Nezworski (1980) found no age difference in adults' temporal knowledge actualization; and Perlmutter, Metzger, Nezworski, and Miller (1979) found no age difference in adults' spatial knowledge actualization.

This pattern of results is in sharp contrast with the findings of most memory experiments. In general, retention of information specifically studied for the laboratory task has been examined, and age-related declines in performance have been observed (see Arenberg, 1973; Arenberg & Robertson-Tschabo, 1977; Botwinick, 1973; Craik, 1977; Horn, 1976; Reese, 1976; Walsh, 1975). Indeed, most of the authors in this volume have presented data that are consistent with this pattern; they reported age-related deterioration of memory performance and enumerated many mechanisms that may contribute to this decline.

We are thus left with rather paradoxical findings about memory aging. While most research has indicated age declines in the memory mechanisms purportedly underlying knowledge actualization, studies that have directly assessed knowledge actualization suggest there may be no age-related decline.

Since knowledge-actualization tasks seem more ecologically valid than standard laboratory memory tasks, it is tempting to conclude that the grim picture of age deterioration of memory so often portrayed is really an experimental artifact. That is, perhaps older adults are simply unfamiliar with and intimidated by laboratory tasks. However, again seemingly paradoxically, older adults report more memory problems in their daily routines than do younger adults (e.g. Perlmutter, 1978; Perlmutter & McGlynn, 1979). Thus, the ecological validity argument appears weak.

Moreover, an informal survey of the real-world memory problems of conference participants (Arenberg, Chapter 3) indicated that the experience of memory failures is more widespread than may have been previously acknowledged, and that this may begin fairly early in adulthood, probably at times when memory demands increase. It is possible, then, that age merely increases sensitivity or awareness and disturbance about memory problems, but perhaps does not actually increase memory failures. In order to assess this possibility, it might be useful to have a broad age range of adults keep records of each time they experience memory failures. We would then be better able to determine whether or not the number of such occurrences of memory failures really increases with age, and also gain insights into the situations that seem to elicit difficulties in knowledge actualization.

Still, I remain rather skeptical that we will find that age deterioration of memory is a myth. Rather, I suspect that the increasing amount, and overlearning, of information in the data base of older adults permits them to perform many ecologically valid memory tasks more competently than younger adults, in spite of less effective memory mechanisms. That is, while older adults' deteriorating memory mechanisms lead to increased memory failures, their enriched data bases still permit them to demonstrate more memory successes than younger adults, at least on some tasks. Thus the paradox may be resolved. If memory tasks are characterized in terms of the *processes* and *knowledge* required for successful performance, the pattern of age effects in developmental studies of adult memory may be predicted. To the degree that task performance depends upon basic memory processes, younger adults will be favored over older adults; but to the degree that task performance depends upon acquired knowledge, older adults will be favored over younger adults.

Of course, an alternative hypothesis is that the deteriorating memory mechanisms implicated in most laboratory memory studies are not relevant to performance on knowledge-actualization tasks. While this suggestion is not especially compelling, it is at least tenable. For example, task analyses of standard laboratory memory tasks and knowledge-actualization tasks point to several important differences. While most laboratory memory studies test retention of experimentally acquired material, knowledge-actualization tasks test retention of previously acquired information. Thus, while encoding and storage processes are central to performance on standard memory tasks, they are less relevant to performance on knowledge-actualization tasks. In addition, while in standard memory tasks episodic memories having specific autobiographical referents are examined, in knowledge-actualization tasks memories that are probably not so specifically time-tagged are examined. Finally, while short-term retrieval mechanisms are critical to performance on standard memory tasks, long-term retrieval mechanisms are required for successful performance on knowledge-actualization tasks.

In light of these discrepancies between standard laboratory memory tasks and knowledge actualization tasks, it may be useful to examine factors that are specifically relevant to successful knowledge actualization. The Lachmans (Lachman & Lachman, Chapter 18) have identified three subcomponents of knowledge actualization: retrieval, inference, and metamemory. *Retrieval processes* permit knowledge actualization of information presumed to be explicitly represented in memory, *inference processes* permit knowledge actualization of information presumed not to be explicitly represented in memory, and *metamemory knowledge* facilitates effective executive control over knowledge actualization. I now briefly discuss adult age change in each of these subcomponents of knowledge actualization. Then I discuss one further factor that may be relevant to knowledge actualization, but that has been largely ignored in considerations of memory aging: that is, *consistency of knowledge processing.*

Retrieval Processes

The first subcomponent of knowledge actualization suggested by the Lachmans is retrieval. This involves search or locative processes needed to access information presumed to be explicitly represented in memory. The Lachmans made the important point that we should concern ourselves with retrieval efficiency, not merely with retrieval quantity. *Retrieval quantity* is the absolute amount of information accessed. It is usually estimated by number recalled. Since it depends upon retrieval mechanisms, as well as the knowledge base supporting them, it cannot give us a clear picture of either. *Retrieval efficiency,* on the other hand, is the amount of information accessed relative to the size of the data base. It is estimated by dividing the number recalled by the size of the knowledge base. Since it in some sense corrects for the knowledge base supporting retrieval mechanisms, it can give us a clearer picture of retrieval processes per se.

However, estimates of retrieval efficiency depend upon knowing the size of the knowledge base, and determining this is by no means trivial. For example, I believe there may be a serious problem with the way the Lachmans estimated the size of the knowledge base. While they suggested that number recalled or recognized is an appropriate estimate of the size of the knowledge base, I believe it is inadequate. If both recall and recognition accuracy decline with age, as I (Perlmutter, 1978; 1979a) and others (e.g., Botwinick & Storandt, 1974; Erber, 1974) have found, then number recalled or recognized may be a systematically conservative estimate of the size of the knowledge base of older adults. That is, it is likely that failing memory mechanisms of older adults result in their making a smaller percentage of correct responses about what is in their knowledge base. This then leads us to underestimate the size of their knowledge base. Moreover, if the knowledge base is underestimated, retrieval efficiency is systematically overestimated. That is, since retrieval is divided by an inappropriately low estimate of the size of the knowledge base retrieval efficiency is inappropriately inflated.

Let me illustrate this fallacy. If the knowledge base is estimated to include 100 items, and 50 items are recalled, retrieval efficiency is estimated at .50. However, if there are really 150 items i n the knowledge base, recall of 50 items would be indicative of a retrieval efficiency of only .33. I suspect retrieval efficiency of the older subjects in the Lachmans' studies was overestimated in this way.

In summary, we are left in a quandary as to whether or not retrieval efficiency actually declines with age. The idea of assessing retrieval relative to the size of the knowledge base is a good one. However, trying to estimate the amount of information in permanent memory is an extremely difficult problem, which I believe must still be resolved.

Inference Processes

The second subcomponent of knowledge actualization suggested by the Lachmans is inference. This involves constructive processes needed to generate information presumed not to be explicitly represented in memory. We presently have no systematic data about the course of inference skills across adulthood; however, I believe this may be a particularly fruitful area of research. For example, in spite of the considerable literature, and prevailing view that cognitive abilities decline with age, there seems to me good reason to believe that some cognitive abilities, perhaps inferencing, improve with age.

Most adults can probably look back on their early adult years as a time when many of their problem-solving and social cognitive skills improved remarkably, and can also look at many who are senior to them but who are valued for their wisdom and perspective. While older adults may have to live with declining memory mechanisms, it seems foolish to believe that this decrement necessarily severely impedes all cognitive performance. Although older adults may be less able to mentally retain relevant information, their "thinking" skills may be as good, or perhaps even better, than younger adults. Moreover, since cognition can involve an interplay between *internal* and *external* information sources, older adults with failing memories could make use of external memory aids, such as written information. They then may be quite able to effectively solve intellective tasks otherwise impeded by poor memory. In addition, since aging is associated with an increasing data base, older adults might actually be prepared to make more inferences, and to do so more accurately.

Metamemory Knowledge

The final subcomponent of knowledge actualization suggested by the Lachmans is metamemory. This involves knowledge about the functioning of the memory system that permits effective executive control over knowledge actualization. Several methods have been developed to assess metamemorial knowledge. Most directly, subjects may be queried about their knowledge of the functioning of their memory systems. Of course, this explicit knowledge measure of metamemory may not be indicative of the knowledge that subjects *can use* in performing knowledge actualization tasks. Therefore, an additional useful way of assessing metamemory is to require subjects to use their knowledge of the functioning of their memory systems by monitoring their performance. However, even such more implicit monitoring measures of metamemory may not be indicative of the knowledge subjects *do use* in performing knowledge actualization tasks. Therefore, another important method of assessing metamemory is to measure some ongoing aspect of knowledge-actualization performance that reflects knowledge of the functioning of the knowledge system.

Perhaps not surprisingly, when subjects are directly queried about the functioning of their memory systems no age declines are noted (Perlmutter, 1978). This sort of questioning would seem to represent an instance where the accumulated experiences of older adults might put them at an advantage over younger adults.

It is somewhat less predictable, however, whether older adults would be as competent as younger adults when required to monitor their memory performance. Some monitoring tasks that seem to be indicative of the ability to use knowledge about one's memory system are memory prediction, confidence rating, and feeling-of-knowing judgments. Available data seem to be quite consistent in portraying stability in these skills across adulthood. For example, Perlmutter (1978) found no age differences in adults' accuracy at predicting recall or recognition, nor in their accuracy in making confidence ratings of recall or recognition responses, and Perlmutter (1976) and Lachman and Lachman (Chapter 18) found no age differences in adults' accuracy at making feeling-of-knowing judgments.

Still, of central interest is whether older adults typically use their knowledge about the functioning of their memory systems as effectively as do younger adults. An index of effective metamemory use that is not contaminated by experimenter elicitation may be the pattern of reaction times on feeling-of-knowing tasks. Accurate monitoring would be indicated by more rapid negative responses to items that are not later correctly recognized than to items that are later correctly recognized, and more rapid positive reponses to items that are later correctly recognized than to items that are not later correctly recognized. Since the Lachmans (Lachman & Lachman, Chapter 18) have found that latencies to respond "I don't know" on feeling-of-knowing tasks are similarly predictive of subsequent recognition accuracy in younger and older adults, it seems that metamemory knowledge is indeed stably used throughout adulthood. However, it would also be useful to know whether latencies to respond "I do know" on feeling-of-knowing tasks are similarly predictive of subsequent recognition accuracy in younger and older adults.

One further point about the metamemory subcomponent of knowledge actualization concerns knowledge of retrieval and inference. Knowledge actualization has been defined to include the actualization of information presumed to be explicitly represented in memory, as well as the actualization of information presumed not to be explicitly represented in memory. An understanding of the metamemory subcomponent of knowledge actualization must therefore include accounts of knowledge of retrieval processes, as well as accounts of knowledge of inference processes. Although we have begun to developmentally investigate adults' knowledge of retrieval processes (Lachman & Lachman, Chapter 18; Perlmutter, 1978; Perlmutter & McGlynn, 1979), to my knowledge no one has yet investigated knowledge of inference processes.

Consistency of Knowledge Processing

A final factor that I believe may play an important role in knowledge actualization is consistency of knowledge processing. Consistency of knowledge processing concerns the likelihood that on repeated occurrences, particular stimuli will elicit consistent information from an individual's knowledge base. The importance of consistency of knowledge processing is related to the state-dependent nature of human memory. That is, retrieval is generally thought to be facilitated by an environment that is similar to the encoding environment.

I believe that on different occasions when an older adult experiences similar external stimulation, that person is less likely to experience similar internal activation of the knowledge base than is a younger adult. This diversity of knowledge processing would result in less consistency in the encoding and retrieval environments, and poorer retention.

Some data that I have collected (Perlmutter, 1979b) on a word association task are relevant to the hypothesis that older adults are less consistent in knowledge processing than are younger adults. Adults 20 and 60 years old generated an association to 24 words on each of four separate trials. The mean number of different associates generated to each word on the four trials was less for younger than older adults. That is, on different occasions, particular words elicited more consistent responses in younger adults and more diverse responses in older adults. This seems to suggest less consistent knowledge processing in older than younger adults.

Some further data that I have collected (Perlmutter, 1979a) on a cued-recall task are relevant to the hypothesis that less consistent knowledge processing in older than younger adults contributes to older adults' poorer memory performance. Adults 20 and 60 years old were given a cued-recall task in which 15 words were cued with normed common associates of the to-be-remembered words (experimenter-provided cues), and 15 words were cued with associates that the subject had him or herself generated to the to-be-remembered words (subject-generated cues). While, as predicted by a state-dependent view of memory, subject-generated cues led to superior recall compared to experimenter-provided cues in younger adults, these two cue types elicited comparable levels of recall in older adults. An overt match between the encoding and retrieval environment did not facilitate retention of older adults. Apparently the reinstatement of the learning situation does not aid older adults in the way it aids younger adults. This might indicate inconsistent and asymmetric knowledge processing. For example, although presentation of stimulus A may lead to associations A_1, A_2, A_3, and A_4, for the older adult, these associations may not be likely to lead back to A.

A final point concerns a possible relationship between older adults' inconsistent knowledge processing and the slower reaction times generally observed with aging. If I may generalize a bit, I believe the Lachmans' (Lachman & Lachman, Chapter 19) picture-naming data from college students indicate that greater diversity of responses is associated with longer reaction times. Analogously, my findings of age-related increases in diversity of responses to a word association task may be associated to the often observed age-related increases in reaction time. Of course, causal factors in slowed reaction times are still unclear. For example, speed changes may be the result of central-nervous-system changes (i.e., change in speed of neural activity), and this speed change may produce greater diversity in responding. On the other hand, a fuller knowledge base may lead to greater diversity in responding, and this may produce loss of speed.

Conclusions

Most researchers have been confident in anecdotal reports of age-related declines in memory, and have been busily carrying out experiments designed to illuminate the mechanisms underlying this deterioration. The results of these experiments have led us to a point of almost complete confidence in the assumption that memory deteriorates with age. It is a bit perplexing then to interpret research, such as that presented by the Lachmans (Lachman & Lachman, Chapter 18), in which age deterioration in memory is not observed. The resolution of this apparent paradox in findings about memory aging should, however, lead to a more accurate understanding about memory aging.

It is my view that a resolution to this apparent paradox about memory aging is possible if we consider the *process* and *knowledge* requirements of memory tasks. While older adults probably do have deteriorating memory mechanisms that lead to increased memory failures, they probably also have enriched data bases that enable them to perform some memory tasks more competently than younger adults, in spite of less effective memory mechanisms. An implication of this position is that we may do well to more explicitly investigate the knowledge actualization functions of memory that have until now been only implicit concerns of our research.

REFERENCES

Arenberg, D. Cognition and aging: Verbal learning, memory, problem solving, and aging. In C. Eisdorfer & M. P. Lawton (Eds.), *The psychology of adult development and aging.* Washington, D.C.: American Psychological Association, 1973.

Arenberg, D., & Robertson-Tchabo, E. A. Learning and aging. In J. E. Birren & K. W. Schaie (Eds.), *The handbook of the psychology of aging.* New York: Van Nostrand Reinhold, 1977.

Botwinick, J. *Aging and behavior.* New York: Springer, 1973.

Botwinick, J. & Storandt, M. *Memory, related functions and age.* Springfield, Ill.: Charles C. Thomas, 1974.

Craik, F. I. M. Age differences in human memory. In J. E. Birren & K. W. Schaie (Eds.), *The handbook of the psychology of aging.* New York: Van Nostrand Reinhold, 1977.

Erber, J. T. Age difference in recognition memory. *Journal of Gerontology,* 1974, *29,* 171-181.

Horn, J. L. Human abilities. A review of research and theory in the early 1970's. *Annual Review of Psychology,* 1976, *27,* 437-485.

Perlmutter, M. *What is memory aging the aging of?* Unpublished doctoral Dissertation, University of Massachusetts, 1976.

Perlmutter, M. What is memory aging the aging of? *Developmental Psychology,* 1978, *14,* 330-345.

Perlmutter, M. Age differences in adults' free recall, cued recall, and recognition. *Journal of Gerontology,* 1979, *34,* 533-539. (a)

Perlmutter, M. Age differences in adults' consistency of associative responding. *Experimental Aging Research,* 1979, *5,* 549–553. (b)

Perlmutter, M. & McGlynn, M. A developmental study of adults' metamemorial knowledge. Manuscript in preparation, 1979.

Perlmutter, M., Metzger, R., Miller, K., Nezworski, T. Memory of historical events. *Experimental Aging Research,* 1980.

Perlmutter, M., Metzger, R., Nezworski, T., & Miller, K. Memory of city locations. Manuscript in preparation, 1979.

Reese, H. W. The development of memory: Life-span perspectives. In H. W. Reese (Ed.), *Advances in child development and behavior* (Vol. 11). New York: Academic Press, 1976.

Walsh, D. A. Age differences in learning and memory. In D. S. Woodruff & J. E. Birren (Eds.), *Aging: Scientific perspectives and social issues.* New York: Van Nostrand, 1975.

21 Retrieval Efficiency, Knowledge Assessment and Age: Comments on Some Welcome Findings

Raymond S. Nickerson
Bolt Beranek and Newman Inc.
Cambridge, Massachusetts

ABSTRACT

This paper comments on the work reported in this volume by Lachman and Lachman. It focuses, in particular, on their major findings with respect to the question of how memory-dependent performance changes with age: (1) that old subjects were as efficient as young subjects in retrieving information from very long term memory and (2) that old subjects were as effective as young subjects in assessing the contents and products of their memories. Some observations are also made with respect to several aspects of the work that are independent of its implications regarding aging: its general focus, the distinction between the possession of knowledge and its use, the importance of inference in memory, and the notion of metamemory.

INTRODUCTION

About three years ago I was invited by Drs. Fozard and Poon to participate in a conference similar in many respects to this one. Knowing almost nothing about the topic of aging, I scurried to become at least casually acquainted with it before the conference was to begin. The main result of this effort was the acquisition of some knowledge that, in retrospect, I would have preferred not to have had. Apparently one's worst fears are well founded: Time is exceedingly unkind to human folk. Decreasing sensory acuity and motor dexterity, decreasing adaptiveness and flexibility, decreasing ability to learn new skills, decreasing inventiveness and creativity, general slowing of mental processes, increasing conservatism and unwillingness to take risks—the list goes on. More recently I have discovered that biologists sometimes *define* aging as functional decrement: "In man and higher vertebrates aging takes the form of morphologic, functional, and biochemical involution—always regressive and often silent—affecting most of the organs and resulting in a gradual decline in performance [Timiras, 1978, p. 606]." Increasing experience and the accumulation of facts (wisdom?) are the great equalizers, we are told, but the evidence is not very convincing. Why anyone should want to do research that can only extend the list of ways in which we succumb to the ravages of time is difficult to understand. The fact that we do engage in such research is testimony to the perversity of human curiosity, a perversity that one must assume can only increase with age.

Having discovered little in the aging literature to heighten the enthusiasm with which one might anticipate those golden years, I find heartwarming indeed the Lachmans' conclusion that old folks are as efficient at retrieving information, and at assessing the contents and outputs of their memories, as are young folks. Unfortunately, I am not sure whether my reaction to this conclusion is best characterized as one of eager credulity or reluctant skepticism. The first finding—that retrieval efficiency is insensitive to age—is suspect, I believe, for reasons that I shall try to make clear. With respect to the second finding—that older people are as good at assessing the contents and products of their memories as are younger people—I happily have no fault to find.

AGING AND RETRIEVAL EFFICIENCY

The finding that older people are as efficient as younger people in retrieving information from memory rests on the validity of the measure of efficiency the Lachmans define. The measure—the ratio of the amount of information that can be produced to the amount that memory possesses—assumes, by analogy with computer data bases, that both the speed and the accuracy with which information can be found in a memory store should decrease as the total amount of information in that store increases. Such a view overlooks the fact that how the speed and accuracy of a search through a data base will relate to the size of that data base will depend on how the data are organized, and the nature of the search process. To be sure, if the search is serial and random, the time required to find a specific item in a data base of size n will be proportional to n. If the search procedure contains some degree of parallel processing, search time may still increase with n, albeit in a nonlinear fashion. If the data are organized categorically, and random searching is done only within appropriate categories, search time may increase with the size of the category within which the search is conducted, but be independent of the size of the entire data base. Finally, there are ways of organizing computer data bases (e.g., content addressing or hash coding) that can reduce search time very considerably, and in some cases effectively eliminate the need for a search altogether (Knuth, 1977). Similar observations may be made with respect to accuracy: Whether a particular sought-for item will be found by a search will depend less on the size of the data base in which it is contained than on the organization of the data and the details of the search procedure.

A second problem with the measure of efficiency defined by the Lachmans has to do with the way the numerator and denominator of the production/possession ratio are determined. Even if one grants that the measure is a reasonable one to use to represent efficiency, the way in which the values of the defining variables are determined is questionable, to my mind. Briefly, the procedure is as follows: Subjects are asked to answer a set of questions in a free-recall situation; later they are asked to answer, in a multiple-choice format, those questions that they could not answer initially. The production/possession ratio is the ratio of the number of items recalled initially to the sum of the number of items recalled and those recognized (corrected for guessing) in the multiple-choice context.

One difficulty with this measure relates to the equating of the total number of items recalled and recognized to the "size of the data base." To see the problem, consider the following case. Suppose that Subject A recalls answers for 5 out of 20 questions correctly and recognizes 5 more, thus yielding a production/possession ratio of .5. Now suppose that Subject B recalls the answers to all 20 questions and hence produces a production/possession ratio of 1. It seems fairly clear that this set of questions would not accurately reflect the size of Subject B's data base. Had additional and more difficult questions been included in the set, there might have been some the answers to which he could have recognized but not recalled. The Lachmans acknowledge this problem, insofar as it may be considered the problem of a ceiling effect, and suggest that the solution to it lies in careful item selection.

A more serious difficulty relates to the justifiability of taking what an individual can recall as an indication of what he can retrieve, and what he can either recall or recognize as an indication of what he knows. Both recall and recognition are memory-dependent activities, and both involve retrieval in some sense. If age has an effect on retrievability for recall purposes, it may also have an effect on retrievability for recognition purposes. The Lachmans have tried to determine how retrieval performance changes with age, and to do so in a way that is insensitive to differences in information content; however, the method by which they measure content may itself be sensitive to differences in retrieval performance if recognition involves retrieval as does recall.

In spite of these problems, I like the finding that older people can retrieve information from memory at least as efficiently as younger people, and, in keeping with Francis Bacon's observation that "what a man had rather were true, that he more readily believes," I am going to believe it whether or not it is a fact.

AGING AND KNOWLEDGE ASSESSMENT

The second question the Lachmans address regarding aging and memory is that of how the ability to assess the performance of one's own memory may change with age. Overconfidence in one's opinions seems to be a rather common failing, at least among people who typically find their way into psychological laboratories to serve as subjects in experiments (Pitz, 1974). Moreover, there is some evidence that the tendency to overestimate what one knows is relatively independent of what one in fact knows. Lichtenstein and Fischhoff (1977), for example, have shown that people are inclined to predict better-than-chance performance when asked to make judgments on matters about which they have virtually no knowledge (identification of nationalities of child artists on the basis of their drawings, prediction of stock price trends) and when their actual performance is at chance levels. At the other end of the confidence scale, Fischhoff, Slovic, and Lichtenstein (1977) have shown that people are often willing to give odds on the accuracy of strongly held—and relatively accurate—opinions that are way out of proportion to the probability that those opinions are in fact correct. A willingness to give 1,000 to 1 odds on opinions that were correct about 80% of the time illustrates this point.

To my knowledge, no one has attempted to determine whether this alleged general predeliction to overestimate what one knows changes in any systematic way with age. One might expect, on the grounds that people tend to become generally more conservative as they grow older, that the tendency toward overconfidence would decrease. On the other hand, because—according to folklore at least—knowledge is expected to increase with age, one might not be surprised to discover an increasing reluctance to admit ignorance—especially of things a person who has lived a long time feels he ought to know.

The Lachmans' results suggest that the ability to assess one's own knowledge is among the things that do not change with age. Perhaps the tendency toward greater conservatism is just sufficient to offset the feeling of obligation to be better informed. Whatever the explanation, the finding of no difference between the performance of old and young subjects in this regard is clearly worthy of attention. One hopes that the reporting of such negative findings might encourage other investigators to report "failures" to find age-related differences in the performance of various tasks. The Lachmans make the excellent point that the fact that the preponderance of studies of effects of aging that find their way into the literature report performance differences may be due in part to the traditional bias against publishing negative results. I, for one, am happy to accept the risk of an occasional Type II error as the price of learning of those attempts to document the various ways in which age incapacitates us that have failed.

There are several aspects of the Lachmans' studies about which I would like to comment that are independent of the relevance of the work to our understanding of aging. These are the general focus of the work, the distinction between the possession of knowledge and its utilization, the importance of inference in memory, and the notion of metamemory.

THE GENERAL FOCUS OF THE WORK

In characterizing their focus of attention, the Lachmans note that they are concerned with memory for information about the world in general that has been acquired during the natural course of life, as opposed to material studied in the laboratory for the purpose of experimental remembering. This is a welcome emphasis. The kinds of questions the Lachmans are asking are representative of a class of questions that have been neglected in spite of their obvious importance: What knowledge do people typically acquire in the normal course of living? How is that knowledge acquired? How is it represented in memory? How is it accessed and used?

The Lachmans have focused especially on the last of these questions, namely that of access and use, which seems the logical place to start if one is interested in the knowledge that people tend to acquire over the course of a lifetime and to retain more or less indefinitely. One seldom has the ability to control conditions of acquisition in such cases, or those prevailing during the retention interval.

KNOWLEDGE VERSUS ITS ACCESS AND USE

The Lachmans make a distinction between possessing knowledge, and being able to access and make effective use of that knowledge. This distinction is fairly generally recognized. Most memory theorists have been willing to assume that information may be stored in memory even though it cannot always be produced on demand. Some have made the assumption that everything that gets into long-term memory is retained and could be retrieved under appropriate conditions. This is not a useful hypothesis inasmuch as there is no way to prove it false if it is false; but it is held nevertheless.

There is an aspect of the distinction between possession and use that has not been widely considered. That is the fact that it seems possible to have information in memory that can be used effectively but cannot be verbalized explicitly under any conditions. An example is the knowledge of strategies in complex cognitive games. One may be able to win consistently at a game without being able to tell someone else how to do so. More generally, people are often able to solve problems without being able to describe the procedures by which they solve them. Perhaps this is why the adage that it is often easier to do something oneself than to tell someone else how to do it seems so obviously true.

THE IMPORTANCE OF INFERENCE IN MEMORY

The Lachmans distinguish three components of knowledge actualization or use: retrieval, inference, and metamemorial processes. Retrieval refers to the direct accessing of information in memory. Inference permits one to go beyond that which is explicitly represented in memory in order to construct or derive new information from information that already exists. Metamemorial processes guide retrieval and inferential activities, and also provide information about the contents of memory—knowledge about one's knowledge, as it were.

The distinction between direct retrieval and inferential processes I find helpful in some respects and misleading in others. It seems helpful to distinguish between situations in which memory appears to be accessed immediately and unconsciously, and those in which an intentional conscious search is required, but this distinction is orthogonal to the question of whether inference is involved. More specifically, inference can be involved when memory is accessed unconsciously, as well as when it is consciously searched. The Lachmans seem to acknowledge this possibility in distinguishing between processes that underlie the apparently effortless and immediate understanding of language and those involved in intense and deliberate efforts to retrieve elusive information, as in tip-of-the-tongue situations. The point is that the amount of inferencing may vary in both of these cases. In particular, it should not be assumed that subjects always intentionally resort to some inferential procedure when in a tip-of-the-tongue state. Sometimes it seems to be quite the reverse: One puts one's mind in neutral, as it were, and waits for the desired word to present itself.

The distinction between information that is explicitly stored in memory and knowledge that is inferentially derived is a very compelling one. Clearly, much of what we know we never learned explicitly. To use an example that I have used elsewhere (Nickerson, 1977), I know that my great-great-grandfather was once a teenager although I doubt that anyone ever explicitly told me so. I suspect that if there were any effective way to measure knowledge, we would discover that what we know implicitly or by inference represents a relatively large proportion of what we know.

Two questions arise about any particular bit of inferentially derived knowledge: (1) From what was that bit of knowledge derived? and (2) what types of inferential procedures were used in its derivation? And in terms of the focus of this conference, it seems reasonable to ask what kinds of changes might occur with age, both with respect to the explicit knowledge base from which implicit knowledge may be derived, and with respect to the inferential procedures that are applied to that base. Presumably, either or both might change with age.

The distinction between explicit and implicit knowledge points up a methodological difficulty in investigating very-long-term memory—namely, the inability sometimes to verify that "remembered" information is in fact remembered. We know from the classic experiments of Bartlett (1932) and others that even in relatively short-term memory, information is modified (simplified, embellished, distorted) in various ways. We know also that the attempt to retrieve information from memory often involves constructive or inferential processes. Even what has sometimes passed for the recall of surface (as opposed to semantic) aspects of sentences can often be attributed to contruction based on memory for meaning coupled with knowledge about linguistic structure (James, Thompson, & Baldwin, 1973).

Sometimes the involvement of inferential procedures is relatively apparent in the performance of memory tasks, when the subject is aware of, and verbalizes, his reasoning process. The degree to which inference is involved is often not apparent, however, from the subject's untutored overt behavior. If asked whether a robin flies, I would say "yes," because I have seen one fly. If asked whether an Arctic tern flies, I would say "yes," because, although I have never, to my knowledge, seen an Arctic tern, I have read of its remarkable migratory journeys. If asked if an ibis flies, I would say "yes"; in fact I know nothing about the ibis except that it is a bird, and having no particular reason to know that it does not fly, I am inclined to impute to it this ability because it is common to most birds of which I have some knowledge. If asked if an emu flies, I would say "no," because I have learned explicitly that ostriches represent exceptions to the rule that birds fly, and I believe that emus are closely related to ostriches and share many of their characteristics. The answer to each of these questions has a rather different basis, and at least in the cases of the ibis and emu, the role of inference is material although not obvious in the simple yes-no answers that might be given, were the questions asked.

The importance of inferential procedures from the point of view of the economics of memory is fairly apparent. If one wants to build a memory system that makes efficient use of limited resources, one must find ways to minimize memory requirements. One wants to store rules and generative procedures whenever possible in preference to specific instantiations. One wants to store closed subroutines that can be paramaterized for specific applications. One wants to store generic, canonical, categorical, default representations of the entities with which the system must deal, and include important idiosyncratic features as exceptions. In short, one wants to provide the system with as much intelligence as possible, thereby precluding the necessity for the encyclopedic accumulation of facts, and to promote effective utilization of such facts as it does retain.

METAMEMORY

One of the functions of metamemory, as the Lachmans use the term, is to evaluate the contents and outputs of our memories. This includes not only the ability to judge the credibility of positive returns from memory but to judge whether a negative return is due to something not being in memory or to its temporary inaccessibility.

The fact that people have different degrees of confidence in the validity of different opinions or beliefs they hold is not only of theoretical interest, but of some practical consequence as well. One assumes, for example, that a person is more likely to act on a belief in which he has high confidence than on one in which his confidence is low. It is of interest, therefore, to determine whether the degree of confidence with which an opinion is held is a good indicator of the probability that the opinion is correct. Several investigators have considered this question and, happily, their results by and large indicate a positive correlation between degree of confidence and probability of correctness.

There are some caveats, however. In particular, there are fairly large differences among people with respect to the extent to which their expressed confidence is indicative of the accuracy of the opinions in which the confidence is expressed. There also can be some fairly strong context effects. For example, the expression of high confidence in the context of a task that requires a subject to try to answer many difficult questions may mean a different thing than an expression of the same degree of confidence in the context of a task that requires the subject to answer generally easier questions (Nickerson & McGoldrick, 1963).

The characteristic of metamemory that has intrigued many investigators is the fact than an individual often can say with confidence that something is in memory even if he is unable at the time to retrieve it. This property of memory, which has been described sometimes as the "tip-of-the-tongue" phenomenon or the "feeling of knowing" has received considerable attention from researchers, beginning with Brown and MacNeill (1966). Most of the research has been designed to demonstrate that the phenomenon exists and to show that the strength of the feeling is a predictor of the probability that one will be able to recall something in time or given appropriate retrieval cues. Relatively little attention has been given to the question of what the feeling of knowing may be based on, and to date there is not a very satisfactory explanation of how it is that one can be sure that something is in memory when one is unable to retrieve it.

There are several things that come to mind as possible bases of the feeling of knowing, among which are the following:

Knowledge That One Once Knew.   One may remember being able to remember what one cannot remember now. I remember, for example, being able to give the names of all the capital cities of the United States, although I probably could not now produce them on demand. If I were asked to name the capital of a particular state and found myself unable to do so, I might be inclined to think that inasmuch as I once knew that name I should be able to retrieve it again under the right circumstances.

Being Able To Infer That One Once Knew.   I do not remember the name of the heroine of George Eliot's *The Mill on the Floss.* Moreover, I do not explicitly remember ever being able to remember that name; however, I do remember having read the book. Therefore, I know that at some time I must have known the name of its heroine. And although my confidence is not great that I could do so, given precisely the right circumstances, I might be able to recognize it or at least to select it from among a set of alternatives. Certainly the probability that I would attach to being able to do so would not be zero.

Knowing That One Should Know.   The high-school graduate who finds himself unable to specify the longest river in the world might feel that he may know the answer to this question (even though he cannot recall it, or even recall having explicitly learned it) because—he might tell himself—this is surely something one should have learned in a basic geography or social science course somewhere along the way.

The Knowledge That One Has An Answer That Could Be, But May Not Be, The Correct One.   If I were asked who was the world's longest reigning female monarch, I would have to say I do not know. I do know, however, that Queen Victoria reigned over the British Empire for more than 60 years. In part because I do not know of any female monarch who has reigned longer, and in part because the likelihood of anyone reigning even that long seems very small, I would consider it not unlikely that the answer to the question is Queen Victoria. It is easy to imagine other examples of cases in which a person may not know the answer to a question, but may know, or feel confident, that the correct answer is one of a small set of possibilities, at least some of which he can identify.

Undoubtedly the reader can think of other reasons why one might feel that one knows some fact that one cannot produce on demand. Studies addressed to the question of whence comes the feeling of knowing might do much to dispell the mystique that surrounds the notion, and make it no less interesting for that.

There are several other processes that relate to the functioning of memory that might be considered metamemory functions. All of these should be fertile ground for the student of aging and memory. The ability to tell the difference between stimulation that originates in the outside world and that which originates from within one's world of memories is a case in point. The loss of that ability typically leads to behavior that is classified as psychotic. There is a closely related ability, however, that one may lose without being obviously insane, namely that of being able to distinguish between memories for experiences and our own embellishments of those memories.

Another aspect of metamemory that seems to me to be especially interesting and particularly relevant to the question of changes that occur with age is that which one might call memory for things future. One often says to oneself, "I must remember to do thus and so at such and such a time." I might say, for example, that I must remember to call John the first thing in the morning, or that I must remember to send off my registration for such and such a conference before next Wednesday. All of us have surely had occasions to remind our memories to remind us of things we must do at some future time. Undoubtedly all of us also know from experience that our memories are not always cooperative in this regard. Somethimes we forget what we have instructed ourselves to remember.

On the other hand, the process also sometimes works. We remember to make that phone call, send off that letter, and so on. It is as though one could set an alarm clock in one's head. Perhaps a better metaphor would be that one can send a message to oneself to be delivered at some specified time in the future. How is it that such a message can lie unobtrusively below the level of consciousness for a while, and what is it that causes it to be delivered at the appropriate time? The forgetfulness that is often alleged to characterize elderly people seems to be a failure of this type of process. People forget to do what they had planned to do. The process seems to be a recursive one that can abort at more than one level. Thus one can find oneself in the embarrassing situation of remembering that one was supposed to remember something but forgetting what it is that one was supposed to remember.

CONCLUDING REMARKS

My final comment is of a general nature and is not focused on the Lachmans' work more than on other work reported in this volume. The comment is really in the nature of a plea; and that is for more attention to factors that can explain changes that tend to accompany age.

As a psychologist whose interest in aging is, in part, professionally motivated, I suppose I should want to know what kinds of performance changes tend to accompany increasing age. I should want to know, for example, whether different kinds of memory (e.g., autobiographical versus encyclopedic) are likely to change differentially with age. I should be curious as to whether memory for facts, for models, for procedures tends to change differentially; whether old people are more or less likely than young people to make use of reconstructive versus reproductive processes; whether different types of retrieval cues tend to be differentially effective at different ages; whether organizational aspects of memory seem to change with age; whether people's information acquisition strategies change over time; whether the accessibility of different types of information varies; whether old people differ from young with respect to the degree to which memories are abstracted, integrated, and fused; whether they differ with respect to their ability to retain surface features of stimuli as well as their meaning; and so on.

But age itself explains nothing. And as a practitioner of aging, I am less interested in knowing that I am likely to deteriorate in this or that way in time, than what I can do about it. Much of what I have learned about aging is among the most eminently forgettable information in my head; I only wish I could forget it. Some things are better permitted to sneak up on us and to take us by surprise.

My plea, then, is for less devotion to the cause of chronicling the numerous ways in which performance decrements can be shown to correlate statistically with age, and more to the task of discovering the concomitants of aging that can account for those decrements in individual cases. There are many physiological and biochemical possibilities that come to mind: cell death, changes in hormonal activity, changes in the ability of the system to manufacture neurotransmitters, changes in its sensitivity to protein-synthesis stimulators, changes in vitamin requirements or intake, changes in the production rate of cyclic AMP or RNA. There is also the possibility of accounting for some performance changes in terms of attitudinal and motivational variables. Old people may differ from young in terms of what they consider to be worth doing and in terms of the amount of effort they are willing to spend on certain types of tasks. They also may utilize different strategies and harbor different expectancies.

Whether physiological or psychological, what we need are constructs that can be related to performance causally. "Aging" will not do. Those among us who intend to fight the aging process, and who appreciate every little bit of encouragement to do so that we can find, can take some comfort in the fact that individuals age functionally at different rates; but it would be nice to know what the determinants of the rate of functional aging are. In the meantime, we can be grateful for findings such as those reported by the Lachmans, that hold out some hope that there may be some important cognitive functions that are relatively independent of age, even correlationally.

Finally, in our pursuit of a fuller understanding of the aging process—and indeed of ourselves and our environment more generally—we might pause occasionally to consider the merits of the advice that Erasmus (1512/1942) has Folly give to her listeners: "If Men would but refrain from all commerce with Wisdom, and give up themselves to be govern'd by me, they should never know what it were to be old, but solace themselves with a perpetual youth[p. 112]."

ACKNOWLEDGMENTS

I am grateful to my ageless friends, Dick Pew, John Swets, and Douwe Yntema, for their most helpful comments on a draft of this paper.

REFERENCES

Bartlett, F. C. *Remembering*. Cambridge: Cambridge University Press, 1932.

Brown, R., & MacNeill, D. The "tip-of-the-tongue" phenomenon. *Journal of Verbal Learning and Verbal Behavior*, 1966, *4*, 325-337.

Erasmus, D. *The praise of folly*. New York: Walter J. Black, 1942. (Published originally circa 1512).

Fischhoff, B., Slovic, P., & Lichtenstein, S. Knowing with certainty: The appropriateness of extreme confidence. *Journal of Experimental Psychology: Human Perception and Performance*, 1977, *3*, 552-564.

James, C., Thompson, J., & Baldwin, J. The reconstructive process in sentence memory. *Journal of Verbal Learning and Verbal Behavior*, 1973, *12*, 51-63.

Knuth, D. E. Algorithms. *Scientific American*, 1977, *236*, 63-80.

Lichtenstein, S., & Fischhoff, B. Do those who know more also know more about how much they know? The calibration of probability judgments. *Organizational Behavior and Human Performance*, 1977, *20*, 159-183.

Nickerson, R. S. Some comments on human archival memory as a very large data base. *Proceedings on Very Large Data Bases*, Third International Conference on Very Large Data Bases, Tokyo, Japan, October 1977, 159-168.

Nickerson, R. S., & McGoldrick, C. C., Jr. Confidence correctness, and difficulty with non-psychophysical comparative judgments. *Perceptual and Motor Skills*, 1963, *17*, 159-167.

Pitz, G. Subjective probability distributions for imperfectly known quantities. In G. W. Gregg, (Ed.), *Knowledge and cognition*. New York: Wiley, 1974, 29-41.

Timiras, P. S. Biological perspectives on aging. *American Scientist*, 1978, *66*, 605-613.

III TESTING AND MNEMONIC STRATEGIES

Edited by
Larry W. Thompson

This section is grouped around three rather distinct topics. One focuses upon issues and problems related to memory assessment and the development of appropriate testing procedures (Chapters 22, 23, 24, and 25). A second views the relation of memory complaints to actual performance (Chapters 24 and 30). The third addresses the use of mnemonics as an aid to offset memory problems, and also the role of individual differences in constructing useful intervention strategies (Chapters 26, 27, 28, & 29). The goal of this introduction is to highlight and to integrate the above topics from the standpoint of memory problems in the clinical arena.

The value of specific memory assessment in clinical work with the elderly has been apparent for many years; recent interest (e.g., Arenberg, 1978; Bernal, Brannon, Belar, Lavigne, & Cameron, 1977; Crook, 1979; Kramer & Jarvik, 1979; Schaie & Schaie, 1977) in the development of adequate testing devices and intervention strategies is most welcome in the clinical world. Issues repeatedly raised in overall assessment include psychometric problems such as improper standardization, lack of normative data, and absence of "ecologically valid" measures of functional capacity; subject factors such as increased between- and within-subject variability, and increased vulnerability to noncognitive influences on performance; and finally, the need for a multifaceted approach in order to capture the range and complexity of behaviors deserving of consideration in a diagnostic formulation. Indeed, when one views the nature of clinical problems experienced by the elderly, it is puzzling that a more concerted effort along this line has not been forthcoming sooner. I would like to mention a few rather specific problems frequently encountered in the clinical setting where memory assessment is helpful.

The first pertains to the concern older individuals have over their general loss of functioning. When confronted with objective evidence of memory slippage, it is not uncommon for elderly individuals to become extremely distressed with the accompanying thought that something is going wrong with their mind or brain. In some instances, this distress can be sufficient to interfere further with memory processes, thereby exacerbating the problem and leading to increased instances of memory impairment. It is not difficult to see how these two factors can be mutually reinforcing, thus triggering a negative spiral effect that culminates with unnecessarily high levels of anxiety and decreased intellectual functioning.

A second problem frequently encountered is the need to differentiate between depression and the early stages of dementia. It is well known that depression, complaints of decreased intellectual performance or memory, and actual performance in everyday situations show substantial interrelationships in the elderly. It is also well established that aging, per se, is associated with decreased performance in some areas. The question often arises as to whether an elderly individual who complains of severe performance decrements is suffering from depression, senile dementia, or is experiencing changes due to normal aging.

A third problem involves the assessment of elderly individuals for placement on a job, in a home setting or for counseling other family members who must provide their care and supervision. In such instances, it is useful to determine the strengths and weaknesses of cognitive function and ascertain how these might interact with other psychological and social-environmental factors, to either minimize or aggravate the individuals' adjustment difficulties.

It is clear that objective memory assessment should be an integral part of any assessment battery employed in addressing such questions. In approaching these problems from a clinical perspective, typically we want to know how a given individual might be different in some way from the majority of older people, what relevance this might have for that person's level of functioning in daily living, and what support systems or environmental manipulations might be needed to optimize level of functioning. In this regard, we must assess a variety of other factors, including other cognitive processes, present and premorbid personality structure, adequacy of the family constellation in providing assistance, level of complexity and hardship of the living situations, level of difficulty of the work situation, availability and quality of community supports, medical history, current health status, etc.

With this background in mind, the remainder of this introduction will deal with each of three topics associated with assessment and mnemonic strategies.

ASSESSMENT OF MEMORY

The chapter by Erickson, Poon, and Walsh-Sweeney (Chapter 22) emphasizes that adequate clinical memory testing of the elderly could play an important role in understanding the nature of memory impairment, and in formulating a plan of remediation for any behavioral deficits. Their analysis of the field, however, reveals considerable shortcomings in the development of a memory test battery. They have proposed that all batteries should be comprehensive, including measures of immediate and delayed memory, verbal and nonverbal visual memory, and tests of motor learning. Specific tests should be "age-fair," and normative data for elderly individuals should be available. Tests should reflect real-life memory problems, and at the same time should emanate from recent theoretical and empirical advances in the field of memory.

In particular, the battery ought to make use of findings in the memory literature that could assist in determining what factors or processes might contribute to the memory impairment. For example, it is often said that older individuals may have memory problems because they utilize inappropriate learning strategies. Research on depth of processing and encoding strategies could be helpful in devising tests to determine the effectiveness of various learning strategies when used by a particular individual.

For the most part, methodological advances suggested in the chapter by Erickson et al. rely heavily on a quantitative approach, using normative data to make inferences regarding an indivdual's performance on a specific test. The chapter by Albert and Kaplan (Chapter 23), on the other hand, emphasizes the value of focusing on qualitative aspects of performance in making inferences about function. In commenting on these chapters, Butters (Chapters 25) also makes the argument that while scores on tests, per se, can provide information about an individual's ability to perform, close scrutiny of the process of performance in attempting to complete a task can provide significantly more information about the nature of the problem the individual is experiencing. His comparison of the performance of two distinct clinical groups on a memory task garners convincing support for the importance of attending to "process achievement" in interpreting test data. While we certainly can applaud the constructive analysis of Butters, it should be pointed out that this approach requires considerable sophistication on the part of those who are doing the assessment. One might wonder whether the average clinician undertaking assessment chores would know how to evaluate the types of errors observed in a "process achievement" approach. It would appear that training in neuropsychology as well as gerontology would be invaluable to the clinician who intends to evaluate memory problems in the elderly.

These brief statements do little justice to the thorough and perceptive discussions presented in the three chapters mentioned, but they do provide a background for some issues in need of further elaboration. As mentioned earlier, memory deficits must be evaluated within the context of other spheres of cognitive functioning. The presence of generalized cognitive deficits plus memory problems, for example, would suggest an entirely different diagnostic formulation than memory problems with no evidence of serious impairment in other cognitive domains. In the first, one might hypothesize extensive brain dysfunction, while in the second a functional disorder or a focal brain lesion might be suggested.

It is also worth mentioning again that just as memory should be evaluated in relation to other cognitive processes, so also should cognitive function, in general, be evaluated in the context of other psychological (e.g., affect level), sociological, and medical factors. As a clinical entity, memory disturbance can be a final common pathway of a variety of psychological and biological complications, and for the most part, a specific etiology is not well established. Therefore, without a comprehensive profile of a particular individual it is difficult to make inferences about etiology or recommend appropriate interventions. In particular, relying solely on normative data for memory tests could present pitfalls. While it is important to generate age norms for tests of memory, as Erickson et al. have argued, comparison of an individual's scores to norms could be misleading in developing a treatment plan if consideration is not given to other factors that might be interfering with memory performance. This would include factors such as level of psychological distress, fatigue, distractibility due to novel situation, medical problems, etc.

One important facet of cognitive function that has been neglected in evaluating individuals with memory disturbance is that of attentional processes. It is quite obvious that if an individual is unable to "pay close attention" to information being presented at any given moment, then that information stands little chance of "being registered" in memory store in a manner that will render it readily retrievable. Researchers have been aware of the importance of attentional factors in memory function in the elderly for some time (Craik, 1977), and it is reassuring to see that attentional processes have not been overlooked in the present volume. Tests of the ability to maintain sustained attention to a task, such as the continuous performance task, and the ability to divide attention between two or more tasks simultaneously (cf. Wingfield & Sandoval, Chapter 12), should shed light on possible mechanisms underlying memory disturbanc.. It is surprising that laboratory procedures used to measure these have not been incorporated into clinical assessment batteries. Now that inexpensive, portable micro-processors are available, it should be relatively easy to develop psychometric measures of sustained and divided attention for use in the evaluation of cognitive processes.

The efficacy of current and proposed assessment procedures in addressing clinical questions about memory in the elderly is as yet controversial and needs further consideration. Some workers have posited that assessment of psychological performance cannot be done adequately independent of the context in which a given individual has to function (cf. Bersoff, 1973). They argue that if you want to determine the performance capability of an individual, you must observe that individual in the environmental context of interest, be it a job setting, a residential home placement, or his or her own familiar life situation. This contention is certainly inclusive of memory assessment, and may be especially applicable for the elderly.

At present, the correspondence between memory tests and memory function in everyday life is not known for the elderly. Therefore, major questions of interest to the clinician revolve around how effective new or old tests can be in predicting performance in the home or work environments; how they can be used effectively as a resource in recommending changes or supports needed to minimize problems; and what can be done to improve the nature of these tools. Several strategies worthy of further exploration are suggested throughout this section. Both Squire (Chapter 24) and Zelinski, Gilewski, and Thompson (Chapter 30) suggest that self-report regarding one's memory function would be helpful. The relation of memory complaint profiles to memory-test performance may provide a clearer picture of daily memory function and problems, as well as assist in delineating various kinds of memory difficulties.

Zelinski et al. mention that the comparison of memory-test performance with a daily log of reporting memory problems would provide information regarding the effectiveness of memory tests. A log of daily memory activities could also be expanded to serve as an excellent assessment device. Borrowing from Kanfer and Saslow's (1969) concept of "functional analysis" and Bersoff's (1973) description of "situational assessment," one could develop a behavioral method of data collection to aid in: (1) documenting the nature of the memory problem; (2) determining possible precipitants of memory disturbance episodes; and (3) identifying environmental and behavioral interventions that might be helpful in treatment.

Observation of elderly individuals in a variety of natural settings could provide important information for the development of "ecologically" valid instruments, but also would enable one to make direct comparisons between laboratory test performance and actual functioning in familiar surroundings. If appropriate tests are or can be made effective in predicting functioning, then expensive observation techniques would be less critical. The use of relatives or significant others as observers has proven to be extremely helpful at times in verifying test results. Several family/observer rating scales and questionnaires are available for measuring other behaviors, and it is likely that similar techniques could be developed for the assessment of memory problems.

The chapters by Albert and Kaplan, by Butters, and by Squire make the point that validation of memory tests on individuals with known clinical entities would strengthen their usefulness in assessment of memory problems. As Butters and Erickson et al. suggest, the effectiveness of memory tests would be particularly high if patterns or types of errors in memory could be associated with specific diagnostic classifications or locus of lesions. Additional neuropsychological tests known to relate to specific diagnostic conditions might also be used in a similar manner to aid in understanding the nature of memory problems in the elderly. Such comparisons may reveal the presence of several subtypes of memory problems in the elderly associated with different types of neuropathology.

MEMORY COMPLAINTS AND PERFORMANCE: THE ROLE OF DEPRESSION

The importance of obtaining specific information about memory complaints as a routine part of the memory assessment process is emphasized in the chapter by Erickson et al. Arguments in support of this position are scattered throughout the clinical literature, but a detailed summary of these by Poon, Fozard, and Treat (1978) has provided convincing rationale for inclusion of such items in a memory battery. It is well known that under certain circumstances, negative self-perceptions can have a remarkable impact on performance; this is especially apparent in the realm of memory abilities. On the other hand, objective evidence of memory problems in an individual also typically precipitates memory complaints. It is not known, however, whether the pattern and quality of the complaints associated with the two conditions are similar. Data presented in Squire's chapter suggests that continued research may result in improved measures for detecting discernible differences. He observed that the memory complaints in depressed individuals prior to and six months following ECT form a different profile than the complaints that occur during and immediately after the course of ECT treatment. This led him to suggest that memory complaints due to depression are distinguishable from those due to amnesic states. Perhaps similar differences in performance may be observed between individuals who have memory problems stemming from depression, and those whose memory problems are due to other factors.

While it is not a major point of discussion in any of the chapters presented in this section, it seems clear that depression should be considered as an important factor in any future studies evaluating the relationship between memory complaints and memory performance. In a recent review, Miller (1975) provided considerable evidence that cognitive deficits are associated with depression, although no particular deficits have been reported to be unique to depression. Kahn and Miller (1978) also argued that cognitive and memory impairment can be especially pronounced in the elderly as a result of depression. Few attempts have been made to investigate the relationship between memory complaints and performance, and even less have included depression as a variable. At the present, the results appear somewhat inconsistent. Kahn, Zarit, Hilbert and Niederehe (1975) and Zarit, Cole, Gallagher, Guider, and Kramer (1978) found a minimal relationship between memory performance and complaints in a clinical sample, but did observe a significant relationship between depression and complaints. No relationship between depression and decreased memory performance was observed in either study. Using a more quantitative measure of memory complaints and a more detailed evaluation of performance, Zelinski et al. (Chapter 30) show a substantial relationship between the two in the elderly group, but their sample is limited to community volunteers. No measure of depression was administered. Clearly, additional research in this area is needed to understand the interactive effect of brain status, affective level, and perception of performance on actual memory processes.

The intricate interrelationship of depression, memory complaints and memory performance has led us (Gallagher & Thompson, 1980) to argue that careful measurement of all three can be especially helpful in assessing and planning treatment for individuals with memory disturbances. Looking just at the results of Kahn et al. (1975), for example, one might emphasize the role depression plays in an individual with memory complaints, whereas the data presented by Zelinski et al. suggests that memory function itself is a more appropriate focus for evaluation and intervention.

If an evaluation of all factors is made, then it is sometimes possible to improve significantly the precision and utility of diagnostic and treatment formulations. For example, if an individual has a high level of memory complaint, normal memory performance, and an elevated level of depression, then this would suggest strongly that depression is a major culprit in the memory problem. Accordingly, one would proceed immediately to treat the depression, probably with time-limited psychotherapy accompanied by appropriate pharmacotherapy, if indicated.

If memory complaints are high, memory performance is normal, and depression is low, then other intervening variables need consideration.

Anxiety, increased concern over age-related changes in cognitive processes, and family- and job-related problems are all likely candidates. Such a constellation can also be seen following an incident causing minimal brain impairment, such as a mild stroke, and occasionally it is observed in the very early states of other pathological conditions that affect brain function. In the latter, other clinical signs and laboratory findings are frequently negative on first examination, and confirm suspicions only upon follow-up examinations.

One of the most difficult diagnostic problems occurs when complaints are high, performance is low, and depression is high. In this situation, particular attention must be paid to the magnitude of the disorder, quality of responses, and other psychological and medical findings before deciding on a diagnosis and focus of intervention. In some instances, without serial testing, it is practically impossible to distinguish between depression, brain impairment, or a combination of both as determinants of the cognitive or memory problems. Treatment frequently focuses initially on depression, irrespective of whether there is confirmatory evidence of brain impairment. If the memory problem is not improved with alleviation of the depression, then the likelihood that brain damage is responsible increases. Follow-up treatment might include training to improve learning strategies, counseling with family or significant others, and environmental changes to minimize complex and stressful situations.

When memory performance, memory complaints, and depression are all low, this is consistent with the development of more severe brain impairment. Given that other treatable causes of brain dysfunction can be ruled out, counseling with the family and environmental modifications can be helpful in minimizing adjustment problems.

Finally, it should be mentioned that the impact of depression on cognitive function in the elderly can at times be so extreme that individuals appear as if they are experiencing extreme dementia. This state has been termed as "pseudodementia" (Post, 1975). As the name implies, it is assumed that the major cause of the disturbance is psychological, even though the behavioral manifestations appear quite organic. Considering the negative implications for treatment when an individual is labeled as having "senile dementia" or "chronic brain syndrome," it becomes increasingly important to evaluate the role of depression. However, as with the milder problems, other factors such as environmental complexities, learned coping skills, etc. can contribute significantly to the impairment. The existence of such a disease entity should serve to remind us of the complex interaction of psychological and social processes, as well as biological factors that underlie the maintenance of adequate cognitive functioning. As Kahn and Miller (1978) have so aptly pointed out:

> Although we are accustomed to think in dichotomous terms with respect to
> 'organic' or 'functional' disorders, in reality we are dealing with total organisms

whose behavior represents a psycho-bio-social interaction. It is the combination of many factors that produces a given behavior pattern, with physiological condition being only one [p. 281].

INTERVENTION

Recently there has been increased interest in whether training can improve cognitive function in elderly individuals. Studies have shown improved performance in intelligence-test scores (Birkhill & Schaie, 1975), performance related to concept formation and abstract reasoning (Hornblum & Overton, 1976; Labouvie-Vief & Gonda, 1976; Sanders & Sanders, 1978), and reaction time (Hoyer, Labouvie & Baltes, 1973). There has even been some suggestion of positive transfer to other classes of tasks (Plemmons, Willis & Baltes, 1978). Similar encouraging results have been reported in attempting to improve memory performance (cf. Poon, Walsh-Sweeney & Fozard, Chapter 26; Zarit et al., 1978). There is controversy, however, regarding what factors might be responsible for positive changes seen in memory function and what particular techniques of cognitive skill training should be the focus of a remedial program. While the few empirical studies in the literature are promising, many questions yet remain unanswered. This should not be surprising in view of the numerous and distinctly different factors that can cause memory disturbance.

The general flavor of controversies in this field are typified in the arguments set forth in this section regarding the use of imagery as a mnemonic device for improving memory function in the elderly. Winograd & Simon (Chapter 27) question the effectiveness of imagery as a mnemonic. Their position stems from evidence in the literature that older individuals have greater declines in visual memory and more difficulty in forming visual codes. While one might question the extent to which visual encoding and imagery reflect identical cognitive processes, their laboratory findings call attention to a need for caution in making inferences about the practical use of imagery. Poon et al. (Chapter 26), on the other hand, provide empirical evidence that visual imagery may be particularly helpful for the elderly. In summarizing these papers, Cermak (Chapter 16) has given us cause for reflection concerning the impact of imagery as a mnemonic, and a welcome admonition that we may not yet have an adequate data base to resolve such controversies or applaud particular intervention techniques. Further, Robertson-Tchabo (Chapter 29) emphasizes the need of considering individual differences and the assessment of whom is likely to benefit from what technique.

At first reading, Chapters 26 and 27, just mentioned, appear to be poles apart, but upon closer examination this is not supported. Winograd and Simon are not completely discarding imagery, and emphasize the importance of attending to individual differences in the use of strategies. Similarly, Poon et al. encourage the clinician to determine in each case whether imagery or verbal mnemonics are more suitable for assisting a particular client. From the clinician's perspective, one might question whether it is productive to be embroiled in such controversies. It seems that both positions can be set in a framework that emphasizes the utility of organizational strategies in memory function; to the extent that particular visual or verbal techniques provide this organizational component, they can be more or less helpful.

The fervor with which these points of view are argued points to an area of tension between the world of the experimentalist and the clinician and encourages us to exhume some time-worn principles that might serve as helpful directives in future research. First, we cannot make the assumption that the cognitive systems mediating the changes we see in laboratory studies are necessarily similar to the processes underlying the longer term change that we are attempting to obtain in a remedial program. It is reasonable to use the extant literature as a point of departure, but it would be premature to rely on this completely when deciding what will be effective in an intervention program. Furthermore, one ought to feel guided by but not wedded to laboratory paradigms in designing research to address issues regarding improved function in practical settings.

Second, there may well be qualitative differences in underlying mechanisms of memory function between individuals who volunteer for studies in a research program and those who are in distress, come to a clinic for help, and are willing to commit themselves to a therapy program. Thus, the generality of current findings may be limited; while useful principles for memory training have been set forth, these may be difficult to apply with a given client. Hopefully, continued dialogue between the laboratory and the clinic will overcome these problems.

Finally, one cannot overlook the possibility that training on a specific technique may improve performance only indirectly by virtue of a more general effect on the individual's appraisal of his or her ability to function effectively. Thus, the specific training technique may not be as critical as the client's subjective evaluation of observed changes. While this point has not been validated empirically, it deserves attention in studies attempting to evaluate the outcome of specific techniques. Zarit et al. (1978) point out that it may also be a particularly critical feature in obtaining positive transfer effects from the clinical setting to the real world. Recall that clients who come for help usually have a set of negative self-perceptions regarding memory function. Improvement in memory function in the clinic may mean little if the client continues to be burdened with the self-fulfilling prophecy that he or she cannot remember anything. Even the most theoretically elegant and empirically effective technique may remain useless if persistent negative self-evaluations are overlooked.

REFERENCES

Arenberg, D. Introduction to a symposium: Toward comprehensive intervention programs for memory problems among the aged. *Experimental Aging Research,* 1978, *4,* 233.

Bernal, G. A. A., Brannon, L. J., Belar, C., Lavigne, J., & Cameron, R. Psychodiagnostics of the elderly. In W. D. Gentry (Ed.), *Gerontology: A model of training and clinical service.* Cambridge: Ballinger Publishing Co., 1977.

Bersoff, D. N. Silk purses into sow's ears: The decline of psychological testing and a suggestion for its redemption. *American Psychologist,* 1973, *28,* 892-899.

Birkhill, W. R., & Schaie, K. W. The effect of differential reinforcement of cautiousness in intellectual performance among the elderly. *Journal of Gerontology,* 1975, *30,* 578-583.

Craik, F. I. M. Age differences in human memory. In J. E. Birren & K. W. Schaie (Eds.), *Handbook of the psychology of aging.* New York: Van Nostrand Reinhold, 1977.

Crook, T. H. Psychometric assessment in the elderly. In A. Raskin & L. F. Jarvik (Eds.), *Psychiatric symptoms and cognitive loss in the elderly: Evaluation and assessment techniques.* Washington, D.C.: Hemisphere, 1979.

Gallagher, D. and Thompson, L. W. Clinical psychological assessment of older adults. In Poon, L. W. (Ed.), *Aging in the 1980's.* Washington, D.C.: American Psychological Association, 1980.

Hornblum, J. N., & Overton, W. F. Area and volume conservation among the elderly: Assessment and training. *Developmental Psychology,* 1976, *12,* 68-74.

Hoyer, W. J., Labouvie, G. V., & Baltes, P. B. Modification of response speed deficits and intellectual performance in the elderly. *Human Development,* 1973, *16,* 233-242.

Kahn, R. L., & Miller, N. E. Adaptational factors in memory function in the aged. *Experimental Aging Research,* 1978, *4,* 273-289.

Kahn, R. L., Zarit, S. H., Hilbert, N. M., & Niederehe, G. Memory complaint and impairment in the aged. *Archives of General Psychiatry,* 1975, *32,* 1569-1573.

Kanfer, F. H., & Saslow, G. Behavioral diagnosis. In C. Franks (Ed.), *Behavior therapy: Appraisal and status.* New York: McGraw-Hill, 1969.

Kramer, N., & Jarvik, L. F. Assessment of intellectual changes in the elderly. In A. Raskin & L. F. Jarvik (Eds.), *Psychiatric symptoms and cognitive loss in the elderly: Evaluation and assessment techniques.* Washington, D.C.: Hemisphere, 1979.

Labouvie-Vief, G., & Gonda, J. N. Cognitive strategy training and intellectual performance in the elderly. *Journal of Gerontology,* 1976, *31,* 327-332.

Miller, W. Psychological deficit in depression. *Psychological Bulletin,* 1975, *82,* 238-260.

Plemmons, J. K., Willis, S. L., & Baltes, P. B. Modifiability of fluid intelligence in aging: A short-term longitudinal approach. *Journal of Gerontology,* 1978, 33, 224-231.

Poon, L. W., Fozard, J. L., & Treat, N. J. From clinical and research findings on memory to intervention programs. *Experimental Aging Research,* 1978, *4,* 235-253.

Post, F. Dementia, depression and pseudodementia. In D. F. Benson & D. Blumer (Eds.), *Psychiatric aspects of neurologic disease.* New York: Grune & Stratton, 1975.

Sanders, R. E., & Sanders, J. A. C. Long-term durability and transfer of enhanced conceptual performance in the elderly. *Journal of Gerontology,* 1978, *33,* 408-412.

Schaie, K. W., & Schaie, J. P. Clinical assessment and aging. In J. E. Birren & K. W. Schaie (Eds.), *Handbook of the psychology of aging.* New York: Van Nostrand Reinhold, 1977.

Zarit, S. H., Cole, K., Gallagher, D., Guider, R., & Kramer, N. *Memory concerns of the aging: Cognitive and affective interventions.* Paper presented at the 11th International Congress of Gerontology, Tokyo, 1978.

Clinical Memory Testing of the Elderly

Richard C. Erickson
Veterans Administration Medical Center
Portland, Oregon

Leonard W. Poon & Leslie Walsh-Sweeney
Veterans Administration Outpatient Clinic
Boston, Massachusetts

Consider these practical questions: What specific criteria should be used to differentiate "normal" age-related memory changes from "abnormal" forgetting? And what diagnostic tests are appropriate to evaluate the memory functioning of the elderly?

At present, there are no cogent answers to these questions. One reason is that the various components of age-related decrements in memory performance are not well understood. Another reason is that no comprehensive and well documented memory battery has been developed.

The important field of memory testing certainly has not suffered from neglect in terms of effort and ingenuity (see Erickson & Scott, 1977; Lezak, 1976, Chapter 13; Poon, 1980). However, it has suffered from a lack of sweeping and systematic reflection on the manifold issues that memory assessment encompasses. The field is littered with half-finished work, leaving the observer with the impression that each investigator has interrupted his or her undertaking once relatively immediate clinical or research needs have been met. The few batteries that are available (see fourth section) tend to rest on partial or ambiguous definitions of memory functioning and as such do not cohere. More often, investigators develop single-faceted tests that serve limited functions and populations. Investigators have not carried through to the end the arduous but necessary task of standardizing their tests on a variety of populations.

As a consequence of this situation, the practicing clinician is confronted with an unorganized test closet filled with the products of others' ingenuity. Given the number of tests and the absence of meaningful guidelines, it is no wonder that many clinicians rely on the frequently criticized Wechsler

Memory Scale (see Erickson & Scott, 1977, for a review) or select and overgeneralize from one or another of the many single-faceted tests.

Experimental psychologists have proposed numerous models of memory functioning (see Baddeley [1976], Craik & Lockhart [1972], and Walsh [1975] for reviews) based on laboratory tasks and procedures, but have given minimal attention to the demands and constraints of clinical settings. However, even though experimental psychologists proceed in ways other than those followed by clinicians (Erickson, 1978), the distance is no longer as great as it once was (Schaie & Schaie, 1977).

In order to develop a valid memory battery appropriate for testing the elderly, a variety of theoretical and clinical issues need to be addressed. This chapter represents one joint effort of clinical and experimental psychologists to consolidate some of the pertinent issues, to highlight some of the questions still in need of answers, to formulate some testing criteria, to evaluate some existing batteries, and to proffer some ideas about the constituents of a viable battery.

In order to carry out these ambitious objectives, we need to appreciate the contributions and claims of several fields of inquiry. Experimental psychologists have postulated a number of theoretical models and procedures which can do much to enlighten clinical procedures. It is they who have done the bulk of the research on normal aging. Neurodiagnosticians have made significant gains in documenting brain-behavior correlates of memory impairment. Practicing clinicians are the possible recipients of this largesse, but at the same time they must respond to situational demands which preclude simply transferring technologies from the laboratory to the clinic (Erickson, 1978).

We start, then, with an overabundance of conflicting demands and a plethora of possible assessment procedures. In order to reduce this data to manageable proportions, we need to summarize the pertinent findings of the experimentalists, neurodiagnosticians, and clinicians, even if the summary is undertaken in the most cursory fashion. The first three sections of this chapter attempt to do this, and such an undertaking is done with full knowledge that we cannot do justice to all the issues. The fourth section presents criteria for reviewing some current clinical tests, followed by a critique of eight batteries. In the fifth section, recommendations for a tripartite assessment approach will be made.

CLINICAL PRIORITIES

It is our contention that the chief justification of a clinical memory test or battery lies in the instrument's ability to contribute to the understanding and remediation of behavioral deficits. The instrument should be comprised of tasks with clear behavioral analogues that can be validated in terms of everyday behavior and translated into meaningful intervention strategies. It may contribute to our experimental and theoretical knowledge of cognition and neuropathology; however, of first-order importance is its effectiveness as a clinical tool to respond to "needed questions" in a nonredundant, cost-effective manner.

"Needed questions" are defined as questions whose answers serve the immediate concerns of the patient[1] (and/or the patient's family) and the various treatment personnel (e.g., psychologists, physicians, rehabilitation nurses, speech pathologists, and physical and occupational therapists) in the intervention setting (hospital, rehabilitation center, outpatient clinic, etc.). The elderly patient who has perceived some memory loss wants to know, in practical terms, what has gone wrong with the ability to attend, learn and remember. This person forgets important events and appointments, has trouble learning new things, can't remember from the past few days or long ago, misplaces possessions, forgets people's names, faces, and the like. These are the lapses that cause the patient inconvenience and embarrassment, and for which he or she would like explanations, a prognosis, and perhaps remedial attention.

In addition to specific patient/family concerns, treatment personnel report[2] a number of typical behaviors which interfere with rehabilitation efforts, daily living, and interpersonal relationships. There are problems of disorientation, including the patient's inability to recall, after an appropriate familiarization interval, the names of friends and treatment staff and the locations of his or her room and treatment areas. The patient may have difficulty providing a sequential report of events that happened during the preceding few hours or days, even to the point of forgetting family visits during the same day. He or she may be unable to take medications on schedule, and may repeatedly ask the same questions about treatment. In attempting to teach the patient needed exercises and skills, therapists report problems of distractibility. Some patients require step-by-step cuing. Even with this assistance, some are still unable to repeat instructions or recall information from one day to the next, or even after a few minutes.

Like the patient, treatment personnel have "needed questions" about etiology and prognosis. In addition, they need information regarding how they should proceed with the patient, and ask questions such as: Is the patient being manipulative? Should they wait until the patient's memory improves before beginning treatment? Should they help the patient with some type of

---

[1]The term patient is used broadly to refer to any person with a memory complaint, irrespective of the intervention setting in which the person is seen.

[2]Personal communication between staff at the Seattle Veterans Administration Hospital and the first author.

memory exercises? Should they confront the patient? Should they provide spoken, written, or gestural input? Should they restrict or change the environment? What can they do to "motivate" the individual? How long should they or will they need to persist before they can expect to see changes? How should the family be trained to work with the patient?

Questions asked by patients and treatment personnel typically are pragmatic and specific, and reflect the need for clear answers to pressing problems. In our judgment, existing memory tests do not do a particularly good job of addressing these practical issues (see Erickson & Scott, 1977; Poon, 1980). In some cases (e.g., the Wechsler Memory Scale), one is left with the sense that memory is an undifferentiated phenomenon. A "memory quotient" tells whether a person's "memory" is good or bad. In most cases, it is unclear from even a conceptual point of view what the behavioral implications of various tests scores might be.

Because many patients present localized brain damage, memory testing must provide for evaluating remaining assets as well as liabilities (see, e.g., Fowler & Fordyce, 1972). Patients unable to process verbal information may be able to learn and recall nonverbal information. Reduced functioning is not always global, which suggests the need for tests of various capabilities as well as tests designed to work around various disabilities (e.g., expressive aphasias, motor control problems) to tap strengths that might otherwise be missed.

For the most part, memory tests have been validated with reference to groups of patients with a variety of neuropathologies or to those who have been globally assessed as "memory impaired" (Inglis, 1957). To the best of our knowledge, however, little research has been directed toward relating memory test scores to commonplace behaviors. If a memory task is valid, it follows that a change in a test score should reflect a change in the patient's ability to respond to particular "real life" memory demands.

One study with which we are familiar (DeLeon, 1974) is relevant to this validation issue. Forty subjects between 60 and 86 years of age were provided with practice in learning paired associates. Although the performance of subjects improved on the paired-associate tasks, there was no transfer to tasks involving the subjects' ability to recall a personal narrative, a grocery list, and the names and occupations of photographed persons. It is possible, of course, that the wrong everyday behaviors were examined. However, these findings suggest that whether our various memory tasks constitute paradigms for everyday behaviors is still a much-neglected question.

An attempt to intuitively relate information-processing theory to everyday clinical problems has been reported by Wolf (1971), a nurse who described three familiar situations requiring nursing action. She cited relevant neuropsychological and information-processing literature, relating it to the kinds of problems confronted by nurses, and made suggestions about the kinds of remedial action nurses might take. Her article is commonsensical, and its uniqueness points out the need for more clinical research in this area.

In summary, the elderly person, that person's family, and treatment personnel have a variety of questions that need to be addressed. These questions include (but are not limited to) concerns about orientation, recent and remote memory, how long it will take the patient to learn, and how well the learned materials will be retained. Memory testing should be designed to respond meaningfully to these "needed questions," and should enable the examiner to make management suggestions that will maximize the person's memory potential. Furthermore, tests should be designed to tap the strengths and weaknesses of persons with and without known central nervous system pathology. Efforts also need to be directed toward validating test tasks in everyday behaviors and toward developing management guidelines for the clinician.

MEMORY TESTING AND AGE-RELATED FACTORS

Recent work (see Craik [1977] for a review) has debunked the notion that aging results in global cognitive deterioration; in some areas people improve with age, while in others they decline. The literature on memory and aging has been fairly extensive, and it is fortunate for our purposes that a number of excellent summaries of the literature have appeared in recent years (Arenberg, 1973; Arenberg & Robertson-Tchabo, 1977; Botwinick, 1973; Botwinick & Storandt, 1974; Craik, 1977; Fozard & Thomas, 1975; and Walsh, 1975). The field is not without controversies. However, the experimental literature has, in a short period of time, given clinicians and experimental investigators alike some notions about which areas to test.

Impact of Individual Differences

It is critically important that we keep in mind that no single pattern is characteristic of all older persons and, if anything, greater individual differences are to be found among older than younger persons (Riegel & Riegel, 1972). On one hand, this increased variability should give us hope as we age. On the other hand, the tremendous variability in individual differences is, at present, a major source of difficulty for experimental psychologists who attempt to describe cross-sectional age differences in cognitive functions among groups of young, middle-aged, and older adults.

Increased variability makes it difficult to establish norms and interpret normative data with confidence. Variability in memory performances has been found to be greater for older than for younger adults (between-group variability); in addition, the performance of an older individual generally is more variable (within-subject variability) (Fozard & Thomas, 1975). This within-subject variability will decrease the reliability and predictive power of a memory test unless factors contributing to this variability are known, evaluated, and used in the decision equation regarding the integrity of memory functioning. Norms become impractical if the range of normal functioning is very large. Furthermore, norms are misleading if abnormal functioning is due to factors other than memory impairment (e.g., depression).

Variability in the memory performances of the elderly has been found to be related to education (Birren & Morrison, 1961; Granick & Friedman, 1967), verbal intelligence (Poon & Fozard, 1978), affective states (Kahn & Miller, 1978), general health status (Birren, Butler, Greenhouse, Sokoloff, & Yarrow, 1963; Hulicka, 1967), environmental stresses, personality, and cognitive styles (Fozard & Costa, in press.) Therefore, in order to assess memory meaningfully, it becomes imperative that information about the "total person" be obtained and used in conjunction with performance data.

Need For And Features Of "Age-Fair" Testing

Increased variability in the gerontological experimental data could be due to the fact that the experimental paradigms designed for and used on younger adults are not suitable for or have not been appropriately adapted for older adults. In recent years, increased attention has been placed on the need for "culture-fair" tests. We think that there is ample evidence to argue that memory must be assessed in an "age-fair" manner.

A review of the aging memory literature shows that (1) the elderly are slower to adapt to experimental tasks than young adults; and (2) the elderly benefit from practice more than the young (Hulicka & Grossman, 1967; Murrell, 1970; Poon, Fozard, & Vierek, 1978; Treat, Poon, & Fozard, 1978). Furthermore, older persons are more cautious (Leech & Witte, 1971), slower in making decisions (Poon & Fozard, 1976), more disadvantaged when the stimuli are presented at a faster pace (Monge & Hultsch, 1971), and sometimes under- (Kahn & Miller, 1978) and over-motivated (Eisdorfer, Nowlin, & Wilkie, 1970; cf. Froehling, 1974).

The magnitude of age decline may be overestimated in tasks that are ecologically unsound to the aged (Poon & Fozard, 1978; Poon, 1980). For example, an elderly subject confronted with a task that he or she considers meaningless or irrelevant may choose to respond more slowly than if the task were perceived positively; or the subject may decide to sacrifice accuracy for speed in order to be able to complete the task as quickly as possible. This is not to suggest that, given ecologically valid tests, older persons necessarily will perform as well as the young. However, performance may be more representative of the memory functions of the individual if this ecological factor is controlled.

Research findings to date suggest that memory testing for the elderly would benefit from at least four specific considerations. First, the test should allow the subject sufficient time to adapt to the experimental environment and procedures (cf. Froehling, 1974). One way to facilitate habituation to the setting and testing routine is to test over two (or more) days, an approach which may be useful for obtaining stable memory test data from the elderly.

Second, the design should be one which makes it possible to adjust the testing procedures for age-related slowing of the sensory and motor systems (cf. Poon & Fozard, 1978). Appropriate baseline measurements should be added to evaluate sensory-motor capacities, independent of cognitive capacities, when speed of memory functioning is being assessed. When speed is not an important variable, it is suggested that self-pacing procedures be used.

Third, since the elderly tend to be more conservative and more cautious in making decision (cf. Leech & Witte, 1971), it is recommended that the patient's decisions criteria be examined by incorporating some mechanism for evaluating qualitative changes in the strategies the patient uses to acquire and retrieve information. And finally, meaningful stimuli and procedures should be utilized (cf. Poon & Fozard, 1978).

In summary, the elderly, both as a group and as individuals within the group, exhibit more variability in memory performance than is the case with younger persons. This variability makes "total person" assessment critical. "Age-fair" tests for the elderly should include provisions for sampling performance over time, for self-pacing, for evaluating the patient's processing strategies, and for controlling the ecological soundness of the tasks.

MEMORY TESTING AND NEURODIAGNOSIS

Memory impairments are common symptoms of a variety of cerebral diseases. Sometimes the impairments are transient, as in the case of toxic and traumatic amnesias, and sometimes they are permanent. Sometimes memory disorders stand in virtual isolation, as with the Korsakoff syndrome, and sometimes they are present as part of a more widespread pattern of cognitive dysfunction. Some appreciation of the disabling effects of memory disorders due to brain disease can be gained by reading fascinating narratives by Barbizet (1970) and Gardner (1974). Interested clinicians have long been able to observe the impact of tumors, head traumas, vascular lesions, surgical interventions, electro-convulsive therapy (ECT), infections, anoxic and toxic states, etc., thus contributing significantly to our current understanding of memory functioning (see Brain, 1969; Williams, 1970).

Confronted with a compromised patient, a clinician would like to know (1) whether memory impairments provide information about the presence and location of neurological lesions; and (2) how current knowledge of brain functioning can contribute to formulating a structure for testing. The following sections will address these two concerns.

Contributions Of Memory Testing To Neurodiagnosis

From a clinical standpoint, the examiner is questioning whether memory testing will yield sensitive and accurate information about the presence and location of possible neurological lesions. At the present time, on the basis of commonly used memory tests, the answer to this question appears to be a qualified "no" (see Erickson & Scott [1977] for a review). Consider, for example, the weaknesses of the Wechsler Memory Scale (WMS), which purports to tap a number of functions associated with memory. Although the WMS was designed to isolate organic problems associated with memory disorders, it has been shown that the test does not differentiate among psychotic, neurotic, and organic patients once age and IQ are controlled (Cohen, 1950). Factor analysis of the WMS (Kear-Colwell, 1973) revealed that only dements exhibited overall memory dysfunction, while some subjects with confirmed lesions produced no measurable memory deficits. Furthermore, in several other attempts to tease out more sensitive portions of the WMS, there has been a notable lack of consistency among investigators with respect to the subtests identified as providing the discriminative power. For example, Bachrach and Mintz (1974) found that the designs subtest provided most of the discrimination, whereas Kljajic (1975), using a small (n = 37) sample, found that the associate learning task distinguished between brain-damaged and normal subjects. In contrast, Russell (1975) identified the logical memory and visual reproduction subtests from the WMS as being discriminative, and used these tasks as the basis of the "six independent memory scales" he developed.

As a screening device for an as yet undiagnosed elderly patient, memory testing alone does not presently appear to be particularly productive in isolating neurological disorders (Erickson & Scott, 1977). General or localized neurological deficits have been implicated in the observed age-related decrement in memory functions (Birren, 1964; Welford, 1969). However, memory testing of geriatric population has not been able to differentiate among patterns of neurological impairment, strategy differences, and cohort factors as reasons for poor performances. Perhaps as we become more sophisticated in devising tests or in revising existing protocols, we may return and find that some new or revised instruments will be more powerful. One attempt to isolate neurological deficits in the aged on the basis of memory testing results is presented in Chapter 23 by Albert and Kaplan.

Contributions Of Neuropsychological Findings To Memory Testing

Although currently available memory tests are not, by themselves, powerful enough to diagnose neuropathologies, the body of neuropsychological knowledge derived from pathological findings has a great deal to suggest about how psychologists should proceed to test and analyze memory functioning. Our understanding of the neuropsychology of memory is certainly more sophisticated now than it was two decades ago, thanks to the careful work of such researchers as Barbizet (1970), Luria (1973), Talland (1965), Milner (1970), and Butters and Cermak (1975), to name a few.

It is now clear that memory is not a localized function, nor is it a product of the brain operating in an undifferentiated fashion. Vast portions of the brain operate as functional systems in acquiring, storing, and retrieving information. Key pathways have been found to involve the main structures in the limbic system containing the Circuit of Papez. Insults to the hippocampus, fornices, mamillary bodies and portions of the thalamus, and the cingulate gyrus suggest these structures form a route for transforming current information into stored memories. Lesions in this pathway may contribute to an inability to process information. This interruption in the information processing sequence seems to be material- (rather than modality-) specific depending on the laterality of the lesion (Milner, 1970), verbal deficits being associated with lesions in the dominant lobe pathway and nonverbal with lesions in the nondominant lobe pathway.

According to Barbizet (1970), hemispheric specialization is also reflected in lesions that produce cortical amnesias. Left retrofrontal lesions result in language disorders and in compromised verbal span, verbal learning, and retention; whereas right retrofrontal lesions result in problems with nonverbal skills, as reflected in a reduced visual span and difficulties learning and retaining visual and tactile information. Split-brain studies highlight the role of the corpus collosum in interhemispheric communications and confirm hemispheric differences. Frontal lesions tend to result in more subtle losses, including difficulty retaining several facts simultaneously as a condition of accomplishing a specific task, difficulty learning unusual associations, and difficulty "learning to learn."

These findings suggest the importance of scrutinizing the acquisition and retention of information using both verbal and nonverbal materials (cf. Baddeley & Warrington, 1970; Butters & Cermak, 1975, 1976; Cermak, 1976; Cermak & Butters, 1973). In addition, two important studies (Corkin, 1968;

Milner, 1970) suggest that the clinician should not only make a distinction between memory for verbal and nonverbal information, but should also assess the patient's ability to acquire and retain motor skills. These studies demonstrated that patients unable to learn and retain verbal and nonverbal materials may well be able to learn and retain motor skills, suggesting the possibility of a third, quite separate information-processing system.

Although we have a grasp of the functional components of the neurological information-processing system in terms of acquisition, we have little neuropsychological data with regard to storage. How and where information is stored is not well understood. Consequently, neuropsychology currently has little to offer the clinician with respect to how to differentiate between memory dysfunction at the storage or retrieval stages.

In our earlier discussion of "age-fair" testing, we suggested repeated testing as an approach to obtaining stable memory data from the elderly. Experience with amnesias resulting from datable traumas also indicates that memory testing needs to provide for repeated assessment over time. Protracted evaluation is important in such cases because, as time passes, a patient's "amnesic zone" usually shrinks until the patient is left with a discrete and permanent memory lacuna (Barbizet, 1970). Barbizet's (1970) work, suggesting that storage of new material is a lengthy process, is a further argument for protracted evaluation of the aged.

Recent work suggesting that inefficient acquisition may be due to inappropriate learning strategies indicates that further attention should be paid to patterns of information processing (Baddeley & Warrington, 1973; Butters & Cermak, 1975; Cermak, 1976; Cermak & Butters, 1973; Cermak, Butters, & Gerrain, 1973; Cermak & Moreines, 1976). Recent studies also suggest that various diseases may result in subtle, but distinctly different patterns of cognitive impairment (Butters & Cermak, 1975, 1976; Lhermitte & Signoret, 1972). Remedial work with the aged (Cole & Guider, 1978; Treat, Poon, & Fozard, 1978; Zarit, Gallagher, Kramer, & Walsh, 1977) and brain-injured patients (Jones, 1974) bolsters the argument that a careful analysis of how the patient processes information should be a part of the clinical analysis. Such data may be of assistance from both a diagnostic and a remedial point of view.

To date, the literature relating aging and brain dysfunction is limited. Work on neuropathologies of the aged, especially of the enlarged ventricles and cortical sulci, has revealed significant relationships between brain atrophy and measures of intelligence (Matthews & Booker, 1972), learning and memory processes (Willanger, Thygesen, Nielsen, & Peterson, 1968), and rate of conditioning (Kiev, Chapman, Guthrie, & Wolff, 1962). A recent dissertation by Kaszniak (1976) further clarifies the relationship between brain atrophy, age, and memory processes, while controlling for education and health status. Kaszniak (1976) found that performance on digit-span forward recall (a test assumed to tap primary memory) was adversely affected by brain atrophy and not by increasing age. In addition, both age and brain atrophy were found to affect paired-associate learning (assumed to be a test of acquisition and secondary memory). This absence of an interaction between age and brain atrophy suggests that variables other than brain atrophy must be sought to account for poor paired-associate learning by elderly normals, and underscores the importance of "total person" assessment.

In summary, memory disorders are associated with a wide variety of brain diseases. Sometimes diminished memory functioning is the main presenting symptom (e.g., the Korsakoff's syndrome) and sometimes it is part of a more global cognitive dysfunction. Currently available memory tests are not sensitive indicators of cerebral dysfunction and thus, by themselves, cannot provide the clinician with information about the presence or location of a lesion. However, current knowledge of brain functioning can contribute to the memory testing process. Some neurological literature suggests that it may be beneficial for the clinician to evaluate the acquisition and retention of verbal and nonverbal information and motor skills, and that repeated testing may be necessary in order to obtain stable memory data. There is also some work which suggests that testing should include an analysis of the processing strategies available to and used by the patient, and other work which indicates that the clinician needs to be prepared to look for variables other than brain atrophy to account for depressed memory functioning.

REVIEW OF SELECTED CLINICAL BATTERIES

In the preceding sections, we discussed clinical priorities, age factors related to memory testing, and the relationships between memory testing and neurodiagnoses. Now, let us turn our attention to some of the instruments available for assessing memory functioning in adults.

There are, we believe, several general features that an adequate instrument should exhibit if the instrument is to contribute meaningfully to answering the "needed questions" discussed earlier:

1. The nature of the clinical questions that typically need to be addressed suggests that the instrument should be structured so that the following memory functions are assessed: orientation, short-term memory, delayed retrieval (long-term memory), and remote (very-long-term) memory.

2. The neuropsychological literature suggests that, in addition to assessing the acquisition and retention of verbal information, it may be useful to evaluate the patient's ability to learn and retrieve nonverbal information and motor skills.

3. The efficiency with which a patient is able to process information should also be evaluated. Learning-to-criterion provides one method of obtaining such information. Qualitative analyses of the strategies used by the patient to acquire information and retrieve previously learned information can also be utilized.

4. The instrument should have alternate procedures that make it possible to test patients unable to execute verbal or motor responses.

5. Both the gerontological and neuropsychological literature suggest that repeated testing of the patient would be advantageous. Delayed retrieval tasks represent one method of obtaining information over time. Alternate forms also make it possible to gather information over time.

6. The instrument should be validated with respect to everyday behaviors.

7. The instrument should include guidelines for further testing and remediation.

8. The instrument should be structured so that it is brief and relatively easy to administer.

9. Elderly norms should be available.

10. The battery should present norms for each subtest instead of combining scores as if memory were a unitary phenomenon. Constructing an instrument in terms of "modules" (Erickson, 1978) with separate norms will make it possible to replace or add new components when warranted by the weight of clinical and experimental evidence.

It was indicated earlier that we believe memory must be assessed in an "age-fair" manner. The fact that a testing instrument has been designed for "adults" does not necessarily make it an appropriate instrument for the elderly. Some of the features that we consider important for an instrument that is to be used with the elderly are as follows:

1. Administration procedures and scoring criteria need to be adjusted to account for age-related slowing in the sensory and motor systems.

2. The administration protocol should allow the elderly patient sufficient time to habituate to the testing environment and procedures.

3. The testing materials and procedures need to be ecologically valid. Procedures that are simple and materials comprised of common stimuli may decrease the possibility that a standardized instrument will be ecologically unsound.

In order to meaningfully interpret the pattern of memory functioning derived from standardized testing, it is critical that concomitant information be obtained to identify pertinent individual differences in education, verbal intelligence, neurophysiological status, health, affective states, environmental stress, personality, and cognitive styles. As we pointed out earlier, the variability among the elderly is greater than among young adults. This increased variability makes it even more important that an instrument's normative information be interpreted in light of concomitant information.

It is beyond the scope of this paper to describe and critique all of the single- and multi-faceted memory tests that are currently available. Eight batteries will be briefly described and evaluated. For more detailed information, the reader is referred to Lezak (1976) and Erickson and Scott (1977).

Brief Description Of The Batteries

The familiar Wechsler Memory Scale (Wechsler, 1945) consists of seven subtests: personal and current information, orientation, mental control, logical memory, digits, visual reproduction, and associate learning. It holds a virtual monopoly in the field of memory testing. It suffers from inadequate conceptualization and is unusable with many impaired patients (see Erickson & Scott [1977] for a review). Approaches which have attempted to structure the scale into more up-to-date terms (e.g., Russell, 1975) appear to get their impetus from the scale's well-entrenched position rather than from more compelling considerations. None of the attempts have been particularly convincing, nor have they enjoyed widespread application.

Cronholm's battery (Cronholm & Ottosson, 1963) consists of three tests: a 30-word-pair test; a 20-item figure test involving presentation of 20 drawings of common objects which subsequently are to be identified in an array of 50 drawings; and a 30-item personal data test featuring drawings of six persons, each associated with five items of information. The test features one-trial learning and delayed recall.

Williams' (1968) Scale for the Measurement of Memory includes simple tests of immediate recall (digit span), verbal learning (word definitions), nonverbal learning (the Rey-Davis task), delayed recall (of nine pictures from an array of 15), and memory for past personal events. Significant problems were unearthed in the course of standardizing the scale.

Barbizet and Cany (1968; also Barbizet, 1970) addressed the problem of adequately evaluating memory disturbances. They made a number of cogent comments about how to study a patient's memory for past events, and described a battery of memory tests they used at the Albert Chenevier Hospital. The battery attempts to analyze immediate evocation, learning, and retention, and it provides for retesting at 1 hr, at 24 hr, and at one week. They also attended to learning modalities. Tests of immediate memory include a verbal and visual span. Immediate evocation is measured by the number of familiar objects recalled from a set of 20 ("KIM" subtest), and by the number of story elements that a patient can recall after one exposure ("Story" subtest). Learning is measured by the number of digits that can be repeated when one new number per trial is added to the sequence, by learning a list of

15 unrelated words over five trials and subsequently recognizing these words when they are presented in a story, and by learning the position of seven chips on a board over 15 trials. Retention is measured by means of a forgetting curve involving the "KIM" and "Story" subtests.

Meyer and Falconer (1960) employed a series of paired-associate tasks, varying receptive and expressive modalities on a small sample of temporal-lobe patients. Patten (1972) has presented a cursory set of tasks (using a "three objects" format) testing verbal, visual, smell, and taste modalities. His article compiled findings from 50 patients, but experienced clinicians might well wonder how he obtained his relatively clearcut results using such simple and familiar items. His test is not sufficient to form a basis for psychometric (as opposed to screening) purposes.

Pershad (Pershad & Wig, 1976) presented 10 subtests of remote and recent memory, mental balance, attention and concentration, immediate and delayed recall, verbal attention for similar and dissimilar pairs, and visual recognition of common objects.

Inglis (1957) compiled a sample battery for research purposes which involved four memory-span tasks and four paired-associate learning tasks involving various modes of presentation and various methods of reproduction. Further developments (Inglis, 1959) in his work only involved the auditory recall approach.

Critique

Table 22.1 summarizes each battery's conformity to some of the features we identified above as desirable. Unfortunately, neither the table nor the cursory descriptions presented earlier convey the richness of conceptualization and the ingenuity of execution reflected in these batteries.

Some general comments are in order. It is evident from Table 22.1 that none of the batteries even approaches including all of the features. When one tallies how many batteries incorporate each of the selected features several commonalities emerge. First, orientation, remote memory, and motor skills typically are not assessed. Second, short-term memory is commonly assessed verbally but not nonverbally. Third, few batteries evaluate learning to criterion. Finally, too few provide alternate forms, standardization, validation on everyday behaviors, or norms for elderly persons.

On the other hand, it is evident that these investigators attempted to use meaningful materials: All of the batteries utilize familiar verbal stimuli, and all but the Wechsler Memory Scale use familiar visual stimuli. In addition, all stress relative brevity and convenience, and all but one provide alternate procedures that allow motor-impaired persons to respond. Furthermore, most batteries provide for delayed retention in one form or another.

Several observations are in order which are not directly reflected in Table 22.1. First, the use of the paired-associate paradigm is pervasive among these

TABLE 22.1
Inventory of Selected Features

	Wechsler Memory Scale	Inglis	Cronholm	Meyer & Falconer	Williams	Barbizet & Cany	Patten	Pershad	Number of Tests Reflecting Each Criterion
Orientation	?ᵃ	No	No	No	No	No	?	?	0+
Remote memory	?	No	No	No	?	?	?	Yes	1+
Short-Term Auditory Memory	Yes	Yes	No	No	Yes	Yes	Yes	Yes	6
Short-Term Visual Memory	No	Yes	No	No	No	Yes	No	No	2
Learning-To—Criterion (Verbal Stimuli)	No	Yes	No	Yes	No	No	?	No	2+
Learning-To-Criterion (Visual Stimuli)	No	No	Yes	Yes	No	Yes	?	No	3+
Delayed Retention (Verbal Stimuli)	No	No	Yes	No	Yes	Yes	Yes	Yes	4
Delayed Retention (Visual Stimuli)	No	No	Yes	No	No	Yes	Yes	Yes	5
Motor Skills Learning	No	No	No	No	No	No	No	No	0
Alternate Procedure For Verbal Response	No	Yes	No	Yes	Yes	Yes	No	No	2
Alternate Procedure For Motor Response	No	Yes	Yes	Yes	Yes	Yes	Yes	Yes	7
Common Verbal Stimuli	Yes	Yes	Yes	Yes	Yes	Yes	Yes	Yes	8
Common Visual Stimuli	No	Yes	Yes	Yes	Yes	Yes	Yes	Yes	7
Brevity And Convenience	Yes	No	Yes	Yes	Yes	No	No	Yes	8
Alternate Forms	Yes	No	?	No	Yes	No	No	No	4
Standardized	Yes	?	No	No	No	No	No	Yes	3+
Validated On Everyday Behaviors	No	No	No	No	No	No	No	No	0+
Elderly Norms Available	Yes	Yes	No	No	Yes	Yes	No	No	4
Number Of Criteria Met On Each Test	6+	10+	7+	8	9+	10+	7+	9+	

ᵃ? = minimal or inadequate.

batteries, as well as among many single-faceted tests for verbal memory (Erickson & Scott, 1977). Second, most tests do not evaluate the acquisition and retrieval of practical everyday information (telephone numbers, names and faces, etc.). Lastly, the patient's processing strategies do not appear to be assessed.

TOWARD A COMPREHENSIVE BATTERY

While present technology can identify gross memory dysfunction, the state of the art has not advanced sufficiently to differentiate the contributions of artifactual and primary factors on memory performances of the aged. We have reviewed the need for "total person" assessment and the need for "age-fair" tests. We have also directed the reader's attention to the need to relate face-validated test results to everyday behavior, and we have discussed the importance of habituation to the test procedure in order to obtain stable and meaningful results. All of these factors can artifactually depress memory performance and result in an inaccurate diagnosis of abnormal memory functioning. Therefore, the assessment process must be designed to take these factors into account.

In the course of this joint effort by experimental and clinical psychologists to define elements of a comprehensive battery, it has become evident that a mutual willingness to understand both clinical diagnostic demands and hypotheses-testing experimental procedures is central to a productive alliance. It has also become apparent that the development of a viable battery ultimately will necessitate a compromise between practical clinical efficiency and comprehensive multifactor evaluation.

Historically, three theoretical vantage points have characterized the experimental literature: stimulus–response (S–R) associationism, information-processing theory, and depth-of-processing theory (see Walsh [1975] for a review). To the uninitiated the literature seems vast, intricate, endlessly laborious, and sometimes contradictory. It is with good reason that some clinicians feel overwhelmed and consequently reject the experimental models and literature as self-serving and irrelevant to their needs. Furthermore, lack of meaningful communication between laboratory and clinical personnel contributes to the practice, by some clinicians, of administering memory tests without knowing the theoretical rationale behind the tests. Likewise, this lack of communication contributes to an insensitivity to and/or an ignorance of clinical problems and procedures on the part of some laboratory researchers (Erickson, 1978).

Confronted with the pressing demands of the intervention setting, clinicians often must make concessions to the realities facing them. In all likelihood, they will not be able to impose the kind of structure on the testing situation that they might wish. Clinicians typically are not able to exercise control over the kinds of persons who will be examined, the examination site, and the kinds of questions that will be addressed to the same degree as experimental personnel. They will often have to accept the fact that they can only note such variables as physical integrity and general health, personality, level of intellectual functioning, and motivation. Patients may present with peripheral sensory and motor deficits, with expressive aphasias, with problems processing elaborate instructions, with fatique negativism, with an unwillingness to participate in esoteric procedures, and the like.

If one hopes to develop a memory battery which will be widely used by clinicians, one must also keep test convenience in mind. If nothing else, convenience explains the durability of the Wechsler Memory Scale. Every proposed task must be functionally nonredundant and no more demanding of the examiner and patient than is absolutely necessary to gain the information needed.

The balance between providing theoretical precision and functional diagnostic information in a memory test is a fine one indeed. It is beneficial for a clinician to employ the latest state of the art memory task if it is one that can provide additional diagnostic insight. We believe that such a diagnostic tool can only be constructed via a close alliance between the clinical and experimental personnel. Judicious use of experimental theories and procedures will not only result in superior examinations, but also offer the hope that clinical work will be able to contribute in some direct way to furthering our knowledge of human memory.

While it is difficult at this stage of development in memory research and memory testing to define the number of memory and related factors for testing, the arbitrary administration of short memory tests for efficiency's sake is not acceptable to clinical and experimental psychologists alike. The debate will continue for some time concerning the number of necessary and sufficient memory subtests, the amount of concomitant information, and the manner of test administration. No single clinical instrument can presently evaluate such complex functioning. As in the case of the Wechsler Adult Intelligence Scale, the Halstead-Reitan Neuropsychological Test Battery, and the Minnesota Multiphasic Personality Inventory, clinicians may employ other tests or clinical observations to take a closer look at issues raised by the initial testing.

The following is a proposed tripartite approach to the assessment process. One area of evaluation involves the examination of the patient's perceptions of his or her memory functioning. The second embraces a consideration of the concomitant factors. The third involves a clinical examination of relevant memory behaviors. Information from all three areas needs to be integrated in order to obtain an adequate picture of the patient's memory abilities and deficits.

Patient's Self-Perception Of Memory Problems

Eisdorfer (1968; Eisdorfer et al., 1970) has demonstrated that high anxiety impedes the performance of older adults on memory tasks. Faulty self-perceptions of memory abilities or generalized feelings of inadequacy may function to heighten the patient's anxiety in a memory-testing situation, so that performance scores do not accurately reflect the patient's abilities. Thus, what a patient believes about the integrity of his or her memory abilities may affect the validity of the test data.

There are few laboratory studies that have evaluated the relationship between a patient's self-perception of memory abilities and level of memory functioning. There is some evidence to suggest that memory complaints and functioning are not highly correlated phenomena (Kahn, Zarit, Hilbert, & Niederehe, 1975; Zarit et al., 1977). However, results from a recent investigation (Gilewski, Zelinski, & Thompson, 1978) questioned the generality of previous findings. The findings of Gilewski et al. suggest that structuring a memory-complaint questionnaire to sort out types and frequencies of memory problems may enable the patient to better articulate memory problems, leading to better congruence between the complaints and actual functioning. In addition, the information derived from such a questionnaire could be used (1) as a basis for selecting auxiliary memory tests; and (2) as one criterion measure to evaluate treatment effectiveness. For a comprehensive discussion of this topic, the reader is referred to Chapter 30 by Zelinski, Gilewski, and Thompson.

Concomitant Factors

As discussed earlier, it is imperative that memory functioning be viewed within the context of the "total person." Information on an individual's health, neurophysiological status, personality, cognitive styles, environmental stresses, education, verbal intelligence, and affective states is needed to provide a perspective for differential diagnosis of memory dysfunction.

Inventory of Memory Behaviors

In the fourth section, we identified some of the features that we believe should be reflected in a comprehensive memory battery. What follows in this section are suggestions for the content of the core components of a memory battery. The core inventory that we propose is designed to tap memory functioning along the information processing continuum, at registration, during learning, and at various retrieval intervals.

Earlier we pointed out that poor memory performances may be a function of inappropriate acquisition and retrieval strategies. Therefore, it is important that qualitative encoding and retrieval analyses be developed and incorporated into the various modules of a comprehensive battery. Qualitative analyses involve consideration of, for example, the types of errors that a patient makes and the order of execution of parts of a task. Demonstration of the clinical usefulness of some qualitative methods are presented in Chapter 23 by Albert and Kaplan.

The quantitative data obtained from the core inventory should yield information about (1) the capacity of the short term memory store and the ability to register information; (2) the efficiency with which the patient learns information; (3) the stability of information learned in the clinical settings; and (4) the integrity of dated information acquired in vivo. The suggestions that follow are presented in the interest of stimulating discussion and research directed toward developing modules of specific tasks capable of differentiating between age-related memory changes and abnormal forgetting.

Short-Term Memory And Registration Of Information. The ability of an individual to register and hold information for a short period of time has been assessed by immediate recall for words, letters, digits, and nonverbal configurations (e.g., Arthur, 1947). The digit span has been one popular instrument for assessing short term memory. The appeal of the digit-span task is that the stimuli are familiar, the task is easy to administer, and the task is relevant to in vivo memory demands (e.g., remembering telephone numbers, zip codes, and street addresses).

Digit span may also yield information about the patient's ability to register information about a sequence of events (Martin, 1978). If so, in addition to providing information about the capacity of short term memory for sequences of discrete items, digit span may also prove useful for evaluating such clinical behaviors as distractability and the inability to execute simple verbal commands.

People frequently have only a single exposure to information that they need or wish to remember (e.g., television news, telephone conversations). We propose that the immediate recall of narrative material (Bates, Masling, & Kintsch, 1978) be used to examine the registration and integrity of gist retention over a short period of time.

Acquisition Efficiency. Because of the slower acquisition rate of the elderly, it is imperative that delayed tests of retrieval from long-term memory be evaluated after the material has been learned to criterion. Establishing the patient's acquisition rate is valuable because it provides the clinician with information about the degree of difficulty in learning new material.

The use of a minimal paired-associate task (Inglis, 1957) is proposed because of its lower correlation with IQ and because the clinician can control the speed of presentation and response. The elderly frequently report difficulty remembering the names of friends and acquaintances. A task that manipulates the concreteness and meaningfulness of the paired stimuli may prove to be sensitive to changes in this ability.

It may also be advantageous to evaluate the acquisition of nonverbal information (e.g., random shapes or familiar but hard-to-label people's faces) and motor skills (Corkin, 1968; Milner, 1970). An example of a motor skill learning task is Milner's (1970) mirror drawing task which is simple and convenient to administer. For this task, the patient is asked to draw a pencil line around the outline of a five-pointed star. The patient's hand and the star are not observed directly but are reflected in a mirror. Number of errors constitutes the measure of learning.

Stability Of Information In Long-Term Memory. Following acquisition, the ability to retrieve the information learned to criterion on one or more subsequent occasions provides an index of the stability of information in long term memory. Recognition as well as recall should be assessed to help the clinician differentiate between storage and retrieval problems (Schonfield & Robertson, 1966).

Integrity Of Dated Information Acquired In Vivo. It has been found that the healthy elderly perform as well as young adults on the recall of recent events. Furthermore, the ability of the healthy, educated elderly to recall familiar remote events has been shown to be fairly intact (Poon & Fozard, 1975).

One way to quantitatively assess recent and remote memory is via the personal history obtained from the patient. However, verification of some of the information may be difficult and time consuming.

Another way to quantitatively assess the ability of the elderly to recall familiar dated information is to employ a questionnaire that presents events from different decades (Albert, Butters, & Levin, 1979; Poon & Fozard, 1975; Squire, 1974; Squire, Chapter 24; Warrington & Sanders, 1971). However, this approach has several limitations that need to be recognized. First, by the time a test of remote and recent public events could be developed and disseminated for clinical use, current events would have become past events, thereby limiting the usability of the normative data. Second, poor performances may not only be due to faulty retrieval, but may also be due to unequal opportunities to be exposed to the events sampled or to lack of interest in the events, despite equivalent exposure opportunities. Last, performances on such instruments can also be affected by the educational level of the individual (Botwinick & Storandt, 1974).

Despite these limitations, we recommend this questionnaire format as one cost-effective way of obtaining verifiable data about recent and remote memory abilities.

CONCLUSION

We have argued for a tripartite approach to memory assessment that, in addition to evaluating pertinent memory functions, attempts to take into account the patient's perception of his or her memory problems and various concomitant factors that have been demonstrated to influence memory performance.

We have also argued that memory should not be regarded as a unidimensional entity, and that various tasks should not be combined in additive fashion to derive a "memory quotient." We have, instead, proposed a module structure to testing. Such a structure permits the selection of a subset of tasks for screening purposes or the selection of various tasks of interest when it is not feasible or desirable to administer an extensive battery.

Obviously, our proposal for a core inventory of memory behaviors constitutes only a modest starting point in what will prove to be a major undertaking. If it stimulates debate and suffers amendment, its purpose will have been served.

Memory is a multidimensional entity that we have just begun to explore and understand. Without the ability to recall information, life loses its meaning. For this reason, advances in memory assessment are imperative, and it is our hope that the ideas we have attempted to set forth will provide some directions for future development.

REFERENCES

Albert, M. S., Butters, N., & Levin, J. Temporal gradients in the retrograde amnesia of patients with alcoholic Korsakoff's syndrome. *Archives of Neurology,* 1979, *36,* 211-216.

Arenberg, D. Cognition and aging: Verbal learning, memory, and problem solving. In C. Eisdorfer & M. P. Lawton (Eds.), *Psychology of adult development & aging.* Washington, D.C.: American Psychological Association, 1973.

Arenberg, D., & Robertson-Tchabo, E. Learning and memory. In J. E. Birren & K. W. Schaie (Eds.), *Handbook of the psychology of aging.* New York: Van Nostrand Reinhold, 1977.

Arthur, G. A. *A point scale of performance tests.* Rev. Form II: Psychological Corporation, 1947.

Bachrach, H., & Mintz, J. The Wechsler Memory Scale as a tool for the detection of mild cerebral dysfunction. *Journal of Clinical Psychology,* 1974, *30,* 58-60.

Baddeley, A. D. *The psychology of memory.* New York: Basic Books, 1976.

Baddeley, A.D., & Warrington, E. K. Amnesia and the distinction between long- and short-term memory. *Journal of Verbal Learning and Behavior,* 1970, *9,* 176-189.

Baddeley, A. D., & Warrington, E. K. Memory coding and amnesia. *Neuropsychologica,* 1973, *11,* 159-165.

Barbizet, J. *Human memory and its pathology.* San Francisco: W. H. Freeman, 1970.

Barbizet, J., & Cany, E. Clinical and psychometrical study of a patient with memory disturbances. *International Journal of Neurology,* 1968, *7,* 44-54.

Bates, E., Masling, M., & Kintsch, W. Recognition memory for aspects of dialogue. *Journal of Experimental Psychology: Human Learning & Memory,* 1978, *4,* 187-197.

Birren, J. E. The psychology of aging in relation to development. In J. E. Birren (Ed.), *Relations of development and aging.* Springfield, Ill.: Charles C. Thomas, 1964.

Birren, J. E., Butler, R. N., Greenhouse, S. W., Sokoloff, L., & Yarrow, M. R. *Human aging: A biological and behavioral study.* U.S. Government Printing Office, 1963.

Birren, J. E., &Morrison, D. F. Analysis of the WAIS subtests in relation to age and education. *Journal of Gerontology,* 1961, *16,* 363-369.

Botwinick, J.*Aging and behavior.* New York: Springer Publishing, 1973.

Botwinick, J., & Storandt, M. *Memory, related functions and age.* Springfield, Ill.: Charles C. Thomas, 1974.

Brain, L. Disorders of memory. In L. Brain & M. Wilkinson (Eds.), *Recent advances in neurology and neuropsychiatry* (8th ed.). Boston: Little Brown, 1969.

Butters, N., & Cermak, L. S. Some analyses of amnesic syndromes in brain damaged patients. In R. L. Isaacson & K. H. Pribram (Eds.), *The hippocampus* (Vol. 2). New York: Plenum, 1975.

Butters, N., & Cermak, L. S. Neuropsychological studies of alcoholic Korsakoff patients. In G. Goldstein & C. Neuringer (Eds.), *Empirical studies of alcoholism.* Cambridge: Ballinger, 1976.

Cermak, L. S. The encoding capacity of a patient with amnesia due to encephalitis. *Neuropsychologia,* 1976, *14,* 311-326.

Cermak, L. S., & Butters, N. Information processing deficits of alcoholic Korsakoff patients. *Quarterly Journal of Studies on Alcohol,* 1973, *34,* 1110-1132.

Cermak, L. S., Butters, N., & Gerrain, J. The extent of verbal encoding ability of Korsakoff patients. *Neuropsychologia,* 1973, *11,* 85-94.

Cermak, L. S., & Moreines, J. Verbal retention deficits in aphasic and amnesic patients. *Brain and Language,* 1976, *3,* 16-27.

Cohen, J. Wechsler Memory Scale performance of psychoneurotic, organic, and schizophrenic groups. *Journal of Consulting Psychology,* 1950, *14,* 371-375.

Cole, K. D., & Guider, R. L. *The effects of specific and nonspecific training on memory and memory complaints in older adults.* Paper presented at the Western Psychological Association Meeting, San Francisco, 1978.

Corkin, S. Acquisition of motor skill after bilateral medial temporal lobe excision. *Neuropsychologia,* 1968, *6,* 255-265.

Craik, F. I. M. Age differences in human memory. In J. Birren & K. Schaie (Eds.), *Handbook of the psychology of aging.* New York: Van Nostrand Reinhold, 1977.

Craik, F. I. M., & Lockhart, R. S. Levels of processing: A framework for memory research. *Journal of Verbal Learning and Verbal Behavior,* 1972, *11,* 671-684.

Cronholm, B., & Ottosson, J. O. Reliability and validity of a memory test battery. *Acta Psychiatrica Scandinavica,* 1963, *39,* 218-234.

DeLeon, J. L.M. *Effects of training in repetition and mediation on paired-associate learning and practical memory in the aged.* Unpublished Ph.D. dissertation, University of Hawaii, 1974.

Eisdorfer, C. Arousal and performance: Experiments in verbal learning and a tentative theory. In G. Talland (Ed.), *Human behavior and aging: Recent advances in research and theory.* New York: Academic Press, 1968.

Eisdorfer, C., Nowlin, J., & Wilkie, F. Improvement in the aged by modification of autonomic nervous system activity. *Science,* 1970, *170,* 1327-1329.

Erickson, R. C. Problems in clinical assessment of memory. *Experimental Aging Research,* 1978, *4,* 255-272.

Erickson, R. C., & Scott, M. Clinical memory testing: A review. *Psychological Bulletin,* 1977, *84,* 1130-1149.

Fowler, R. S., & Fordyce, W. E. Adapting care for the brain-damaged patient. *American Journal of Nursing,* 1972, *72,* 1832-1835, 2056-2059.

Fozard, J. L., & Costa, P. T. Age differences in memory and decision-making in relation to personality, ability, and endocrine function: Implications for clinical practice and health planning policy. *Proceedings of Aging: A Challenge for Science and Social Policy,* Vichy, France. London: Pergammon Press, in press.

Fozard, J. L., & Thomas, J. C. Psychology of aging: Basic findings and some psychiatric implications. In J. G. Howells (Ed.), *Modern perspectives in the psychiatry of old age.* New York: Brunner/Mazel, 1975.

Froehling, S. *Effects of propranolol on behavioral and physiological measures of elderly males.* Unpublished Ph.D. dissertation, Duke University, 1974.

Gardner, H. *The shattered mind.* New York: Vintage Books, 1974.

Gilewski, M. J., Zelinski, E. M., & Thompson, L. W. *Remembering forgetting: Age differences in metamemorial processes.* Paper presented at the American Psychological Association Meeting, Toronto, Canada, 1978.

Granick, S., & Friedman, A. S. The effect of education on the decline of psychometric test performance with age. *Journal of Gerontology,* 1967, *22,* 191-195.

Hulicka, I. M. Short-term learning and memory efficiency as a function of age and health. *Journal of American Geriatric Society,* 1967, *15,* 285-294.

Hulicka, I. M., & Grossman, J. L. Age-group comparisons for the use of mediators in paired-associate learning. *Journal of Gerontology,* 1967, *22,* 46-51.

Inglis, J. An experimental study of learning and memory function in elderly psychiatric patients. *Journal of Mental Science,* 1957, *103,* 796-803.

Inglis, H. Learning, retention, and conceptual usage in elderly patients with memory disorder. *Journal of Abnormal and Social Psychology,* 1959, *59,* 210-215.

Jones, M. K. Imagery as a mnemonic aid after left temporal lobectomy: Contrast between material-specific and generalized memory disorders. *Neuropsychologia,* 1974, *12,* 21-30.

Kahn, R. L., & Miller, N. E. Adaptational factors in memory impairment in the aged. *Experimental Aging Research,* 1978, *4,* 273-290.

Kahn, R. L., Zarit, S. H., Hilbert, N. M., & Niederehe, M. A. Memory complaint and impairment in the aged: The effect of depression and altered brain function. *Archives of General Psychiatry,* 1975, *32,* 1569-1573.

Kasniak, A. W. *Effects of age and cerebral atrophy upon span of immediate recall and paired-associate learning in older adults.* Unpublished Ph.D. dissertation, University of Illinois, Chicago, 1976.

Kear-Colwell, J. J. The structure of the Wechsler Memory Scale and its relationship to "brain damage." *British Journal of Social and Clinical Psychology,* 1973, *12,* 384-392.

Kiev, A., Chapman, L. F., Guthrie, T. C., & Wolff, H. G. The highest integrative functions of diffuse cerebral atrophy. *Neurology,* 1962, *12,* 385-393.

Kljajic, I. Wechsler memory scale indices of brain pathology. *Journal of Clinical Psychology,* 1975, *31,* 698-701.

Leech, S., & Witte, K. L. Paired associate learning in elderly adults as related to pacing and incentive conditions. *Developmental Psychology,* 1971, *5,* 180.

Lezak, M. D. *Neuropsychological assessment.* New York: Oxford, 1976.

Lhermitte, F., & Signoret, J. L. Analyse neuropsychologique et differentiation des syndromes amnesiques. *Revue Neurologique,* 1972, *126,* 161-178.

Luria, A. R. *The working brain.* New York: Basic Books, 1973.

Martin, M. Memory span as a measure of individual differences in memory capacity. *Memory & Cognition,* 1978, *6,* 194-198.

Matthews, C. G., & Booker, H. E. Pneumoencephalographic measurements of test performance in human adults. *Cortex,* 1972, *8,* 69-92.

Meyer, V., & Falconer, M. A. Defects of learning ability with massive lesions of the temporal lobe. *Journal of Mental Science,* 1960, *106,* 472-477.

Milner, B. Memory and the medial temporal region of the brain. In K. Pribram & D. E. Broadbent (Eds.), *Biology of memory.* New York: Academic Press, 1970.

Monge, R. H., & Hultsch, D. F. Paired associate learning as a function of adult age and the length of the anticipation and inspection intervals. *Journal of Gerontology*, 1971, *26*, 157-162.

Murrell, F. H. The effect of extensive practice on age differences in reaction time. *Journal of Gerontology*, 1970, *25*, 268-274.

Patten, B. M. Modality specific memory disorders in man. *Acta Neurologica Scandinavica*, 1972, *48*, 69-86.

Pershad, D., & Wig, N. M. A battery of simple tests of memory for use in India. *Neurology India*, 1976, *24*, 86-93.

Poon, L. W. A systems approach for the assessment and treatment of memory problems. In J. Ferguson & C. B. Taylor (Eds.), *Comprehensive handbook of behavioral medicine (Vol. 1)*. New York: Spectrum Publications, 1980.

Poon, L. W., & Fozard, J. L. Age differences in remembering dated information. *Xth International Congress of Gerontology*, 1975, *2*, 161. (Abstract)

Poon, L. W., & Fozard, J. L. *Design conference on decision making and aging*. Veterans Administration Technical Report 76-01, 1976.

Poon, L. W., & Fozard, J. L. Speed of retrieval from long term memory in relation to age, familiarity and datedness of information. *Journal of Gerontology*, 1978, *33*, 711-717.

Poon, L. W., Fozard, J. L., & Vierck, B. Effects of extensive practice and information feedback on age-related differences in a two-choice decision task. *XIth International Congress of Gerontology*, 1978, 185. (Abstract)

Riegel, K. F., & Riegel, R. M. Development, drop, and death. *Developmental Psychology*, 1972, *6*, 306-319.

Russell, E. W. A multiple scoring method for the assessment of complex memory functions. *Journal of Consulting and Clinical Psychology*, 1975, *43*, 800-809.

Schaie, K. W., & Schaie, J. P. Clinical assessment and aging. In J. Birren & K. W. Schaie (Eds.), *Handbook of the psychology of aging*. New York: Van Nostrand Reinhold, 1977.

Schonfield, D., & Robertson, B. A. Memory storage and aging. *Canadian Journal of Psychology*, 1966, *20*, 228-236.

Squire, L. R. Remote memory as affected by aging. *Neuropsychologia*, 1974, *12*, 429-435.

Talland, G. A. *Deranged memory*. New York: Academic Press, 1965.

Treat, N. J., Poon, L. W., & Fozard, J. L. Age, practice, and imagery in paired associate learning. *The Gerontologist*, 1978, *18*, 134. (Abstract)

Walsh, D. A. Age differences in learning and memory. In D. S. Woodruff & J. E. Birren (Eds.), *Aging: Scientific perspectives and social issues*. New York: Van Nostrand Reinhold, 1975.

Warrington, E. K., & Sanders, H. I. The fate of old memories. *Quarterly Journal of Experimental Psychology*, 1971, *23*, 432-442.

Wechsler, D. A standardized memory scale for clinical use. *Journal of Psychology*, 1945, *19*, 87-95.

Welford, A. T. Age and skill: Motor, intellectual and social. In A. T. Welford & J. E. Birren (Eds.), *Decision making and age*. New York: Karger, 1969.

Willanger, R., Thygesen, P., Nielson, R., & Peterson, O. Intellectual impairment and cerebral atrophy: A psychological, neurological and radiological investigation. *Danish Medical Bulletin*, 1968, *15*, 65-93.

Williams, M. The measurement of memory in clinical practice. *British Journal of Social and Clinical Psychology*, 1968, *7*, 19-34.

Williams, M. *Brain damage and the mind*. Baltimore: Penguin, 1970.

Wolf, V. C. Some implications of short term, long term memory theory. *Nursing Forum*, 1971, *10*, 150-165.

Zarit, S. H., Gallagher, D., Kramer, N., & Walsh, D. *The effects of group training on memory & memory complaints*. Paper presented at the American Psychological Association Meeting, San Francisco, 1977.

23 Organic Implications of Neuropsychological Deficits in the Elderly

Marilyn S. Albert
Edith Kaplan
Boston Veterans Administration Medical Center and
Boston University School of Medicine

There is extensive evidence to indicate that as people age they demonstrate alterations in performance on a wide variety of behavioral and physiological measures. Investigations of learning and memory reflect the scope of this age-related change and, therefore, are briefly reviewed, along with several theoretical interpretations of age declines. The primary focus of this paper, however, is an examination of the neurophysiological correlates of these behavioral alterations. Particular emphasis will be placed upon areas of dysfunction in the elderly that may signal focal neuropathological change. In addition, an approach to neuropsychological testing of the elderly will be suggested that stresses the importance of evaluating the process underlying both adequate and inadequate final achievement.

INTELLECTUAL DEFICITS

It has long been apparent that on intelligence tests such as the WAIS (Wechsler Adult Intelligence Scale), the scores on the performance scale decline with age, whereas the verbal scores do not (Wechsler, 1958). Since this finding has been repeatedly replicated, the demonstration of higher verbal than performance scores is now referred to as the "classic aging pattern." The degree of decrement observed is determined by the method of population sampling. Both cross-sectional and longitudinal sampling show little or no decline in performance for subjects until the age of approximately 50 (Schaie, Labouvie, & Buech, 1973). The cross-sectional method shows a greater age decline for individuals aged 53 to 67 (Botwinick, 1977). However, among subjects aged 67 to 81, decrements in performance are shown by both sampling methods.

Several factors appear to account for these differences. The cross-sectional method seems to maximize age differences because of cohort, or generational, effects. Older persons tend to have either a poorer quality education or fewer years of formal schooling, in addition to poorer nutrition and health care. These limitations appear to exaggerate their deficits when they are compared with younger individuals. Longitudinal testing, on the other hand, probably minimizes age differences because a subset of the test population, people who perform poorly, tend to be less available for longitudinal retesting than those who perform well (Kleemier, 1962). Nevertheless—regardless of sampling method—after age 60, individuals perform better on the traditional tests of verbal ability than on the so-called performance items (Eisdorfer, Busse, & Cohen, 1959).

Several explanations for this verbal-performance discrepancy have implied that it is an artifactual result. One argument concerns the fact that most performance subtests are scored for speed of response in addition to accuracy. Recent experiments indicate that removing the criterion of speed may reduce, but does not eliminate, this aging pattern. Doppelt and Wallace (1955) and Klodin (1975) gave timed and untimed versions of WAIS subtests to both young and old subjects. Despite the fact that older subjects improved their performance on some tasks with additional time at their disposal, they never performed as well as the younger ones.

The verbal and performance items also differ from one another in the nature of the information that they test. The verbal items, as Birren, Botwinick, Weiss, and Morrison (1963) have pointed out, deal with stored, highly overlearned information. They seem to measure the manipulation of familiar materials in familiar ways. In addition, they appear unambiguous, in that the subject usually has a clear idea of what he does and doesn't know. The performance items, on the other hand, often employ novel material which must be manipulated in an unfamiliar manner (Schonfield & Robertson, 1966).

The verbal-performance differences may be further exaggerated by the fact that verbal items are rarely subjected to a qualitative analysis. Thus, familiarity of verbal materials may enable the individual to compensate for decreases in quality of response. Since performance tasks may be less familiar and not overlearned, deficits may be more easily detected, despite the absence of a qualitative analysis.

Botwinick and Storandt (1974) examined this possibility by scoring responses to the WAIS vocabulary subtest both qualitatively and quantitatively. Young and old adults were first matched on the basis of their regular "quantitative" scores. Then their responses were rescored on the basis of six qualitative criteria. An excellent synonym received the highest score, while an illustration (e.g., use of the word in a sentence) received the lowest score. The results showed that when these qualitative criteria were employed, a decline with age was apparent. This decline was not evident when the usual scoring system was used because the answers had been acceptable, though of a lesser quality. This suggests the possibility that qualitative analyses of verbal as well as visual tasks may reveal an underlying mechanism that is not test-specific, and that the verbal-performance discrepancies on the WAIS may be an artifact of the scoring system.

LEARNING DEFICITS

Learning tasks have also shown a decline in performance with age. Since several paradigms have been administered, with and without time constraints, to populations sampled cross-sectionally and longitudinally, it is instructive to compare these results to those just reported with regard to intelligence testing. Arenberg (1967) administered paired-associate and serial-performance tasks at two different anticipation intervals to groups of increasing age. He found that large age differences appeared on both tasks after age 60, particularly at the short anticipation interval. Later, Arenberg and Robertson-Tchabo (1977) reported some results from the Baltimore Longitudinal Study in which similar tasks were used. Although the magnitude of change was different as a function of the sampling technique, the oldest subjects in both studies (approximately 60 to 76 years old) showed significant mean declines. Even within-cohort comparisons showed that the younger members of the cohort performed better than older ones (Arenberg & Robertson-Tchabo, 1977).

Since paired-associate and serial-learning tasks are generally paced according to the experimenter's, rather than the subjects' convenience, the effect of pacing and response speed was carefully investigated, as it had been with regard to IQ testing. Older individuals are thought to be particularly disadvantaged by a paced task because of the motor element involved. It has been suggested that what appears to be a deficit in learning capacity (Canestrari, 1963; Eisdorfer, Axelrod & Wilkie, 1963) might only be an age-related performance deficit: that if time constraints are removed, older individuals would be capable of performing as well as younger ones. This possibility was examined by varying the length of the inspection and anticipation interval in a paired-associate task. In such a paradigm, each item in the list is presented in two parts: The stimulus is presented together with its response in the original presentation. (The amount of time the stimulus is exposed is the inspection interval.) Later, the stimulus is presented alone and the subject is asked to produce the response. (The amount of time that transpires before the subject responds is the anticipation interval.) The results of several studies indicate that increasing either the inspection interval (Kinsbourne & Berryhill, 1972; Monge & Hultsch, 1971) or the anticipation interval (Canestrari, 1963; Monge & Hultsch, 1971) improves the performance of both old and young subjects. However, neither this technique nor a self-paced condition (Arenberg, 1965) eliminates the difference between the old and the young. Thus, eliminating speed variables in these test situations reduces, but does not eliminate, the age decline. Age differences exist even under self-paced conditions.

Several other learning paradigms have consistently shown deficits with elderly subjects as well. The dichotic listening paradigm (Clark & Knowles, 1973; Craik, 1965; Inglis, 1964; Schonfield, Trueman & Kline, 1972), the supraspan technique (Craik, 1968; Drachman & Leavitt, 1972; Friedman, 1966), and single-trial free recall (Laurence, 1967; Raymond, 1971; Schonfield & Robertson, 1966) have repeatedly shown deficits with elderly subjects. As in all the instances previously described, pacing and speed variables do not account for the age-declines reported.

THEORETICAL ISSUES

Under the weight of this evidence, it is hard to avoid concluding that as men and women age, a wide variety of their abilities become compromised. Yet despite decades of research, the explanation for this decline has not yet been established.

For many years, the most frequent explanation for age-related declines in performance was that the elderly are particularly susceptible to the effects of interference (Arenberg, 1973; Botwinick, 1973; Jerome, 1959; Schonfield, 1969; Welford, 1958). It was proposed that proactive or retroactive interference (i.e., prior or subsequent learning) disrupted the processes of learning and memory more easily in the elderly than the young. However, a review of the literature provides little evidence for this explanation. As Craik's excellent review (1977) pointed out, a number of early studies of long-term memory failed to equate the initial learning of the old and young groups. When this was done, the performance of the elderly and the young did not differ (Hulicka, 1967; Kausler, 1970; Moenster, 1972; Wimer & Wigdor, 1958). Altering the required speed of response eliminated differences that had originally been attributed to interference effects (Arenberg, 1967; Arenberg & Robertson-Tchabo, 1977; Wimer & Wigdor, 1958).

Two other testing paradigms that are known to maximize interference in short-term memory have also produced strikingly negative support for the interference hypothesis. One of these is the recognition probe task. In this task, a list of numbers are presented orally, followed by a probe number. The subjects task is to decide whether the test number has occurred in the preceding series. Craik (1971), Binks and Sutcliffe (1972), and Wickelgren (1975) have all shown that older subjects perform as well as younger subjects on such high interference tasks. These findings were interpreted to indicate that older individuals are not more prone to the effects of interference.

In the Peterson paradigm (Peterson & Peterson, 1959), the subject is presented with a consonant trigram (e.g., X–R–C) and then asked to count backwards for varying lengths of time until recall of the letters is requested. Several studies have reported that performance is the same for all age groups (Keevil-Rogers & Schnore, 1969; Kriauciunas, 1968; Schonfield, 1969; Talland, 1967). Thus it would appear that interference does not differentially affect elderly subjects in tests of either long- or short-term memory. However, several points need to be made with regard to these findings. First, qualitative analyses (e.g., omission, perseverative and sequencing errors) were not carried out. Such an analysis has proven fruitful in differentiating the performance of amnesic and dementing patients on this task (Meudell & Butters, 1978), and may yet reveal differences between young and old individuals. Secondly, negative findings (i.e., finding no difference between the performance of the young and the old) cannot conclusively prove that interference is not a factor in age declines. A more definitive test of this issue would be to find a high-interference task on which elderly subjects are impaired and, by reducing interference directly, show that performance does not improve.

A second theory of age decline states that age differences in verbal learning are a function of the exaggerated cautiousness of the elderly. This has been based on the fact that tests of cautiousness correlate with age and that the elderly make more omission errors than the young. Performance in the elderly has been improved by encouraging people to be less cautious (i.e., by paying them for incorrect responses). Okun , Siegler, and George (1978) have recently reported results that support the finding that excessive cautiousness is causally related to number of omission errors. However, their results cast doubt on the assumption that the rate of omission errors is a factor in the performance declines observed in the elderly. They correlated performance on verbal learning tasks with two widely used measures of cautiousness. They report that measures of cautiousness correlate highly with age differences in omission errors but that age differences in omission errors do not account for the significant age differences in performance on the serial learning tasks. Thus, the cautiousness of the elderly does not appear to be the entire explanation for their impairment in performance.

Craik (1977) has contributed a third theoretical interpretation to the aging literature. He reevaluated earlier research in terms of a three-stage memory model and concluded that, though there are age decrements in secondary memory, primary memory functioning in the elderly is unimpaired when material does not require reorganization. These data are discussed at length elsewhere in these proceedings and therefore are not debated here.

Finally, it has been proposed that old people suffer particular disabilities with perceptual organization. One of the earliest examples of this was an experiment by Clay (1956) in which subjects had to fill cells in a 5 × 5 matrix with numbers that gave specified row and column totals. By manipulating the perceptual complexity of the task, she demonstrated that the perceptual organization of a display may affect speed and accuracy of problem solving. She concluded that old people find complex perceptual tasks more difficult than the young. Even in very simple visual perceptual tasks, older subjects are deficient. They do not show as many reversals of the classic ambiguous figures (Botwinick, Robbin & Brinley, 1959; Heath & Orbach, 1963), nor do they perform as well as young people on the children's embedded figures test (Axelrod & Cohen, 1961). Simple auditory tasks reveal an equivalent phenomenon. Welsh, Laterman, and Bell (1969) showed that old people recognize words less well than do the young when speech is presented through high or low band-pass filters. Obusek and Warren (1973) reported an unusual break-down in the perception of an undistorted message. When a single word on a tape-loop is continually repeated, young subjects report that the perceived word seems to change from one word into another. Old subjects not only experience fewer of these transformations but they report shifts of individual phonemes rather than shifts to entirely new words.

At this juncture, it seems important to ask whether these impairments in perceptual organization are related to the deficits seen on the performance items of the WAIS. Since the WAIS performance items appear to be more dependent on perceptual integration, this explanation seems reasonable. It is possible that fundamental neurological changes may produce perceptual changes, that then result in the deficits in perceptual organization just described. It is important to know what brain structures underly these processes and whether age deficits are the result of diffuse or focal damage to structures in the central nervous system. Are changes widespread or are there a small number of neural circuits that can explain most of the performance decrements? In order to examine this possibility more closely, some of the physiological correlates of aging are now described.

BRAIN-BEHAVIOR RELATIONSHIPS

It is known that, as people age, changes occur in the central nervous system. Senile plaques and neurofibrillary tangles are found in greater concentrations in the elderly than the young (Brody, Harman, & Ordy, 1978). Alterations in neuronal metabolism, such as changes in the concentration of transmitter substances, occur as well (Bondareff, 1977). In terms of behavior, the important question seems to be whether these changes are diffuse or localized.

The first matter that should be considered with regard to this issue is whether physiological changes in the cortex occur unilaterally or bilaterally. Since functional hemisphere asymmetry is a fundamental aspect of normal brain function, it must be understood before this question can be answered. Fortunately, it has been extensively studied in the last quarter century. Studies of normal and brain-damaged subjects have indicated that the left hemisphere and right hemisphere predominate according to the activity that is being carried out. In general, researchers agree that the left hemisphere is clearly dominant in the processing of verbal material. It deals with language and with stimuli that can be verbally labeled without difficulty. The right hemisphere, by contrast, is predominant in tasks requiring spatial orientation (e.g., drawings, constructions, spatial memory, etc.) and the perception or recall of nonverbal material, particularly material that cannot be verbally labeled with ease. Several investigators (Bogen, 1969; Levy-Agresti & Sperry, 1968; Nebes, 1974) have proposed models of hemispheric function that elaborate on these differences. The right, or minor hemisphere, is said to act as a synthesizer, organizing data in terms of complex wholes. It is predominant when fragmentary perceptual information must be used to generate an idea of the whole. Nebes (1974), in particular, emphasizes that the type of information processing required determines which hemisphere is dominant. If identification of the external appearance of something is called for (as in visual recognition), the right hemisphere is dominant, even if the material is verbal. On the other hand, if abstracting or analyzing the parts that make up a whole is required, the left hemisphere is predominant. The left hemisphere uses verbal symbols in order to label and manipulate information. Of course it is dominant in any task requiring a verbal transformation of material. Because most of the performance items of the WAIS relate to the visuospatial functions for which the right hemisphere is dominant, it has been hypothesized that aging affects the right hemisphere more than the left.

A few neuropsychologists have attempted to address this issue by statistically analyzing performance scores on two test batteries. Overall and Gorham (1972) administered the WAIS to men between 45 and 84. They compared the performance of men with a diagnosis of chronic brain disease to normal controls. A multiple discriminant analysis on the subtest scores indicated that the performance of the older controls did not resemble that of the brain-damaged subjects. Goldstein and Shelly (1975), using the Halstead–Reitan Neuropsychological Test Battery, compared elderly normal controls to subjects with a diagnosis of diffuse brain damage. They also found that the performance of normal older people did not resemble that of diffusely brain-damaged individuals. A more selective analysis by Schaie and Schaie (1977), on the other hand, demonstrated the similarity between the performance pattern of older people on the WAIS and that found in patients with acute or chronic right-hemisphere damage. Klisz (1978) has recently reported similar evidence. She reanalyzed early data of Reed and Reitan (1963) and found that subtests of the Halstead–Reitan Battery that are indicators of right-hemisphere damage discriminate middle-aged controls from older controls better than subtests that are indicators of either left-hemisphere or diffuse brain damage.

Other researchers have attempted to localize brain changes by giving elderly people tests that correlate with more circumscribed cortical lesions. Some researchers have speculated that the right or left parietal lobes are particularly affected in the process of aging. Deficits on the Bender–Gestalt Visual Motor Test and the Archimedes Spiral Test (Gilbert & Levee, 1965), the Embedded Figures Test with vision or touch (Axelrod & Cohen, 1961), and figure drawings (Plutchik, Conte, Weiner, & Teresi, 1978) have all been reported. Recently, Farver (1975) conducted a study in which healthy, nonhospitalized elderly subjects were given tasks that are associated with right and left parietal-lobe function. She found no impairments on tasks of map location, arithmetic, or right-left orientation: functions that have been shown to depend on an intact left parietal lobe (Critchley, 1953/1966; Gerstmann, 1930/1971; Strub & Geschwind, 1974). On the other hand, Farver (1975) found age-related changes on recall of stick constructions, block constructions, clock setting, and the Hooper Visual Organization Test. These are tasks with a strong visuospatial component, and most of them are usually associated with right parietal lobe functions. Therefore, Farver concluded that right parietal lobe functions decline with age but left parietal lobe functions do not. Her conclusions reemphasize Klisz' (1978) findings that Halstead–Reitan indicators of right-hemisphere damage discriminate the elderly better than indicators of either left-hemisphere or diffuse brain damage. They also are reminiscent of the verbal-performance discrepancy on the WAIS. Many of the performance items consist of visuospatial tasks that are thought to rely heavily on an intact right hemisphere (Levy-Agresti & Sperry, 1968), while the verbal items are thought to rely on left hemisphere function.

Nevertheless, a recent reanalysis of Farver's data (Kaplan, in preparation) has suggested that right frontal, rather than right parietal, pathology may explain the deficits observed in Farver's elderly subjects. Patients with lesions circumscribed to the right parietal area usually show evidence of neglect for the left side of space (e.g., they may not attend to the left side of a drawing), closing in (e.g., drawing on top of the lines of the figure to be copied), and conglomeration (e.g., taking the blocks from the experimenter's model to make the copy). These symptoms were conspicuously absent in Farver's population. The segmentation and right-left reversals she reports in her elderly subjects are often seen in patients with frontal-system pathology

(Kaplan, in preparation). The aforementioned symptoms that are pathognomonic of right parietal damage are absent in patients with focal frontal lesions.

In addition to differences in laterality, there are also anterior–posterior differences within the brain that are of importance. Although these are less clearly understood, many aspects of frontal function have become delineated in recent years. The most important neuroanatomical information has come from Nauta (1971, 1972), who demonstrated that there are complex interconnections between the frontal lobes and many other areas of the brain. This "frontal system" extends from the reticular formation to the frontal cortex via limbic structures and the thalamus. There are also reciprocal connections between the frontal cortex and the inferior parietal and rostral temporal areas. This input makes the frontal association areas unique, in that they receive an input that has been modified by processing in many important cortical and sub-cortical structures along the way. As a result of this evidence, and neuropsychological data as well, Nauta (1971) has proposed that the frontal system is centrally involved in anticipatory processes. Building on Teuber's (1964) concept of "corollary discharge," he suggests that since the frontal lobes receive input from so many other structures, they are ideally suited to anticipate sensory input and cognitive activity. By presetting either sensory systems, association areas, or limbic structures for events that are about to occur, the frontal system allows them to compare the actual result of an action with the result intended. This helps establish a temporal sequence of reference points that have subjective significance for the individual, and therefore can help guide complex goal-directed activity. Such a model would predict that subjects with frontal-lobe damage experience disorders in the regulation of their activity and the correction of errors. This, in fact, is what has been found by Milner (1971). In many of her cases with frontal-lobe lesions, the patients demonstrate difficulty in the temporal ordering of events. They cannot distinguish the degree of recency of one item among a series of many, whether the task requires a verbal or nonverbal recency judgment. They are impaired on the Wisconsin Card Sorting Test (Milner, 1963), which requires the individual to repeatedly change his hypothesis according to the experimenter's response to his action.

There is evidence of disturbances in sensory–motor integration and sensory processing in subjects with frontal lesions. Visual search is impaired, and visuospatial tasks, such as the perception of reversible figures, are not performed well (Teuber, Battersby, & Bender, 1960). Heilman and Valenstein (1972) have described a number of cases of unilateral neglect in frontal patients which they ascribe to an attentional defect. Changes in arousal are also frequently associated with frontal damage (Nauta, 1972), and one of the most characteristic clinical features of frontal patients is their lack of initiative or spontaneity. It thus appears that a disruption in the frontolimbic–reticular activating systems does not produce deficits in primary motor, sensory, or language activity. Instead, there appears to be a disturbance in the appropriate regulation of these functions (Luria, 1966).

"FRONTAL SYSTEM" EFFECTS: AROUSAL AND ATTENTION

Since Nauta (1971) has demonstrated that the reticular activating system provides one of the primary inputs to the frontal system, changes in arousal may be considered to reflect an impairment in frontal function. Only a few studies have specifically examined the correspondence between the deficits of normal aging and frontal lobe lesions. Nevertheless, in examining the aging literature, a surprisingly large number of studies report deficits that indicate a degradation in frontal system function.

A number of studies have reported changes in arousal in the elderly, although there have been large differences of opinion regarding the mechanisms involved. Bioelectric measures of autonomic nervous system (ANS) function have tended to support the hypothesis that the elderly are underaroused, while the biochemical measures of ANS function have tended to support the notion of overarousal. Botwinick and Kornetsky (1960) measured the galvanic skin response (GSR), as a reflection of ANS activation in a classical conditioning situation, and found reduced GSR in the elderly. Reduced GSR responsivity has also been reported during vigilance tasks (Surwillo, 1966). Skin conductance responses (SCR) have been correlated with depth of processing on a recall task (Zelinski, Walsh & Thompson, 1978). Though the elderly were impaired on both measures, depth of processing and level of responsivity were not correlated with one another. On the other hand, telemetric recordings of EEG, EKG, EMG, and EOG over an 8-hr period of normal daily activity have been correlated with scores on the Stockton Geriatric Rating Scale, the Benton Visual Retention Test, and the Trail Making Test, Part A, from the Halstead–Reitan battery (Poitrenaud, Hazemann & Lille, 1978). The authors report that the correlations between telemetric and behavioral data support the hypothesis that a disturbance in mental abilities may be due to variations in level of arousal.

The average evoked potential (AEP) has been useful as a measure of central nervous system activity (CNS) and is known to be sensitive to attention and/or activation (Karlin, 1970). The late components (P_3 or P_{300}) of the AEP have consistently been shown to decrease with age (Dustman & Beck, 1969; Lüders, 1970; Schenkenberg, 1970), and Schenkenberg (1970) has suggested that the decrease in the amplitude of the late components is due to a diminished effectiveness of the reticular activating system.

Another bioelectric index of attention or arousal that has been shown to decrease in the elderly is the CNV (contingent negative variation). The CNV is recorded in the interval between two stimuli that have been previously repeated, and is thought of as a bioelectric correlate of preparatory set. Loveless and Sanford (1974) argue that the reduction of the CNV in the elderly, particularly in long preparatory intervals, is a reflection of a difficulty in initiating a preparatory set at an appropriate time.

Biochemical studies that have evaluated ANS arousal have used free fatty acid (FFA) mobilization as their primary measure. Studies with this technique have shown that the elderly have higher FFA levels than the young during serial learning and monitoring tasks (Powell, Eisdorfer, & Bogdonoff, 1964; Troyer, Eisdorfer, Wilkie, & Bogdonoff, 1966). Eisdorfer (1967) has therefore argued that the performance decrement seen in learning studies with the elderly may be attributed to autonomic overarousal.

There are several possibilities for these conflicting results. One is that the measures of arousal used (FFA mobilization, GSR, etc.) may no longer be adequate reflections of arousal because end organs change with age. The second alternative is that measures indicative of underarousal are generally taken when the subject is not actively engaged in performing a task, but is merely a passive participant in a controlled situation—whereas overarousal has been found in tasks which provide a high level of cognitive stress. The third possibility is one first proposed by Thompson and Marsh (1973). They suggest that the critical issue may not be the absolute level of arousal but the congruence between the degree of arousal in the CNS and the ANS. In support of this, Thompson and Nowlin (1973) found that elderly subjects did not show a significant relationship between an ANS measure (heart rate change) and a CNS measure (CNV amplitude), whereas young people did. However these issues are resolved, it is clear that elderly people have changes in their arousal mechanisms which may be reflected in behavior. The recent study by Poitrenaud et al. (1978) is helpful in that its authors monitored bioelectric measures of arousal in a task with neuropsychological relevance. It would be nice to see such a paradigm accompanied by simultaneous biochemical measures. Because changes in arousal have been associated with frontal-system involvement (due to its interconnections with the reticular activating system), it would be particularly interesting if these measures of arousal could be correlated with performance on a task that has been shown to tap frontal functions. In any case, these reports are clearly supportive of a frontal-system disturbance in the elderly.

Behavioral studies have also reflected a disturbance of attentional mechanisms in aging populations. As pointed out by Craik (1977), "One of the clearest results in the experimental psychology of aging is the finding that older subjects are more penalized when they must divide their attention, either between two input sources, input and holding or holding and responding." Studies by Kirchner (1958), Brinley and Fichter (1970) and Craik (1973) used paradigms that required the subject to divide their attention between a detection task and a memory task, while Broadbent and Gregory (1965) and McGhie, Chapman and Lawson (1965) used a bisensory paradigm that required the subject to simultaneously attend to an auditory and visual input. In all instances the elderly subjects were impaired with respect to the younger ones, though when the memory task was presented auditorily the deficits were less marked. In this regard, it is of interest that elderly subjects are also impaired in dichotic listening tasks (Clark & Knowles, 1973; Craik, 1965; Inglis, 1964; Schonfield, Trueman, & Kline, 1972).

Attentional mechanisms have also been implicated by studies in which accurate performance by the subjects depends on their ability to ignore irrelevant cues. Simple perceptual tasks, such as the detection of a target stimulus in a large array, have shown that elderly people are more distracted by irrelevant stimuli (Layton, 1975). More complex perceptual tasks, such as multiple-recognition learning (Kausler & Kleim, 1978) and hidden-word identification (Schneider, Gritz & Jarvik, 1977), reveal similar impairments. In the former task, subjects are shown a series of lists, each containing a right word and one or more wrong words. They are later asked to pick out the correct word from the original array. In the latter task, the subject must detect four-letter words on a sheet that contains lines of letters. These tests require the scanning and subsequent screening out of irrelevant material. Both studies report that tests with fewer attentional and perceptual demands are performed well by the elderly. This should be kept in mind with regard to remedial training techniques.

A recent study of evoked potentials provides evidence that these sorts of attentional tasks are related to frontal function. Tecce (1978) first administered a reaction-time task (flash–tone–key-press) to elderly subjects for 30 "control" trials. It has been shown that when two stimuli are presented as a pair and the subject must perform some action to the second stimulus (as in the above task), a sustained negative shift (i.e., CNV) occurs in the recorded evoked potential. Tecce (1978) reported that all subjects, young and old, displayed similar CNV patterns in this control situation. He then introduced a distracting memory task into the reaction time experiment. Consonant trigrams (e.g., L–P–M) were flashed on a screen prior to the sound of the tone in half of the subsequent trials. The CNV was reduced for all subjects when these letters appeared; this reduction was interpreted as a distraction effect. However, during the trials in which no letters were presented, the young subjects responded differently from the older ones. The young individuals showed a dramatic increase in the CNV (a CNV rebound). However, the rebound effect of the elderly subjects was significantly smaller than that of the younger controls. This appeared frontocentrally but not parietally. Tecce concluded that a CNV rebound reflects a response to change and that the reduced rebound seen frontally in the elderly subjects signals an inability to change set or attention on the part of these individuals.

Learning to attend to relevant cues is critical to the mastery of a wide variety of tasks. Information-processing theorists have demonstrated (Craik & Lockhart, 1972; Tulving & Thompson, 1973) that the organization imposed by an individual on a set of items depends on his perception of the structure of the material. The ability to impose structure on incoming information (whether it be a visual pattern, a list of words or a prose passage), in turn, enables the individual to attend to the most relevant aspects of a task. Thus, the development of relevant categories (be they perceptual, semantic, or conceptual) has an impact on what information is stored. This, in turn, influences the cues that might be effective in retrieval of that information. It may be that aging decrements develop because elderly subjects are less able to perceptually organize and encode information, which then makes storage, and therefore retrieval of the data, unreliable. If attentional mechanisms, in particular, are impaired in the elderly, one might expect that requiring subjects to verbalize the relevant dimensions of a task would enable them to focus their attention and thereby process information more effectively.

There are numerous examples of testing situations in which the elderly have improved their performance by verbalizing the critical dimensions of the stimuli to be discriminated. Crovitz (1966) found that on the Wisconsin Card Sorting Test (which, as was pointed out earlier, is thought to reflect adequacy of frontal system function), age differences are sharply reduced by training older subjects to verbalize the sequence and nature of their decisions. Hultsch (1971) had half of his subjects sort 52 words into categories while the other half merely inspected the word list for the same length of time. An age decrement was evident on the retention test and was most marked for subjects who were not told to sort the words into categories. A similar finding was reported by Baddeley (1966). He presented subjects with groups of random letters one card at a time. Age deficits in immediate recall were found. However, Rabbitt, Clancy, and Vyas (1969) presented the random letters simultaneously on cards and did not find age differences. They hypothesized that the young subjects had spontaneously treated the string of letters as pronounceable nonsense words, whereas older subjects did not do this unless all the letters were displayed simultaneously. In other words, conditions that encourage subjects to verbalize the meaningful dimensions of a stimulus situation, so that it can be attended to and organized, improve the performance of elderly people.

There are a number of studies on the use of mnemonics (i.e., verbal or imaginal mediators) that parallel this finding. The evidence indicates that older subjects tend not to use mnemonics spontaneously (Hulicka & Grossman, 1967; Rowe & Schnore, 1971) but that if instructed to use mediators, the old improve more than the young (Hulicka, Sterns, & Grossman, 1967; Knill, 1966). This differential age benefit remains controversial (see Winograd & Simon, Chapter 27, and Poon, Walsh-Sweeney, & Fozard, Chapter 26, for a more detailed analysis of this issue); nevertheless, it is similar to the improvement in performance that occurs when subjects are asked to verbalize the relevant dimensions of a task. Older subjects are able to perform the mental operation required, but do not carry it out spontaneously.

Taken as a whole, these data suggest that elderly people do not develop adequate techniques for selectively attending to material unless a task is constructed in such a way that this necessity is minimized. Since adequate selective attention and set are usually thought to require an intact frontal system, it is not surprising that some theories of frontal function resemble some theories of aging. In discussing their theory that aging produces a misalignment of CNS and ANS function, Marsh and Thompson (1977) state that a sensitive alignment of such activity may be crucial in developing "preparatory set." Nauta (1971) describes the frontal system as preeminently important in matters relating to "presetting activity".

"FRONTAL SYSTEM" EFFECTS: VISUOSPATIAL PERFORMANCE

Preliminary results of a large normative aging study[1] demonstrate another means of identifying areas of dysfunction in the elderly that may signal focal neuropathological change. A unique aspect of the study was its quantification of naturalistic observations of test behavior. Though both language and visuospatial behavior were examined in this manner, only visuospatial performance is reported here.

The analysis that is described here utilized a set of controlled tasks that were administered to large numbers of elderly subjects. Individuals were asked to copy and recall simple figures, assemble blocks and sticks in predetermined patterns, and rearrange parts of objects to form wholes. Trained observers recorded the order or sequence in which each task was performed in order to plot the way in which each individual proceeded and to permit an examination of the processs underlying both adequate and inadequate final achievement.

---

[1]Individuals participating in this normative aging study are also subjects in the Framingham Heart Study. In this latter capacity, they have received biannual medical examinations for the past 28 years for the purpose of examining risk factors in the development of heart disease and stroke. All 2,242 individuals in the project were administered a brief neuropsychological screening battery on the basis of which they were divided, for the purpose of future testing, into high, medium, and low scorers. The evaluation of normative aging is being directed by Drs. Martin Albert and Edith Kaplan in association with P. Wolf, A. E. Veroff, W. Rosen, T. Dawber, W. Kannel, and P. Macnamara. We particularly acknowledge Amy Veroff for her sequential analyses of the Wechsler Memory Scale Visual Reproductions.

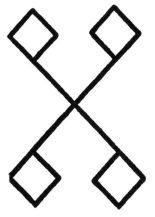

FIG. 23.1. The first stimulus figure on the visual reproduction subtest of the Wechsler Memory Scale.

This approach derives directly from the work of Werner. In his early paper on process and achievement (Werner, 1937) he demonstrated that individuals may succeed or fail on a task for a variety of reasons. An identical outcome may be achieved in multiple ways. Impairment in function may be evident in the strategy that a given individual employs even though the final product

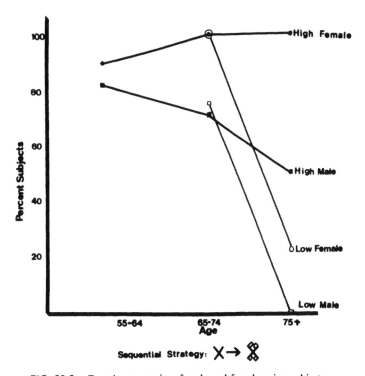

FIG. 23.2. Drawing strategies of male and female aging subjects.

may be correct. An incorrect final solution may reflect either varying degrees of dysfunction or, more importantly, differential focal pathology.

An analysis of the immediate recall of the first stimulus figure in the visual reproduction subtest of the Wechsler Memory Scale (WMS), Form I, serves to illustrate this mode of approach (Fig. 23.1). Preliminary results of the normative aging study indicate that the strategy employed in the reproduction of Fig. 23.1 changes with age (Fig. 23.2). Young, healthy adults typically reproduce this figure by drawing the crossed lines first and then adding the "flags" or squares, while elderly adults who scored highly on a neuropsychological screening battery utilized this strategy with less frequency. By and large, the men continued to produce the figure accurately, but it was drawn in many segments and with a variety of sequences.

The high-scoring women, on the other hand, did not show the same pattern of change in approach. This poses interesting questions with regard to brain lateralization and sex differences which will not be pursued here. However, it should be noted that the performance of both men and women would have appeared identical had only the final scores been examined. By analyzing the sequence of the production of the drawn features, significant differences were revealed.

There were, in fact, few overt errors made by the high-scoring subjects on this task. As Fig. 23.3 shows, the errors were primarily ones in which the

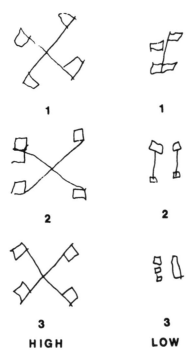

1   **1**

2   **2**

3   **3**

HIGH   **LOW**

FIG. 23.3. Sample errors of aging individuals on the visual reproduction subtest of the Wechsler Memory Scale.

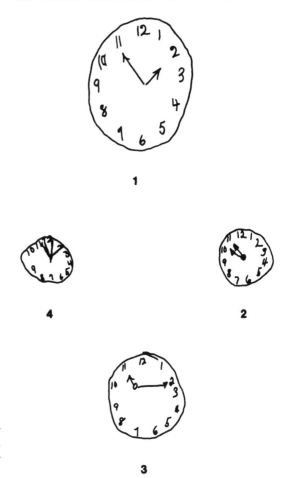

FIG. 23.4. Clock drawings by elderly subjects with high scores on a neuropsychological screening battery.

"flags" or squares were oriented incorrectly. This may be a function of the temporal order in which the flags were drawn. Drawings 1 and 2 for the high-scoring subjects are examples of figures in which the subject started in the right visual field and proceeded in a counter clockwise direction, orienting the flags in a similar manner at each point. It is interesting to note that patients with cortical damage lateralized to the left hemisphere tend to proceed in the opposite manner (Kaplan, in preparation). That is, they begin in the left visual field and move counter clockwise. In general, patients with focal damage typically begin in the visual field contralateral to the one that receives projections from the non-lesioned hemisphere (e.g., the left hemisphere projects to the right visual field, therefore a patient with left-hemisphere damage would begin in the left half of space.)

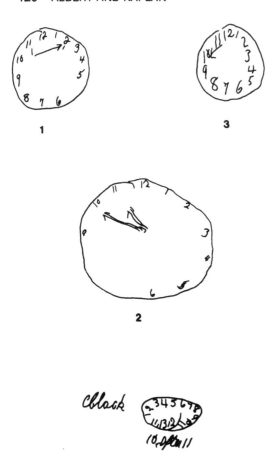

FIG. 23.5. Clock drawings by elderly subjects with low scores on a neuropsychological screening battery.

The low scorers on the neuropsychological screening battery show a much more dramatic breakdown in performance (Fig. 23.3). They retain the knowledge that the original figure consisted of lines and squares, but the juxtaposition and orientation of these subunits is lost, and the drawings reveal massive segmentation. It should be noted that if the overall configuration of the figure, rather than just its subwholes, is appreciated, the task becomes much easier. If the individual encodes the original drawing as two crossed lines with squares on the insides, the task can be correctly remembered with essentially two bits of information. If, on the other hand, the individual does not organize the subunits into a whole in this manner, six or more bits of information may be needed to complete the task accurately. This tendency to perceive the units of a drawing accurately but reproduce them in a segmented way is most typical of patients with frontal system damage (Kaplan, in preparation).

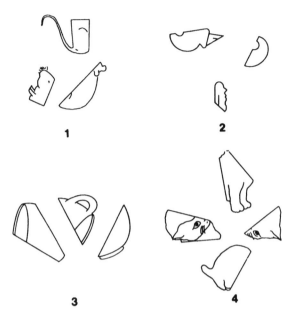

FIG. 23.6.   Selected items from the Hooper Visual Organization Test.

The clock drawings of elderly individuals demonstrate a pull to salient segments of the configuration. Fig. 23.4 shows the errors made by the high scorers in the Framingham Normative Aging Study when they were told: "Draw a clock. Set the hands at 10 after 11." The length of the hands are inappropriately drawn (Fig. 23.4, numbers 1 and 4), the center of the clock is pulled over toward the 11 (Fig. 23.4, number 3), and the subject sets one hand on the 10 and one on the 11 (Fig. 23.4, number 2).

The low scorers are more severely impaired, but the errors are surprisingly similar (Fig. 23.5). In both populations, there are productions where the point at which the hands meet is pulled to the 11 (Fig. 23.5, number 1) and the hands are pointed to the 10 and 11 (Fig. 23.5, number 2). This tendency to be pulled to the two most salient bits of information is most evident in clock number 3, where the subject merely drew a line from the 11 to the 10. Clock 4 demonstrates that these errors are not based on a failure to comprehend the command; the writing of "cllock" and "10 after 11" reveal a reception of the information.

These errors in clock setting are similar to the errors made by elderly individuals on the Wechsler figure. The subjects thus appear to segment the stimulus information, whether it is verbal or visual. Their errors often seem to be the result of a pull to the most prominent bits of information and a failure to appreciate the relationships between the parts and of the parts to the whole.

These characteristics are again evident in the performance of the elderly on the Hooper Visual Organization Test. This task consists of showing the subject a line drawing of an object that has been cut up and rearranged. The individual is asked to mentally rearrange the pieces so the object can be identified (a mental object-assembly test).

Elderly subjects typically focus on a single piece of the puzzle, especially if it appears as if it may itself be a complete whole. Fig. 23.6 shows selected stimulus items from the Hooper Visual Organization Test. Elderly individuals often give "isolate" responses: For example, they report that item number 1 is a pipe, number 2 is a knife, number 3 is a suitcase. A focus on a segment, internal detail, or feature may produce a correct answer if the prominent segment or feature contains salient information such that the whole can be inferred from the part (e.g., the eye and whiskers in Fig. 23.6, number 4).

A final example of segmentation in the visuospatial performance of the elderly is found on a task designed by Bowman and Grünbaum (1930) to test motor agraphia. This task has been found to be sensitive to frontal pathology (Luria, 1966). The subject is merely asked to copy a three-looped figure for 90 sec: first with the right hand and then with the left. A pull to the stimulus is evident in production number 1 (Fig. 23.7), where the loops are correctly drawn but divided into groups of threes. Segmentation is found in number 2 (Fig. 23.7). A number of loops are disconnected from one another and four,

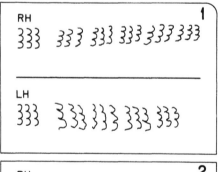

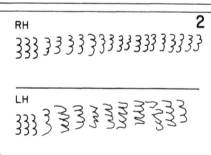

FIG. 23.7. Multiple loops by elderly subjects with high scores on a neuropsychological screening battery.

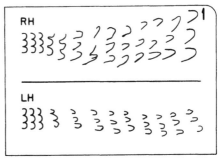

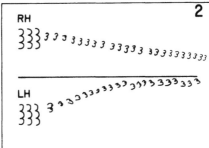

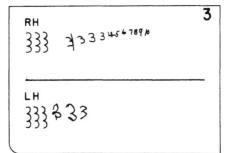

FIG. 23.8. Multiple loops by elderly subjects with low scores on a neuropsychological screening battery.

rather than three, loops are consistently produced by the left hand (two three-loop productions may be a consequence of a verbal encoding strategy).

The errors of the low scorers are shown in Fig. 23.8. Segmentation is profound in number 1, while slope changes are evident in number 2. The subject seems pulled to the line, which is then used as a guide. The verbal encoding strategy of the subject appears to be reflected in the fact that a "3" rather than a three-looped figure has been drawn. It should be noted that the inability to produce writing on a straight line and the use of verbal encoding strategies on this task are frequently noted in patients with right-hemisphere lesions (Kaplan, in preparation). These errors, in their extreme, appear in Fig. 23.8, number 3. After writing a series of threes, the subject loses track of the task entirely and slips into a highly practiced, automatized series.

In sum, the quality of the degraded drawings of these elderly subjects is consonant with the productions of brain damaged patients with lesions lateralized to the right hemisphere and focalized to the frontal system.

SUGGESTED NEUROPSYCHOLOGICAL BATTERY

Before one can convincingly argue that aging implicates the brain selectively and focally, as opposed to all areas of the brain equally, it is necessary to administer a comprehensive battery of tests sensitive to the measurement of brain–behavior relationships. This would then enable the investigator to develop a profile of spared and impaired functions which could be contrasted with the profiles obtained from younger controls, on the one hand, and a population of brain damaged patients (below the age of 60) with verified focal lesions.

To this end, tests should be included that best tap functions of the frontal, temporal, and parietal lobes and subcortical structures. These tests should be appropriate for the assessment of attention, memory, language, and visuospatial ability. Such a battery should also examine the qualitative as well as quantitative changes that occur during aging, so that the strategies and structure an individual imposes on a task himself (not just those created by the experimenter) can be evaluated. Few existing tests fully satisfy these criteria. However, with emendations and careful observation of the process by which tasks are solved, some standardized and experimental tests should shed light on brain–behavior changes in the elderly.

Outlined next are a number of tests that meet these criteria. This suggested battery does not presume to be exhaustive. Rather, it is intended to reflect an approach that it is felt may be productive. The aim is to describe tests which may prove useful in the neuropsychological assessment of the elderly. The purpose of the evaluation, the needs of the subject, and the constraints of time will all be factors in determining the ultimate selection of the tests to be used.

Wechsler Adult Intelligence Scale. This widely used test of intelligence (Wechsler, 1955) provides an estimate of the general level of present intellectual functioning. Selected subtests, with additions, lend themselves to a finer analysis of strategies and elucidate impairments that reflect brain-behavior relationships while still permitting standard scoring. For example, on the arithmetic subtest, failure may result from impaired computational ability (acalculia), difficulty in organization of the elements of the orally presented problem for the application of the appropriate computations, or from an inability to retain all of the critical information. To identify the source of error, two changes have been made: (1) to remove the memory component, problems failed on oral presentation are readministered in written form; and (2) to remove the organizational component, basic arithmetic problems (addition, subtraction, etc.) from the parietal lobe battery of the Boston Diagnostic Examination for Aphasia are presented for written calculation. Analysis of errors adds another dimension to the understanding of the nature of the disorder. Similarly, on the digit–symbol subtest, reduction in the number of correct digit–symbol pairs produced within the 90-

sec time limit may be due to a number of problems, most notable of which are psychomotor retardation and an inability to incidentally learn the digit–symbol pairs. Allowing the completion of three rows of digit–symbol pairs, with the reference key available, while the fourth row is completed from memory, permits the determination of the source of the problem underlying poor digit–symbol performance (within the 90-sec period of the standard administration time). Finer analyses of graphomotor features further aid in focalization of impairment.

Performance on the block design subtest of the WAIS provides additional information for localization of cerebral dysfunction. Here, plotting the sequence of block placement en route to the solution may reveal errors pathognomonic of given focal pathology, even though the errors may be self-corrected within the time limit. The direction in which the subject works (right to left, instead of left to right; bottom to top, instead of top to bottom), the inability to retain the square matrix (2 × 2 or 3 × 3 configuration), working on discrete subwholes in a segmented manner, and preponderance of block errors on the left side of the design are all characteristic of patients with pathology focalized to the right frontal lobe (Fig. 23.9). Similar errors are seen in the performance of the elderly. Patients with left-frontal or right-parietal pathology produce error patterns that are distinctly different (Fig. 23.9).

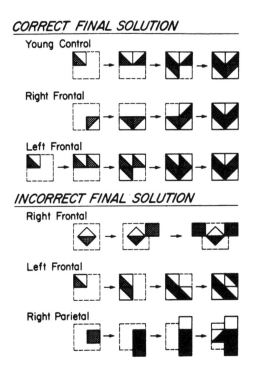

FIG. 23.9.   Sample flow charts of the performance of control and brain-damaged subjects on the block design subtest of the Wechsler Adult Intelligence Test.

Boston Neuropsychological Adaptation Of The Wechsler Memory Scale. The original Wechsler Memory Scale (Wechsler, 1945) combines a brief survey of public information, orientation in place and time, and sustained attention (mental control) with new learning of factual material, verbal paired-associates, and memory for designs. The Boston Neuropsychological Adaptation of the original Wechsler Memory Scale corrects for the underrepresentation of items of information from the recent past, questions that tap orientation in place and time, and mental control. The revised test also corrects for the absence of remote memory items and the ability to retain newly acquired verbal and nonverbal information over time (delayed recall). The addition of design recognition and copy and matching tasks permits a finer analysis of the contribution of such underlying components as perception, motor execution, memory and attention. Reverse-recall and free-recall tasks are also included to test the associative strength of newly learned paired associates under varying cue conditions.

Short-Term Memory Tasks.   Verbal, visual, and auditory tests of short-term memory can also be administered to subjects. The basic paradigm of such tasks is as follows: The subject is presented with the to-be-remembered stimulus; a time delay ensues (from 0 to 30 sec), during which the subject must engage in some sort of distractor activity; and recall is required at the end of the delay period (Peterson & Peterson, 1959). Consonant trigrams (e.g., X–R–C) and word triads (e.g., bring, stain, vegetable) are examples of stimuli that are commonly used. Retention scores are compared on the basis of modality of presentation (visual versus auditory) and mode of presentation (sequential versus simultaneous: X,R,C versus XRC). An error analysis (e.g., omission errors, sequencing errors, perseveration errors) also yields valuable information.

Remote Memory Tests.   Several tests of remote memory are available. Albert (Albert, Butters, & Levin, 1979) has developed a test comprised of three parts: a famous faces test, a recall questionnaire, and a recognition questionnaire. It contains questions about famous people and events from the 1920s to the 1970s and is sensitive to differences between the remote memory patterns of amnesic and dementing patients of varying etiologies (Albert, Butters, & Levin, 1980). Squire (Squire & Slater, 1975) has created two types of multiple-choice tests. One contains questions about television shows aired from 1955 to 1975; the other is composed of questions about events, persons, and places prominent in the news during the four decades from 1930 to 1969. The current events test has three alternate forms that can be given to the same subject at different time intervals.

Parietal-Lobe Battery.   This test, devised and described by Goodglass and Kaplan (1972), can be used to evaluate drawing and constructional ability, as well as other tasks thought to be affected by parietal-lobe dysfunction (e.g., calculation, right–left orientation, and finger localization). It should be noted that the qualitative analysis of performance on these tests is of greater relevance than the absolute score.

Frontal-System Battery.   A frontal-system battery should include tests which evaluate abstracting and conceptual ability (e.g., proverb interpretation), inhibition, attention, fluency, and motor-programming capacities. The Wisconsin Card Sort, Gorham Proverbs, Shipley–Hartford Institute of Living Scale, and Ravens Progressive Matrices examine different aspects of abstracting and conceptual ability (Drewe, 1974; Hécaen & Albert, 1975; Milner, 1963, 1964). The Stroop and the Porteus Mazes (Perret, 1974) test inhibitory capacities. Continuous performance tests evaluate attention and vigilance (Drewe, 1975). A controlled word-association test (known colloquially as the FAS test) is an excellent measure of verbal fluency (Benton, 1968; Milner, 1964), while a variety of repetitive, sequential tasks evaluate motor programming ability (Drewe, 1975; Luria, 1966).

It is hoped that when a well chosen battery of selected tests is analyzed with the aforementioned approach, a better understanding of the nature of the aging process will ensue. Such an analysis may ultimately have significance with regard to the development of appropriate support systems for the elderly. Thus, an understanding of the strategies that elderly individuals impose on incoming information may enable researchers to plan an environment in which the strengths of the elderly can be exploited. If such spared functions can be used in dealing with the exigencies of daily living, we may hope to improve the quality of life for a rapidly enlarging population of elderly people.

REFERENCES

Albert, M. S., Butters, N, & Levin, J. Retrograde amnesia in alcoholic Korsakoff patients. *Archives of Neurology,* 1979, *36,* 211-216.

Albert, M. S., Butters, N., & Levin, J. Memory for remote events in chronic alcoholics and alcoholic Korsakoff patients. In H. Begleiter & B. Kissen (Eds.), *Alcohol intoxication and withdrawal.* New York: Plenum Press, 1980.

Arenberg, D. Anticipation interval and age difference in verbal learning. *Journal of Abnormal Psychology,* 1965, *70,* 419-425.

Arenberg, D. Age differences in retroaction. *Journal of Gerontology.* 1967, *22,* 88-91.

Arenberg, D. Cognition and Aging: Verbal learning memory and problem solving. In E. Eisdorfer & M. P. Lawton (Eds.), *The psychology of adult development and aging.* Washington, D.C.: American Psychological Association, 1973.

Arenberg, D. and Robertson-Tchabo, E. A. Learning and aging. In J. E. Birren & K. Schaie (Eds.), *Handbook of the psychology of aging.* New York: Von Nostrand Reinhold, 1977.

Axelrod, S., & Cohen, L. D. Senescence and embedded figure performances in vision and touch. *Perceptual Motor Skills,* 1961, *12,* 283–288.

Baddeley, A. D. The influence of acoustic and semantic similarity on long-term memory for word sequences. *Quarterly Journal of Experimental Psycholgy,* 1966, *18,* 302–309.

Benton, A. L. Differential behavioral effects in frontal lobe disease. *Neuropsychologia,* 1968, *6,* 53–60.

Binks, M. G. & Sutcliffe, J. *The effects of age and verbal ability on short-term recognition memory.* Paper presented at the annual conference of the British Psychological Society, Nottingham, 1972.

Birren, J. E., Botwinick, J., Weiss, A., & Morrison, D. F. Interrelations of mental and perceptual tests given to healthy elderly men. In J. E. Birren, R. N. Butler, S. W. Greenhouse, L. Sokoleff, & M. Yarrow (Eds.), *Human Aging: A biological and behavioral study.* Washington, D.C. Government Printing Office, 1963.

Bogen, J. E. The other side of the brain: An appositional mind. *Bulletin of the Los Angeles Neurological Society,* 1969, *34,* 135–162.

Bondareff, W. The neural basis of aging. In J. E. Birren & K. W. Schaie (Eds.), *Handbook of the psychology of aging.* New York: Van Nostrand Reinhold, 1977.

Botwinick, J. *Aging and behavior,* New York: Springer, 1973.

Botwinick, J. Intellectual abilities. In J. E. Birren & K. W. Schaie (Eds.), *Handbook of the psychology of aging.* New York: Van Nostrand Reinhold, 1977.

Botwinick, J., & Kornetsky, C. Age differences in the acquisition and extinction of GSR. *Journal of Gerontology,* 1960, *15,* 83–84.

Botwinick, J., & Storandt, M. *Memory related functions and age.* Springfield, Ill: Charles C. Thomas, 1974.

Botwinick, J., Robbin, J. S., & Brinley, J. F. Reorganization of perceptions with age. *Journal of Gerontology,* 1959, *14,* 85–88.

Bowman, L., & Grünbaum, A. A. Über motorische momente der agraphie. *Monatschrift Psychiatrie und Neurologie,* 1930, *77,* 223.

Brinley, J., & Fichter, J. Performance deficits in the elderly in relation to memory load and set. *Journal of Gerontology,* 1970, *25,* 30–35.

Broadbent, D. E., & Gregory, M. Some confirmatory results on age differences in memory for simultaneous stimulation. *British Journal of Psychology,* 1965, *56,* 77–80.

Brody, J., Harman, T., & Ordy, L. *Clinical, morphological and neurochemical aspects in the aging CNS.* New York: Raven Press, 1978.

Canestrari, R. E. Paced and self-paced learning in young and elderly adults. *Journal of Gerontology,* 1963, *18,* 165–168.

Clark, L., & Knowles, J. Age differences in dichotic listening performance. *Journal of Gerontology,* 1973, *28,* 173–178.

Clay, H. M. An age difference in separating spatially contiguous data. *Journal of Gerontology,* 1956, *11,* 318–322.

Craik, F. I. M. The nature of the age decrement in performance on dichotic listening tasks. *Quarterly Journal of Experimental Psychology,* 1965, *17,* 227–240.

Craik, F. I. M. Short-term memory and the aging process. In G. A. Talland (Ed.), *Human aging and behavior.* New York: Academic Press, 1968.

Craik, F. I. M. Age differences in recognition memory. *Quarterly Journal of Experimental Psychology,* 1971, *23,* 316–323.

Craik, F. I. M. *Signal detection analysis of age differences in divided attention.* Paper presented at the meeting of the American Psychological Association, Montreal. 1973.

Craik, F. I. M. Age differences in human memory. In J. E. Birren & K. W. Schaie (Eds.), *Handbook of the psychology of aging.* New York: Van Nostrand Reinhold, 1977.

Craik, F. I. M., & Lockhart, R. S. Levels of processing: a framework for memory research. *Journal of Verbal Learning and Verbal Behavior,* 1972, *11,* 671–684.

Critchley, M. *The parietal lobes.* London: Arnold, 1966. (Originally published, 1953.)

Crovitz, B. Recovering a learning deficit in the aged. *Journal of Gerontology,* 1966, *21,* 236–238.

Doppelt, J. E. & Wallace, W. L. Standardization of the Wechsler Adult Intelligence Scale for older persons. *Journal of Abnormal Social Psychology,* 1955, *51,* 312–330.

Drachman, D. A., & Leavitt, J. Memory impairment in the aged: Storage versus retrieval deficits. *J. Exp. Psychol.,* 1972, *93,* 302–308.

Drewe, E. A. The effect of type and area of brain lesion on Wisconsin Card Sorting Test performance. *Cortex,* 1974, *10,* 159–170.

Drewe, E. A. An experimental investigation of Luria's theory on the effects of frontal lobe lesions in man. *Neuropsychologia,* 1975, *13,* 421–429.

Dustman, R. E., & Beck, E. C. The effects of maturation and aging on the wave form of visually evoked potentials. *Electroencephalography and Clinical Neurophysiology,* 1969, *26,* 2–11.

Eisdorfer, C. New dimensions and a tentative theory. *Gerontologist,* 1967, *7,* 14–18.

Eisdorfer, C., Axelrod, S., & Wilkie, F. L. Stimulus exposure time as a factor in serial learning in an aged sample. *Journal of Abnormal Social Psychology,* 1963, *67,* 594–600.

Eisdorfer, C., Busse, E. W., & Cohen, L. D. The WAIS performance of an aged sample: The relationship between verbal and performance I.Q.s. *Journal of Gerontology,* 1959, *14,* 197–201.

Farver, P. Performance of normal older adults on a test battery designed to measure parietal lobe functions. Unpublished master's thesis, Boston University, 1975.

Friedman, H. Memory organization in the aged. *Journal of Genetic Psychology,* 1966, *109,* 3–8.

Gerstmann, J. On the symptomatology of cerebral lesions in the transitional area of the lower parietal and middle occipital convolutions. In M. D. Wilkins & I. A. Brody, Gerstmann's Syndrome. *Archives of Neurology,* 1971, 475–476. (Originally published, 1930.)

Gilbert, J. G., & Levee, D. F. Age differences on the Bender Visual-Motor Gestalt Test and the Archimedes Spiral Test. *Gerontology,* 1965, *2,* 196–198.

Goldstein, G., & Shelly, C. H. Similarities and differences between psychological deficit in aging and brain damage. *Journal of Gerontology,* 1975, *30,* 448–455.

Goodglass, H., & Kaplan, E. F. *The assessment of aphasia and related disorders.* Philadelphia: Lea and Febiger, 1972.

Heath, H. A., & Orbach, J. Reversibility of the Necker-cube: IV. Responses of elderly people. *Perceptual Motor Skills,* 1963, *17,* 625–626.

Hécaen, H., & Albert, M. L. Disorders of mental functioning related to frontal lobe pathology. In D. F. Benson & D. Blumer (Eds.), *Psychiatric aspects of neurologic disease.* New York: Grune and Stratton, 1975.

Heilman, K., & Valenstein, E. Frontal lobe neglect in man. *Neurology,* 1972, *22,* 660–664.

Hooper, H. E. *Visual Organization Test.* Los Angeles: Western Psychological Services, 1951.

Hulicka, I. M. Age differences in retention as a function of interference. *Journal of Gerontology,* 1967, *22,* 180–184.

Hulicka, I. M., & Grossman, J. L. Age-related comparisons for the use of mediators in paired-associate learning. *Journal of Gerontology,* 1967, *22,* 46–51.

Hulicka, I. M., Sterns, H., & Grossman, J. Age group comparisons of paired-associate learning as a function of paced and self-paced association and response times. *Journal of Gerontology,* 1967, *22,* 274–280.

Hultsch, D. F. Adult age differences in free classification and free recall. *Developmental Psychology,* 1971, *4,* 338–342.

Inglis, J. Influence of motivation, perception and attention on age-related changes in short-term memory. *Nature,* 1964, *204,* 103–104.

Jerome, E. A. Age and learning-experimental studies. In J. E. Birren (Ed.), *Handbook of aging and the individual: Psychological and biological aspects.* Chicago: University of Chicago Press, 1959.

Kaplan, E. *Neuropsychological assessment of the elderly.* In preparation.

Karlin, L. Cognition, preparation, and sensory-evoked potentials. *Psychological Bulletin,* 1970, *73,* 122–136.

Kausler, D. H. Retention-forgetting as a nomological network for developmental research. In L. R. Goulet & P. B. Baltes (Eds.), *Life-span developmental psychology.* New York: Academic Press, 1970.

Kausler, D. H., & Kleim, D. M. Age differences in processing relevant versus irrelevant stimuli in multiple-item recognition learning. *Journal of Gerontology,* 1978, *33,* 87–93.

Keevil-Rogers, P., & Schnore, M. Short-term memory as a function of age in persons of above average intelligence. *Journal of Gerontology,* 1969, *24,* 184–188.

Kinsbourne, M., & Berryhill, J. The nature of the interaction between pacing and the age decrement in learning. *Journal of Gerontology,* 1972, *27,* 471–477.

Kirchner, W. K. Age differences in short-term retention of rapidly changing information. *Journal of Experimental Psychology,* 1958, *55,* 352–358.

Kleemier, R. W. *Intellectual change in the senium.* Proceedings of the social statistics section of the American Statistical Association, 1962.

Klisz, D. Neuropsychological evaluation of older persons. In M. Storandt, E. C. Siegler, & M. F. Elias (Eds.), *The clinical psychology of aging.* New York: Plenum Press, 1978.

Klodin, V. M. Verbal facilitation of perceptual-integrative performance in relation to age. Unpublished doctoral dissertation, Washington University, St. Louis, 1975.

Knill, F. P. *The effect of visual and verbal mnemonic devices on the paired-associate learning of aged population.* Unpublished master's thesis, University of Richmond, 1966.

Kriauciunas, R. The relationship of age and retention interval activity in short-term memory. *Journal of Gerontology,* 1968, *23,* 169–173.

Laurence, M. W. Memory loss with age: a test of two strategies for its retardation. *Psychonomic Science,* 1967, *9,* 209–210.

Layton, B. Perceptual noise and aging. *Psychological Bulletin,* 1975, *82,* 875–883.

Levy-Agresti, J., & Sperry, R. W. Differential perceptual capacities in major and minor hemispheres. *Proceedings of the National Academy of Sciences of the United States of America.* 1968, *61,* 1151.

Loveless, N. E., & Sanford, A. J. Effects of age on the contingent negative variation and preparatory set in a reaction-time task. *Journal of Gerontology,* 1974, *29,* 52–63.

Lüders, H. The effects of aging on the wave form of the somatosensory cortical evoked potential. *Electroencephalography and Clinical Neurophysiology,* 1970, *29,* 450–460.

Luria, A. R. *The higher cortical function in man.* New York: Basic Books, 1966.

Marsh, G. R., & Thompson, L. W. Psychophysiology of aging. In J. E. Birren & K. W. Schaie (Eds.), *Handbook of the psychology of aging.* New York: Van Nostrand Reinhold, 1977.

McGhie, A., Chapman, T., & Lawson, T. Changes in immediate memory with age. *British Journal of Psychology,* 1965, *56,* 69–75.

Meudell, P., & Butters, N. The role of rehearsal in the short-term memory performance of patients with Korsakoff's and Huntington's Disease. *Neuropsychologia,* 1978, *16,* 507–510.

Milner, B. Effects of different brain lesions on card sorting. *Journal of Experimental Psychology (Chicago),* 1963, *9,* 90–100.

Milner, B. Some effects of frontal lobectomy in man. In J. M. Warren & K. Akert (Eds.), *The frontal granular cortex and behavior.* New York: McGraw-Hill, 1964.

Milner, B. Interhemispheric differences in the localization of psychological processes in man. *British Medical Bulletin,* 1971, *27,* 272–277.

Moenster, P. A. Learning and memory in relation to age. *Journal of Gerontology,* 1972, *27,* 361–363.

Monge, R., & Hultsch, D. Paired-associate learning as a function of adult age and the length of the anticipation and inspection intervals. *Journal of Gerontology,* 1971, *26,* 157–162.

Nauta, W. J. H. The problem of the frontal lobe: A reinterpretation. *Journal of Psychiatric Research*, 1971, *8*, 167–187.

Nauta, W. J. H. Neural associations of the frontal cortex. *Acta Neurobiol. Exp.*, 1972, *32*, 125–140.

Nebes, R. D. Hemispheric specialization in commissurotomized man. *Psychological Bulletin*, 1974, *81*, 1–14.

Obusek, C. J., & Warren, R. M. Comparison of speech perception in senile and well-preserved aged by means of the verbal transformation effect. *Journal of Gerontology*, 1973, *28*, 184–188.

Okun, M. A., Siegler, I. C., & George, L. K. Cautiousness and verbal learning in adulthood. *Journal of Gerontology*, 1978, *33*, 94–97.

Overall, J. E., & Gorham, D. R. Organicity versus old age in objective and projective test performance. *Journal of Consulting Clinical Psychology*, 1972, *39*, 98–105.

Perret, E. The left frontal lobe of man and the suppression of habitual responses in verbal categorical behavior. *Neuropsychologia*, 1974, *12*, 323–330.

Peterson, L. R., & Peterson, M. J. Short-term retention of individual verbal items. *Journal of Experimental Psychology*, 1959, *58*, 193–198.

Plutchik, R., Conte, H. R., Weiner, M. B., & Teresi, J. Studies of body image. IV. Figure drawings in normal and abnormal geriatric and nongeriatric groups. *Journal of Gerontology*, 1978, *33*, 68–75.

Poitrenaud, J., Hazemann, P., & Lille, F. Spontaneous variations in level of arousal among aged. *Gerontology*, 1978, *24*, 241–249.

Powell, A. H., Eisdorfer, C., & Bogdonoff, M. D. Physiologic response patterns observed in a learning task. *Archives of General Psychiatry*, 1964, *10*, 192–195.

Rabbitt, P. M. A., Clancy, M. C., & Vyas, S. M. Proceedings of XVII International Congress of Gerontology, Washington, D.C., 1969.

Raymond, B. Free recall among the aged. *Psychological Reports*, 1971, *29*, 1179–1182.

Reed, H. B. C., & Reitan, R. M. A comparison of the effects of the normal aging process with the effects of organic brain damage on adaptive abilities. *Journal of Gerontology*, 1963, *18*, 177–179.

Rowe, E. J., & Schnore, M. M. Item concreteness and reported strategies in paired-associate learning as a function of age. *Journal of Gerontology*, 1971, *26*, 470–478.

Schaie, K. W., Labouvie, O. U., & Buech, V. U. Generation and cohort-specific differences in adult cognitive functioning: a fourteen year study of independent samples. *Developmental Psychology*, 1973, *9*, 151–166.

Schaie, K. W., & Schaie, T. P. Clinical assessment and aging. In J. E. Birren & K. W. Schaie (Eds.), *Handbook of the psychology of aging*. New York: Van Nostrand Reinhold, 1977.

Schenkenberg, T. *Visual, auditory, and somatosensory, evoked responses of normal subjects from childhood to senescence.* Unpublished doctoral dissertation, University of Utah, 1970.

Schneider, N. G., Gritz, E. R., & Jarvik, M. E. Age differences in simple paced tasks of attention and perception. *Gerontology*, 1977, *23*, 142–147.

Schonfield, D. Learning and retention. In J. E. Birren (Ed.), *Contemporary gerontology: Issues and concepts.* Los Angeles: University of Southern California Press, 1969.

Schonfield, D., & Robertson, E. A. The coding and sorting of digits and symbols by an elderly sample. *Journal of Gerontology*, 1966, *23*, 318–323.

Schonfield, D., Trueman, V., & Kline, D. Recognition tests of dichotic listening and the age variable. *Journal of Gerontology*, 1972, *27*, 487–493.

Squire, L. R., & Slater, P. C. Forgetting in very long-term memory as assessed by an improved questionnaire technique. *Journal of Experimental Psychology*, 1975, *104*, 50–54.

Strub, R., & Geschwind, N. Gerstmann syndrome without aphasia. *Cortex*, 1974, *10*, 378–387.

Surwillo, W. W. The relation of autonomic activity to age differences in vigilance. *Journal of Gerontology*, 1966, *21*, 257–260.

Talland, G. A. Age and the immediate memory span. *Gerontologist,* 1967, *7,* 4–9.

Tecce, J. J. Contingent negative variation and attention functions in the aged. In E. Callaway, P. Tueting, & S. H. Koslow (Eds.), *Event-related brain potentials in man.* New York: Academic Press, 1978.

Teuber, H. L. The riddle of frontal lobe function in man. In J. M. Warren & K. Akert (Eds.), *The frontal granular cortex and behavior.* New York: McGraw-Hill, 1964.

Teuber, H. L., Battersby, W. S., & Bender, M. B. *Visual field defects after penetrating missile wounds of the brain.* Cambridge: Harvard University Press, 1960.

Thompson, L. W., & Marsh, G. R. Psychophysiological studies of aging. In C. Eisdorfer & M. P. Lawton (Eds.), *The psychology of adult development and aging.* Washington, D.C.: American Psychological Association, 1973.

Thompson, L. W., & Nowlin, J. B. Relation of increased attention to central and autonomic nervous system states. In L. Jarvik, C. Eisdorfer, & J. Blum (Eds.), *Intellectual functioning in adults: Psychological and biological influences.* New York: Springer, 1973.

Troyer, L. W., Eisdorfer, C., Wilkie, F., & Bogdonoff, M. D. Free fatty acid responses in the aged individual during performance of learning tasks. *Journal of Gerontology,* 1966, *21,* 45–51.

Tulving, E., & Thomson, D. M. Encoding specificity and retrieval process in episodic memory. *Psychological Review,* 1973, *80,* 352–373.

Wechsler, D. A standardized memory scale for clinical use. *Journal of Psychology,* 1945, *19,* 87–95.

Wechsler, D. *Wechsler Adult Intelligence Scale, manual.* New York: Psychological Corp., 1955.

Wechsler, D. *The measurement and appraisal of adult intelligence* (4th ed.). Baltimore: Williams and Wilkins, 1958.

Welford, A. T. *Aging and human skill.* London: Oxford University Press, 1958.

Welsh, O. L., Laterman, D. M., & Bell, B. The effects of aging on responses to filtered speech. *Journal of Gerontology,* 1969, *24,* 189–192.

Werner, H. Process and achievement: A basic problem of education and developmental psychology. *Harvard Educational Review,* May 1937.

Wickelgren, W. A. Age and storage dynamics in continuous recognition memory. *Developmental Psychology,* 1975, *11,* 165–169.

Wimer, R. E., & Wigdor, B. T. Age differences in retention of learning. *Journal of Gerontology,* 1958, *13,* 291–295.

Zelinski, E. M., Walsh, D. A., & Thompson, L. W. Orienting task effects on EDR and free recall in three age groups. *Journal of Gerontology,* 1978, *33,* 239–245.

24

The Neuropsychology of Amnesia: An Approach to the Study of Memory and Aging

Larry R. Squire

Veterans Administration Medical Center
San Diego, California and
University of California, San Diego

Memory dysfunction can occur in conjunction with head trauma (Russell & Nathan, 1946), temporal lobe dysfunction (Milner, 1972), Korsakoff psychosis (Talland, 1965; Butters & Cermak, 1975), electroconvulsive therapy (ECT) (Squire, 1977), dorsal thalamic lesions (Squire & Moore, 1979), encephalitis (Starr & Phillips, 1970; Rose & Symonds, 1960), third ventricle tumors (Williams & Pennybacker, 1954; Ignelzsi & Squire, 1976), occlusion of the posterior artery (Benson, Marsden, & Meadows, 1974), and as part of a broad pattern of cognitive decline in conjunction with Alzheimer's disease and the other dementias (Wells, 1977). Memory problems are also frequently reported by psychiatric patients and by healthy aged persons. Since memory problems often occur in the context of various cognitive defects, e.g., defects in mood, attention, vigilance, language, or general intellectual capacity, formal memory testing can sometimes lead to uncertain results. Thus, if an individual patient scores poorly on a memory test, it is often difficult to know whether performance was influenced more by mood, motivation, or by a specific memory disorder. Similarly, if an aged person scores poorly on a memory test, it may be difficult to know whether performance was influenced primarily by memory or by some cognitive deficit other than amnesia.

Some examples of memory dysfunction occur in striking isolation from other cognitive defects, and therefore are particularly amenable to experimental study. Here some recent studies of anterograde and retrograde amnesia are described, drawing from the amnesia associated with ECT and case N.A., who has chronic amnesia for verbal material. Then, the memory complaints associated with ECT are considered, using a newly developed self-rating instrument to evaluate their severity, as well as some of their qualitative features. Finally, the neuropathology of amnesia is reviewed, with special reference to the problem of aging. It is proposed that information obtained in this way about relatively circumscribed amnesias can provide a perspective from which to explore instances of memory dysfunction, like that associated with aging, that occur in the context of broader neuropsychological impairment.

The amnesia associated with ECT is particularly favorable for exploring memory dysfunction. Because ECT is a scheduled event, the time of onset of amnesia can be specified, and before–after studies can be conducted with each patient serving as his own control. After a postictal confusional period of about 30 min, patients exhibit an amnesic syndrome in the absence of general confusion or impaired intellectual capacity. The amnesia diminishes gradually following each treatment in a series and is cumulative across treatments. Amnesia for both verbal and nonverbal material is greater following bilateral ECT than folllowing right unilateral ECT (Squire & Slater, 1978b).

ANTEROGRADE AMNESIA

Figure 24.1 illustrates the anterograde amnesia associated with ECT, and makes several points about memory and neuropsychological testing. Here patients were read a short story and immediately thereafter asked to recall it. Recall was tested again the following day and again two weeks later for some of the groups. Three of the groups had received bilateral ECT, right unilateral ECT, or hospitalization without ECT six to nine months previously. The fourth group (D) learned the same story 6 to 10 hr after the fifth bilateral treatment of the series. On immediate recall, performance of all groups was about the same, and ECT exerted no measurable effect on memory. One day later, however, only two patients in group D could remember any of the story, and the average score of this group was significantly poorer than the scores of the other groups. These results make the point that the anterograde amnesia associated with ECT affects delayed recall but has little effect on immediate recall. This same conclusion seems to apply to all of the amnesias that cause memory problems out of proportion to other cognitive dysfunction (Milner, 1972; Ignelzi & Squire, 1976). Clearly, the most sensitive tests for assessing anterograde amnesia are ones that assess delayed recall. It is therefore most appropriate that memory test batteries recently designed for the aged population have included tests of delayed recall (Erickson, Poon, & Walsh-Sweeney, Chapter 22). Memory tests have not always incorporated this important feature (Wechsler, 1945).

FIG. 24.1. Recall of a short story learned 6 to 10 hr after the fifth treatment of a prescribed course of electroconvulsive therapy (Group D, N = 15). Control groups learned the same story six to nine months after bilateral treatment (N = 16), right unilateral treatment (N = 10), or psychiatric hospitalization without ECT (N = 12). Retention was tested immediately after learning, and again one day and two weeks later. From Squire and Chace, 1975.

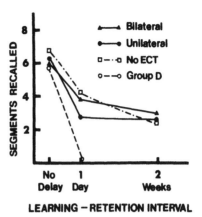

LEARNING – RETENTION INTERVAL

RETROGRADE AMNESIA

Until recently, assessment of remote memory capacity depended on informal interviews. Objective tests of remote memory were first developed by Botwinick and Storandt (1974) and Warrington and Silberstein (1970); and these methods have been applied extensively to the study of amnesia. Remote memory defects can occur in amnesia (Sanders & Warrington, 1971), but there has been uncertainty as to whether all remote memories are affected to about the same extent regardless of their age, or whether older memories are relatively preserved.

A large literature of animal studies (McGaugh & Herz, 1972; Squire, 1975b) indicates that retrograde amnesia can be temporally graded, and that recently formed memories are more vulnerable to disruption than older memories. The time course of this temporally graded amnesia is typically minutes or hours. Yet in man, clinical reports have suggested that memory of the previous few years can sometimes be lost without disturbing older memories (Barbizet, 1970; Russell & Nathan, 1946). In such cases, however, it has been difficult to know whether amnesia is temporally graded or whether all memories are affected equally. That is, when an informal memory interview covers a period of many years, questions about remote events tend to be more general and to cover more salient material than questions about recent events. Thus, loss of memory for recent events is easier to detect than loss of memory for remote events, and a hypothetical patient with a loss of 10% of all his memories might give the appearance of having lost recent memories to a greater extent than remote memories.

To clarify this issue, we have constructed a series of remote memory tests designed to sample equivalently from past time periods (Squire, Chace, &

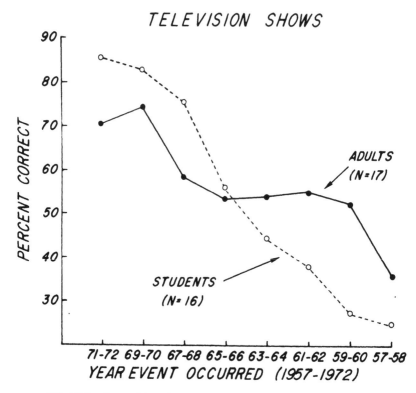

FIG. 24.2. Recognition of the names of former television programs that broadcast for only one season beginning in autumn 1957 to autumn 1972. Adults aged 26–71 years (mean = 51) and 17-year-old high school students took this test in late 1973. From Squire and Slater, 1975.

Slater, 1975; Squire & Slater, 1975). These tests ask subjects questions about television programs that were broadcast for no more than one season during the past several years. Fig. 24.2 shows results with normal subjects using one such test. Here, subjects selected from four alternatives the correct name of a former television program, and incorrect choices were fabricated with the intent of imitating the style of television program names. There were five programs for each year, 1957–1972, and the test was administered in the autumn of 1973. Adults did best answering questions about programs that were broadcast recently, and more poorly answering questions about programs that were broadcast long ago. Students, not old enough to have viewed all the programs appearing on the test, did somewhat better than adults on questions about recent programs, but scored close to chance on questions about programs that were broadcast when they were small children.

In early 1974 we prepared two equivalent forms of this test and administered them to psychiatric patients receiving prescribed bilateral ECT

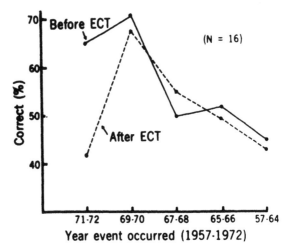

FIG. 24.3. A test of remote memory based on former one-season television programs was given to psychiatric patients receiving a prescribed course of bilateral ECT. Testing occurred before the first treatment and one hour after the fifth treatment. The study was conducted in early 1974. From Squire, Slater, and Chace, 1975.

for depressive illness (Squire, Slater, & Chace, 1975). Patients were tested before the first treatment, and then again 1 hr after the fifth treatment of the series. By 1 hr after treatment, patients have recovered from the postictal confusional state and can obtain normal scores on conventional tests of adult intelligence (Squire, 1975a). Fig. 24.3 shows that before ECT, patients exhibited a normal forgetting curve and performed rather well across the time span covered by the test. After ECT, there was a selective defect in the ability to recognize the names of programs that began in the autumn of 1971 or 1972, approximately 1½ to 2½ years before testing. Recognition of programs broadcast prior to that time was normal. Fig. 24.4 provides results of follow-up of these patients on two separate occasions: one week after the completion of ECT (mean 7.6 treatments), and eight months later. These results were based on their performance on both forms of the test, and indicate that this retrograde amnesia is transient. Recently completed long-term follow-up studies with more sensitive memory tests also suggest that retrograde amnesia for remote events substantially recovers by six months after ECT (Squire, Slater, & Miller, 1980).

Fig. 24.5 presents the results for a more recently developed test that asks patients to recall everything that they can remember about 25 former television programs (Squire & Cohen, 1979). Such tests of detailed recall are known to be particularly sensitive to remote memory defects (Squire & Slater, 1978). Before ECT, patients could recall considerable detail about programs that broadcast only a few years ago, and less detail about programs that broadcast many years ago. After ECT, there was a selective loss in the ability to recall recently acquired memories. Information about programs broadcast many years ago was not affected by ECT. Thus, results from this test also provided strong evidence that retrograde amnesia can be temporally graded, and that this gradient can cover a period of several years.

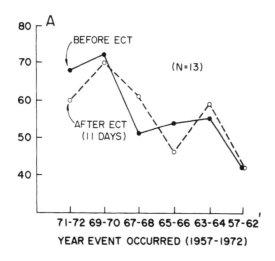

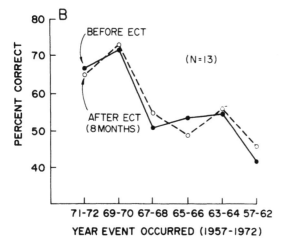

FIG. 24.4. Recovery from retrograde amnesia. Recognition of former television programs (a) before and one to two weeks after completion of a course of bilateral ECT (mean = 7.6 treatments); and (b) before and eight months after completion of treatment. The results shown are for thirteen out of sixteen patients who were available for follow-up.

These finding have several implications for the structure of memory and its neurological basis (Squire & Schlapfer, 1980). First, temporal gradients of retrograde amnesia are real and seem to be the typical pattern of memory dysfunction when amnesia for remote events occurs. This pattern of impairment has now been described for four different tests, in the case of ECT (Squire, Slater & Chace, 1975; Squire, Chace & Slater, 1976; Squire & Cohen, 1979; Squire & Cohen, 1980), and recently has been extended to the Korsakoff syndrome (Albert, Butters, & Levin, 1979; Seltzer & Benson, 1974). Possible reasons for two failures to find a temporally graded defect (Sanders & Warrington, 1971; Squire, 1975a) have been considered elsewhere (Squire, Chace, & Slater, 1976; Squire & Cohen, 1980). Second, we infer from the phenomenon of temporally graded retrograde amnesia that some change must occur beyond the acquisition process that renders memory gradually

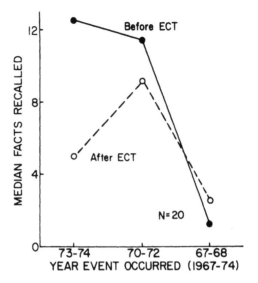

FIG. 24.5. Patients recalled all they could remember about former television programs that broadcast for only one season, 1967–1974. Testing occurred before ECT and one hour after the fifth treatment of the series. There were 10 programs in the 1973–74 period, seven in 1970–72, and eight in 1967–68. The results have been presented to show the number of facts recalled per 10 ducted during 1976. From Squire and Cohen, 1979.

resistant to disruption. In this sense, the results constitute strong confirmation of Ribot's Law which was formulated in 1882 (Ribot, 1882), and which stated that memory grows stronger and more resistant with the passage of time. Since forgetting occurs while resistance develops, the changes that occur as time passes might provide the basis for gradual reorganization and restructuring in memory storage (cf. Bartlett, 1932; Norman & Rumelhart, 1975).

Although it now seems clear that remote memory loss can be temporally graded in the organic amnesias, the character of remote memory impairment in aging is still uncertain. The results of two studies using tests of current events suggested that remote memory loss may occur equivalently across all time periods (Squire, 1974; Warrington & Sanders, 1971). However, tests of the type used in these studies do not yield forgetting curves in normal memory and have not yielded temporal gradients in the retrograde amnesia associated with ECT (Squire, 1975a). Memory tests of the type which do yield temporal gradients of retrograde amnesia in ECT patients have not yet been applied to the aged population. If gradients of amnesia indeed reflect a process of increasing resistance in normal memory that develops with time, then it seems reasonable to suspect that this process might be revealed through the aging process as well as through the amnesias.

CASE N.A.

To develop a general understanding of memory and memory dysfunction, it is important to evaluate amnesias with diverse etiologies. In this way it becomes possible to ask whether there is one amnesia or many. Here the patient N.A.

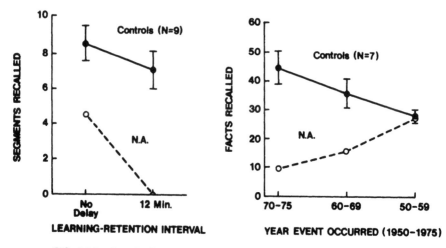

FIG. 24.6. Recall of a short story by the patient N.A., who has chronic amnesia for verbal material, and by a group of control subjects. (Right) Performance on a test that asked subjects to recall everything they could remember about events that were in the news 1950–1975. From Squire and Slater, 1978a.

(Squire & Slater, 1977, 1978a; Teuber, Milner, & Vaughan, 1968) is considered in the context of ECT amnesia and some data from Korsakoff amnesia. In 1960, at the age of 22, N.A. sustained a stab wound to the brain with a miniature fencing foil. Since that time he has had chronic amnesia, primarily for verbal material. Formal testing indicates that his I.Q. is 124, and that he has no known cognitive defect other than amnesia. Fig. 24.6 presents results for two memory tests. The left panel demonstrates this individual's difficulty in new learning, as assessed by the test of short story recall described above. His immediate recall of the story was poorer than the immediate recall of matched control subjects, and his defect was even clearer after a 12-min delay.

The right panel presents results for a test of past news events, in which N.A. and matched control subjects were asked to tell as much as they could remember about events that occurred from 1950 to 1975. N.A. was markedly deficient at recalling details about events that had occurred since his accident in 1960, but recalled details from the 1950s as well as normal subjects. This discontinuity between premorbid and postmorbid memory has also been reported for the well studied and severely amnesic patient, H.M. (Marslen-Wilson & Teuber, 1975). Clinical interviews have suggested that both H.M. and N.A. have some retrograde amnesia covering a period of perhaps a few months in the case of N.A. to perhaps a few years in the case of H.M. These results suggest that these amnesias cannot be characterized as retrieval defects, since a general defect in retrieval should affect premorbid memories along with postmorbid memories (Squire, 1980). The available evidence is consistent with the view that these amnesias involve a defect in the formation of enduring memories. In this respect, the amnesic syndrome exhibited by N.A. and by H.M. seems to resemble the amnesia associated with ECT.

We have recently analyzed this defect further by evaluating the ability of ECT patients and N.A. to accomplish three kinds of encoding (Wetzel & Squire, 1980). Following the Craik-Tulving procedure (Craik & Tulving, 1975), amnesic patients were induced to engage in semantic, phonemic, or graphic encoding and then were given a recognition memory test. On the retention test, patients performed more poorly than controls, but they exhibited a qualitatively normal pattern of performance that included superior retention of semantically encoded words. By contrast, in agreement with previous work (Cermak & Reale, 1978), Korsakoff patients failed to exhibit this semantic superiority, and obtained similar recognition scores for all words regardless of the nature of encoding.

Results with the Craik-Tulving procedure suggest that amnesia is not a unitary disorder. Korsakoff patients are reported to have cognitive defects (e.g., deficient perception of embedded figures; impaired performance in the digit symbol substitution test [Talland, 1965]) not exhibited by ECT patients (McAndrew, Berkey, & Matthews, 1967), or by N.A. (Teuber, Milner, & Vaughan, 1968). The amnesia associated with ECT and the amnesia exhibited by N.A. may reflect a relatively circumscribed memory impairment in which encoding is qualitatively normal, but subsequent consolidation processes are defective. The amnesia associated with the Korsakoff syndrome may depend on defects at an earlier stage of information processing that affect registration and the elaborateness of encoding.

MEMORY COMPLAINTS

Another way to compare kinds of memory dysfunction is to evaluate the subjective experiences that underlie them. Recently, we have developed a new self-rating scale for memory complaints and have used it to evaluate the memory complaints associated with ECT. We began this inquiry with the observation that at six months after ECT about 65% of patients tested said that their memory was not as good as it used to be (Squire, 1977; Squire & Chace, 1975). Taken at face value, it has been difficult to know whether these complaints are related to ECT, to depression, to chronic low self-esteem, or to other factors. Since depression and the acute amnesia associated with ECT can affect memory test scores differently (Cronholm & Ottoson, 1961; Sternberg & Jarvik, 1976), we thought that memory complaints might also differ in some measurable way, depending on their cause. A self-rating scale was developed that could be given to psychiatric patients before and after ECT. Eighteen test items were included, each asking about different aspects of memory functions: immediate memory, new learning ability, recent memory, and remote memory. Each item asked patients to judge their memory "now compared to how it was before you began to feel bad and came to the hospital." Ratings were made on a nine-point scale from –4 (worse than ever before), through 0 (same as before), to +4 (better than ever before). Thirty-five patients filled out the scale before ECT, one week after ECT (mean = 11.1 treatments, range = 5–21), and six months after treatment. A detailed description of the test and a list of the 18 items can be found elsewhere (Squire, Wetzel, & Slater, 1979).

Figure 24.7 shows the results for before and one week after ECT. The data have been ordered so that the item yielding the largest difference between the before-ECT condition and the after-ECT condition appears to the extreme left. The item yielding the smallest difference is to the extreme right. Before ECT, patients rated their memory as equivalently poor across all items. The average self-rating score was –.8, confirming the expectation that depression is associated with memory complaints. When we gave this same rating scale to 20 hospital employees of the same age and educational level as the patients, and asked them to rate their memory "now compared to one year ago," the average rating was close to zero (–.05), a value significantly different from the score of the psychiatric patients before ECT.

After ECT, memory complaints were more severe than before ECT (mean = –1.4). More important, the qualitative nature of the memory complaints after ECT was different than before ECT. That is, patients rated themselves about the same on all items before ECT, but they rated themselves as more impaired on some items than on others after ECT. This point follows from the significant interaction of test occasion × items (p < .01). Memory complaints reported before ECT were presumably related to depressive illness. Since memory dysfunction can easily be demonstrated one week after a course of bilateral treatment (Cronholm & Blomquist, 1959), and since ECT is effective in relieving depressive illness (Fink, 1979), it seems reasonable to

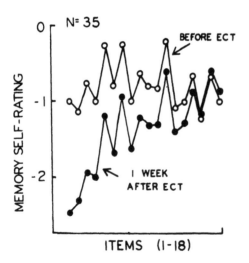

FIG. 24.7. Psychiatric patients filled out a memory complaints self-rating scale before and one week after a prescribed course of bilateral ECT. The scale consisted of 18 items, each to be rated from –4 to + 4. Here the scores for the 18 items appear from left to right in order of the magnitude of the before-ECT–after-ECT difference in score. From Squire, Wetzel, and Slater, 1979.

FIG. 24.8. Memory complaints determined by an 18-item self-rating scale before, one week after, and six months after a prescribed course of bilateral ECT. For each item patients rated themselves from -4 (worse than ever before), to + 4 (better than ever before). Regression lines have been constructed through the average scores for each test item. At six months after treatment, memory complaints were diminished, compared to one week after treatment, and resembled the after-ECT pattern of complaints rather than the before-ECT pattern. From Squire, Wetzel, and Slater, 1979.

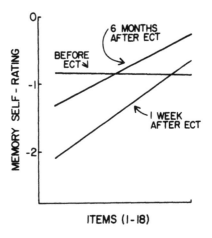

suppose that the altered pattern of memory complaints observed one week after ECT was largely related to amnesia.

We next asked whether memory complaints occurring many months after ECT resembled the before-ECT pattern or the after-ECT pattern. Fig. 24.8 shows the results. For clarity, we have constructed the best fitting line (method of least squares) through the 18 scores for before ECT, one week after ECT, and six months after ECT. These results indicated that (1) memory complaints six months after ECT were diminished relative to memory complaints one week after ECT ($p < .05$); (2) memory complaints six months after ECT qualitatively differed from the complaints reported before ECT. This point follows from the finding of a significant interaction between the six-month results and the before-ECT results ($p < .01$, test occasion × items). There was no significant interaction between the results at six months and the results at one week after ECT. Because complaints about memory long after ECT differed from the before-ECT pattern of complaints, the results suggest that complaints long after ECT cannot be attributed primarily to recurring depressive illness, to chronic low self-esteem or to other feelings about memory that were present before ECT.

One possible interpretation of these findings is that amnesia persists long after ECT. This possibility seems unlikely, because formal tests have suggested that memory has substantially recovered by six months after a typical course of treatment (Squire & Chace, 1975; Squire, Slater, & Miller, 1980). This recovery extends to both new learning capacity and remote memory, but not to events that occurred quite close to the time of treatment. In addition, some amnesia may remain for events that occurred during the one or two years prior to treatment. An alternative interpretation is that the amnesia initially associated with ECT affects a patient's perception of his memory abilities for a long time after these abilities have largely recovered. This perception may persist in gradually diminishing form for several months after a typical course of treatment. In any case, since the rating scale described here seems to differentiate between the effects of depression and the effects of amnesia, it might be useful in evaluating other instances of memory complaint, such as those that occur in the aged.

NEUROPATHOLOGY

Study of the amnesias has also provided information about neuroanatomical aspects of memory. From this point of view, the best studied of the amnesias is the alcoholic Korsakoff syndrome. Neuropathological material has indicated that the mammillary bodies and dorsal medial thalamus are the most affected structures in Korsakoff amnesia, though there are typically symmetrical lesions all along the third and fourth ventricles (Brierley, 1970). There has been disagreement as to whether the dorsal thalamus or the mammillary bodies is the more critical structure. The older literature describes at least four cases of Korsakoff amnesia with damage reportedly limited to the mammillary bodies (Gruner, 1956; Grunthal, 1939; Delay & Brion, 1954; Remy, 1942). In their recent monograph Victor and his colleagues described five cases with damage confined to the mammillary bodies, in which patients did not exhibit memory problems (Victor, Adams, & Collins, 1971). These authors emphasized the role of the dorsal medial thalamus in Korsakoff amnesia.

We have recently obtained CAT (computer assisted tomography) scans for the patient N.A. (Squire & Moore, 1979). The only consistent abnormality in three scans taken during 1977 was a small lucency to the left of the third ventricle at the level of the pineal calcification. The position of the lucency corresponds precisely to the location of the left dorsomedial thalamic nucleus. Of course, these data identify only the minimal extent of the lesion, and it is possible that scar tissue, isolucent to normal tissue, is present to some extent in adjacent regions. Nevertheless, the results suggest that the mammillary bodies may not be preeminent in diencephalic amnesia and indicate that damage confined to the region of the dorsomedial thalamic nucleus is sufficient to cause amnesia. Other data pertaining to this view have been reviewed elsewhere (Squire & Moore, 1979).

Another brain region having an important role in memory is the medial portion of the temporal lobe. This conclusion derives in large part, though not entirely, from study of the noted patient H.M., who in 1953 sustained bilateral removal of the anterior two-thirds of the hippocampus, as well as the parahippocampal gyrus, uncus, and amygdala (Scoville & Milner, 1957). Following surgery, H.M. exhibited an above-average intellectual capacity and intact immediate memory. However, he exhibited a severe impairment in the ability to learn new material, which has continued to the present time (Milner, 1972).

It is generally believed that the hippocampus is the critical structure in bitemporal amnesia, and a considerable body of literature exists in support of this conclusion (Milner, 1972; Penfield & Milner, 1958; Van Buren & Borke, 1972). The amnesic syndrome has also been investigated in subhuman primates, using tasks that rather closely resemble ones that are sensitive to human amnesia. In the rhesus monkey, memory was severely impaired by combined removal of hippocampus and amygdala, but only moderately impaired by removal of either structure alone (Mishkin, 1978). Since in the patient H.M. the amygdala was removed together with the hippocampus, this finding in monkeys is consistent with the view that both the hippocampus and the amygdala are involved in bitemporal amnesia. Still another point of view is that the albal stalk or temporal stem, which lies adjacent to the hippocampus, is the critical structure in bitemporal amnesia (Horel, 1978). The temporal stem has direct connections to the dorsomedial thalamic nucleus, whereas connections between the hippocampus and dorsal thalamus are sparse (but see Valenstein & Nauta, 1959). This view of amnesia would require that temporal stem damage must have occurred in the patient H.M. and also in the monkeys sustaining hippocampal–amygdala damage. Although it seems unlikely that temporal stem damage occurred in all these cases, further work is clearly needed to evaluate these alternative views of bitemporal amnesia.

Taken together, evidence from amnesia indicates that the dorsal thalamus, possibly the mammillary bodies, and the medial temporal region constitute an essential neuroanatomical system for the formation of new memories. Because memory for events that occurred prior to amnesia can be relatively unaffected compared to memory for events that happened after the onset of amnesia, these structures cannot be the sites of memory storage. These regions appear to function as a control system that regulates the establishment of memory. The plastic changes in neural connectivity that represent memory must occur in other regions of the nervous system.

In long-term mammalian memory, it has never been possible to dissociate the location of memory storage from the location of those mental operations required to perform the task under study (Lashley, 1950). For example, memory for the delayed-response task in monkeys can be effectively destroyed by excising a small amount of cortical tissue along the depths and banks of the middle third of the sulcus principalis in the frontal lobe (Butters & Pandya, 1969). Yet it is not correct to conclude that memory for delayed response is stored in this region, since the excision also makes the animal unable to ever learn the task again. The defect also cannot reflect a general memory impairment, since even monkeys with much larger lesions in the frontal lobes can learn and remember a variety of visual discriminations (Warren & Akert, 1964). One possibility is that this region is involved both in performing the delayed response task and in storing memory for the results of this activity. In any case, the brain regions that store memory have never been clearly separated from brain regions required to perform the task that is to be remembered.

An example of the same thing in a simpler nervous system can be found in the mollusc *Aplysia*. In *Aplysia,* memory for habituation of the gill withdrawal reflex involves alterations in synaptic connectivity along the same pathways that are normally involved in performing gill withdrawal (Kandel, 1976). Perhaps this organizing principle is preserved in vertebrates, so that memory involves synaptic alterations along neural pathways that ordinarily have a role in the behavior of the animal. By this view, there is no reason to believe in the existence of memory centers or memory neurons. The distribution of memory for newly acquired information is probably as broad as the distribution of the neural machinery needed to perceive, think about, and act on new information.

Given this hypothesis about memory and brain function, it is perhaps surprising that disorders of learning and memory can ever occur in isolation, rather than in the context of a general impairment affecting many functions. The notion of a control system, however, that functions to establish enduring memories in other locations, can satisfactorily explain how disorders of memory are sometimes as circumscribed as they are observed to be. It follows from these same ideas that, whenever there is cognitive dysfunction in addition to disorders of learning and memory, the neuropathological correlates of that condition should extend beyond the brain regions associated with amnesia and into other regions.

Aging appears to be such a condition, in that the memory defect occurs in the context of diverse neuropsychological impairment. Aging is associated with measurable loss in a variety of cognitive tasks, particularly those requiring speed (Jarvik, Eisdorfer, & Blum, 1973). Aging is also associated with defects in several attentional tasks including tasks of divided attention (Waugh & Barr, Chapter 15). Accordingly, one might suppose that the neuropathological correlates of aging might correspond to those of amnesia, insofar as the defects in memory resemble those in amnesia, but can be expected to involve other brain regions, insofar as there are other cognitive defects.

The neuropathological correlates of aging have been studied rather extensively, and the findings generally fit these expectations. Neurofibrillary tangles, together with senile plaques and granulovacuolar changes, constitute the neuropathological signs of Alzheimer's disease, the most common cause of presenile and senile dementia. These abnormalities are present, to some extent, in healthy, nondementing aged (Tomlinson, 1972). Neurofibrillary tangles and senile plaques are evident by the fifth decade of life. In the nondemented aging brain, neurofibrillary tangles occur almost exclusively in the hippocampus (Tomlinson, 1972). In later life, and especially in senescense, they are evident in neocortex (Scheibel & Scheibel, 1975), in prefrontal pyramidal cells, and in superior temporal cortex. Senile plaques are densest in the hippocampus but are also abundant in frontal, temporal, and occipital cortex (Brizee, Harkin, Ordy, & Kaack, 1975). An inverse correlation between neocortical plaque concentration and performance on cognitive tests has also been reported (Tomlinson, 1972; Tomlinson, Blessed & Roth, 1968). Granulovacuolar changes are largely limited to pyramidal cells of the hippocampus (Scheibel & Scheibel, 1975). Cell loss (Critchley, 1942; Scheibel & Scheibel, 1975) occurs most prominently in prefrontal areas and in the superior temporal region. A sequence of age-related changes in dendritic architecture has also been described (Scheibel & Scheibel, 1975). These changes involve a progressive loss of horizontally oriented dendrites, particularly in the basilar shafts, that lead to a loss of dendritic mass and eventual cell death. These changes are most prominent in the pyramidal cells of prefrontal and superior temporal cortex.

Although the neuropathological data reviewed here comes from both healthy and demented populations, it seems clear that the neuropathological changes accompanying aging do not constitute a global, diffuse process but one that involves some brain regions more than others. The hippocampal region seems more reactive to the aging process than any other structure. This finding is consistent with the neuropsychological observation that aging is accompanied by difficulty in forming new memories (Craik, 1977), and with the clinical observation that complaints about memory functions are common in the aged population. In cortex, the prefrontal and superior temporal regions appear to be disproportionately involved. Since a considerable body of information is available concerning the behavioral topography of focal brain dysfunction, the neuropsychological investigation of aging by Albert and Kaplan (Chapter 23) promises to teach us a great deal about how the neuropathology of aging reveals itself in behavior.

This brief discussion of memory and memory pathology has focused on anterograde and retrograde amnesia, memory complaints, and neuro-pathology. It seems reasonable that when this information has been assembled in the case of relatively pure amnesias, it can be useful in the exploration of memory dysfunction like that associated with aging, which occurs in the context of other cognitive defects. When considering the problem of memory and aging, it seems clear that there is much to recommend an interdisciplinary approach that includes neuroscience and neuropsychology along with experimental psychology.

ACKNOWLEDGMENTS

The work reported here was supported by the Medical Research Service of the Veterans Administration, by NIMH Grant MH24600, and by NIMH Mental Health Clinical Research Center Grant 1 P50 MH 30914 01. I thank Pamela Slater, Mary Fox, and Joy Beck for research assistance, and Dr. Douglas Wetzel and Neal Cohen for stimulating discussion.

REFERENCES

Albert, M. S., Butters, N., & Levin, J. Temporal gradients in the retrograde amnesia of patients with alcoholic Korsakoff disease. *Archives of Neurology,* 1979, *36,* 211-216.

Barbizet, J. *Human memory and its pathology.* Translated by D. K. Jardine. San Francisco: W. H. Freeman, 1970.

Bartlett, F. C. *Remembering.* Cambridge: Cambridge University Press, 1932.

Benson, D. F., Marsden, C. D., & Meadows, J. C. The amnesic syndrome of posterior cerebral artery occlusion. *Acta Neurologica Scandinavica,* 1974, *50,* 133-145.

Botwinick, J., & Storandt, M. *Memory, related functions and age.* Springfield, Ill.: Charles C. Thomas, 1974.

Brierly, J. B. Neuropathology of amnesic states. In C. W. M. Whitty & O. L. Zangeill (Eds.), *Amnesia.* London: Butterworths, 1970.

Brizee, K. R., Harkin, J. C., Ordy, J. M., & Kaack, B. Accumulation and distribution of lipofusin, amyloid and senile plaques in the aging nervous system. In H. Brody, D. Harman, & J. M. Ordy (Eds.), *Aging* (Vol. 1). New York: Raven Press, 1975.

Butters, N., & Cermak, L. S. Some analyses of amnesic syndromes in brain-damaged patients. In *The hippocampus, Vol. 2: Neurophysiology and behavior.* New York: Plenum Press, 1975.

Butters, N., & Pandya, D. Retention of delayed-alteration: Effect of selective lesions of sulcus principalis. *Science,* 1969, *165,* 1271-1273.

Cermak, L. S., & Reale, L. Depth of processing and retention of words by alcoholic Korsakoff patients. *Journal of Experimental Psychology: Human Learning and Memory,* 1978, *4,* 165-174.

Craik, F. I. M. Age differences in human memory. In J. E. Birren & K. W. Schaie (Eds.), *Handbook of the Psychology of Aging.* New York: Van Nostrand Reinhold Company, 1977.

Craik, F. I. M., & Tulving, E. Depth of processing and the retention of words in episodic memory. *Journal of Experimental Psychology,* 1975, *104,* 268-294.

Critchley, M. Aging of the nervous system. In E. V. Cowdrey (Ed.), *Problems of aging* (2nd ed.). Baltimore: Williams & Wilkins, 1942.

Cronholm, B., & Blomquist, C. Memory disturbances after electroconvulsive therapy. 2. Conditions one week after a series of treatments. *Acta Psychiatrica Scandinavica,* 1959, *34,* 18-25.

Cronholm, B., & Ottosson, J. O. Memory functions in endogenous depression. *Archives of General Psychiatry,* 1961, *5,* 101-107.

Delay, J., & Brion, S. Syndrome de Korsakoff et corps mamillaires *Encephale,* 1954, *43,* 193-200.

Fink, M. *Convulsive Therapy: Theory and Practice.* Raven Press, New York, 1979.

Gruner, J. E. Sur la pathologie des encephalopthies alcooliques. *Revue Neurologique,* 1956, *94,* 682-689.

Grunthal, E. Ueber das corpus mamillare und den Korsalowschen symtomenkomplex. *Confinia Neurologica,* 1939, *2,* 64-95.

Horel, J. The neuroanatomy of amnesia. *Brain,* 1978, *101,* 403-445.

Ignelzi, R. J., & Squire, L. R. Recovery from anterograde and retrograde amnesia after percutaneous drainage of a cystic craniopharyngioma. *Journal of Neurology, Neurosurgery, and Psychiatry,* 1976, *39,* 1231-1235.

Jarvik, L. F., Eisdorfer, C., & Blum, J. E. *Intellectual functioning in adults.* New York: Springer, 1973.

Kandel, E. R. *Cellular basis of behavior.* New York: Freeman, 1976.

Lashley, K. S. In search of the engram. *Symposia of the Society for Experimental Biology,* 1950, *4,* 454–482.

Marslen-Wilson, W. D., & Teuber, H. L. Memory for remote events in anterograde amnesia: Recognition of public figures from newsphotographs. *Neuropsychologia,* 1975, *13,* 353–364.

McAndrew, J., Berkey, B., & Matthews, C. The effects of dominant and nondominant unilateral ECT. *American Journal of Psychiatry,* 1967, *124,* 483–490.

McGaugh, J. L., & Herz, M. J. *Memory consolidation.* San Francisco: Albion, 1972.

Milner, B. Disorders of learning and memory after temporal lobe lesions in man. *Clinical Neurosurgery,* 1972, *19,* 421–446.

Mishkin, M. Memory in monkeys severely impaired by combined but not by separate removal of amygdala and hippocampus. *Nature,* 1978, *273,* 297–298.

Norman, D. A., & Rumelhart, D. E. *Explorations in cognition.* San Francisco: Freeman, 1975.

Penfield, W., & Milner, B. Memory deficit produced by bilateral lesions in the hippocampal zone. *A.M.A. Archives of Neurology and Psychiatry,* 1958, *79,* 475–497.

Remy, M. Contribution a l'étude de la maladie de Korsakow. *Monatsschrift fuer Psychiatrie und Neurologie,* 1942, *106,* 128–144.

Ribot, T. *Diseases of memory.* New York: Appleton, 1882.

Rose, F. C., & Symonds, C. P. Persistent memory defect following encephalitis. *Brain,* 1960, *83,* (part 2), 195–212.

Russell, W. R., & Nathan, P. W. Traumatic amnesia. *Brain,* 1946, *69,* 280–300.

Sanders, H., & Warrington, E. K. Memory for remote events in amnesic patients. *Brain,* 1971, *94,* 661–668.

Scheibel, M. E., & Scheibel, A. B. Structural changes in the aging brain. In H. Brody, D. Harman, & J. M. Ordy (Eds.), *Aging.* New York: Raven Press, 1975.

Scoville, W. B., & Milner, B. Loss of recent memory after bilateral hippocampal lesions. *Journal of Neurology, Neurosurgery and Psychiatry,* 1957, *20,* 11–21.

Seltzer, B., & Benson, D. F. The temporal pattern of retrograde amnesia in Korsakoff's disease. *Neurology,* 1974, *24,* 527–530.

Squire, L. R. A stable impairment in remote memory following electroconvulsive therapy. *Neuropsychologia,* 1975, *13,* 51–58. (a)

Squire, L. R. Remote memory as affected by aging. *Neuropsychologia,* 1974, *12,* 429–435.

Squire, L. R. Short-term memory as a biological entity. In J. A. Deutsch, & D. Deutsch (Eds.), *Short-term memory.* New York: Academic Press, 1975. (b)

Squire, L. R. ECT and memory loss. *American Journal of Psychiatry,* 1977, *134,* 997–1001.

Squire, L. R. Specifying the defect in human amnesia: storage, retrieval and semantics. *Neuropsychologia,* 1980, in press.

Squire, L. R., & Chace, P. M. Memory functions six to nine months after electroconvulsive therapy. *Archives of General Psychiatry,* 1975, *32,* 1557–1564.

Squire, L. R., Chace, P. M., & Slater, P. C. Assessment of memory for remote events. *Psychology Reports,* 1975, *37,* 223–234.

Squire, L. R., Chace, P. M., & Slater, P. C. Retrograde amnesia following electroconvulsive therapy. *Nature,* 1976, *260,* 775–777.

Squire, L. R., & Cohen, N. Memory and amnesia: resistance to disruption develops for years after learning. *Behavioral and Neural Biology,* 1979, in press.

Squire, L. R., & Cohen, N. Remote memory, retrograde amnesia, and the neuropsychology of memory. In L. Cermak (Ed.), *Memory and Amnesia,* Lawrence Erlbaum Associates, Hillsdale, N.J., 1980, in press.

Squire, L. R., & Moore, R. Y. Dorsal thalamic lesion in a noted case of human memory dysfunction. *Annals of Neurology,* 1979, *6,* 503–506.

Squire, L. R., & Schlapfer, W. T. Memory and memory disorders: A biological and neurological perspective. In H. M. Van Praag, M. H. Lader, O. J. Rafaelsen, & E. J. Sachar (Eds.),

Handbook of biological psychiatry: Brain mechanisms and abnormal behavior (Vol. 2). Netherlands: Marcel Dikker, 1980.

Squire, L. R., & Slater, P. C. Forgetting in very long-term memory as assessed by an improved questionnaire technique. *Journal of Experimental Psychology: Human Learning and Memory,* 1975, *104,* 50–54.

Squire, L. R., & Slater, P. C. Remote memory in chronic anterograde amnesia. *Behavioral Biology,* 1977, *20,* 398–403.

Squire, L. R., & Slater, P. C. Verbal and non-verbal memory as affected by bilateral and unilateral ECT. *American Journal of Psychiatry,* 1978, *135:11,* 1316–1320. (b)

Squire, L. R., & Slater, P. C. Anterograde and retrograde memory impairment in chronic amnesia. *Neuropsychologia,* 1978, *16,* 313–322. (a)

Squire, L. R., Slater, P. C., & Chace, P. M. Retrograde amnesia: Temporal gradient in very long-term memory following electroconvulsive therapy. *Science,* 1975, *187,* 77–79.

Squire, L. R., Slater, P. C., & Miller, P. L. Retrograde amnesia following ECT: long-term follow-up studies. *Archives of General Psychiatry,* 1980, in press.

Squire, L. R., Wetzel, C. D., & Slater, P. C. Memory complaint after electroconvulsive therapy: assessment with a new self-rating instrument. *Biological Psychiatry, 14,* 1979, 791–801.

Starr, A., & Phillips, L. Verbal and motor memory in the amnestic syndrome. *Neuropsychologia,* 1970, *8,* 75–88.

Sternberg, D. E., & Jarvik, M. E. Memory functions in depression. *Archives of General Psychiatry,* 1976, *33,* 219–224.

Talland, G. A. *Deranged memory.* New York: Academic Press, 1965.

Teuber, H. L., Milner, B., & Vaughan, H. G. Persistent anterograde amnesia after stab wound of the basal brain. *Neuropsychologia,* 1968, *6,* 267–282.

Tomlinson, B. E. Morphological brain changes in non-demented old people. In H. M. Van Praag & A. K. Kalverbocr (Eds.), *Aging of the central nervous system* (Vol. 1). New York: De Evron F. Bohn, 1972.

Tomlinson, B. E., Blessed, G., & Roth, M. Observations in the brain of nondemented old people. *Journal of Neurological Science,* 1968, *7,* 331–356.

Valenstein, E. S., & Nauta, W. J. H. A comparison of the fornix system in the rat, guinea pig, cat and monkey. *Journal of Comparative Neurology,* 1959, *113,* 337–363.

Van Buren, J. M., & Borke, R. C. The mesial temporal substratum of memory. Anatomical study in three individuals. *Brain,* 1972, *95,* 599–632.

Victor, M., Adams, R., & Collins, G. In F. Plum & F. H. McDowell (Eds.), *The Wernicke-Korsakoff syndrome.* Philadelphia: F. A. Davis, 1971.

Warren, J. M., & Akert, K. *The frontal granular cortex and behavior.* New York: McGraw-Hill, 1964.

Warrington, E. K., & Sanders, H. The fate of old memories. *Quarterly Journal of Experimental Psychology,* 1971, *23,* 432–442.

Warrington, E. K., & Silbertstein, M. S. A questionnaire technique for investigating very long-term memory. *Quarterly Journal of Experimental Psychology,* 1970, *22,* 508–512.

Wechsler, D. A standardized memory scale for clinical use. *Journal of Psychology,* 1945, *19,* 87–95.

Wells, C. E. *Dementia.* Philadelphia: F. A. Davis, 1977.

Wetzel, C. D. and Squire, L. R. Encoding in anterograde amnesia. *Neuropsychologia,* 1980, in press.

Williams, M., & Pennybacker, J. Memory disturbances in third ventricle tumours. *Journal of Neurology, Neurosurgery and Psychiatry,* 1954, *17,* 115–123.

25

Potential Contributions of Neuropsychology to our Understanding of the Memory Capacities of the Elderly

Nelson Butters
Boston Veterans Administration Medical Center and
Boston University School of Medicine

On a superficial level the preceding chapters by Erickson, Poon, and Walsh-Sweeney (Chapter 22) and Albert and Kaplan (Chapter 23) would seem unrelated to each other. Erickson et al. lament the current status of memory assessment in the elderly and offer a list of admonishments to those who would intrepidly approach this problem. On the other hand, Albert and Kaplan provide us with a prescription, along with some provoking illustrations, for the neuropsychological assessment of cognitive changes in the elderly. Fortunately, the unrelatedness or conflict between these two chapters is more apparent than real, and it will be my contribution to demonstrate that these chapters actually complement each other and to illustrate from studies of amnesia and dementia how Albert and Kaplan's neuropsychological prescription can cure the ills so clearly delineated by Erickson et al.

Erickson and his colleagues note three disturbing and valid problems that now characterize clinical evaluations of aging populations. One, the results of such testing do not answer "needed questions" about etiology, prognosis, and remediation. An M.Q. (based on the Wechsler Memory Scale) of 75 tells us nothing about the source of this memory dysfunction, the future course of the impairment, or the appropriate therapeutic strategies for relieving or circumventing the patient's deficit. Such a score only informs us that the patient cannot learn some new materials at the present time. Two, the specific tests used with the elderly have often ignored "total person assessment," and there has been a lack of development of "age-fair" tests. The elderly exhibit a great deal of between- and within-individual variability on memory tests due to a number of social and physical factors and are generally disadvantaged on memory tests that stress their speed of sensory and motor functioning. An elderly individual with intact retention and retrieval capacities might perform poorly on a given memory task because of a depressed mood or because the stimulus materials were presented too rapidly to allow proper encoding. Three, the memory batteries that have been employed have focused on a restricted segment of the total memory spectrum. No single battery includes verbal, nonverbal, and motor learning, long-term retention, iconic memory, short-term memory, memory for remote events, and encoding strategies. As Erickson et al. note, only such a complete battery, presented in an "age-fair" manner, can provide a thorough assessment of memory processes in aging populations.

While Albert and Kaplan's chapter deals with neuropsychological testing in general, its emphasis upon process-achievement analyses may be applied specifically to the evaluation of memory. For a neuropsychological test to illuminate underlying processes (neuroanatomical and psychological), it must be sensitive to disruption of specific hemispheres, lobes, and subcortical structures and must allow "qualitative" analyses of both successes and failures. As a hypothetical example of a process-achievement approach to memory, let us assume that three elderly patients all perform poorly on a memory-for-designs task. Knowledge that all three individuals earned low scores relates nothing about the processes involved in their failures, and thereby illustrates the very problems discussed by Erickson et al. However, if the test has been properly designed and analyzed, important distinctions among the "memory deficits" of the three individuals may emerge. One patient's impairment may reflect an inability to remember the internal details of the figures while accurately reproducing the overall configuration or "gestalt" of the design. A second individual may accurately remember many of the internal features but fail to reproduce the external configuration or general shape of the design. In contrast to the other two patients, the third individual may encounter no difficulty with either the internal or external features of the designs, but may fail because of his perseverative tendencies. That is, when asked to reproduce the fifth design on the test, the third patient may accurately reproduce the fourth design in the series.

Such differences in the three patients' performances provide us with important clues as to the nature of their "memory" deficits. The first patient may have a left-hemisphere lesion that limits his encoding and analysis of internal details, while the second individual may have some right-hemisphere abnormality that prevents a full synthesis of detailed stimuli. If one accepts the validity of much of the amnesia literature (Butters & Cermak, 1975, 1976; Warrington & Weiskrantz, 1970, 1973), the third patient may have a subcortical limbic lesion that has left him very sensitive to proactive interference.

The example just cited was by necessity hypothetical because such analyses of the memory problems of the aged have not been attempted. Happily this dearth of analyses focusing upon underlying processes does *not* extend to the general study of amnesia. Many investigators have been attempting to uncover the nature of amnesia by applying concepts and tests borrowed from studies of normal information processing (for review, see Piercy, 1978). While these studies have been motivated by theoretical issues, the results have had important clinical implications directly related to the issues raised by Erickson et al. and by Albert and Kaplan. To provide the reader with some indication of what these process-achievement analyses might accomplish if applied to the memory problems of the aged, I now quickly review some recent studies comparing the memory impairments of amnesic and dementing patients.

The amnesic patients used in these studies were alcoholic Korsakoffs; the dementing patients had Huntington's Disease (HD). Both of these groups have been described extensively in previous publications (Butters & Cermak, 1976; Butters, Sax, Montgomery, & Tarlow, 1978). Briefly, the Korsakoff patients had severe anterograde and retrograde amnesias related to long-term alcohol abuse and malnutrition but were otherwise intellectually intact as judged by standardized psychometric tests (e.g., WAIS). The HD patients also evidenced severe memory problems on clinical examination, but their memory disorder was only one feature of a general intellectual decline (i.e., progressive dementia). HD is genetically transmitted and also characterized by involuntary choreic movements. The two patient groups were matched for age and educational background.

Fig. 25.1 shows the performance of HD and alcoholic Korsakoff patients and of a group of alcoholic (non-Korsakoff) control subjects on a test of short-term memory that employed the Peterson distractor technique (Peterson & Peterson, 1959). The patients were presented with the to-be-recalled material (a single word) and then distracted from rehearsing this information until recall was signalled. The distractor task was counting backwards from 100 by two's or three's for 0, 3, 9, or 18 sec. It is evident in Fig. 25.1 that both HD patients and the amnesic Korsakoffs were severely impaired in comparison to the alcoholic control subjects. Similar results were found when three words (word triads) and three consonants (consonant trigrams) were the to-be-remembered materials (Butters, Tarlow, Cermak, & Sax, 1976).

Despite the quantitative similarity in their short-term memory (STM) scores, an analysis of the types of errors made by the two patient groups indicated that their failures may reflect different processing problems. Meudell, Butters, and Montgomery (1978) distinguished three types of errors—omission errors, prior-item intrusions, extra-list intrusions—on a distractor task using word triads as the stimulus material. An omission error was a failure to respond with any words ("I can't remember the words"). A prior-item intrusion was a word(s) that had been presented on a previous trial. For example, if "fish" was one of the to-be-remembered words on Trial 1 but

SINGLE WORDS

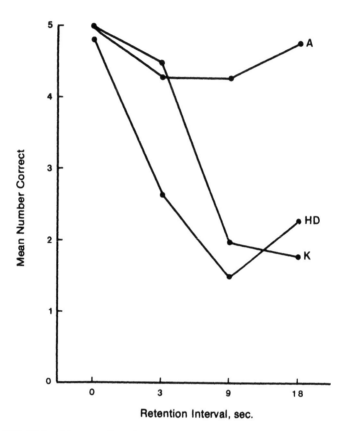

FIG. 25.1.   Mean number of words recalled on Peterson distractor task with single words as the to-be-recalled materials. A = alcoholic controls, HD = patients with Huntington's Disease, K = amnesic alcoholic Korsakoff patients.

continued to be given as an answer on Trials 2 and 3, the patient was credited with two prior-item intrusion errors. Errors labeled extra-list intrusions were responses that were not among the stimulus words comprising the test. As shown in Fig. 25.2, the HD and Korsakoff patients accumulated approximately the same number of total errors on this short-term memory task, but the two groups can be dissociated according to the types of errors they made. While the amnesic Korsakoff patients had many prior-item intrusions, the HD patients made primarily omission errors. Neither patient group produced many extra-list intrusions.

This dissociation of the two groups provides some hints as to the nature of their short-term memory impairments. The Korsakoffs' intrusion errors suggest that their memory deficits are related to an increased sensitivity to

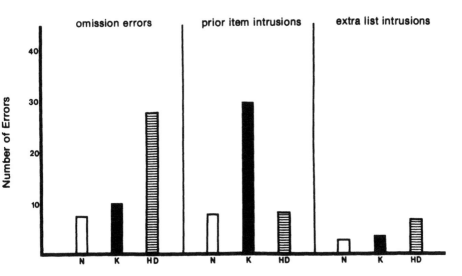

FIG. 25.2.   Types of errors on Peterson distractor task with word triads as the to-be-recalled materials. N = normal controls, K = amnesic alcoholic Korsakoff patients, HD = patients with Huntington's Disease.

proactive interference (PI), while the lack of prior-item intrusions for the HD patients indicates that interference may not be an important factor in their impaired memory performance.

Two experiments in which the amount of PI in the test situation was manipulated offer further confirmation that the dementing HD patients' memory impairment is not related to interference (Butters et al., 1976). Fig. 25.3 shows the results of a study in which short-term memory (with the Peterson technique) was evaluated under massed (high PI) and distributed (low PI) presentation conditions. During massed presentation, a 6-sec rest interval was interspersed between trials, and during distributed presentation, a 1-min rest interval intervened between Peterson trials. It is well known from studies of normal human learning that distributed practice allows interference to dissipate and to have little effect upon new learning. The results of this experiment show that with distributed presentation the Korsakoff patients did significantly better than did the HD patients, but with massed presentation the HD patients recalled more items than did the Korsakoff patients, although both groups were impaired in comparison to the alcoholic controls. The Korsakoffs and the alcoholic controls, but not the HD patients, were aided by the reduction in interference with distributed presentation of the stimuli.

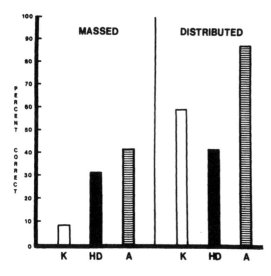

FIG. 25.3. Performance of amnesic Korsakoff patients (K), patients with Huntington's Disease (HD), and alcoholic controls (A) on a Peterson distractor task with massed (6-sec) and distributed (1-min) presentation of trials.

An identical outcome occurred in a second experiment manipulating the amount of PI in the learning situation (Butters et al., 1976). On this occasion, the Peterson trials were divided into blocks of two with a 6-sec interval between trials. By varying the similarity of the material presented on the two trials, it was possible to manipulate the amount of PI influencing the patients' recall on the second trial of each block. For instance, with high PI conditions, word triads were the materials presented on the first and second trials of each block. With low PI conditions, a consonant trigram (e.g., "JQL") was presented on the first trial and a word triad on the second trial of each block. In comparison to the three words, three consonants on the first trial of each block are less likely to interfere with the recall of the three words on the second trial. The results of this second experiment (i.e., the subjects' performance on the second trial of each block) showed again that the Korsakoff patients performed very poorly under high PI conditions (word triads on both trials) but improved significantly with conditions that minimized PI (consonant trigrams on the first trial, word triads on the second). However, the HD patients did not demonstrate a similar improvement. Although the Korsakoff and HD patients recalled the same number of words with high PI conditions, the Korsakoffs recalled significantly more words than did the HD patients with low PI conditions.

Amnesic Korsakoff and HD patients also differ in the degree to which rehearsal will benefit their performance on a Peterson short-term memory task. Butters and Grady (1977) employed a modified Peterson task in which a delay of 0, 2, or 4 sec intervened between presentation of the to-be-recalled word triads (three words) and the beginning of the distractor procedure. Thus, on a given trial, a word triad was presented and then a delay interval of 0, 2, or 4 sec passed before the subject started the distractor task. The 2-sec and 4-sec predistractor delays were used to allow the patients additional time to rehearse the verbal stimuli. The results (Fig. 25.4) indicated that while the predistractor delays led to improved recall for the amnesic Korsakoff patients, this experimental manipulation had virtually no effect upon the HD patients. It appears then that the dementing HD patients could not utilize a predistractor delay for productive rehearsal that would improve their recall.

The findings of these studies strongly suggest that the information-processing deficits underlying the HD patients' anterograde amnesia are qualitatively different from those involved in the impairments of amnesic Korsakoff patients. While it is evident that the amnesic patients are highly sensitive to proactive interference and have serious limitations in their analyses of stimulus materials, the specific nature of the HD patients' processing problems is not clear. One possibility is that the HD patients simply cannot store (i.e., consolidate) new information. The HD patients' failure to improve with low interference conditions and with increased time for rehearsal is consistent with the notion that these dementing patients may

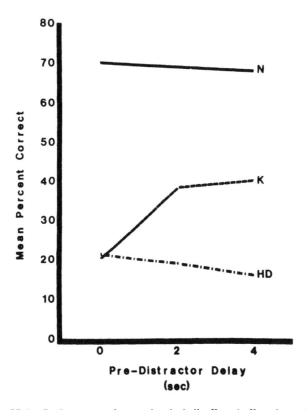

FIG. 25.4. Performance of amnesic alcoholic Korsakoff patients (K), patients with Huntington's Disease (HD), and normal controls (N) on short-term memory test with predistractor delays of 0, 2, and 4 sec.

lack some of the neuroanatomical structures necessary for storing new information.

This example of an information-processing approach to memory has focused upon the performance of only two patient groups (alcoholic Korsakoffs, patients with HD) on a single task (Peterson distractor technique). These limitations were deliberate to underline what a process-achievement analysis can accomplish when applied to abnormal memory. While both the amnesic and dementing populations were severely impaired on short-term memory tasks, a search for the processes underlying their deficits illuminated important qualitative differences in the patients' memory disorders. When one attempted to analyze types of errors and to manipulate the learning conditions, it became evident that the amnesic and the dementing patients failed the Peterson task for different reasons. Such information provides us not only with new theoretical knowledge but also with some clinical insights for diagnosis and rehabilitation.

The extrapolation of this process-achievement approach to the clinical assessment of memory disorders in the elderly is obvious. As Erickson et al. have noted, a simple quantitative score or M.Q. provides little insight into the nature of the elderly individual's memory problems. If the clinician is to answer "needed questions" about etiology, prognosis, and remediation, he must know whether a low M.Q. or failure on a short-term memory task is due to problems with interference, encoding, retrieval, or storage. It is now possible to construct the battery of memory tests suggested by Erickson et al., but it is imperative that these tests be analyzed in the manner described by Albert and Kaplan. If the cautiousness of Erickson et al. is combined with the innovative neuropsychological approach of Albert and Kaplan, we may not have to bemoan much longer our evaluations of the memory disorders of the elderly.

ACKNOWLEDGMENT

The research reported in these studies was supported by funds from the Veterans Administration Medical Research Service from NIAAA Grant 00187 to Boston University.

REFERENCES

Butters, N., & Cermak, L. Some analyses of amnesic syndromes in brain-damaged patients. In K. Pribram & R. Isaacson (Eds.), *The hippocampus.* New York: Plenum Press, 1975.

Butters, N., & Cermak, L. Neuropsychological studies of alcoholic Korsakoff patients. Edited by G. Goldstein & C. Neuringer (Eds.), *Empirical studies of alcoholism.* Cambridge: Ballinger Press, 1976.

Butters, N., Tarlow, S., Cermak, L., & Sax, D. A comparison of the information processing deficits of patients with Huntington's Chorea and Korsakoff's syndrome. *Cortex*, 1976, *12*, 134–144.

Butters, N., & Grady, M. Effect of predistractor delays on the short-term memory performance of patients with Korsakoff's and Huntington's Disease. *Neuropsychologia*, 1977, *13*, 701–705.

Butters, N., Sax, D., Montgomery, K., & Tarlow, S. Comparison of the neuropsychological deficits associated with early and advanced Huntington's Disease. *Archives of Neurology*, 1978, *35*, 585–589.

Meudell, P., Butters, N., & Montgomery, K. Role of rehearsal in the short-term memory performance of patients with Korsakoff's and Huntington's Disease. *Neuropsychologia*, 1978, *16*, 507–510.

Peterson, L. R., & Peterson, M. J. Short-term retention of individual verbal items. *Journal of Experimental Psychology*, 1959, *58*, 193–198.

Piercy, M. Experimental studies of the organic amnesic syndrome. In C. W. M. Whitty & O. L. Zangwill (Eds.), *Amnesia* (2nd ed.). London: Butterworths, 1978.

Warrington, E. K., & Weiskrantz, L. Amnesic syndrome: Consolidation or retrieval? *Nature*, 1970, *228*, 628–630.

Warrington, E. K., & Weiskrantz, L. An analysis of short-term and lone-term memory defects in man. In J. A. Deutsch (Ed.), *The physiological basis of memory*. New York: Academic Press, 1973.

26 Memory Skill Training for the Elderly: Salient Issues on the Use of Imagery Mnemonics

Leonard W. Poon
Leslie Walsh-Sweeney
James L. Fozard
Veterans Administration Outpatient Clinic, Boston

The experimental data reviewed in the previous chapters show measurable age-related decline in the acquisition, storage, and retrieval of information. In view of this general decreased functioning of the memory system, a question of considerable practical importance needs to be addressed: Can the elderly learn memory techniques to sustain and improve their memory abilities?

Available memory techniques can be divided into verbal and visual (or imagery) mnemonics. This chapter is limited to a consideration of the application of the latter to the memory problems of the elderly.

The mental image has been conceptualized as functioning in two ways. First, it has been hypothesized (cf. Plato and Aristotle in Boring, 1950; Titchner, 1909) that memorized information is stored holistically as stimulus traces or images on a "wax tablet." Second, images have been conceptualized as having associative value for mediating various ideas and thoughts. Roman and Greek orators and messengers used this association concept to learn and retrieve long and complicated speeches by relating specific information with a sequence of familiar loci, such as the rooms in their houses.

The study of imagery waned in the early 1900s. The loss of interest was due partly to the downfall of introspectionalism and structuralism and the ascendance of Watson's (1928) empiricism. The decline was due also, in part, to the wide range of individual differences found in the quality of imagery and imagery abilities (Galton, 1880). Watson (1928) criticized imagery as being a mere "ghost of sensation" because of the lack of empirical evidence that images have any functional significance.

The incorporation of imagery as a theoretical construct in behavioral theories emerged again in the 1930s. The notion of memory traces was evident in classical learning theories such as Hull's (1931) postulation of a fractional anticipatory goal response, and in Tolman's (1932) cognitive map theory. Imagery concepts enjoyed a full revival when Neisser (1972) stated that imagery is germane to both perception and memory. Recent experimental data (Kosslyn, Reiser, & Ball, 1978; Podgorny & Shepard, 1978) have shown that imagery and actual perception share common psychological and physiological pathways.

Although the importance of imagery as a crucial construct in memory, perception, and problem-solving behavior has come full circle since the early part of the 20th century, the investigation of memory techniques has remained a peripheral area of interest among psychologists. Recently, however, Murdock (1974) suggested that the study of individuals with exceptionally good memories and the evaluation of mnemonic methods effectively utilized by people with normal memories would help pave the way toward understanding the mechanics of memory.

The importance of the study of mnemonics for both practical and theoretical concerns has been stated most succintly by Norman (1969):

> Throughout the centuries man has been concerned with the practical art of memory. Everyone knows that normally it is difficult to memorize things. Yet a few people have always known special techniques that make the task possible with apparent ease. We tend to ignore these techniques today because they are mere tricks and sophistry—the practitioners exhibit themselves as stage entertainers or advertise themselves and their methods in unrespectable classified advertisements-- but we cannot deny that the techniques work. In fact, we ought to examine procedures that simplify the job of memorizing with great care. Not only might they be useful in our lives, but the secrets of those who practice the art of memory ought to shed some light on the organization and operation of the mechanisms involved in memory [p. 98].

Norman's comments are pertinent to the identification of memory improvement techniques for the aged. It is important to identify changes in the processes that lead to age-related decline in memory performance. It is also important to isolate mnemonics that can sustain and improve the memory functioning of the elderly. Description, explanation, and optimization of behavior in aging adults are three interrelated goals that may substantially assist the development of psychological theories of aging (Baltes & Willis, 1977).

Elderly individuals are usually aware of their memory loss (Lowenthal, Berkman, Buehler, Pierce, Robinson, & Trier, 1967). Declining memory abilities may serve to compound and magnify other existing or developing problems. Application of effective mnemonic methods not only may serve to improve the memory of the elderly but also could have an important impact on their standard of daily functioning.

This chapter examines the effectiveness of visual mnemonics for responding to the memory problems of the elderly. Toward this end, a review of both published and unpublished research efforts is presented first. Then several salient issues associated with utilizing imagery as a clinical tool are identified and discussed.

EXPERIMENTAL EVIDENCE OF IMAGERY EFFECTS

General Findings. The imagery effect primarily has been demonstrated with college subjects (cf. Bower, 1970). In contrast, only a comparatively small number of mnemonic studies have been carried out with children, elderly persons, or with patients with memory disorders.

The exceptional retention capability of young adults using imagery techniques was demonstrated in a study by Wallace, Turner, and Perkins (1960), using a paired-associate learning paradigm. Subjects using visual mnemonics could recall 99% of 500 pairs of associates each seen only once. When the number of pairs was increased to 700, subjects could identify 95% of the pairs.

The type of imagery used by a learner has been shown to have an impact on memory performance. Bower (1970) reported that subjects using interacting images[1] recalled 53% of the paired associates; subjects using non-interacting images[2] recalled 27%, while subjects using a rote repetition learning strategy recalled 30%. However, when a recognition procedure was used, there was no between-group difference: All subjects correctly recognized about 87%. Bower (1970) interpreted the data as support for the hypothesis that interactive imagery enhances the "associative effectiveness" during the retrieval process.

A review of the literature shows that the performance of subjects given visual mnemonics instruction for learning concrete information is reliably facilitated compared to the performance of subjects not provided with imagery instructions. Furthermore, the effects of interactive imagery instruction on recall have been shown to be about twice as large as noninteractive instruction. The mnemonic advantage of interactive imagery seems to be fairly reliable for imagined configurations and experimenter-provided drawings (Bower, 1970, 1972; Bower & Winzenz, 1970; Wollen, Weber, & Lowry, 1972), for intentional and incidental learning (Rowe &

---

[1]An interacting image depicts (1) flow of action between elements of the image—e.g., a dog chewing a ball; or (2) structural unity between the elements of the image—e.g., a dog made out of wood.

[2]A noninteracting or spatially separate image depicts two or more elements which are not in physical contact, and between which little or no action is evident—e.g., a dog is sitting next to a ball.

Paivio, 1971; Sheehan, 1971), and for cued recall and cued recognition (Bower, 1972; Winograd, Karchner, & Russell, 1971).

In three experiments, Buggie (1974) systematically evaluated the mnemonic advantage of interactive imagery. In one experiment, he varied the number of different mediators[3] in the lists of noun pairs to be learned by the subjects. He found that recall improved when a different mediator was used to learn each noun pair, compared to when the same mediator was used throughout the list or when several mediators were used repetitively in the list.

In a second experiment, Buggie used different mediators for each noun pair and manipulated the degree of action transfer indicated by the mediator. He found that any degree of action transfer between the nouns pairs was a more effective mnemonic than a spatially separate mediator.

The third experiment replicated the design of the second, except that one interactive mediator or one spatially separate mediator was used repetitively. Under these conditions, interactive mediators were no more effective in assisting recall than spatially separate mediators.

Buggie concluded that his set of experiments suggested an explanation for the mnemonic advantage of interactive imagery. According to Buggie, there are hundreds of verbs potentially available to convey an interacting relationship, whereas there is only a small set of words (usually prepositions and conjunctions) appropriate for conveying a spatially separate relationship. Moreover, the number of spatially separate mediators is restricted even further by the fact that several members of the set (e.g., beside, to the left of, next to) convey similar meanings. Consequently, it is easier for a person to employ a unique interactive mediator than it is to employ a unique spatially separate mediator. Buggie suggested that the uniqueness of the relationship yields the better performance because the association is less prone to interference by other associations.

Patient Populations. Because imagery mnemonics facilitate recall of single items and paired associates for healthy college individuals, it is reasonable to investigate whether imagery techniques can improve the memory functioning of patients with dominant hemispheric lesions. The literature reviewed provides encouraging evidence that visual mnemonics can improve the memory abilities of patients with unilateral brain damage; however, only limited success has been reported with patients with generalized amnesic syndromes.

Patten (1972) investigated the facilitative effects of a peg-word mnemonic in a case study of seven adult patients with diagnosed memory deficits. First, patients memorized a peg-word list (e.g., *one* is a *radio, two* is an

---

[3]A mediator is a word or phrase (usually a verb, preposition or conjunction) used to establish relationship(s) between elements to be imagined.

airplane, . . . ten is a *watch).* Once the list was memorized, the patients were taught to associate each peg-word with a to-be-remembered item by forming a bizarre interacting image. This method was used to teach the patients to remember lists of U.S. Presidents, grocery items, etc. The recall sequence started with the number (e.g., one); the number was linked with a peg-word (e.g., radio) which was then linked to the peg image (e.g., George Washington changing the station on a radio). Once the patient mastered the basic system, the patient was taught additional peg-words linked to numbers from 11 to 100, and subsequently was tested for recall of longer lists of items. Patients were encouraged to show off their new memory skills once they had mastered the system.

Four patients with dominant hemispheric lesions and poor verbal memory were able to master the system and improve their memory performances. Initial memory testing of these patients revealed:

1. A general pattern of disorientation for time and dates.
2. A forward digit span of about seven and difficulty with backward digits.
3. Ineffective utilization of cues.
4. Fairly good memory for colloquial information, but poor recall of work-related information.
5. Poor recall of verbal information when a distraction task was interposed between presentation and retrieval.

After four weeks of memory therapy, these patients showed improvement in their ability to remember series of items. (Some could master up to 100 items.) Furthermore, they generalized and transferred the system to everyday memory demands such as grocery lists and appointments. In addition, improvement in other impaired abilities (e.g., in the ability to communicate verbally) and improvement in the patients' self-esteem were reported.

Three other patients with poor performances on memory tests did not improve significantly. One patient had diagnosed Alzheimer's disease, one had a third ventricular tumor, and the other had problems with recent memory after operative clipping of an aneurysm located in an anterior communicating artery. It was observed that these patients could not form vivid images. Furthermore, they were not aware of their memory deficits or interested in improving memory functioning.

Patten (1972) showed that memory therapy using the peg-word system could help improve the memory for some patients with abnormal memory functioning. These case studies, however, did not adequately differentiate the effects of visual mnemonics, the amount of attention, the duration of practice, and the motivation and background of the patients.

A systematic, controlled study was reported by Jones (1974), who examined the effect of imagery mnemonics on paired associate learning with adult left- and right-temporal-lobectomy patients and patients with bilateral mesial temporal lobe lesions. Normal subjects matched on age and sex were used as controls.

Three lists of 10 paired associates were used for each group. The first list was used for baseline assessment. The second was used with imagery instructions and pictures depicting the paired associates. The subjects generated their own images on the third list with no imagery instructions. Recall on all three lists was measured 2 hr after each task commenced.

As expected, the left-temporal-lobe group performed significantly worse than both the right-temporal lobe and control groups on all of these paired associate tasks. Interestingly, the left-temporal-lobe group significantly improved and maintained their improved performance level after receiving imagery instructions. The performance of these patients with left-temporal-lobe damage indicates that imagery may facilitate recall of verbal information.

Because their spatial abilities were impaired, the right-temporal-lobe group was expected to perform significantly worse compared to normal controls with imagery instructions. However, the results showed that their performance was equal to or slightly worse than that of the controls. Jones (1974) postulated that the paired-associate learning list might have been too easy for right-temporal-lobe subjects, with the result that a significant performance difference could not be obtained between patients and normals. It also is possible that these subjects used verbal mnemonics to compensate for the lack of spatial and imagery abilities.

Although patients with bilateral mesial-temporal-lobe lesions understood the imagery instructions and could describe the images, they were unable to improve their performances on immediate-recall tasks with imagery instructions. These patients could not retrieve any items in any lists for immediate or delayed recall.

Baddeley and Warrington (1973) substantiated Jones' (1974) findings with bilateral-lesion patients in a list-learning study with adult amnesic patients with no impairment other than memory dysfunction. The performance of these amnesic subjects was compared to that of control subjects with peripheral nerve lesions. Control and experimental subjects were matched on age, sex, and intelligence. The subjects performed the following tasks: recall of phonemic and taxonomic clustered lists, recall of lists from different categories, and recall of an unrelated list of words using visual images.

The overall performance of the amnesic subjects was significantly worse than the control subjects. All subjects performed significantly better with the phonemically and taxonomically clustered lists. Two pertinent findings were specifically relevant to the amnesic subjects. First, although the amnesics could form visual images, they derived no benefit from the imagery instruction in recall tasks. Second, these subjects could take advantage of phonemic and category cueing to improve their memory. Verbal mnemonics were shown to be beneficial for the subjects, a finding consistent with those reported by Warrington and Weiskrant (1971).

Lewinsohn, Danaher, and Kikel (1977) have reported imagery facilitation effects with brain-damaged adult patients. In addition, imagery facilitation effects have been reported with the educable mentally retarded (Lebrato & Ellis, 1974; Paris, Mahoney, & Buckhalt, 1974).

The duration of imagery effects in facilitating recall is not clear from most studies with patient groups. With the exception of Patten's (1972) study in which subjects maintained their mnemonic skills over several months, most studies either failed to evaluate long term benefits or showed no benefit (e.g., Glasgow, Zeiss, Barrera, & Lewinsohn, 1977; Lewinsohn, Danaher, & Kikel, 1977). Thus, advances in techniques suitable for long-term maintenance of imagery facilitation effects are pertinent to the remediation of memory problems for these patient groups.

Elderly Populations.   Despite the successful demonstration of the imagery effects with younger adults and the documented finding that the elderly can improve their abilities to memorize when provided with appropriate organizational methods (Hulicka & Grossman, 1967; Hultsch, 1969, 1971), there are very few studies that have evaluated the effectiveness of visual mnemonics with elderly subjects. Our literature search revealed 17 studies in this area, with 14 reporting a facilitative imagery effect for the elderly. This handful of studies indicates imagery mnemonics may be a viable memory technique for the elderly.

As in studies with younger adults, most studies with the elderly have used a paired-associate learning procedure. Five pioneer studies are frequently referred to as exemplars of the effectiveness of visual mnemonics for the elderly. These are Caird and Hannah (1964), Hulicka and Grossman (1967), Canestrari (1968a,b), and Rowe and Schnore (1971).

It was found that elderly subjects given pictorial elaborations or verbal instructions to form images of both items in the paired associates performed better than control subjects with standard paired-associate instructions. Hulicka and Grossman (1967) found that the elderly tended to use either verbal mediators or inappropriate strategies. However, when they were instructed to use an appropriate mnemonic strategy, performance improved. Furthermore, the elderly have reported using visual mnemonic strategies more frequently with concrete stimuli as compared with abstract pairs (Rowe & Schnore, 1971).

The method of loci was successfully employed to help the older learners in serial recall (Robertson-Tchabo, Hausman, & Arenberg, 1976). In this method, the learner takes a mental trip through his or her residence, stopping at 16 locations. These locations serve as cues to elicit the appropriate responses. The method of loci capitalizes on the familiarity and natural order of the stopping places.

The results of this study demonstrated three important points. First, there were large individual differences in retrieval performances among the elderly. Second, the use of the method of loci over three consecutive days for memorizing different lists did not produce proactive interference for the elderly. And third, although the elderly successfully employed the method during the three training days, they did not spontaneously use it on the posttest, which was presented without specific instructions to use the method.

Thomas and Ruben (1973) evaluated age differences among young adult, middle-aged, and elderly groups in paired-associate learning, either under interacting imagery instructions or cartoon mnemonics that depicted a bizarre interacting relationship between the stimulus and response items. Groups of control subjects received standard paired-associate learning instructions. The study is particularly noteworthy because it tested retention at 1 hr and at four, eight, and 16 months after learning to criterion, testing intervals much longer than those employed by most paired-associate learning studies. As expected, a substantial decline in retrieval performance was found for all groups over the retention periods. However, subjects in the imagery instruction and cartoon mnemonics groups performed very similarly, and both groups performed better than the standard instruction controls at the four-, eight-, and 16-month retention intervals. The elderly performed at a lower level at all testing intervals under standard instructions; but no age difference was found with the imagery instructions or cartoon mnemonics at any test interval, an encouraging result. On the other hand, the marked decline in performance following the 1-hr test is not an encouraging finding, for it provides evidence that mnemonic strategies do not assist recall for any substantial length of time, even when immediate recall is facilitated.

The stimuli employed in the study may limit the study's generalizations. The study employed 12 paired associates composed of three-letter words in which the stimulus and response words were arranged in a sequential alphabetic order (ace–boy, cow–dog, eel–fox, etc.). These stimuli may have contributed to what seemed to be large variability in the performances at the longer retention intervals. Subjects in any of the groups may have utilized the alphabetic and three-letter structure to reconstruct the response word, either in combination with or to the exclusion of the experimental instructions.

Three studies by Treat and her colleagues contributed to the understanding of the effect of mnemonics on the acquisition rate of the elderly in paired-associate learning tasks. Treat and Reese (1976) demonstrated that with self-generated images and longer anticipation time, the elderly can learn as rapidly as the young. On the other hand, with no imagery instructions and a shorter anticipation time, the young performed as poorly as the old. It was concluded that in order to facilitate performance the young needed the longer anticipation time only when imagery instructions were not provided, but the elderly needed the time to benefit from imagery instructions. In her unpublished dissertation (Treat, 1977), it was further demonstrated that imagery can facilitate acquisition when an elderly person generates images compatible with that person's own style.

The effects of practice on paired-associate learning with the elderly were evaluated in a recently completed experiment (Treat, Poon, & Fozard, 1978). In a subject-paced factorial design using young and elderly community-dwelling adults, four instructional techniques for learning paired asssociates were evaluated over three training-testing sessions spaced two weeks apart. Subjects in each age group were divided into five different groups. Subjects in Group 1 were instructed to use self-generated images to learn two lists of paired associates in each of the three sessions. In Group 2, subjects were given experimenter-generated images to use when learning the lists. Subjects in Group 3 were taught to learn the first list by employing images provided by the experimenter, and then were instructed to learn the second list by generating their own images, a sequence that was followed in each of the three sessions. Group 4 subjects were asked to generate their own images to learn the first list, and then were instructed to use the experimenter-provided images to learn the second list. Finally, Group 5, the control group, was provided with standard paired-associate learning instructions during each session.

The young learned the paired associates much faster than the elderly in all learning sessions, and no difference was found among the treatment groups. There was a slight improvement in learning rate across sessions for all young subjects.

In all three sessions, Group 1 (self-generated imagery) elderly subjects learned the paired associates much faster than subjects in the other groups. In the first session, elderly Groups 2, 3, and 4 performed similarly, and performance of Group 5 (controls) was significantly poorer than the other elderly groups. The elderly in all groups improved their performance in Sessions 2 and 3, so that by the end of Session 3 there was no statistically significant difference in performance among the treatment and control groups.

The study demonstrated the following:

1. Young subjects spontaneously used efficient strategies; imagery instructions or practice did not serve to enhance acquisition to any significant degree.
2. Self-generated images assisted the elderly in learning tasks.
3. Organizational techniques may be developed spontaneously by the elderly, given sufficient experience with a task.

The finding that, with practice, the elderly develop mediation strategies in paired-associate learning was corroborated in a dissertation by DeLeon

(1974). Elderly subjects matched on initial performance on a paired-associate learning task were divided into five groups. The groups were provided with training either in a mediational strategy or in a repetition strategy, practice in learning paired associates, social attention, or no treatment. Subjects in the four treatment groups performed the paired-associate tasks for five days. The mediational and repetition groups showed immediate facilitation. However, at the end of five days, all five groups performed at similar levels. At the end of training, some subjects in groups that were not provided with specific mediational strategies indicated that they adopted mediational strategies on their own.

Based on subjects' reports of their use of mediational strategies, independent of treatment group, two groups of subjects were identified: those who used mediation and those who did not. DeLeon (1974) found that mediators performed significantly better than the nonmediators, corroborating the results of the facilitation effect of self-generated images reported by Treat (1977).

DeLeon could find no evidence of generalization from training on paired associates to performance on three practical memory tests: recall of (1) a personal narrative, (2) a grocery list, and (3) the names and occupations of photographed persons. Thus, it is possible that paired associates do not have an analogue in everyday memory behaviors, and will ultimately prove to be inappropriate to use in memory intervention programs. However, it is also possible that a relationship does exist between paired associates and in vivo memory behaviors but that, in the DeLeon study, the wrong behaviors were identified.

Another study demonstrated the facilitative effects of imagery mnemonics on the memory performance of the elderly. Zarit, Gallagher, Kramer, and Walsh (1977) evaluated the effects of group training on memory complaints, memory performance, and affective status. The training program spanned five weeks, with two sessions per week (one pretest session, seven instructional sessions, and two posttest sessions).

The subjects, all community-dwelling women over 50 years of age, were divided into three groups. The first group was given training in memory techniques (grouping, categorization, visual mediators, semantic encoding of personal and general information, visual mediators for names and faces, integrative recall, and provoked integration). The second group was given training on increasing concentration and personal effectiveness (social skills, problem solving, cognitive reappraisal, unpleasant activities, relaxation and personal rights, differentiation of rejection and compliments). These two groups also were given memory tests after each training session. The third group was given no training and was put on a waiting list.

Memory performance, memory complaints, and depression were evaluated in all three groups after the treatment groups completed their respective training programs. Tests of memory performance involved the recall of a phone number, a shopping list, noncategorizable items, personal events, names associated with photographs of faces, and identification of material presented in a photograph.

The results showed that both training groups significantly reduced their concern about memory functions after training, and that there were no differences among the three groups in affective status. Significantly better memory performances were found only after training on tasks involving novel visual mediators. However, with the exception of the visual mediation tasks, there was no statistical difference among the treatment and control groups in posttraining memory performances. On the visual mediation tasks, the memory-training group (given visual mediation training) performed significantly better than the personal-effectiveness-training group which, in turn, performed better than the control group.

This study conducted by Zarit and his colleagues replicated the results of Kahn, Zarit, Hilbert, and Niederehe (1975) with respect to the impact of depression on an individual's concern about personal memory functioning, and provides evidence that memory complaints may be independent of memory functions. More importantly, the study showed that specific training in visual mnemonics is effective in improving the memory performance of the aged. This finding was replicated in a second study (Cole & Guider, 1978). Further treatment of this topic can be found in Zelinski, Gilewski and Thompson (Chapter 30).

Negative results on three imagery mnemonic experiments with the elderly were reported from the laboratory of Smith and his associates: one study on the effects of imagery on free recall and two on the use the peg-word system. Mason and Smith (1977, Experiment II) reported no facilitative effects with younger and older subjects given instructions to form "a mental picture" with a list of 20 words, compared to subjects given standard free-recall instructions. The facilitative effect was found, however, with a group of middle-aged subjects.

Smith (1975) evaluated the effectiveness of the peg-word system in improving item recall with groups of young, middle-aged and elderly subjects. The system is very similar to that used by Patten (1972), reported earlier, except that a number–word rhyme is used (e.g., one is a bun; two is a shoe; . . . ; ten is a hen). After a subject learned the number–word rhymes, the subject formed discrete visual images of the peg words with the to-be-remembered items (e.g. bun–orange; shoe–apple, etc.). On the recall trial, only a number was given (e.g., one) and the subjects were given 5 sec to respond with the appropriate word (e.g., orange). Eight different lists of paired associates with eight pairs per list were presented to the subjects at a 5-sec rate. The stimulus words were always the peg words, and the response words were chosen from different conceptual categories. The recall tests were given immediately after presentation. The control groups were not taught the mnemonic system. The results showed no performance difference between the mnemonic and no-mnemonic middle-aged and elderly groups. However, a mnemonic facilitation effect was found for the young adults.

Mason and Smith (1977, Experiment I) essentially replicated the design and procedure of the Smith (1975) study for evaluating the peg-word system. Young, middle-aged, and elderly adults matched on vocabulary level and digit-span recall ability were employed. Abstract (e.g., one is fun) in addition to concrete (e.g., one is a bun) peg-word rhymes and word lists were evaluated. A self-paced and a 5-sec presentation rate were employed. Eight different 10-item lists were presented.

The data showed no performance difference between the concrete and abstract mnemonic peg-word rhymes. More importantly, the results replicated the Smith (1975) study; i.e., the mnemonic effect was found with the young and not with the elderly. No control group was provided for the middle-aged mnemonic group in the study.

The remaining results were found in the predicted direction: Concrete lists and self-paced presentation rate facilitated performance over abstract lists and the 5-sec rate, and younger subjects performed better than the old.

In contrast, successful application of the peg-word system with the elderly was demonstrated by Hellebusch (1976). The study evaluated the effects of the standard peg-word system (e.g., one is a bun), sentence generation, and first-letter strategies on learning 10-item and 20-item self-paced lists and recalling them at 3 min and two weeks after learning. The results showed that both the peg-word and sentence-generation systems aided retrieval 3 min after presentation for both young and elderly adults. For the two-week recall, the mnemonic strategies were found to benefit the young but not the old.

To evaluate whether or not subjects transferred the strategies learned earlier, the subjects were presented another self-paced list of 30 items to learn without specific instructions. By their own report, most of the young (83%) attempted to use the mnemonic strategies, while only a minority (44%) of the elderly did. Self-report data also indicated that 36% of the young subjects generalized their strategies from the unpaced tasks to a paced laboratory task. In contrast, only one older subject (out of the 48) generalized his mnemonic strategy.

SALIENT ISSUES

The laboratory studies just reviewed provide encouraging evidence that imagery mnemonics can improve the acquisition and immediate recall of item information and paired associates. Aside from a few techniques (e.g., method of loci and peg-word) popularized in courses offered by mnemonists (e.g., Lorayne & Lucas, 1974), the application of visual mnemonics for remembering practical information (e.g., names, faces, dates, events, shopping lists, telephone numbers) has received limited laboratory attention. Furthermore, the long-term retention benefits of imagery mnemonics have only been examined in a few studies. Among those that have evaluated the long-term retention of practical information (e.g., names and faces), most have found that subjects could not retain the information acquired in the initial training (cf. Glasgow, Zeiss, Barrera, & Lewinsohn, 1977; Lewinsohn, Danaher & Kikel, 1977).

If visual mnemonics are to help elderly individuals cope with in vivo memory demands, three issues need to receive careful scrutiny: First, the effects of individual differences in imagery abilities need to be explored. In particular, the relationship between imagery ability and memory performance needs to be understood. Second, imagery mnemonic training procedures appropriate for the elderly must be developed and tested. Finally, because long-term effectiveness is an important criterion for viable memory intervention, techniques for preventing decay of clinically acquired or reestablished strategies must be sought.

Individual Differences In Imagery And Memory Abilities.   The first factor which can contribute to the success of visual mnemonic training is a better understanding of the relationship between individual differences in imagery ability and acquisition and retrieval performance. In order to do this, we need to address three questions: First, how are imagery abilities evaluated? Second, do individuals with good imagery abilities tend to acquire and retrieve information faster and more accurately? Last, on the basis of imagery ability or aptitude, can we make a judgment about whether imagery mnemonics are an appropriate memory training method for an individual?

Ernest (1977) reviewed the past 10 years of literature on individual differences in imagery abilities related to learning, memory, and perceptual and conceptual processes. Her review pointed to the multidimensionality of individual differences in imagery ability and to the need for future investigations. It is noted that most studies of imagery ability employed young adults and children. There is very limited information on the imagery ability of the elderly.

Three procedures currently are available to evaluate imagery abilities: (1) self-ratings that attempt to identify the presence, vividness and degree to which individuals manipulate images; (2) tests of spatial abilities; and (3) direct measures of the use of imagery in various cognitive tasks. Examples of self-report imagery tests are: the Sheehan version of the Betts Questionnaire (Sheehan, 1967), the Gordon Scale of Imagery Control (Gordon, 1949), the Vividness of Visual Imagery Questionnaire (VVIQ) (Marks, 1973), and the Individual Differences Questionnaire (IDQ, Paivio, 1971). The test–retest (two to six weeks) reliability of the IDQ (.84, on imagery scale; .88, on verbal scale) was comparable to that of the Betts (Sheehan, 1967) and Marks (1973) instruments (Hiscock, 1978). The correlation between imagery scores from the Betts and IDQ scales was found to be 0.49; the relationship between the Betts and Gordon scales did not exceed 0.20 (Richardson, 1969).

Examples of spatial ability tests with satisfactory reliabilities include the Primary Mental Abilities Spatial Ability Test (Thurstone, 1938), the Visual Manipulation Scale (Hiscock, 1978) and the Minnesota Paper Form Board Test (Ernest & Paivio, 1969, 1971). Hiscock (1978) found correlations among performances on imagery self-assessments and spatial abilities tests in the range of .01 to .16.

Given the low correlations among the various imagery ability tests, it is not surprising to find variability in results relating imagery abilities and memory performances. In a review of the literature, Ernest (1977) found the following relationships. First, spatial tests of imagery ability are predictive of paired-associate learning performances when imagery mnemonic strategies are encouraged and when pictorial stimuli are used. On the other hand, self-reported ratings of imagery appear not to be related to learning performance. Second, imagery abilities measured by self-report tests are predictive of performances in incidental recall. Third, imagery vividness measured by self-report is not predictive of memory abilities for block designs, faces, and dot patterns, while imagery abilities measured by objective tests are. Ernest's (1977) review did not address the issue of age differences in imagery ability and performance, possibly due to the sparseness of literature.

The low correlations among various imagery ability tests and the variability among scores in different imagery tests and cognitive performances suggest that there may be different types of imagery ability, and that different abilities are associated with different cognitive and task demands. A great amount of investigation is needed to better understand the role of imagery in memory performance. Consequently, to use an imagery test to predict success in an imagery mnemonic training program would be premature at this time.

Features Of Mnemonic Training Programs For The Elderly.   This section reviews the various elements of imagery mnemonic techniques that were found to facilitate acquisition and retrieval of information by the elderly. In addition, other features of mnemonic training that deserve further investigation and development are discussed.

Real-life situations demand that an individual generate images on one's own if visual mnemonics are to be utilized. A question of considerable importance is whether certain kinds of instructions may be needed by (some) elderly persons to enable them to generate suitable and efficient images. The failure of Mason and Smith (1977, Experiment II) to obtain an imagery effect with the elderly suggests that some people may not be able to respond to instructions to "form a mental picture of the words" without some type of training that focuses on how to form a useful image.

In order to provide such training and to design specific imagery techniques, it is necessary to identify whether a particular set of characteristics is likely to make an image more effective for the elderly. Catino, Taub, and Borkowski (1977) found that the elderly could not form associations with novel stimuli; however, the elderly spontaneously formed effective associations with familiar mediators. Robertson-Tchabo, Hausman, and Arenberg (1976) utilized the familiar surroundings of their elderly subjects' residences in their successful application of the method of loci. Thus, these two studies suggest that prior familiarity with stimuli or cues may be helpful to the elderly.

Smith (1975) and Mason and Smith (1977) failed to produce a facilitating effect with the elderly using the peg-word method. However, it is possible that the peg-word system, which is fairly complicated and unfamiliar to most individuals, takes longer to master than was provided for in the design of the study. The learner must first master a list of novel pairs of peg-words and then use this system to remember new information. Patten (1972) took up to four weeks to successfully train brain-damaged subjects to use the peg-word system. Hellebusch (1976) taught and tested his elderly subjects within the same session but only was able to obtain a minimal facilitation effect. Thus, the evidence suggests that expectations of the time needed by the elderly to acquire and demonstrate proficiency with a mnemonic technique may need to be extended, particularly if the technique and stimuli are novel to the elderly learner.

It is clear that interacting images can facilitate memory performance (Buggie, 1974). The nature of this interaction (bizarre versus plausible) on memory performance is not clear. Classical (Yates, 1966) and modern (Bower, 1978; Lorayne & Lucas, 1974; Miller, Gallanter, & Pribram, 1960) mnemonists advocate the formation of illogical, implausible, or bizarre interacting images. However, studies evaluating images along the bizarre and plausible dimension on retrieval accuracy with college subjects are inconclusive. Collyer, Jonides, and Bevan (1972) found plausible images were superior, while Andreoff and Yarmey (1976) showed that bizarre images were more effective. Wollen, Weber, and Lowry (1972), on the other hand, found no performance difference between bizarre and plausible images. It remains to be demonstrated whether the plausibility or bizarreness of an image has an effect on the memory performance of the elderly, and/or on the willingness of the elderly to utilize such images in memory tasks.

The relationship between image complexity and effective utilization of the image is not well understood. In the clinical literature (Lewinsohn, Glasgow, Barrera, Danaher, Alperson, McCarty, Sullivan, Zeiss, Nyland, & Rodrigues, 1977), it has been reported that both young and elderly patients often generate images that are too complex to assist memory. In contrast, many young and elderly subjects seen in the authors' laboratory have generated images with a surprising amount of detail, without any observable negative effect on memory performance. These contrasting observations suggest that imagery complexity needs to be explored not only to evaluate its impact on optimal acquisition and retrieval, but also to try to determine the extent to which variations in complexity might be influenced by individual differences and situational demands.

The mnemonic effects of single versus multiple coding of information may also be pertinent to the investigation of image complexity. Individuals with exceptional memory (cf. Luria, 1968) tend to encode information through different modalities (visual, auditory, olfactory, etc.) as well as to encode the same information with multiple codes within the same modality. Differential encoding models (e.g., Garskoff, 1969; Martin, 1968) hypothesize that multiple associative links among the items to be recalled may strengthen the retrieval pathways and increase the probability of recall. A research program evaluating the efficacy of multiple coding strategies using visual mnemonics with the elderly may be a fruitful avenue to explore.

Conditions that will enable the elderly to use imagery effectively are important to identify. One procedural issue received concensus in the literature: The performance of the elderly is better when information is presented at a slower pace (Monge & Hultsch, 1971) or when it is self-paced (Treat & Reese, 1976; Mason & Smith, 1977). Since it may be difficult to know what constitutes a "slower pace" for a particular clinical task, it may be advantageous to allow the elderly individual to proceed at that person's own pace, at least during the initial learning phase. This is not to suggest, however, that an increase in response speed should never be a goal of intervention, because life situations may be contingent upon the learner's ability to respond within a certain time frame.

The affective state of an individual during acquisition and retrieval may have an important impact on the outcome of mnemonic training. Learning and memory performances can be artificially depressed when the learner is under- or over-motivated or very depressed (Eisdorfer, 1968; Kahn & Miller, 1978). Consequently, a clinician should be particularly aware of the affective states of the learner during mnemonic training.

In any learning situation, the learning and response set ("social desirability") of the learner (White, Sheehan, & Ashton, 1977) may interact with the instructional format, the amount of attention given by the experimenter (clinician), and the face validity of the learning material. Attempts to operationalize the effects of these influences ("social desirability" effects) on cognitive performances (Ashton & White, 1975) with college students have been inconclusive. The impact of these peripheral influences on mnemonic training with the elderly has not been explored extensively.

Zarit et al. (1977) demonstrated that clinically associated training, whether it is specific or nonspecific to memory problems, tends to improve an individual's self-concept about his or her memory functioning. This finding suggests that the elderly need to have someone pay attention to their memory problems. However, it was also found that visual mediation training enhanced performance on some tasks, indicating that further investigation is needed to differentiate the amount of specific versus generalized training the elderly require.

The acquisition of imagery mnemonic skills, like the acquisition of other skills, requires a commitment of effort and time. The development of memory skills is analagous in some ways to the acquisition of tennis-playing skills. Proper tennis techniques frequently feel awkward to students because the target behaviors are in conflict with playing habits that are inefficient. Similarly, mnemonic techniques initially may feel awkward to the learner. In both learning situations, the student may require many hours of instruction and practice until the target behaviors are integrated into the student's repertoire.

However, the amount of effort and time needed to acquire a memory strategy is a critical issue in the case of the elderly learner. It seems unlikely that a memory "payoff" far down the road and/ or requiring extensive energy to attain will be particularly appealing to the elderly. Nor is such a memory technique considered to be clinically sound. Imagery mnemonic techniques must be reasonable in terms of effort and time demands to be viable strategies for the elderly.

Maintenance Of Memory Skills.   Not only is it important to develop viable methods to help an individual improve his memory, but it is also necessary to develop satisfactory methods of preventing these newly acquired or reestablished strategies from decaying over time. Therefore, future laboratory and clinical endeavors need to address the following: First, what can be done within the framework of the clinical program to increase the likelihood that the learner will continue to apply what he or she has learned? Secondly, can post-training decay be prevented or slowed by the application of some schedule of periodic intervention or via some sort of self-administered program?

Long-term success of memory intervention requires that learners leave the program equipped with strategies that will allow them to accurately evaluate as well as modify their own behavior. Consequently, good self-monitoring skills are not only important for the acquisition stages of a memory training program, but are also critical to successful post-treatment maintenance. Therefore when discrepancies exist between self-report information and objective performance measures, it needs to be determined whether the discrepancies are indicative of self-monitoring skills that are underdeveloped or underutilized.

One way to develop self-monitoring skills may be via self-instructional training (Meichenbaum, 1974; Meichenbaum & Cameron, 1973), based on a modeling and overt to covert rehearsal paradigm. The procedure consists of a series of successive approximations designed to provide the learner with an opportunity to actively rehearse each component of a task, first aloud and then to oneself. According to Meichenbaum (1974), self-instruction assists the learner in organizing input, in evaluating feedback, in reinforcing and maintaining task-relevant behaviors, and in coping with failure.

Meichenbaum (1974) suggested that self-instruction is particularly appropriate for the elderly. This view has evolved, at least in part, from his observations that elderly persons frequently talk to themselves and repeat instructions out loud, behaviors he feels may represent some sort of compensatory mechanism. Self-instructional training, he believes, may be able to overcome age-related deficits by capitalizing on this "natural mechanism."

In the preceding subsection, it was pointed out that new behaviors need to be practiced. Recently, it has been shown (Murrell, 1970; Poon, Fozard, & Vierck, 1978) that the elderly profit more than the young from practice. Furthermore, it has been demonstrated that the magnitude of performance decay may be overestimated by tasks that the elderly consider meaningless or irrelevant (Botwinick, 1973). These findings not only provide a rationale for the inclusion of homework assignments in a memory-skill training program but also suggest that it may be even more critical that "ecologically sound" materials (i.e., materials appropriate for and meaningful to the learner) be utilized in the design of tasks that are to be self-administered.

One practical problem for the clinician is that the preparation of individualized materials can be very time consuming. In fact, it recently has been reported (Lewinsohn, Glasgow, et al., 1977) that the development of individualized memory intervention materials has, in some cases, necessitated long intervals between consecutive treatment sessions, a rather undesirable consequence.

One strategy for dealing with the materials problem might be to involve the learner in the development of his or her materials. Such a strategy would seem valuable for four reasons: First, the materials are more likely to be appropriate for and of interest to the learner if the learner actively participates in the selection process. Second, learners sometimes view intervention as something that is "done" to them rather than as something they do. Shared responsibilities for materials may help such a learner feel more responsible for the behavior changes that occur (or do not occur) as the result of his or her participation in the program.

Third, this strategy provides the learner with an opportunity to develop a valuable self-help skill that may assist the learner in continuing to practice after the training program is completed. Finally, the kinds of materials that a learner selects may yield some clues relative to the features that are apt to make a task unreasonable from the learner's point of view. The authors concur with Lewinsohn, Glasgow, et al. (1977), who note the importance of providing the learner with techniques that are not "too demanding, obtrusive, or time consuming to be applied in an ongoing fashion [p. 9]."

It might also be advantageous for the clinician to provide the learner's spouse or friend with training so that someone can help the learner practice at home. After the clinical program has ended, involved family members and friends may function as valuable external sources of support for the learner which, in turn, may enhance the probability that the learner will continue to apply the new memory strategies.

Self-help programs abound in the current marketplace. Their apparent popularity makes it reasonable to consider whether such a format might serve as a vehicle for presenting a program to prevent or retard post-treatment decay of memory skills.

Some programs are of the single-component (or isolated technique) variety, and some attempt to address the area of need with a broader (or multicomponent) design. Some programs are self-administered, others require some contact with an instructor, and others are entirely administered by an instructor.

Recently, Glasgow and Rosen (1978) reviewed 75 self-help programs designed to meet consumer needs in a variety of areas (phobias, smoking, obesity, sexual dysfunction, assertiveness, child behavior problems, study skills, and physical fitness). According to the authors, long-term effects generally have not been demonstrated with single-component programs. Multicomponent programs appear more promising; however, the authors indicate that it may prove difficult to successfully translate broad approaches into written self-help formats. When one considers that a self-help program for an overt behavior such as smoking has not been successfully developed to date (Glasgow & Rosen, 1978), the magnitude of the problem facing the field of memory-skill training becomes still more apparent.

The development of memory self-help programs is contingent on the identification of the "relevant and effective components [p. 16]" (Glasgow & Rosen, 1978), something that we have yet to do fully in either the laboratory or the clinic. In order to provide the user with orderly steps to follow, it first is necessary to identify these steps.

Although short-term effects have been demonstrated for some self-help programs (for the treatment of obesity, phobias, physical fitness, and study skills), long-term effects generally have been difficult to assess because of lack of follow-up studies and/or because of high user drop-out (Glasgow & Rosen, 1978). The high attrition suggests that programs are failing to meet the need and/or expectations of users and underscores the importance of clarifying process issues such as type of instructional format, sequencing of tasks, level(s) of task difficulty, length of program, spacing of instruction, and amount of practice. Furthermore, attention needs to be directed to the question of whether cost-effective, ecologically sound self-help materials can be developed given the variability among the elderly. This variability may necessitate more individualization than is possible in a published self-help format.

At this point in time, it is premature to tell whether self-help programs can function as a viable vehicle for memory skill maintenance. At best, the prospect of utilization seems to be distant.

CONCLUSION

The elderly commonly describe two signs of aging: (1) gradual loss of energy; and (2) gradual loss of memory for names, faces, dates, and events (Lowenthal et al., 1967). This chapter has focused on evaluating the state of the art of imagery mnemonics as a tool for responding to memory concerns.

The data reviewed suggest that imagery mnemonics may be useful in memory intervention programs for the elderly. However, because relatively few researchers have evaluated this approach with the elderly, the efficacy of imagery mnemonics will need to be explored further.

One of the challenges that lies ahead is to determine the extent to which imagery can be applied to in vivo memory demands. In addition, we need to know more about (1) the *characteristics* of imagery that are likely to assist the acquisition and retrieval of information; (2) the types of *memory tasks* to which these characteristics can meaningfully be applied; and (3) the learning and retrieval *conditions* that will enable an elderly person to utilize imagery. Furthermore, it needs to be determined whether imagery techniques can be devised that are realistic for the elderly both in terms of ease of mastery and the time and effort needed to maintain positive changes in memory functioning.

Even if the efficacy of imagery as a clinical tool can be demonstrated, it is reasonable to expect that imagery will be appropriate for some elderly persons and not for others. Procedures capable of differentiating between those elderly individuals who are likely to benefit from imagery training and those individuals who are likely to benefit from other mnemonic techniques would be of significant clinical value, and currently await development.

Ultimately, it is the clinician who selects the intervention strategy to be employed. The selection of imagery should be contingent not only on a judgment of the probability of success but also on whether imagery appears to be the most *appropriate* and the most *efficient* strategy for the specific memory problem(s) presented by the elderly complainant. Much work lies ahead to determine if the promise that imagery mnemonics has at this time will be realized.

ACKNOWLEDGMENTS

Preparation of this chapter was supported in part by the Medical Research Service of the Veterans Administration and in part by Grants AG 00738 and AG 00467 from the National Institute on Aging. The authors are grateful to W. R. Poon and S. Carroll for manuscript preparation.

REFERENCES

Andreoff, G. R., & Yarmey, D. Bizarre Imagery and Associative Learning: A Confirmation. *Perceptual and Motor Skills,* 1976, *43,* 143-148.

Ashton, R., & White, K. The effects of instructions on subjects' imagery questionnaire scores. *Social Behavior,* 1975, *3,* 41-43.

Baddeley, A. D., & Warrington, E. K. Memory coding and amnesia. *Neuropsychologia,* 1973, *11,* 159-165.

Baltes, P. B., & Willis, S. L. Toward psychological theories of aging and development. In J. E. Birren & K. W. Schaie (Eds.), *Handbook of the psychology of aging.* New York: Van Nostrand Reinhold, 1977.

Boring, E. G. *A history of experimental psychology.* New York: Appleton-Century-Crofts, 1950.

Botwinick, J. *Aging and behavior.* New York: Springer, 1973.

Bower, G. H. Analysis of a mnemonic device. *American Scientist,* 1970, *58,* 496-510.

Bower, G. H. A selective review of organizational factors in memory. In E. Tulving & W. Donaldson (Eds.), *Organization and memory.* New York: Academic Press, 1972.

Bower, G. H. Improving memory. *Human Nature,* 1978, *2,* 64-72.

Bower, G. H., & Winzenz, D. Comparison of associative learning strategies. *Psychonomic Science,* 1970, *20,* 119-120.

Buggie, S. E. *Imagery and relational variety in associative learning.* Unpublished Ph.D. dissertation, University of Oregon, 1974.

Caird, W. K., & Hannah, F. Short-term memory disorder in elderly psychiatric patients. *Diseases of the Nervous System,* 1964, *25,* 564-568.

Canestrari, R. E. Age changes in acquisition. In G. A. Talland (Ed.), *Human aging and behavior.* New York: Academic Press, 1968. (a)

Canestrari, R. E. Age differences in verbal learning and verbal behavior. In S. S. Chown & K. F. Riegal (Eds.), *Psychological functioning in the normal aging and senile aged.* New York: Karger, 1968. (b)

Catino, C., Taub, S. I., & Borkowski, J. G. Mediation in children and the elderly as a function of memory capabilities. *Journal Genetic Psychology,* 1977, *130,* 35-47.

Cole, K. D., & Guider, R. L. *The effects of specific and nonspecific training on memory and memory complaints in older adults.* Paper presented at the meeting of the Western Psychology Association, San Francisco, 1978.

Collyer, S. C., Jonides, J., & Bevan, W. Images as memory aids: is bizarreness helpful? *American Journal of Psychology,* 1972, *85,* 31-38.

DeLeon, J. M. *Effects of training in repetition and mediation on paired-associate learning and practical memory in the aged.* Unpublished Ph.D. dissertation, University of Hawaii, 1974.

Eisdorfer, C. Arousal and performance: Experiments in verbal learning and a tentative theory. In G. A. Talland (Ed.), *Human aging and behavior.* New York: Academic Press, 1968.

Ernest, C. Mental imagery and cognition: A critical review. *Journal of Mental Imagery*, 1977, *1*, 181-216.

Ernest, C. H., & Paivio, A. Imagery abilities in paired-associate and incidental learning. *Psychonomic Science*, 1969, *15*, 181-182.

Ernest, C. H., & Paivio, A. Imagery and sex differences in incidental recall. *British Journal of Psychology*, 1971, *62*, 67-72.

Galton, F. Statistics of mental imagery. *Mind*, 1880, *5*, 301-318.

Garskoff, M. H. *The effect of spacing and variation in short-term memory*. Unpublished Ph.D. dissertation, University of Michigan, 1969.

Glasgow, R. E., & Rosen, G. M. Behavioral bibliotherapy: A review of self-help behavior manuals. *Psychological Bulletin*, 1978, *85*, 1-23.

Glasgow, R. E., Zeiss, R. A., Barrera, M., Jr., & Lewinsohn, P. M. Case studies on remediating memory deficits in brain-damaged individuals. *Journal of Clinical Psychology*, 1977, *33*, 1049-1054.

Gordon, R. An investigation into some factors that favour the formation of stereotyped images. *British Journal of Psychology*, 1949, *39*, 156-167.

Hellebusch, S. J. *On improving learning and memory in the aged: The effects of mnemonics on strategy, transfer, and generalization*. Dissertation Abstract (1459-B Order No. 76-19, 496), University of Notre Dame, 1976.

Hiscock, M. Imagery assessment through self-report: What do imagery questionnaires measure? *Journal of Consulting and Clinical Psychology*, 1978, *46*, 223-230.

Hulicka, I. M., & Grossman, J. L. Age group comparisons for the use of mediators in paired-associate learning. *Journal of Gerontology*, 1967, *22*, 46-51.

Hull, C. L. Goal attraction and directing ideas conceived as habit phenomena. *Psychological Review*. 1931, *38*, 487-506.

Hultsch, D. F. Age differences in the organization of free recall. *Developmental Psychology*, 1969, *1*, 673-678.

Hultsch, D. F. Organization and memory in adulthood. *Human Development*. 1971, *14*, 16-29.

Jones, M. K. Imagery as a mnemonic aid after left temporal lobectomy: Contrast between material-specific and generalized memory disorders. *Neuropsychologia*, 1974, *12*, 21-30.

Kahn, R., & Miller, N. Adaptational factors in memory impairment in the aged. *Experimental Aging Research*, 1978, *4*(4), 273-290.

Kahn, R. L., Zarit, S. H., Hilbert, N. M., & Niederehe, M. A. Memory complaint and impairment in the aged: The effect of depression and altered brain function. *Archive of General Psychiatry*, 1975, *32*, 1569-1573.

Kossyln, S. M., Reiser, B. J., & Ball, T. M. Visual images preserve metric spatial information: Evidence from studies of image scanning. *Journal of Experimental Psychology: Human Perception and Performance*, 1978, *4*, 47-60.

Lebrato, M. T., & Ellis, N. R. Imagery mediation in paired-associate learning by retarded and non-retarded subjects. *American Journal of Mental Deficiency*, 1974, *78*, 704-713.

Lewinsohn, P. M., Danaher, B. G., & Kikel, S. Visual imagery as a mnemonic aid for brain-injured persons. *Journal of Consulting and Clinical Psychology*, 1977, *45*, 717-723.

Lewinsohn, P. M., Glasgow, R. E., Barrera, M., Danaher, B. G., Alperson, J., McCarty, D. L., Sullivan, J. M., Zeiss, R. A., Nyland, J., & Rodriques, M. R. P. Assessment and treatment of patients with memory deficits: Initial studies. *JSAS Catalog of Selected Documents in Psychology* (ms. no. 1538), 1977, *1*, 79.

Lorayne, H., & Lucas, J. *The memory book*. New York: Ballantine Books, 1974.

Lowenthal, M. F., Berkman, P. L., Buehler, J. A., Pierce, R. C., Robinson, B. C., & Trier, M. L. *Aging and mental disorder in San Francisco*. San Francisco: Jossey-Bass, Inc., 1967.

Luria, A. R. *The mind of a mnemonist*. New York: Basic Books, 1968.

Marks, D. F. Visual imagery differences in the recall of pictures. *British Journal of Psychology*, 1973, *64*, 17-24.

Martin, E. Stimulus meaningfulness and paired-associate transfer: An encoding variability hypothesis. *Psychological Review*, 1968, *75*, 421-441.

Mason, S. E., & Smith, A. D. Imagery in the aged. *Experimental Aging Research*, 1977, *3*, 17-32.

Meichenbaum, D. Self-instructional strategy training: A cognitive prosthesis for the aged. *Human Development*, 1974, *17*, 273-280.

Meichenbaum, D., & Cameron, R. Training schizophrenics to talk to themselves: A means of developing attentional controls. *Behavior Therapy*, 1973, *4*, 515-534.

Miller, G. A., Gallanter, E., & Pribram, K. H. *Plans and the structure of behavior.* New York: Henry Holt, 1960.

Monge, R. H., & Hultsch, D. F. Paired-associate learning as a function of adult age and the length of the anticipation and inspection intervals. *Journal of Gerontology*, 1971, *26*, 157-162.

Murdock, B. B. *Human memory.* New York: Wiley, 1974.

Murrell, F. H. The effects of extensive practice on age differences in reaction time. *Journal of Gerontology*, 1970, *25*, 268-274.

Neisser, U. Changing conception of imagery. In P. W. Sheehan (Ed.), *The functions and nature of imagery.* New York: Academic Press, 1972.

Norman, D. A. *Memory and attention.* New York: Wiley, 1969.

Paivio, A. *Imagery and verbal processes.* New York: Holt, Rhinehart & Winston, 1971.

Paris, S. G., Mahoney, G. J., & Buckhalt, J. Facilitation of semantic integration in sentence memory of retarded children. *American Journal of Mental Deficiency*, 1974, *78*, 714-720.

Patten, B. M. The ancient art of memory—usefulness in treatment. *Archives of Neurology*, 1972, *26*, 25-31.

Podgorny, P., & Shepard, R. N. Functional representations common to visual perception and imagination. *Journal of Experimental Psychology: Human Perception and Performance*, 1978, *4*, 21-35.

Poon, L. W., Fozard, J. L., & Vierck, B. Effects of extensive practice and information feedback on age-related differences in a two-choice decision task. *11th International Congress of Gerontology Abstract*, 1978, 185.

Richardson, A. *Mental imagery.* London: Routledge & Kegan Paul, 1969.

Robertson-Tchabo, E. A., Hausman, C. P., & Arenberg, D. A classical mnemonic for older learners: A trip that works. *Educational Gerontology*, 1976, *1*, 215-226.

Rowe, E., & Paivio, A. Imagery and repetition instructions in verbal discrimination and incidental paired-associate learning. *Journal of Verbal Learning and Verbal Behavior*, 1971, *10*, 668-672.

Rowe, E., & Schnore, M. M. Item concreteness and reported strategies in paired-associate learning as a function of age. *Journal of Gerontology*, 1971, *26*, 470-475.

Sheehan, P. W. A shortened form of Betts' questionnaire upon mental imagery. *Journal of Clinical Psychology*, 1967, *23*, 386-389.

Sheehan, P. W. Individual differences in vividness of imagery and the function of imagery in incidental learning. *Australian Journal of Psychology*, 1971, *23*, 279-288.

Smith, A. D. Interaction between human aging and memory. *Georgia Institute of Technology Progress Report #2*, 1975.

Thomas, J. C., & Ruben, H. *Age and mnemonic techniques in paired associate learning.* Presented at the Gerontological Society meeting, Miami, Florida, 1973.

Thurstone, L. L. Primary mental abilities. *Psychometrika Monographs*, 1938, *1*.

Titchener, E. B. *Lectures on the experimental psychology of the thought processes.* New York: Macmillan, 1909.

Tolman, E. C. *Purposive behavior in animals and men.* New York: Appleton-Century, 1932.

Treat, N. J. *Age, imagery, focused attention, and egocentricism in paired-associate learning.* Unpublished Ph.D. dissertation, University of West Virginia, 1977.

Treat, N. J., Poon, L. W., & Fozard, J. L. From clinical and research findings on memory to intervention programs. *Experimental Aging Research,* 1978, *4,* 235-253.

Treat, N. J., & Reese, H. W. Age, pacing and imagery in paired-associate learning. *Developmental Psychology,* 1976, *12,* 119-124.

Wallace, W. H., Turner, S. H., & Perkins, C. C. Preliminary studies of human information storage. In G. A. Miller, E. Galanter, & K. H. Pribram (Eds.), *Plans and the structure of behavior.* New York: Henry Holt & Co., 1960.

Warrington, E. K., & Weiskrantz, L. Organizational aspects of memory in amnesic patients. *Neuropsychologia,* 1971, *9,* 67-73.

Watson, J. B. *The ways of behaviorism.* New York: Harper, 1928.

White, K., Sheehan, P. W., & Ashton, R. Imagery assessment: A survey of self-report measures. *Journal of Mental Imagery.* 1977, *1,* 145-170.

Winograd, E., Karchner, M. A., & Russell, I. S. Role of encoding unitization in cued recognition memory. *Journal of Verbal Learning and Verbal Behavior,* 1971, *10,* 199-206.

Wollen, K. A., Weber, A., & Lowry, D. H. Bizarreness versus interaction of mental images as determinants of learning. *Cognitive Psychology,* 1972, *3,* 518-523.

Yates, F. A. *The art of memory.* London: Routledge & Kegan Paul, 1966.

Zarit, S., Gallagher, D., Kramer, N., & Walsh, D. *The effects of group training on memory and memory complaints.* Presented at the meeting of the American Psychology Association, San Francisco, 1977.

27 Visual Memory and Imagery in the Aged

Eugene Winograd
Elliott W. Simon
Emory University

A recurring note in the literature on aging and memory is that the age-related decline in memory for nonverbal information, usually taken to be memory for visual information, is steeper than the decline for verbal information. More recently, there has been a revival of interest within psychology in the study of mental imagery and how it facilitates memory, and this interest has been taken up by psychologists interested in aging. The import of this development for the psychology of aging is to attempt remediation of memory problems in the aged by means of training in imagery-based mnemonic techniques (see Poön, Walsh-Sweeney, & Fozard, Chapter 26, for a statement of this position). The point of departure for the present contribution is the potential conflict between these two notions. If older people in general do indeed manifest special problems with visual memory, then perhaps we are playing to cognitive weakness in applying traditional mnemonics training. In short, if visual memory, the capacity to store and/or retrieve information about the appearance of things, and mental imagery, the capacity to manipulate internal visual representations, decline markedly with age, might it not be unrealistic to rely on visualization as the core of a cognitive training program?[1] Before returning to this question, we need to examine what we

---

[1]Of course, in principle we may be lumping together what are, in fact, psychologically independent abilities. That is, visual memory may be quite distinct from visual imagery; the first concerns remembering episodes in their visual aspects, while the second involves generation and manipulation of stored visual information from memory. But note that mnemonic systems depend on remembering the product of this generation, and may therefore be another form of visual memory.

know about visual memory and imagery among the aged, what we need to know, and how we might go about finding it out.

Evidence for a decline in visual memory and imagery processes comes from a variety of sources. Craik (1977) has recently reviewed much of the earlier work on age differences in nonverbal memory and cited a number of studies showing a decline in recall and recognition of pictorial material. The most frequently cited finding is a steeper age-related decline in the performance than the verbal tests of the Wechsler Adult Intelligence Scale (Botwinick, 1973). Performance on the perceptual Embedded Figures Test has been recently shown to decline with age by Lee and Pollack (1978). McGhie, Chapman, and Lawson (1965) found poorer short-term memory for digits presented visually as compared to aural presentation. However, there are serious methodological problems in interpreting these differences. Recent investigators who have raised serious questions about the comparability of scores from different psychometric instruments of laboratory tests of memory include Gaylord and Marsh (1975) and Kinsbourne (1977). Among the methodological problems encountered in comparing scores from tests measuring memory for different kinds of information are the following:

1. Tests and tasks have differed in their demands on attention as well as on memory.
2. The mode of response has been inconsistent; in some instances verbal recall has been required, in others pressing a button to indicate that a picture is the same as one seen earlier, and, in other studies, drawing a design seen earlier.
3. Experience with the type of stimulus has varied from life-long familiarity with words to little or no previous exposure to geometric forms and unfamiliar faces.
4. Time constraints have varied widely.
5. Other stimulus characteristics than familiarity, such as complexity, have been confounded with the verbal–nonverbal dimension.

Problems inherent in comparing declines in verbal and visual memory can be illustrated by examining some recent studies selected for their sophistication. In a particularly well-done study, Arenberg (1978) has included some methodological refinements in approaching the question of whether there is an across-the-board decline in cognitive skills as opposed to a more specific decline in nonverbal memory. The tasks studied by Arenberg were the Benton Visual Retention Test, in which subjects are asked to reproduce from memory a geometric design after 10 seconds of study, and the vocabulary subtest of the WAIS. Arenberg employed a combined longitudinal and within-cohort experimental design and obtained measures on the Benton test and the vocabulary test from the same subjects. These are commendable features of his study. Both within-cohort and longitudinal estimates agreed on a decline with age on memory for designs, the rate of decline increasing considerably for men over 70 years of age. For our purposes, the interesting findings accompanying this decline in visual memory were, first, neither the cross-sectional nor longitudinal method found a vocabulary decline, and second, the correlation between memory for designs and vocabulary performance was essentially zero at all ages.

It is instructive to compare Arenberg's findings of an age-related loss in visual memory with the findings of Schaie and Labouvie-Vief (1974), who used a combined longitudinal and cross-sectional design similar to that of Arenberg, but tested performance on the spatial visualization test from the Primary Mental Abilities battery. While Schaie and Labouvie-Vief found cross-sectional losses on the spatial visualization test, as they did on a verbal meaning test, the longitudinal data showed a signficant decrement only past the age of 70. On the verbal meaning test, Schaie and Labouvie-Vief found no decline with age. The discrepancy between this study and Arenberg's lies in the finding of a clear decline at all ages in memory for designs by Arenberg, even when cohort effects were controlled for, whereas Schaie and Labouvie-Vief found no decline until around age 70 in a spatial visualization test.

A possible reconciliation between the two studies is that the Arenberg study tested memory while Schaie and Labovie-Vief's spatial visualization task did not involve memory. Schaie (1975) describes the test as follows:

> This test consists of geometric figures, some of which have been rotated clockwise and others counter-clockwise. The subject must pick the ones that have been rotated clockwise. It is a novel and complex task for most people and is a good measure of spatial visualization [p. 118].

The finding of a decline only past 70 in the spatial task when a longitudinal study was carried out should be kept in mind by the reader when the section on studies of information processing tasks is encountered. It may be that the studies presented there have overestimated effects associated with age due to reliance on cross-sectional designs.

As discussed above, there are certain inherent problems in drawing strong conclusions about differential decline in types of stored information, although one is tempted to infer from Arenberg's data that visual memories are more susceptible to aging than verbal memories. Two major difficulties are, first, the response mode differs drastically across tasks, and second, so does the amount of previous learning and knowledge about the class of stimuli. With regard to the first point, one could argue that Arenberg's data support the hypothesis that the aged suffer from a motor-output deficit which makes the drawing of even well remembered patterns inordinately difficult. Ideally, retired draftsmen should have been studied. On the other hand, perhaps the same pattern of decline would be found even if the forms remained in front of the subject, removing the inclination to consider it a memory task altogether. (We note, however, that Tesch, Whitbourne, & Nehrke [1978] found no decline from 45 to 75 years of age in recognizing a checkerboard pattern which matched a sample perceptually present.) As for the second point, one could view these data as consistent with a deficit for newly learned material of some complexity and novelty and conclude that linguistic information is more resistant to the ravages of time than visual memory not because it is verbal but because it was acquired early in life and is overlearned. The reader should note that these observations are not meant as criticisms of Arenberg, who avoided making conclusions about differential rates of loss associated with different kinds of information, but as problems to deal with if one seeks such comparisons.

Clearly, it is highly desirable to compare memory for different kinds of information without confounding type of information or psychological process with other factors. This is not easily achieved, but we examine some attempts later on to overcome these difficulties. First, we consider some research on memory for faces, an almost pure form of visual memory.

MEMORY FOR FACES

Consider the following advantages of using pictures of unfamiliar faces as stimuli in memory experiments:

1. They are visual patterns which do not easily lend themselves to verbal coding without special training.
2. There are a great many of them.
3. Unlike many other kinds of visual patterns which have been employed in memory research (e.g., nonsense shapes made up of random dot patterns), they have unity in that they can be apprehended as a whole.
4. As unfamiliar events, novel faces are not represented in semantic memory, and hence afford a way to test episodic memory, in terms of Tulving's useful distinction (1972).
5. Recognition of faces is difficult enough to allow experimental sensitivity to variables of interest, thereby avoiding the common problem in recognition memory of ceiling effects.

Smith and Winograd (1978) compared memory for faces between young and elderly adults in a study whose focus was on the nature of the orienting task employed by the subject at encoding. (See Chapter 1 by Smith in this volume for a discussion of this study emphasizing encoding factors in recognition.) Independent groups at two ages were given one of three tasks to perform while studying a set of 50 adult faces. One group, the standard condition, were told only to try to remember the faces; a second group judged whether each face had a big nose; a third group judged whether each face appeared friendly or not. All subjects expected a subsequent memory test and were tested on recognition immediately after studying the last face.

The results are shown in Fig. 1.6 of Smith's chapter in this volume. At both ages, judgments of friendliness lead to significantly better memory than for the other two encoding conditions. As can be seen from the figure, while there was no interaction of task with age, there was a sizeable decrement in recognition memory associated with aging. Note that the highest score for the older subjects, obtained when faces were judged with respect to friendliness, is lower than the lowest score for the younger group. Two aspects of the experiment which we regard as noteworthy are, first, the response mode is simply an indication of yes or no—all that is asked of the subject is whether the face is one that was shown earlier—and second, the stimuli are unquestionably nonverbal in nature. In addition, it should be noted that while the individual faces were chosen to be unfamiliar, the class of stimuli to which they belong—human faces—is highly familiar.

There is a large decline, then, in recognition memory for unfamiliar faces associated with aging in this study. With regard to the question of cognitive-skills training, there is a clear prescription for improving the ability of the aged (as well as the young) to remember new faces. As the figure shows, memory was markedly aided by judging each face with respect to friendliness as compared to the usual condition in which subjects were simply urged to try to remember the faces. In this connection, it should be pointed out that there seems to be nothing especially important about the friendliness dimension. Other research (Bower & Karlin, 1974; Warrington & Ackroyd, 1975; Winograd, 1976) has shown that a considerable number of trait dimensions (e.g., honesty, friendliness, intelligence) produce equivalent facilitation of face recognition, whereas questions about physical features produce performance at the same level as the standard instructions. The practical point of significance is that trait questions posed at the time of encountering a face serve as a mnemonic aid, in that memory is facilitated as compared to "normal" strategies. This mnemonic effect has so far been found with young children (Blaney & Winograd, 1978), as well as college students and older people (Smith & Winograd, 1978), and is discussed elsewhere by Winograd (1978).

For the purposes of this chapter, the finding of a decrement in this type of visual memory adds to the accumulated evidence of such loss with aging, although it does not speak to the question of whether the memory loss observed for faces is steeper than verbal memory loss. Indeed, it is hard to conceive of an experiment with verbal material which would afford a satisfactory comparison. However, an ingenious experiment on very-long-term memory for faces and names carried out on a large sample of people at different ages by Bahrick, Bahrick, and Wittlinger (1975) is worth serious consideration in this regard.

Bahrick et al. were interested in the time course of forgetting for information acquired in everyday experience rather than the psychology laboratory. To this end, they tested adults who had graduated from high school at different times and were, therefore, of different ages. Rather than testing these individuals on general information that could be dated (e.g., Who won the World Series your senior year? or Who was the drummer in Benny Goodman's sextet?), an approach recently used to advantage by Warrington and Sanders (1971) and Squire (1975), Bahrick et al. tested their subjects on biographically specific information. They accomplished this by taking the test information from the high-school yearbooks of their subjects, a rich source of names, faces, and activities. Among other kinds of tests, they constructed five-alternative forced-choice recognition tests for faces and names. A test for faces contained one face from the subject's graduating class along with four foils of the same period taken from yearbooks of other schools. Similar recognition tests were constructed for names. The retention of information about faces was virtually unchanged for 35 years, a decline showing only past the age of 52 years. The verbal information concerning names showed a small decline 15 years after graduation, after about 32 years of age. Forty-seven years after graduation, both names and faces were recognized at about the 70% level. It should be clear to the reader that, in contrast to the data of Smith and Winograd (1978) on memory for unfamiliar faces seen recently for one exposure, these data concern memory for faces seen countless times over a period stretching over many years in some cases and then not seen for periods as long as 48 years. It might be said that the memories and the subjects are aging together.

A neuropsychological case has been seriously made during the past decade by many competent investigators (Benton & Van Allen, 1968; Milner, 1968; Yin, 1970) that the process of facial recognition is lateralized in the right cerebral hemisphere. Recently, a developmental version of this lateralization hypothesis has been extended by Carey and Diamond (1977) to the development of the capacity of children to remember faces (Blaney & Winograd, 1978; Goldstein & Chance, 1964). Carey and Diamond suggest that maturational changes in the right hemisphere, which underlie facial recognition, are not complete until around age 10 in children. As evidence, they point to studies showing improvement in recognition of unfamiliar faces up to that age and their own finding that, below the age of 10 years, children remember inverted faces as well as upright faces. Normal adults are seriously impaired when faces are upside down, but Yin (1970) found that adult patients with lesions in the right posterior cortex were not sensitive to facial inversion. If insensitivity to facial inversion is an indicator of right hemisphere problems, then a correlation should be found between the extent to which older people are impaired in facial recognition and the extent to which they are insensitive to facial inversion. Here is a possible direction for neuropsychological research to take.

MEMORY FOR PICTURES AND WORDS

It was emphasized earlier that a comparison of verbal and nonverbal memory in which other important task characteristics are not confounded with the kind of information to be remembered would be desirable. We have attempted such an experiment in collaboration with Anderson D. Smith and now report our progress so far. The emphasis is on our method and its relevance to mnemonic training, as our results, while interesting, require further clarification. Our reading of the literature on the use of mnemonic techniques as remediation leaves us with the impression of mixed findings (see Chapter 26 for a review of that work). Results range from considerable success (Robertson-Tchabo, Hausman, & Arenberg, 1976) to success under restricted parameter values (Treat & Reese, 1976) to no success at all (Mason & Smith, 1977). Our thinking has also been influenced by the sizeable aging deficit found by Smith and Winograd (1978) for recognition memory of faces.

Consider the following simple, but probably wrong, hypothesis: The aging deficit found in memory is largely due to the relative difficulty that older people have in forming or utilizing visual codes. This is essentially an application of Paivio's dual-code hypothesis to the aging problem. Paivio (1971) has offered a simple notion to account for a variety of memory effects associated with word concreteness, pictures, and induced mental imagery. Paivio and Csapo (1973) found a 2:1 ratio in recall in favor of pictures over words. Paivio argues that pictures are better remembered than corresponding word lists because subjects (invariably young adults) store the picture name as well as a visual representation in their memories. For words, on the other hand, they are less likely to store the visual code as well as the verbal code. Two codes are better than one, hence the better memory for pictures. In fact, Paivio and Csapo (1973) suggest that the relative contributions of verbal and visual codes of words to memory are unequal, with pictorial codes being more memorable.

We proposed to compare recall for lists of pictures and words between an aged sample and a younger control group. The question was whether a picture superiority would be found among the aged at all, and if so, would it be less than among the young. What if the elderly show no picture superiority at all in recall and the younger subjects do? Such an interaction would be consistent with a deficiency hypothesis that assumes the absence of, or failure to retrieve, visual codes. The more modest hypothesis that the aged are at a greater disadvantage with visual than with verbal memory predicts an interaction such that the increment gained from studying pictures over words would be less for the elderly.

In terms of the methodological strictures discussed earlier, this procedure has much to commend it. Since subjects recalled by saying words for both kinds of lists (for word lists the words they had seen; for picture lists the names of the pictures they had seen), output mode was the same in both conditions. There were no time pressures at output, so that if translation from a stored image to its name took more time for the aged, they should not have been penalized. All subjects named the pictures at input (or read the word aloud) to make storage of both a verbal and visual code more likely with the picture lists. We do not think it likely that familiarity differs in any significant way between line drawings of everyday objects and their names; granting that the pictures are relatively less familiar, in terms of absolute familiarity both kinds of lists should be highly familiar. What we see as a particular advantage of this experiment is that we are looking for differences in improvement in memory due to the addition of a nonverbal code to the verbal code. Based on the work of Paivio and Csapo (1973), a sizeable increment in memory for pictures was expected; the question is what the size of the increment will be. The extent to which it is smaller for older than younger people can be interpreted in terms of dual-coding theory. A deficit would be inferred on the basis of the size of the increment in recall associated with pictures.[2]

Some procedural details of the experiment are necessary at this point. The elderly sample were all females between 60 and 80 years of age. Sixteen of them were tested at a club meeting under the auspices of the Cobb County, Georgia, Young Women's Christian Association (YWCA). The organization was paid an amount determined by the number of volunteers. An additional six women who live in the New York City area were tested, all of whom were friends or relations of the second author. The 22 subjects in the young group were undergraduate students (seven males and 15 females) enrolled in psychology courses during the 1978 summer session at Emory, and they were paid for their participation. The materials consisted of two lists of black-and-white line drawings of 24 common objects and two lists of the names of these objects printed on index cards in large letters. Subjects were tested one at a time, with half of the subjects tested on a picture list followed by a different word list and the other half tested in the reverse order. Subjects were told to try to remember as many of the items as they could. Each item was shown for about 5 sec, with subjects asked to say the name of the picture or to read the word aloud. Following the last of the 24 cards, the subject was shown a pencil maze and asked to trace his or her way through it. One minute was allowed for this filler task. A 2-min recall test followed this filler task immediately. The subject was asked to recall as many items as possible by saying the word (or the names of the objects for the picture list) aloud.

---

[2]This point is relevant to Crowder's observation at the Talland Conference (Chapter 11) to the effect that most aging research can be summarized by the following generalization: The more difficult the task, the poorer the performance of older relative to younger subjects. In this experiment, the opposite is hypothesized, namely, a greater disadvantage for the older subjects when the memory task is easier, as it is with remembering pictures.

TABLE 27.1
Mean Recall For All Subjects

	Pictures	Words
Young, n = 22	13.50	11.77
Old, n = 20	8.95	9.20

Data for one old subject were discarded because she appeared to be upset when attempting recall of her word list and ended up finally recalling only two items. All other subjects recalled a minimum of four items. Mean recall is shown in Table 27.1. It can be seen that the young subjects recalled more pictures, but the older group recalled slightly more words. The interaction between age and type of list is significant, $F(1,38) = 5.03, p < .05$, as is the main effect of age, $F(1,38) = 34.00$. The effect of type of list is marginally significant, $F(1,38) = 3.50, p < .07$. (The difference between picture and word recall is significant by t-test for the younger group.)

The noteworthy feature of the data is the interaction between age and type of list. Not only is the interaction significant, but there is no evidence of facilitation of recall with the picture list among the aged. This observation would have greater force, however, if the picture superiority were greater among the young group. A relative measure of picture superiority was obtained by calculating the index, $(P-W)/W$, for each subject, where P is the number of pictured items recalled and W the number of words recalled. The mean value on this index for the young group is 15% compared to 5% for the older subjects, but the difference between these relative measures is not significant. It should be noted that the relative measure is highly susceptible to variability when the denominator is low, as it is with the aged.

Before making too much of the interaction observed with the absolute scores, we should point out that there were no males in the older sample. Therefore, we examined the data for only female subjects (that is, we excluded the younger males) for the first list studied and, with this reduced sample, found a marginally significant interaction (see Table 27.2 for the data from female subjects), $F(1,31) = 3.57, p < .07$.

TABLE 27.2
Mean Recall For Female Subjects

	Pictures	Words
Young	14.00	12.11
	(n = 6)	(n = 9)
Old	8.89	10.09
	(n = 9)	(n = 11)

The outcome of this experiment is consistent with the hypothesis that older people have difficulty in forming pictorial codes, in utilizing them effectively at retrieval, or both. Support for this statement comes from the finding that, for older subjects, presenting the items in pictorial form did not significantly improve recall over when the items were verbally presented. Furthermore, the memory of younger subjects was facilitated when the lists were shown pictorially. In studies which have shown less reliance on imaginal mediators by old people (Hulicka & Grossman, 1967; Hulicka, Sterns, & Grossman, 1967), or studies showing essentially no facilitation of recall following instruction in the use of a mnemonic system involving imagery (Mason & Smith, 1977), investigators have tended to favor an interpretation in terms of a production deficiency. The elderly, it has been suggested, are less disposed to use imaginal codes for their own good reasons. In the present experiment, where pictures were explicitly shown to the subject and attention was compelled by the requirement that the picture be named by the subject, visual encoding seems more obligatory and less optional than in the work just referred to.

CONCRETE VERSUS ABSTRACT WORDS

Let us consider only recall of the word lists for a moment. A dual-code theorist might well argue that the age difference in recall for the word lists, as for the picture lists, is due to a deficiency in forming a visual second code. To a dual-code theorist, memory for concrete words is enhanced because of the high probability of storing two codes. If the aged do not form visual codes, then they should be at a disadvantage in recalling concrete words when compared to a population which does engage in imaginal coding. According to this reasoning, just as we have found an interaction between age and stimuli for picture and word lists, so should an interaction be found between age and word concreteness. That is, older subjects should be at a greater disadvantage with concrete words than with abstract words. The available data offer little support for this line of argument. Neither Mason & Smith (1977) with free recall nor Rowe and Schnore (1971) with paired-associate learning have found any evidence that older subjects are at a greater disadvantage with concrete than with abstract words. Our tentative suggestion is that the role of imaginal codes in accounting for the greater recall of concrete words may have been overestimated. Full discussion of the reasons for this statement would take us too far afield, but the interested reader is referred to work by Bransford and McCarrell (1974, pp. 220–227) and Rowe and Schnore (1971). It is not comforting to dual-code theory that Rowe and Schnore (1971) found better recall for concrete words, whether verbal or imaginal mediation was reported by the subject as the strategy for that pair. We suggest that it is wiser to use pictorial material or imagery instructions when pursuing imaginal processes, rather than assume that concrete words reliably lead to visualization.

IMPLICATIONS FOR
COGNITIVE-SKILL TRAINING

We admit to being rather taken aback at the outcome of this experiment. While we had anticipated an interaction such as the one obtained, we did not expect that the older subjects would show no facilitation at all from a picture list. However, we think it would be mistaken, based on these data, to conclude that the aged have such a marked deficit for visual memory that any skill training based on encouraging mental imagery is doomed to failure. There are several reasons for this caution. First, the review by Poon et al. in Chapter 26 shows that a number of investigators have produced facilitation by encouraging older people to form their own images. Second, we must always bear in mind that there are different kinds of mental imagery. The generation of one's own internal representations may produce beneficial memory outcomes, even if externally provided pictures do not. Factor analytic studies (DiVesta, Ingersoll, & Sunshine, 1971, Paivio, 1971, pp. 490–497) have shown that there are different aspects to imagery, including the kind of manipulation of spatial representations measured by the Spatial Relations Test, and that proficiency at this kind of imagery is factorially independent of reports of vividness of imagery. A third reason for caution has to do with this particular experiment. Pictures only facilitated recall by 15% for the younger group, a result quite different from the remarkable facilitation obtained by Paivio and Csapo (1973) but, we point out, a finding in line with earlier work by Paivio, Rogers, and Smythe (1968), who also found a recall increment of 15% for pictures. It would be useful to determine the conditions which produce robust picture superiority effects in the young and then determine whether, under such optimal circumstances, the aged benefit from pictorial representation. Until then, these findings should be taken as a first attempt.

DOES PICTORIAL INTERACTION HELP?

On the basis of the picture–word experiment just described, we asked ourselves what would be the elaboration condition with which we would be most confident of a facilitative effect on memory. To put it another way, what test would old people, or any population, have to fail for us to seriously reconsider the usefulness of any remediation training which derives from experimental work on mnemonic techniques? The answer was easy for us to agree on. If old people did not show considerably higher recall following the study of pictures of two objects interacting than when the pictures of the objects were not depicted as interacting, then the situation would be grim. There is general agreement with Bower (1972) that mnemonic techniques such as visualization are effective because they enhance the associative integration of what were psychologically isolated items prior to application of the method. Bower calls the process "relational organization"; others have called it "unitization" or "functional integration" (Begg, 1978). The point is that, as the Gestalt psychologists argued, interacting imagery confers unity on what were separate psychological elements.

To reduce the cognitive demands of the task, we showed our subjects two decks of ten cards each. On each card were drawings of two common objects. In one deck, the objects were shown side by side, while in the other deck, the objects were depicted as interacting. This comparison has been carried out with young adults by Epstein, Rock, and Zuckerman (1960) and Wollen, Weber, and Lowry (1972) and has been found to result in about twice the recall with the interactive depiction. Our subjects served in both conditions in a counterbalanced order with different objects drawn in each deck and saw each card for about 5 sec at study. They knew that their memory would be tested with the method of cued recall and were tested on one practice card for each deck. The participants were volunteers from a high-rise residence for senior citizens in which residents are free to come and go. All participants were over 70, with five over 80 and one over 90. There were four males and six females; three of the four males were over 80.

We are pleased to report that performance was twice as good when the pairs were depicted as interacting. Mean recall (of 10) was 5.00 and 2.40 items for the interactive and separate pairs, respectively, $t(9) = 4.99, p < .01$. Nine of the 10 subjects recalled more items shown as interacting, while the remaining subject recalled no words at all in either condition although he appeared to know what the objects were and claimed that he recognized the cues when they were shown. The results of this small study probably speak more to the importance of unitization in associative recall than to the role of visual factors.

EVIDENCE FROM
INFORMATION-PROCESSING RESEARCH

Innovative methods taken from the study of information processing have recently been applied to the question of an age-related decline in visual performance. These experiments have in common the goal of examining processes which occur early on in the flow of information within the organism. Typically, the problem is approached as either one of attention or short-term memory and may be contrasted with the previous studies reviewed in this chapter which have dealt primarily with long-term memory. There are two studies in particular which we think repay close analysis because of their careful attention to methodological problems as well as their interesting findings. Elias and Kinsbourne (1974) were concerned with the speed of same–different judgments when the two stimuli were either verbal or visual in nature, while Gaylord and Marsh (1975) examined the performance of older subjects in a mental rotation task employing purely visual figures.

[Elias and Kinsbourne (1974) were interested in exploring] age-cohort differences in the processing of verbal and non-verbal stimuli. Therefore, a task was selected in which the role of long-term memory was minimized and the mode of responding was held constant. The verbal stimuli used in the experiment were pairs of letters which served as abbreviations of verbal messages. The non-verbal stimuli were arrows which provided a graphic representation of the verbal stimuli [p. 162].

Two stimuli were presented in succession and the subject's task was to respond by pressing the "same" button as rapidly as possible if the second stimulus belonged to the same set as the first, and the "different" button when it did not. Items belonged to the same set if they described the same spatial orientation—that is, if both stimuli rotated in the same direction. For example, two verbal items which are not physically identical but belonged to the same set because they rotate in a common direction would be DR (for "down right") and UL (for "upper left"). If the reader imagines a clock face, he will see that both stimuli refer to rotation in a clockwise direction. Visual stimuli represented these rotations by means of arrows.

Although the reader might assume that both the verbal and visual stimuli in this experiment would require essentially the same kind of visual transformation in order to determine whether they are the same or different with respect to rotation, Elias and Kinsbourne found an undeniable difference between the two kinds of stimuli. For our purposes, the important outcome was an age × sex × stimulus interaction for the error measure (no such interaction was found for speed). For both males and females, the difference in errors between visual and verbal stimuli was greater, with more errors for visual stimuli for the older subjects; furthermore, this effect was particularly pronounced for the older women. In short, the error measure revealed a differential degree of difficulty among the aged in dealing with visual stimuli as compared to verbal stimuli, with a strong interaction with sex. In the words of Elias and Kinsbourne (1974):

Inferiority of women for the non-verbal material suggests a relative inferiority on their part for information processing tasks which involve non-verbal as opposed to verbal mediation. The generality of this conclusion must rely on a demonstration of a similar relationship between processing of non-verbal and verbal stimuli in laboratory paradigms which carefully separate stimulus characteristics, mode of response, and the conceptual nature of the task [p. 170].

MENTAL ROTATION AND MEMORY SCANNING

In an interesting study, Gaylord and Marsh (1975) have applied the technique developed by Shepard and Metzler (1971) to older subjects. The basic procedure involves showing two pictures of the same three-dimensional shape and asking the subject to make a same–different judgment with respect to the congruence of the two shapes. An example of an incongruent pair used by Gaylord and Marsh is shown in Fig. 27.1. On half the trials, the objects were identical in three-dimensional shape but differed in their angular difference in orientation; on the remaining trials, not only was the difference in orientation manipulated, but the figures were mirror images of each other. Shepard and Metzler (1971) found that the time to decide if the two figures were the same in orientation or were mirror images increased linearly with the angular difference in orientation. On the basis of this finding and others reviewed by Cooper and Shepard (1973), including subjects' reports that they made their decision about the identity of the shapes by mentally rotating one figure,

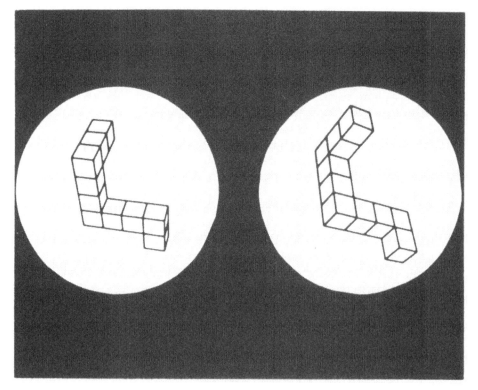

FIG. 27.1.   Example of one of the pairs of figures used by Gaylord and Marsh (1975).

Shepard and his associates argue that subjects are manipulating an internal representation of the stimulus and that the speed of this manipulation is proportional to the distance this representation is rotated. The slope of the function relating time for the same–different judgment to the angular difference between the two figures being compared is taken to be a relatively uncontaminated measure of the speed of mental rotation. The intercept of the function, or the residual time, is interpreted as the sum of the times taken to carry out such processes as encoding the stimuli and pressing a button to convey the outcome of the decision.

Gaylord and Marsh (1975) compared the performance of young and old adults with the Shepard–Metzler paradigm. It should be noted that the task was made comprehensible to their subjects by ample practice, first with wooden models of the figures and then with visually presented practice figures. The slope obtained for the older group yielded a mental rotation rate of 17.7 msec per degree, compared with a rate of 9.6 msec per degree for the younger group, a ratio of 1.84:1. Associated with this finding were greater variability for the older subjects and an intercept more than 2 sec higher. The reader should bear in mind that the slope and intercept are independent; that is, the fact that the older subjects have a greater intercept does not compel their mental rotation rate, as read from the slope, to be slower. As Gaylord and Marsh put it, "Thus it would appear that apart from any slowing of motor response or sensory encoding process there is a slowing in those aspects of cognitive processing related to mentally manipulating the figures [p. 677]." The significance of this finding is that the marked slowing down observed here in the internal manipulation of visual representations can be separated out from the more general slowing down generally associated with age. In addition to the slowing of what they identified as the rate of mental rotation, Gaylord and Marsh also found a significantly higher error rate in their older sample; the average error rate was 11% for the older group compared with 5% for the younger group. As Elias and Kinsbourne (1974) found, the decline in performance with age was manifested not only by a slowing down of cognitive processing but by more errors as well.

RELATIONSHIP TO MEMORY SCANNING

The reader will no doubt have noticed a similarity between this analysis of the mental rotation task and Sternberg's (1975) analysis of retrieval from short term memory, usually called "memory scanning". Briefly, in Sternberg's procedure the subject is presented with a small set of items, usually digits or letters, to hold in memory and is then presented with either one of the memorized set or a new item for test. The task is to respond as rapidly as possible, positively if the test item was a member of the set, negatively if it was not. On the basis of a linear slope increase with the size of the memory set,

Sternberg concluded that the memory scan was exceedingly rapid for young adults (between 35–40 items per second) and could be characterized as an exhaustive, serial search.

The memory-scanning paradigm has been applied to the aged in several experiments (Anders & Fozard, 1973; Anders, Fozard, & Lillyquist, 1972; Eriksen, Hamlin, & Daye, 1973) with a common outcome. Compared to young adults, the slope for older subjects has been steeper by a ratio of about 2:1; translated into rate, the younger subjects, on the average, are scanning the contents of short-term memory twice as fast as the older subjects. In terms of absolute scanning rates, the estimates obtained for the older subjects in the three experiments just cited are between 12 and 23 items per sec. It should be emphasized that the qualitative aspects of performance do not differ as a function of age. At all ages tested, memory scan shows the characteristics found by Sternberg; aging is manifested solely by a slower rate of scan and a higher intercept. As with the mental rotation study of Gaylord and Marsh (1975), the reader should bear in mind that the measurement of the speed of memory scanning is independent of other kinds of slowing down. In fact, Sternberg (1975) reviews studies comparing populations of alcoholics, schizophrenics, and children, in which the slope parameter does not differ at all from young adults. In these groups, slower performance is manifested only in a higher intercept, suggesting impairment of perception and encoding, output time, or both, but not in speed of memory search. The aged, on the other hand, are slower in both measurable aspects of performance, slope and intercept.

To review, at this point we have examined findings from mental rotation and memory search tasks showing nearly identical outcomes. In both tasks, when compared with young adults, older subjects are slower by half in the purely cognitive aspect of the task. What should be made of this? Gaylord and Marsh (1975) conclude from the constancy of the slope ratios in both tasks that "there might be the same rate-limiting mechanisms in both verbal and non-verbal cognitive processing systems [p. 678]." It is on this point that we take issue with Gaylord and Marsh. The problem, as we see it, is that Gaylord and Marsh presuppose that the memory scan in the Sternberg task involves verbal processing, an assumption which is doubtful. Sternberg (1970, 1975) has concluded that, even when the contents of primary memory are verbal items such as digits or letters, the representation or code used in carrying out the memory search is visual. His reasons may be briefly mentioned. Estimates of the speed of covert articulatory rehearsal give values not nearly rapid enough in the face of the observed very rapid search rates. Also, similar scanning phenomena to those obtained with alphanumeric stimuli are obtained when such nonverbal material as faces and nonsense forms are presented. Further evidence for the position that the usual memory scan is carried out on a visual rather than a verbal representation of the stimuli is to be found in a discussion by Klatzky (1975, pp. 119–122).

To step back for a moment, a persistent problem throughout this chapter has been to distinguish, where necessary, between the type of stimulus presented to the subject and the type of code or process he uses in dealing with that stimulus. Thus, in the context of memory for concrete and abstract words, the stimuli are words, but theorists such as Paivio (1971) hypothesize that concrete words lead to visual representations whereas abstract words are represented in verbal codes. In the context of Gaylord and Marsh's comparison between mental rotation of geometric forms and memory scanning of digits, it is clear that the stimuli in the former case are nonverbal and, in the latter, verbal, but we have tried to convince the reader that the information in neither case is dealt with verbally by the subject. This leads us to contest Gaylord and Marsh's conclusion about "the same rate-limiting mechanisms in both verbal and cognitive processing systems" as not proven, since we are suggesting that, in point of fact, the rate-limiting mechanism, whatever it may be, is one and the same in both the rotation and scanning experiments. The grounds for this assertion are that both tasks produce reliance on nonverbal codes. In our opinion, then, these studies do not afford a comparison between verbal and nonverbal processing. What they do show, however, is a marked slowing down with age of cognitive functions involving manipulation of visual representations.

SIGNIFICANCE OF INFORMATION-PROCESSING FINDINGS FOR COGNITIVE-SKILLS TRAINING IN THE ELDERLY

The most reliable finding of this selective review of studies of information processing is that with aging, not only are general reactions slowed down, but more purely cognitive skills as well. In particular, experimental analysis of a simple decision as to whether two figures are identical into its cognitive and perceptual–motoric components has been applied to the aged, with the result that they have been shown to be much slower than young adults on the purely cognitive aspect of the task. The error data are consistent with the speed data. Furthermore, we have argued that the small literature available at present suggests clearly that the cognitive component which has been assessed has to do with visually coded information. The only comparison attempted between verbal and nonverbal information we are aware of which meets strict methodological criteria, that of Elias and Kinsbourne (1974), complicates matters by not having found an interaction of age and type of stimulus for the speed measure, but does report an interaction for errors which includes sex as a major factor.

It will be recalled that it was elderly women who were found to be at a particular disadvantage with nonverbal information by Elias and Kinsbourne. These authors cited work by other investigators showing a male superiority in dealing with nonverbal information, particularly when the nonverbal task has a predominately spatial manipulation aspect. (See Coltheart, Hull, & Slater [1975] for a recent example of a comparable finding among college students.) It so happens that Gaylord and Marsh's subjects were all males, as were the older subjects in the memory scanning studies reviewed above. Since the pattern of sex differences in the literature leads one to expect poorer performance by females on visuospatial tasks, it would be useful to have comparisons which include sex as a factor in future research. (Our own work on picture–word differences in free recall described earlier is deficient in this regard in only having females as subjects in the older group.) Of course, it is anticipated that any sex difference found will not change conclusions based on the studies discussed here, because they were done with males and, according to the literature, males would be expected to perform better than females on these visual tasks.

Another direction for research on modes of processing information would be to apply selective interference paradigms to research with the aged. Rather sophisticated paradigms have been developed which, by systematically manipulating the type of information to be processed in conjunction with the type of information serving as the interference tasks, allow one to make conclusions about representational modes on the basis of the interactions observed. An instructive application of one such design in an attempt to compare verbal and nonverbal memory loss among Korsakoff patients is to be found in a recent study by Cermak, Reale, and De Luca (1977).

IMPLICATIONS FOR MEMORY TRAINING

We have reviewed evidence in this chapter from a variety of tasks, including memory for designs, faces, and pictures, as well as studies of visual information processing. In virtually all of these studies, support has been found for the hypothesis of an age-related decline in the capacity to deal with visual information. Whether this decline is steeper than the decline in verbal memory remains a difficult question, as we have seen. However, the evidence surveyed leaves us with little confidence that memory for visual information is immune to the processes associated with aging. This brings us back to the point we started with, that it might be unwise to build a memory remediation program on a weak foundation. Because mnemonics training based on mental imagery obviously relies on encouraging visualization in order to aid verbal memory—after all, to remember an image is to rely on visual memory—and because the ability to manipulate and remember visual representations is apparently declining, the prescription of imagery for memory ills would seem to be on shaky ground. We propose a way out of this dilemma.

To retrace our steps a bit, why has so much reliance been placed on mental imagery as an aid to memory? The answer is simply because it has been shown to work, particularly with younger adults. The next question is especially important. Why does mental imagery work? The answer which seems to have the broadest agreement is because mental imagery organizes information very effectively. This conclusion has been reached independently by Bower, Bransford and McCarrell, and Begg, among others. Thus, as discussed earlier, Bower (1972) argues that imagery facilitates associative recall not because it produces distinctive representations but because it confers relational organization on otherwise separate psychological elements. Bower points out that this argument derives from the Gestalt thinkers who emphasized the central role of perceptual unity in cognition. Similarly, in a discussion of why concrete words are more memorable than abstract words, Bransford and McCarrell (1974) emphasize that one is more likely to find a meaningful relation with concrete material; the emphasis here is on finding relations rather than visualizing. In a similar vein, Begg (1978) concludes that imagery is effective in facilitating memory only when it promotes organization or integration. The shared insight of these theorists is that imagery is effective because some kinds of visualization promote the efficient organization of stored information. An important consequence of this view is that anything which is conducive to organization at the time of encoding should help memory. With reference to the aged, if it seems unlikely that they will benefit from using visual organization, then we should look for other methods which will help them organize information. It should be noted that there are descriptions in the literature of people with exceptional memories who do not rely on visual imagery, notwithstanding Luria's (1968) famous mnemonist who relied most exclusively on an incredible capacity for visual imagery. Thus, Hunt and Love (1972) have described VP, an extraordinary verbal mnemonist, while Hunter (1977) has described the abilities of the late Professor Aitken, both of whom developed their own nonvisual techniques leading to remarkable mnemonic achievements.

To be more specific, we are suggesting that many older adults who are experiencing memory problems might benefit more from verbal mnemonic aids than reliance on mental imagery. In Hulicka and Grossman's (1967) well known study, there was no difference following the use of verbal and imaginal mediation among older adults, while both strategies led to significantly better recall than the use of no mediation at all. Such mnemonic aids as memorizing the notes of the treble clef with "Every Good Boy Does Fine" or the number of days in each month by means of the rhyme beginning "Thirty days hath September, April, June, and November" are familiar examples of verbal mnemonics which elaborate the information to be remembered with verbal devices such as rhyme and meter. In his recent book on memory training, Cermak (1975) includes a separate chapter on such purely verbal devices. In short, memory training can employ techniques which do not depend on imagery.

In addition, the great amount of variability shown by older people on cognitive tasks must be kept in mind when remediation is under consideration. Undoubtedly some people can and will benefit from mental imagery, while others will benefit more from verbal elaboration. Can we foresee the day when the memory therapist will be able to prescribe memory remediation training tailored for his client on the basis of a cognitive test profile? We can all agree that a lot of work lies between present capabilities and that state of affairs. The cautionary note sounded by this chapter is that it is conceivable that imagery training may not be the single road toward memory remediation in the elderly and that, by a premature commitment to imagery training, failure could lead to the false conclusion that the memory problems associated with aging are not remediable.

In conclusion, we see three directions for research related to memory remediation. First, research related to visual and verbal information processing and memory in the aged is needed, informed by the recent advances in cognitive psychology. We have reviewed some of this work in this chapter and pointed to some possible directions for it to take. Second, we urge that, at the same time, research on memory skill training employ broader techniques than the traditional imagery device. Third, and perhaps most difficult, the importance of individual differences in preferred modes of representation of information must be kept in mind, so that the future memory trainer can be diagnostician as well as teacher.

REFERENCES

Anders, T. R., & Fozard, J. L. Effects of age upon retrieval from primary and secondary memory. *Developmental Psychology,* 1973, *9,* 411–415.

Anders, T. R., Fozard, J. L., & Lillyquist, T. D. Effects of age upon retrieval from short-term memory. *Developmental Psychology,* 1972, *6,* 214–217.

Arenberg, D. Differences and changes with age in the Benton Visual Retention Test. *Journal of Gerontology,* 1978, *33,* 534–540.

Bahrick, H. P., Bahrick, P. P., & Wittlinger, R. P. Fifty years of memory for names and faces: A cross-sectional approach. *Journal of Experimental Psychology: General,* 1975, *104,* 54–75.

Begg, I. Imagery and organization in memory: Instructional effects. *Memory & Cognition,* 1978, *6,* 174–183.

Benton, A. L. & Van Allen, M. W. Impairment of facial recognition of patients with cerebral disease. *Cortex,* 1968, *4,* 344–358.

Blaney, R. L. & Winograd, E. Developmental differences in children's recognition memory for faces. *Developmental Psychology,* 1978, *14,* 441–442.

Botwinick, J. *Aging and behavior.* New York: Springer, 1973.

Bower, G. H. Mental imagery and associative imagery. In L. W. Gregg (Ed.), *Cognition in learning and memory.* New York: Wiley, 1972.

Bower, G. H., & Karlin, M. B. Depth of processing pictures of faces and recognition memory. *Journal of Experimental Psychology,* 1974, *103,* 751–757.

Bransford, J. D., & McCarrell, N. S. A sketch of a cognitive approach to comprehension. In W. B. Weimer & D. S. Palermo (Eds.), *Cognition and the symbolic processes.* Hillsdale, N.J.: Lawrence Erlbaum Associates, 1974.

Carey, S., & Diamond, R. From piecemeal to configurational representation of faces. *Science,* 1977, *193,* 312–313.

Cermak, L. S. *Improving your memory.* New York: McGraw-Hill, 1975.

Cermak, L. S., Reale, L. & Deluca, D. Korsakoff patients' non-verbal vs. verbal memory: Effects of interference and mediation on rate of information loss. *Neuropsychologia,* 1977, *15,* 303–310.

Coltheart, M., Hull, E., & Slater, D. Sex differences in imagery and reading. *Nature,* 1975, *253,* 438–440.

Cooper, L. A., & Shepard, R. N. Chronometric studies of the rotation of mental images. In W. G. Chase (Ed.), *Visual information processing.* New York: Academic Press, 1973.

Craik, F. I. M. Age differences in human memory. In J. E. Birren & K. W. Schaie (Eds.), *Handbook of the psychology of aging.* New York: Van Nostrand and Reinhold, 1977.

DiVesta, F. J., Ingersoll, G., & Sunshine, P. A factor analysis of imagery tests. *Journal of Verbal Learning and Verbal Behavior,* 1971, *10,* 471–479.

Elias, M. F., & Kinsbourne, M. Age and sex differences in the processing of verbal and non-verbal stimuli. *Journal of Gerontology,* 1974, *29,* 162–171.

Epstein, W., Rock, I., & Zuckerman, C. B. Meaning and faimilarity in associative learning. *Psychological Monographs,* 1960, *74,* No. 491.

Eriksen, C. W., Hamlin, R. M., & Daye, C. Aging adults and rate of memory scan. *Bulletin of the Psychonomic Society,* 1973, *1,* 259–260.

Gaylord, S. A., & Marsh, G. R. Age differences in the speed of a spatial cognitive process. *Journal of Gerontology,* 1975, *30,* 674–678.

Goldstein, A. G., & Chance, J. E. Recognition of children's faces. *Child Development,* 1964, *35,* 129–136.

Hulicka, I. M., & Grossman, J. L. Age-group comparisons for the use of mediators in paired-associate learning. *Journal of Gerontology,* 1967, *22,* 46–51.

Hulicka, I. M., Sterns, H., & Grossman, J. L. Age-group comparisons of paired-associate learning as a function of paced and self-paced association and response times. *Journal of Gerontology,* 1967, *22,* 274–280.

Hunt, E., & Love, T. How good can memory be? In A. W. Melton & E. Martin (Eds.), *Coding processes in human memory.* Washington, D.C.: V. H. Winston, 1972.

Hunter, I. M. L. An exceptional memory. *British Journal of Psychology,* 1977, *68,* 155–164.

Kinsbourne, M. Cognitive decline with advancing age: An interpretation. In W. L. Smith, & M. Kinsbourne (Eds.), *Aging and dementia.* New York: Spectrum, 1977.

Klatzky, R. L. *Human memory: Structures and processes.* San Francisco: W. H. Freeman, 1975.

Lee, J. A., & Pollack, R. H. The effects of age on perceptual problem-solving strategies. *Experimental Aging Research,* 1978, *4,* 37–54.

Luria, A. R. *The mind of a mnemonist.* New York: Basic Books, 1968.

McGhie, A., Chapman, T., & Lawson, J. S. Changes in immediate memory with age. *British Journal of Psychology,* 1965, *56,* 69–75.

Mason, S. E., & Smith, A. D. Imagery in the aged. *Experimental Aging Research,* 1977, *3,* 17–32.

Milner, B. Visual recognition and recall after right temporal lobe excision in man. *Neuropsychologia,* 1968, *6,* 191–209.

Paivio, A. *Imagery and verbal processes.* New York: Holt, Reinhart, & Winston, 1971.

Paivio, A., & Csapo, K. Picture superiority in free recall: Imagery or dual coding? *Cognitive Psychology,* 1973, *5,* 176–206.

Paivio, A., Rogers, T. B., & Smythe, P. C. Why are pictures easier to recall than words? *Psychonomic Science,* 1968, *11,* 137–138.

Robertson-Tchabo, E. A., Hausman, C. P., & Arenberg, D. A classical mnemonic for older learners: A trip that works! *Educational Gerontology,* 1976, *1,* 215–226.

Rowe, E. J., & Schnore, M. M. Item concreteness and reported strategies in paired associate learning as a function of age. *Journal of Gerontology,* 1971, *26,* 470–475.

Schaie, K. W. Age changes in adult intelligence. In D. S. Woodruff & J. E. Birren (Eds.), *Aging.* New York: Van Nostrand, 1975.

Schaie, K. W., & Labouvie-Vief, G. Generational versus ontogenetic components of change in adult cognitive behavior: A fourteen-year cross-sectional sequence. *Developmental Psychology,* 1974, *10,* 305–320.

Shepard, R. N., & Metzler, J. Mental rotation of three-dimensional objects. *Science,* 1971, *171,* 701–703.

Smith, A. D., & Winograd, E. Adult age differences in remembering faces. *Developmental Psychology,* 1978, *14,* 443–444.

Squire, L. R. A stable impairment in remote memory following electroconvulsive therapy. *Neuropsychologia,* 1975, *13,* 51–58.

Sternberg, S. Memory-scanning: Mental processes revealed by reaction-time experiments. In J. S. Antrobus (Ed.), *Cognition and affect.* Boston: Little, Brown, 1970.

Sternberg, S. Memory scanning: New findings and current controversies. *Quarterly Journal of Experimental Psychology,* 1975, *27,* 1–32.

Tesch, S., Whitbourne, S. K., & Nehrke, M. Cognitive egocentrism in institutionalized males. *Journal of Gerontology,* 1978, *33,* 546–552.

Treat, N. J., & Reese, H. W. Age, pacing, and imagery in paired-associate learning. *Developmental Psychology,* 1976, *12,* 119–124.

Tulving, E. Episodic and semantic memory. In E. Tulving & W. Donaldson (Eds.), *Organization of memory.* New York: Acacemic Press, 1972.

Warrington, E. K., & Ackroyd, C. The effect of orienting tasks on recognition memory. *Memory and Cognition,* 1975, *3,* 140–142.

Warrington, E. K. & Sanders, H. I. The fate of old memories. *Quarterly Journal of Experimental Psychology,* 1971, *21,* 432–442.

Winograd, E. Recognition memory for faces following nine different judgments. *Bulletin of the Psychonomic Society,* 1976, *8,* 419–421.

Winograd, E. Encoding operations which facilitate memory for faces across the life span. In Gruneberg, M. M., Morris, P. E., & Sykes, R. (Eds.), *Practical aspects of memory.* London: Academic Press, 1978.

Wollen, K. A., Weber, A., & Lowry, D. H. Bizarreness versus interaction of mental images as determinants of learning. *Cognitive Psychology,* 1972, *3,* 518–523.

Yin, R. K. Face recognition by brain-injured patients: a dissociable ability? *Neuropsychologia,* 1970, *8,* 395–402.

28 Comments on Imagery as a Therapeutic Mnemonic

Laird S. Cermak
Boston Veterans Administration Medical Center and
Boston University School of Medicine

The conflict which exists between the optimistic fervor displayed in proposing the application of imagery as a mnemonic technique and the limited success of the procedure which is seen under rigorous analysis is quite apparent in the two chapters just presented. Poon, Walsh-Sweeney, and Fozard (Chapter 26) almost appear to want to will the success of imagery as an aid improving memory in the elderly. To their credit, their arguments are extremely convincing and they leave one with the feeling that it could be pulled off despite the obstacles which they keenly depict in their literature review. Winograd and Simon (Chapter 27), however, appear less willing to leap into this Camelot of imagination, and they state their reservations succinctly. Nevertheless, like most of us, they stolidly refuse to give up hope and pray in the end that imagery will prove to be the savior of fading memory abilities, even though it must rise out of the ashes of objectivity to fulfill its destiny.

This author is going to choose (I could have gone either way, I suppose) to sound an empty note into this arena of illusions and propose that imagery might best have remained relegated to its place in history rather than being elevated to a lofty place alongside verbal mnemonics. There are essentially two reasons why I have taken this rather barren attitude: one quite personal, the other completely objective.

Ever since the time I wrote the book (1976) referred to in Winograd and Simon's chapter, I have felt a sort of personal obligation to try to "master" those techniques I so confidently presented as mnemonic aids in the text. Those aids which were primarily verbal in nature proved to be easy skills to learn and even in a limited fashion to apply. Thus, I can now retain telephone numbers by converting them first to predesignated letters and then combining these letters into words through the appropriate insertion of meaningful vowels. Furthermore, I can remember names better by forming nonsense phrases out of the name (e.g., Chowmentowski becomes "show men to ski"). But I have been dramatically unsuccessful in applying pure imagery as a mnemonic aid. It serves well as an interactive supplement or as a way to retain pictorial material (I'll come back to this), but in its pure form its use has been disastrous as a mechanism for retaining verbal information.

It is perfectly true that the "one is a bun" procedure works well for learning a short series of unrelated items. But, beyond the classroom demonstration or occasional parlor game, the skill to use such a device has not stood me in good stead in the real world. Under what circumstances does one feel required to memorize an unrelated list? The only "lists" we tend to memorize are shopping lists or lists of things to do. In both these cases, the items are related and their images are as easily confused as the items themselves. Try the "one is a bun" technique with all the list items being vegetables; some say it's easier to just remember that they are vegetables.

I have tried to imagine other circumstances under which imagery might be useful, but in each instance found it interfering at best. I watched a mechanic fix my carburetor and tried to remember how it would go back together by imagery. There was a complete loss of information. I've tried remembering names paired with faces by pairing a salient facial feature with an image suggested by the person's name. Except for rare instances, the most I could remember was that I performed the process. Lastly, I have tried to remember the story line of a book by making an imagined movie of the plot, but again found myself trying to remember what the book "said" when my mental movie needed splicing.

In short, then, I have not found imagery to be terribly useful in my own life, despite, I believe, more genuine attempts to apply it than is generally the norm. Each time I come back to the realization that the use of imagery to remember verbal materials is less useful than the use of verbal mnemonics. True, it is dramatically useful under specialized circumstances, but then so are specialized verbal mnemonics, especially those designed to remember large numbers. The problem is that imagery is just not highly applicable to real life situations. I believe that if it were, it would have evolved as a social skill long ago. The fact that it has not, indeed has at various times gone out of vogue, attests to its nonutilitarian nature.

This is not meant to imply that we do not use imagery as a mode for retention of pictorial information—e.g., pictures, faces, etc. Retention of this material is extremely good, as evidenced by Shephard's (1967) classic experiments on picture retention, and by the fact that all of us realize that we can remember faces very well. This matching of images seems to be a highly developed skill in humans. But it must be remembered that all these tasks are recognition tasks in which a picture is rated as old or new, familiar or unfamiliar. Reconstruction of a picture or a face is difficult and, in fact, we find that we do not carry around a photograph of the desired stimulus at all, but merely an impression. It is hard to "visualize" the face of one's spouse or close friend whom one sees daily. How is the hair parted, where are the freckles, which tooth is crooked? Reconstruction is terrible, especially when compared to reconstruction of a poem one has learned, or a paired-associate once formed. The point is that even in its own mode, imagery is not tremendously powerful as a "reconstructive" device.

Why then should we expect imagery will aid the verbal retentive ability of an individual who possesses less than the normal armada of information-processing skills? Imagery skills, weak as they are normally, could hardly be expected to suddenly subsume previously latent functions. The previous two papers present the hope that imagery would somehow remain stable and become, in the final stage, the only mechanism whereby information could be retained. However, such has not proven to be the case in my own objective observations, at least with amnesic patients.

Amnesic patients' use of imagery did facilitate learning and "temporarily" aided the retrievability of paired-associate (P–A) information, but only when the patient was continuously reminded that an image had in fact been formed. Specifically, alcoholic Korsakoff patients were instructed to learn the correct response to each of five stimuli in a P–A list using either rote learning, mediation or imagery. Under both the mediation and imagery conditions, the patients were given explicit instructions to mediate using a particular word, or to remember using a particular image. In both cases, learning and retention exceeded rote memorization levels. However, and this is what is of greatest import here, the patients had to be reinstructed with regard to the appropriate mediator or image on each learning trial *and* they had to be reminded to use the aid during retrieval. Furthermore, left to themselves they were unable to use the techniques with new materials. They simply "forgot" what to do from trial to trial or forgot how to retrieve the mediator or image they had been asked to learn.

It is true that these patients do represent the ultimate form of retrieval deficiency, but their case seems to highlight what might well occur among the less afflicted: namely, that with aging the ability to remember a specific image, or to remember that an image had been formed at all, or even to remember how to use imagery is going to deteriorate quite possibly at a rate comparable to the rest of the individual's cognitive and mnemonic skills.

Consequently, lest we promise more than can be delivered, let's be cautious and not yet proclaim imagery as even a potential therapeutic device for the elderly. To do so, prior to several replicated successes over a broad spectrum of real world situations, would be to place imagery on the same level with "hypnosis," "ESP," "miracle drugs," and "divine intervention." Additionally, and as a final note, I wonder if any therapist ought to attempt to teach any mnenonic as utilitarian when, in fact, he finds it difficult, even unnecessary, to apply it himself.

REFERENCES

Cermak, L. S. *Improving Your Memory.* New York: Norton, 1976.

Shepherd, R. N. Recognition memory for words, sentences and pictures. *Journal of Verbal Learning and Verbal Behavior,* 1976, *6,* 156–163.

29

Cognitive-Skill Training for the Elderly: Why Should "Old Dogs" Acquire New Tricks

Elizabeth Anne Robertson-Tchabo
Department of Human Development, University of Maryland

Experimental psychologists are beginning to accept the challenge to develop practical memory remediation techniques for the elderly that have broad applicability in non-laboratory situations. Poon, Walsh-Sweeney, and Fozard (Chapter 26) have suggested that imagery mnemonics seem to be a potentially useful aid to improve learning and memory performance of the elderly. However, Winograd and Simon (Chapter 27) have sounded a cautionary note and have concluded that imagery training may not be the optimal path toward memory remediation.

Before considering the essential features of a mnemonic tailored to meet the special needs of the elderly, it would be prudent to answer two important and related questions. First, for whom are these mnemonics being developed; and second, why is a mnemonic needed or with which specific task(s) is the technique to be used? Since we do not know the impact of an age-related decrease in free-recall performance on the daily activities of an older individual (Erickson, Poon, & Walsh-Sweeney, Chapter 22), we may not evaluate accurately the significance of the problem for an older individual.

Perhaps a needs assessment for memory performance of specific tasks should be considered an essential first step in cognitive skill training. Of course, it is entirely possible that an individual (or professional) might fail to recognize a particular difficulty as a memory problem—for example, noncompliance with a drug regimen. Moreover, memory complaint may not be correlated highly with the level of objective memory performance which has been found to relate to the affective state of the individual (Kahn, Zarit, Hilbert, & Niederehe, 1975). The well established association between depression and chronic disease (Botwinick, 1973) suggests that health status is a variable which may be related systematically to both memory complaint and to memory performance. In any case, since self-reported memory problems have not been a criterion for a subject's participation in most memory-intervention studies, perhaps we should not be surprised that most "normal" older individuals do not continue to use a mnemonic outside of the laboratory. Moreover, for the type of task typically used in the laboratory, memory for a list of unrelated, discrete items or pairs of items, there is a more efficient memory aid—preparing a written list to which one may refer when necessary, thereby precluding the memory requirement of search and retrieval of specific items. Undoubtedly, it is time to examine the predictive validity of tasks typically used in the experimental laboratory. Moreover, priority should be given to age-related health, personality, and environmental factors that are associated with memory problems.

Despite my opinion that difficulties in the acquisition and retention of lists of "new" items will prove not to be the most serious memory problem of "seasoned" citizens, there are some individuals, for example, the elderly blind, for whom an efficient and accurate memory is a necessity to carry out daily activities and to avoid institutionalization. Since no comparable aid to making lists exists for the adventitiously blind adult who has not learned Braille, a blind person must commit to memory a myriad of details to perform tasks for which sighted individuals need not rely on memory: for example, the number of steps in a flight of stairs or the order of pill bottles in the medicine cabinet. Even a modest decline in memory performance can have a profound and far-reaching effect on the older blind person's quality of life, including the ability to benefit from rehabilitation training programs. Only 16% of the 484,000 Americans who are legally blind were congenitally blind, and approximately 75% of those who are legally blind are at least 40 years old (Hatfield, 1973). The National Center for Health Statistics (1971) reported that there were 909,000 individuals with severe visual disability 65 years or older, a prevalence rate of 47 per 1,000. Almost no research has addressed memory-skill training for adventitiously blind adults. However, Raia (1979) used a procedure reported by Robertson-Tchabo, Hausman, and Arenberg (1976) and found that, with training and practice in the method of loci, recall performance of elderly adventitiously blinded women was facilitated. The elderly adventitiously blind may well afford psychologists a unique opportunity to investigate memory complaint, memory performance, and cognitive-skill training in an ecologically valid context. Hopefully, it is not overly optimistic to predict that experimental psychologists will begin to apply their knowledge of age differences in cognitive functioning to develop more successful rehabilitation programs for the adventitiously blind.

Having addressed the issues of the characteristics of the learner and of the task to be learned, a consideration of the essential features of a mnemonic tailored to meet the needs of older individuals is in order. It is accepted generally that the amount of information retained by an individual is a function of the organization of the material at the time of input (Bower, 1970). Any age-related decrease in the amount of information encoded, whether due to the pacing of the input (Treat & Reese, 1976) or to an inability to devise an encoding strategy (Hulicka & Rust, 1964; Hulicka & Weiss, 1965; Rowe & Schnore, 1971) will limit the variety of retrieval cues available to direct the search process at the time of recall. Elaboration encoding, adding a visual image or a verbal association to the item information, does make material more memorable; however, the additional information initially will increase the storage load and indeed may overload some older individuals' information-processing capacity. Until older individuals have practiced using an unfamiliar mnemonic technique, such as the "peg-word" system (Mason & Smith, 1977), there is *more* information to remember. Older learners may be unable to make optimal use of the additional cues provided by a mnemonic to direct a subsequent search. Thus, while mnemonics benefit all learners, older learners have more difficulty using and maintaining them, because the techniques typically used in laboratory experiments necessitate the acquisition of two new sets of information at the same time. Thus, an appropriate mnemonic for an older subject probably is one in which the components are overlearned already.

Robertson-Tchabo, Hausman, and Arenberg (1976) employed somewhat successfully a mnemonic procedure, the method of loci, to facilitate the free recall performance of elderly men and women. Using this method, a subject takes a mental trip through his residence stopping *in order* at 16 places. When he learns a list of words, he retraces the trip visualizing one of the items in association with each stopping place. This method was selected because it capitalizes on the familiarity of the stopping places and their natural order–attributes that provide strong retrieval cues that can be applied without adding to the information overload typically experienced by older learners. Using familiar spatial locations capitalizes on self-generated mediators, reduces the interference from dividing attention between input and storage, and reduces search failure as a subject knows where to resume a "trip."

Unfortunately, despite the marked improvement in recall performance and the subjects' recognition of the efficacy of the "trip," some of the subjects did not apply the mnemonic on the posttest, free-recall trial unless there was a specific instructional set to use the mnemonic. Apparently the subjects did not perceive that using the method of loci was appropriate on the posttest. Of course, outside of a laboratory setting a subject must recognize when application of a particular mnemonic would be appropriate and must generate his own instructions. Additional practice with a mnemonic would likely improve performance for many subjects, but the possibility of age differences in nonspecific transfer effects (Goulet, 1972) cannot be ignored.

It should be noted that this study of training in the method of loci was conducted in three sessions each of approximately 20 min on three consecutive days, whereas the training component in other intervention studies (for example, Mason & Smith, 1977) was conducted as part of a single testing session. Practice in using a mnemonic would be expected to improve performance.

Furthermore, there is no direct evidence that subjects formed a mental image or pictorial representation of a particular locus and its to-be-remembered item. The elaborative encoding generated in using the method of loci may be verbally mediated for some subjects. The nature of the elaboration undoubtedly reflects individual differences in modality preference, and it is possible that there are cohort differences in the relative proportions of visualizers and verbalizers (Richardson, 1969, 1977). This may perhaps be due, in part, to prevailing pedagogical techniques at the time when individuals were involved in formal education. The key to method-of-loci recall facilitation may well be that elaborative encoding operations are used, and the use of visual imagery may not be essential to the successful application of the method. However, for some tasks, such as memory for faces or the acquisition of the 30 symbols of Grade I Braille, visual imagery may prove to be indispensible.

There are some general observations with respect to cognitive-skill training for the elderly which might be mentioned. To some extent, the issues reflect differences in the respective purposes of basic and applied research. Investigators who are interested in age differences in the relative efficacy of a training procedure frequently employ somewhat arbitrarily lists of 10 or more items, usually to avoid a ceiling effect in young subjects' recall. It may be that these list lengths exceed the information-processing capacity required to perform a desired task by an older individual. In any case, it may be advisable to begin training with a list length which an individual can master successfully and then to progress to more difficult tasks. Moreover, voluntary imagery seems to be used most effectively when a task is relatively easy (Costello & McGregor, 1957; Sutcliffe, in Richardson, 1969, p. 66). Some techniques that have been rejected as ineffective in the laboratory may still be useful for some subjects when employed in a different setting with a different task.

The second point is related to the criterion of success. Frequently, in the experimental laboratory the criterion is one of a statistically significant change (gain) relative to that for a control group (which frequently is *not* a "no-treatment" group; that is, control subjects may have *practiced* a task without specific instructions). Whether or not the change criterion is met, one needs also to consider the final level of performance. To the extent that a particular cognitive process is an essential component of task performance, it is likely to be the level of memory performance (rather than change) that will be correlated with successful task performance. Again, there is a danger of premature rejection of a particular technique.

The third point is that clinicians must consider individual preferences in the choice of treatment. Both Poon, Walsh-Sweeney, and Fozard (Chapter 26) and Winograd and Simon (Chapter 27) have cited as priorities for future research a consideration of individual differences in preferred encoding strategies.

Costa and Fozard (1978) have pointed out that the ways in which stable individual differences in adult personality traits are related to differences in characteristic ways of thinking, learning, and remembering have received relatively little scientific study. Further, they have suggested that a consideration of such psychological processes underlying cognitive performance may help to provide a better understanding of the possibilities for intervention in cognitive problems of the elderly. Robertson-Tchabo, Arenberg, and Costa (1979) reported an exploratory study to examine personality (measured by the Guilford Zimmerman Temperament Survey) predictors and correlates of residualized change in visual memory performance for men aged 70–79 years old at the time of the initial administration of the Benton Revised Visual Retention Test. Despite the small sample size ($N = 52$) and the need to control for the effects of other variables (for example, health), the consistency with which some scales (general activity, restraint, and masculinity) emerged as important predictors of residualized change in Benton performance was encouraging. It is interesting to consider the personal characteristics reflected by high scores on general activity, restraint, and masculinity: Men who maintained their memory performance were generally more active, energetic and productive (high general activity); more responsible, more serious, more self-restrained, and less impulsive (high restraint); and more analytic and task-oriented (high masculinity). Again, there is no direct evidence that individuals with these personality characteristics approach the task or process information in a particular manner. An interesting empirical question is whether men with high scores on these traits encode visual information in a characteristically different way than men with low socres on general activity, restraint, and masculinity. In this regard, Meichenbaum's (1977) cognitive functional approach or Rundus and Atkinson's (1970) overt rehearsal procedure may be informative.

Historically, research in cognitive styles has been concerned with the manner in which stable differences in adult personality might be related to differences in characteristic ways of processing information. Previous cross-sectional studies in the aging literature have found significant relationships between personality dimensions and task performance (Heron & Chown, 1967; Botwinick & Storandt, 1974; Costa & Fozard, 1978; Fozard & Costa, in press), though none of these studies provides evidence as to how personality traits might influence performance.

For the psychologists interested in memory intervention, another important question is whether individual differences in personality traits are related to differences in expressed need for participation in a memory improvement program if it were available.

The answer to the question, "Why should old dogs learn new tricks?" is the same as that for younger dogs—because they want and need to learn new behaviors. Although imagery mnemonics may not be the answer for everyone, with appropriate consideration of age-related differences in cognitive processing, imagery does facilitate recall performance. Of course, this does not mean that other techniques should not be explored. Moreover, we may advance the field of cognitive-skill training more quickly if we are more sensitive to the external validity of our experimental tasks.

REFERENCES

Botwinick, J. *Aging and behavior: A comprehensive integration of research findings.* New York: Springer, 1973.

Botwinick, J., & Storandt, M. *Memory, related functions and age.* Springfield, Ill.: Charles C. Thomas, 1974.

Bower, G. H. Organizational factors in memory. *Cognitive Psychology,* 1970, *1,* 18–46.

Costa, P. T. Jr., & Fozard, J. L. Remembering the person: Relations of individual difference variables to memory. *Experimental Aging Research,* 1978, *4,* 291–304.

Costello, C. G., & McGregor, P. The relationship between some aspects of visual imagery and the alpha rhythm. *Journal of Mental Science,* 1957, *103,* 786–795.

Fozard, J. L., & Costa, P. T. Jr. Age differences in memory and decision making in relation to personality, abilities, and endocrine function. In Aging: A challenge for science and social policy. Oxford: Oxford University Press, in press.

Goulet, L. R. New directions for research on aging and retention. *Journal of Gerontology,* 1972, *27,* 52–60.

Hatfield, E. M. Estimates of blindness in the United States. *Sight Saving Review,* 1973, *43,* 69–80.

Heron, A., & Chown, S. *Age and function.* London: J. and A. Churchill, 1967.

Hulicka, I. M., & Rust, L. D. Age-related retention deficit as a function of learning. *Journal of the American Geriatrics Society,* 1964, *11,* 1061–1065.

Hulicka, I. M., & Weiss, R. L. Age differences in retention as a function of learning. *Journal of Consulting Psychology,* 1965, *29,* 125–129.

Kahn, R. L., Zarit, S. H., Hilbert, N. M., & Niederehe, M. A. Memory complaint and impairment in the aged: The effect of depression and altered brain function. *Archives of General Psychiatry,* 1975, *32,* 1569–1573.

Mason, S. E., & Smith, A. D. Imagery in the aged. *Experimental Aging Research,* 1977, *3,* 17–32.

Meichenbaum, D. Cognitive behavior modification. New York: Plenum Press, 1977.

National Center for Health Statistics. *Estimates on blindness in the United States by age and sex groups.* (Series 99). Washington, D.C.: Government Printing Office, 1971.

Raia, P. A. *Cognitive skill training of adventitiously blinded elderly women: The effects of training in the method of loci on free recall performance.* Unpublished dissertation, University of Maryland, College Park, 1979.

Richardson, A. *Mental imagery.* London: Routledge and Kegan Paul, 1969.

Richardson, A. Verbalizer-visualizer: A cognitive style dimension. *Journal of Mental Imagery,* 1977, *1,* 109–126.

Robertson-Tchabo, E. A., Hausman, C. P., & Arenberg, D. A classical mnemonic for older learners: A trip that works! *Educational Gerontology,* 1976, *1,* 215–226.

Robertson-Tchabo, E. A., Arenberg, D., & Costa, P. T., Jr. Temperamental predictors of longitudinal change in performance on the Benton Revised Visual Retention Test among seventy-year-old men: An exploratory study. In Hoffmeister, F., & Müller, C. (Eds.), *Bayer Symposium VII. Brain Function in Old Age.* Berlin: Springer-Verlag, 1979.

Rowe, E. J., & Schnore, M. M. Item concreteness and reported strategies in paired-associate learning as a function of age. *Journal of Gerontology,* 1971, *26,* 470-475.

Rundus, D., & Atkinson, R. C. Rehearsal processes in free recall: A procedure for direct observation. *Journal of Verbal Learning and Verbal Behavior,* 1970, *9,* 99-105.

Treat, N. J., & Reese, H. W. Age, pacing, and imagery in paired-associate learning. *Developmental Psychology,* 1976, *12,* 119-124.

30 Do Laboratory Tests Relate to Self-Assessment of Memory Ability in the Young and Old?

Elizabeth M. Zelinski, Michael J. Gilewski,
and Larry W. Thompson
Pitzer College and the University of Southern California

Erickson, Poon, and Walsh-Sweeney (Chapter 22) as well as Albert and Kaplan (Chapter 23) have made it clear that the currently available methods of memory assessment of aged patients are inadequate. Moreover, both clinicians and researchers agree that the experimental paradigms used to evaluate memory processes in the elderly do not readily lend themselves to assessment-related applications. These issues were the focus of a symposium discussing the problems of memory assessment recently published in *Experimental Aging Research* (Arenberg, 1978). In one of the symposium papers, Poon, Fozard, and Treat (1978) indicated the need for realistic evaluation methods in assessing memory in the aged, and specifically emphasized the role of self-evaluation of memorial processes as a useful assessment procedure. Our purpose in this chapter is to review research in progress in our laboratory examining the relationship between one's self-evaluation of everyday memory functioning and performance in a variety of memory tasks, as well as the role of inter- and intra-age differences in self-assessment and performance.

THE EVIDENCE FOR METAMEMORY

Although some researchers argue that self-assessment of psychological functioning is not always a reliable index of actual behavior (Mischel, 1968; Nisbet & Wilson, 1977), this does not appear to be the case with self-assessment of memory. According to Flavell (1971), metamemory, which includes knowledge of one's memory, plays a critical role in remembering. His model of memory (Flavell, 1977) involves four essential processes: basic memory, the automatic memory functions which manifest from neonatal stages on; knowledge, information about the world; memory strategies, deliberate storage and retrieval schemes which assist in effecting efficient memory performance; and metamemory. While metamemory involves several different control processes, the one with which we will concern ourselves comprises the characteristics of the individual as a rememberer.

Evidence that individuals are aware of their ability to remember in various situations comes from several sources. Hart (1965) studied the "feeling-of-knowing" phenomenon, the subjective feeling that the individual can recognize, and thus demonstrate, his knowledge of something he cannot readily recall. He had subjects attempt to recall answers to general information questions, such as "Who wrote *The Tempest?*" For any question they could not answer, they judged the feeling of certainty they had that they could recognize the correct response from several alternatives. Subjects then took a multiple-choice test which included all the items judged. Results showed that when subjects thought that they could correctly recognize answers, they selected more correct than incorrect responses. When they felt that they would not recognize the correct answer, they were more likely to make errors than correct responses. Flavell and Wellman (1976) asked children of different ages to predict whether they would be able to recall serially lists ranging from two to 10 items. They then tested serial recall span, and found that older children were fairly accurate in predicting their spans, while younger ones overestimated span considerably.

Studies similar to the two just cited show that older adults are also capable of assessing their memory abilities adequately. Lachman and Lachman described their replication of Hart's (1965) study with young and old subjects in Chapter 18.

Briefly, they found no substantial age differences in the accuracy of "feeling-of-knowing," and obtained some data which may suggest that older people are somewhat more accurate than the young in this ability. Perlmutter (1978) employed a metamemory technique similar to the one introduced by Flavell and Wellman (1976). She had young and old subjects predict the number of words they would recall and recognize in a subsequent test, and found no age differences in prediction accuracy. These studies suggest that from childhood, people of all ages can predict memory performance in laboratory testing with some accuracy. However, behavior in the laboratory should be generalizable to everyday phenomena if it is to have clincal applicability.

Memory Complaint And Memory Performance

Several investigations have attempted to relate assessment of everyday memory functioning to memory test performance. Lowenthal and her associates (Lowenthal, Berkman, Buehler, Pierce, Robinson, & Trier, 1967) investigated correlates of mental health in a large sample of elderly subjects. One question they asked in the interview phase of the study involved self-assessment of memory: "Would you say your memory is as good as it used to be, or that it is not so good anymore?" Response patterns to this question indicated that complaints of memory declines increased with age. Yet in this sample, there were no age differences in digit span and general information, which are thought to reflect memory processes. This study did not attempt to categorize subjects into groups reporting complaints versus those with no complaints, and then directly compare performance. As Poon et al. (1978) indicated in their critique of this paper, it does not provide strong evidence against a relationship between self-assessment of everyday memory and test performance.

In an investigation specifically designed to examine the self-assessment/test-performance relationship, Kahn and his colleagues (Kahn, Zarit, Hilbert, & Niederehe, 1975) had subjects indicate whether they had any memory problems, and then rate any specific complaints on a five-point scale. Subjects also rated relative quality of their recent and past memory abilities to index perceived changes in memory performance with age. Finally, subjects were assessed for performance in digit span, story recall, paired associates, and knowledge of recent and remote personal and general information. Results showed that over half the subjects indicated that "the complaint was more than minimal [p. 1571]." However, memory complaint was not systematically correlated with performance on any of the memory measures. A possible explanation for the negative findings is that the open-ended nature of the questions used to elicit responses about memory complaints may introduce an element of response bias. Responses to their questions may be state-dependent—i.e., biased as a function of affective state. Other problems are that subjects might respond to the questions with complaints most salient at the moment, but omit discussing other memory failures which may occur frequently, but have not come to mind at the time. Some failures may be omitted because they appear trivial, or because they may not even be considered to be memory failures by the individual. There may also be age differences in considering memory failures to be an index of memory ability. For instance, older people may be more likely than the young to concede that failures indicate memory problems because of prevailing cultural expectations of memory decline with age. We explored response bias in open-ended interviews in a pilot study. It consisted of an open-ended questionnaire on memory problems and complaints and a checklist of possible memory failures. Older people reported far more complaints in the open-ended questionnaire than the young. However, the majority of subjects in both age groups indicated experiencing failures in over 50% of those possibilities listed. There were no age differences in the number of failures reported when subjects were presented with specific situations. As a result of these findings, we decided to investigate self-assessment of memory performance in a host of situations to eliminate potential biases in assessing memory complaint and to provide a clearer picture of the relationship between complaint and performance than was found in earlier studies.

QUANTIFYING SELF-ASSESSMENT: THE METAMEMORY QUESTIONNAIRE

Memory Failures

A wide range of situations involving remembering and forgetting were used in our scales. Situations included forgetting appointments, losing the thread of thought in conversation, forgetting important personal dates such as birthdays, and so on. A complete list of all questionnaire items is found in the Appendix.

To obtain a more complete picture of the individual's perceived memory functioning, three scales were used: (1) frequency of failures; (2) importance of memory failures; and (3) the amount of effort made by the individual to avoid failures. These three dimensions are not necessarily related to one another. For instance, one might forget car keys very infrequently, consider that a serious failure, and yet expend little effort to remember them. Alternatively, one might forget his intention in going to a room to obtain something quite frequently, consider such occurrences trivial, and also make no effort to alleviate the situation. Subjects rated each remembering or forgetting situation on the individually administered frequency, importance, and effort scales.

Awareness of Memory Ability

Perception of ability to remember recent and remote events and assessment of current versus previous overall memory functioning were investigated to suggest perceived changes in function, with respect to specific reference points. Subjects rated their ability to recall events which occurred one month, six months, one year, two to five years ago, and so on. They compared current functioning to previous functioning within similar time frames.

Frequency of usage of various mnemonics in everyday life was obtained from an extensive list of mnemonics, such as making notes and using an appointment book, to determine how mnemonics usage relates to memory complaint. This would have implications for memory intervention programs.

The questionnaire also included a general rating of memory functioning, and sections on memory difficulties, if any, in reading various kinds of prose. All ratings were on seven-point scales.

MEASURES OF MEMORY PERFORMANCE

To investigate whether evaluation of memory in everyday situations is related to memory performance, we selected measures which are thought to reflect somewhat different processes. These included immediate and delayed free recall of a word list, recognition of the free recall list items, recall of a prose passage, and general knowledge.

List Recall. Immediate free recall of a word list is a standard procedure for testing memory. Delayed recall of the same list was also used, because this appears to be a good index of memory pathology. As Erikson and Scott (1977) pointed out, subjects with amnesia may perform at the same level as those without memory deficits in immediate recall tests. However, after a delay, amnesics demonstrate greater deficit than normals.

List Recognition. Although there is some controversy as to whether recognition reflects similar or different processes than recall, many researchers agree that recognition requires less retrieval than recall. Recognition tests are frequently used to assess memory, and given the potential differences between recall and recognition, recognition of the above word list was included. Synonym distractors were included in the recognition test to determine whether subjects with memory deficits would incorrectly recognize them as original list words. This would suggest that they encoded the concept underlying the list item, but could not retrieve its exact form. Another purpose in using synonym distractors was to make the recognition test somewhat difficult, and thereby avoid ceiling effects.

Prose Recall. Essay recall was included in the memory tests for several reasons. The most obvious is that prose material is a more "ecologically valid" source of information than a word list. Subjects might find such material more meaningful and familiar than a list of words, and be motivated to remember it to a greater extent than a word list. This test would also insure that at least one of the memory measures had some applicability to a real-world memory phenomenon.

Using the essay grammar developed by Meyer (1975), recall would be scored for the presence of propositions or "content units," the correctness of relations between propositions, and the level of importance of each proposition in the essay. The concept of level originates from the notion that recall of prose material is based on a reconstruction of details from an outline or schema (Bartlett, 1932). The schema is the backbone of the passage, in that it provides its organizational framework, which cues the reconstruction process. Statements central to the information presented in the passage have an important place in the schema, while details and less critical information have subsidiary roles. Prose grammars define the level, or relative importance, of propositions in the schema. Propositions at high levels are more critical, and therefore more likely to be recalled, than those at low levels (cf. Thorndyke, 1977).

Level of a recalled proposition is essentially qualitative, while the number of propositions recalled overall is a quantitative measure. We were interested in using both a quantitative and a qualitative approach to evaluate recall as a function of memory complaint. We wished to determine whether an interaction between level of proposition and complaint would be observed. We expected all subjects to recall the same amount of information at high levels, but only those with little deficit to recall propositions at low levels. This interaction would suggest that those with memory difficulties may have problems encoding and/or retrieving detail information obtained from prose, and would be helpful in indicating the nature of possible intervention strategies.

General Information.   A measure of general information was used to determine whether subjects with complaints would differ from those with none in world knowledge. Since this measure does not assess memory following acquisition of information in the laboratory, scores for general information and other memory measures were analyzed separately.

Specific procedures for each measure are described next.

List Recall Procedure.   Subjects were given a list of 20 common nouns with concreteness and imagery ratings of 5.6 and above from the Paivio, Yuille, and Madigan (1968) norms. They studied the list for 3.5 min, then wrote their free recall. The total number of words correctly recalled was the dependent measure.

Subjects free-recalled the same list approximately 20 min after the first recall.

List Recognition Procedure.   The recognition test followed delayed recall. It consisted of the 20 original items studied, 10 synonym distractors, and 10 unrelated distractors.

Prose Recall Procedure.   Subjects were given a copy of a 227-word version of an essay originally used by Meyer (1975, pp. 203–204). They silently read the essay twice at their own pace, then wrote their recall. They were not required to recall it verbatim.

General Information Test Procedure.   Following the test developed by Botwinick and Storandt (1974) as our model, we examined knowledge of information about six 15-year periods ranging from 1886 to 1975. There were 48 multiple-choice questions, eight from each period. Of these, four referred to news and four to popular events and personalities.

All the memory evaluation measures described above were completed at the subjects' own pace.

SUBJECTS

The subject sample included 123 young adults, ranging in age from 18 to 40 years. Undergraduates numbered 104 while 19 were graduate students. The elderly sample totaled 73, and ranged in age from 60 to 82 years. Seventeen were members of the Andrus Volunteers, a highly educated service auxiliary of the Andrus Gerontology Center. Fifty-six were members of a senior citizens' recreation center in Culver City. All volunteered to participate in the study. Demographic information indicates that young and old samples had similar socioeconomic backgrounds.

Subjects completed the metamemory and demographic questionnaires, then took the memory tests in the following order: immediate recall, essay recall, delayed recall, recognition, and general information. Subjects were run in groups ranging in size from five to 20. There were no differences in performance as a function of group size.

ANALYSIS PROCEDURES

Data analyses were aimed at (1) defining memory evaluation groups as a function of response patterns to the metamemory questionnaire; (2) determining whether memory evaluation groups differed in performance on the memory measures; and (3) investigating whether a correlational relationship existed between memory evaluation and test performance. The rationales and sequence of specific analyses are outlined below.

Defining Memory Evaluation Groups

Data Reduction.   Before categorizing subjects into memory evaluation groups, it was necessary to reduce the metamemory questionnaire data. There were too many questionnaire variables for initially grouping subjects meaningfully, and since there were insufficient observations for factor analysis, scores on the questionnaire were averaged across scale categories. For instance, scores for the memory failure questions dealing with frequency of occurrence were averaged into one frequency-of-failure score, while scores for the questions dealing with importance of failures were averaged into another.

Cluster Analysis. The first analysis involved using the nine metamemory-scale category scores as the basis for grouping individuals. Cluster analysis was employed to determine which individuals had similar response patterns and to indicate the number of different types of response patterns or clusters found in the data. However, since clustering procedures are mathematical and not statistical in nature, it is advisable to use an alternative procedure to test the adequacy of the cluster solution and to describe which variables were critical in differentiating clusters. The next analysis was used to do this.

Discriminant Analysis. Using membership in one of the subject clusters as the grouping variable, and the nine metamemory-scale categories as dependent variables, discriminant analysis was performed. By determining which linear combinations of dependent variables differentiated the cluster groups on discriminant functions, the analysis would indicate which metamemory-scale categories were most informative in defining memory evaluation clusters. Centroids, or the means of the clusters on the discriminant functions, would be interpreted to suggest how members of the clusters described their memory abilities. Finally, predicting cluster-group membership for individuals on the basis of their discriminant function scores, and examining the proportion of individuals correctly predicted to be members of their clusters, would indicate whether a cluster actually contained individuals with similar response patterns, and whether individuals within a cluster responded differently from those in other clusters.

Analysis Of Variance. As a further check on the nature of differences in response patterns in the cluster groups, one-way analysis of variance was performed on each metamemory scale category, with cluster membership as the factor. This would indicate whether groups differed significantly from one another in responses to a given scale category. To confirm the interpretation of the memory-evaluation clusters based on their centroids, means for each cluster on each metamemory-scale category would be examined.

Chi Square. To test whether there were differences in the proportion of young and old members in the memory evaluation groups, chi-square analysis was carried out.

Memory Performance As A Function Of Evaluation Groups

Once the metamemory evaluation groups were identified through cluster analysis, the identification confirmed with discriminant analysis, and the groups described by discriminant analysis, analysis of variance, and chi square analysis, they would be used to determine whether differences in memory evaluation would be mirrored in patterns of performance.

Multivariate Analysis Of Variance (MANOVA). Using memory evaluation group and age as between-subjects factors, and scores on the memory measures as dependent variables, MANOVA was employed. This analysis was to indicate the effects of memory evaluation, age, and their interaction on performance. The purpose of examining age as a factor was to control for the possibility that age imbalances might exist in the membership in metamemory evaluation groups, and that possible group differences might be more a function of age than memory evaluation. Post hoc tests following *F* ratios would indicate the nature of specific effects.

Investigating The Relationship Between Evaluation And Performance

Regression And Canonical Correlation. Regression of the performance measures on membership in one of the memory evaluation groups would indicate the power of a combination of the memory performance scores to predict group membership. In this analysis, the single index of metamemory evaluation, the group to which the individual belonged, was predicted by performance. An alternative approach which would yield more information about the relationship between evaluation and performance would be to use canonical correlation to correlate the combined effect of the metamemory scale category scores with the combined effect of memory performance measures.

Results from the regression and canonical correlation analyses would be contrasted to indicate whether the single index of memory evaluation group or the multiple indices of scale category scores were more useful in accounting for variance in memory performance.

RESULTS

Cluster Analysis

Results of the cluster analysis revealed that a three-cluster solution fit the data. Adequacy of this solution and interpretation of the cluster groups was tested in a discriminant analysis using Mahalanobis distance functions. Table 30.1 presents the results of the discriminant analysis. Six of the nine categories included in the metamemory questionnaire contributed significantly to the two discriminant functions obtained. The frequency of memory failures and the frequency of forgetting during reading had salient loadings on the first function, while usage of mnemonics, ability to recall recent and remote occurrences, importance of memory failures, and reliance on memory during daily activities were salient on the second function. Centroids, or the means of the three clusters on the two functions are shown in the lower half of Table

TABLE 30.1

Loadings Of Metamemory Scale Categories And Centroids Of The Groups On
The Discriminant Functions

Metamemory Scale Category	Function I	Function II
Frequency Of Memory Failures	.92*	–.05
Frequency Of Forgetting During Reading	.28*	.08
Frequency Of Usage Of Various Mnemonics	.09	.64*
Ability To Remember Occurrences Recent And Remote In Time	–.20	.63*
Importance Of Forgetting When It Occurs In Various Situations	.36	.47*
Frequency Of Reliance On Memory Alone In Various Situations	–.05	.38*
Centroids of Memory Evaluation Groups		
Cluster 1	2.52	2.50
Cluster 2	.42	–.25
Cluster 3	–2.92	–1.22

*Indicates a variable salient on the discriminant function.

30.1. The first cluster has a high positive centroid on both functions. This suggests that members of the first cluster responded to the questions of the scale categories salient on both functions fairly positively. The second cluster has a low positive centroid on Function I and a low negative one on Function II. The absolute value of the centroids, which tend toward zero, suggest moderate responses to the category scales in each function. The third cluster has a high negative centroid on the first function and a moderate negative one on the second. This suggests that for the variables salient on both functions, these individuals rated themselves quite negatively. Next, we examined the predicted classification of individuals into clusters, based on their discriminant function scores, and found that 93% of individuals were correctly predicted to be members of the clusters to which they actually belonged. This hit rate was interpreted as evidence that we could differentiate individuals based on their responses to the metamemory questionnaire. To verify that the three clusters of subjects were defined into positive, moderate, and negative memory evaluation groups, we examined F ratios and means of each cluster group on the nine scale categories of the metamemory questionnaire. These are seen in Table 30.2. The F ratios for all comparisons are highly significant. The means for the three clusters fit the description given in the interpretation of their centroids. Thus, the data indicate that the first cluster is positive, the second moderate, and the third negative in memory evaluation.

TABLE 30.2

F Ratios, Means And Standard Deviations Of Ratings On Metamemory Scales By Positive Moderate, And Negative Evaluation Groups

| | | Evaluation Groups | | | | | |
| | | Positive | | Moderate | | Negative | |
	F^* (df = 2,193)	$\bar{X}$	SD	$\bar{X}$	SD	$\bar{X}$	SD
General Rating Of Memory	27.22	5.64	.87	4.64	1.15	3.62	1.27
Frequency Of Reliance On Memory Alone In Various Situations[a]	8.75	5.19	1.70	3.95	1.69	3.61	1.29
Retrospective Evaluation Of Memory[b]	5.37	4.73	.91	4.33	1.00	3.89	1.32
Frequency Of Forgetting In Various Situations[a]	187.20	5.77	.42	4.91	.53	3.36	.68
Frequency of Forgetting During Reading[a]	67.60	6.16	.16	5.20	.79	3.89	1.04
Ability To Remember Occurrences Recent And Remote In Time[c]	26.53	5.86	1.04	4.54	.92	4.13	1.21
Importance Of Forgetting When It Occurs In Various Situations[d]	49.31	5.87	.91	4.50	.99	3.54	.90
Frequency Of Usage Of Various Mnemonics[a]	27.68	5.18	1.00	3.82	.99	3.40	1.09
Effort To Avoid Forgetting In Various Situations[e]	79.01	5.91	.62	4.64	.76	3.53	.92

*All *F* values reported were statistically reliable. Level of significance for this and all analyses was s at $p < .05$.
[a]Scale: 1 = always; 4 = sometimes; 7 = never.
[b]Scale: 1 = much worse; 4 = same; 7 = much better.
[c]Scale: 1 = very bad; 4 = fair; 7 = very good.
[d]Scale: 1 = very serious; 4 = somewhat serious; 7 = not very serious.
[e]Scale: 1 = great effort; 4 = some effort; 7 = no effort.

Table 30.3 shows the breakdown of subpopulations for each of the three groups. The positive and moderate groups consist chiefly of young individuals, while there is a majority of elderly subjects in the negative evaluation group. The differences in frequency of young and old individuals in the groups were significant ($\chi^2 = 10.64$, $df = 2$, $p < .005$). Within the young sample, the proportion of individuals in the three memory groups approaches normality, with roughly equivalent and small proportions of individuals in the extreme positive and negative categories, and the majority in the middle moderate category. The proportions of the elderly sample in the extreme

TABLE 30.3
Composition of Memory Evaluation Groups by Population[a]

| | Memory Evaluation | | | | | |
| | Positive | | Moderate | | Negative | | Marginal |
Group	N	%	N	%	N	%	
Undergraduates	17	16.3	72	69.2	15	14.4	104
Graduate Students	5	26.3	11	57.9	3	15.8	19
Young Subjects, Total	22	17.9	83	67.5	18	14.6	123
Senior Recreation Members	5	8.9	30	53.6	21	37.5	56
Andrus Volunteers	1	5.9	13	76.5	3	17.6	17
Old Subjects, Total	6	8.2	43	58.9	24	32.9	73

[a]χ^2 for age × evaluation group = 10.64 with 2 degrees of freedom, $p < .005$.

categories, however, show skewing. A relatively small proportion of elderly subjects rated their memory positively enough to belong to the positive group, while almost one-third of them fell into the negative group. Over half of the elderly sample, though, rated themselves well enough to be categorized into the moderate evaluation group.

Education and age means for the memory evaluation groups reflect the population biases in group constituencies. Mean ages for the positive, moderate, and negative groups are 33.68, 38.22, and 49.76, respectively, and differ significantly [$F(2,193) = 4.83$, $MS_e = 571.93$]. Mean education for the three groups are 14.29, 13.91, and 12.45 years for the positive, moderate, and negative groups, which differ reliably [$F(2,193) = 5.43$, $MS_e = 7.39$]. Newman–Keuls contrasts for mean differences indicate that for age and education, the positive and moderate groups do not differ from one another, but both are reliably different from the negative group.

Although the cells ranged considerably in size, for the evaluation group × age MANOVA design, we report findings from the total sample of subjects, because we found identical results from two partial samples. Despite the cell size problem, the data appear reliable.

Multivariate analysis of variance was used to examine the effects of memory evaluation, age, and their interaction on immediate and on delayed free recall, recognition of list items, and the total propositions and relations correctly recalled from the essay. (Although cell size was substantially different across the sample, analysis with two partial samples yielded identical results.) A significant multivariate effect for evaluation groups obtained $F(8, 374) = 5.24$. Univariate tests revealed reliable memory evaluation group effects on immediate [$F(2, 190) = 15.22$, $MS_e = 8.60$] and on delayed free recall [$F(2, 190) = 18.37$, $MS_e = 14.07$]; on recognition [$F(2, 190) = 5.12$,

TABLE 30.4
Mean Scores of Memory Evaluation Groups on Memory Measures

	Positive	Moderate	Negative	Marginal
Immediate Free Recall				
Young	16.27	17.01	16.72	16.84
Old	11.33	12.02	9.29	11.07
Marginal	15.21	15.31	12.48	—
Delayed Free Recall				
Young	15.40	15.76	14.94	15.58
Old	8.17	9.52	5.79	8.19
Marginal	13.86	13.63	9.71	—
List Recognition				
Young	18.91	19.22	18.78	19.10
Old	17.67	17.63	16.46	17.25
Marginal	18.64	18.67	17.45	—
Essay Recall				
Young	49.27	57.08	54.94	55.37
Old	37.83	40.88	30.71	37.29
Marginal	46.82	51.56	41.10	—
General Information				
Young	29.50	27.00	29.17	27.76
Old	31.83	32.19	26.08	30.15
Marginal	30.00	28.77	27.40	—

MS_e = 4.77]; and on essay recall [$F(2, 190)$ = 8.99, MS_e = 197.74]. Table 30.4 shows means for the three evaluation groups on the various measures. In all cases, contrasts reveal that the positive and moderate groups do not differ from one another, while their performance is superior to that of the negative group.

A separate univariate analysis of variance on the general information measure revealed borderline differences across the three evaluation groups [$F(4, 190)$ = 2.86, MS_e = 39.28, $p < .06$].

Multivariate analysis of the memory measures revealed a reliable age effect [$F(4, 187)$ = 46.39]. Univariate tests of age on each dependent measure indicated reliable differences for immediate free recall [$F(1, 190)$ = 155.89]; delayed free recall [$F(1, 190)$ = 152.75]; recognition of list items [$F(1, 190)$ = 27.02]; and essay recall [$F(1, 190)$ = 8.99]. In all cases, the young recalled or recognized significantly more items than the elderly.

The multivariate test of the memory evaluation group × age interaction was not reliable [$F(8, 374)$ = 1.04], nor were any of the tests on the dependent measures: immediate recall [$F(2, 190)$ = 2.73]; delayed recall [$F(2, 190)$ = 2.27]; recognition [$F(2, 190)$ = .55]; or total essay recall [$F(2, 190)$ = 1.74]. This interaction was apparent, however, for the test of performance on the general information questionnaire [$F(2, 190)$ = 6.59]. Simple effects tests revealed no age differences in the positive group, better performance by the old than the young in the moderate group, and better performance by the young than the old in the negative group.

The next analysis focused on recall of propositions from the various levels of the essay schema as a function of memory evaluation group and age. This was a repeated-measures analysis of variance of the proportion of correctly recalled propositions from each level. Results indicated that the interaction of amount recalled at each level with memory evaluation group did not obtain significance [$F(10, 950) = .51$]. However, the age × level interaction was reliable [$F(5, 950) = 2.74$, $MS_e = .047$], and is illustrated in Fig. 30.1. Simple effects tests for repeated measures (Boik, 1978), examining age differences in recall at each level, indicated no age differences in recall of propositions from Levels 1 and 2. Age deficits were reliable at all other levels.

The three-way interaction of memory evaluation group × age levels was not statistically significant.

Since the main effects for age on performance were significant, it was decided that the correlational analyses of evaluation with performance would be conducted separately for young and old subjects. Results of the regression analyses revealed that performance accounted for a minimal amount of variance in predicted group membership. For the old sample, the R^2 value was .18; for the young, it was .05. The second set of correlational analyses, the canonical correlations, showed that the relationship between metamemory scale categories and performance was not statistically reliable for the young. This was not the case for old subjects' data. For the older group, the canonical correlation between the sets of memory evaluation and performance scores was .67, and accounted for 45% of the variance. Variables salient for this correlation are seen in Table 30.5. In the evaluation set, these were the general ratings of memory, frequency of reliance on memory in everyday situations, frequency of memory failures, frequency of forgetting during reading, and

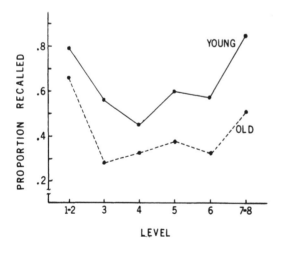

FIG. 30.1. Mean proportion of propositions recalled as a function of their level in the structure of the essay, "Parakeets: Ideal Pets." Functions are plotted by age (young versus old).

TABLE 30.5
Loadings of Metamemory Scale Categories and Memory
Performance Measures

Metamemory Scale Category	Loading
General rating of memory	.35*
Frequency of reliance on memory alone in various situations	.91*
Retrospective evaluation of memory	− .21
Frequency of forgetting in various situations	− .69*
Frequency of forgetting during reading	.30*
Ability to remember occurrences recent and remote in time	.29
Importance of forgetting when it occurs in various situations	.04
Frequency of usage of various mnemonics	.06
Effort to avoid forgetting in various situations	− .50*

Memory Measure	
List Memory:	
Immediate Recall	− .20
Delayed Recall	.36*
Recognition	− .04*
Essay Propositions Recalled:	
Levels 1–2	.13
Level 3	− .38*
Level 4	−1.02*
Level 5	.61*
Level 6	− .21
Levels 7–8	.41*

*Indicates a variable salient in the canonical correlation.

effort to avoid memory failures. In the performance set, these were delayed recall, and propositions recalled from Levels 3, 4, 5, and 7-8 of the essay structure.

DISCUSSION

In general, the data suggest that subjects' evaluation of everyday memory functioning are related to performance in laboratory tasks in the old sample, but not in the young. This may suggest that older people are more accurate in evaluating their memory functioning levels relative to performance than the young. This conclusion has also been suggested by Lachman and Lachman (Chapter 18). They found that older people might better predict their "feeling of knowing" than the young. Our data, which are based on much more global indices of memory functioning than theirs, support their findings. This may indicate that metamemory accuracy in the elderly is a robust phenomenon.

Our results show that in the elderly sample, the relationship between evaluation and performance is more complex than earlier researchers thought it would be. Merely asking older people to list and rate complaints in an open-ended format is perhaps fruitful in predicting depression, but not memory performance, as the data of Kahn et al. (1975) suggest. Our findings of a relationship between performance and evaluation in the elderly may be more definitive than theirs because of the extensive and specific nature of the questionnaire. This becomes clear when we examine the percentage of variance accounted for by the canonical correlation, which indexes the relationship between one linear combination of measures, the metamemory scale categories, and another, the memory performance measures. In the data of the elderly, the amount of variance accounted for was .45, which was reasonably large. On the other hand, consider the results of the regression analysis, in which the value of R^2, the amount of variance accounted for, was .18, which is considerably lower than the value of .45 obtained in the canonical correlation. This indicates the importance of using multiple indices of memory, instead of a single index: The scale categories cover sufficiently nonredundant aspects of memory that a global and fairly adequate evaluation of everyday memory functioning can be made. Multiple indices of memory evaluation definitely improve prediction of memory performance. These findings coincide with the analysis of information necessary in memory evaluation suggested by Poon et al. (1978). Profiles of memory evaluation are apparently critical in predicting performance in normal, healthy, noninstitutionalized older individuals. Once the questionnaire is streamlined and adapted for clinical use, we will determine how useful evaluation profiles are for predicting performance in various aged clinical populations.

In the data of the young, the relationship between evaluation and performance is virtually nonexistent. At first glance this might suggest that, even with our extensive assessment questionnaire, young individuals are unable to describe their everyday memory functioning as accurately as the old. We do not think that this is really the case, and instead suggest several likely inadequacies of the measurement techniques which may have obscured the relationship between evaluation and performance in the young.

The first possible difficulty is that the metamemory questionnaire was used differently by the young and the old as an evaluation metric. Since the scales are relative measures, we do not know whether there are age-related criterion differences in response selection. Although most people may experience memory failures, the relative frequency of occurrence may be perceived differentially as a function of age. An older person who is presumably sensitized to memory failures may be more realistic in evaluating whether memory difficulties for specific occurrences exist or not. Young people, on the other hand, may be less aware of memory problems and be less able to differentiate frequent from infrequent memory failures. If there are age differences in the criteria used for selecting responses, the relative nature of the questionnaire would serve to obfuscate those differences. One solution to the criterion problem is to have young and old subjects complete the questionnaire, and then to collect data on the frequency of actual memory failures, actual use of mnemonics, and so on. This would indicate whether there is an age-related discrepancy between metamemory evaluation and actual occurrences of responses to memory failures. Such data would also provide a measure of validation for the metamemory questionnaire.

A second reason for the absence of a relationship between evaluation and performance in the young sample is that the memory measures are irrelevant to everyday remembering in the young subjects of this study. A problem plaguing researchers who study age differences in cognitive functioning is that college students whose performance is usually compared with that of the elderly are in a sense professional test-takers, and are probably better trained to score well on cognitive measures than the older subjects, who are no longer students. College students may be especially able to perform well on cognitive measures as the result of continual practice in examination-taking, and individual differences may wash out because of this. Practice in test-taking would explain why there is usually relatively little variance in performance in the young, compared with that of the aged. The memory measures used in this study may be insensitive to individual differences in memory evaluation in the young sample. Replicating this study with a young nonstudent population will indicate whether practice in test-taking obscures memory differences in young subjects.

A third alternative explanation is that everyday memory evaluation predicts performance only when performance is below the peak level observed in the young sample. A glance at Table 30.4 indicates that elderly subjects in the positive and moderate groups perform at about 60 to 80% of the level of the young in the various recall measures. If memory declines with age, then the evaluation–performance relationship will hold only when the individual had reached an age where decline is appreciable. Longitudinal data we are collecting in collaboration with K. W. Schaie from a large sample of elderly will indicate whether or not this is true.

Let us now turn to a discussion of the usefulness of the questionnaire and memory measures in determining the relationship of performance and evaluation. If the canonical correlation results were used as our guide, five of the nine category scales and five of the eight performance measures were salient on the canonical variate. The other scales and memory measures contributed less to the correlation, suggesting that they were intercorrelated with the other variables. Rather than ruling out the use of the nonsalient variables in future research, it may be beneficial to first determine whether the scales salient in this analysis are also salient in replication studies with similar base populations. This will be critical in ultimately determining which scales and performance measures play informative roles in the evaluation—performance relationship, and therefore may be useful in developing a metamemory instrument for clinical use.

It is worthwhile to note that the total essay recall measure was not as informative as the levels scores in the canonical correlation analysis. When essay recall was included with immediate and delayed recall, and recognition scores in the correlation with scale categories, the eigenvalue was .31. In the analysis with the levels scores substituting for the essay recall measure, the eigenvalue was .45. This indicates that in the elderly population studied, the essay grammar provides more informative measures than the quantitative total essay recall score. This was also true in the repeated measures analysis of levels recalled, in which age interacted with recall at the various levels. Recall between the young and old was similar at the highest level, but showed age deficits at lower levels. This suggests that older individuals are able to recall the most critical information in the essay, but are more likely than the young to forget the less central ideas. The use of prose grammars may be helpful in determining the nature of memory differences within the elderly and between different age groups.

Thus far, we have given little attention to the possibility of clinical applicability of the results. Clearly, we are not at a point to offer either of our sets of measures of metamemory evaluation scales or of memory performance to the clinical community as assessment tools. However, there are some practical implications of our data. The results show that self-assessment of memory functioning is related to performance on objective measures when the subjects are elderly. This suggests that normal, healthy, noninstitutionalized older persons are aware of memory problems, or the lack of them, and that their complaints are realistic. Those working with the elderly should not ignore complaints by considering them to be the result of cultural expectations of memory loss. However, specific extensive measures are warranted in assessment, as our findings indicate.

With respect to intervention, these preliminary findings do not allow us to pinpoint the exact nature of memory differences in elderly individuals with varying memory evaluations. Therefore, we feel it is premature to suggest specific intervention strategies. Since mnemonics usage, one of the metamemory scale categories, was not salient in the canonical correlation, and was not highly correlated with any individual performance measures, we cannot recommend the particular mnemonics covered in our questionnaire as appropriate memory improvement strategies. Exploration of other types of mnemonics such as imagery, however, may prove to be more useful.

How adequate the metamemory questionnaire is as an assessment instrument is an open question at this time. We are currently collecting more data on the questionnaire and memory measures described here, as part of a collaborative study with K. W. Schaie. These data, obtained from approximately 500 noninstitutionalized individuals ranging in age from 55 to 85 years, will be used to evaluate the metamemory questionnaire in a factor-analytic framework. The results of this study will then be used to indicate how the questionnaire can be shortened and improved for clinical use.

Three-year longitudinal data are also to be collected from the participants in this collaborative study, and this will indicate whether short-term age changes occur in self-evaluation of memory, and in performance on memory measures.

We will also be examining how clinical populations respond to the questionnaire and to the performance measures in studies still in the planning stages. We think the approach we are using will eventually be useful in assessment and in planning intervention strategies for clinical application, and are continuing our efforts toward that goal.

ACKNOWLEDGMENTS

Preparation of this chapter was supported in part by postdoctoral fellowship AG05140 to Elizabeth M. Zelinski, and by training grant AG00037 and program grant AG000133 to the Andrus Gerontology Center, from the National Institute on Aging.

REFERENCES

Arenberg, D. Introduction to a symposium: Toward comprehensive intervention programs for memory problems among the aged. *Experimental Aging Research,* 1978, *4,* 233-234.

Bartlett, F. C. *Remembering: A study in experimental and social psychology.* Cambridge: Cambridge University Press, 1932.

Boik, R. J. Personal communication. December 1978.

Botwinick, J., & Storandt, M. *Memory, related functions, and age.* Springfield, Ill.: Charles C. Thomas, 1974.

Erickson, R. C., & Scott, M. Clinical memory testing: A review. *Psychological Bulletin,* 1977, *84,* 1130-1149.

Flavell, J. H. First discussant's comments: What is memory development the development of? *Human Development,* 1971, *14,* 272-278.

Flavell, J. H. *Cognitive development.* Englewood Cliffs, N.J.: Prentice-Hall, 1977.

Flavell, J. H., & Wellman, H. M. Metamemory. In R. V. Kail & J. W. Hagen (Eds.), *Memory in cognitive development.* Hillsdale, N.J.: Lawrence Erlbaum Associates, 1976.

Hart, J. T. Memory and the feeling-of-knowing experience. *Journal of Educational Psychology,* 1965, *56,* 208-216.

Kahn, R. L., Zarit, S. H., Hilbert, N. M., & Niederehe, G. A. Memory complaint and impairment in the aged: The effect of depression and altered brain function. *Archives of General Psychiatry,* 1975, *32,* 1560-1573.

Lowenthal, M. F., Berkman, P. L., Buehler, J. A., Pierce, R. C., Robinson, B. C., & Trier, M. L. *Aging and mental disorder in San Francisco.* San Francisco: Jossey Bass, 1967.

Meyer, B. J. F. *The organization of prose and its effects on memory.* New York: American Elsevier, 1975.

Mischel, W. *Personality and assessment.* New York: Wiley, 1968.

Nisbett, R. E., & Wilson, T. D. Telling more than we know: Verbal reports on mental processes. *Psychological Review,* 1977, *84,* 231-259.

Paivio, A., Yuille, J. C., & Madigan, S. A. Concreteness, imagery, and meaningfulness values for 925 nouns. *Journal of Experimental Psychology Monograph Supplement,* 1968, *76* (1), Part 2.

Perlmutter, M. What is memory aging the aging of? *Developmental Psychology,* 1978, *14,* 330-346.

Poon, L. W., Fozard, J. L., & Treat, N. J. From clinical and research findings on memory to intervention programs. *Experimental Aging Research,* 1978, *4,* 235-255.

Thorndyke, P. W. Cognitive structures in comprehension and memory of narrative discourse. *Cognitive Psychology,* 1977, *9,* 77-110.

APPENDIX

Metamemory Questionnaire Items

1. How would you rate your memory in terms of the kinds of problems that you have?

1	2	3	4	5	6	7
major problems			some minor problems		no problems	

2. How often do you need to rely on your memory without the use of remembering techniques such as making lists when your are engaged in...

	very frequently			usually		never
a. social activities	1	2	3	4	5	6	7
b. at work	1	2	3	4	5	6	7
c. household chores ..	1	2	3	4	5	6	7
d. hobbies	1	2	3	4	5	6	7
e. conversations with others	1	2	3	4	5	6	7

3. How is your memory compared to the way it was...

		much worse			same			much better
a.	one month ago	1	2	3	4	5	6	7
b.	one year ago	1	2	3	4	5	6	7
c.	five years ago......	1	2	3	4	5	6	7
d.	ten years ago	1	2	3	4	5	6	7
e.	twenty years ago ...	1	2	3	4	5	6	7
f.	when you were eighteen	1	2	3	4	5	6	7

4. How often do these present a memory problem to you...

		always			sometimes			never
a.	names	1	2	3	4	5	6	7
b.	faces	1	2	3	4	5	6	7
c.	appointments......	1	2	3	4	5	6	7
d.	where you put things (e.g., keys) ..	1	2	3	4	5	6	7
e.	performing house- hold chores	1	2	3	4	5	6	7
f.	directions to places	1	2	3	4	5	6	7
g.	phone numbers you've just checked...........	1	2	3	4	5	6	7
h.	phone numbers used frequently	1	2	3	4	5	6	7
i.	things people tell you	1	2	3	4	5	6	7
j.	keeping up correspondence	1	2	3	4	5	6	7
k.	personal dates (e.g., birthdays)	1	2	3	4	5	6	7
l.	words	1	2	3	4	5	6	7
m.	going to the store and forgetting what you wanted to buy	1	2	3	4	5	6	7
n.	taking a test.......	1	2	3	4	5	6	7
o.	beginning to do something and forgetting what you were doing	1	2	3	4	5	6	7

	always			sometimes			never
p. losing the thread of thought in conversation.......	1	2	3	4	5	6	7
q. losing the thread of thought in public speaking	1	2	3	4	5	6	7
r. knowing whether you've already told someone something.........	1	2	3	4	5	6	7

5. As you are reading a novel, how often do you have trouble remembering what you have read...

	always			sometimes			never
a. in the opening chapters once you have finished the book	1	2	3	4	5	6	7
b. three or four chapters before the one you are currently reading...	1	2	3	4	5	6	7
c. the chapter before the one you are currently reading...	1	2	3	4	5	6	7
d. the paragraph just before the one you are currently reading	1	2	3	4	5	6	7
e. the sentence before the one you are currently reading	1	2	3	4	5	6	7

6. How well do you remember things which occurred...

	very bad			fair			very good
a. last month is	1	2	3	4	5	6	7
b. between six months and one year ago is	1	2	3	4	5	6	7

c. between one and						
five years ago is....	1	2	3	4	5	6	7
d. between six and						
ten years ago is	1	2	3	4	5	6	7
e. when I was a child	1	2	3	4	5	6	7
f. when I was a						
teenager	1	2	3	4	5	6	7

7. When you actually forget in these situations, how serious of a problem do you consider the memory failure to be...

	very serious			somewhat serious			not serious
a. names	1	2	3	4	5	6	7
b. faces	1	2	3	4	5	6	7
c. appointments......	1	2	3	4	5	6	7
d. where you put things (e.g., keys) ..	1	2	3	4	5	6	7
e. performing household chores	1	2	3	4	5	6	7
f. directions to places	1	2	3	4	5	6	7
g. phone numbers you've just checked..........	1	2	3	4	5	6	7
h. phone numbers used frequently	1	2	3	4	5	6	7
i. things people tell you	1	2	3	4	5	6	7
j. keeping up correspondence	1	2	3	4	5	6	7
k. personal dates (e.g., birthdays)	1	2	3	4	5	6	7
l. words	1	2	3	4	5	6	7
m. going to the store and forgetting what you wanted to buy	1	2	3	4	5	6	7
n. taking a test.......	1	2	3	4	5	6	7
o. beginning to do something and forgetting what you were doing	1	2	3	4	5	6	7

	very serious		somewhat serious		not serious		
p. losing the thread of thought in conversation.......	1	2	3	4	5	6	7
q. losing the thread of thought in public speaking	1	2	3	4	5	6	7
r. knowing whether you've already told someone something.........	1	2	3	4	5	6	7

8. When you are reading a newspaper or magazine article, how often do you have trouble remembering what you have read ...

	always		sometimes		never		
a. in the opening paragraphs, once you have finished the article........	1	2	3	4	5	6	7
b. three or four paragraphs before the one you are currently reading...	1	2	3	4	5	6	7
c. the paragraph before the one you are currently reading	1	2	3	4	5	6	7
d. three or four sentences before the one you are currently reading...	1	2	3	4	5	6	7
e. the sentence before the one you are currently reading	1	2	3	4	5	6	7

9. How often do you use these techniques to remind yourself about things ...

	always		sometimes		never		
a. keep an appointment book	1	2	3	4	5	6	7
b. write yourself reminder notes.....	1	2	3	4	5	6	7

c.	make lists of things to do	1	2	3	4	5	6	7
d.	make grocery lists	1	2	3	4	5	6	7
e.	have others remind you........	1	2	3	4	5	6	7
f.	plan your daily schedule in advance...........	1	2	3	4	5	6	7
g.	mental repetition...	1	2	3	4	5	6	7
h.	associations with other objects	1	2	3	4	5	6	7
i.	keep objects in the identical place so you always know where to find them .	1	2	3	4	5	6	7
j.	keep things you need to do in a prominent place where you will notice them	1	2	3	4	5	6	7

10. How much of an effort do you usually have to make to remember in these situations...

		great effort				some effort		no effort
a.	names	1	2	3	4	5	6	7
b.	faces	1	2	3	4	5	6	7
c.	appointments	1	2	3	4	5	6	7
d.	where you put things (e.g., keys) ..	1	2	3	4	5	6	7
e.	performing house-hold chores	1	2	3	4	5	6	7
f.	directions to places	1	2	3	4	5	6	7
g.	phone numbers you've just checked..........	1	2	3	4	5	6	7
h.	phone numbers fre-quently used.......	1	2	3	4	5	6	7
i.	things people tell you	1	2	3	4	5	6	7

		great effort			some effort			no effort
j.	keeping up with correspondence	1	2	3	4	5	6	7
k.	personal dates (e.g., birthdays)	1	2	3	4	5	6	7
l.	words	1	2	3	4	5	6	7
m.	going to the store and forgetting what you wanted to buy	1	2	3	4	5	6	7
n.	taking a test	1	2	3	4	5	6	7
o.	beginning to do something and forgetting what you were doing	1	2	3	4	5	6	7
p.	losing the thread of thought in conversation.......	1	2	3	4	5	6	7
q.	losing the thread of thought in public speaking	1	2	3	4	5	6	7
r.	knowing whether you've already told someone something.........	1	2	3	4	5	6	7

Epilogue:
New Directions in Memory and Aging Research

Leonard W. Poon
James L. Fozard
Veterans Administration Outpatient Clinic, Boston

This book is designed to stimulate future research in memory and aging by providing testable concepts and hypotheses which have the potential of serving as viable basis for programs of research.

A wide range of substantive issues have been examined by investigators from different theoretical and clinical persuasions in the preceding chapters. Among the examined topics which included memory theories, memory testing, mnemonic aids, and strategies in localizing memory loss, we believe the following six areas could provide new directions for future research.

1. Memory Functions And Neurological Changes.   One important question of concern in memory aging is, how much of the observed age decline in memory functioning is attributable to changes in neurological functions? This question has been addressed by several contributors from three different directions.

One proposed direction is to compare qualitative memory deficit patterns of aged individuals with those from patients with known neurological disorders. Cermak (Chapter 16) and Butters (Chapter 25) have illustrated some known memory deficit patterns for Korsakoff and Huntington disease patients. Squire (Chapter 24) provided examples of anterograde and retrograde amnesia patterns following ECT which could be compared with memory decline patterns with the elderly.

A second direction was presented by Kinsbourne (Chapter 6), who postulated that both focal and diffuse neuronal damage that impair remembering can be diagnosed through the inspection of behavioral patterns of attentional dysfunction. He described possible mechanisms of attention dysfunction due to diffuse and uneven cerebral damage.

Finally, Albert and Kaplan (Chapter 23) also identified selective attention as an important landmark in identifying neurological impairment loci with the aged. On the basis of existing data from biochemical, electrocortical, behavioral, and neuropsychological studies, they hypothesized that age-related changes in cognitive functioning can be primarily localized in changes in the frontal lobe.

Past efforts attempting to identify similarities between cognitive deficit patterns in the aged and brain-damage have not met with much success. For example, Goldstein and Shelly (1975) in a factor-analysis study examined the hypothesis that if the effects of aging are similar to those of diffuse brain damage, then the magnitude of performance difference between normal and brain-damaged persons should diminish with age. The results did not support the hypothesis except for a set of abilities associated with motor-perceptual functioning. The magnitude of performance difference between normal and brain-damaged subjects was similar for young and elderly alike.

It can be anticipated that the road will be a long one in identifying the amount of the observed age decline in memory functioning which can be attributable to neurological changes. However, the extant technology has advanced sufficiently since the study performed by Goldstein and Shelly (1975) with the diffuse brain-damaged. The ability to utilize computerized axial tomography provides us with a more accurate and detailed neurological diagnosis of impairment. More information has been accumulated on the neuroanatomical aspects of memory, specifically with amnesic patients with known neurological damage and the elderly (Cermak, Chapter 16; Albert & Kaplan, Chapter 23; Butters, Chapter 25; Squire, Chapter 26). The challenge to the psychologist is to document as carefully as possible the cognitive performance patterns associated with the normal, patients with specific lesions, and the elderly. This information together with more accurate neurodiagnosis could provide a more focused picture of the neurological correlates of age-related memory decline.

2. Complexity Of Memory-Aging Functions.   Considerable effort has been expended in the identification of norms for different types of memory functions for individuals of different ages (e.g., age-appropriate Wechsler Memory Test scores). The question of how fast memory declines has no simple answers at present.

Barr (Chapter 9) and Crowder (Chapter 11) examined data from studies using different cognitive tasks and concluded independently that different tasks produced different magnitudes of age effect. Crowder posited that much of the published data on cognitive aging demonstrated that older individuals, compared to their younger cohorts, performed relatively worse on more difficult tasks, but less so on easier tasks. Different aging functions can be obtained depending on the difficulty of the task employed.

From the preliminary work of Barr and Crowder, one can conceptualize families of aging functions. These functions could be identified by the factors (or tasks) that influence their rates of change. Some functions may improve with age. Some may not change with age until the later decades, and some may show different rates of decline over the adult age span. Examination of these different functions could identify factors that are vulnerable to aging.

3. *Defining Sufficient Conditions For Memory Aging.* First, consider "process" and "knowledge" requirements in memory tasks. Although findings of age decrement are quite common in laboratory tasks, the report of either no age decline or superior performances by the aged is the exception (e.g., Lachman & Lachman, Chapter 18; Perlmutter, Chapter 20; Poon & Fozard, 1978; Poon, Fozard, Paulshock, & Thomas, 1979). Perlmutter (Chapter 20) differentiated between "process" and "knowledge" requirements in memory tasks. She postulated that if successful performance of a task depends on efficient utilization of basic memory processes, the young typically are favored over the elderly; whereas, if task performance is dependent upon previously acquired knowledge, older adults may be superior. This postulation reminded us that one purpose of doing aging research is to identify cognitive processes that improve as well as decline with increasing age. Future work directed toward identifying the process and knowledge requirements of memory tasks will help further our understanding of the behavioral loci of memory aging. Developing information acquisition and retrieval techniques that are based on previously acquired knowledge may help minimize the difficulty the elderly exhibit in learning or using new processes.

Next, consider capacity for resource allocation. There is a general concensus among contributors in this volume that a principle factor influencing memory aging is the decreased availability of processing resources. Craik and Simon (Chapter 5) hypothesized that poorer performance of the elderly could be due to lower attentional capacity, which in turn causes a lower level of processing of input stimuli. Barr (Chapter 9) came to similar conclusions and added that as the processing demands of any task increase, the aging function should approximate linear aging functions found in divided attention tasks.

Crowder (Chapter 11) proposed an attention allocation framework to account for the age/task-difficulty phenomenon. He postulated that in easy tasks, younger subjects tend to underallocate attention, while elderly subjects need to work closer to their attention capacities to "catch up" to the young. For easy tasks, there may be minimal or no age difference in performance. When the task difficulty is increased, younger subjects work closer to capacity while elderly subjects fail to keep up with the young because they are already operating at capacity. Crowder further postulated that if his framework is correct, it should not make any difference whether task difficulty is increased via additional information-processing stages or via additions to the processing load.

Divided or selective attentional deficits are frequently identified as a locus of memory problems for the elderly. While this deficit may be manifested by age-related changes in the biological system (Kinsbourne, Chapter 6; Albert & Kaplan, Chapter 23; Squire, Chapter 24), its impact has been attributed to the observed age decrement in sensory memory (Walsh & Prasse, Chapter 10; Crowder, Chapter 11) and information processing (Smith, Chapter 1; Craik & Simon, Chapter 5; Wingfield & Sandoval, Chapter 12; Wingfield, Chapter 8). Tichtner's observation (cited by Wingfield & Sandoval) in 1908 that the discovery of attention is something like the discovery of a hornet's nest is still true today. As evidenced by the work of Wingfield and Sandoval, and Walsh and Prasse, much theorizing has been done, yet no one attentional model is adequate to operationally define the influence of attentional cognitive performance. The outstanding challenge is to define the phenomenon of attention (Fredericksen, Chapter 7). Further work in defining the phenomenon in terms of capacity, allocation and flexibility characteristics, particularly how they change with age, should greatly contribute toward understanding the loci of loss.

4. Memory Tempo. Two chapters in this volume have postulated that most age-related memory impairments can be parsimoniously accounted for by the slowing of mental operations. Waugh and Barr (Chapter 15) documented that it takes the elderly longer to perceive, to register, and to recall. They posited that a general theory identifying those functions that slow down with age, and their rates of slowing, could supplement existing theoretical dichotomies such as "episodic," "primary" and "secondary," and "deep" and "superficial" processing.

Salthouse (Chapter 2) also capitalized on the general slowing of behavior as an aging phenomenon. He extended Birren's hypothesis (cited by Salthouse) that the loss of speed not only is a performance factor but also is an indicator of fundamental change in the nervous system activity. Salthouse advanced a "rehearsal speed" hypothesis which is supported by data showing that increased age and increased number of syllables to be processed had very similar effects on rehearsal time and recall accuracy. The postulation implied that the elderly have poorer memory because they are slower and take longer to rehearse.

The postulations by Waugh and Barr and by Salthouse deserve careful consideration as theories to account for speed of behavior. However, a note of caution is sounded here for theories based on description of output responses. The observed slowing of memory tempo may be the cause and/or consequence of memory dysfunction among the aged (Arenberg, Chapter 3).

It is possible for two individuals to produce similar latency patterns. However, the underlying mechanisms that produce the similar patterns may be very different, and use of the same remediation procedure could produce very different results for the two individuals. It is important to quantify output responses, for only they can reflect underlying mechanisms.

5. Memory Diagnosis. There is concensus among contributors in the section on memory diagnosis that the time is ripe to develop more focused diagnostic instruments which encompass the extant findings and the many factors involved in memory dysfunction. Recommendations from both quantitative (Erickson, Poon, & Walsh-Sweeney, Chapter 22) and qualitative, process-achievement (Albert & Kaplan, Chapter 23; Butters, Chapter 25) approaches were made. Furthermore, accurate diagnosis leading to effective remediation must involve examination of memory complaints (Erickson et al., Chapter 22; Lachman & Lachman, Chapter 18; Nickerson, Chapter 21; Perlmutter, Chapter 20; and Zelinski, Gilewski, & Thompson, Chapter 30), memory performance, and the affective state of the individual. It is hoped that these recommendations will provide the impetus for meaningful changes in memory diagnosis.

6. Mnemonic Strategies And Individual Differences. Two perspectives on memory improvement were presented in this volume. Poon, Walsh-Sweeney, and Fozard (Chapter 26) presented evidence that visual mnemonics facilitated learning and retrieval for the elderly. They discussed limitations that must be overcome in order to obtain meaningful results with the visual mnemonic technique. Winograd and Simon (Chapter 27) presented a review suggesting that the spatial abilities of the elderly decline more rapidly than verbal abilities. They argued that effective mnemonic training should start with an individual's strength, which is more verbally oriented than visually oriented. The question of the applicability of visual mnemonics for memory improvement for the elderly is indeed a controversial one. Investigators are divided into pro (see Arenberg, Chapter 3; Poon et al., Chapter 26; and Robertson-Tchabo, Chapter 29) and con (see Cermak, Chapter 28; and Winograd & Simon, Chapter 27). Review of available research has shown that the appropriateness of a mnemonic is situation-, individual-, and technique-specific (Poon et al., Chapter 26; Robertson-Tchabo, Chapter 29). The field of memory remediation is very much in its infancy, and it is expected that such controversy will lead to beneficial advances in treatment for the aged.

Given the wide range of possible areas for advances in memory and aging research, it appears appropriate to conclude this volume by sharing Professor A. T. Welford's advice at the memorial conference. Professor Welford proposed that gerontologists can do well to follow the procedure that has proved highly rewarding in certain areas of applied psychological research in the past. We need to forget about the conventionally advocated hypothetico-deductive method, and proceed instead by three stages:

1. Careful observation of everyday behavior in all its complexity, without being frightened of including anecdotal evidence and our own introspective experiences.
2. Use of the full inductive capacities of our "neural computers" to pinpoint seemingly key issues which can be brought into the laboratory for intensive, experimental scrutiny.
3. Application of laboratory findings to real-life situations. Such applicability is the acid test of theorizing as well as the ultimate justification of our research efforts.

Professor Welford further offered a crumb of comfort to our fellow gerontological researchers and those who have contributed in this volume honoring George A. Talland. If one is a gerontologist, any misgivings about signs of aging in oneself are outweighed by gratification that one's theories have been justified; and if the signs fail to appear, it is not distressing that one's theories have not been upheld.

REFERENCES

Goldstein, G. & Shelly, C. H. Similarities and differences between psychological deficit in aging and brain damage. *Journal of Gerontology,* 1975, *30,* 448–455.

Poon, L. W. & Fozard, J. L. Speed of retrieval from long-term memory in relation to age, familiarity, and datedness of information. *Journal of Gerontology,* 1978, *33,* 711–717.

Poon, L. W., Fozard, J. L., Paulshock, D., & Thomas, J. C. A questionnaire assessment of age differences in retention of recent and remote events. *Experimental Aging Research,* 1979, *5,* 401–411.

Author Index

551

.

Subject Index

Echoic memory *(cont.)*
  stage analysis of aging, 191–193
    added stages that are beneficial, 192, 197
    added stage that complicates, 192, 197
    ceiling effect, 193
    recognition and retrieval, 192–193
ECT, 433–439, 441–443
Effort, 218–219, 223, 228, 233
Elaboration, 20, 21, 34–42, 97, 107, 265, *see also* Imagery; Information processing, encoding, and strategies; Memory, models of, serial; Organization
  instructions, 36
  orienting task procedures, 36–37
Embedded Figures Test, 486
Encoding, *see* Information processing

F

Feeling-of-knowing, *see* Metamemory
Filter theory, 206–208, 210–217, *see also* Attention, models of, time-sharing

H

Hooper Visual Organization Test, *see* Visuospatial performance
Hippocampus, 444–447
Huntington's Disease, *see* Dementia

I

Iconic memory, 151, 244, 330–333, *see also* Perception; Memory, sensory
  and aging, 164–170, 177–179
  and attentional processes, 157, 160, 170–172, 177–179
  confounded with other processes, 244
  definition of, 153
  duration of, 160–161, 163
    age differences, 167–170
  locus of, 155, 159, 162–164, 168
  measures of
    auditory click adjustment, 163
    oscillating slit, 161
    partial report, *see* Partial report procedure

Iconic memory *(cont.)*
  persistence of form, 161–162, 167–169
  stimulus halves, 160–161, 169–170
  nature of, 155–157, 167–168, 171, 179
  readout rate, 172–177
  research history, 153–157
Imagery, 13, 34–39, 507–509, *see also* Elaboration; Information processing, encoding, and strategies; Memory, models of serial; Organization; Recall, free
  concepts of, 461
  concrete vs. abstract words, 39–40, *see also* Memory
  dual-code theory, 39, 491–492, 501
  with elderly, 467–472
  instructions, 40
  mediators, *see* Mediators
  as mnemonic device
    bizarre vs. plausible, 475
    complexity, 475–476
    effects of practice, 469
    for elderly, 474–477
    individual differences, 468, 473–474, 514
    interacting, 463, 468, 475, 495–496
    learning rates, 468–469
    method of loci, 461, 467–468, 472, 513
    noninteracting, 463
    peg-word method, 464–465, 471–472, 475
    self-help, 477–480
    skill maintenance, 477–480
    with patient groups, 464–467
  production time, 256
  single vs. multiple coding of, 476
  subject- vs. experimentor-generated, 39, 254, 469
  tests, 473–480, 503–504, 511–514, 549, *see also* Memory, training
  and verbal learning, 256
  and visual memory, 485–488
    decline with age, 486–488
    with young adults, 463–464
Inference, *see* Knowledge
Information processing, 452, 453, 457, 458, 496–502, *see also* Knowledge, Learning, Paired-associate learning, Recall, Recognition, Retrieval, Serial learning
  approaches, *see* Memory, models of
  auditory integration, 253